Contents at a Glance

Table of Contents

About the Author

Steven Holzner is an award-winning author who has written 80 computing books. He has been writing about XML since it first appeared and is one of the foremost XML experts in the United States, having written several XML bestsellers and being a much-requested speaker on the topic. He's also been a contributing editor at *PC Magazine*, has been on the faculty of Cornell University and MIT, and teaches corporate programming classes around the United States.

Dedication

To Nancy, as always and forever—for all the reasons she already knows!

Acknowledgments

A book like the one you're reading is the product of many people's hard work. I'd especially like to thank Todd Green, the acquisitions editor; Songlin Qiu, the development editor; Matt Purcell, the project editor; and Christian Kenyeres, the tech editor.

We Want to Hear from You!

As the reader of this book, *you* are our most important critic and commentator. We value your opinion and want to know what we're doing right, what we could do better, what areas you would like to see us publish in, and any other words of wisdom you're willing to pass our way.

As an associate publisher for Sams Publishing, I welcome your comments. You can email or write me directly to let me know what you did or didn't like about this book—as well as what we can do to make our books better.

Please note that I cannot help you with technical problems related to the topic of this book. We do have a User Services group, however, where I will forward specific technical questions related to the book.

When you write, please be sure to include this book's title and author as well as your name, email address, and phone number. I will carefully review your comments and share them with the author and editors who worked on the book.

Email: feedback@samspublishing.com

Mail: Michael Stephens
Associate Publisher
Sams Publishing
800 East 96th Street
Indianapolis, IN 46240 USA

For more information about this book or another Sams Publishing title, visit our Web site at `http://www.samspublishing.com`. Type the ISBN (0672325764) or the title of a book in the Search field to find the page you're looking for.

Introduction

Welcome to Extensible Markup Language (XML), the most influential innovation the Internet has seen in years. XML is a powerful, very dynamic topic, spanning dozens of fields, from the simple to the very complex. This book opens up that world, going after XML with dozens of topics—and hundreds of examples.

Unlike other XML books, this book makes it a point to show how XML actually works, making sure that you see everything demonstrated with examples. The biggest problem with most XML books is that they discuss XML and its allied specifications in the abstract, which makes it very hard to understand what's going on. This book, however, illustrates every XML discussion with examples. It shows all that's in the other books and more besides, emphasizing seeing things at work to make it all clear.

Instead of abstract discussions, this book provides concrete working examples because that's the only way to really learn XML. You're going to see where to get a lot of free software on the Internet to run the examples you create—everything from XML browsers to XPath visualizers to XQuery processors to XForms handlers, which you don't find in other books. You'll create XML-based documents that display multimedia shows you can play in RealPlayer, use browser plug-ins to handle XML-based graphics in the popular Hypertext Markup Language (HTML) browsers, enable Web pages to load and handle XML, and much more. XML can get complicated, and seeing it at work is the best way to understand it.

What This Book Covers

This book covers XML as thoroughly as any book you'll find: It goes from the most basic up through the advanced. XML ranges over many disciplines, and this book tracks it down where it lives. Part I, "Creating XML Documents," shows how to use XML in both current Web browsers as well as specialized XML-only browsers. Part I works through every part of an XML document to show how to construct such documents. You'll see how to use online XML validators to check XML and where to find software that lets you check an XML document's schema to make sure the document works as it should. You'll see how to format XML by using cascading style sheets (CSS), Extensible Stylesheet Language Transformations (XSLT), and XML-based formatting objects.

You don't need any programming skills to work with XML in Part I of this book. However, there's no way to ignore the terrific amount of XML support in programming languages such as JavaScript, Java, and the .NET programming languages. Later in the book, you'll see how to use those languages with XML, navigating through XML documents, extracting data, formatting data, and even creating your own simple XML browsers.

Here's an overview of some of the topics covered in this book:

- The basics of XML
- Displaying XML in browsers
- Writing XML
- Creating well-formed and valid XML documents
- Working with XML validators
- Finding XML resources on the Internet
- Creating Document Type Definitions (DTDs)
- Creating XML schema
- Using XML schema-generating tools
- Using CSS with XML documents
- Displaying images
- Using XSLT to transform XML in the server, in the client, and with standalone programs
- Creating XSLT stylesheets
- Working with XPath
- Using the XSL formatting language
- Introducing Extensible HTML (XHTML)
- Validating XHTML
- Drawing basic shapes in Scalable Vector Graphics (SVG)
- Using SVG hyperlinks, animation, scripting, and gradients
- Creating SMIL documents
- Using Synchronized Multimedia Integration Language (SMIL)
- Creating XLinks, XPointers, and XForms
- Separating data and presentations in XForms
- Handling XML with JavaScript
- Using Java and the XML Document Object Model (DOM)
- Using XML data islands
- Parsing XML documents

- Navigating through an XML document by using Java
- Creating graphical XML browsers by using Java
- Using Java and the Simple API for XML (SAX)
- Using Simple Object Access Protocol (SOAP) to communicate between Web applications
- Binding XML data to HTML controls
- Navigating through XML data
- Displaying XML data in tables
- Managing XML databases
- Working with XML database storage in .NET
- Using XQuery to query an XML document
- Editing XML documents and XML schemas in .NET
- Writing and reading XML documents from code
- Creating XML Web services

As you can see, this book covers many facets of XML.

Who This Book Is For

This book is for anyone who wants to learn XML and how it is used today. This book assumes that you've had some experience with HTML, but that's about all it assumes. In Part IV, "Programming and XML," knowledge of JavaScript and Java helps, although the chapters in Part IV discuss where you can find free online tutorials on these subjects. The .NET programming discussed on Day 21, "Handling XML in .NET," may be a little hard to follow unless you've worked with Visual Basic .NET before.

Note that this book is as platform-independent as possible. XML is not the province of any one particular operating system, so this book does not lean one way or another on that issue. This book aims to show you as much of XML as it can, in the greatest depth possible. However, it's a fact of life that a great deal of XML software these days is targeted at Windows. And among the standard browsers, Internet Explorer has many times more XML support than any other browser does. This book doesn't have any special pro- or anti-Microsoft bias, but in order for this book to cover what's available for XML these days, you're going to find yourself in Microsoft territory fairly often; there's no getting around it.

Conventions Used in This Book

The following conventions are used in this book:

- Code lines, commands, statements, and any other code-related terms appear in a `monospace` typeface. Placeholders (which stand for what you should actually type) appear in *`italic monospace`*. Text that you should type appears in **`bold`**.
- When a line of code is too long to fit on one line of this book, it is broken at a convenient place and continued to the next line. The continuation is preceded by a special code continuation character (➥).
- New lines of XML or programming code that are added and are being discussed appear shaded, and when there's more code to come, you see three vertical dots. Here's how these features look:

```
<?xml version="1.0" encoding="UTF-8"?>
<document>
      .
      .
      .
</document>
```

- Throughout the book are notes that are meant to give you something more. This is what a note looks like:

NOTE

> A note presents interesting information related to the discussion—a little more insight or a pointer to some new technique.

- This book also contains tips. This is what a tip looks like:

TIP

> A tip offers advice or shows you an easier way of doing something.

- This book also contains cautions. This is what a caution looks like:

CAUTION

> A caution alerts you to a possible problem and gives you advice on how to avoid it.

- Each day's lesson ends with questions pertaining to that day's subject matter, with answers from the book's author. Each day's discussion also includes a quiz that is designed to test your knowledge of the day's concepts. The answers to these quiz questions are provided in Appendix A, "Answers to Quiz Questions." Many lessons conclude with exercises that give you an opportunity to practice what you've learned in the lesson.

Where to Download the Book's Code

You can download all the code examples used throughout this book from `http://www.samspublishing.com`. Simply enter this book's ISBN without the hyphens (**0672325764**) in the Search box and click Search. When the book's title is displayed, click it to go to a page where you can download the code.

PART I

At a Glance

Creating XML Documents

Part I provides an overview of XML and many of the popular ways it's used. You'll take a look at the various markup languages that have been created using XML and how they work.

You'll also begin creating your own XML documents in this part, and in the process you'll get all the basics down. you're going to see how to create both well-formed and valid XML documents.

Well-formed documents obey a number of rules, and before an XML document can be considered "official," it must be well-formed. To be valid, an XML document must specify a set of syntax rules, and XML processors can use these rules to check whether that document adheres to those rules. You're going to see the two ways of specifying the syntax of XML documents in this part—by using document type declarations (DTDs) and XML schemas.

PART I

DAY 1

Welcome to XML

Welcome to Extensible Markup Language, XML, the language for handling data in compact, easy-to-manage form—not to mention the most powerful advance the Internet has seen for years. The XML world is a large and ever-expanding one, full of complex and unpredictable innovations, and this book is your guided tour to that world. We're going to go just about everywhere XML goes these days, and that's going to include some pretty amazing territory. Today, we'll get our start with XML and see what it's good for. Here are today's topics in overview:

- Markup languages
- Introducing XML
- Seeing XML in a browser
- Well-formed and valid XML documents
- Extracting data from XML documents
- Working with XML validators
- Seeing XML at work
- Finding XML resources on the Internet

The name of the game in XML is *data*, because XML is all about storing your data—phone directories, business orders, book lists, anything you like. Unlike HTML, XML is *not* about displaying your data—it's about packaging that data to transport it easily. The main reason XML has experienced such popularity is that it stores its data as text, meaning that XML documents can be transferred using the already-existing Web technology, which was built to transfer HTML documents as text.

We'll start today's work by taking a look at the languages designed to let you store and handle text, called *markup languages*, and there are plenty of them out there. As we're going to see, XML is both different and more powerful than most other markup languages.

All About Markup Languages

The term *markup* refers to codes or tokens you put into a document to indicate how to interpret the (non-markup) data in the document. In other words, markup describes the data in the document and how it should be interpreted. For example, a markup language most people have heard of is HTML for creating Web pages, and you can see a sample HTML Web page in Listing 1.1.

LISTING 1.1 A Sample HTML Web Page (`ch01_01.html`)

```
<HTML>
    <HEAD>
        <TITLE>Hello From HTML</TITLE>
    </HEAD>
    <BODY>
        <CENTER>
            <H1>
                An HTML Document
            </H1>
        </CENTER>
        This is an HTML document!
    </BODY>
</HTML>
```

The markup in this HTML document is there to tell a browser how to interpret the document's data—which data is a header, which is text for the body of the document, and so on. This HTML markup is made up of HTML *tags* such as `<HEAD>`, `<BODY>`, and so on, and those tags give directions to the browser. You can see this HTML page in the Netscape Navigator in Figure 1.1. Note in particular that because the HTML markup in this document is only there to give directions to the browser, none of the markup itself appears directly in the browser's display of this document.

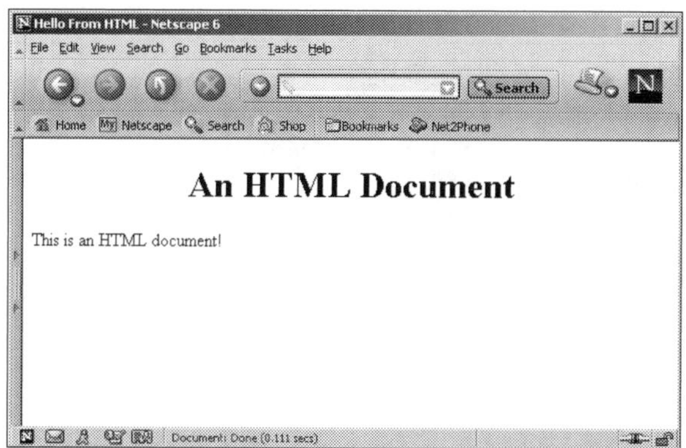

FIGURE 1.1
An HTML page in a browser.

When you think of it, there are already many markup languages around. For example, you might use a word processor like Microsoft Word, or a text editor like Windows WordPad, which can store text in Rich Text Format (RTF) files. RTF files are usually filled with markup indicating how to display text and holding directions to the word processor. For example, here's the RTF markup for a file created with Microsoft Word holding the text "No worries!" in bold (hint: the "No worries!" text is at the very end) :

```
{\rtf1\ansi\ansicpg1252\uc1 \deff0\deflang1033\deflangfe1033
{\fonttbl{\f0\froman\fcharset0\fprq2{\*\panose 02020603050405020304}
Times New Roman;}{\f153\froman\fcharset238\fprq2 Times New Roman CE;}
{\f154\froman\fcharset204\fprq2 Times New Roman Cyr;}
{\f156\froman\fcharset161\fprq2 Times New Roman Greek;}
{\f157\froman\fcharset162\fprq2 Times New Roman Tur;}
{\f158\froman\fcharset177\fprq2 Times New Roman (Hebrew);}
{\f159\froman\fcharset178\fprq2 Times New Roman (Arabic);}
{\f160\froman\fcharset186\fprq2 Times New Roman Baltic;}}
{\colortbl;\red0\green0\blue0;\red0\green0\blue255;\red0\green255\blue255;
\red0\green255\blue0;\red255\green0\blue255;\red255\green0\blue0;
\red255\green255\blue0;\red255\green255\blue255;\red0\green0\blue128;
\red0\green128\blue128;\red0\green128\blue0;\red128\green0\blue128;
\red128\green0\blue0;\red128\green128\blue0;\red128\green128\blue128;\
red192\green192\blue192;}{\stylesheet{\ql \li0\ri0\widctlpar\aspalpha
\aspnum\faauto\adjustright\rin0\lin0\itap0 \fs24\lang1033\langfe1033
\cgrid\langnp1033\langfenp1033 \snext0 Normal;}{\*\cs10 \additive
Default Paragraph Font;}}{\info{\title No worries}{\author Steven Holzner}
{\operator Steven Holzner}{\version1}{\edmins0}{\nofpages1}{\nofwords0}
{\nofchars0}{\*\company Your Company Name}{\nofcharsws0}{\vern8269}}
\widowctrl\ftnbj\aenddoc\noxlattoyen\expshrtn\noultrlspc\dntblnsbdb
\nospaceforul\formshade\horzdoc\dgmargin\dghspace180\dgvspace180
\dghorigin1701\dgvorigin1984\dghshow1\dgvshow1
{\*\pnseclvl1\pnucrm\pnstart1\pnindent720\pnhang{\pntxta .}}
{\*\pnseclvl2\pnucltr\pnstart1\pnindent720\pnhang{\pntxta .}}
{\*\pnseclvl3\pndec\pnstart1\pnindent720\pnhang{\pntxta .}}
{\*\pnseclvl4\pnlcltr\pnstart1\pnindent720\pnhang{\pntxta )}}{\*\pnseclvl5
```

```
\pndec\pnstart1\pnindent720\pnhang{\pntxtb (}{\pntxta )}}
{\*\pnseclvl6\pnlcltr\pnstart1\pnindent720\pnhang{\pntxtb (}{\pntxta
➥ )}}{\*\pnseclvl7\pnlcrm\pnstart1\pnindent720\pnhang{\pntxtb (}{\pntxta
➥)}}{\*\pnseclvl8\pnlcltr\pnstart1\pnindent720\pnhang
{\pntxtb (}{\pntxta )}}{\*\pnseclvl9\pnlcrm\pnstart1\pnindent720\pnhang
{\pntxtb (}{\pntxta )}}\pard\plain \ql \li0\ri0\widctlpar\aspalpha\aspnum
\faauto\adjustright\rin0\lin0\itap0 \fs24\lang1033\langfe1033\cgrid
\langnp1033\langfenp1033 {\b No worries!\par }}
```

All the codes you see here are markup. As you can see, markup is just the general name for directives indicating how you want your data treated.

You might think of HTML (which, of course, stands for Hypertext Markup Language) first when someone mentions markup languages, but the fact is that HTML is a very limited language. It's OK for creating standard Web pages, but it can't go much farther than that.

For example, HTML is great for creating Web pages that display standard text and some images, and the HTML tags like `<img>`, `<table>`, and others are fine for that. But as things got more complex, HTML couldn't keep up—in the original HTML version, 1.0, there were only about a dozen tags. In the current version, HTML 4.01, there are nearly 100 tags—and still many more are needed (if you add the nonstandard ones that various browsers support to fill in some holes, there are over 120 HTML tags in current use).

Even so, to really fill the needs of Web developers, HTML could use hundreds of additional tags. But there's no way those additional tags could handle all kinds of situations—for example, what if you wanted to store information about your close friends instead? There are no HTML tags like `<firstname>`, `<lastname>`, `<phone>`, or `<age>`. What if you are a bank that offers loans and you want tags like `<amount>`, `<term>`, `<rate>`, and `<accountID>`? There's no way HTML could fit in all these kinds of tags. In other words, there are as many reasons to create markup as there are ways of handling data—and that's infinite. That's where XML comes in, because the whole idea behind XML is to let you create *your own* markup.

All About XML

Extensible Markup Language, XML, is really all about creating your own markup (technically, XML is a meta-language, which means it's a language that lets you create your own markup languages). Unlike HTML, XML is meant for *storing* data, not *displaying* it. XML provides you with a way of structuring your data in documents, and as mentioned at the beginning of today's discussion, the reason it's taken off so quickly is it's perfect for the Internet—because XML documents are text, you can send them using the existing Internet technology that was built for HTML.

1

You can package your great books collection as XML, or list all the books in a library, or all the types of fish in the sea; that's what XML is all about, and it's popular largely because restricted markup languages like HTML can't do that. Once you've packaged your data, you can send it over the Internet, and either other people or dedicated software you or others have created can understand it. There's an immense need to communicate data these days, from real estate listings to bank holdings, and XML is proving to be the way to do it.

XML was actually derived from Standard Generalized Markup Language, SGML, in 1998. SGML is a complex language, and was around for a long time without gaining widespread acceptance—but XML hasn't suffered from that problem. XML just turned five years old shortly before this book was written, and Jon Bosak, one of the people instrumental in XML's creation, wished XML happy birthday by saying, *"The five years since XML was released have seen XML become the lingua franca of the Web."* And it's true—using the markup you develop with XML, you can package your data so that data can be read by others. HTML is limited by having a limited amount of available markup; XML is limitless, because the markup you can create with it is also limitless.

XML is a creation of the World Wide Web Consortium (W3C) `http://www.w3.org`, which is the same group responsible for HTML and many other such specifications. W3C publishes its specifications (they're not called standards, technically, because W3C is not a government-sponsored body) using four types of documents, and if you want to work with XML and all its allied specifications, you have to be familiar with them:

- *Notes*—Specifications that were submitted to the W3C by an organization that is a member of the World Wide Web Consortium. W3C makes these specifications public, although doesn't necessarily endorse them, by publishing them as a note.
- *Working drafts*—A working draft is a specification that is under consideration, and open to comment. This is the first stage that W3C specifications must go through on their way to becoming recommendations.
- *Candidate recommendations*—Working drafts that the W3C has accepted become candidate recommendations, which means they're still open for comment. This is the second stage that W3C specifications must go through on their way to becoming recommendations.
- *Recommendations*—Candidate recommendations that the W3C has accepted become recommendations, which is the term the W3C uses when it publishes its specifications it considers ready for general use.

XML version 1.0 is in recommendation form, and has been since October 6, 2000, which means it's an established standard. You can find the formal XML 1.0 recommendation at http://www.w3.org/TR/REC-xml. There's a new version of XML now in candidate recommendation form, XML 1.1 (the latest version is October 15, 2002). You can find the XML 1.1 candidate recommendation at http://www.w3.org/TR/xml11/. As we'll discuss tomorrow, XML 1.1 improves on XML 1.0 by fixing a few errors, and by making the support for Unicode stronger.

NOTE The formal specifications themselves are not easy to read—our guided tour of the subject in this book is designed to unravel them and make them accessible.

What does an XML document actually look like? Let's take a look at one to get an idea of what's going on and how XML works. You can see a sample XML document, ch01_02.xml, in Listing 1.2.

LISTING 1.2 A Sample XML Document (ch01_02.xml)

```
<?xml version="1.0" encoding="UTF-8"?>
<document>
    <heading>
        Hello From XML
    </heading>
    <message>
        This is an XML document!
    </message>
</document>
```

We're going to dissect the kind of XML document you see in Listing 1.2 in detail tomorrow, but we'll get familiar with its structure today.

Like all XML documents, this one starts with an *XML declaration*, <?xml version="1.0" encoding="UTF-8"?>. This XML declaration indicates that we're using XML version 1.0, and using the UTF-8 *character encoding*, which means that we're using an 8-bit condensed version of Unicode (more on this tomorrow):

```
<?xml version="1.0" encoding="UTF-8"?>
<document>
    <heading>
        Hello From XML
    </heading>
    <message>
        This is an XML document!
    </message>
</document>
```

1

This XML declaration, `<?xml?>`, uses two *attributes*, `version` and `encoding`, to set the version of XML and the character set we're using (XML declarations also have other attributes, as you'll see tomorrow). XML attributes are much like HTML attributes—they hold additional information, and you create them by assigning a quoted value to the attribute as here: `version = "1.0"`. (Unlike HTML attributes, you must always assign a value to an XML attribute if you use that attribute—there are no standalone attributes as in HTML.)

NOTE

> Most of the examples in this book will use version 1.0 of XML, because XML 1.1 is still in candidate recommendation form, which means that it hasn't been granted full status yet, and most software (like Microsoft's Internet Explorer) won't recognize or even open XML 1.1 documents yet. In practical terms, the differences between XML 1.0 and 1.1 are small, and we'll see them tomorrow.

Next in `ch01_02.xml`, we create a new XML element named `<document>`. As in HTML, an *element* is the fundamental unit that you use to hold your data—all data in an XML document must be inside an element. Elements always start with an *opening tag*, which is the actual text `<document>` in this case, and end with a *closing tag*, which will be `</document>` here. (Note that this is similar to, but different from, HTML, where you don't always need a closing tag.) XML tags themselves always start with `<` and end with `>`. You create an XML element by pairing an opening tag with a closing tag, as we've done here to create the `<document>` element:

```
<?xml version="1.0" encoding="UTF-8"?>
<document>
    .
    .
    .
</document>
```

Now you're free to store other elements in our `<document>` element, or text data, as we wish.

You're free to make up your own element names in XML, and that's XML's whole power—the capability to create your own markup. You don't have to call this new element `<document>`; you could have named it `<data>`, or `<record>`, or `<people>`, or `<movies>`, or `<planets>`, or many other things. As you'll see tomorrow, in XML 1.0, an element's name can start with a letter or underscore, and the characters following the first one are made up of letters, digits, underscores, dots (`.`), or hyphens (`-`)—but no spaces. XML 1.1 is more flexible about names, as you'll also see. Unlike HTML, the case of a tag is important—`<DOCUMENT>` is not the same tag as `<document>`, for example.

In between an element's opening tag and its closing tag, you can place the element's content, if there is any. An element's content can be made up of simple text or other elements. Like XML declarations, XML elements can support attributes.

When you create an XML document, you must enclose all elements inside one overall element, called the *root element*, also called the *document element*. The root element contains all the other elements in your XML document, and in this case, we've named the root element `<document>`. XML documents always need a root element, even if they don't have any other elements or text (that is, even if the root element doesn't have any other content).

Inside the root element, we'll add a new element, `<heading>`, to our XML document, like this:

```
<?xml version="1.0" encoding="UTF-8"?>
<document>
    <heading>
        .
        .
        .
    </heading>
    .
    .
    .
</document>
```

This new element will contain data in the form of text—"Hello from XML":

```
<?xml version="1.0" encoding="UTF-8"?>
<document>
    <heading>
        Hello from XML
    </heading>
    .
    .
    .
</document>
```

We will also add another element, which we'll name `<message>`, to the root element (there is no limit to the number of subelements an element can hold), holding the text data "This is an XML document!":

```
<?xml version="1.0" encoding="UTF-8"?>
<document>
    <heading>
        Hello From XML
    </heading>
    <message>
        This is an XML document!
    </message>
</document>
```

And that completes our first XML document. In this case, the root element, <document>, contains two elements, <heading> and <message>, both of which contain text (although they could contain other elements).

As you can see, this XML document looks like the HTML document we created earlier—the elements we've created here are surrounded by tags, just as in the HTML document. However, we just created the elements in the XML document out of thin air; we didn't have to stick to a predefined set. Being able to create your own elements from scratch like this has advantages and disadvantages—you're not restricted to a predefined and limited set of tags, but on the other hand, a standard Web browser can understand HTML tags but will have no idea what to do with a <message> tag.

We've stored our data in an XML document; to start interpreting that data, we'll begin by simply opening it in a browser.

Looking at XML in a Browser

Some browsers, such as Microsoft Internet Explorer version 5 or later, let you display XML documents directly. For example, if you download the code for this book, you can browse to `ch01_02.xml` in Internet Explorer, as you see in Figure 1.2. As you see in the figure, the whole XML document we've created is displayed. You can even click the – sign in front of the <document> element to collapse all the contents of that element into a single line (which will have a + sign in front of it, indicating that that line may be expanded). In this way, you can display a raw XML document in Internet Explorer.

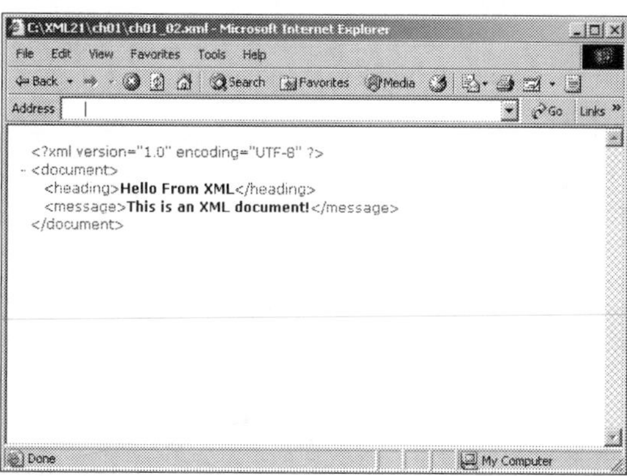

FIGURE 1.2
Viewing an XML document in Internet Explorer.

Note, however, that Internet Explorer hasn't done anything more than display our raw XML here—it hasn't interpreted that XML in any way, because browsers are specialists at displaying data, not interpreting XML tags.

In fact, if you're only interested in displaying your data, you can use your XML tags to tell the browser how to do that by using style sheets. For example, you might want to create an element named `<red>` that specifies to the browser that all enclosed text should be displayed in red. Using style sheets, you can let a browser interpret your XML if you just want to use that XML to tell a browser how to display your data visually.

NOTE

> One of the most popular reasons for using style sheets with XML is that you store your data in an XML document, and specify how to display that data using a separate document, the style sheet. This separates your data from the presentation details, unlike HTML, where the tags that specify how to display your data are mixed in with that data. By separating the presentation details from the data, you can change the entire presentation with a few changes in the style sheet, instead of making multiple changes in your data itself.

There's plenty of support for working with XML documents and style sheets in both Internet Explorer and Netscape Navigator. There are two kinds of style sheets you can use with XML documents—cascading style sheets (CSS), which you can also use with HTML documents, and Extensible Stylesheet Language style sheets (XSL), designed to be used only with XML documents.

We'll cover both CSS and XSL in this book (see Days 8–10), but you'll also get an idea of what you can do using style sheets today. As an example, we'll use CSS to format our XML sample document. To do that, we'll use an XML *processing instruction*, `<?xml-stylesheet?>`, supported by both Internet Explorer and Netscape Navigator, to associate a CSS style sheet with an XML document.

As you can guess from their name, processing instructions are instructions to the software processing the XML; all XML processing instructions like this one start with `<?` and end with `?>`. Processing instructions might appear throughout an XML document, and like XML elements themselves, they may have attributes. As with XML elements, you're free to make up your own processing instructions—the `<?xml-stylesheet?>` processing instruction is not built into XML, it just happens to be one supported by both Netscape Navigator and Internet Explorer. More on processing instructions tomorrow.

In this case, this processing instruction will have its `type` attribute set to `"text/css"` to indicate that we're using a CSS style sheet, and its `href` attribute set to the location of the CSS style sheet (much like the way the `href` attribute of an HTML `<a>` element specifies the target of a hyperlink), as you see in `ch01_03.xml` in Listing 1.3.

1

LISTING 1.3 An XML Document Using a Style Sheet (ch01_03.xml)

```
<?xml version="1.0" encoding="UTF-8"?>
<?xml-stylesheet type="text/css" href="ch01_04.css"?>
<document>
    <heading>
        Hello From XML
    </heading>
    <message>
        This is an XML document!
    </message>
</document>
```

In this case, we've named the CSS style sheet `ch01_04.css`, and you can see the entire contents of this file in Listing 1.4. In `ch01_04.css`, we're telling the browser how to display our XML elements' content. In particular, we're saying that we want the text content of `<heading>` elements to appear centered in the browser, 24 points high (a point is 1/72 of an inch), and colored red (you specify colors as you would in an HTML page—#ff0000 is bright red, for example; more on setting colors like these when we discuss CSS in detail in Day 8, "Formatting XML with Cascading Style Sheets"), and the text content of `<message>` elements in centered 18 point blue text.

LISTING 1.4 A CSS Style Sheet (ch01_04.css)

```
heading {display: block; font-size: 24pt; color: #ff0000; text-align: center}
message {display: block; font-size: 18pt; color: #0000ff; text-align: center}
```

You can see the results in Netscape Navigator in Figure 1.3, and in Internet Explorer in Figure 1.4. In this way, we've been able to tell a browser how we want our data formatted, using XML elements to format that data, and a style sheet to tell the browser how to interpret those XML elements.

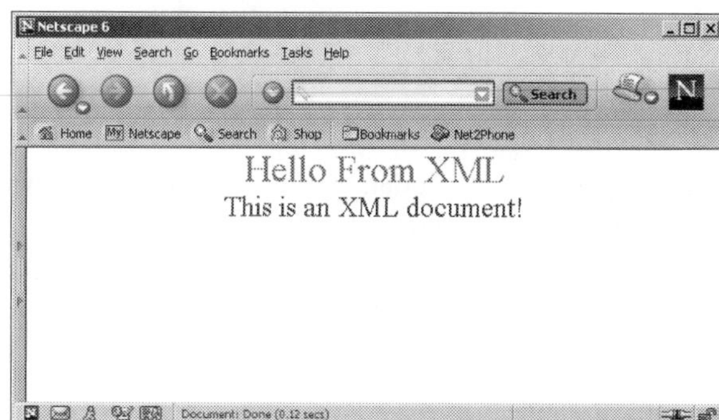

FIGURE 1.3

Viewing an XML document in Netscape Navigator.

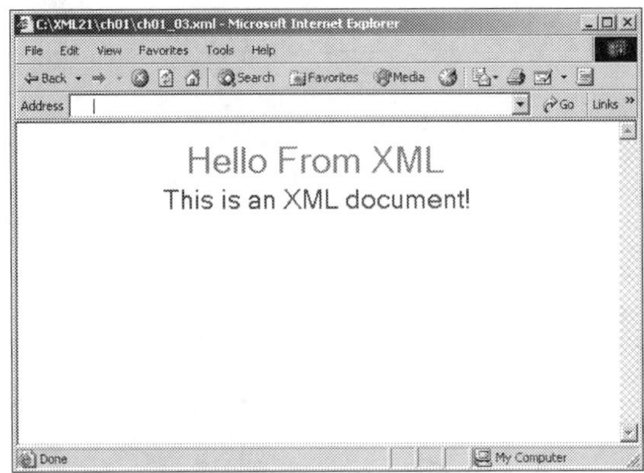

FIGURE 1.4
Viewing an XML document in Internet Explorer.

That's about as far as a browser can go with XML unless you do more yourself. However, using XML to indicate how your data should be displayed is only the beginning. You can extract data from an XML document yourself, and we'll see how to do that in detail toward the end of this book. For example, you might use a scripting language like JavaScript to tell a browser how to extract data from the elements in an XML document, and we'll take a look at how that might work next.

Working with XML Data Yourself

Say that you want to extract the data from an XML document yourself, and to work with that data, rather than simply telling a browser how to display it. For example, suppose you want to extract the text from our `<heading>` element:

```
<?xml version="1.0" encoding="UTF-8"?>
<?xml-stylesheet type="text/css" href="ch01_04.css"?>
<document>
    <heading>
        Hello From XML
    </heading>
    <message>
        This is an XML document!
    </message>
</document>
```

One way of gaining access to that data in a browser is to use JavaScript, which browsers like Internet Explorer and Netscape Navigator support. We'll work through that process step by step in Day 15, "Using JavaScript and XML," but you can see a sample HTML page with embedded JavaScript that will do the trick in Listing 1.5.

LISTING 1.5 Extracting Data from an XML Document Using JavaScript (`ch01_05.html`)

```
<HTML>
    <HEAD>
        <TITLE>
            Retrieving data from an XML document
        </TITLE>

        <XML ID="firstXML" SRC="ch01_02.xml"></XML>

        <SCRIPT LANGUAGE="JavaScript">
            function getData()
            {
                xmldoc= document.all("firstXML").XMLDocument;

                nodeDoc = xmldoc.documentElement;
                nodeHeading = nodeDoc.firstChild;

                outputMessage = "Heading: " +
                      nodeHeading.firstChild.nodeValue;
                message.innerHTML=outputMessage;
            }
        </SCRIPT>
    </HEAD>

    <BODY>
        <CENTER>
            <H1>
                Retrieving data from an XML document
            </H1>

            <DIV ID="message"></DIV>
            <P>
            <INPUT TYPE="BUTTON" VALUE="Read the heading"
                ONCLICK="getData()">
        </CENTER>
    </BODY>
</HTML>
```

When you open this example in Internet Explorer, it displays a button with the caption `"Read the heading"`, as you see in Figure 1.5. When you click that button, the JavaScript reads the text in the `<heading>` element in our sample XML document, `ch01_02.xml`, and displays that text, as you see in the figure. In this way, we've been able to extract data from an XML document—and when you've extracted your data from an XML document, you're free to work on it as you like.

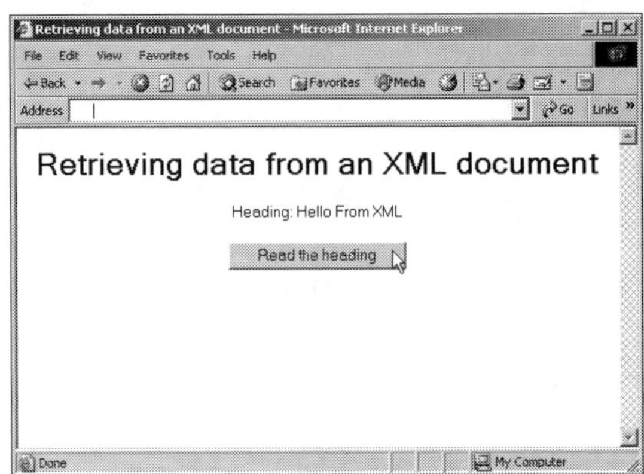

FIGURE 1.5
Extracting data from an XML document in Internet Explorer.

We'll also take a look at using the Java programming language to handle XML in Day 16, "Using Java and .NET: DOM," and Day 17, "Using Java and .NET: SAX." Java has all kinds of built-in support for working with XML, and you can see a sample Java program in Listing 1.6. Like our JavaScript example, this example reads the text content of the `<heading>` element in our sample XML document, `ch01_02.xml`, and displays that text.

LISTING 1.6 Extracting Data from an XML Document Using Java (`ch01_06.java`)

```
import javax.xml.parsers.*;
import org.w3c.dom.*;
import java.io.*;

public class ch01_06
{
    static public void main(String[] argv)
    {
        try {

        DocumentBuilderFactory dbf =
            DocumentBuilderFactory.newInstance();

        DocumentBuilder db = null;
        try {
            db = dbf.newDocumentBuilder();
        }
        catch (ParserConfigurationException pce) {}

        Document doc = null;
            doc = db.parse("ch01_02.xml");

            for (Node node = doc.getDocumentElement().getFirstChild();
```

LISTING 1.6 continued

```
                    node != null; node = node.getNextSibling()) {

                    if (node instanceof Element) {
                        if (node.getNodeName().equals("heading")) {

                            StringBuffer buffer = new StringBuffer();

                            for (Node subnode = node.getFirstChild();
                                subnode != null; subnode = subnode.
➥getNextSibling()){
                                if (subnode instanceof Text) {
                                    buffer.append(subnode.getNodeValue());
                                }
                            }
                            System.out.println(buffer.toString());
                        }
                    }
                }
            } catch (Exception e) {
                e.printStackTrace();
            }
        }
    }
```

When you run this program (see Day 16 for the details), the output looks like this:

```
%java ch01_06
        Hello From XML
```

NOTE

> In this book, we'll use `%` to stand for the command-line prompt. For example, if you're using Unix, this prompt might look familiar, or your prompt might look something like `\home\xml21:`, or `\user\steve`, or something similar. If you're using Windows, you get a command-line prompt by opening an MS DOS window, and your prompt might look something like `C:\XML21>`.

As you can see, it's possible to extract data from an XML document, so someone else can write such a document using tags you both agree on, send you that document over the Internet, and you can extract the data you need from the document by searching for elements with specific names. There are thousands of Web-based applications these days, and they've sent and interpreted thousands of XML documents in the time it took you to read this sentence.

Structuring Your Data

An XML document actually can do more than just hold your data; it can let you specify the *structure* of that data as well, and that's our next topic. This structuring is very important when you're dealing with complex data. For example, you could store a long account statement in HTML, but after the first ten pages or so, that data would be prone to errors. But in XML, you can actually build in the syntax rules that specify the structure of the document so that the document can be checked to make sure it's set up correctly.

This emphasis on the correctness of your data's structure is strong in XML, and it makes it easy to detect problems. In HTML, a Web author could (and frequently did) write sloppy HTML, knowing that the Web browser would take care of any syntax problems. In fact, some people estimate that 50% or more of the code in modern browsers is there to take care of sloppy HTML in Web pages. But things are different in XML. The software that reads your XML—called an *XML processor*—is supposed to check your document; if there's a problem, the processor is supposed to quit. It should let you know about the problem, but that's as far as it's supposed to go, according to W3C.

So how does an XML processor check your document? There are two main checks that XML processors make: checking that your document is *well-formed* and checking that it's *valid*. You'll see what these terms mean in more detail over the next few days, but you'll also take a look at them in overview here.

Creating Well-Formed XML Documents

What does it mean for an XML document to be well-formed? Formally, it means that the document must follow the syntax rules specified for XML by the W3C in the XML 1.0 recommendation or the XML 1.1 candidate recommendation. Although there are a fair number of requirements for a document to be well-formed, informally, the main requirements are that the document must contain one or more elements, and one element, the root element, must contain all the other elements. In addition, each element must nest inside any enclosing elements properly.

Here's an example of a nesting error—this document is not well-formed because the `</heading>` closing tag comes after the `<message>` opening tag, mixing up the `<heading>` and `<message>` elements:

```
<?xml version="1.0" encoding="UTF-8"?>
<?xml-stylesheet type="text/css" href="ch01_04.css"?>
<document>
```

```
    <heading>
        Hello From XML
    <message>
    </heading>
        This is an XML document!
    </message>
</document>
```

Creating well-formed documents is what Day 3, "Creating Well-Formed XML Documents," is all about.

Creating Valid XML Documents

An XML processor will usually check whether your XML document is well-formed, but only some are also capable of checking whether it's valid. An XML document is valid if it adheres to the syntax you've specified for it, and you can specify that syntax in either a *Document Type Definition (DTD)* or an *XML schema*. We'll see DTDs in Days 4 and 5, and XML schemas in Days 6 and 7.

As an example, you can see how you add a DTD to our XML document in Listing 1.7. DTDs can be separate documents, or they can be built into an XML document as we've done here using a special element named `<!DOCTYPE>`.

LISTING 1.7 An XML Document with a DTD (`ch01_07.xml`)

```
<?xml version="1.0" encoding="UTF-8"?>
<?xml-stylesheet type="text/css" href="ch01_04.css"?>
<!DOCTYPE DOCUMENT [
    <!ELEMENT document (heading, message)>
    <!ELEMENT heading (#PCDATA)>
    <!ELEMENT message (#PCDATA)>
]>
<document>
    <heading>
        Hello From XML
    </heading>
    <message>
        This is an XML document!
    </message>
</document>
```

We'll create DTDs like this one in Day 4, "Creating Valid XML Documents: Document Type Definitions"; briefly, the DTD in Listing 1.7 is the `<!DOCTYPE>` element, which specifies that the root element, `<document>`, should contain a `<heading>` element and a

`<message>` element. We're also specifying that the `<heading>` and `<message>` elements may contain text data. Using a DTD like this, you're able to specify the syntax your XML document should obey—what elements should be inside what other elements, what attributes an element can have, and so on—and if an XML processor can perform *validation*, it can check your document and head off problems (we'll validate this document tomorrow).

Today's discussion has introduced us to the basic XML concepts that we'll need for the coming days. Now it's time to start taking an in-depth look at how XML is used in the real world and what it's good for.

How XML Is Used in the Real World

As you already know, XML is designed to help store, structure, and transfer data; because it's written using plain text, it can be sent on the Internet and handled by software on many different platforms. XML was designed to let people circulate data. In its five years, hundreds of XML sublanguages—that is, sets of predefined XML elements—have appeared.

For example, suppose you want to perform genealogical research. To search through many genealogical records rapidly, you would need to have those records in a predetermined form, not just in any order in a simple text file. To do that, you could use a specialized XML sublanguage, Genealogical Data Communication (GEDCOM), which defines its own tags for storing names, dates, marriages, and so on. Using GEDCOM, people from all over the world can search genealogical databases rapidly.

XML sublanguages like GEDCOM are called *XML applications* (the term is a little unfortunate, because software packages are also called applications, but the idea is that these sublanguages are applications of XML). There are hundreds of XML applications, allowing various groups of people to communicate and exchange data. Here's a list of a few of these applications:

- Application Vulnerability Description Language (AVDL)
- Bank Internet Payment System (BIPS)
- Banking Industry Technology Secretariat (BITS)
- Common Business Library (xCBL)
- Connexions Markup Language (CNXML) for Modular Instructional Materials
- Electronic Business XML Initiative (ebXML)
- Extensible Access Control Markup Language (XACML)

- Financial Exchange (IFX)
- Financial Information eXchange protocol (FIX)
- Financial Products Markup Language (FpML)
- Genealogical Data Communication (GEDCOM)
- Geography Markup Language (GML)
- Global Justice's Justice XML Data Dictionary (JXDD)
- Human Resources Background Checks and Payroll Deductions Language (HR-XML)
- Product Data Markup Language (PDML)
- Schools Interoperability Framework (SIF)
- Telecommunications Interchange Markup (TIM)
- The Text Encoding Initiative (TEI)
- Windows Rights Management Services (RMS) by Microsoft
- XML Common Biometric Format (XCBF)
- XML Process Definition Language (XPDL) for workflow management

You can find information about XML applications like these by watching the XML news releases from W3C. The Web site `http://www.xml.org/xml/marketplace_company.jsp` also lists many XML applications. To get an idea of what's going on in XML these days, we'll take a look at a few of these applications next—and we're going to see more throughout this book.

Using XML: Mathematical Markup Language

Mathematical Markup Language, MathML, was designed to let people embed mathematical and scientific equations in Web pages (in fact, Tim Berners-Lee first developed the World Wide Web so that physicists could exchange papers and documents).

MathML is itself a W3C specification, and you can find it at `http://www.w3.org/TR/MathML2/`. Using MathML, you can display all kinds of equations, but there's only one commonly used Web browser that supports MathML—the Amaya browser, which is W3C's own testbed browser for testing new HTML elements. You can download Amaya for free from `http://www.w3.org/Amaya/`.

You can see a MathML document, `ch01_08.ml`, in Listing 1.8. This document just displays the equation $4x^2 - 5x + 6 = 0$.

LISTING 1.8 A MathML Document (ch01_08.ml)

```
<?xml version="1.0"?>
<math xmlns="http://www.w3.org/1998/Math/MathML">
    <mrow>
        <mrow>
            <mn>4</mn>
            <mo>&InvisibleTimes;</mo>
            <msup>
                <mi>x</mi>
                <mn>2</mn>
            </msup>
            <mo>-</mo>
            <mrow>
                <mn>5</mn>
                <mo>&InvisibleTimes;</mo>
                <mi>x</mi>
            </mrow>
            <mo>+</mo>
            <mn>6</mn>
        </mrow>
        <mo>=</mo>
        <mn>0</mn>
    </mrow>
</math>
```

You can see how this document looks in the Amaya browser in Figure 1.6.

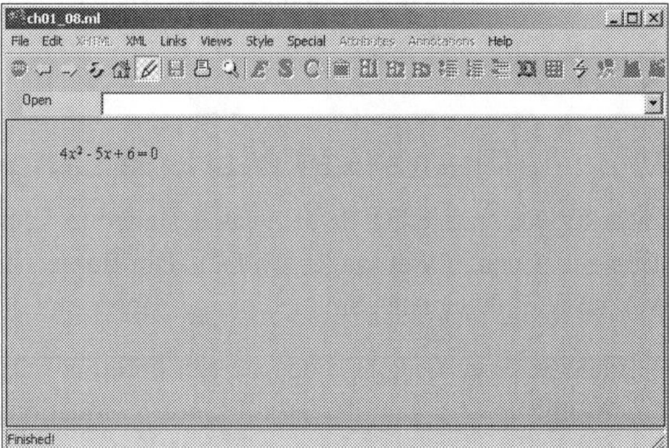

FIGURE 1.6
A MathML document displayed by the Amaya browser.

Using XML: Chemical Markup Language

Chemical Markup Language (CML) was developed by Peter Murray-Rust and lets you view three-dimensional representations of molecules in a Jumbo browser. Using CML, one chemist can publish a visual model of a molecule and exchange that model with others.

For example, this CML document, from the CML Web site at `http://www.xml-cml.org`, displays the formamide molecule:

```
<molecule xmlns="http://www.xml-cml.org" id="formamide">
<atomArray>
  <stringArray builtin="atomId">H1 C1 O1 N1 Me1 Me2</stringArray>
  <stringArray builtin="elementType">H C O N C C</stringArray>
  <integerArray builtin="hydrogenCount">0 1 0 1 3 3</integerArray>
  </atomArray>
  <bondArray>
  <stringArray builtin="atomRef">C1 C1 C1 N1 N1</stringArray>
  <stringArray builtin="atomRef">H1 O1 N1 Me1 Me2</stringArray>
  <stringArray builtin="order">1 2 1 1 1</stringArray>
  </bondArray>
  <h:html xmlns:h="http://www.w3.org/TR/html20">
  <p>Formamide is the simplest amide ...</p>
  <p>
  This represents a
  <emph>connection table</emph>
  for formamide. The structure corresponds to the diagram:
  </p>
  <pre>H3 H1 \ / N1-C1=O1 / H2</pre>
  </h:html>
  <float title="molecularWeight" units="g">45.03</float>
 <list title="local information">
 <!--
    <link title="safety" href="/safety/chemicals.xml#formamide">
    </link>
  -->
  <string title="location">Storeroom 12.3</string>
  </list>
</molecule>
```

We'll see CML at work tomorrow when we take a look at the Jumbo CML browser.

Using XML: Synchronized Multimedia Integration Language

Synchronized Multimedia Integration Language (SMIL, pronounced "smile") lets you customize multimedia presentations, and we'll take a look at SMIL in depth in this book. We'll even be able to create SMIL files that can be run in RealNetwork's RealPlayer (now called RealOne). SMIL is a W3C standard, and you can find more about at `http://www.w3.org/AudioVideo/#SMIL`.

For example, here's the beginning of a SMIL document that plays background music and displays a slide show of images and text:

```
<?xml version="1.0"?>
<!DOCTYPE smil PUBLIC "-//W3C//DTD SMIL 1.0//EN"
```

```
  "http://www.w3.org/TR/REC-smil/SMIL10.dtd">
<smil>
    <body>
        <par id="show">
            <audio src="river.wav" region="background_audio"
            type="audio/x-wav" dur="20s"/>
            <seq id="slides">
            <par id="slide01">
                <img src="mountain.jpg" type="image/jpeg" dur="5s"/>
                <text src="welcome.txt" type="text/plain" dur="5s"/>
            </par>
        .
        .
        .
```

Using XML: XHTML

Despite its popularity, W3C thinks there are a lot of problems with HTML—and, having created it, they should know. For example, some HTML elements don't need closing tags, but may be used with them, while others require closing tags. Many Web pages have all kinds of HTML errors, like overlapping elements, that Web browsers struggle to fix. To make HTML more rigorous, and in an attempt to let you extend it with your own tags, W3C introduced Extensible Hypertext Markup Language, or XHTML. XHTML is HTML 4.01 (the current version of HTML) in XML form. We'll be seeing XHTML in depth in Day 11, "Extending HTML with XHTML," and Day 12, "Putting XHTML to Work."

In other words, XHTML is simply an XML application that mimics HTML 4.0 in such a way that you can display the results—true XML documents—in today's Web browsers, as well as extending it with your own new elements. Here are some XHTML resources online:

- `http://www.w3.org/MarkUp/Activity.html`—The W3C Hypertext Markup activity page, which has an overview of XHTML
- `http://www.w3.org/TR/xhtml1/`—The XHTML 1.0 specification (in more common use than XHTML 1.1 today)
- `http://www.w3.org/TR/xhtml11/`—The XHTML 1.1 working draft of the XHTML 1.1 module-based specification

XHTML 1.0 comes in three different versions: transitional, frameset, and strict. The transitional version is the most popular version of XHTML because it supports HTML as it's used today. The frameset version supports XHTML documents that display frames. The strict version omits all the HTML elements considered obsolete in HTML 4.0 (of which there were quite a few).

XHTML 1.1 is a form of the XHTML 1.0 strict version made a little more strict by omitting support for some elements and adding support for a few more (such as `<ruby>` for annotated text). You can find a list of the differences between XHTML 1.0 and XHTML 1.1 at `http://www.w3.org/TR/xhtml11/changes.html#a_changes`.

As an example, you can see an XHTML 1.0 transitional document in Listing 1.9 called `ch01_09.html` (XHTML documents use the extension .html so they can appear in standard Web browsers—note that all the element names are in lowercase). We're going to take XHTML documents like this apart piece by piece in Days 11 and 12.

LISTING 1.9 An XHTML Document (`ch01_09.html`)

```
<?xml version="1.0"?>
<!DOCTYPE html PUBLIC "-//W3C//DTD XHTML 1.0 Transitional//EN"
"http://www.w3.org/TR/xhtml1/DTD/xhtml1-transitional.dtd">
<html xmlns="http://www.w3.org/1999/xhtml" xml:lang="en" lang="en">
    <head>
        <title>
            An XHTML Page
        </title>
    </head>

    <body>
        <h1>
            Welcome to XHTML!
        </h1>
        <center>
        <p>
        This is an XHTML document.
        </p>
        <p>
        Pretty cool, eh?
        </p>
        </center>
    </body>
</html>
```

You can see the results of this XHTML in Figure 1.7. Writing XHTML is a lot like HTML, except that you have to adhere to XML syntax (which means, for example, that every element has a closing tag) .

FIGURE 1.7

Displaying an XHTML page in Internet Explorer.

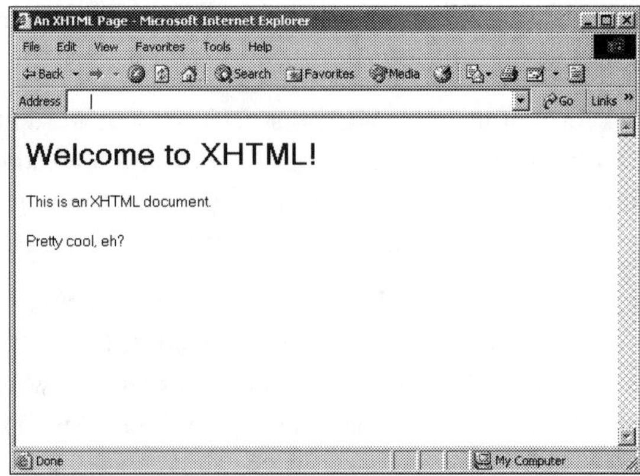

Using XML: HTML+TIME

Here's another XML application—HTML+TIME. This one was created by Microsoft, Macromedia, and Compaq as an alternative to SMIL for multimedia alternative. You can find out about HTML+TIME at `http://msdn.microsoft.com/workshop/Author/behaviors/time.asp`.

You can see a sample HTML+TIME document that displays the words `Welcome`, `to`, `HTML+TIME`, in Listing 1.10. If you open this document in Internet Explorer, you'll see that the words appear one at a time, separated by two seconds, and then the whole process repeats.

LISTING 1.10 An HTML+TIME Document (`ch01_10.html`)

```
<HTML>
    <HEAD>
        <TITLE>
            Using HTML+TIME
        </TITLE>
        <STYLE>
            .time {behavior: url(#default#time);}
        </STYLE>
    </HEAD>

    <BODY>
        <DIV CLASS="time" t:REPEAT="5" t:DUR="10" t:TIMELINE="par">
            <DIV CLASS="time" t:BEGIN="0" t:DUR="10">Welcome</DIV>
            <DIV CLASS="time" t:BEGIN="2" t:DUR="10">to</DIV>
            <DIV CLASS="time" t:BEGIN="6" t:DUR="10">HTML+TIME.</DIV>
        </DIV>
    </BODY>
</HTML>
```

You can see the results of this HTML+TIME document in Figure 1.8.

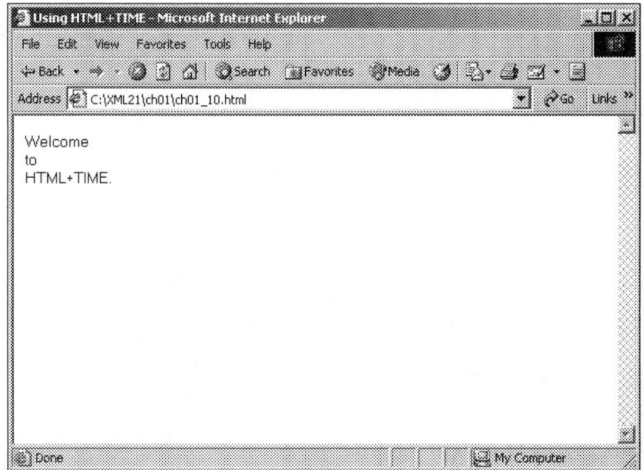

FIGURE 1.8
Viewing an HTML+TIME document in Internet Explorer.

Using XML: Microsoft's .NET

Microsoft's .NET initiative took what had been local Windows functionality to the Internet. Components in .NET use XML to communicate, often even when they're on the same machine. You don't usually see the XML in .NET, but each time you communicate between components, it's there.

For example, ADO.NET (ActiveX Data Objects) is the .NET protocol for working with databases, and all communication between your code and the data provider that hosts the database uses XML. You can see an example demonstrating how ADO.NET works using in Visual Basic .NET, one of the programming languages in Visual Studio .NET, in Figure 1.9.

When the user clicks the Write Data to XML Document button, the code connects to the SQL Server data provider, opens the sample database named `pubs` that comes with SQL Server, and reads the data in the employee table from that database using XML. It'll then write that data out to an XML document, `data.xml`. When the user clicks the Get Data from XML Document button, the code reads in that XML and displays the data in it in the grid you see in Figure 1.9.

Here is the Visual Basic .NET code that handles the button clicks and that does the actual work:

```
Private Sub Button1_Click(ByVal sender As System.Object, _
    ByVal e As System.EventArgs) Handles Button1.Click
    DataSet11.Clear()
    OleDbDataAdapter1.Fill(DataSet11)
```

```
    DataSet11.WriteXml("data.xml")
End Sub

Private Sub Button2_Click(ByVal sender As System.Object, _
    ByVal e As System.EventArgs) Handles Button2.Click
    Dim dataset As New DataSet()
    ds.ReadXml("data.xml")
    DataGrid1.SetDataBinding(dataset, "employee")
End Sub
```

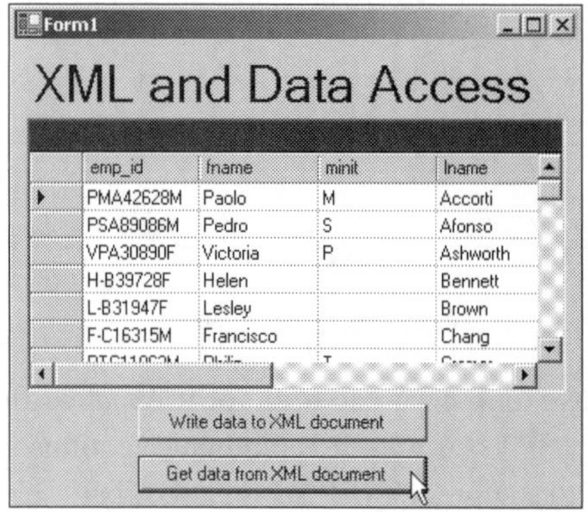

FIGURE 1.9
Writing data in XML in Visual Basic .NET.

And here is the XML that was written out to disk in `data.xml`—note that it matches the data you see in Figure 1.9:

```
<?xml version="1.0" standalone="yes"?>
<DataSet1 xmlns="http://www.tempuri.org/DataSet1.xsd">
  <employee>
    <emp_id>PMA42628M</emp_id>
    <fname>Paolo</fname>
    <minit>M</minit>
    <lname>Accorti</lname>
    <job_id>13</job_id>
    <job_lvl>35</job_lvl>
    <pub_id>0877</pub_id>
    <hire_date>1992-08-27T00:00:00.0000000-04:00</hire_date>
  </employee>
  <employee>
    <emp_id>PSA89086M</emp_id>
    <fname>Pedro</fname>
    <minit>S</minit>
    <lname>Afonso</lname>
    <job_id>14</job_id>
    <job_lvl>89</job_lvl>
```

```
    <pub_id>1389</pub_id>
    <hire_date>1990-12-24T00:00:00.0000000-05:00</hire_date>
  </employee>
        .
        .
        .
```

That's what the XML that's used to move data between components in XML looks like behind the scenes.

Using XML: Scalable Vector Graphics

A number of popular XML applications revolve around graphics, and one of these applications is Scalable Vector Graphics (SVG), a W3C-based XML application. Until recently, SVG found only limited support, notably because Microsoft had its own XML-style graphics language for Internet Explorer, Vector Markup Language (VML), followed by its DirectAnimation tools. Now, however, Adobe has created an SVG viewer as a browser plug-in, and we'll take a look at SVG and that plug-in in Day 13, "Creating Graphics and Multimedia: SVG and SMIL." You can find the SVG specification itself at `http://www.w3.org/TR/SVG11/`, and an SVG overview at `http://www.w3.org/Graphics/SVG/Overview.htm8`.

Millions of SVG viewers from Adobe have already been downloaded (Adobe calls SVG "the future of Web graphics") and you can get the SVG viewer at `http://www.adobe.com/svg/`. You can see a sample SVG document in Listing 1.11, which draws a blue ellipse filled in with light blue color.

LISTING 1.11 An SVG Document (`ch01_11.svg`)

```
<?xml version="1.0" encoding="UTF-8"?>
<svg xmlns="http://www.w3.org/2000/svg">
    <title>SVG Example</title>
    <ellipse cx="200" cy="100" rx="100" ry="60"
        style="fill:lightblue; stroke:blue; stroke-width:6"/>
</svg>
```

You can see `ch01_11.svg` at work in Figure 1.10, where we're using the Adobe SVG plug-in in Internet Explorer.

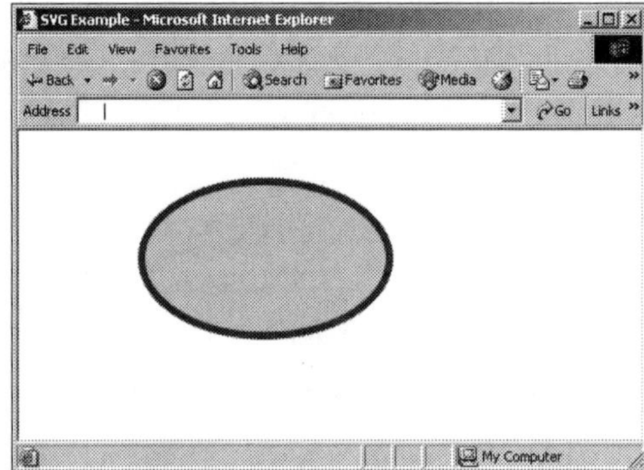

FIGURE 1.10
Viewing an SVG example.

Using XML: SOAP

These days, more and more Web applications are appearing every day. Based on the Internet, these programs can communicate with each other, transferring data back and forth as needed. For example, a Web application might provide real estate agents in the field with today's real estate listings, which they can download into their laptops.

One problem with Web applications is that they can end up using their own XML element sets only, making it difficult for a Web application written in Java to communicate with one written in a .NET language like Visual Basic .NET or C# .NET. To make communication between Web applications easier, the XML-based Simple Object Access Protocol (SOAP, which you can read about at `http://www.w3.org/TR/SOAP/`) was created. SOAP defines a widely accepted lightweight XML protocol that lets you send messages between Web applications, no matter what language such Web applications might have been written in.

You'll see more about SOAP in Day 18, "Working with SOAP and RDF," when you take a look at some examples. SOAP messages contain a SOAP envelope that acts like the root element of the message, a SOAP header that tells the recipient what kind of message this is, and a SOAP body that holds the message. For example, if you wanted to tell a Web application that there are currently 200 desks in stock in your warehouse, you might send a SOAP message like this:

```
<?xml version="1.0" encoding="UTF-8"?>
<soap:Envelope
    xmlns:soap="http://schemas.xmlsoap.org/soap/envelope/">
    <soap:Header>
        SOAP Example
    </soap:Header>
    <soap:Body>
        <desks:NumberInStock>
```

```
            200
        </desks:NumberInStock>
    </soap:Body>
</soap:Envelope>
```

NOTE

If you're a programmer familiar with object-oriented programming (OOP), you might be interested to know that another place SOAP is used when two different .NET applications—which might be written in different languages—want to send objects back and forth across application boundaries (a process called *remoting*). In that case, one application sends a SOAP message to the other describing the object that will be transferred.

That gives us a taste of how XML is put to use these days. Before finishing up today, we'll take a quick look at some of the rich XML resources available online—there's a great deal of free stuff out there for you.

Online XML Resources

There are plenty of XML resources available free on the Internet. For example, the XML specifications themselves are online, and although they are hard to read, they're the place to check if you want the ultimate answer on an XML question. Here's a list of official W3C Web sites on various XML topics (note that we won't see some of these topics until later in the book):

- `http://www.w3c.org/xml`—W3C's main XML site. A good place to start.
- `http://www.w3.org/XML/Activity`—The W3C activity page listing what's going on with XML these days.
- `http://www.w3.org/XML/1999/XML-in-10-points`—Features a mini-tutorial called "XML in 10 Points" (really only seven). Provides an XML overview.
- `http://www.w3.org/TR/REC-xml`—The official W3C recommendation for XML 1.0. Not easy to read. We're going to cover nearly all of this specification in this book.
- `http://www.w3.org/TR/xml11/`—The official W3C XML 1.1 candidate recommendation, which turns out to be still evolving (more than most W3C candidate recommendations at this stage have done in the past).
- `http://www.w3.org/Style/CSS/`—The W3C outline and overview of CSS programming.

- `http://www.w3.org/TR/REC-CSS1/`—The W3C CSS1 specification.
- `http://www.w3.org/TR/REC-CSS2/`—The W3C CSS2 specification.
- `http://www.w3.org/Style/XSL/`—The W3C XSL page.
- `http://www.w3.org/TR/xml-stylesheet/`—A resource on style sheets and XML.
- `http://www.w3.org/TR/REC-xml-names/`—An XML namespaces resource.
- `http://www.w3.org/Style/XSL/`—The details on Extensible Stylesheet Language.
- `http://www.w3.org/TR/xslt`—The details on XSL Transformations (XSLT).
- `http://www.w3.org/XML/Schema`—XML schema activity page.
- `http://www.w3.org/TR/xmlschema-0/`, `http://www.w3.org/TR/xmlschema-1/`, and `http://www.w3.org/TR/xmlschema-2/`—All about XML schemas.
- `http://www.w3.org/TR/xhtml1/`—The XHTML 1.0 specification.
- `http://www.w3.org/TR/xhtml11/`—The XHTML 1.1 specification.
- `http://www.w3.org/XML/Linking`—All about XML Pointer, XML Base, and XML Linking.
- `http://www.w3.org/TR/xlink/`—The XLinks specification.
- `http://www.w3.org/TR/xptr`—The XPointers specification.
- `http://www.w3.org/DOM/`—The W3C Document Object Model (DOM).
- `http://www.w3.org/MarkUp/Forms/`—XForms, a new version of Web forms of the kind that currently appear in HTML documents.
- `http://www.w3.org/TR/xmlbase/`—All about the XML Base specification.
- `http://www.w3.org/Encryption/2001/`—Discussion on XML encryption.
- `http://www.w3.org/2001/XKMS/`—The XML Key Management Working Group.
- `http://www.w3.org/XML/Query`—The XML Query specification.
- `http://www.w3.org/Signature/`—Deals with XML signature, an XML-compliant syntax used for representing the signature of Web resources.
- `http://www.w3.org/TR/xpath`—The XPath 1.0 recommendation.
- `http://www.w3.org/TR/xpath20/`—The XPath 2.0 working draft.

There are many, many non-W3C XML resources available as well, of course—just searching for "XML" on the Internet gives you about 18,300,000 matches, and more appear every day. Here's a list of some of the best of the non-W3C resources:

- `http://www.xml.com`—Packed with XML resources, discussions, and schedules of public events.

- `http://www.xml.org`—Carries information about XML in industrial and commercial settings. A reference site for XML vocabularies, DTDs, schemas, and namespaces.
- `http://www.oasis-open.org`—The Organization for the Advancement of Structured Information Standards, OASIS, hosting many XML application specifications.
- `http://msdn.microsoft.com/xml/default.asp`—Microsoft's own page on XML (note that Microsoft URLs are very volatile, and this URL might have changed by the time you look for it).

XML tutorials are also easy to find—a search for "XML Tutorial" turns up about 14,000 matches. Here's a starter list:

- `http://www.w3schools.com/xml/default.asp`—A free XML tutorial.
- `http://msdn.microsoft.com/xml/tutorial/default.asp`—Microsoft's XML tutorial in ten lessons (again, watch out—this URL might have changed by the time you read this).
- `http://xmlfiles.com/xml/`—An XML tutorial from XMLFiles.com.
- `http://www.webdeveloper.com/html/html_xml_1.html`—Webdeveloper.com's XML tutorial.
- `http://www.ucc.ie/xml/`—A comprehensive Frequently Asked Questions (FAQ) list about XML, maintained by some of the members of the W3C's XML Working Group.
- `http://www.xfront.com`—An XML schema tutorial by Roger L. Costello.

You might also find some Usenet newsgroups on XML to be helpful; here are a few (note that not all news servers will carry all these groups):

- `comp.text.xml`—A good, free-floating XML newsgroup. If you want answers, try posting your questions here.
- `microsoft.public.dotnet.xml`—Discussion on using XML in Microsoft's .NET initiative.
- `microsoft.public.xml`—The general XML newsgroup hosted by Microsoft.

That completes your introduction to XML today. Tomorrow, we'll start taking a look at creating XML documents in depth.

Summary

Today, you've gotten your introduction to XML and built the foundation you'll need in the coming days. We've covered a lot of ground, starting with a discussion of markup languages in general, seeing how "markup" refers to the codes that structure the data in a document.

XML was created in 1998 from an earlier markup language, SGML. XML is a specification of the World Wide Web Consortium, W3C, and the current form is XML 1.0, which became a W3C recommendation on October 6, 2000. XML 1.1 is now in candidate recommendation form.

The main reason XML has taken off is that it's great for storing data, in particular, for transferring data on the Internet. It's written in text form, which means it can be sent using existing Internet protocols. Unlike HTML, XML is meant for storing data, not displaying it.

XML documents begin with an XML declaration and can contain XML elements and text data. (Even so, you just got an introduction to the structure and components of an XML document today—that's what tomorrow's discussion is all about.) You also took a look at XML in browsers, and used Cascading Style Sheets to format XML for display in those browsers.

Besides using style sheets to format XML data, you also saw that XML processors can read and work with the data in XML documents. You got a quick look at working with XML using both JavaScript and Java today, and you'll get more details near the end of this book.

To be useful, XML documents must be well-formed so they can be read; being well-formed means obeying some basic rules of syntax, such as not overlapping elements. XML documents can also specify their own syntax with a Document Type Definition, DTD, or an XML schema. A document that adheres to its specified syntax is called valid.

You also spent much of today taking a look at XML applications—languages created using XML for specific purposes, such as MathML, Chemical Markup Language, SMIL, SVG, XHTML, and others, providing a real-world snapshot of how XML is used today, and how powerful it can be.

Q&A

Q Can I mix HTML and XML in the same Web page?

A Only one browser really supports mixed HTML/XML documents: Internet Explorer. You can embed XML in HTML pages using XML islands when you use Internet Explorer. We'll take a look at this in detail in Day 15.

Q Must a valid XML document also be well-formed?

A Yes. For an XML document to be well-formed, it has to satisfy the syntax you specify for it, and the first step in satisfying that syntax is to make sure that it satisfies the basic syntax rules for an XML document, which means it must be well-formed. However, a well-formed XML document isn't necessarily valid.

Workshop

This workshop tests whether you understand the concepts you saw today. It's a good idea to make sure you can answer these questions before pressing on to tomorrow's work.

Quiz

1. What's the main reason XML has become so popular in the last five years?
2. What are the four different types of specifications that W3C publishes?
3. What's an XML element? What's an XML attribute?
4. What are some of the requirements for an XML document to be well-formed?
5. What are two XML constructs that let you specify an XML document's syntax so it can be checked for validity?

PART I

DAY 2

Creating XML Documents

Yesterday you got an introduction to XML; today, you're going to get down to work by creating XML documents piece by piece. Here's an overview of today's topics:

- Writing XML
- The parts of an XML document
- XML prologs
- XML declarations
- Comments
- Processing instructions
- Elements
- CDATA sections
- Entities
- XML tools
- XML validators

You'll start creating XML documents at the logical beginning point—by choosing the correct software for this task.

Choosing an XML Editor

To create XML documents, you'll need a text editor of some kind, such as vi, emacs, pico, Macintosh's BBEdit or SimpleText, Windows Notepad, or WordPad. If you're using a fancy word processor like Microsoft Word, make sure that you save your XML documents in *plain text format*, not in some other format like .doc (for example, in Microsoft Word, you would select the "Text Only" option from the Save As Type drop-down list box in the Save As dialog). By default, XML files are given the extension .xml.

NOTE

Windows WordPad has the annoying habit of appending the extension .txt to a filename if it doesn't understand the extension you've given the file. That's not a problem with .xml files, because WordPad understands the extension .xml. However, if you try to save, for example, an XML-based Math Markup Language (MathML) document with the extension .ml, WordPad will give it the extension .ml.txt. To avoid that, surround the name of the file with quotation marks when you save it, as in `"equation5.ml"`. Also note that by default, WordPad saves files in rich text format (.rtf files) or as Microsoft Word .doc files, depending on your version of Windows. To make sure you save your XML documents in plain text format, select the Text Document option in the Save As Type drop-down list box in the Save As dialog.

As you advance in XML, however, you might find it easier to use a dedicated XML editor to create your XML documents. XML editors can check the syntax of your document as you create it, for example, or help you create DTDs and XML schemas. Here's a starter list of XML editors:

- Adobe FrameMaker (`http://www.adobe.com`)—Adobe includes good XML support in FrameMaker (but it's expensive).
- XML Pro (`http://www.vervet.com/`)—A powerful but fairly expensive XML editor.
- XML Writer (`http://xmlwriter.net/`)—An XML editor with a good interface.
- XML Notepad—Microsoft's free XML editor, no longer available from Microsoft, but still available from some other sites, such as `http://www.webattack.com/get/xmlnotepad.shtml`.

- Microsoft's Visual Studio .NET (the development environment for .NET languages like C# .NET and Visual Basic .NET) includes a powerful XML editor.
- XML Spy (`http://www.xmlspy.com/`)—One of the premier XML editors, with a good user interface, but also not free.
- XMLmind (`http://www.xmlmind.com/xmleditor/`)—Includes DTD- and XML Schema-aware editing commands, and a word processor-like view.

What do these XML editors look like in action? You can see XML Spy in Figure 2.1, XML Writer in Figure 2.2, XML Notepad in Figure 2.3, and an XML designer in Visual Studio .NET in Figure 2.4 (we're going to take a look at editing XML documents and creating XML schema in Visual Studio .NET in more detail in Day 21). If you're interested in XMLmind, you can find a screenshot at `http://www.xmlmind.com/xmleditor/`. Using one of these editors can help you a great deal in the long run, but to start, you only need a simple text editor that can store plain text files.

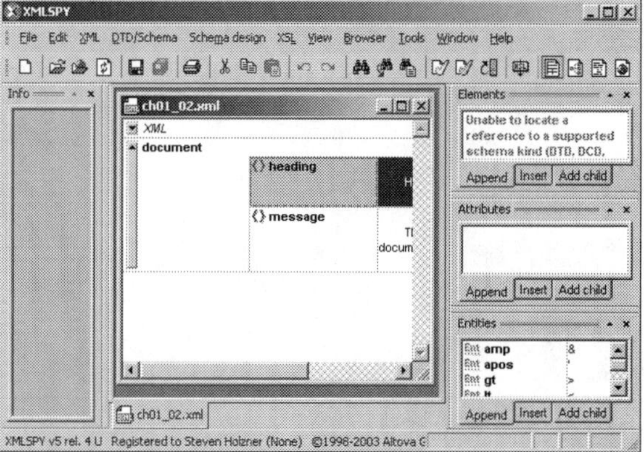

FIGURE 2.1
Using the XML Spy application.

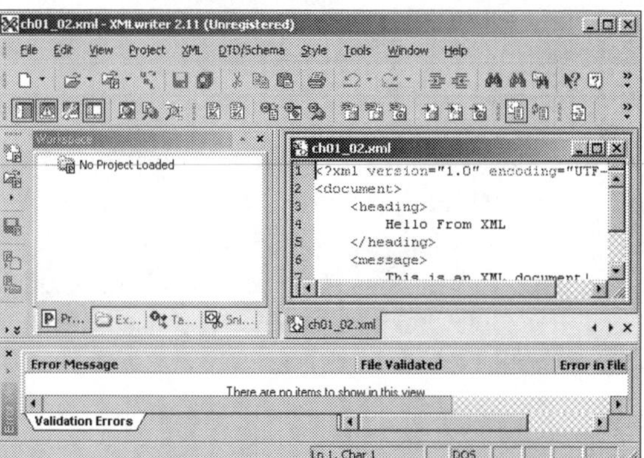

FIGURE 2.2
Using the XML Writer application.

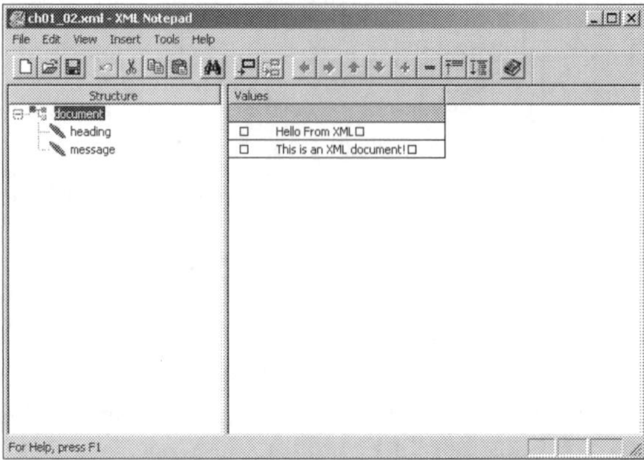

FIGURE 2.3
Using the XML Notepad application.

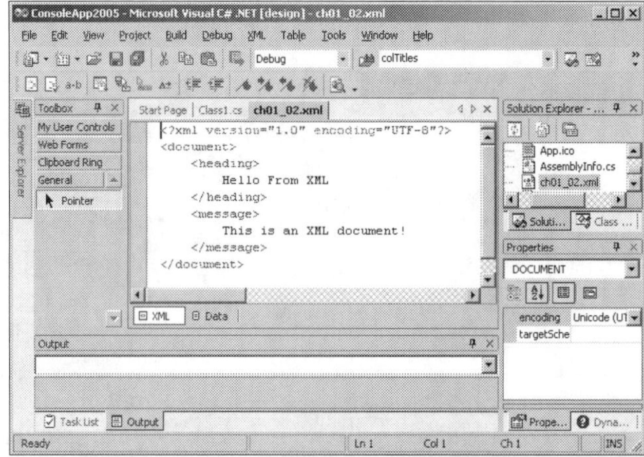

FIGURE 2.4
Using a Visual Studio XML designer.

After you've created your XML, you can take a look at it in XML-enabled browsers, as we'll do next.

Using XML Browsers

Calling a browser an XML browser means one of two things. As we've seen, a browser like Internet Explorer can display XML documents, and you can even use CSS or XSL to format those documents for display. However, displaying an XML document's data is one thing—making use of that data is another, and you do that in the second type of XML browser.

For example, with JavaScript you can access the data in an XML document in a browser like Internet Explorer, and you can also rewrite the HTML the browser will display. There are also dedicated XML browsers for some XML applications, and they can go far beyond HTML. We'll see one such example of a dedicated XML browser today—Jumbo, which displays XML documents using Chemical Markup Language (CML) to represent chemical molecules (and we'll build our own visual XML browser later in this book). We'll take a look at a few XML browsers now.

Using XML in Internet Explorer

Whether you love it or hate it, Microsoft's Internet Explorer is by far the most powerful general-purpose XML browser available today. You can get it at `http://www.microsoft.com/windows/ie/default.asp`.

The current version of Internet Explorer, version 6, is strongly XML-enabled, so we're going to see it frequently in this book. This doesn't imply a bias for or against Microsoft; it just means that there's no way to ignore this browser in a book on XML that aims to be as complete as possible. Internet Explorer can display XML documents directly, as we've already seen. It can use scripting languages like JavaScript (technically JScript, Microsoft's version of JavaScript) to access the data in an XML document and let you handle that data in code (including rewriting the HTML the browser displays, creating your own XML browser that displays your numeric data using bar graphs, and so on). It can also handle XML with both CSS and XSL style sheets, allowing you to format and display XML data as you like. It can validate XML documents using both DTDs and XML schemas (it's the only widely available browser that can use schemas). It can bind XML data to HTML controls like text boxes and buttons. There's even a special element, `<XML>`, that can load in XML documents automatically. We're going to see all this and more in this book.

Internet Explorer is not the only program that Microsoft has enabled for XML—XML is also used throughout the Microsoft Office suite of applications, and it's fundamental to the .NET initiative, as we're going to see towards the end of this book.

Using XML in Netscape Navigator

There's also some support for XML in the Netscape Navigator browser, which you can get at `http://channels.netscape.com/ns/browsers/default.jsp`. The current version is 7.0, and although this browser doesn't display raw XML documents in the same way that Internet Explorer does, you can use CSS style sheets to display XML documents in the Netscape Navigator, just as you can in Internet Explorer.

Using CML in Jumbo

Jumbo is a dedicated XML browser designed to display CML documents. You can get Jumbo free at `http://www.xml-cml.org/`. Jumbo can display XML (but not with style sheets), as well as using CML to draw molecules. There's an online version of Jumbo at `http://www.xml-cml.org/jumbo3/jumbo3-JS/jumbo.html`, and you can see it at work in Figure 2.5, drawing a picture of the ethanol molecule from CML.

FIGURE 2.5

Using the XML browser Jumbo to display the ethanol molecule.

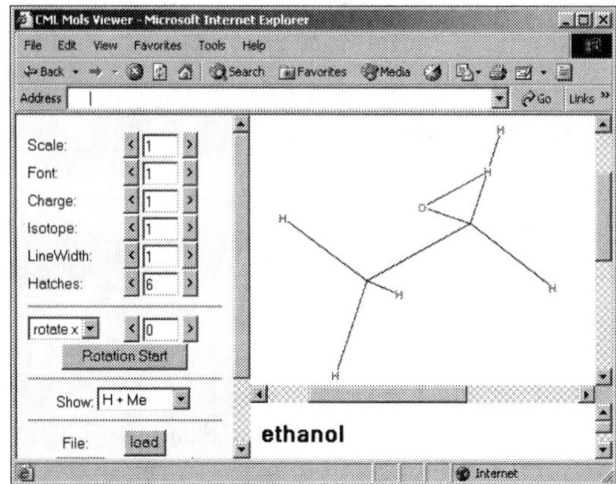

Besides XML browsers like these, other tools called validators let you check your XML after you've written it.

Using XML Validators

An XML *validator* checks your XML to make sure it's well formed and valid, giving you feedback if there's a problem. Here's a starter list of some validators on the Internet—note that your XML document must be online to use any of these validators, except for the Scholarly Technology Group validator, which can upload your XML document from your hard disk:

- `http://validator.w3.org/`—This is the official W3C HTML validator. It's designed for HTML, but also includes some XML support.
- `http://tidy.sourceforge.net/`—Tidy is a popular utility for cleaning up and repairing Web pages. It also includes some support for XML.
- `http://www.xml.com/pub/a/tools/ruwf/check.html`—This is XML.com's XML validator, based on the Lark XML processor.

- `http://www.ltg.ed.ac.uk/~richard/xml-check.html`—The Language Technology Group at the University of Edinburgh's validator, based on the RXP XML parser.
- `http://www.stg.brown.edu/service/xmlvalid/`—The home of the very useful XML validator from the Scholarly Technology Group at Brown University. This is one of only a few online XML validators that allows you to check XML documents that are not online—you can browse to your document on your hard disk and this validator will upload it.

2

You can see the Scholarly Technology Group's validator at work in Figure 2.6. To give it something to chew on, we'll send it the XML document from yesterday's work, where we've exchanged the `<message>` and `</heading>` tags like this:

```
<?xml version="1.0" encoding="UTF-8"?>
<?xml-stylesheet type="text/css" href="ch01_04.css"?>
<!DOCTYPE document [
    <!ELEMENT document (heading, message)>
    <!ELEMENT heading (#PCDATA)>
    <!ELEMENT message (#PCDATA)>
]>
<document>
    <heading>
        Hello From XML
    <message>
    </heading>
        This is an XML document!
    </message>
</document>
```

Note also that to let the validator actually validate the document, you have to let it know what the document's syntax is. To do that, we've included a DTD in this document specifying that syntax (DTDs are coming up in Day 4, "Creating Valid XML Documents: Document Type Definitions," and Day 5, "Handling Attributes and Entities in DTDs."

When you click the Validate button in the validator, you get the results that appear in Figure 2.7. As you see in the figure, the validator indicates that these two tags are indeed swapped, causing a validation error.

There's a built-in validator for documents with XML schema in Microsoft's Visual Studio .NET, and Internet Explorer can also validate documents with XML schemas. (As you'll see in more depth in Day 6, "Creating Valid XML Documents: XML Schemas," Visual Studio lets you generate an XML schema for an XML document with the XML, Create Schema menu item.) You can use the XML, Validate XML Data menu item to validate an XML document that uses a schema, as you see in Figure 2.8. Note the text `No validation errors were found` at the lower left, which is Visual Studio .NET's subtle way of telling you that the document is OK.

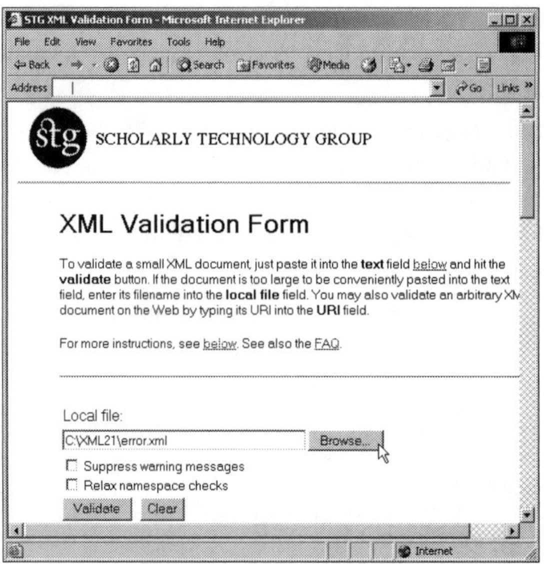

FIGURE 2.6

Using an XML validator.

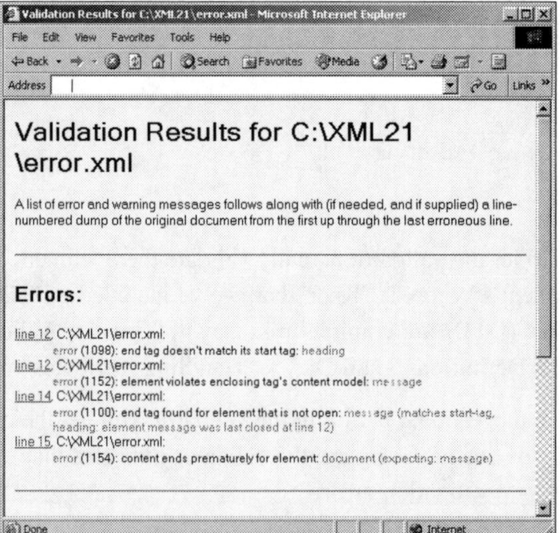

FIGURE 2.7

The results from an XML validator.

That gives you a good overview of the kinds of tools available to help you develop your XML these days—editors, browsers, and validators. Now it's time to get down to brass tacks and understand what makes an XML document tick, piece by piece.

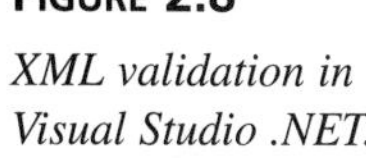

FIGURE 2.8

XML validation in Visual Studio .NET.

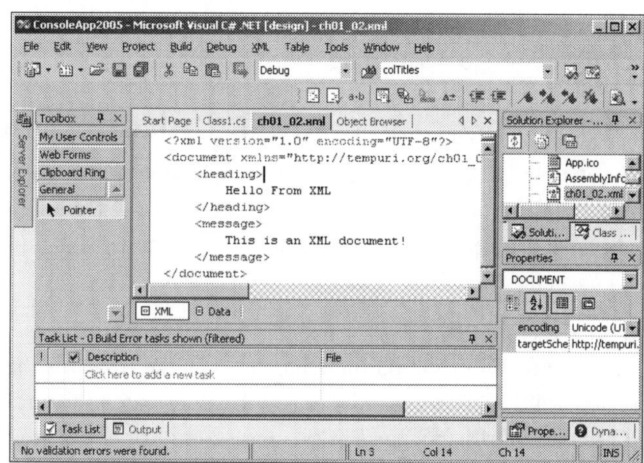

Creating XML Documents Piece by Piece

Yesterday, you created this example XML document:

```
<?xml version="1.0" encoding="UTF-8"?>
<document>
    <heading>
        Hello From XML
    </heading>
    <message>
        This is an XML document!
    </message>
</document>
```

That's a fully-functional XML document, but it's only an example. Today, we're going to be more systematic about what goes into an XML document, discussing all the possible parts of such documents. You'll take a look at these parts of an XML document in the coming sections:

- Prologs
- XML declarations
- Processing instructions
- Elements and attributes
- Comments
- CDATA sections
- Entities

W3C defines everything that can go into XML documents in the XML 1.0 and 1.1 specifications, right down to our starting point—the character set you use.

Character Encodings: ASCII, Unicode, and UCS

The characters in an XML document are stored using numeric codes. That can be an issue, because different character sets use different codes, which means an XML processor might have problems trying to read an XML document that uses a character set—called a *character encoding*—other than what it's used to.

For example, a common character encoding used by text editors is the American Standard Code for Information Interchange (ASCII). ASCII is the default for plain text files created with Windows WordPad. ASCII codes extend from 0 to 255—for example, the ASCII code for *A* is 65, for *B* is 66, and so on. So, if you stored the word *cat* in an XML document written in ASCII, the numbers 67, 65, and 84 are what would actually be stored. On the other hand, the World Wide Web is just that—worldwide. Plenty of character sets can't fit into the 256 characters of ASCII, such as Cyrillic, Armenian, Hebrew, Thai, Tibetan, and so on.

For that reason, W3C turned to Unicode (`http://www.unicode.org`), which holds 65,536 characters, not just 256 (although only about 40,000 Unicode codes are reserved at this point). To make things easier, the first 256 Unicode characters correspond to the ASCII character set.

There's another character encoding available that has even more space than Unicode—the Universal Character System (UCS, also called ISO 10646) uses 32 bits—two bytes—per character. This gives it a range of two billion symbols—and a good thing, too, since there are more Chinese characters alone than there is space in Unicode. UCS also encompasses the smaller Unicode character set—each Unicode character is represented by the same code in UCS, in much the same way that Unicode encompasses the smaller ASCII character set.

So which character sets are supported in XML? ASCII? Unicode? UCS? Unicode uses two bytes for each character, so a Unicode file would be twice as long as an ASCII file. For that and other reasons, it's difficult to convert much of the available software to Unicode. XML actually supports a compressed version of Unicode created by the UCS group called UCS Transformation Format-8 (UTF-8). UTF-8 includes all the ASCII codes unchanged, and uses a single byte for the most common Unicode characters. Any other Unicode characters need more than one byte (and can use up to six)—for example, the Unicode for Π is 03C0 in hexadecimal (960 in decimal), which you need to store in two bytes.

To make it easier to handle, UCS itself has also been compressed in the same way into a character set named UTF-16, which uses two bytes (instead of the normal four that UCS uses) for the most common characters, and more bytes for the less common characters.

W3C requires all XML processors to support both UTF-8 (compressed Unicode, including the full ASCII set), and UTF-16 (compressed UCS, including the full ASCII set), and those are the only two W3C requires. The UTF-8 encoding is the most popular one today in XML documents, because you can store documents in ASCII using a text editor and they can be treated, without any changes, as UTF-8 by an XML processor (ASCII uses one byte for characters, and UTF-8 uses one byte for the most common characters, including all the characters in the ASCII set). In fact, we've been using UTF-8 since our first XML example, as you can see where we've specified the character encoding for a document with the `encoding` attribute in the XML declaration:

```
<?xml version="1.0" encoding="UTF-8"?>
<document>
    <heading>
        Hello From XML
    </heading>
    <message>
        This is an XML document!
    </message>
</document>
```

UTF-8 is so widespread that an XML processor will assume you're using it if you omit the encoding attribute. Although W3C requires all XML processors to support UTF-16 and UTF-8 (so you can assign these values to the `encoding` attribute), most don't support UTF-16 yet.

NOTE

If you expressly save your documents in Unicode format (which a text editor like Windows WordPad will let you do), your text will use two bytes per character. This means you should specify UTF-16 encoding so that XML processors will be prepared to use two bytes for each character.

Although only UTF-8 and UTF-16 are required, there are many character encodings that an XML processor can support, such as the following:

- US-ASCII—U.S. ASCII
- UTF-8—Compressed Unicode
- UTF-16—Compressed UCS
- ISO-10646-UCS-2—Unicode

- ISO-10646-UCS-4—UCS
- ISO-2022-JP—Japanese
- ISO-2022-CN—Chinese
- ISO-8859-5—ASCII and Cyrillic

NOTE There are many more character sets available than mentioned here. For a more complete list, visit the Internet Assigned Numbers Authority (IANA) at `http://www.iana.org/assignments/character-sets`.

The increasing adoption of Unicode is the main driving force behind XML 1.1. There are three main areas in which XML 1.1 differs from XML 1.0, all having to do with characters:

- XML 1.1 accepts more Unicode characters than were available when XML 1.0 was created. (XML 1.0 was created when Unicode version 2.0 was current; now version 4.0 is being tested.)
- XML 1.1 relaxes some rules of creating names (as used for elements and attributes) to allow more Unicode characters, and to permit for Unicode expansion in the future.
- XML 1.1 permits more legal characters you can use to end a line.

You'll see these various points in more depth today. However, note that most of these differences are technical, and won't concern you a great deal. For example, XML 1.0 and 1.1 differ slightly in what character references you can use. As in HTML, *character reference* stands for a Unicode character and begins with `&`, followed by a numeric code specifying a character, and ends with `;`. You can either enter a Unicode character in an XML document as the character itself or as a character reference, which the XML processor will convert into the corresponding character.

For example, the Unicode for Π is 960 in decimal, so you can embed Π in your XML document by entering Π (if your text editor supports Unicode), or as the character reference `π` (if your text editor doesn't support Unicode). The XML processor will replace the character reference with Π. (You can also give the Unicode in hexadecimal if you preface it with an x, which would be `π` in this case.)

The difference between XML 1.0 and XML 1.1 as far as character references go is that XML 1.1 allows the use of character references `` through ``, most of which are forbidden in XML 1.0. Conversely, the character references `` through `Ÿ`, which were allowed as characters or character references in XML 1.0 documents, might only appear as character references in XML 1.1. These kinds of relatively small differences aren't going to concern us a great deal. For all these details, check the XML 1.1 candidate recommendation itself.

That's given us a handle on the character encodings you can use to create XML documents. The next step is to see just how you put those characters to work in XML as you create markup and text data.

Understanding XML Markup and XML Data

At their most basic level, XML documents are combinations of markup and text data. They might also include binary data one day, but there's no way to include binary data in an XML document at the moment. (If you want to associate binary data with an XML document, you keep that data external to the document and use an entity reference, as you'll see later today and in Day 5 in detail.)

The markup in a document gives it its structure. *Markup* includes start tags, end tags, empty element tags, entity references, character references, comments, CDATA section delimiters (more about CDATA sections in a few pages), document type declarations, and processing instructions. What about the data in an XML document? All the text in an XML document that is not markup is data.

Although the markup we've seen has mostly consisted of tags up to this point, there's another type of markup that doesn't use tags—*general entity references* and *parameter entity references*. Whereas tags begin with < and end with >, general entity references start with `&` and end with ; (as with the character references we've already seen, which are general entity references—for example, if you're using the UTF-16 encoding, `π` is a character reference for Π). General entity references are replaced by the entity they refer to when the document is parsed. *Parameter entity references*, which start with `%` and end with ;, are used in DTDs, as we'll see in Days 4 and 5.

For example, the markup `<` is a general entity reference that is turned into a < (less than) symbol when parsed by an XML processor, and the general entity reference `>` is turned into a > (greater than) symbol when parsed by an XML processor. You can see an example using these general entity references in Listing 2.1.

LISTING 2.1 Using an Entity Reference (ch02_01.xml)

```
<?xml version="1.0" encoding="UTF-8"?>
<document>
    <heading>
        Hello From XML
    </heading>
```

LISTING 2.1 continued

```
    <message>
        This text is inside a &lt;message&gt; element.
    </message>
</document>
```

You can see ch02_01.xml in Internet Explorer in Figure 2.9. As you can see in the figure, the markup < was turned into a <, and the markup > was turned into a > by the XML processor.

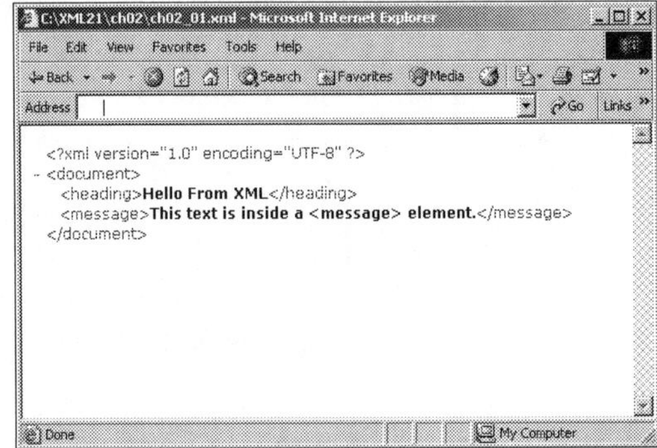

FIGURE 2.9
Using markup in Internet Explorer.

Besides character entity references, where a character code is replaced by the character it stands for, there are five predefined general entity references in XML, which are used when browsers might otherwise assume that they're part of markup to be interpreted:

- <—Replaced with <
- >—Replaced with >
- &—Replaced with &
- "—Replaced with "
- '—Replaced with '

You can also create your own general entity references, which we'll do in Day 5.

When an XML processor parses your XML, it replaces general entity references like > with the entity those references stand for, which is > in this case. Before it's parsed, text data is called *character data*; after it's been parsed and general entity references have been replaced with the entities they refer to, the text data is called *parsed character data*.

2

Using Whitespace and Ends of Lines

Spaces, carriage returns, line feeds, and tabs are all treated as *whitespace* in XML. That means that to an XML processor, this XML document:

```
<?xml version="1.0" encoding="UTF-8"?>
<document>
<heading>
Hello From XML
</heading>
<message>
This is an XML document!
</message>
</document>
```

is the same as this one, in terms of content:

```
<?xml version="1.0" encoding="UTF-8"?>
<document>heading>Hello From XML</heading>
<message>This is an XML document!</message></document>
```

You can use a special attribute named `xml:space` in an element to indicate that you want whitespace to be preserved by XML processors (not all XML processors will support this attribute). You can set this attribute to `"default"` to indicate that the default handling of whitespace is OK for the current element and all contained elements, or `"preserve"` to indicate that you want all applications to preserve whitespace as it is in the document. This is useful if the XML processor is going to display the XML document visually:

```
<?xml version="1.0" encoding="UTF-8"?>
<document xml:space="preserve">
    <heading>
        Hello From XML
    </heading>
    <message>
        This is an XML document!
    </message>
</document>
```

NOTE

> When you start using JavaScript or Java code that supports the W3C Document Object Model (DOM, which you can read about at `http://www.w3.org/DOM/`) to navigate through an XML document, you'll see that the whitespace between the elements in a document also counts (it's considered a whitespace *node*, and to get to a following element node, you have to navigate past whitespace nodes).

In XML 1.0, lines officially end with a linefeed character (ASCII and UTF-8 code 10—the Unix way of ending lines). In MS DOS and some Windows programs, lines can end with a carriage return (ASCII and UTF-8 code 13) linefeed pair, but when parsed by an XML processor, that pair (codes 13 and 10) is converted into a single linefeed (ASCII and UTF-8 code 10). In XML 1.1, which is mostly about expanding the character sets you can use, XML 1.0 was considered to discriminate against the conventions used on IBM and IBM-compatible mainframes. That means that in XML 1.1, the acceptable line endings that XML processors are supposed to convert to `
` are expanded to include the following:

- The two-character sequence `

`
- The two-character sequence `
 …` (`…` is the New Line (NEL) character in many mainframes.)
- The single character `…`
- The single character ` ` (This is the Unicode line separator character.)
- Any `
` character not immediately followed by `
` or `…`.

That brings us up through the basic structure of an XML document—markup and data. Now it's time to actually start putting markup and data to work as you start creating XML documents.

Creating Prologs

Prologs appear at the beginning of XML documents, and contain information about the rest of the document. A prolog can contain XML declarations, XML comments (which describe the document), processing instructions, whitespace, and doctype declarations (doctype declarations are DTDs, which we'll see in Days 4 and 5). You don't need a prolog in an XML document for the document to be well formed. However, W3C says you should include at least an XML declaration in all XML documents.

There's a sample prolog at the beginning of this XML document containing an XML declaration, a processing instruction, and a DTD (which is stored in a `<!DOCTYPE>` element):

```
<?xml version = "1.0"?>
<?xml-stylesheet type="text/css" href="ch_02.css"?>
<!DOCTYPE document [
<!ELEMENT document (employee)*>
<!ELEMENT employee (name, hiredate, projects)>
<!ELEMENT name (lastname, firstname)>
<!ELEMENT lastname (#PCDATA)>
<!ELEMENT firstname (#PCDATA)>
```

```
<!ELEMENT hiredate (#PCDATA)>
<!ELEMENT projects (project)*>
<!ELEMENT project (product,id,price)>
<!ELEMENT product (#PCDATA)>
<!ELEMENT id (#PCDATA)>
<!ELEMENT price (#PCDATA)>
]>
<document>
    <employee>
        <name>
            <lastname>Kelly</lastname>
            <firstname>Grace</firstname>
        </name>
        <hiredate>October 15, 2005</hiredate>
        <projects>
            <project>
                <product>Printer</product>
                .
                .
                .
```

The first item in a prolog should always be an XML declaration, and you'll take a look at this item next.

Creating an XML Declaration

XML declarations tell XML processors what version of XML you're using, what character encoding the document is written in, and so on. According to W3C, all XML documents should start with an XML declaration, which should be the first line in an XML document. You can also have XML document *fragments* in some cases, which don't start with an XML declaration, although such fragments are losing support. Here's a sample XML declaration:

```
<?xml version = "1.0" standalone="yes" encoding="UTF-8"?>
```

The XML declaration uses the `<?xml?>` element. In earlier drafts of XML, it was `<?XML?>`, but was made lowercase in the final recommendation—it's an error to use uppercase. There are three possible attributes you can use in the XML declaration:

- `version`—The XML version; currently, only 1.0 or 1.1 is possible here, and most XML processors do not support 1.1 yet. This attribute is required if you use an XML declaration.
- `encoding`—The language encoding for the document. As discussed earlier today, the default here is UTF-8. You can also use Unicode, UCS, and many other character sets, such as ISO character sets. This attribute is optional.

- `standalone`—Set to `"yes"` if the document does not refer to any external documents or entities, `"no"` otherwise. This attribute is optional.

NOTE

> Theoretically, the `encoding` attribute in an XML declaration lets the XML processor know what character encoding you're using, but that raises an obvious problem—to determine the character encoding, you must be able to read the document, at least as far as the `encoding` attribute in the XML declaration. In practice, XML processors sometimes scan XML documents that they can't figure out, searching for typical character sequences when an unusual character encoding is used. W3C respects that, and is sometimes careful about what character sequences it allows in XML to avoid confusing XML processors scanning documents to determine character encoding.

Creating XML Comments

You can use *comments* to include explanatory and descriptive notes in a document. Comments are ignored by XML parsers and may appear anywhere in a document outside other XML markup. XML comments look very much like HTML comments. As in HTML, you start a comment with `<!--` and end it with `-->`. Here's an example:

```
<?xml version="1.0" encoding="UTF-8"?>
    <!--Here comes the document element...-->
<document>
    <!--The next element contains a heading.-->
    <heading>
        Hello From XML
    </heading>
    <!--The next element contains the actual message.-->
    <message>
        This is an XML document!
    </message>
</document>
```

The text inside a comment is ignored by XML processors (unless, with some XML processors, that text includes markup, which is sometimes mistakenly treated as markup).

You're only supposed to use comments outside markup—for example, this is not legal:

```
<?xml version="1.0" encoding="UTF-8"?>
<document >
    <heading <!--This is the heading element-->>
        Hello From XML
    </heading>
    <message>
        This is an XML document!
    </message>
</document>
```

You should not use the character sequence -- in the text of a comment, because when some XML processors see that sequence, they assume the comment is ended. For example, don't do this:

```
<?xml version="1.0" encoding="UTF-8"?>
<document >
    <heading>
        Hello From XML
    </heading>
    <!--This is our--friendly--message element-->
    <message>
        This is an XML document!
    </message>
</document>
```

In particular, the XML 1.0 specification says that comments cannot end with the sequence --->. Also, comments cannot come before an XML declaration (nothing can). So this usage is not legal:

```
<!--This document contains a message.-->
<?xml version="1.0" encoding="UTF-8"?>
<document >
    <heading>
        Hello From XML
    </heading>
    <message>
        This is an XML document!
    </message>
</document>
```

It's also worth knowing that in most XML processors, you can use comments to exclude sections of a document from being treated as markup. For example, here's how you might remove the <heading> element as far as an XML processor is concerned:

```
<?xml version="1.0" encoding="UTF-8"?>
<document >
<!--
    <heading>
        Hello From XML
    </heading>
-->
    <message>
        This is an XML document!
    </message>
</document>
```

2

As far as most XML processors are concerned, here's what the content of this XML document looks like:

```
<?xml version="1.0" encoding="UTF-8"?>
<document >
    <message>
        This is an XML document!
    </message>
</document>
```

Creating Processing Instructions

As you can gather from their names, processing instructions are instructions to the XML processor, not general data-handling items like elements. XML doesn't come with any processing instructions built-in; it's up to your XML processor to support the ones it uses. For example, a common processing instruction is `<?xml-stylesheet?>` (supported by browsers like Netscape Navigator and Internet Explorer), but that's not an official W3C processing instruction built into XML. In other words, processing instructions must be understood by the XML processor, so they're processor-dependent.

Processing instructions start with `<?` and end with `?>`. The only restriction here is that you can't use `<?xml?>` (or `<?XML?>`, which is also reserved). We saw an example processing instruction yesterday in `ch01_03.xml`, where we used `<?xml-stylesheet?>` to connect a CSS style sheet to that XML document:

```
<?xml version="1.0" encoding="UTF-8"?>
<?xml-stylesheet type="text/css" href="ch01_04.css"?>
<document>
    <heading>
        Hello From XML
    </heading>
    <message>
        This is an XML document!
    </message>
</document>
```

Keep in mind that processing instructions like this one are not built into XML, but have been agreed upon by various browser manufacturers.

Now we've seen all that an XML prolog can contain, except for DTDs: XML declarations, comments, processing instructions, and whitespace. Next up is the actual meat of XML documents—storing your data using tags and elements.

Creating Tags and Elements

You give structure to the data in an XML document using elements. An XML element consists of a start tag and an end tag—except in the case of elements that are defined to be empty, which consist only of one tag—and might include character data and/or other elements. We've already seen both tags and elements in action.

Creating Tag Names

In XML 1.0, the names you give to a tag, like "message" in the tag <message>, are tightly controlled. You can start a tag name with a letter, an underscore, or a colon. The next characters might be letters, digits, underscores, hyphens, periods, and colons (but no whitespace).

In XML 1.1, things have changed. Instead of saying that everything not permitted is forbidden, XML 1.1 names are designed so that everything that is not forbidden is permitted. The idea is that because Unicode will continue to grow, further changes to XML can be avoided by allowing almost any character, including those not yet assigned, in names.

Formally speaking, in XML 1.1 you can start a name with :, A to Z, _, a to z, or the Unicode characters À to ˿, Ͱ to #x37D;, Ϳ to ῿, ‌ to #x200D;, ⁰ to ↏, Ⰰ to ⿯, 、 to ퟿, and 豈 to . This excludes -, ., and digits. The next characters in a name may include all the characters you can start a name with, as well as -, ., 0 to 9, ·, ̀ to ͯ, and ‿ to ⁀.

TIP

Although the XML 1.0 recommendation doesn't say so, it's best to avoid using colons in tag names, because you use a colon when specifying namespaces in XML, as you'll see tomorrow.

For example, here are some allowable XML tags:

```
<DOCUMENT>
<document>
<Chapter15>
<Section-19>
<_text>
```

Bear in mind that tag names are case sensitive, so <PUMPKIN> is not the same as <pumpkin>, which is not the same as <PuMpKiN>. Actually, your document can have <PUMPKIN>, <pumpkin>, and <PuMpKiN> tags at the same time, and they would all be considered different. Here are some tags that are not legal in XML:

```
<2005>
<Loan Number>
<.text>
<*yay*>
<EMPLOYEE(ID)>
```

So far, the elements you've seen have all contained data or other elements, but elements don't need to contain any content at all if they're empty.

Creating Empty Elements

In XML, *empty elements* only have one tag, not a start and end tag. You might be familiar with empty elements from HTML; for example, the HTML `<img>`, `<li>`, `<hr>`, and `<br>` elements are empty, which is to say that they do not enclose any content (either character data or markup). Empty elements are represented with only one tag (in HTML, there is no closing `</img>`, `</li>`, `</hr>`, and `</br>` tags).

In XML, you close an empty element with `/>`, not just `>`. For example, if the `<heading>` element were an empty element, it might appear like this in an XML document:

```
<?xml version="1.0" encoding="UTF-8"?>
<document>
    <heading/>
    <message>
        This is an XML document!
    </message>
</document>
```

Empty elements can have attributes, as in this case, where we're using an attribute named `text` to hold the text content of this element:

```
<?xml version="1.0" encoding="UTF-8"?>
<document>
    <heading text = "Hello From XML"/>
    <message>
        This is an XML document!
    </message>
</document>
```

The `<.../>` syntax is XML's way of making sure that an XML processor isn't left searching for a nonexistent closing tag. In fact, in XHTML, which is the derivation of HTML in XML, the `<img>`, `<li>`, `<hr>`, and `<br>` elements are used as `<img />`, `<li />`, `<hr />`, and `<br />`, and HTML browsers don't have a problem with that.

Creating a Root Element

If you want your document to be well formed, it must have one element that contains all the other elements and text data in the document—the root element, also called the document element. In our sample XML file, the document element happens to be named `<document>`, although you can use any legal name.

Each well-formed XML document must contain one element that contains all the other elements, and the containing element is called the *root element*. The root element is a very important part of XML documents, especially when you look at them from an XML processor's point of view, because you parse XML documents starting with the root element. In `ch02_01.xml`, developed at the start of this chapter, the root element is the `<document>` element (although you can give the root element any name):


```
<?xml version="1.0" encoding="UTF-8"?>
<?xml-stylesheet type="text/css" href="ch01_04.css"?>
<document>
    <heading>
        Hello From XML
    </heading>
    <message>
        This is an XML document!
    </message>
</document>
```

Creating Attributes

XML attributes, which can appear in elements, processing instructions, and XML declarations, work much like attributes in HTML. In XML, you use them in pairs like this: `attributename = "value"` in opening tags. Unlike HTML, note that the values you assign to attributes must be quoted (even if they're numbers), and that if you use an attribute, it must be assigned a value. (Some HTML attributes, like `BORDER`, don't need to be assigned a value.) Using DTDs or XML schemas, you can make an attribute required or optional—if required, you must use the attribute when you use the corresponding element, and you must assign the attribute a value. You can also specify what values an attribute may be assigned, if you want to.

You can see an example in Listing 2.2, where we've given each `<employee>` element an attribute named `status`, and are assigning the text `"retired"`, `"active"`, and `"leave"` to that attribute in various places in the document.

Listing 2.2 Using Attributes in an XML Document (`ch02_02.xml`)

```
<?xml version = "1.0" standalone="yes"?>
<document>
    <employee status="retired">
        <name>
            <lastname>Kelly</lastname>
            <firstname>Grace</firstname>
        </name>
```

LISTING 2.2 continued

```
            <hiredate>October 15, 2005</hiredate>
            <projects>
                <project>
                    <product>Printer</product>
                    <id>111</id>
                    <price>$111.00</price>
                </project>
                <project>
                    <product>Laptop</product>
                    <id>222</id>
                    <price>$989.00</price>
                </project>
            </projects>
        </employee>
        <employee status="active">
            <name>
                <lastname>Grant</lastname>
                <firstname>Cary</firstname>
            </name>
            <hiredate>October 20, 2005</hiredate>
            <projects>
                <project>
                    <product>Desktop</product>
                    <id>333</id>
                    <price>$2995.00</price>
                </project>
                <project>
                    <product>Scanner</product>
                    <id>444</id>
                    <price>$200.00</price>
                </project>
            </projects>
        </employee>
        <employee status="leave">
            <name>
                <lastname>Gable</lastname>
                <firstname>Clark</firstname>
            </name>
            <hiredate>October 25, 2005</hiredate>
            <projects>
                <project>
                    <product>Keyboard</product>
                    <id>555</id>
                    <price>$129.00</price>
                </project>
                <project>
                    <product>Mouse</product>
                    <id>666</id>
                    <price>$25.00</price>
```

LISTING 2.2 continued

```
            </project>
        </projects>
    </employee>
</document>
```

You can see this XML document in Internet Explorer, including the attributes and their values, in Figure 2.10.

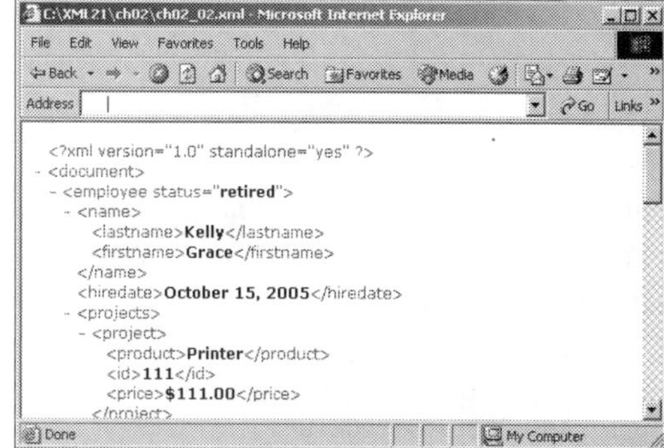

FIGURE 2.10
Viewing element attributes in Internet Explorer.

Just like the data in an element, an XML processor can retrieve the values you've assigned to an element's attributes. We'll see how to do that in both JavaScript and Java later in this book.

Attributes hold data, and elements hold data—so when should you use which? It's up to you, but practically speaking, there are two things to take into account. The first is that you can't specify document structure using attributes. For example, this `<employee>` element makes it clear what data you're storing about an employee:

```
<employee status="retired">
    <name>
        <lastname>Kelly</lastname>
        <firstname>Grace</firstname>
    </name>
    <hiredate>October 15, 2005</hiredate>
    <projects>
        <project>
            <product>Printer</product>
            <id>111</id>
            <price>$111.00</price>
        </project>
        <project>
            <product>Laptop</product>
            <id>222</id>
```

```
            <price>$989.00</price>
        </project>
    </projects>
</employee>
```

A good rule to follow, therefore, is to use elements to structure your document, and to use attributes when you have more information to include *about* a specific element, as when you want to indicate the language the enclosed text is in. Here's an example where we're storing the standard abbreviation for U.S. English, `"en-US"`, in an attribute:

```
<text language="en-US">
It was a dark and stormy night. A shot rang out!
.
.
.
</text>
```

Also, it's worth noting that using too many attributes can make a document hard to read, something you'll readily see if you start converting the earlier `<employee>` element to use attributes rather than subelements to hold its data:

```
<employee status="retired">
    <name lastname="Kelly" firstname="Grace"/>
    <hiredate>October 15, 2005</hiredate>
    <projects>
        <project product="Printer" id="111" price="$111.00"/>
            .
            .
            .
```

Naming Attributes

In XML, attribute names must follow the same rules as those for element names. That means in XML 1.0 you can start an attribute name with a letter, an underscore, or a colon, and the next characters may be letters, digits, underscores, hyphens, periods, and colons (but no whitespace). In XML 1.1, you follow the rules for XML 1.1 names, as discussed earlier today.

Here are some legal attribute name examples:

```
<brush width="10" height="5" color="cyan"/>
<point x="10" y="100"/>
<book title="My Sweet Summer" review="Yuck!"/>
<vegetable name="broccoli" color="green"/>
```

Here are some attribute names that are not legal:

```
<fish measured length="500"/>
<friend 1stPhone="555.2222" 2ndPhone="555.3333"/>
<application .NET="yes"/>
<person name(or nick name)="sammy"/>
```

Assigning Values to Attributes

As noted, all data in XML documents is text, including the data you assign to attributes. Even when you assign a number to an attribute, you treat that number as if it were text:

```
<constant name="pi" value="3.1415926"/>
```

You can use single or double quotation marks when quoting an attribute's value. By convention, double quotation marks are usually used, but if the value you're quoting contains double quotation marks—for example, `He said, "No worries."`—you can't just surround that value with double quotation marks, because the XML processor won't understand where the quotation begins and ends. Instead, you can use single quotation marks to begin and end the attribute's value like this:

```
<citation text='He said, "No worries."' />
```

What if the attribute value contains both single *and* double quotes, as when you want to say `The tree was 16' 3" tall`? In this case, you can use the XML-defined general entity references for a single quotation mark, `'` and for a double quotation mark, `"`, like this:

```
<citation text="The tree was 16&apos; 3&quot; tall" />
```

The XML processor will turn this back into `The tree was 16' 3" tall` when it parses this text.

Specifying Language with the `xml:lang` Attribute

Besides `xml:space`, there's one more attribute that comes built into XML—`xml:lang`, which lets you specify the language of a document, such as English, German, and so on. Although `xml:space` and `xml:lang` are "built into" XML, and so should be usable with any element, some XML processors will not support these attributes.

You can set the `xml:lang` attribute to these values:

- A two-letter language code as defined by the International Organization for Standardization (ISO) document 639:1988, "Code for the Representation of Names of Languages."
- A language identifier registered with the Internet Assigned Numbers Authority (IANA) in the document "Registry of Language Tags." See `http://www.isi.edu/in-notes/iana/assignments/languages/`. Such identifiers begin with the prefix "i-" (or "I-").
- A language identifier assigned by you, or for private use. Such identifiers should begin with "x-" or "X-".

2

Here is an example; in this case, we're specifying that the language of an element should be English, using the `xml:lang` attribute and the ISO language code `"en"`:

```
<p xml:lang="en">The quick brown fox jumped over the lazy dog.</p>
```

Besides specifying the language, you can also specify a language subcode to indicate a regional variation or dialect, such as U.S. English. These subcodes are two characters each, and they're also defined by the International Organization for Standardization in the document ISO 3166-1:1997, "Codes for the Representation of Names of Countries and Their Subdivisions—Part 1: Country Codes." For example, here's how you might specify that one element holds British English content, and one American English:

```
<p xml:lang="en-GB">What colour is the sky?</p>
<p xml:lang="en-US">What color is the sky?</p>
```

Note that `xml:lang` specifies the language used in both the element's content (including all text data, if you use `xml:lang` in the document element), as well as an element's attribute values, as here, where we're using German in an element's attributes:

```
<p farbe="weiss" xml:lang="de">
```

Creating CDATA Sections

When an XML processor parses an XML document, it interprets the markup in that document and replaces entity references (like the built-in general entity reference `"`) with whatever those entity references refer to (which is a double quotation mark, `"`, for the general entity reference `"`). On the other hand, sometimes you might not want text data parsed—for example, what if your text contains many `<` and `&` characters? When parsed, those characters will be interpreted as part of the markup unless you convert them to `<` and `&`, which is called *escaping* them. To avoid that, you can specify that you don't want the XML processor to parse part of your text data by placing it in a *CDATA section*. CDATA stands for character data, as opposed to parsed character data, which is PCDATA.

You use the CDATA section to tell the XML processor to leave the enclosed text alone, and pass it on unchanged. You start a CDATA section with the markup `<![CDATA[` and end it with `]]>`.

> **NOTE**
>
> Note that CDATA sections *are* read by the XML processor, but only because it searches for the ending text `]]>`. Among other things, this means that you cannot include the text `"]]>"` inside a CDATA section—and it also means that you cannot nest CDATA sections.

For example, suppose you are documenting how your XML application works, and want to say this:

```
Here's how the element starts:

    <employee status="retired">
        <name>
            <lastname>Kelly</lastname>
            <firstname>Grace</firstname>
        </name>
        <hiredate>October 15, 2005</hiredate>
        <projects>
            <project>
                <product>Printer</product>
                <id>111</id>
                <price>$111.00</price>
            </project>
                .
                .
                .
```

This partial `<employee>` element without a closing `</employee>` tag would drive an XML processor crazy, so you should enclose this text in a CDATA section to tell the XML processor not to parse it, as you see in Listing 2.3. When an XML processor parses this document, it is supposed to place the text in the CDATA section directly into the output it produces, without trying to interpret that text (as well as removing the `<![CDATA[` and `]]>` markup).

LISTING 2.3 Using a CDATA Section in an XML Document (`ch02_03.xml`)

```
<?xml version = "1.0" standalone="yes"?>
<document>
    <text>
    Here's how the element starts:
    <![CDATA[
        <employee status="retired">
            <name>
                <lastname>Kelly</lastname>
                <firstname>Grace</firstname>
            </name>
            <hiredate>October 15, 2005</hiredate>
            <projects>
                <project>
                    <product>Printer</product>
                    <id>111</id>
                    <price>$111.00</price>
                </project>
                    .
                    .
```

LISTING 2.3 continued

```
            .
        ]]>
    </text>
</document>
```

You can see that Internet Explorer treats this CDATA section as unparsed text in Figure 2.11. (If it had parsed the text, you would see an error instead of the display you see in the figure.)

FIGURE 2.11
Viewing a CDATA section in Internet Explorer.

Here's another example using XHTML, the version of HTML that is written in XML. XHTML pages can be parsed like other XML documents, but that can cause problems if you've included certain characters that a scripting language like JavaScript uses, such as the less than (<) JavaScript operator. To avoid confusing an XML processor reading an XHTML page with this embedded JavaScript operator, you can enclose that JavaScript in a CDATA section:

```
<?xml version="1.0"?>
<!DOCTYPE html PUBLIC "-//W3C//DTD XHTML 1.0 Transitional//EN"
"http://www.w3.org/tr/xhtml1/DTD/xhtml1-transitional.dtd">
<html xmlns="http://www.w3.org/1999/xhtml" xml:lang="en" lang="en">
    <head>
        <title>
            Checking the temperature
        </title>
    </head>

    <body>
```

```
        <script language="javascript">
            <![CDATA[
                var temperature
                temperature = 234.77
                if (temperature < 32) {
                    document.writeln("Below freezing!")
                }
            ]]>
        </script>

        <center>
            <h1>
                Checking the temperature
            </h1>
        </center>
    </body>
</html>
```

2

Unfortunately, there's a problem here—the markup `<![CDATA[` and `]]>`, confuses HTML browsers, which means you can't use syntax like this until those browsers are fully equipped to handle XHTML. You can, however, include JavaScript in XHTML pages like this one if they're intended only for HTML browsers, not XML processors, by omitting the markup `<![CDATA[` and `]]>`.

Handling Entities

There's another type of item you can work with in XML documents—entities, which can be *parsed* or *unparsed*. An *entity* simply means a data item, such as a section of text or binary data. There are various ways to use entities, or to associate them with an XML document, as we'll be covering in the coming days, and it's appropriate to mention that now that we're discussing the parts of an XML document.

A parsed entity is one that you refer to with an *entity reference*. Entity references are replaced with the entities they refer to by the XML processor. There are two types of entity references: general entity references (starting with `&` and ending with `;`) and parameter entity references (used in DTDs and starting with `%` and ending with `;`). These references, such as one of the five predefined general entity references like `"`, will be replaced by the item the reference refers to. You can also specify characters with a general entity reference using the character's Unicode code—you saw that `π` is replaced by Π by an XML processor, for example.

You can define your own general entity references, as you're going to see in Day 5. For example, you could assign the general entity reference `©right;` the text `"(c)2005 Don't copy without permission."`, and from then on, whenever you use `©right;` in your XML document, the XML processor will replace it with `(c)2005 Don't copy without permission.`.

Unparsed entities can be binary data that you don't want parsed, or even non-XML text, and they're usually external to your XML document. You don't refer to an unparsed entity with an entity reference (which the XML processor will replace with the entity itself), but by a *name*. When you refer to an entity by name instead of with an explicit entity reference, that entity will not be parsed or placed into your XML document directly. We'll see how this works in Day 5.

More on all this is coming up—for the purposes of our present discussion on the structure of XML documents, however, what's important to note is that you can come across entity references in an XML document, and that it is possible to associate named external data, including binary data, with an XML document.

That's it—we've covered the items that can go into an XML document now, completing today's discussion. We're ready to start creating real XML documents now, which are well-formed documents (for an XML processor to read your documents, they must be well-formed). We're going to turn to that tomorrow.

Summary

Today, you took a look at how to create XML documents in general. You saw various ways of writing XML to files, and worked with a few XML editors.

You also took a look at the parts of an XML document—XML prologs, XML declarations, comments, processing instructions, comments, processing instructions, elements, CDATA sections, and entities. You're going to get more familiar with all these items in the days to come.

You can use XML validators to check your XML documents, and there are a number of free ones online. However, you need a way of specifying how that document's syntax is supposed to work, such as a Document Type Definition (DTD) or XML schema.

Most of today's work centered around the creation of XML documents and what's legal to put in them and what's not. You'll see more details in the Days to come, but we've gotten a good foundation here.

Q&A

Q What's the difference between character data and parsed character data?

A Character data is simply verbatim text data from an XML document. Parsed character data is text data where the XML processor has replaced any entity references with the entities themselves. Character data is referred to as CDATA (as in CDATA sections), and parsed character data is referred to as PCDATA (as we'll see when we create DTDs in Day 4).

Q My text editor says it can save documents in plain text format, but says nothing about Unicode or UCS. Will that be OK when I write my XML documents?

A Yes, your text editor is most likely writing documents in ASCII, which is a subset of Unicode, which itself is a subset of UCS. ASCII characters use the same codes in compressed Unicode, UTF-8, so you should specify the UTF-8 encoding and an XML processor should have no trouble reading your document if you save it as plain text.

Workshop

This workshop tests whether you understand the concepts you saw today. It's a good idea to make sure you can answer these questions before pressing on to tomorrow's work.

Quiz

1. What two character encodings are all XML processors supposed to implement?
2. If you wanted to include the text data `"This is a <message> element"` in an element named `<message>`, how could you do it without confusing an XML processor?
3. What items can be contained in an XML prolog?
4. What three attributes can appear in an XML declaration?
5. What processing instructions are built into XML already?

PART I

DAY 3

Creating Well-Formed XML Documents

Yesterday, you took a look at the various parts of XML documents—prologs, elements and attributes, processing instructions, and so forth. Today, you're going to start putting those items to work as you create well-formed documents.

Why is it so important to make an XML document well-formed? For one thing, W3C doesn't consider an XML document to be XML unless it's well-formed. For another, XML processors won't read XML documents unless those documents are well-formed. All of which is to say that making your XML well-formed is integral to creating XML documents—software isn't even going to be able to read your documents unless they are. Here's an overview of today's topics:

- Well-formed XML documents
- The W3C Well-formedness constraints
- Nesting constraints
- Element and attribute constraints

- Namespaces
- Local and default namespaces
- XML Infosets
- Canonical XML

To some extent, the current loose state of HTML documents is responsible for the great emphasis W3C puts on making sure XML documents are well-formed. HTML browsers have become more and more friendly to HTML pages as time has gone on, which means a Web page can have dozens of errors and still be displayed by a browser. That's not such a problem when it comes to simply displaying a Web page, but when it comes to handling what might be crucial data, it's a different story.

So W3C changed the rules from HTML to XML—unlike an HTML browser, an XML processor is *never* supposed to guess when it reads an XML document. If it finds an error (if the document is not well-formed, or if it uses a DTD or XML schema and it's not valid), the XML processor is supposed to inform you of the error, but then it can quit immediately. Ideally, according to W3C, a validating XML processor should list all the errors in an XML document and then quit; a non-validating one doesn't even have to do that—it can quit the first time it sees an error.

This enforced precision has two sides to it—there's no doubt that your data is transferred more faithfully using XML, but because XML processors make no guesses as to what you're trying to do, XML and XML processors can come across as non-user friendly, and not as generous or as easy to work with as HTML. On the other hand, you don't end up with the many possible errors that can creep into HTML, and that's important. XML authors have to be aware of the constraints on what they write, which is why we spend time in this book on document well-formedness and validity. In fact, in the XML 1.0 specification, W3C says that you can't even call a data object an XML document unless it's well-formed:

> A data object is an XML document if it is well-formed, as defined in this specification. A well-formed XML document may in addition be valid if it meets certain further constraints.

What Makes an XML Document Well-Formed?

The W3C, which is responsible for the term *well-formedness*, defines it this way in the XML 1.0 recommendation:

A textual object is a well-formed XML document if:

- Taken as a whole, it matches the production labeled *document*.
- It meets all the well-formedness constraints given in this specification (that is, the XML 1.0 specification, `http://www.w3.org/TR/REC-xml`).
- Each of the parsed entities, which is referenced directly or indirectly within the document, is well-formed.

Because the major differences between XML 1.0 and XML 1.1 have to do with what characters are legal, you probably won't be surprised to learn that a well-formed XML 1.0 document is also a well-formed XML 1.1 document, as long as it avoids certain characters. From the XML 1.1 specification:

> If a document is well-formed or valid XML 1.0, and provided it does not contain any characters in the range [#x7F-#x9F] other than as character escapes, it may be made well-formed or valid XML 1.1 respectively simply by changing the version number.

3

Let's get into three conditions that make an XML document well-formed, starting with the requirement that the document must match the production named `document`.

Matching the Production Labeled `document`

W3C calls the individual specifications within a working draft or recommendation *productions*. In this case, to be well-formed, a document must follow the `document` production, which means that the document itself must have three parts:

- a prolog (which can be empty)
- a root element (which can contain other elements)
- a miscellaneous part (unlike the preceding two parts, this part is optional)

You've seen XML prologs yesterday; they can contain an XML declaration (such as `<?xml version = "1.0"?>`), as well as comments, processing instructions, and doctype declarations (that is, DTDs).

You've also seen root elements; the root element is the XML element that contains all the other elements in your document. Each well-formed XML document must have one, and only one, root element.

The optional miscellaneous part can be made up of XML comments, processing instructions, and whitespace, all items you saw yesterday.

In other words, this first requirement says that an XML document must be made up of the parts you saw yesterday. So far, so good.

Meeting the Well-Formedness Constraints

The next requirement is a little more difficult to track down, because it says that to be well-formed, XML documents must also satisfy the well-formedness constraints in the XML 1.0 specification. This means that your XML documents should adhere to the syntax rules specified in the XML 1.0 recommendation. You'll discuss those rules, which are sprinkled throughout the XML 1.0 specification, in a few pages.

Making Parsed Entity Must Be Well-Formed

The final requirement is that each parsed entity in a well-formed document must itself be well-formed. When an XML document is parsed by an XML processor, entity references (such as `π`) are replaced by the entities they stand for (such as Π in this case). The requirement that all parsed entities must be well-formed simply means that when you replace entity references with the entities they stand for, the result must be well-formed.

That's the W3C's definition of a well-formed document, but you still need more information. What are the well-formedness constraints given throughout the XML specification? You're going to go over these constraints today; to start, you'll create an XML document that you'll use as we discuss what it means for a document to be well-formed.

Creating an Example XML Document

The sample document you'll use today, and which you'll also see tomorrow when working with DTDs, will store data about a set of employees, such as their names, projects they're working on, and so on. This document will start, as all XML documents should, with an XML declaration:

```
<?xml version = "1.0"?>
```

Because all the documents you'll see today are self-contained (they don't refer to or include any external entities), you'll also add the `standalone` attribute, setting it to `"yes"`, and specify that we're using UTF-8 encoding:

```
<?xml version = "1.0" encoding="UTF-8" standalone="yes"?>
```

And you'll also add a root element, called `<document>` in this case, although you can use any legal name:

```
<?xml version = "1.0" encoding="UTF-8" standalone="yes"?>
<document>
    .
    .
    .
</document>
```

The root element will contain all the other elements in the document. In this case, that will be three <employee> elements:

```
<?xml version = "1.0" encoding="UTF-8" standalone="yes"?>
<document>
    <employee>
    .
    .
    .
    </employee>
    <employee>
    .
    .
    .
    </employee>
    <employee>
    .
    .
    .
    </employee>
</document>
```


For each employee, we can store a name in a <name> element, which itself encloses a <lastname> and <firstname> element:

```
<?xml version = "1.0" encoding="UTF-8" standalone="yes"?>
<document>
    <employee>
        <name>
            <lastname>Kelly</lastname>
            <firstname>Grace</firstname>
        </name>
    .
    .
    .
    </employee>
    .
    .
    .
</document>
```

We'll also store each employee's hire date, as well as the projects they're working on. For each project, we can store the product name, ID, and price:

```
<?xml version = "1.0" encoding="UTF-8" standalone="yes"?>
<document>
    <employee>
        <name>
            <lastname>Kelly</lastname>
            <firstname>Grace</firstname>
        </name>
```

```
        <hiredate>October 15, 2005</hiredate>
        <projects>
            <project>
                <product>Printer</product>
                <id>111</id>
                <price>$111.00</price>
            </project>
            <project>
                <product>Laptop</product>
                <id>222</id>
                <price>$989.00</price>
            </project>
        </projects>
    </employee>
    .
    .
    .
</document>
```

That's what the data looks like for one employee; you can see the full document, `ch03_01.xml`, in Listing 3.1. Documents like this one can grow very long, but that presents no problem to XML processors—as long as the document is well-formed.

LISTING 3.1 Sample Well-Formed XML Document (`ch03_01.xml`)

```
<?xml version = "1.0" encoding="UTF-8" standalone="yes"?>
<document>
    <employee>
        <name>
            <lastname>Kelly</lastname>
            <firstname>Grace</firstname>
        </name>
        <hiredate>October 15, 2005</hiredate>
        <projects>
            <project>
                <product>Printer</product>
                <id>111</id>
                <price>$111.00</price>
            </project>
            <project>
                <product>Laptop</product>
                <id>222</id>
                <price>$989.00</price>
            </project>
        </projects>
    </employee>
    <employee>
        <name>
            <lastname>Grant</lastname>
```

Listing 3.1 continued

```
            <firstname>Cary</firstname>
        </name>
        <hiredate>October 20, 2005</hiredate>
        <projects>
            <project>
                <product>Desktop</product>
                <id>333</id>
                <price>$2995.00</price>
            </project>
            <project>
                <product>Scanner</product>
                <id>444</id>
                <price>$200.00</price>
            </project>
        </projects>
    </employee>
    <employee>
        <name>
            <lastname>Gable</lastname>
            <firstname>Clark</firstname>
        </name>
        <hiredate>October 25, 2005</hiredate>
        <projects>
            <project>
                <product>Keyboard</product>
                <id>555</id>
                <price>$129.00</price>
            </project>
            <project>
                <product>Mouse</product>
                <id>666</id>
                <price>$25.00</price>
            </project>
        </projects>
    </employee>
</document>
```

Today's work gets us into the structure of XML documents, and there's some terminology we should get to know at this point having to do with the relative position of elements in an XML document. As an example, take a look at an employee element in `ch03_01.xml`.

Elements on the same level, such as `<name>`, `<hiredate>`, and `<projects>` in an `<employee>` element, are all called *siblings*. Similarly, the two `<project>` elements in each `<projects>` element are siblings.

This family-type relationship is also continued with *child* and *parent* relationships. For example, the parent of the two `<project>` elements is the `<projects>` element. And the two `<project>` elements are children of the `<projects>` element.

You can always count on every non-root element to have exactly one, and only one, parent element. And a parent element can enclose an indefinite number of child elements (which can also mean zero child elements). You can continue the analogy to multiple generations as well; for example, the two `<project>` elements in this case are also *grandchildren* of the `<employee>` element.

That gives us the example document and terminology we'll need; now let's take a look at the well-formedness constraints you'll find in XML.

Understanding the Well-Formedness Constraints

The well-formedness constraints in the XML 1.0 specification are sprinkled throughout the document, and some of them are hard to dig out because they're not clearly marked. You'll get a look at the well-formedness constraints here, although note that some of them have to do with DTDs and entity references, and those will appear in Day 4, "Creating Valid XML Documents: Document Type Definitions," and Day 5, "Handling Attributes and Entities in DTDs."

Beginning the Document with an XML Declaration

The first well-formedness structure constraint is to start the document with an XML declaration. Even though some XML processors won't insist on it, W3C says you should always include this declaration first thing:

```
<?xml version = "1.0" encoding="UTF-8" standalone="yes"?>
<document>
    <employee>
    .
    .
    .
```

TIP

> Although the XML 1.0 specification says that only the `version` attribute is required here, some software—notably including W3C's own Amaya testbed browser—will consider XML documents as not well-formed if you don't also include the `encoding` attribute.

Using Only Legal Character References

Another well-formedness constraint is that character references, which are character codes enclosed in & and ;, and which are replaced by the characters that code stands for, must only refer to characters supported by the XML specification.

This constraint is more or less obvious—it simply means that you have to stick to the established character set for the version of XML you're using. Note that, as you saw yesterday, the characters that are legal in XML 1.0 differ somewhat from what's legal in XML 1.1.

Including at Least One Element

3

To be a well-formed document, a document must include *one or more* elements. The first element, of course, is the root element, so to be well-formed, a document must contain at least a root element. In other words, an XML document must contain more than just a prolog. Of course, your documents will usually contain many elements, as in our example document:

```
<?xml version = "1.0" encoding="UTF-8" standalone="yes"?>
<document>
    <employee>
        <name>
            <lastname>Kelly</lastname>
            <firstname>Grace</firstname>
        </name>
        <hiredate>October 15, 2005</hiredate>
        <projects>
            <project>
            .
            .
            .
            </project>
        </projects>
    </employee>
        .
        .
        .
</document>
```

Structuring Elements Correctly

HTML browsers are pretty easygoing about how you structure HTML elements in a Web page as long as they can understand what you're doing. For example, you can often omit closing tags in elements—you might use a <p> tag and then follow it with another <p> tag—without using a </p> tag—and the browser will have no problem.

That's not the way things work in XML. In XML, every non-empty element must have both a start tag and an end tag, as in our example document:

```
<employee>
    <name>
        <lastname>Gable</lastname>
        <firstname>Clark</firstname>
    </name>
    <hiredate>October 25, 2005</hiredate>
    <projects>
        <project>
            <product>Keyboard</product>
            <id>555</id>
            <price>$129.00</price>
        </project>
        <project>
            <product>Mouse</product>
            <id>666</id>
            <price>$25.00</price>
        </project>
    </projects>
</employee>
```

Besides making sure that every non-empty element has an opening tag and a closing tag, another well-formedness constraint says that end tags must match start tags, and both must use the same name.

Some elements—empty elements—don't have closing tags. These tags have no content of any kind (although they can have attributes), which means that they do not enclose any character data or markup. Instead, these elements are made up entirely of one tag like this:

```
<?xml version = "1.0" standalone="yes"?>
<document>
    <heading text = "Hello From XML"/>
</document>
```

In XML, empty elements must always end with `/>`.

TIP

> HTML elements can also be ended with `/>`, such as `<BR/>`, and HTML browsers will not have a problem with them. That's good, because the alternative is to write `<BR></BR>`, which some browsers, such as Netscape Navigator, interpret as two `<BR>` elements.

Using the Root Element to Contain All Other Elements

Another well-formedness constraint is that the root element must contain all the other elements in the document, as in our sample XML document, where we have three <employee> elements, which themselves contain other elements, in the document element:

```
<?xml version = "1.0" encoding="UTF-8" standalone="yes"?>
<document>
    <employee>
        .
        .
        .
    </employee>
    <employee>
        .
        .
        .
    </employee>
    <employee>
        .
        .
        .
    </employee>
</document>
```


That's how a well-formed XML document works—you start with a prolog, followed by the root element, which contains all the other the elements, if there are any. Among other things, containing all elements in a root element makes it easier for an XML processor to understand the structure of an XML document—starting at the single root element, it can navigate the entire document.

Nesting Elements Properly

Nesting elements correctly is a big part of well-formedness; the requirement here is that if an element contains a start tag for a non-empty tag, it must also contain that element's end tag. In other words, you cannot spread an element over other elements at the same level. For example, this XML is nested properly:

```
<employee>
    <name>
        <lastname>Kelly</lastname>
        <firstname>Grace</firstname>
    </name>
    <hiredate>October 15, 2005</hiredate>
    <projects>
        <project>
            <product>Printer</product>
            <id>111</id>
```

```
            <price>$111.00</price>
        </project>
        <project>
            <product>Laptop</product>
            <id>222</id>
            <price>$989.00</price>
        </project>
    </projects>
</employee>
```

But as you can see, there's a nesting problem in this next element, because an XML processor will encounter a new `<project>` tag before finding the closing `</project>` tag it's looking for at the end of the current `<project>` element:

```
<employee>
    <name>
        <lastname>Kelly</lastname>
        <firstname>Grace</firstname>
    </name>
    <hiredate>October 15, 2005</hiredate>
    <projects>
        <project>
            <product>Printer</product>
            <id>111</id>
            <price>$111.00</price>
        <project>
        </project>
            <product>Laptop</product>
            <id>222</id>
            <price>$989.00</price>
        </project>
    </projects>
</employee>
```

In fact, this nesting requirement is where the whole term *well-formed* comes from—the original idea was that a document where the elements were not garbled and mixed up with each other was well-formed.

There are other well-formedness constraints that have nothing to do with elements, however—for example, the next two concern attributes.

Making Attribute Names Unique

Another well-formedness constraint is that you can't use the same attribute more than once in one start-tag or empty-element tag. This is another well-formedness constraint that seems more or less obvious, and it's hard to see how you might violate this one except by mistake, as in this case:

```
<message text="Hi there!" text="Hello!">
```

XML is case sensitive, so you could theoretically do something like this:

```
<message Text="Hi there!" text="Hello!">
```

Obviously, that's not a very good idea, however; attribute names that differ only in capitalization are bound to be confusing.

Enclose Attribute Values in Quotation Marks

One well-formedness constraint that trips up most XML novices sooner or later is that you must quote every value you assign to an attribute, using either single quotation marks or double quotation marks. This trips many people up because you don't have to quote attribute values in HTML, as in this HTML example (which also doesn't have a closing tag):

```
<img src=mountains.jpg>
```

An XML processor would have problems with this element, however. Here's what it would look like properly constructed:

```
<img src="mountains.jpg" />
```

If you prefer, you could use single quotation marks:

```
<img src=mountains.jpg' />
```

As you've seen, using single quotation marks helps when an attribute's value contains quoted text:

```
<message text='I said, "No, no, no!"' />
```

And as you've also seen, in worst-case scenarios, where an attribute value contains both single and double quotation marks, you can escape " as " and ' as '—as here, where you're reporting the height of a tree as 50' 6" :

```
<tree type="Maple" height="50&apos;6&quot;" />
```

Avoiding Entity References and < in Attribute Values

Also, W3C makes it an explicit well-formedness constraint that you should avoid references to external entities (this means XML-style references—general entity references or parameter entity references, not just, for example, using an image file's name) in attribute values. This means that an XML processor doesn't have to replace an attribute value with the contents of an external entity.

In addition, another constraint says that you are not supposed to use < in attribute values, because an XML processor might mistake it for markup. If you really have to use the text <, use < instead, which will be turned into < when parsed. For example, this XML:

```
<project note="This is a <project> element.">
```

should be written as this, where you're escaping both < and >:

```
<project note="This is a &lt;project&gt; element.">
```

In fact, < is a particularly sensitive character to use anywhere in an XML document, except as markup, and that's another well-formedness constraint concerning <, coming up next.

Avoiding Overuse of < and &

XML processors assume that < starts a tag and & starts an entity reference, so you should avoid using those characters for anything else. Sometimes, this is a problem, as in the JavaScript example you saw yesterday, which uses the JavaScript < operator that enclosed in a CDATA section:

```
<?xml version="1.0"?>
<!DOCTYPE html PUBLIC "-//W3C//DTD XHTML 1.0 Transitional//EN"
"http://www.w3.org/tr/xhtml1/DTD/xhtml1-transitional.dtd">
<html xmlns="http://www.w3.org/1999/xhtml" xml:lang="en" lang="en">
    <head>
        <title>
            Checking the temperature
        </title>
    </head>

    <body>
        <script language="javascript">
            <![CDATA[
                var temperature
                temperature = 234.77
                if (temperature < 32) {
                    document.writeln("Below freezing!")
                }
            ]]>
        </script>

        <center>
            <h1>
                Checking the temperature
            </h1>
        </center>
    </body>
</html>
```

However, because modern Web browsers don't understand CDATA sections, this solution (which was suggested by W3C) doesn't really work. And if you escape the > operator as <, very few browsers will understand what you're doing.

There are two main ways of handling the < JavaScript operator in XML with today's browsers. You can reverse the logical sense of the test—for example, in this case, instead of checking whether the temperature is below 32, you would check to make sure it isn't above or equal to 32, which lets you use > instead of < (note that the JavaScript ! operator, the Not operator, reverses the logical sense of an expression) :

```
<script language="javascript">
    var temperature
    temperature = 234.77
    if (!(temperature >= 32)) {
        document.writeln("Below freezing!")
    }
</script>
```

Practically speaking, the best way is usually to remove the whole problem by placing the script code in an external file, which you'll name `script.js` here, so the browser won't parse it as XML in the first place. You can do that like this in JavaScript (more on JavaScript and how to use it in XML is coming up in Day 15, "Using JavaScript and XML"):

```
<?xml version="1.0"?>
<!DOCTYPE html PUBLIC "-//W3C//DTD XHTML 1.0 Transitional//EN"
"http://www.w3.org/tr/xhtml1/DTD/xhtml1-transitional.dtd">
<html xmlns="http://www.w3.org/1999/xhtml" xml:lang="en" lang="en">
    <head>
        <title>
            Checking the temperature
        </title>
    </head>

    <body>
        <script language="javascript" src="script.js">
        </script>
        <center>
            <h1>
                Checking the temperature
            </h1>
        </center>
    </body>
</html>
```

That completes today's discussion of well-formedness, although you'll see more in the next two days as we discuss the well-formedness constraints that have to do with DTDs.

As your XML documents evolve and become more complex, it's also going to be increasingly important to understand namespaces, which are the second major topic for today.

Using XML Namespaces

There's a lot of freedom in XML, because you get to create your own markup. As time went on, however, XML authors started noticing a problem that the original creators of XML hadn't really anticipated—conflicting tag names.

For example, you've already seen that two popular XML applications are XHTML, which is the derivation of HTML in XML, and MathML, which lets you format and display math equations. Suppose that you want to display an equation in an XHTML Web page. That could be a problem, because because the tag set in XHTML and MathML overlap—in particular, each XML application defines a `<var>` and `<select>` element.

The way to solve this problem is to use *namespaces*. Namespaces give you a way to make sure that one set of tags will not conflict with another. You prefix a name to tag and attribute names. Changing the resulting names won't conflict with others that have a different prefix.

XML namespaces are one of those XML companion recommendations that keep being added to the XML specification. You can find the specification for namespaces at `http://www.w3.org/TR/REC-xml-names/`. There's still a lot of debate about this one (mostly because namespaces can make writing DTDs difficult), but it's an official W3C recommendation now.

Creating Namespaces

An example will make namespaces and why they're important clearer. For example, suppose you're the boss of one of the employees in our sample document, `ch03_01.xml`:

```
<employee>
    <name>
        <lastname>Kelly</lastname>
        <firstname>Grace</firstname>
    </name>
    <hiredate>October 15, 2005</hiredate>
    <projects>
        <project>
            <product>Printer</product>
            <id>111</id>
            <price>$111.00</price>
        </project>
        <project>
```

```
            <product>Laptop</product>
            <id>222</id>
            <price>$989.00</price>
        </project>
    </projects>
</employee>
```

Now suppose that you want to add your own comments to this employee's data in a `<comment>` element. The problem with that is that the XML data on this employee comes from the Human Resources department, and they haven't created an element named `<comment>`. You can indeed create your own `<comment>` element, but first you should confine the human resource's department's XML data to its own namespace to indicate that your comments are not part of the Human Resource Department's set of XML tags.

3

To define a new namespace, use the `xmlns:`*`prefix`* attribute, where *`prefix`* is the prefix you want to use for the namespace. In this case, you'll define a new namespace called `hr` for the Human Resources department:

```
<employee>
   xmlns:hr="http://www.superduperbigco.com/human_resources">
    <name>
        <lastname>Kelly</lastname>
        <firstname>Grace</firstname>
    </name>
    <hiredate>October 15, 2005</hiredate>
    <projects>
        <project>
            <product>Printer</product>
            <id>111</id>
            <price>$111.00</price>
        </project>
        <project>
            <product>Laptop</product>
            <id>222</id>
            <price>$989.00</price>
        </project>
    </projects>
</employee>
```

To define a namespace, you assign the `xmlns:`*`prefix`* attribute to a unique identifier, which in XML is usually a URI that might direct the XML processor to a DTD for the namespace (but doesn't have to). So what's a URI?

Defining Namespaces with URIs

The XML specification expands the idea of standard URLs (Uniform Resource Locators) into *URIs (Uniform Resource Identifiers)*. In HTML and on the Web, you use URLs; in

XML, you use URIs. URIs are supposed to be more general than URLs, as we'll see when we discuss XLinks and XPointers in Day 14, "Handling XLinks, XPointers, and XForms."

For example, in theory, a URI can point not just to a single resource, but to a cluster of resources, or to *arcs* of resources along a path. The truth is that the whole idea of URIs as the next step after URLs is still being developed, and in practice, URLs are almost invariably used in XML—but you still call them URIs. Some software accepts more general forms of URIs, letting you, for example, access only a specific section of an XML document, but such usage and the associated syntax is far from standardized yet.

TIP

> You might want to look up the current formal definition of URIs, which you can find in its entirety at `http://www.ics.uci.edu/pub/ietf/uri/rfc2396.txt`.

When you define a namespace with the `xmlns:`*`prefix`* attribute, you usually assign a URI to that attribute (in practice, this URI is always a URL today). The document that URI points to can describe more about the namespace you're creating; an example of this is the XHTML namespace, which uses the namespace `http://www.w3.org/1999/xhtml`:

```
<?xml version="1.0"?>
<!DOCTYPE html PUBLIC "-//W3C//DTD XHTML 1.0 Transitional//EN"
"http://www.w3.org/tr/xhtml1/DTD/xhtml1-transitional.dtd">
<html xmlns:xhtml="http://www.w3.org/1999/xhtml" xml:lang="en" lang="en">
        .
        .
        .
```

A namespace's URI can also hold a DTD or XML schema that defines the syntax for the XML elements you can use in that namespace (then it's up to the XML processor to use that DTD or XML schema, if it's been written to be smart enough to interpret namespaces in this way—most aren't). All that's really necessary, however, is that you assign a unique identifier, which can be any text, to the `xmlns:`*`prefix`* attribute.

After defining the `hr` namespace in our example, you can preface every tag and attribute name in this namespace with `hr:` like this:

```
<hr:employee
   xmlns:hr="http://www.superduperbigco.com/human_resources">
    <hr:name>
        <hr:lastname>Kelly</hr:lastname>
        <hr:firstname>Grace</hr:firstname>
    </hr:name>
```

```
    <hr:hiredate>October 15, 2005</hr:hiredate>
    <hr:projects>
        <hr:project>
            <hr:product>Printer</hr:product>
            <hr:id>111</hr:id>
            <hr:price>$111.00</hr:price>
        </hr:project>
        <hr:project>
            <hr:product>Laptop</hr:product>
            <hr:id>222</hr:id>
            <hr:price>$989.00</hr:price>
        </hr:project>
    </hr:projects>
</hr:employee>
```


Now you've made it clear that all these tags come from the Human Resources department. Note how this works—the actual tag names themselves have been changed, because a colon is a legal character to use in tag names. (Now you know why you shouldn't use colons in tag names, although they're legal—they can make it look like you're using namespaces when you're not.) For example, the `<product>` tag has now become the `<hr:product>` tag. In other words, using namespaces keeps elements separate by actually changing tag and attribute names. This was a clever solution to the problem of tag and attribute name conflicts, because this way, even XML processors that have never heard of namespaces can still "support" them.

At this point, all tag and attribute names from the `hr` namespace are in their own namespace, so you can add your own namespace to the document, allowing you to use your own elements without fear of conflict. Since you're the boss, you might start by defining a new namespace named `boss`:

```
<hr:employee
   xmlns:hr="http://www.superduperbigco.com/human_resources"
   xmlns:boss="http://www.superduperbigco.com/big_boss">
    <hr:name>
        <hr:lastname>Kelly</hr:lastname>
        <hr:firstname>Grace</hr:firstname>
    </hr:name>
    <hr:hiredate>October 15, 2005</hr:hiredate>
    <hr:projects>
        <hr:project>
            <hr:product>Printer</hr:product>
            <hr:id>111</hr:id>
            <hr:price>$111.00</hr:price>
        </hr:project>
        <hr:project>
            <hr:product>Laptop</hr:product>
            <hr:id>222</hr:id>
            <hr:price>$989.00</hr:price>
```

```
        </hr:project>
    </hr:projects>
</hr:employee>
```

Now you can use the new boss namespace to add your own markup to the document, as you see in Listing 3.2.

LISTING 3.2 XML Document with Namespaces (ch03_02.xml)

```
<hr:employee
   xmlns:hr="http://www.superduperbigco.com/human_resources"
   xmlns:boss="http://www.superduperbigco.com/big_boss">
    <hr:name>
        <hr:lastname>Kelly</hr:lastname>
        <hr:firstname>Grace</hr:firstname>
    </hr:name>
    <hr:hiredate>October 15, 2005</hr:hiredate>
    <boss:comment>Needs much supervision.</boss:comment>
    <hr:projects>
        <hr:project>
            <hr:product>Printer</hr:product>
            <hr:id>111</hr:id>
            <hr:price>$111.00</hr:price>
        </hr:project>
        <hr:project>
            <hr:product>Laptop</hr:product>
            <hr:id>222</hr:id>
            <hr:price>$989.00</hr:price>
        </hr:project>
    </hr:projects>
</hr:employee>
```

You can also add your own attributes in the boss namespace as long as you prefix them with boss: this way:

```
<hr:employee>
   xmlns:hr="http://www.superduperbigco.com/human_resources"
   xmlns:boss="http://www.superduperbigco.com/big_boss">
    <hr:name>
        <hr:lastname>Kelly</hr:lastname>
        <hr:firstname>Grace</hr:firstname>
    </hr:name>
    <hr:hiredate>October 15, 2005</hr:hiredate>
    <boss:comment boss:date="10/15/2006">
        Needs much supervision.
    </boss:comment>
    <hr:projects>
        <hr:project>
            <hr:product>Printer</hr:product>
            <hr:id>111</hr:id>
```

LISTING 3.2 continued

```
            <hr:price>$111.00</hr:price>
        </hr:project>
        <hr:project>
            <hr:product>Laptop</hr:product>
            <hr:id>222</hr:id>
            <hr:price>$989.00</hr:price>
        </hr:project>
    </hr:projects>
</hr:employee>
```

And that's how namespaces work—you can use them to separate tags, even tags with the same name, so there's no conflict. As you can see, using multiple namespaces in the same document is no problem at all—just use the `xmlns:prefix` attribute in the enclosing element to define the appropriate namespace. In fact, you can use this attribute attribute in child elements to redefine an enclosing namespace, if you want to.

Namespace prefixes are really just text prefixed to (*prepended* is the offical term) tag and attribute names. They follow the same rules for naming tags and attributes. For example, in XML 1.0, a namespace name can start with a letter or an underscore. The following characters can include underscores, letters, digits, hyphens, and periods. Note also that although colons are legal in tag names, you can't use a colon in a namespace name, for obvious reasons. Also, there are two namespace names that are reserved: `xml` and `xmlns`.

Creating Local Namespaces

The `xmlns:prefix` attribute can be used in any element, not just the document element. Just bear in mind that this attribute defines a namespace for the current element and any enclosed element, which means you shouldn't use the namespace prefix until you've defined the namespace with an attribute like `xmlns:prefix`.

For example, you can create the `boss:` namespace prefix and use it in the same element, as you see in Listing 3.3.

LISTING 3.3 XML Document with a Local Namespaces (`ch03_03.xml`)

```
<hr:employee
   xmlns:hr="http://www.superduperbigco.com/human_resources">
    <hr:name>
        <hr:lastname>Kelly</hr:lastname>
        <hr:firstname>Grace</hr:firstname>
    </hr:name>
    <hr:hiredate>October 15, 2005</hr:hiredate>
    <boss:comment
```

LISTING 3.3 continued

```
        xmlns:boss="http://www.superduperbigco.com/big_boss"
        boss:date="10/15/2006">
        Needs much supervision.
    </boss:comment>
    <hr:projects>
        <hr:project>
            <hr:product>Printer</hr:product>
            <hr:id>111</hr:id>
            <hr:price>$111.00</hr:price>
        </hr:project>
        <hr:project>
            <hr:product>Laptop</hr:product>
            <hr:id>222</hr:id>
            <hr:price>$989.00</hr:price>
        </hr:project>
    </hr:projects>
</hr:employee>
```

You can see `ch03_03.xml` in the Internet Explorer, complete with namespaces, in Figure 3.1.

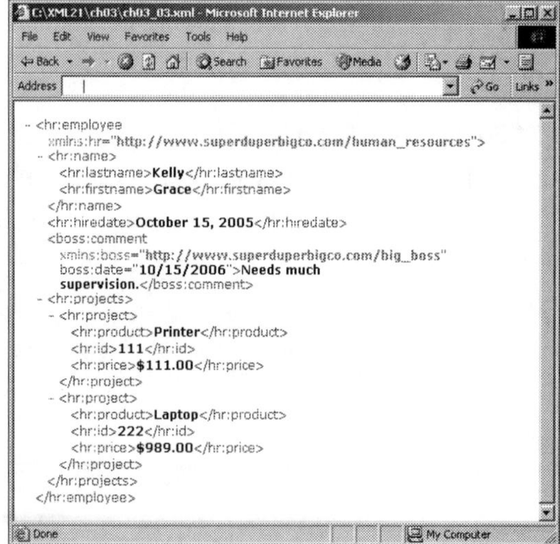

FIGURE 3.1
Viewing an XML document with local namespaces.

Creating Default Namespaces

You can use the `xmlns:prefix` attribute to define a namespace, or you can use the `xmlns` attribute by itself to define a *default* namespace. When you define a default namespace, elements and attributes without a namespace prefix are in that default namespace.

To see how this works, we'll come full circle and put to work the example that introduced our discussion of namespaces in the first place—mixing XHTML with MathML. We'll start with some XHTML (all the details on XHTML are coming up in Day 11, "Extending HTML with XHTML," and Day 12, "Putting XHTML to Work"), like this:

```
<?xml version="1.0" encoding="UTF-8"?>
<!DOCTYPE html PUBLIC "-//W3C//DTD XHTML 1.0 Transitional//EN"
"http://www.w3.org/tr/xhtml1/DTD/xhtml1-transitional.dtd">
<html xmlns="http://www.w3.org/1999/xhtml" xml:lang="en" lang="en">
    <head>
        <title>
            Using XHTML and MathML Together
        </title>
    </head>

    <body>
        <center>
            <h1>
                Using XHTML and MathML Together
            </h1>
        </center>
        <br/>
        Consider the equation
        .
        .
        .
    </body>
</html>
```


You'll see what you need to create XHTML documents like this, such as the `<!DOCTYPE>` element, in Day 11. Note in particular here that in the `<html>` element, the `xmlns` attribute defines a default namespace for the `<html>` and all enclosed elements. (This namespace is the XHTML namespace, which W3C defines as `"http://www.w3.org/1999/xhtml"`.) When you use the `xmlns` attribute alone this way, without specifying any prefix, you are defining a default namespace. The current element and all child elements are assumed to belong to that namespace. Making use of a default namespace in this way, you can use the standard XHTML tag names without any prefix, as you see here.

However, we also want to use MathML markup in this document, and to do that, we add a new namespace, named `m` to this document, using the namespace W3C has specified for MathML, `"http://www.w3.org/1998/Math/MathML"`:

```
<?xml version="1.0" encoding="UTF-8"?>
<!DOCTYPE html PUBLIC "-//W3C//DTD XHTML 1.0 Transitional//EN"
"http://www.w3.org/tr/xhtml1/DTD/xhtml1-transitional.dtd">
<html xmlns="http://www.w3.org/1999/xhtml" xml:lang="en" lang="en"
    xmlns:m="http://www.w3.org/1998/Math/MathML">
    <head>
```

```
        <title>
            Using XHTML and MathML Together
        </title>
    </head>

    <body>
        <center>
            <h1>
                Using XHTML and MathML Together
            </h1>
        </center>
        <br/>
        Consider the equation
        .
        .
        .
    </body>
</html>
```

Now you can use MathML as you like, as long as you prefix it with the `m` namespace. You can see this at work in `ch03_04.html` (XHTML documents use the extension `.html`), shown in Listing 3.4, where we're using the MathML we developed in Day 1 to display an equation.

LISTING 3.4 An XML Document Combining XHTML and MathML (`ch03_04.html`)

```
<?xml version="1.0" encoding="UTF-8"?>
<!DOCTYPE html PUBLIC "-//W3C//DTD XHTML 1.0 Transitional//EN"
"http://www.w3.org/tr/xhtml1/DTD/xhtml1-transitional.dtd">
<html xmlns="http://www.w3.org/1999/xhtml" xml:lang="en" lang="en"
    xmlns:m="http://www.w3.org/1998/Math/MathML">
    <head>
        <title>
            Using XHTML and MathML Together
        </title>
    </head>

    <body>
        <center>
            <h1>
                Using XHTML and MathML Together
            </h1>
        </center>
        <br/>
        Consider the equation
        <m:math>
            <m:mrow>
                <m:mrow>
                <m:mn>4</m:mn>
```

Listing 3.4 continued

```
                    <m:mo>&InvisibleTimes;</m:mo>
                    <m:msup>
                        <m:mi>x</m:mi>
                        <m:mn>2</m:mn>
                    </m:msup>
                    <m:mo>-</m:mo>
                    <m:mrow>
                        <m:mn>5</m:mn>
                        <m:mo>&InvisibleTimes;</m:mo>
                        <m:mi>x</m:mi>
                    </m:mrow>
                    <m:mo>+</m:mo>
                    <m:mn>6</m:mn>
                </m:mrow>
                <m:mo>=</m:mo>
                <m:mn>0.</m:mn>
            </m:mrow>
        </m:math>
        <br/>
        What, you may ask, are this equation's roots?
    </body>
</html>
```

Thanks to namespaces, this XHTML/MathML document works just as it should, as you can see in the W3C Amaya browser in Figure 3.2.

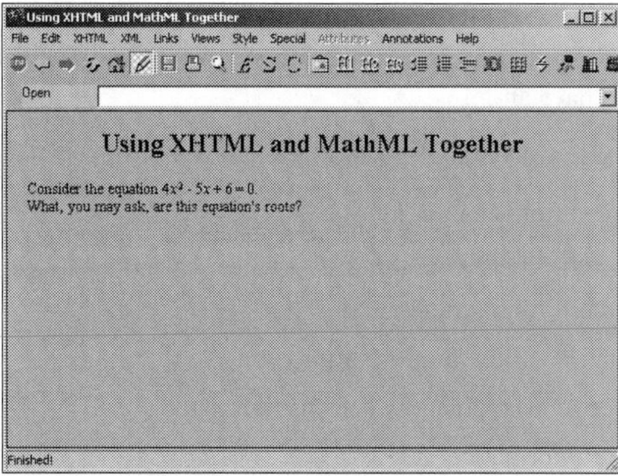

Figure 3.2

Viewing an XML document with local namespaces.

You'll be seeing XML namespaces throughout this book, especially when we use the popular XML applications available, such as XHTML.

That finishes the main topics for today's discussion—well-formed documents and namespaces. Before getting into validation in tomorrow's work, however, we'll round off our discussion of XML documents by taking a look at XML infosets and canonical XML. These two topics are worth discussing before we start talking about validation, because they're terms you'll run across as you work with XML, but we're going to consider them optional topics—if you want to skip them and get directly to DTDs, just turn to Day 4.

Understanding XML Infosets

The inspiration behind both *XML infosets* (formally named *XML information sets*) and canonical XML is to make handling the data in XML documents easier. Reducing an XML document down to its infoset is intended to make comparisons between all kinds of XML documents easier by presenting the data in those documents in a standard way. You can find the official XML Information Set specification at `http://www.w3.org/TR/xml-infoset`.

To understand what infosets are and what they're used for, imagine searching for data on the World Wide Web. You might want to search for a particular topic, such as XML, and you would turn up millions of matches. How could you possibly write software to compare those documents? The data in those documents isn't stored in any way that's directly comparable.

That's where infosets come in, because the idea is to regularize how data is stored in an XML document that, ultimately, is designed to let you work with thousands of such documents. The idea behind infosets is to set up an abstract way of looking at an XML document that allows it to be compared to others. (Note that documents need to be well-formed to have an infoset.)

An XML infoset can contain fifteen different types of information items:

- A document information item
- Element information items
- Attribute information items
- Processing instruction information items
- Reference to skipped entity information items
- Character information items
- Comment information items
- A document type declaration information item
- Entity information items

- Notation information items
- Entity start marker information items
- Entity end marker information items
- CDATA start marker information items
- CDATA end marker information items
- Namespace declaration information items

So what software works with infosets? None, really—infosets are primarily theoretical constructs, and the infoset specification is mostly designed to provide a set of definitions that other XML specifications can use when they need to refer to the information in an XML document. Although the term *infoset* has entered common usage as a way to refer to the information in an XML document, it's not a specific enough specification to allow any real implementation. The closest you can come these days to truly regularizing the data in XML documents to make it easy to compare them is to use canonical XML, coming up next.

Understanding Canonical XML

Infosets are only abstract formulations of the information in an XML document. So without reducing an XML document to its infoset, how can you actually approach the goal of being able to actually compare XML documents character by character? You can write your documents in canonical XML.

TIP

> You can find a canonical XML tutorial at `www.xfront.com/canonical/CanonicalXML.html`.

Canonical XML is a companion specification to XML, and you can read all about it at `http://www.w3.org/TR/xml-c14n`. Canonical XML is a very strict XML syntax, which lets documents in canonical XML be compared directly.

Using this strict syntax makes it easier to see whether two XML documents are the same. For example, a section of text in one document might read `Black & White`, whereas the same section of text might read `Black & White` in another document, and even `<![CDATA[Black & White]]>` in another. If you compare those three documents byte by byte, they'll be different. But if you write them all in canonical XML, which specifies every aspect of the syntax you can use, these three documents would all have the same version of this text (which would be `Black & White`) and could be compared without problem.

As you might imagine, the canonical XML syntax is very strict; for example, canonical XML uses UTF-8 character encoding only, carriage-return linefeed pairs are replaced with linefeeds (that is, `
`), tabs in CDATA sections are replaced by spaces, all entity references must be expanded, and much more, as specified in `http://www.w3.org/TR/xml-c14n`.

TIP

In their canonical form, documents can be compared directly, and any differences will be readily apparent. Because canonical XML is intended to be byte-by-byte correct, it's often a good idea to use software to convert your XML documents to that form. One such package that will convert valid XML documents to canonical form comes with the XML for Java software that you can get free from IBM's AlphaWorks (`http://www.alphaworks.ibm.com/tech/xml4j`). The actual program is named DOMWriter, and it's part of the XML for Java package.

That completes today's discussion on constructing XML documents. We've covered everything we need to know before we start discussing how to create valid XML documents—and we're going to start doing that tomorrow.

Summary

Today, you took a look at how to create well-formed XML documents. W3C doesn't even consider an XML document to be XML unless it's well-formed. W3C considers an XML document well-formed if it meets three criteria:

- Taken as a whole, it matches the production labeled *document*.
- It meets all the well-formedness constraints given in this specification (that is, the XML 1.0 specification, `http://www.w3.org/TR/REC-xml`).
- Each of the parsed entities, which is referenced directly or indirectly within the document, is well-formed.

The most general of these items says that an XML document must meet the well-formedness constraints in the XML specification, and you took a look today at what that meant.

Those constraints include beginning a document with an XML declaration, using only legal character references, the document must include at least one element, elements must be structured and nested correctly, the root element must contain all other elements, attribute names must be unique, attribute values must be quoted, and so on.

You also took a look at creating namespaces, and how namespaces help you avoid conflicts in XML. To define a namespace, you can assign the `xmlns:prefix` attribute to a unique identifier (usually a URI), or you can use the `xmlns` attribute to define a default namespace.

Q&A

Q Can I use an XML validator to test an XML document's well-formedness?

A Yes, if you have a DTD or XML schema for the document—an XML validator will also report whether the document is well-formed or not. However, you do need a DTD or XML schema if you want to use a validator—very few will check a document without one. One program that will check an XML document's well-formedness without a DTD or XML schema is Internet Explorer. If the document is not well-formed, you'll see the message `"The XML page cannot be displayed"`, and Internet Explorer will tell you the exact problem with the document.

Q Do I need to use namespaces if there's no chance of tag name conflicts with other XML applications?

A Often, yes. Namespaces aren't used solely to avoid tag (and attribute) name conflicts—using a namespace also indicates to an XML processor what XML application you're using. For example, if you're using MathML, you must use the current MathML namespace or most MathML-enabled XML processors will complain.

Workshop

This workshop tests whether you understand the concepts you saw today. It's a good idea to make sure you can answer these questions before pressing on to tomorrow's work.

Quiz

1. To be well-formed, what's the least number of elements an XML document can contain?
2. Why is the following XML document not well-formed?

```
<?xml version = "1.0" standalone="yes"?>
<employee>
    <name>Frank</name>
    <position>Chef</position>
</employee>
<employee>
    <name>Ronnie</name>
    <position>Chef</position>
</employee>
```

3. Why is the following XML document not well-formed?

```
<?xml version = "1.0" standalone="yes"?>
<employee>
    <kitchen_staff/>
    <name language=en>Frank</name>
    <new_hire />
    <position language=en>Chef</position>
</employee>
```

4. How can you create a namespace named `service` whose URI is `http://www.superduperbigco.com/customer_service`?

5. How could you set the default namespace in a set of XML elements to the URI `http://www.superduperbigco.com/customer_returns`?

PART I

DAY 4

Creating Valid XML Documents: DTDs

The past couple days have prepared you for what's coming up now—the creation of *valid* XML documents. Unlike with HTML, where a browser can check HTML because it knows all about legal HTML, you create your own markup in XML, which means that an XML processor can't check your markup unless you let it know how to. In XML, you define what's legal and what's not by specifying the syntax you're going to allow for an XML document. There are two ways to validate XML documents—with document type definitions (DTDs) and with XML schemas. Today and tomorrow cover DTDs, and Days 6, "Creating Valid XML Documents: XML Schemas," and 7, "Creating Your Own Types in XML Schemas," cover XML schemas.

Here's an overview of today's topics:

- Creating DTDs
- Using validators
- Declaring elements
- Using `ANY` to allow any content

- Declaring child elements
- Declaring parsed character data
- Creating child sequences
- Using DTD choices
- Using internal and external DTDs
- Using DTDs and namespaces

DTDs provided the original way to validate XML documents, and the syntax for DTDs is built right in to the XML 1.0 specification. Tons of XML processors out there use DTDs in XML documents, and DTDs are the first step in any discussion on validation. But it's also true that DTDs are limited compared to XML schemas, and with the vast support Microsoft is pouring into XML schemas, schemas are really taking off these days. The details on schemas are provided on Days 6 and 7.

All About DTDs

Yesterday we discussed creating well-formed XML documents, and while an XML document needs to be well-formed to be considered a true XML document, that's only part of the story. In real life, we also need to give an XML processor some way of checking the syntax (also called the *grammar*) of an XML document to make sure the data remains intact. For example, take a look at the XML document you created yesterday that contains data about employees:

```
<?xml version = "1.0" standalone="yes"?>
<document>
    <employee>
        <name>
            <lastname>Kelly</lastname>
            <firstname>Grace</firstname>
        </name>
        <hiredate>October 15, 2005</hiredate>
        <projects>
            <project>
                <product>Printer</product>
                <id>111</id>
                <price>$111.00</price>
            </project>
            <project>
                <product>Laptop</product>
                <id>222</id>
                <price>$989.00</price>
            </project>
        </projects>
    </employee>
```

```
    .
    .
    .
</document>
```

Say we've expanded to 5,000 employees, and that we have a team of typists typing in all that employee data. The likelihood is high that there are going to be errors in all that data entry. But how will an XML processor know that a `<project>` element must contain at least one `<product>` element unless we tell it so? How do we tell an XML processor that each `<employee>` element must contain one `<name>` element? To do this and more, we can use a DTD. DTDs are all about specifying the *structure* of an XML document, not the data in that document. The formal rules for DTDs are available in the XML 1.0 recommendation, `http://www.w3.org/TR/REC-xml`. (Note that the XML 1.1 candidate recommendation has nothing to add about DTDs as of this writing.)

We define the syntax of an XML document by using a DTD, and we declare that definition in a document by using a document type *declaration*. We can use a `<!DOCTYPE>` element to create a DTD, and the DTD appears in that element. The element can take many different forms, including the following (where *`URI`* is the URI of a DTD outside the current XML document and *`rootname`* is the name of the root element) :

- `<!DOCTYPE` *`rootname`* `[`*`DTD`*`]>`
- `<!DOCTYPE` *`rootname`* `SYSTEM` *`URI`*`>`
- `<!DOCTYPE` *`rootname`* `SYSTEM` *`URI`* `[`*`DTD`*`]>`
- `<!DOCTYPE` *`rootname`* `PUBLIC` *`identifier URI`*`>`
- `<!DOCTYPE` *`rootname`* `PUBLIC` *`identifier URI`* `[`*`DTD`*`]>`

4

To use a DTD, we need a DTD, which means we need a `<!DOCTYPE>` element. The `<!DOCTYPE>` element is part of a document's prolog. For example, here's how we would add a `<!DOCTYPE>` element to the employees example:

```
<?xml version = "1.0" standalone="yes"?>
<!DOCTYPE document [
        .
        .
    <!-- DTD goes here! -->
        .
        .
]>
<document>
    <employee>
        <name>
            <lastname>Kelly</lastname>
            <firstname>Grace</firstname>
        </name>
```

```
        <hiredate>October 15, 2005</hiredate>
        <projects>
            <project>
                <product>Printer</product>
                <id>111</id>
                <price>$111.00</price>
            </project>
            <project>
                <product>Laptop</product>
                <id>222</id>
                <price>$989.00</price>
            </project>
        </projects>
    </employee>
        .
        .
        .
</document>
```

So what does a DTD look like? The actual XML syntax for DTDs is pretty terse, so today's discussion is dedicated to unraveling that terseness. To get started, Listing 4.1 shows a full `<!DOCTYPE>` element that contains a DTD for the employee document. We're going to dissect that DTD today.

LISTING 4.1 A Sample XML Document with a DTD (`ch04_01.xml`)

```
<?xml version = "1.0" standalone="yes"?>
<!DOCTYPE document [
<!ELEMENT document (employee)*>
<!ELEMENT employee (name, hiredate, projects)>
<!ELEMENT name (lastname, firstname)>
<!ELEMENT lastname (#PCDATA)>
<!ELEMENT firstname (#PCDATA)>
<!ELEMENT hiredate (#PCDATA)>
<!ELEMENT projects (project)*>
<!ELEMENT project (product,id,price)>
<!ELEMENT product (#PCDATA)>
<!ELEMENT id (#PCDATA)>
<!ELEMENT price (#PCDATA)>
] >
<document>
    <employee>
        <name>
            <lastname>Kelly</lastname>
            <firstname>Grace</firstname>
        </name>
        <hiredate>October 15, 2005</hiredate>
        <projects>
            <project>
```

LISTING 4.1 continued

```
                <product>Printer</product>
                <id>111</id>
                <price>$111.00</price>
            </project>
            <project>
                <product>Laptop</product>
                <id>222</id>
                <price>$989.00</price>
            </project>
        </projects>
    </employee>
    <employee>
        <name>
            <lastname>Grant</lastname>
            <firstname>Cary</firstname>
        </name>
        <hiredate>October 20, 2005</hiredate>
        <projects>
            <project>
                <product>Desktop</product>
                <id>333</id>
                <price>$2995.00</price>
            </project>
            <project>
                <product>Scanner</product>
                <id>444</id>
                <price>$200.00</price>
            </project>
        </projects>
    </employee>
    <employee>
        <name>
            <lastname>Gable</lastname>
            <firstname>Clark</firstname>
        </name>
        <hiredate>October 25, 2005</hiredate>
        <projects>
            <project>
                <product>Keyboard</product>
                <id>555</id>
                <price>$129.00</price>
            </project>
            <project>
                <product>Mouse</product>
                <id>666</id>
                <price>$25.00</price>
            </project>
        </projects>
    </employee>
</document>
```

Validating a Document by Using a DTD

Before you create DTDs of the kind shown in `ch04_01.xml` (refer to Listing 4.1), let's take a look at how to use DTDs to check an XML document's validity by using an XML validator. We discussed and used XML validators on Day 1, "Welcome to XML," and that discussion provides a list of online XML validators that make use of DTDs. One of the easiest to use is the Scholarly Technology Group's XML validator at Brown University, `http://www.stg.brown.edu/service/xmlvalid`; although it's online, it lets you browse to XML documents on your hard drive to check them. Figure 4.1 shows the results of validating today's first DTD example, `ch04_01.xml`; as we can see, the document validates correctly.

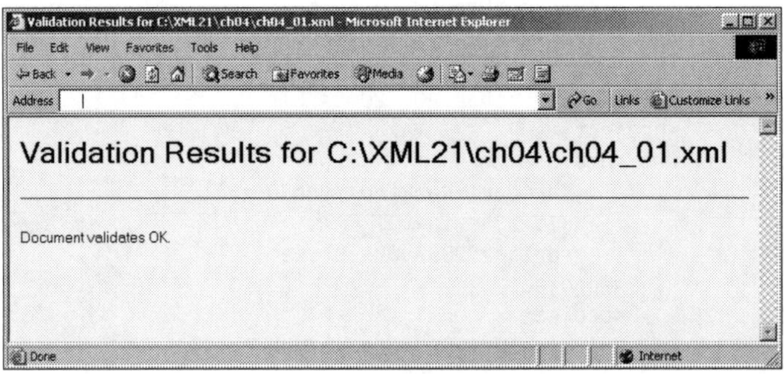

FIGURE 4.1
Validating an XML document by using a DTD.

On the other hand, say that our data-entry team made a mistake and someone typed `<nane>` instead of `<name>` in an element:

```
<document>
    <employee>
        <nane>
            <lastname>Kelly</lastname>
            <firstname>Grace</firstname>
        </name>
        <hiredate>October 15, 2005</hiredate>
        <projects>
            <project>
                <product>Printer</product>
                <id>111</id>
                <price>$111.00</price>
            </project>
            <project>
                <product>Laptop</product>
                <id>222</id>
                <price>$989.00</price>
            </project>
        </projects>
```

```
</employee>
    .
    .
    .
```

This error would not be easy to catch if you were trying to check all 5,000 employee records by eye, but it's no problem at all for an XML validator. Figure 4.2 shows how the Scholarly Technology Group's XML validator catches this error and others.

FIGURE 4.2

Catching an error in an XML document by using a DTD.

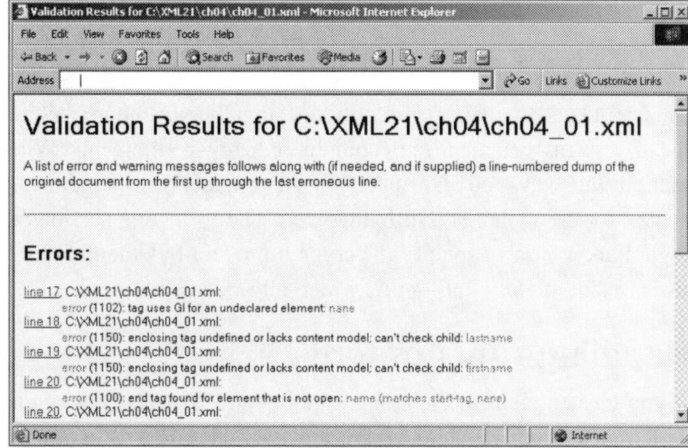

TIP

> Can a browser such as Internet Explorer use DTDs to validate XML documents? Yes, but not by default. By default, Internet Explorer can use XML schemas and displays the results when loading a document. But if we want to validate by using DTDs in Internet Explorer, we can only check whether the validation went well by using a scripting language such as JavaScript. Day 15, "Using JavaScript and XML," describes how to handle DTDs in Internet Explorer.

Let's start creating DTDs like the one shown in `ch04_01.xml`. You've seen that a DTD goes in a `<!DOCTYPE>` element, but what does the actual DTD itself look like? The first step in creating that DTD is to declare the elements that appear in the XML document, as described in the following section.

Creating Element Content Models

To declare the syntax of an element in a DTD, we use the `<!ELEMENT>` element like this: `<!ELEMENT` *`name content_model`*`>`. In this syntax, *`name`* is the name of the element we're declaring and *content_model* is the content model of the element. A *content model* indicates what content the element is allowed to have—for example, you can allow child elements or text data, or you can make the element empty by using the EMPTY keyword, or you can allow any content by using the ANY keyword, as you'll soon see. Here's how to declare the <document> element in ch04_01.xml:

```
<!DOCTYPE document [
<!ELEMENT document (employee)*>
          .
          .
          .
]>
```

This <!ELEMENT> element not only declares the <document> element, but it also says that the <document> element may contain <employee> elements. When you declare an element in this way, you also specify what contents that element can legally contain; the syntax for doing that is a little involved. The following sections dissect that syntax, taking a look at how to specify the content model of elements, starting with the least restrictive content model of all—ANY, which allows any content at all.

Handling Any Content

If you give an element the content model ANY, that element can contain any content, which means any elements and/or any character data. What this really means is that you're turning off validation for this element because the contents of elements with the content model ANY are not even checked. Here's how to specify the content model ANY for an element named <document>:

```
<!DOCTYPE document [
<!ELEMENT document ANY>
          .
          .
          .
]>
```

As far as the XML validator is concerned, this just turns off validation for the <document> element. It's usually not a good idea to turn off validation, but you might want to turn off validation for specific elements, for example, if you want to debug a DTD that's not working. It's usually far preferable to actually list the contents you want to allow in an element, such as any possible child elements the element can contain.

Specifying Child Elements

You can specify what child elements an element can contain in that element's content model. For example, you can specify that an element can contain another element by explicitly listing the name of the contained element in parentheses, like this:

```
<!DOCTYPE document [
<!ELEMENT document (employee)*>
        .
        .
        .
]>
```

This specifies that a `<document>` element can contain `<employee>` elements. The `*` here means that a `<document>` element can contain any number (including zero) `<employee>` elements. (We'll talk about what other possibilities besides `*` are available in a few pages.) With this line in a DTD, you can now start placing an `<employee>` element or elements inside a `<document>` element, this way:

```
<?xml version = "1.0" standalone="yes"?>
<!DOCTYPE document [
<!ELEMENT document (employee)*>
]>
<document>
    <employee>
        .
        .
        .
    </employee>
</document>
```

Note, however, that this is no longer a valid XML document because you haven't specified the syntax for individual `<employee>` elements. Because `<employee>` elements can contain `<name>`, `<hiredate>`, and `<projects>` elements, *in that order*, you can specify a content model for `<employee>` elements this way:

```
<?xml version = "1.0" standalone="yes"?>
<!DOCTYPE document [
<!ELEMENT document (employee)*>
<!ELEMENT employee (name, hiredate, projects)>
<!ELEMENT name (lastname, firstname)>
<document>
    <employee>
        <name>
            <lastname>Kelly</lastname>
            <firstname>Grace</firstname>
        </name>
        <hiredate>October 15, 2005</hiredate>
        <projects>
            <project>
                <product>Printer</product>
                <id>111</id>
                <price>$111.00</price>
            </project>
            <project>
```

4

```
                <product>Laptop</product>
                <id>222</id>
                <price>$989.00</price>
            </project>
        </projects>
    </employee>
</document>
```

Listing multiple elements in a content model this way is called creating a *sequence*. You use commas to separate the elements you want to have appear, and then the elements have to appear in that sequence in our XML document. For example, if you declare this sequence in the DTD:

```
<!ELEMENT employee (name, hiredate, projects)>
```

then inside an `<employee>` element, the `<name>` element must come first, followed by the `<hiredate>` element, followed by the `<projects>` element, like this:

```
<employee>
    <name>
        <lastname>Kelly</lastname>
        <firstname>Grace</firstname>
    </name>
    <hiredate>October 15, 2005</hiredate>
    <projects>
        <project>
            <product>Printer</product>
            <id>111</id>
            <price>$111.00</price>
        </project>
        <project>
            <product>Laptop</product>
            <id>222</id>
            <price>$989.00</price>
        </project>
    </projects>
</employee>
```

This example introduces a whole new set of elements—`<name>`, `<hiredate>`, `<lastname>`, and so on—that don't contain other elements at all—they contain text. So how can you specify that an element contains text? Read on.

Handling Text Content

In the preceding section's example, the `<name>`, `<hiredate>`, and `<lastname>` elements contain text data. In DTDs, non-markup text is considered parsed character data (in other words, text that has already been parsed, which means the XML processor shouldn't touch that text because it doesn't contain markup). In a DTD, we refer to parsed character data as #PCDATA. Note that this is the only way to refer to text data in a DTD—you can't say anything about the actual format of the text, although that might be important if you're dealing with numbers. In fact, this lack of precision is one of the reasons that XML schemas were introduced.

Here's how to give the text-containing elements in the PCDATA content model example:

```
<?xml version = "1.0" standalone="yes"?>
<!DOCTYPE document [
<!ELEMENT document (employee)*>
<!ELEMENT employee (name, hiredate, projects)>
<!ELEMENT name (lastname, firstname)>
<!ELEMENT lastname (#PCDATA)>
<!ELEMENT firstname (#PCDATA)>
<!ELEMENT hiredate (#PCDATA)>
<!ELEMENT projects (project)*>
<!ELEMENT project (product,id,price)>
<!ELEMENT product (#PCDATA)>
<!ELEMENT id (#PCDATA)>
<!ELEMENT price (#PCDATA)>
]>
<document>
    <employee>
        <name>
            <lastname>Kelly</lastname>
            <firstname>Grace</firstname>
        </name>
        <hiredate>October 15, 2005</hiredate>
        <projects>
            <project>
                <product>Printer</product>
                <id>111</id>
                <price>$111.00</price>
            </project>
            <project>
                <product>Laptop</product>
                <id>222</id>
                <price>$989.00</price>
            </project>
        </projects>
    </employee>
</document>
```

NOTE

Can you mix elements and PCDATA in the same content model? Yes, you can. This is called a *mixed content model*, and you'll see how to work with such models in a few pages.

4

You're almost done with the sample DTD—except for the `*` symbol. The following section takes a look at `*` and the other possible symbols to use.

Specifying Multiple Child Elements

There are a number of options for declaring an element that can contain child elements. You can declare the element to contain a single child element:

```
<!ELEMENT document (employee)>
```

You can declare the element to contain a list of child elements, in order:

```
<!ELEMENT document (employee, contractor, partner)>
```

You can also use symbols with special meanings in DTDs, such as `*`, which means "zero or more of," as in this example, where you're allowing zero or more `<employee>` elements in a `<document>` element:

```
<!ELEMENT document (employee)*>
```

There are a number of other ways of specifying multiple children by using symbols. (This syntax is actually borrowed from regular expression handling in the Perl language, so if you know that language, you have a leg up here.) Here are the possibilities:

- **x+**—Means x can appear one or more times.
- **x***—Means x can appear zero or more times.
- **x?**—Means x can appear once or not at all.
- **x, y**—Means x followed by y.
- **x | y**—Means x *or* y—but not both.

The following sections take a look at these options.

Allowing One or More Children

You might want to specify that a `<document>` element can contain between 200 and 250 `<employee>` elements, and if you do, you're out of luck with DTDs because DTD syntax doesn't give us that kind of precision. On the other hand, you still do have some control here; for example, you can specify that a `<document>` element must contain one or more `<employee>` elements if you use a + symbol, like this:

```
<!ELEMENT document (employee)+>
```

Here, the XML processor is being told that a `<document>` element has to contain at least one `<employee>` element.

Allowing Zero or More Children

By using a DTD, you can use the `*` symbol to specify that you want an element to contain any number of child elements—that is, zero or more child elements. You saw this in action earlier today, when you specified that the `<document>` element may contain `<employee>` elements in the `ch04_01.xml` example:

```
<!ELEMENT document (employee)*>
```

Allowing Zero or One Child

When using a DTD, you can use `?` to specify zero or one child elements. Using `?` indicates that a particular child element *may* be present once in the element you're declaring, but it need not be. For example, here's how to indicate that a `<document>` element may contain zero or one `<employee>` elements:

```
<!ELEMENT document (employee)?>
```

Using `+`, `*`, and `?` in Sequences

You can use the `+`, `*`, and `?` symbols in content model sequences. For example, here's how you might specify that there can be one or more `<name>` elements for an employee, an optional `<hiredate>` element, and any number of `<project>` elements:

4

```
<?xml version = "1.0" standalone="yes"?>
<!DOCTYPE document [
<!ELEMENT document (employee)*>
<!ELEMENT employee (name+, hiredate?, projects*)>
<!ELEMENT name (lastname, firstname)>
<!ELEMENT lastname (#PCDATA)>
<!ELEMENT firstname (#PCDATA)>
<!ELEMENT hiredate (#PCDATA)>
<!ELEMENT projects (project)*>
<!ELEMENT project (product,id,price)>
<!ELEMENT product (#PCDATA)>
<!ELEMENT id (#PCDATA)>
<!ELEMENT price (#PCDATA)>
]>
<document>
    <employee>
        <name>
            <lastname>Kelly</lastname>
            <firstname>Grace</firstname>
        </name>
        <hiredate>October 15, 2005</hiredate>
        <projects>
            <project>
                <product>Printer</product>
                <id>111</id>
                <price>$111.00</price>
```

```
            </project>
            <project>
                <product>Laptop</product>
                <id>222</id>
                <price>$989.00</price>
            </project>
        </projects>
    </employee>
</document>
```

Using +, *, and ? inside sequences provides a lot of flexibility because it means you can specify how many times an element can appear in a sequence—and even whether the element can be absent altogether.

In fact, you can get even more powerful results by using the +, *, and ? operators inside sequences. By using parentheses, we can create *subsequences*—that is, sequences inside sequences. For example, say that we wanted to allow each employee to list multiple names (including nicknames and so on), possibly list his or her age, and give multiple phone numbers. You can do that by using the subsequence shown in Listing 4.2.

LISTING 4.2 A Sample XML Document That Uses Subsequences in a DTD (ch04_02.xml)

```
<?xml version = "1.0" encoding="UTF-8" standalone="yes"?>
<!DOCTYPE document [
<!ELEMENT document (employee)*>
<!ELEMENT employee ((name, age?, phone*)+, hiredate, projects)>
<!ELEMENT name (lastname, firstname)>
<!ELEMENT lastname (#PCDATA)>
<!ELEMENT firstname (#PCDATA)>
<!ELEMENT hiredate (#PCDATA)>
<!ELEMENT projects (project)*>
<!ELEMENT project (product,id,price)>
<!ELEMENT product (#PCDATA)>
<!ELEMENT age (#PCDATA)>
<!ELEMENT phone (#PCDATA)>
<!ELEMENT id (#PCDATA)>
<!ELEMENT price (#PCDATA)>
]>
<document>
    <employee>
        <name>
            <lastname>Kelly</lastname>
            <firstname>Grace</firstname>
        </name>
        <phone>
            555.2345
        </phone>
        <hiredate>October 15, 2005</hiredate>
```

LISTING 4.2 continued

```
        <projects>
            <project>
                <product>Printer</product>
                <id>111</id>
                <price>$111.00</price>
            </project>
            <project>
                <product>Laptop</product>
                <id>222</id>
                <price>$989.00</price>
            </project>
        </projects>
    </employee>
    <employee>
        <name>
            <lastname>Grant</lastname>
            <firstname>Cary</firstname>
        </name>
        <age>
            32
        </age>
        <phone>
            555.2346
        </phone>
        <hiredate>October 20, 2005</hiredate>
        <projects>
            <project>
                <product>Desktop</product>
                <id>333</id>
                <price>$2995.00</price>
            </project>
            <project>
                <product>Scanner</product>
                <id>444</id>
                <price>$200.00</price>
            </project>
        </projects>
    </employee>
    <employee>
        <name>
            <lastname>Gable</lastname>
            <firstname>Clark</firstname>
        </name>
        <age>
            46
        </age>
        <phone>
            555.2347
        </phone>
```

LISTING 4.2 continued

```
        <hiredate>October 25, 2005</hiredate>
        <projects>
            <project>
                <product>Keyboard</product>
                <id>555</id>
                <price>$129.00</price>
            </project>
            <project>
                <product>Mouse</product>
                <id>666</id>
                <price>$25.00</price>
            </project>
        </projects>
    </employee>
</document>
```

Getting creative when defining subsequences and using the +, *, and ? operators allows us to be extremely flexible in DTDs.

Allowing Choices

DTDs can support *choices*. By using a choice, we can specify one of a group of items. For example, if you want to specify that one (and only one) of either <x>, <y>, or <z> will appear, use a choice like this:

```
(x | y | z)
```

Listing 4.3 shows an example of using choices in the document `ch04_03.xml`. In that example, each product is allowed to contain *either* a `<price>` element *or* a `<discountprice>` element. To indicate that that's what you want, you only need to make this change to the DTD (as well as declare the new `<discountprice>` element):

```
<!ELEMENT project (product, id, (price | discountprice))>
```

LISTING 4.3 A Sample XML Document That Uses Choices in a DTD (`ch04_03.xml`)

```
<?xml version = "1.0" standalone="yes"?>
<!DOCTYPE document [
<!ELEMENT document (employee)*>
<!ELEMENT employee (name, hiredate, projects)>
<!ELEMENT name (lastname, firstname)>
<!ELEMENT lastname (#PCDATA)>
<!ELEMENT firstname (#PCDATA)>
<!ELEMENT hiredate (#PCDATA)>
<!ELEMENT projects (project)*>
<!ELEMENT project (product, id, (price | discountprice))>
```

LISTING 4.3 continued

```
<!ELEMENT product (#PCDATA)>
<!ELEMENT id (#PCDATA)>
<!ELEMENT price (#PCDATA) >
<!ELEMENT discountprice (#PCDATA)>
]>
<document>
    <employee>
        <name>
            <lastname>Kelly</lastname>
            <firstname>Grace</firstname>
        </name>
        <hiredate>October 15, 2005</hiredate>
        <projects>
            <project>
                <product>Printer</product>
                <id>111</id>
                <discountprice>$111.00</discountprice>
            </project>
            <project>
                <product>Laptop</product>
                <id>222</id>
                <price>$989.00</price>
            </project>
        </projects>
    </employee>
        .
        .
        .
    <employee>
        <name>
            <lastname>Gable</lastname>
            <firstname>Clark</firstname>
        </name>
        <hiredate>October 25, 2005</hiredate>
        <projects>
            <project>
                <product>Keyboard</product>
                <id>555</id>
                <price>$129.00</price>
            </project>
            <project>
                <product>Mouse</product>
                <id>666</id>
                <discountprice>$25.00</discountprice>
            </project>
        </projects>
    </employee>
</document>
```

You can also use the +, *, and ? operators with choices. For example, to allow multiple discount prices and to insist that at least one element from the choice appear in the XML document, you can do something like this:

```
<!ELEMENT project (product, id, (price | discountprice*)+)>
```

As you can see, there are plenty of options available when it comes to specifying elements or text content in DTDs (although XML schemas allow us to be even more precise, specifying numeric formats for numbers and so on). But what if we want a content model to let an element contain both elements and text? That's coming up next.

Allowing Mixed Content

When using a DTD, you can allow an element to contain text or child elements, giving it a mixed content model. Note that even with a mixed content model, an element can't contain child elements and text data at the same level at the same time (unless you use the content model ANY). For example, this doesn't work:

```
<product>
    Keyboard
    <stocknumber>1113</stocknumber>
<product>
```

However, you can set up a DTD so that an element can contain *either* child elements *or* text data. To do that, we treat #PCDATA as we would any element name in a DTD choice. Listing 4.4 shows an example of this; in this example, the <product> element is declared so that it can have text content *or* it can contain a <stocknumber> element.

LISTING 4.4 A Sample XML Document That Uses a Mixed Content Model (ch04_04.xml)

```
<?xml version = "1.0" encoding="UTF-8" standalone="yes"?>
<!DOCTYPE document [
<!ELEMENT document (employee)*>
<!ELEMENT employee (name, hiredate, projects)>
<!ELEMENT name (lastname, firstname)>
<!ELEMENT lastname (#PCDATA)>
<!ELEMENT firstname (#PCDATA)>
<!ELEMENT hiredate (#PCDATA)>
<!ELEMENT projects (project)*>
<!ELEMENT project (product, id, price)>
<!ELEMENT product (#PCDATA | stocknumber)*>
<!ELEMENT id (#PCDATA)>
<!ELEMENT price (#PCDATA)>
<!ELEMENT stocknumber (#PCDATA)>
]>
<document>
    <employee>
```

LISTING 4.4 continued

```
        <name>
            <lastname>Kelly</lastname>
            <firstname>Grace</firstname>
        </name>
        <hiredate>October 15, 2005</hiredate>
        <projects>
            <project>
                <product>
                    <stocknumber>1111</stocknumber>
                </product>
                <id>111</id>
                <price>$111.00</price>
            </project>
            <project>
                <product>
                    Laptop
                </product>
                <id>222</id>
                <price>$989.00</price>
            </project>
        </projects>
    </employee>
        .
        .
        .
    <employee>
        <name>
            <lastname>Gable</lastname>
            <firstname>Clark</firstname>
        </name>
        <hiredate>October 25, 2005</hiredate>
        <projects>
            <project>
                <product>
                    <stocknumber>1113</stocknumber>
                </product>
                <id>555</id>
                <price>$129.00</price>
            </project>
            <project>
                <product>Mouse</product>
                <id>666</id>
                <price>$25.00</price>
            </project>
        </projects>
    </employee>
</document>
```

There are plenty of restrictions when we use a mixed content model like this in a DTD. We cannot specify the order of the child elements, and we cannot use the +, *, or ? operators. In fact, there's usually very little reason to use mixed content models at all in XML. We're almost always better off being consistent and declaring a new element that can contain our text data than using a mixed content model.

Allowing Empty Elements

Elements don't need to have any content at all, of course; they can be empty. As you would expect, you can support empty elements by using DTDs. In particular, you can create an empty content model with the keyword `EMPTY`, like this:

```
<!ELEMENT intern EMPTY>
```

This declares an empty element named `<intern/>` that you can use to indicate that an employee is an intern. Listing 4.5 shows this new empty element at work in `ch04_05.xml`. As you can see, this example allows each `<employee>` element to contain an `<intern/>` element—and makes that element optional.

LISTING 4.5 A Sample XML Document That Uses an Empty Element (`ch04_05.xml`)

```
<?xml version = "1.0" encoding="UTF-8" standalone="yes"?>
<!DOCTYPE document [
<!ELEMENT document (employee)*>
<!ELEMENT employee (intern?, name, hiredate, projects)>
<!ELEMENT name (lastname, firstname)>
<!ELEMENT lastname (#PCDATA)>
<!ELEMENT firstname (#PCDATA)>
<!ELEMENT hiredate (#PCDATA)>
<!ELEMENT projects (project)*>
<!ELEMENT project (product, id, price)>
<!ELEMENT product (#PCDATA)>
<!ELEMENT id (#PCDATA)>
<!ELEMENT price (#PCDATA)>
<!ELEMENT intern EMPTY>
]>
<document>
    <employee>
        <intern/>
        <name>
            <lastname>Kelly</lastname>
            <firstname>Grace</firstname>
        </name>
        <hiredate>October 15, 2005</hiredate>
        <projects>
            <project>
                <product>Printer</product>
```

LISTING 4.5 continued

```
                <id>111</id>
                <price>$111.00</price>
            </project>
            <project>
                <product>Laptop</product>
                <id>222</id>
                <price>$989.00</price>
            </project>
        </projects>
    </employee>
        .
        .
        .
    <employee>
        <intern/>
        <name>
            <lastname>Gable</lastname>
            <firstname>Clark</firstname>
        </name>
        <hiredate>October 25, 2005</hiredate>
        <projects>
            <project>
                <product>Keyboard</product>
                <id>555</id>
                <price>$129.00</price>
            </project>
            <project>
                <product>Mouse</product>
                <id>666</id>
                <price>$25.00</price>
            </project>
        </projects>
    </employee>
</document>
```


Empty elements can't contain any content, but they can contain attributes, and tomorrow we'll talk about how to support attributes in DTDs.

Commenting a DTD

DTDs can get long and involved in complex XML documents. You can use standard XML comments in DTDs, just as you can throughout the body of an XML document, to clarify what you're doing. Here's an example of comments in a DTD:

```
<!DOCTYPE document [
<!--Create the document element first -->
```

```
<!ELEMENT document (employee)*>
<!--Each employee needs a name, hire date, and projects -->
<!ELEMENT employee (name, hiredate, projects)>
<!-- Should we reverse the order of these two? -->
<!ELEMENT name (lastname, firstname)>
<!ELEMENT lastname (#PCDATA)>
<!ELEMENT firstname (#PCDATA)>
<!--Use standard date format for the hiredate element -->
<!ELEMENT hiredate (#PCDATA)>
<!ELEMENT projects (project)*>
<!ELEMENT project (product, id, price)>
<!--Product name should match catalog 8547382 -->
<!ELEMENT product (#PCDATA)>
<!ELEMENT id (#PCDATA)>
<!ELEMENT price (#PCDATA)>
]>
```

As in any standard XML document, comments in a DTD are stripped out of the DTD by the XML processor. Some XML processors pass those comments on to us, but some don't.

Supporting External DTDs

So far, we've stored DTDs internally in XML documents, using `<!DOCTYPE>` elements. But we can also store DTDs externally, in entirely separate files (which usually use the extension `.dtd`). It's often a good idea to use an external DTD with an XML application that is shared by many people. That way, if you want to make changes in the XML application, you only need to change the DTD once, not in dozens of separate files. (In fact, that's the way many XML applications, such as XHTML, are implemented.)

Private and Public DTDs

There are two ways to support external DTDs—as private DTDs for personal or limited use and as public DTDs for public use. We'll start with private DTDs.

Creating Private DTDs

You specify that we're using an external private DTD by using the `SYSTEM` keyword in the `<!DOCTYPE>` element, like this:

```
<!DOCTYPE document SYSTEM "ch04_07.dtd">
```

This example specifies the name of the document element (which is just `<document>` in this example), the `SYSTEM` keyword to indicate that the example is using a private external DTD, and the name of the external DTD file. Note that because the XML document now depends on an external file, the external DTD file, we must also change the `standalone` attribute from "yes" to "no", as shown in ch04_06.xml in Listing 4.6. The external DTD here is in ch04_07.dtd, which is shown in Listing 4.7. Note that the external DTD simply holds the part of the document that was originally between the [and] in the earlier versions of the <!DOCTYPE> element.

LISTING 4.6 A Sample XML Document That Uses a Private External DTD (ch04_06.xml)

```
<?xml version = "1.0" encoding="UTF-8" standalone="no"?>
<!DOCTYPE document SYSTEM "ch04_07.dtd">
<document>
    <employee>
        <name>
            <lastname>Kelly</lastname>
            <firstname>Grace</firstname>
        </name>
        <hiredate>October 15, 2005</hiredate>
        <projects>
            <project>
                <product>Printer</product>
                <id>111</id>
                <price>$111.00</price>
            </project>
            <project>
                <product>Laptop</product>
                <id>222</id>
                <price>$989.00</price>
            </project>
        </projects>
    </employee>
        .
        .
        .
</document>
```

LISTING 4.7 An External DTD (ch04_07.dtd)

```
<!ELEMENT document (employee)*>
<!ELEMENT employee (name, hiredate, projects)>
<!ELEMENT name (lastname, firstname)>
<!ELEMENT lastname (#PCDATA)>
<!ELEMENT firstname (#PCDATA)>
<!ELEMENT hiredate (#PCDATA)>
<!ELEMENT projects (project)*>
<!ELEMENT project (product,id,price)>
<!ELEMENT product (#PCDATA)>
<!ELEMENT id (#PCDATA)>
<!ELEMENT price (#PCDATA) >
```

The example shown in Listing 4.7 assumes that the external DTD is in the same directory as the XML document itself, so you just need to give the name of the external DTD file in the <!DOCTYPE> element:

```
<?xml version = "1.0" standalone="no"?>
<!DOCTYPE document SYSTEM "ch04_07.dtd">
```

On the other hand, you can place the external DTD anywhere, as long as you give its full URI (in this case, that's just the full URL, as far as most XML processors are concerned) in the <!DOCTYPE> element, as in this example:

```
<?xml version = "1.0" standalone="no"?>
<!DOCTYPE document SYSTEM "http://www.xmlpowercorp.com/dtds/ch04_07.dtd">
```

You need to supply a URL like this for an external DTD if you want to use an online XML validator.

Creating Public DTDs

As discussed so far today, it's easy to create and use a private external DTD. Creating and using a public external DTD can take a little more work. In this case, you use the `PUBLIC` keyword instead of `SYSTEM` in the <!DOCTYPE> DTD. To use the `PUBLIC` keyword, you must also create a *formal public identifier (FPI)*, which is a quoted string of text, made up of four fields separated by `//`. For example, the official FPI for transitional XHTML 1.0 is `-//W3C//DTD XHTML 1.0 Transitional//EN`. Here are the rules for creating the fields in FPIs:

- The first field indicates whether the DTD is for a formal standard. For DTDs you create on your own, this field should be `-`. If a non-official standards body has created the DTD, you use `+`. For formal standards bodies, this field is a reference to the standard itself (such as `ISO/IEC 19775:2003`).
- The second field holds the name of the group or person responsible for the DTD. You should use a name that is unique (for example, W3C just uses `W3C`).
- The third field specifies the type of the document the DTD is for and should be followed by a unique version number of some kind (such as `Version 1.0`).
- The fourth field specifies the language in which the DTD is written (for example, `EN` for English) .

When you use a public external DTD, we can use the <!DOCTYPE> element like this: `<!DOCTYPE` *`rootname`* `PUBLIC` *`FPI URI`*`>`. Listing 4.8 shows an example, `ch04_08.xml`, which uses the made-up FPI `-//DTDS4ALL//Custom DTD Version 1.0//EN`. This document uses `ch04_07.dtd` as the external DTD, as in the previous example, but as we can see, it treats that DTD as a public external DTD, complete with its own FPI.

LISTING 4.8 A Sample XML Document That Uses a Public External DTD (ch04_08.xml)

```
<?xml version = "1.0" standalone="no"?>
<!DOCTYPE document PUBLIC "-//DTDS4ALL//Custom DTD Version 1.0//EN"
"http://www.xmlpowercorp.com/dtds/ch04_07.dtd">
<document>
    <employee>
        <name>
            <lastname>Kelly</lastname>
            <firstname>Grace</firstname>
        </name>
        <hiredate>October 15, 2005</hiredate>
        <projects>
            <project>
                <product>Printer</product>
                <id>111</id>
                <price>$111.00</price>
            </project>
            <project>
                <product>Laptop</product>
                <id>222</id>
                <price>$989.00</price>
            </project>
        </projects>
    </employee>
        .
        .
        .
</document>
```


Using Internal and External DTDs at the Same Time

So far, you've seen these versions of the `<!DOCTYPE>` element:

- `<!DOCTYPE *rootname* [*DTD*]>`
- `<!DOCTYPE *rootname* SYSTEM *URI*>`
- `<!DOCTYPE *rootname* PUBLIC *identifier URI*>`

However, you can also use *both* internal and external DTDs if you use these forms of the `<!DOCTYPE>` element:

- `<!DOCTYPE *rootname* SYSTEM *URI* [*DTD*]>`
- `<!DOCTYPE *rootname* PUBLIC *identifier URI* [*DTD*]>`

In this case, the external DTD is specified by *URL* and the internal one by *DTD*. Listing 4.9 shows an example in ch04_09.xml, where the external DTD—ch04_10.xml in Listing 4.10—specifies the syntax of all elements in ch04_09.xml except the `<price>` element, which is specified in the `<!DOCTYPE>` element in the XML document ch04_09.xml.

LISTING 4.9 A Sample XML Document That Uses an Internal DTD and an External DTD (`ch04_09.xml`)

```
<?xml version = "1.0" encoding="UTF-8" standalone="no"?>
<!DOCTYPE document SYSTEM "http://www.lightlink.com/steve/ch04_10.dtd" [
<!ELEMENT price (#PCDATA)>
]>
<document>
    <employee>
        <name>
            <lastname>Kelly</lastname>
            <firstname>Grace</firstname>
        </name>
        <hiredate>October 15, 2005</hiredate>
        <projects>
            <project>
                <product>Printer</product>
                <id>111</id>
                <price>$111.00</price>
            </project>
            <project>
                <product>Laptop</product>
                <id>222</id>
                <price>$989.00</price>
            </project>
        </projects>
    </employee>
        .
        .
        .
</document>
```

LISTING 4.10 The External DTD for ch04_09.xml (`ch04_10.xml`)

```
<!ELEMENT document (employee)*>
<!ELEMENT employee (name, hiredate, projects)>
<!ELEMENT name (lastname, firstname)>
<!ELEMENT lastname (#PCDATA)>
<!ELEMENT firstname (#PCDATA)>
<!ELEMENT hiredate (#PCDATA)>
<!ELEMENT projects (project)*>
<!ELEMENT project (product,id,price)>
<!ELEMENT product (#PCDATA)>
<!ELEMENT id (#PCDATA) >
```

Combining internal and external DTDs like this is a good idea if you have a standard DTD that we share with other XML documents but also want to do some customization in certain XML documents. Theoretically, if you specify the syntax for an element or attribute in both an internal and external DTD, the internal DTD is supposed to take precedence. Unfortunately, however, most XML processors these days just treat conflicts in an internal and external DTD as errors.

Handling Namespaces in DTDs

Another important topic when it comes to working with DTDs is how to handle namespaces. As we already know, a *namespace* name is really just a name prepended to an element or attribute name with a colon. That means that as far as a DTD is concerned, those new names have to be declared.

For example, if we want to put our employees document into a namespace named `emp`, our elements would change from `<name>` to `<emp:name>`, from `<hiredate>` to `<emp:hiredate>`, and so on. And to make the document valid, we would have to declare those new names in the DTD.

To see how this works, you can start by declaring the namespace `emp`, using the attribute `xmlns:emp` in the document element, and then using that namespace throughout the document:


```
<emp:document xmlns:emp="http://www.xmlpowercorp.com/dtds/">
    <emp:employee>
        <emp:name>
            <emp:lastname>Kelly</emp:lastname>
            <emp:firstname>Grace</emp:firstname>
        </emp:name>
        <emp:hiredate>October 15, 2005</emp:hiredate>
        <emp:projects>
            <emp:project>
        .
        .
        .
```

Now construct the DTD to match. Start with the `xmlns:emp` attribute itself. As you'll see tomorrow, if you use attributes in an XML document with a DTD, you have to declare them in that DTD. Here's how to do that:

```
<?xml version = "1.0" encoding="UTF-8" standalone="yes"?>
<!DOCTYPE document [
<!ELEMENT document (employee)*>
<!ATTLIST document
    xmlns:emp CDATA #FIXED "http://www.xmlpowercorp.com/dtds/">
<!ELEMENT employee (name, hiredate, projects)>
<!ELEMENT name (lastname, firstname)>
<!ELEMENT lastname (#PCDATA)>
```

```
<!ELEMENT firstname (#PCDATA)>
<!ELEMENT hiredate (#PCDATA)>
<!ELEMENT projects (project)*>
<!ELEMENT project (product, id, price)>
<!ELEMENT product (#PCDATA)>
<!ELEMENT id (#PCDATA)>
<!ELEMENT price (#PCDATA)>
]>
```

Now you're free to use the `emp` namespace when you declare each element in the DTD:

```
<?xml version = "1.0" encoding="UTF-8" standalone="yes"?>
<!DOCTYPE emp:document [
<!ELEMENT emp:document (emp:employee)*>
<!ATTLIST emp:document
    xmlns:emp CDATA #FIXED "http://www.xmlpowercorp.com/dtds/">
<!ELEMENT emp:employee (emp:name, emp:hiredate, emp:projects)>
<!ELEMENT emp:name (emp:lastname, emp:firstname)>
<!ELEMENT emp:lastname (#PCDATA)>
<!ELEMENT emp:firstname (#PCDATA)>
<!ELEMENT emp:hiredate (#PCDATA)>
<!ELEMENT emp:projects (emp:project)*>
<!ELEMENT emp:project (emp:product, emp:id, emp:price)>
<!ELEMENT emp:product (#PCDATA)>
<!ELEMENT emp:id (#PCDATA)>
<!ELEMENT emp:price (#PCDATA)>
]>
```

That's all there is to it. Now you can use the `emp` namespace throughout the document, as shown in `ch04_11.xml` in Listing 4.11.

LISTING 4.11 Using a Namespace in an XML Document with a DTD (`ch04_11.xml`)

```
<?xml version = "1.0" encoding="UTF-8" standalone="yes"?>
<!DOCTYPE emp:document [
<!ELEMENT emp:document (emp:employee)*>
<!ATTLIST emp:document
    xmlns:emp CDATA #FIXED "http://www.xmlpowercorp.com/dtds/">
<!ELEMENT emp:employee (emp:name, emp:hiredate, emp:projects)>
<!ELEMENT emp:name (emp:lastname, emp:firstname)>
<!ELEMENT emp:lastname (#PCDATA)>
<!ELEMENT emp:firstname (#PCDATA)>
<!ELEMENT emp:hiredate (#PCDATA)>
<!ELEMENT emp:projects (emp:project)*>
<!ELEMENT emp:project (emp:product, emp:id, emp:price)>
<!ELEMENT emp:product (#PCDATA)>
<!ELEMENT emp:id (#PCDATA)>
<!ELEMENT emp:price (#PCDATA)>
]>
<emp:document xmlns:emp="http://www.xmlpowercorp.com/dtds/">
```

LISTING 4.11 continued

```
    <emp:employee>
        <emp:name>
            <emp:lastname>Kelly</emp:lastname>
            <emp:firstname>Grace</emp:firstname>
        </emp:name>
        <emp:hiredate>October 15, 2005</emp:hiredate>
        <emp:projects>
            <emp:project>
                <emp:product>Printer</emp:product>
                <emp:id>111</emp:id>
                <emp:price>$111.00</emp:price>
            </emp:project>
            <emp:project>
                <emp:product>Laptop</emp:product>
                <emp:id>222</emp:id>
                <emp:price>$989.00</emp:price>
            </emp:project>
        </emp:projects>
    </emp:employee>
        .
        .
        .
    <emp:employee>
        <emp:name>
            <emp:lastname>Gable</emp:lastname>
            <emp:firstname>Clark</emp:firstname>
        </emp:name>
        <emp:hiredate>October 25, 2005</emp:hiredate>
        <emp:projects>
            <emp:project>
                <emp:product>Keyboard</emp:product>
                <emp:id>555</emp:id>
                <emp:price>$129.00</emp:price>
            </emp:project>
            <emp:project>
                <emp:product>Mouse</emp:product>
                <emp:id>666</emp:id>
                <emp:price>$25.00</emp:price>
            </emp:project>
        </emp:projects>
    </emp:employee>
</emp:document>
```

As today's discussion shows, supporting namespaces in DTDs is not difficult; you just treat the namespace and colon as part of the name of an element. In fact, as shown here, you also treat attributes the same way. Tomorrow we'll talk about the idea of declaring attributes in DTDs.

Summary

Today you practiced validating XML documents with DTDs and specified the syntax of XML documents for XML processors to check. In a perfect world, there would be no data-entry errors in XML documents, but real life is a different story. If you specify the syntax of an XML document, you can let an XML processor check that document automatically.

There are two ways to specify the syntax of XML documents—by using DTDs and XML schemas, both of which have syntaxes of their own. You saw today that you use the <!DOCTYPE> element to enclose a DTD and that DTD can either be internal to the XML document (in which case you set the XML declaration's standalone attribute to "yes"), external to the XML document (in which case you provide the DTD's URI and set the XML declaration's standalone attribute to "no"), or a combination of the two. You saw that XML validators can work with either type of DTD.

Today's discussion focuses on writing DTDs and using <!ELEMENT> to declare XML elements. You can use <!ELEMENT>, to use the following syntax for elements: <!ELEMENT *name content_model*>. Today you saw that there are various content models possible. You can use the content model ANY to allow any content and to turn off syntax checking, or use EMPTY to declare an empty element. You can list possible child elements by using <!ELEMENT document (employee)>, which allows a <document> element to contain an <employee> element.

You can also list the child elements an element can contain, in order, like this: <!ELEMENT employee (name, hiredate, projects)>. Such a list is called a *sequence*. You can also specify that an element contains text content—parsed character data—by using the term #PCDATA.

You saw today that you can use the symbols + (one or more), * (zero or more), ? (one or none), and | (choices) in DTDs so that you can work with multiple child elements. You can also use these symbols in sequences to specify exactly what child elements or combinations of child elements an element can contain.

Finally, you took a look at working with namespaces in DTDs. Because using a namespace changes the names of elements and attributes, you have to take the new names into account when we're writing a DTD with namespaces. You even have to declare the xmlns attribute that creates the namespace in the first place—and that's a topic we'll hear more about tomorrow.

Q&A

Q We've been using elements such as `<!DOCTYPE>` and `<!ELEMENT>` today. Is it okay to use lowercase for these element names?

A No. You need to call them `<!DOCTYPE>` and `<!ELEMENT>`, not `<!doctype>` and `<!element>`. The capitalization is specified in the XML 1.0 specification, and XML processors accept only the versions in the XML 1.0 specification.

Q Is there any way to create a mixed content model by using a DTD where you can mix both text data and elements on the same level (that is, as siblings), like this: `<document>Here is an element:<element>Hello!</element></document>`?

A Yes, you can use the `ANY` keyword. Beyond that, there's no way to do this. The XML 1.0 specification only allows you to create mixed content models by using choices, which means that in mixed content models, you can have *either* text data *or* elements, but not both at the same time (the elements themselves can contain text, of course).

Workshop

4

This workshop tests whether you understand the concepts discussed today. It's a good idea to make sure you can answer these questions before pressing on to tomorrow's work. Answers to the quiz can be found in Appendix A, "Quiz Answers."

Quiz

1. What's wrong with this XML document?

```
<?xml version = "1.0" encoding="UTF-8" standalone="yes"?>
<!DOCTYPE document [
<!ELEMENT document (employee)*>
<!ELEMENT employee (hiredate, name)>
]>
<document>
    <employee>
        <hiredate>October 15, 2005</hiredate>
        <name>
            Grace Kelly
        </name>
    </employee>
</document>
```

2. Where do you see a problem with this XML document?

```
<?xml version = "1.0" encoding="UTF-8" standalone="yes"?>
<!DOCTYPE document [
<!ELEMENT document (employee)*>
```

```
<!ELEMENT employee (name, hiredate)>
<!ELEMENT name (#PCDATA)>
<!ELEMENT hiredate (#PCDATA)>
]>
<document>
    <employee>
        <hiredate>October 15, 2005</hiredate>
        <name>
            Grace Kelly
        </name>
    </employee>
</document>
```

3. What error is in this XML document?

```
<?xml version = "1.0" encoding="UTF-8" standalone="yes"?>
<!DOCTYPE document [
<!ELEMENT document (employee)*>
<!ELEMENT employee (hiredate+ | name+)>
<!ELEMENT hiredate (#PCDATA)>
<!ELEMENT name (#PCDATA)>
]>
<document>
    <employee>
        <hiredate>October 15, 2005</hiredate>
        <name>
            Grace Kelly
        </name>
    </employee>
</document>
```

4. There's a problem in this XML document, too. What is it?

```
<?xml version = "1.0" encoding="UTF-8" standalone="yes"?>
<!DOCTYPE document [
<!ELEMENT document (employee)?>
<!ELEMENT employee (hiredate+, name*, phone+)>
<!ELEMENT hiredate (#PCDATA)>
<!ELEMENT name (#PCDATA)>
<!ELEMENT phone (#PCDATA)>
]>
<document>
    <employee>
        <hiredate>October 15, 2005</hiredate>
        <name>
            Grace Kelly
        </name>
        <phone>
            555.8888
        </phone>
    </employee>
    <employee>
        <hiredate>October 16, 2005</hiredate>
        <name>
```

```
            Myrna Loy
        </name>
        <name>
            Muriel Blandings
        </name>
        <phone>
            555.9999
        </phone>
    </employee>
</document>
```

5. What's wrong with this XML document?

```
<?xml version = "1.0" encoding="UTF-8" standalone="yes"?>
<!DOCTYPE document SYSTEM "employee.dtd">
<document>
    <employee>
        <name>
            Grace Kelly
        </name>
        <hiredate>October 15, 2005</hiredate>
    </employee>
</document>
```

Exercises

1. Create a new XML document that holds the names of your relatives by using elements such as `<brother>`, `<sister>`, `<mother>`, and `<father>`, as well as `<name>`, `<age>`, and `<address>` elements. Next, add a DTD to the document and use an XML validator such as the Scholarly Technology Group's XML validator, at `http://www.stg.brown.edu/service/xmlvalid`, to check whether your document is valid. Alternatively, add to the well-formed XML document you created in Exercise 1 at the end of yesterday's discussion a DTD that holds the available menu items and their prices at a favorite restaurant of yours.
2. Convert the XML document you created in Exercise 1 to make the DTD external. If you can upload the external DTD file to a Web server and include its URI in the `<!DOCTYPE>` element (for example, `<!DOCTYPE document SYSTEM "http://www.`*`server`*`.com/`*`username`*`/relatives.dtd">`), use an online XML validator such as the Scholarly Technology Group's XML validator to check the new document's validity.

4

PART I

DAY 5

Handling Attributes and Entities in DTDs

Yesterday you got your start with DTDs by seeing how to declare and handle elements. But that's only part of the story. Today's discussion continues with DTDs, explaining how to handle the other items you can declare in DTDs—attributes and entities. Both attributes and entities are essential parts of XML, and today's discussion will explain how to support them in valid XML documents. Here's an overview of the topics covered in today's discussion:

- Declaring attributes
- Understanding legal attribute types
- Using default values for attributes
- Making attributes required
- Giving attributes fixed values
- Working with entities
- Using general and parameter entities

- Working with internal and external entities
- Handling binary data

The term *entity* might seem worrisome, but it's actually very simple: In an XML document, an *entity* is simply a data item. In other words, *entity* is simply XML's way of referring to a piece of data. And you already know about the other big topic for today—attributes, which we'll start discussing now.

Declaring Attributes in DTDs

As in HTML, an *attribute* is a name-value pair that you can use in a start tag or an empty tag to provide additional information for an element. For example, say you want to add an attribute to an `<employee>` element named `supervisor`, which indicates whether an employee is a supervisor and which may be set to `"yes"` or `"no"`. Here's what that would look like in an XML document:

```
<document>
    <employee supervisor="no">
        <name>
            <lastname>Kelly</lastname>
            <firstname>Grace</firstname>
        </name>
    .
    .
    .
```

It's easy enough to add attributes to XML documents, but if you don't declare them in a DTD or an XML schema, your document won't be valid. You can declare a list of attributes for an element by using the `<!ATTLIST>` element in the DTD. Here's the general syntax of an `<!ATTLIST>` element:

```
<!ATTLIST element_name
    attribute_name type default_value
    attribute_name type default_value
    .
    .
    .
    attribute_name type default_value>
```

Here, *`element_name`* is the name of the element for which you're declaring attributes, *`attribute_name`* is the name of an attribute you want to declare, *`type`* is the attribute's type, and *`default_value`* specifies the default value of the attribute. Today's discussion describes what types and kinds of default values are possible in DTDs.

What does an attribute declaration look like? Listing 5.1 shows an example, in `ch05_01.xml`. In this example, the type of the supervisor attribute is `CDATA`, which stands for *character data*, and the default value is #IMPLIED, which means that you can use this attribute or not in <employee> elements.

LISTING 5.1 A Sample XML Document with an Attribute Declared in a DTD (ch05_01.xml)

```
<?xml version = "1.0" encoding="UTF-8" standalone="yes"?>
<!DOCTYPE document [
<!ELEMENT document (employee)*>
<!ELEMENT employee (name, hiredate, projects)>
<!ELEMENT name (lastname, firstname)>
<!ELEMENT lastname (#PCDATA)>
<!ELEMENT firstname (#PCDATA)>
<!ELEMENT hiredate (#PCDATA)>
<!ELEMENT projects (project)*>
<!ELEMENT project (product, id, price)>
<!ELEMENT product (#PCDATA)>
<!ELEMENT id (#PCDATA)>
<!ELEMENT price (#PCDATA) >
<!ATTLIST employee supervisor CDATA #IMPLIED>
]>
<document>
    <employee supervisor="no">
        <name>
            <lastname>Kelly</lastname>
            <firstname>Grace</firstname>
        </name>
        <hiredate>October 15, 2005</hiredate>
        <projects>
            <project>
                <product>Printer</product>
                <id>111</id>
                <price>$111.00</price>
            </project>
            <project>
                <product>Laptop</product>
                <id>222</id>
                <price>$989.00</price>
            </project>
        </projects>
    </employee>
    <employee supervisor="yes">
        <name>
            <lastname>Grant</lastname>
            <firstname>Cary</firstname>
        </name>
        <hiredate>October 20, 2005</hiredate>
        <projects>
            <project>
                <product>Desktop</product>
```

LISTING 5.1 continued

```
                <id>333</id>
                <price>$2995.00</price>
            </project>
            <project>
                <product>Scanner</product>
                <id>444</id>
                <price>$200.00</price>
            </project>
        </projects>
    </employee>
</document>
```

As its name implies, you can use <!ATTLIST> to declare an entire list of attributes for an element. For example, you might want an <employee> element to have multiple attributes—say, supervisor, division (indicating the division of the company that the employee works in), and fullTime (set to "yes" if the employee is full time, "no" if part time). Listing 5.2 shows how such an example would look, in the valid document ch05_02.xml.

LISTING 5.2 A Sample XML Document with Multiple Attributes Declared in a DTD (ch05_02.xml)

```
<?xml version = "1.0" encoding="UTF-8" standalone="yes"?>
<!DOCTYPE document [
<!ELEMENT document (employee)*>
<!ELEMENT employee (name, hiredate, projects) >
<!ELEMENT name (lastname, firstname)>
<!ELEMENT lastname (#PCDATA)>
<!ELEMENT firstname (#PCDATA)>
<!ELEMENT hiredate (#PCDATA)>
<!ELEMENT projects (project)*>
<!ELEMENT project (product, id, price)>
<!ELEMENT product (#PCDATA)>
<!ELEMENT id (#PCDATA)>
<!ELEMENT price (#PCDATA)>
<!ATTLIST employee
    supervisor CDATA #IMPLIED
    division CDATA #IMPLIED
    fullTime CDATA #IMPLIED
>
]>
<document>
    <employee supervisor="no" division="plastics" fullTime="yes">
        <name>
            <lastname>Kelly</lastname>
```

LISTING 5.2 continued

```
            <firstname>Grace</firstname>
        </name>
        <hiredate>October 15, 2005</hiredate>
        <projects>
            <project>
                <product>Printer</product>
                <id>111</id>
                <price>$111.00</price>
            </project>
            <project>
                <product>Laptop</product>
                <id>222</id>
                <price>$989.00</price>
            </project>
        </projects>
    </employee>
    <employee supervisor="yes" division="metals" fullTime="yes">
        <name>
            <lastname>Grant</lastname>
            <firstname>Cary</firstname>
        </name>
        <hiredate>October 20, 2005</hiredate>
        <projects>
            <project>
                <product>Desktop</product>
                <id>333</id>
                <price>$2995.00</price>
            </project>
            <project>
                <product>Scanner</product>
                <id>444</id>
                <price>$200.00</price>
            </project>
        </projects>
    </employee>
</document>
```

These examples provide an introduction to declaring attributes in DTDs. As you can see, all you have to do is use an `<!ATTLIST>` element to declare the attributes for an element. It's a little more involved to use this element than to use `<!ELEMENT>`, however, because you're restricted to certain types and default values for attributes in DTDs, as described in the following section.

Using the Legal Default Values and Attribute Types

When you're declaring attributes in DTDs, these are the possible *`default_value`* settings you can use in `<!ATTLIST>` elements:

- ***value***—Specifies a text value and must be enclosed in quotes.
- **#IMPLIED**—Makes an attribute optional.
- **#FIXED *value***—Sets the attribute's value to *value*.
- **#REQUIRED**—Means that this attribute is required and must be given a value.

These are the possible *type* values you can use:

- **CDATA**—Specifies character data, which is just text without markup.
- **ENTITY**—Specifies an entity name.
- **ENTITIES**—Specifies multiple entity names, which are separated by whitespace in the attribute value, like this: *entity1 entity2 entity3*.
- **Enumerated**—Specifies one value from a list of values (that is, an enumeration).
- **ID**—Specifies an ID attribute, which holds a proper XML name (which must not be shared by any other attribute of the ID type).
- **IDREF**—Holds the ID value of some other element.
- **IDREFS**—Holds multiple ID values of elements, separated by whitespace.
- **NMTOKEN**—Specifies text made up of XML name characters, or *tokens*. This text may be made up of one or more letters, digits, hyphens, underscores, colons, and periods.
- **NMTOKENS**—Specifies multiple NMTOKEN items, separated by whitespace.
- **NOTATION**—Specifies a notation name that holds a format description (such as a MIME type).

You'll see these various values at work today.

Specifying Default Values

The most common attribute type, as you've seen in the examples so far in this book, is CDATA, which is just character data. Before working through all the types of attributes you can use, you'll use CDATA attributes for a few more pages as you take a look at what kinds of default values you can specify for attributes. The first, and most common, type of default values are immediate values, and you'll begin with them.

Immediate Values

You can specify a default value for an attribute simply by listing that value, in quotes, in the attribute's declaration in the <!ATTLIST> element, making it an *immediate value*. If you give an attribute a default value and then don't use that attribute in an element, the attribute is automatically given the default value. The following example specifies a default value of "no" for the supervisor attribute, "plastics" for the division attribute, and "yes" for the fullTime attribute:

```
<?xml version = "1.0" encoding="UTF-8" standalone="yes"?>
<!DOCTYPE document [
<!ELEMENT document (employee)*>
<!ELEMENT employee (name, hiredate, projects)>
<!ELEMENT name (lastname, firstname)>
<!ELEMENT lastname (#PCDATA)>
<!ELEMENT firstname (#PCDATA)>
<!ELEMENT hiredate (#PCDATA)>
<!ELEMENT projects (project)*>
<!ELEMENT project (product, id, price)>
<!ELEMENT product (#PCDATA)>
<!ELEMENT id (#PCDATA)>
<!ELEMENT price (#PCDATA)>
<!ATTLIST employee
    supervisor CDATA "no"
    division CDATA "plastics"
    fullTime CDATA "yes"
>
    .
    .
    .
```

Now each of these three attributes has a default value that will be assigned to it if you don't specifically assign another value.

The #REQUIRED Default Value

5

You can specify a default value of #REQUIRED to indicate that an attribute is required. For example, if you want to specify that all <employee> elements needed to have supervisor attributes, you can do so like this:

```
<?xml version = "1.0" encoding="UTF-8" standalone="yes"?>
<!DOCTYPE document [
<!ELEMENT document (employee)*>
<!ELEMENT employee (name, hiredate, projects)>
<!ELEMENT name (lastname, firstname)>
<!ELEMENT lastname (#PCDATA)>
<!ELEMENT firstname (#PCDATA)>
<!ELEMENT hiredate (#PCDATA)>
<!ELEMENT projects (project)*>
<!ELEMENT project (product, id, price)>
<!ELEMENT product (#PCDATA)>
<!ELEMENT id (#PCDATA)>
<!ELEMENT price (#PCDATA)>
<!ATTLIST employee supervisor CDATA #REQUIRED>
]>
```

```
<document>
    <employee supervisor="no">
        <name>
            <lastname>Kelly</lastname>
            <firstname>Grace</firstname>
        </name>
        .
        .
        .
    </employee>
</document>
```

`#REQUIRED` is useful, for example, when you have an attribute whose data is essential, such as when an XML author needs to supply the URI of an image in an attribute named `uri`.

The `#IMPLIED` Default Value

Attributes declared with `#IMPLIED` are optional. For example, you can use the `#IMPLIED` default value if you want to allow the document author to include an attribute, but you don't want to require it. Here's an example that declares the `supervisor` attribute with `#IMPLIED`:

```
<?xml version = "1.0" encoding="UTF-8" standalone="yes"?>
<!DOCTYPE document [
<!ELEMENT document (employee)*>
<!ELEMENT employee (name, hiredate, projects)>
<!ELEMENT name (lastname, firstname)>
<!ELEMENT lastname (#PCDATA)>
<!ELEMENT firstname (#PCDATA)>
<!ELEMENT hiredate (#PCDATA)>
<!ELEMENT projects (project)*>
<!ELEMENT project (product, id, price)>
<!ELEMENT product (#PCDATA)>
<!ELEMENT id (#PCDATA)>
<!ELEMENT price (#PCDATA)>
<!ATTLIST employee supervisor CDATA #IMPLIED>
]>
<document>
    <employee supervisor="no">
        <name>
            <lastname>Kelly</lastname>
            <firstname>Grace</firstname>
        </name>
        .
        .
        .
    </employee>
    <employee>
```

```
        <name>
            <lastname>Grant</lastname>
            <firstname>Cary</firstname>
        </name>
        .
        .
        .
    </employee>
</DOCUMENT>
```

Using `#IMPLIED` this way means that an attribute can appear in elements or not, as the document author prefers.

The `#FIXED` Default Value

The final default value is `#FIXED`, which you use when you want to assign a fixed value to an attribute—a value that the attribute will always have. For instance, the following example ensures that an attribute named `language` will always have the value `"en"`, to specify that a document is in English:

```
<?xml version = "1.0" encoding="UTF-8" standalone="yes"?>
<!DOCTYPE document [
<!ELEMENT document (employee)*>
<!ELEMENT employee (name, hiredate, projects)>
<!ELEMENT name (lastname, firstname)>
<!ELEMENT lastname (#PCDATA)>
<!ELEMENT firstname (#PCDATA)>
<!ELEMENT hiredate (#PCDATA)>
<!ELEMENT projects (project)*>
<!ELEMENT project (product, id, price)>
<!ELEMENT product (#PCDATA)>
<!ELEMENT id (#PCDATA)>
<!ELEMENT price (#PCDATA)>
<!ATTLIST employee language CDATA #FIXED "en">
]>
<document>
    <employee>
        <name>
            <lastname>Kelly</lastname>
            <firstname>Grace</firstname>
        </name>
        <hiredate>October 15, 2005</hiredate>
        <projects>
            <project>
                <product>Printer</product>
                <id>111</id>
                <price>$111.00</price>
            </project>
            <project>
                <product>Laptop</product>
```

5

```
                <id>222</id>
                <price>$989.00</price>
            </project>
        </projects>
    </employee>
</document>
```

When you make an attribute fixed, you don't even have to give it a value, as in this example. In this case, even though you haven't used the `language` attribute in the `<employee>` element, an XML processor will report a `language` attribute with the value `"en"` for the `<employee>` element.

TIP

> You can set the value of a fixed attribute in an element like this: `<employee language="en">`. But there's little point in doing this because if you don't set the value to the fixed value (that is, the value it already has), an XML processor will consider that an error.

Specifying Attribute Types

Although `CDATA` is the most common attribute type, DTDs support other types as well. These types are not specific enough to let you declare, say, the format of numbers (such as integer, floating point, and so on—which you would be able to declare in XML schemas), but they do let you check the syntax of XML documents to some extent. The following sections describe some of the attribute type possibilities.

The `CDATA` Attribute Type

As you've already seen, the `CDATA` data type stands for *character data*. Unlike *parsed* character data (`PCDATA`), which is assumed to have already been parsed, the character data in attribute values is read and parsed by the XML processor. Among other things, that means that you should avoid using the characters `<`, `"`, and `&` in `CDATA` attribute values because those characters look like markup. If you want to use those characters, you should use their predefined entity references (`<`, `"`, and `&`) instead because these entity references will be parsed and replaced with the corresponding characters.

You've already been using `CDATA` attributes, the most basic type of attributes, in examples, such as this one:

```
<?xml version = "1.0" encoding="UTF-8" standalone="yes"?>
<!DOCTYPE document [
<!ELEMENT document (employee)*>
<!ELEMENT employee (name, hiredate, projects)>
<!ELEMENT name (lastname, firstname)>
```

```
<!ELEMENT lastname (#PCDATA)>
<!ELEMENT firstname (#PCDATA)>
<!ELEMENT hiredate (#PCDATA)>
<!ELEMENT projects (project)*>
<!ELEMENT project (product, id, price)>
<!ELEMENT product (#PCDATA)>
<!ELEMENT id (#PCDATA)>
<!ELEMENT price (#PCDATA)>
<!ATTLIST employee supervisor CDATA #IMPLIED>
]>
<document>
    <employee supervisor="no">
        <name>
            <lastname>Kelly</lastname>
            <firstname>Grace</firstname>
        </name>
        .
        .
        .
</document>
```

The CDATA type is the most general type of attribute. From this point on, however, you'll get into increasingly more specific types.

Enumerated Types

An *attribute enumeration* is just a list of possible values that an attribute can take. Each possible value must be a valid XML name. In the following example, the supervisor attribute has two possible values—"yes" and "no"—and a default value of "no":

```
<?xml version = "1.0" encoding="UTF-8" standalone="yes"?>
<!DOCTYPE document [
<!ELEMENT document (employee)*>
<!ELEMENT employee (name, hiredate, projects)>
<!ELEMENT name (lastname, firstname)>
<!ELEMENT lastname (#PCDATA)>
<!ELEMENT firstname (#PCDATA)>
<!ELEMENT hiredate (#PCDATA)>
<!ELEMENT projects (project)*>
<!ELEMENT project (product, id, price)>
<!ELEMENT product (#PCDATA)>
<!ELEMENT id (#PCDATA)>
<!ELEMENT price (#PCDATA)>
<!ATTLIST employee supervisor (yes | no) "no">
]>
<document>
    <employee supervisor="no">
        <name>
            <lastname>Kelly</lastname>
            <firstname>Grace</firstname>
```

```
        </name>
        <hiredate>October 15, 2005</hiredate>
    </employee>
        .
        .
        .
</document>
```

Using an enumeration is a good choice if you want to restrict an attribute to a set of allowed values. For example, if you have an attribute named `month`, you might want to allow only values such as `"January"`, `"February"`, `"March"`, `"April"`, and so on.

The NMTOKEN Attribute Type

The attribute type NMTOKEN stands for *name token*, and it lets you assign to an attribute any value made up of legal XML name characters. Attributes of this type can only take values that are made up of characters that can be used in legal XML names (this excludes the restrictions that beginning characters in names must obey, such as no numbers, periods, and so on). For example, in XML 1.0, NMTOKEN characters are letters, digits, hyphens, underscores, colons, and periods. (Note that NMTOKEN characters cannot include whitespace.) In XML 1.1, the characters are the same as in XML 1.0, except for the differences in the characters that are considered legal, as discussed on Day 2, “Creating XML Documents.”

In other words, the idea behind the NMTOKEN type is to let you use any standard nonwhitespace character in attributes. The following example adds a `state` attribute of the NMTOKEN type to hold a two-letter state abbreviation:

```
<?xml version = "1.0" encoding="UTF-8" standalone="yes"?>
<!DOCTYPE document [
<!ELEMENT document (employee)*>
<!ELEMENT employee (name, hiredate, projects)>
<!ELEMENT name (lastname, firstname)>
<!ELEMENT lastname (#PCDATA)>
<!ELEMENT firstname (#PCDATA)>
<!ELEMENT hiredate (#PCDATA)>
<!ELEMENT projects (project)*>
<!ELEMENT project (product, id, price)>
<!ELEMENT product (#PCDATA)>
<!ELEMENT id (#PCDATA)>
<!ELEMENT price (#PCDATA)>
<!ATTLIST employee
    state NMTOKEN #REQUIRED>
]>
<document>
    <employee state="NY">
        <name>
```

```
            <lastname>Kelly</lastname>
            <firstname>Grace</firstname>
        </name>
        <hiredate>October 15, 2005</hiredate>
        <projects>
        .
        .
        .
    </employee>
</document>
```

The NMTOKENS Attribute Type

The preceding section describes the NMTOKEN attribute type—so what's NMTOKENS? You can use the NMTOKENS attribute type when you want to list multiple values made up of NMTOKEN values, separated by whitespace. The following example allows whitespace in attribute values because you want to store the first and last names of supervisors, making supervisors a required NMTOKENS attribute:

```
?xml version = "1.0" encoding="UTF-8" standalone="yes"?>
<!DOCTYPE document [
<!ELEMENT document (employee)*>
<!ELEMENT employee (name, hiredate, projects)>
<!ELEMENT name (lastname, firstname)>
<!ELEMENT lastname (#PCDATA)>
<!ELEMENT firstname (#PCDATA)>
<!ELEMENT hiredate (#PCDATA)>
<!ELEMENT projects (project)*>
<!ELEMENT project (product, id, price)>
<!ELEMENT product (#PCDATA)>
<!ELEMENT id (#PCDATA)>
<!ELEMENT price (#PCDATA)>
<!ATTLIST employee supervisor NMTOKENS #REQUIRED>
]>
<document>
    <employee supervisor="Tom Brown">
        <name>
            <lastname>Kelly</lastname>
            <firstname>Grace</firstname>
        </name>
        <hiredate>October 15, 2005</hiredate>
        .
        .
        .
    </employee>
</document>
```

5

The ID Attribute Type

An important attribute type is the ID type. There's a special meaning to an element's ID value because sometimes XML processors use an ID attribute to identify an element. (They don't have to, but some XML processors pass on ID values of XML elements to underlying software.) Therefore, XML processors are supposed to make sure that no two elements have the same value for the attribute that is of the type ID in a document; in addition, you can give an element only one attribute of this type.

The value you assign to an attribute of the ID type must be a proper XML name. The following example adds an ID attribute to a DTD:

```
<?xml version = "1.0" encoding="UTF-8" standalone="yes"?>
<!DOCTYPE document [
<!ELEMENT document (employee)*>
<!ELEMENT employee (name, hiredate, projects)>
<!ELEMENT name (lastname, firstname)>
<!ELEMENT lastname (#PCDATA)>
<!ELEMENT firstname (#PCDATA)>
<!ELEMENT hiredate (#PCDATA)>
<!ELEMENT projects (project)*>
<!ELEMENT project (product, id, price)>
<!ELEMENT product (#PCDATA)>
<!ELEMENT id (#PCDATA)>
<!ELEMENT price (#PCDATA)>
<!ATTLIST employee id ID #REQUIRED>
]>
<document>
    <employee id="A1112">
        .
        .
        .
    </employee>
    <employee id="A1114">
        .
        .
        .
    </employee>
    <employee id="A1115">
        .
        .
    </employee>
</document>
```

You can give ID attributes default values of #REQUIRED or #IMPLIED, but note that you wouldn't usually use explicit default values or a #FIXED value because each ID attribute must have a unique value.

TIP

> Because ID values must be proper XML names, and because XML names can't start with numbers, ID values in XML can't start with numbers (as, for example, Social Security numbers do) .

The IDREF Attribute Type

DTDs let you do more than specify ID values by using attributes. We can also use IDREF (which stands for ID reference) attributes to tie an element to another element, using the other element's ID value as a reference. For example, if we wanted to store genealogical data in an XML document, we could store a child's data by using an IDREF attribute to hold the ID value of a parent's data.

The following example gives each employee an id attribute and also creates an optional supervisor attribute of type IDREF, which will store the ID value of an employee's supervisor:

```
<?xml version = "1.0" encoding="UTF-8" standalone="yes"?>
<!DOCTYPE document [
<!ELEMENT document (employee)*>
<!ELEMENT employee (name, hiredate, projects)>
<!ELEMENT name (lastname, firstname)>
<!ELEMENT lastname (#PCDATA)>
<!ELEMENT firstname (#PCDATA)>
<!ELEMENT hiredate (#PCDATA)>
<!ELEMENT projects (project)*>
<!ELEMENT project (product, id, price)>
<!ELEMENT product (#PCDATA)>
<!ELEMENT id (#PCDATA)>
<!ELEMENT price (#PCDATA)>
<!ATTLIST employee
    id ID #REQUIRED
    supervisor IDREF #IMPLIED>
]>
<document>
    <employee id="A1112" supervisor="A1114">
        <name>
            <lastname>Kelly</lastname>
            <firstname>Grace</firstname>
        </name>
        <hiredate>October 15, 2005</hiredate>
        .
        .
        .
    </employee>
    <employee id="A1114">
        <name>
```

5

```
            <lastname>Grant</lastname>
            <firstname>Cary</firstname>
        </name>
        <hiredate>October 20, 2005</hiredate>
        .
        .
        .
    </employee>
</document>
```

Note that attributes of ID and IDREF are allowed in XML, but they don't have any more special meaning than is discussed here. If you want to do more with these attributes, it's up to you to create or use an XML processor that can handle ID and IDREF data as you want it handled.

The ENTITY Attribute Type

The ENTITY type lets you assign to an attribute the name of an entity you've declared. Later on today we'll talk about how to handle entities; the idea is that we can handle data, such as an external image file, in an XML document by using the <!ENTITY> element. The following example gives the entity name PHOTO1221 to the image file 1221.gif and the entity name PHOTO1222 to the image file 1222.gif:

```
<!ENTITY PHOTO1221 SYSTEM "1221.gif">
<!ENTITY PHOTO1222 SYSTEM "1222.gif">
```

Now you can use these entity names, PHOTO1221 and PHOTO1222, as attribute values in attributes of type ENTITY. For example, if 1221.gif and 1222.gif held the photos of various employees, you could indicate that this is the case by using an ENTITY attribute named photo, like this (note that you don't have to use ENTITY attributes to do this—you could just set a CDATA attribute to 1221.gif, for example):

```
<?xml version = "1.0" encoding="UTF-8" standalone="no"?>
<!DOCTYPE document [
<!ELEMENT document (employee)*>
<!ELEMENT employee (name, hiredate, projects)>
<!ELEMENT name (lastname, firstname)>
<!ELEMENT lastname (#PCDATA)>
<!ELEMENT firstname (#PCDATA)>
<!ELEMENT hiredate (#PCDATA)>
<!ELEMENT projects (project)*>
<!ELEMENT project (product, id, price)>
<!ELEMENT product (#PCDATA)>
<!ELEMENT id (#PCDATA)>
<!ELEMENT price (#PCDATA)>
<!ENTITY PHOTO1221 SYSTEM "1221.gif">
<!ENTITY PHOTO1222 SYSTEM "1222.gif">
<!ATTLIST employee
```

```
    photo ENTITY #IMPLIED>
]>
<document>
    <employee photo="PHOTO1221">
        <name>
            <lastname>Kelly</lastname>
            <firstname>Grace</firstname>
        </name>
        <hiredate>October 15, 2005</hiredate>
        .
        .
        .
    </employee>
    <employee photo="PHOTO1222">
        <name>
            <lastname>Grant</lastname>
            <firstname>Cary</firstname>
        </name>
        <hiredate>October 20, 2005</hiredate>
        .
        .
        .
    </employee>
</document>
```

Using ENTITY attributes is a good way of working with entities, and we'll talk about how that works later today. As part of that discussion, we'll talk about how to indicate to an XML processor what the format of the external data is; for instance, we'll elaborate on this example to indicate that the external entity uses the GIF image format.

The ENTITIES Attribute Type

Like the NMTOKEN attribute type, which has a plural type, NMTOKENS, the ENTITY attribute type also has a plural type, ENTITIES. Attributes of this type can hold lists of entity names, separated by whitespace. For example, to associate not just one photo but multiple photos with an employee, you could change the ENTITY attribute photo created in the previous example to an ENTITIES attribute named photos, like this:

```
<?xml version = "1.0" encoding="UTF-8" standalone="no"?>
<!DOCTYPE document [
<!ELEMENT document (employee)*>
<!ELEMENT employee (name, hiredate, projects)>
<!ELEMENT name (lastname, firstname)>
<!ELEMENT lastname (#PCDATA)>
<!ELEMENT firstname (#PCDATA)>
<!ELEMENT hiredate (#PCDATA)>
<!ELEMENT projects (project)*>
<!ELEMENT project (product, id, price)>
<!ELEMENT product (#PCDATA)>
```

```
<!ELEMENT id (#PCDATA)>
<!ELEMENT price (#PCDATA)>
<!ENTITY PHOTO1221 SYSTEM "1221.gif">
<!ENTITY PHOTO1222 SYSTEM "1222.gif">
<!ATTLIST employee
    photos ENTITIES #IMPLIED>
]>
<document>
    <employee photos="PHOTO1221 PHOTO1222">
        <name>
            <lastname>Kelly</lastname>
            <firstname>Grace</firstname>
        </name>
        <hiredate>October 15, 2005</hiredate>
        .
        .
        .
    </employee>
</document>
```

The NOTATION Attribute Type

The last legal attribute type is NOTATION. You can assign to NOTATION attribute values that you have declared to be notations. *Notations* specify the format of non-XML data, and they're typically used to describe the storage format of external entities such as image files. For example, one popular type of notations is Multipurpose Internet Mail Extension (MIME) types, such as application/xml, text/html, image/jpeg, and so forth, which are often used to specify data storage formats.

TIP

There's a list of all the available MIME types at ftp://ftp.isi.edu/in-notes/iana/assignments/media-types/media-types.

When you want to declare a notation, you use the <!NOTATION> element in a DTD like this:

```
<!NOTATION name SYSTEM "external_id">
```

Here, *name* is the name of the notation and *external_id* is the identification you want to use for the notation, such as a MIME type.

You can also use the PUBLIC keyword for public notations if you supply a formal public identifier (FPI; see Day 4, "Creating Valid XML Documents: DTDs," for the rules on constructing FPIs), like this:

```
<!NOTATION name PUBLIC FPI "external_id">
```

The following example declares three standard notations—`jpg`, `gif`, and `text`, which stand for the MIME types `image/jpeg`, `image/gif`, and `text/plain`:

```
<?xml version = "1.0" encoding="UTF-8" standalone="no"?>
<!DOCTYPE document [
<!ELEMENT document (employee)*>
<!ELEMENT employee (name, hiredate, projects)>
<!ELEMENT name (lastname, firstname)>
<!ELEMENT lastname (#PCDATA)>
<!ELEMENT firstname (#PCDATA)>
<!ELEMENT hiredate (#PCDATA)>
<!ELEMENT projects (project)*>
<!ELEMENT project (product, id, price)>
<!ELEMENT product (#PCDATA)>
<!ELEMENT id (#PCDATA)>
<!ELEMENT price (#PCDATA)>
<!NOTATION jpg SYSTEM "image/jpeg">
<!NOTATION gif SYSTEM "image/gif">
<!NOTATION text SYSTEM "text/plain">
    .
    .
    .
```

Now you can create an attribute named, say, `imagetype`, of type `NOTATION`. You can then assign either the `gif` or `jpg` notations to `imagetype`:

```
<?xml version = "1.0" encoding="UTF-8" standalone="yes"?>
<!DOCTYPE document [
<!ELEMENT document (employee)*>
<!ELEMENT employee (name, hiredate, projects)>
<!ELEMENT name (lastname, firstname)>
<!ELEMENT lastname (#PCDATA)>
<!ELEMENT firstname (#PCDATA)>
<!ELEMENT hiredate (#PCDATA)>
<!ELEMENT projects (project)*>
<!ELEMENT project (product, id, price)>
<!ELEMENT product (#PCDATA)>
<!ELEMENT id (#PCDATA)>
<!ELEMENT price (#PCDATA)>
<!NOTATION jpg SYSTEM "image/jpeg">
<!NOTATION gif SYSTEM "image/gif">
<!NOTATION text SYSTEM "text/plain">
<!ATTLIST employee
    photo NMTOKEN #IMPLIED
    imagetype NOTATION (jpg | gif) #IMPLIED>
]>
    .
    .
    .
```

5

Now that you have declared a new attribute, `imagetype`, of the `NOTATION` type, you can put this attribute to work, like this:

```
<?xml version = "1.0" encoding="UTF-8" standalone="yes"?>
<!DOCTYPE document [
<!ELEMENT document (employee)*>
<!ELEMENT employee (name, hiredate, projects)>
<!ELEMENT name (lastname, firstname)>
<!ELEMENT lastname (#PCDATA)>
<!ELEMENT firstname (#PCDATA)>
<!ELEMENT hiredate (#PCDATA)>
<!ELEMENT projects (project)*>
<!ELEMENT project (product, id, price)>
<!ELEMENT product (#PCDATA)>
<!ELEMENT id (#PCDATA)>
<!ELEMENT price (#PCDATA)>
<!NOTATION jpg SYSTEM "image/jpeg">
<!NOTATION gif SYSTEM "image/gif">
<!NOTATION text SYSTEM "text/plain">
<!ATTLIST employee
    photo NMTOKEN #IMPLIED
    imagetype NOTATION (jpg | gif) #IMPLIED>
]>
<document>
    <employee photo="1221.gif" imagetype ="gif">
        <name>
            <lastname>Kelly</lastname>
            <firstname>Grace</firstname>
        </name>
        <hiredate>October 15, 2005</hiredate>
        <projects>
            <project>
                <product>Printer</product>
                <id>111</id>
                <price>$111.00</price>
            </project>
            <project>
                <product>Laptop</product>
                <id>222</id>
                <price>$989.00</price>
            </project>
        </projects>
    </employee>
</document>
```

Handling Entities

An *entity* in XML is simply a data item. Entities are usually text in common usage, but they can also be binary data. If you want an XML document that uses entities to be valid, you can declare an entity in a DTD and refer to it in the document (for text entities, the entity reference is replaced by the entity itself when parsed by an XML processor).

There are many different ways of dealing with data, so you probably won't be surprised to learn that there are different ways of working with entities. DTDs know about two types of entities: general entities and parameter entities. *General entities* are for use in the body of XML documents, and *parameter entities* are for use in a document's DTD. You'll see both today. General entity references start with & and end with ;, and parameter entity references start with % and end with ;.

> **NOTE**
>
> Because *entity* is simply XML's term for a data item, you might wonder where entities leave off and the rest of the document starts. Can the text in an element be considered an entity? Yes, it can, and so can fragments of XML documents. In fact, technically speaking, an entire XML document may be called an entity. All this is to reiterate that *entity* is XML's general term for any data item.

Entities can also be internal or external. An *internal entity* is defined completely inside the XML document that uses it. An *external entity*, on the other hand, is stored externally, such as in a file; to refer to an external entity in XML, you can use a URI.

Here's how it works: You declare an entity in a DTD, and then you can refer to it with an entity reference in the rest of the XML document. In fact, you've already seen that there are five general entity references that are predefined in XML—<, >, &, ", and ', which stand for the characters <, >, &, ", and ', respectively. Because these entities are predefined in XML, you don't need to define them in a DTD; you can just use the entity references; for example, you can see all five predefined entity references at work in Listing 5.3.

LISTING 5.3 A Sample XML Document That Uses Predefined General Entity References (ch05_03.xml)

```
<?xml version = "1.0" encoding="UTF-8" standalone="yes"?>
<!DOCTYPE data [
<!ELEMENT data (#PCDATA)>
]>
<data>
    Welcome to Marge &amp; Maggie&apos;s XML document!
    Marge says, &quot;Do you like your &lt;data&gt; element&quot;?
</data>
```

An XML processor will replace each of the entity references in `ch05_03.xml` with the corresponding character. Figure 5.1 shows the results of Listing 5.3 in Internet Explorer.

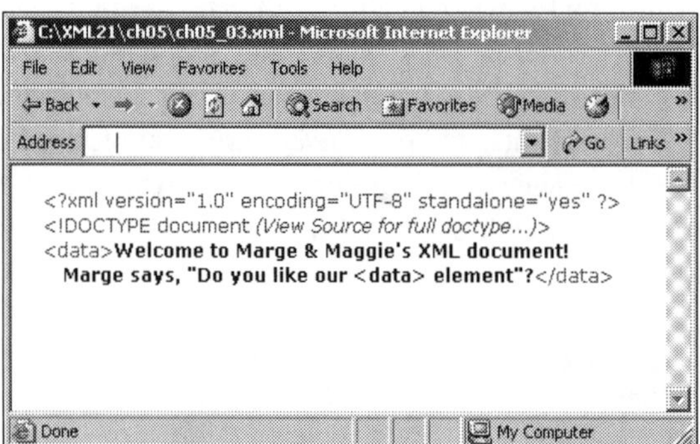

FIGURE 5.1
Using the predefined entity references.

Although the five predefined general entity references are useful when you want to make sure text isn't interpreted as markup, they're very limited. When it is time to create your own entities, it's time to use the `<!ENTITY>` element, as described in the following section.

Creating Internal General Entity References

In much the same way that you use the `<!ELEMENT>` element to declare an element in a DTD, you use the `<!ENTITY>` element to declare an entity. You declare a general entity like this:

```
<!ENTITY name definition>
```

In this case, *`name`* is the entity's name and *`definition`* is its definition. The name of the entity is just the name you want to use to refer to the entity, but an entity's definition can take several different forms. The simplest way of defining an entity is just to use the text that you want XML processors to replace entity references with. For example, here's how you might create a new entity named `copyright` that will be replaced with the text "(c) XML Power Corp. 2005":

```
<!ENTITY copyright "(c) XML Power Corp. 2005">
```

Now when you declare this entity in a DTD and refer to it in your document as `©right;`, that entity reference will be replaced with the text "(c) XML Power Corp. 2005". Listing 5.4 shows an example, `ch05_04.xml`, which declares this entity in the DTD and uses it in the body of the XML document in an element named `<copy>`. (Note that you also have to declare `<copy>` in the DTD.)

LISTING 5.4 Defining a General Entity (ch05_04.xml)

```
<?xml version = "1.0" encoding="UTF-8" standalone="yes"?>
<!DOCTYPE document [
<!ELEMENT document (employee)*>
<!ELEMENT employee (copy, name, hiredate, projects)>
<!ELEMENT name (lastname, firstname)>
<!ELEMENT lastname (#PCDATA) >
<!ELEMENT firstname (#PCDATA)>
<!ELEMENT hiredate (#PCDATA)>
<!ELEMENT projects (project)*>
<!ELEMENT project (product, id, price)>
<!ELEMENT product (#PCDATA)>
<!ELEMENT id (#PCDATA)>
<!ELEMENT price (#PCDATA)>
<!ELEMENT copy (#PCDATA)>
<!ATTLIST employee supervisor CDATA #IMPLIED>
<!ENTITY copyright "(c) XML Power Corp. 2005">
]>
<document>
    <employee supervisor="no">
        <copy>&copyright;</copy>
        <name>
            <lastname>Kelly</lastname>
            <firstname>Grace</firstname>
        </name>
        <hiredate>October 15, 2005</hiredate>
        <projects>
            <project>
                <product>Printer</product>
                <id>111</id>
                <price>$111.00</price>
            </project>
            <project>
                <product>Laptop</product>
                <id>222</id>
                <price>$989.00</price>
            </project>
        </projects>
    </employee>
    <employee supervisor="yes">
        <copy>&copyright;</copy>
        <name>
            <lastname>Grant</lastname>
            <firstname>Cary</firstname>
        </name>
        <hiredate>October 20, 2005</hiredate>
        <projects>
            <project>
                <product>Desktop</product>
```

LISTING 5.4 continued

```
                    <id>333</id>
                    <price>$2995.00</price>
                </project>
                <project>
                    <product>Scanner</product>
                    <id>444</id>
                    <price>$200.00</price>
                </project>
            </projects>
        </employee>
    </document>
```

Figure 5.2 shows the document `ch05_04.xml` in Internet Explorer. Note that `©right;` has indeed been replaced by the text "(c) XML Power Corp. 2005".

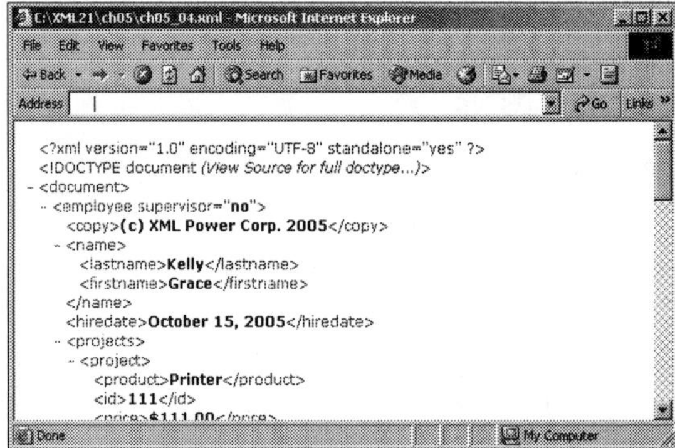

FIGURE 5.2

Creating and using a user-defined entity.

The replacement text for internal general entity references doesn't have to be quoted text; you can use UTF-8 (or other) character codes directly. For example, here's how to modify the example that uses the predefined general entities `quot`, `amp`, `lt`, and so on by defining your own internal general entities `quot2`, `amp2`, `lt2`, and so on, using UTF-8 character codes:

```
<?xml version = "1.0" standalone="yes"?>
<!DOCTYPE TEXT [
<!ENTITY amp2 "&#38;#38;">
<!ENTITY apos2 "&#39;">
<!ENTITY gt2 "&#62;">
<!ENTITY lt2 "&#38;#60;">
<!ENTITY quot2 "&#34;">
<!ELEMENT data (#PCDATA)>
]>
<data>
```

```
    Welcome to Marge &amp2; Maggie&apos2;s XML document!
    Marge says, &quot2;Do you like our &lt2;data&gt2; element&quot2;?
</data>
```

This XML gives the same results as the previous example, which simply uses the predefined general entities `quot`, `amp`, `lt`, and so on.

What's happening here is that when you use an entity reference such as `>2;`, it's replaced with the entity reference `>` which the XML processor then replaces with ">". Among other things, this indicates that you can *nest* entity references.

The following is another example, in which the entity reference `&me;` in the second entity declaration will be replaced with "Ferdinand Magellan" from the first entity declaration:

```
<!ENTITY me "Ferdinand Magellan">
<!ENTITY copyright "(c) &me; 1519">
```

Note that although you can nest entity references, they can't be circular, or the XML processor will go nuts. For example, this isn't legal:

```
<!ENTITY me "&copyright; Ferdinand Magellan">
<!ENTITY copyright "(c) &me; 1519">
```

Circular entity references like this one are illegal in valid documents.

General entity references, such as `©right;`, are valid only in the body of the XML document, not in the DTD itself. For example, this is not legal:

```
<!ENTITY employeeContent "(copy, name, hiredate, projects)">
<!ELEMENT employee &employeeContent;>
```

The way you should handle a situation like this, where an entity reference is used in the DTD itself, is by using parameter entities, which you'll take a look at later today.

5

Creating External General Entity References

In addition to the internal general entities just described, you can also work with external general entities. In this case, you use a URI to direct the XML processor to the external entity. As you're going to see, you can also indicate that such an entity should not be parsed, which is how to associate binary data with an XML document; it's something like associating images with an HTML document. (Note that even though you don't want the XML processor to parse the external entity, most processors will still check to make sure the external entity exists and is at the URI you've given.)

Just as you can with external DTDs, you can use the `SYSTEM` keyword or the `PUBLIC` keyword when declaring external general entities. As with external DTDs, you use `SYSTEM` when working with an external entity that's private to you or your organization, and you use `PUBLIC` when you're using an external entity that's public. As with external DTDs, when you use a public external entity, you need to use an FPI when you refer to it. Here's the syntax for declaring an external general entity:

```
<!ENTITY name SYSTEM URI>
<!ENTITY name PUBLIC FPI URI>
```

For example, you can place the text "(c) XML Power Corp. 2005" for the copyright general entity in the file `ch05_05.xml`, which appears in Listing 5.5.

LISTING 5.5 Storing Text as an External General Entity (`ch05_05.xml`)

```
<?xml version = "1.0" encoding="UTF-8"?>
"(c) XML Power Corp. 2005"
```

You use the following to create an external general entity reference named `copyright` that refers to the external document `ch05_05.xml`:

```
<!ENTITY copyright SYSTEM "ch05_05.xml">
```

Now you can use the `©right;` external entity reference just as you did before, when it was an internal entity reference. You can see this at work in `ch05_06.xml`, which is shown in Listing 5.6. (Note that you also have to change the value of the `standalone` attribute in the XML declaration from `"yes"` to `"no"`.)

LISTING 5.6 Using an External General Entity (`ch05_06.xml`)

```
<?xml version = "1.0" encoding="UTF-8" standalone="no"?>
<!DOCTYPE document [
<!ELEMENT document (employee)*>
<!ELEMENT employee (copy, name, hiredate, projects)>
<!ELEMENT name (lastname, firstname)>
<!ELEMENT lastname (#PCDATA)>
<!ELEMENT firstname (#PCDATA)>
<!ELEMENT hiredate (#PCDATA)>
<!ELEMENT projects (project)*>
<!ELEMENT project (product, id, price)>
<!ELEMENT product (#PCDATA)>
<!ELEMENT id (#PCDATA)>
<!ELEMENT price (#PCDATA)>
<!ELEMENT copy (#PCDATA)>
<!ATTLIST employee supervisor CDATA #IMPLIED>
<!ENTITY copyright SYSTEM "ch05_05.xml">
]>
<document>
    <employee supervisor="no">
        <copy>&copyright;</copy>
        <name>
```

LISTING 5.6 continued

```
            <lastname>Kelly</lastname>
            <firstname>Grace</firstname>
        </name>
        <hiredate>October 15, 2005</hiredate>
        <projects>
            <project>
                <product>Printer</product>
                <id>111</id>
                <price>$111.00</price>
            </project>
            <project>
                <product>Laptop</product>
                <id>222</id>
                <price>$989.00</price>
            </project>
        </projects>
    </employee>
    <employee supervisor="yes">
        <copy>&copyright;</copy>
        <name>
            <lastname>Grant</lastname>
            <firstname>Cary</firstname>
        </name>
        <hiredate>October 20, 2005</hiredate>
        <projects>
            <project>
                <product>Desktop</product>
                <id>333</id>
                <price>$2995.00</price>
            </project>
            <project>
                <product>Scanner</product>
                <id>444</id>
                <price>$200.00</price>
            </project>
        </projects>
    </employee>
</document>
```

If you open this new XML document, `ch05_06.xml`, in Internet Explorer, you'll see the same results shown in Figure 5.2. The external entity (that is, the text in `ch05_05.xml`) is picked up, and its text appears in the resulting display.

By using external general entities in this way, you can assemble XML documents together from various pieces stored in their own files. That can be very useful if, for example, you have standard headers or footers or copyright notices that you want to use.

Note that if you need to change those items (such as the date in a copyright notice), you need to make your changes only in one file.

TIP

It's not uncommon for nonvalidating XML processors to scan DTDs to pick up external general entity references. So even if an XML processor you're working with doesn't perform validation, it still might read your DTD to let you include external general entities in the document.

Associating Non-XML Data with an XML Document

Earlier in today's discussion, you saw that you can associate non-XML data—an image file, in fact—by using an external entity. You created an entity named `PHOTO1221` that referred to an external file named `1221.gif` and an attribute of the `ENTITY` type to which you could assign `PHOTO1221`:

```
<!ENTITY PHOTO1221 SYSTEM "1221.gif">
<!ATTLIST employee
    photo ENTITY #IMPLIED>
        .
        .
        .
<employee photo="PHOTO1221">
```

This associates the image file `1221.gif` with the current XML document, but you can make things even clearer to the XML processor. In particular, you can indicate that `1221.gif` is an external entity that *should not be parsed.* That's the way you normally associate binary data with an XML document—by treating it as an unparsed external entity.

To declare an external unparsed entity, you use an `<!ENTITY>` element with either the `SYSTEM` keyword or the `PUBLIC` keyword, like this (note the keyword `NDATA`, which indicates that you're referring to an unparsed entity):

```
<!ENTITY name SYSTEM value NDATA type>
<!ENTITY name PUBLIC FPI value NDATA type>
```

Here, *`name`* is the name of the external unparsed entity, *`value`* is the value of the entity, such as the name of an external file (for example, 1221.gif), and *`type`* is a declared notation (which you create by using a `<!NOTATION>` element). For example, to explicitly indicate that `1221.gif` is an external entity that should not be parsed, you can create a notation named `gif` for GIF files:

```
<!NOTATION gif SYSTEM "image/gif">
```

Next, you can declare `1221.gif` as an unparsed entity that uses the `gif` notation:

```
<!NOTATION gif SYSTEM "image/gif">
<!ENTITY PHOTO1221 SYSTEM "1221.gif" NDATA gif>
```

And you can create an `ENTITY` attribute named `photo` for the `<employee>` element:

```
<!NOTATION gif SYSTEM "image/gif">
<!ENTITY PHOTO1221 SYSTEM "1221.gif" NDATA gif>
<!ATTLIST employee
    photo ENTITY #IMPLIED>
```

Finally, you can assign the `photo` attribute the value `PHOTO1221`:

```
<?xml version = "1.0" encoding="UTF-8" standalone="no"?>
<!DOCTYPE document [
<!ELEMENT document (employee)*>
<!ELEMENT employee (name, hiredate, projects)>
<!ELEMENT name (lastname, firstname)>
<!ELEMENT lastname (#PCDATA)>
<!ELEMENT firstname (#PCDATA)>
<!ELEMENT hiredate (#PCDATA)>
<!ELEMENT projects (project)*>
<!ELEMENT project (product, id, price)>
<!ELEMENT product (#PCDATA)>
<!ELEMENT id (#PCDATA)>
<!ELEMENT price (#PCDATA)>
<!NOTATION gif SYSTEM "image/gif">
<!ENTITY PHOTO1221 SYSTEM "1221.gif" NDATA gif>
<!ATTLIST employee
    photo ENTITY #IMPLIED>
]>
<document>
    <employee photo="PHOTO1221">
        <name>
            <lastname>Kelly</lastname>
            <firstname>Grace</firstname>
        </name>
        <hiredate>October 15, 2005</hiredate>
        <projects>
            <project>
                <product>Printer</product>
                <id>111</id>
                <price>$111.00</price>
            </project>
            <project>
                <product>Laptop</product>
                <id>222</id>
                <price>$989.00</price>
            </project>
        </projects>
    </employee>
</document>
```

5

Note that in this example, you do *not* use an entity reference (that is, `&PHOTO1221;`) because you do not want the XML processor to parse `1221.gif`. Note also that when you use external unparsed entities like this, validating XML processors won't try to read and parse them, but they will usually check to make sure that the entities exist at the URI you specify to ensure that the whole XML document is considered complete.

You can also associate multiple unparsed external entities with an XML document if you create an attribute of the `ENTITIES` type, like this:

```
<?xml version = "1.0" encoding="UTF-8" standalone="no"?>
<!DOCTYPE document [
<!ELEMENT document (employee)*>
<!ELEMENT employee (name, hiredate, projects)>
<!ELEMENT name (lastname, firstname)>
<!ELEMENT lastname (#PCDATA)>
<!ELEMENT firstname (#PCDATA)>
<!ELEMENT hiredate (#PCDATA) >
<!ELEMENT projects (project)*>
<!ELEMENT project (product, id, price)>
<!ELEMENT product (#PCDATA)>
<!ELEMENT id (#PCDATA)>
<!ELEMENT price (#PCDATA)>
<!NOTATION gif SYSTEM "image/gif">
<!ENTITY PHOTO1221 SYSTEM "1221.jpg" NDATA gif>
<!ENTITY PHOTO1222 SYSTEM "1222.jpg" NDATA gif>
<!ATTLIST employee
    photos ENTITIES #IMPLIED>
]>
<document>
    <employee photo="PHOTO1221 PHOTO1222">
        <name>
            <lastname>Kelly</lastname>
            <firstname>Grace</firstname>
        </name>
        <hiredate>October 15, 2005</hiredate>
        <projects>
            <project>
                <product>Printer</product>
                <id>111</id>
                <price>$111.00</price>
            </project>
            <project>
                <product>Laptop</product>
                <id>222</id>
                <price>$989.00</price>
            </project>
        </projects>
    </employee>
</document>
```

Now that you've discussed general entities, let's take a look at entities that are specially designed to be used in DTDs only: parameter entities.

Creating Internal Parameter Entities

General entities are limited when it comes to working with DTDs. You can declare general entities in DTDs, but you can't use general entity references that the XML processor will expand in a DTD. However, it turns out that it can be useful to use parameters in DTDs, and you use parameter entities and parameter entity references (which can only be used in DTDs) for that. In fact, there's one more restriction on DTDs: Parameter entity references that you use inside an already existing DTD declaration can appear only in the DTD's *external subset*, which means the part of the DTD that is external. You'll discuss what this means in a few pages.

Unlike entity references, parameter references don't start with `&`; they start with `%` instead. Like general entities, you can declare a parameter entity by using the `<!ENTITY>` element, but you include a `%` to show that you're declaring a parameter reference. Here's the syntax for declaring an internal parameter entity:

```
<!ENTITY % name definition>
```

As you might expect, when you declare an external parameter entity, you can use the `SYSTEM` and `PUBLIC` keywords, like this:

```
<!ENTITY % NAME SYSTEM URI>
<!ENTITY % NAME PUBLIC FPI URI>
```

5

The following is an example that shows how to use an internal parameter entity. In this case, you just declare the parameter entity `project` to refer to the standard declaration of the `<project>` element in the sample XML document:

```
<!ENTITY % project "<!ELEMENT project (product, id, price)>">
```

Now when you use the parameter entity reference `%project;` in the DTD, it will be replaced with the text "`<!ELEMENT project (product, id, price)>`". Listing 5.7 shows this at work in `ch05_07.xml`.

Listing 5.7 Using an Internal Parameter Entity (`ch05_07.xml`)

```
<?xml version = "1.0" encoding="UTF-8" standalone="yes"?>
<!DOCTYPE document [
<!ENTITY % project "<!ELEMENT project (product, id, price)>">
<!ELEMENT document (employee)*>
<!ELEMENT employee (name, hiredate, projects)>
<!ELEMENT name (lastname, firstname)>
<!ELEMENT lastname (#PCDATA)>
```

LISTING 5.7 continued

```
<!ELEMENT firstname (#PCDATA)>
<!ELEMENT hiredate (#PCDATA)>
<!ELEMENT projects (project)*>
%project;
<!ELEMENT product (#PCDATA)>
<!ELEMENT id (#PCDATA)>
<!ELEMENT price (#PCDATA)>
<!ATTLIST employee supervisor CDATA #IMPLIED>
]>
<document>
    <employee supervisor="no">
        <name>
            <lastname>Kelly</lastname>
            <firstname>Grace</firstname>
        </name>
        <hiredate>October 15, 2005</hiredate>
        <projects>
            <project>
                <product>Printer</product>
                <id>111</id>
                <price>$111.00</price>
            </project>
            <project>
                <product>Laptop</product>
                <id>222</id>
                <price>$989.00</price>
            </project>
        </projects>
    </employee>
</document>
```

This turns out to be about as far as you can go with internal parameter entities because you can't use them *inside* other declarations. To see how parameter entities can really be useful, you have to turn to external parameter entities, which are described in the following section.

Creating External Parameter Entities

When you use a parameter entity in a DTD's external subset, you can refer to that entity anywhere in the DTD, including inside other element declarations. To see an example, you need an XML document that uses an external DTD, like `ch05_08.xml`, which uses an external DTD named `ch05_09.dtd` (see Listing 5.8).

LISTING 5.8 Using External Parameter Entities (ch05_08.xml)

```
<?xml version = "1.0" encoding="UTF-8" standalone="no"?>
<!DOCTYPE document SYSTEM "ch05_09.dtd">
<document>
    <employee supervisor="no">
        <name>
            <lastname>Kelly</lastname>
            <firstname>Grace</firstname>
        </name>
        <hiredate>October 15, 2005</hiredate>
        <projects>
            <project>
                <product>Printer</product>
                <id>111</id>
                <price>$111.00</price>
            </project>
            <project>
                <product>Laptop</product>
                <id>222</id>
                <price>$989.00</price>
            </project>
        </projects>
    </employee>
</document>
```

Let's say that in an external DTD, you want to create three elements that might appear in <employee> elements to record comments about the employee: <supervisorComment>, <customerComment>, and <employeeComment>. All three of these elements have the same content model. Say that each of these elements has the content model (date, text), where <date> contains the date of the comment and <text> contains the text of the comment. You can create a new parameter entity named record for this content model:

```
<!ENTITY % record "(date, text)">
```

Now in the external DTD, you can use a reference to this entity when you want to use the content model for the <supervisorComment>, <customerComment>, and <employeeComment> elements:

```
<!ELEMENT supervisorComment %record;>
<!ELEMENT customerComment %record;>
<!ELEMENT employeeComment %record;>
```

That's all it takes; Listing 5.9 shows the entire external DTD, which uses the record parameter entity.

5

LISTING 5.9 An External DTD That Uses Parameter Entities (ch05_09.dtd)

```
<?xml version = "1.0" encoding="UTF-8"?>
<!ENTITY % record "(date, text)">
<!ELEMENT document (employee)*>
<!ELEMENT employee (name, hiredate, projects,
supervisorComment*, customerComment*,
employeeComment*)>
<!ELEMENT name (lastname, firstname)>
<!ELEMENT lastname (#PCDATA)>
<!ELEMENT firstname (#PCDATA)>
<!ELEMENT hiredate (#PCDATA)>
<!ELEMENT projects (project)*>
<!ELEMENT supervisorComment %record;>
<!ELEMENT customerComment %record;>
<!ELEMENT employeeComment %record;>
<!ELEMENT project (product, id, price)>
<!ELEMENT product (#PCDATA)>
<!ELEMENT id (#PCDATA)>
<!ELEMENT price (#PCDATA)>
<!ELEMENT date (#PCDATA)>
<!ELEMENT text (#PCDATA)>
<!ATTLIST employee supervisor CDATA #IMPLIED>
```

Using parameter entities as in this example can be very useful because it means you can store all the content models you use in one location and change them in that one place as needed rather than having to hunt through an entire document. You can also use parameter DTDs to centralize your attribute declarations in the same way. You can even collect attribute declarations into groups and use them in element declarations as needed. For example, you might decide that a new element named `<imager>` should support both hyperlink attributes (such as a `targetURI` attribute) and image attributes (such as an `imageURI` attribute), and if you've grouped your attributes by functionality, here's how you could add those attributes to this element:

```
<!ATTLIST imager %hyperlink_attributes; %image_attributes;>
```

Using `INCLUDE` and `IGNORE` to Parameterize DTDs

There are two important directives that you need to know about when it comes to working with DTDs: `INCLUDE` and `IGNORE`. *Directives* are special commands to the XML processor, and `INCLUDE` and `IGNORE` are specially designed to customize a DTD by including or omitting sections of that DTD. The following is the syntax of `INCLUDE` and `IGNORE`:

```
<![ INCLUDE [DTD Section]]> and <![ IGNORE [DTD Section]]>
```

Here are two examples of what these directives might look like in action:

```
<![ INCLUDE [
<!ELEMENT lastname (#PCDATA)>
<!ELEMENT firstname (#PCDATA)>
]]>

<![ IGNORE [
<!ELEMENT lastname (#PCDATA)>
<!ELEMENT firstname (#PCDATA)>
]]>
```

In the first of these examples, the contained DTD fragment will be included by the XML processor, and in the second example, the contained DTD fragment will be ignored.

So why are `INCLUDE` and `IGNORE` useful? Can't you just include or ignore sections of DTDs ourselves, by adding or deleting them as needed? Can't you just use standard XML comments to hide sections of DTDs if you need to? Yes, you can. The reason you see `INCLUDE` and `IGNORE` in DTDs is that by using these directives, you can create *parameterized DTDs*. DTDs can be dozens of pages long (like the ones for XHTML), and you might miss some sections you want to exclude if you just rely on XML comments. But when you parameterize a DTD, you can just set a parameter entity to `"INCLUDE"` or `"IGNORE"` to include or ignore many DTDs sections at once.

Let's use the DTD for XHTML 1.1, which is a parameterized DTD, as an example. The main DTD for XHTML 1.1 is set up to include or ignore other sections of the DTD (a DTD that works like this is sometimes called a *DTD driver*), depending on how you want to customize the DTD. For example, some devices that can support some XHTML can't support everything. Cell phones might be fine with bold text and hyperlinks but might have trouble displaying tables, for instance. For that reason, you can customize the XHTML 1.1 DTD to include or ignore the DTD section that has to do with tables. In particular, the XHTML 1.1 DTD declares a parameter entity named `xhtml-table.module` that is set to `"INCLUDE"` by default and includes the table DTD module with an `INCLUDE` section, like this:

5

```
<!ENTITY % xhtml-table.module "INCLUDE" >
        .
        .
        .
<![%xhtml-table.module;[
<!ENTITY % xhtml-table.mod
    PUBLIC "-//W3C//ELEMENTS XHTML 1.1 Tables 1.0//EN"
        "xhtml11-table-1.mod" >
%xhtml-table.mod;]]>
]]>
```

If you wanted to, you could exclude all reference to XHTML tables in your own version of the XHTML 1.1 DTD just by setting `xhtml-table.module` to `"IGNORE"` to exclude support for tables. In this way, you can centralize control over a parameterized DTD, which might be dozens of pages long, simply by changing the values of a few parameter entities in one location. The XHTML 1.1 DTD is written in modules that can be expressly included or ignored if you want, making the entire XHTML 1.1 DTD fully parameterized.

Summary

Today's discussion describes how to use attributes and entities with DTDs. You saw that you declare attributes in a DTD by using an `<!ATTLIST>` element.

You can assign various default values to attributes when you declare them. You can assign an explicit default value—`#IMPLIED` to make the attribute optional, `#FIXED` to give it a fixed value, and `#REQUIRED` to make an attribute required —enclosed in quotation marks,.

You can also declare the type of an attribute in an `<!ATTLIST>` element. The various attribute types are `CDATA`, which means character data; `ENTITY`, which means you can assign an entity name to an attribute; `ENTITIES`, which you can use to assign a list of entity names to an attribute; an enumeration, which specifies a list of possible values for an attribute; an `ID` value; an `IDREF` value, which holds the `ID` of another element; `IDREFS`, which holds multiple `ID` values; `NMTOKEN`, which can hold text made up of XML name characters; `NMTOKENS`, which can hold multiple `NMTOKEN` items; and `NOTATION`, which holds the name of a notation (that is, a format description).

In this discussion you also saw how to work with entities. You saw that you can declare entities by using the `<!ENTITY>` element. And you saw that *entity* is XML's term for a data item, and when you declare entities in a DTD, you can refer to them in the rest of the XML document.

In general, entity references in an XML document will be replaced by the entity they stand for when the entity is text. However, you can also create unparsed entities that will not be parsed by the XML processor; for example, external image files in binary format are usually unparsed external entities.

DTDs were introduced when XML was, and they haven't really grown since that time. They're still the technique of choice for validating XML documents with much of the software out there, but the real growth these days is in XML schemas. XML schemas give you the ability to pinpoint the format of your data in a way that DTDs can't, and you'll be hearing more about XML schemas over the next two days.

Q&A

Q These days, DTDs and XML schemas are both popular. Which should I use?

A The answer depends on several factors. Which does your target XML processor support? Which are you more comfortable with? Can DTDs give you the precision you want, or do you need to turn to schemas? DTDs have been around longer than schemas. A casual Web search turns up 1.9 million matches to "DTD" but only 385,000 to "XML schema." And many beginning XML authors find DTDs easier to work with than schemas. Nonetheless, XML schemas are where the growth is these days. Microsoft has thrown its weight behind schemas, so the industry as a whole is shifting toward them.

Q The DTD syntax is just too complex. Isn't there some way to make writing a DTD easier?

A Take a look at the automatic DTD generators available online. You just navigate to a DTD generator on the Web, click a button to browse to the XML document on your disk for which you want a DTD, and click a button to upload the document; the DTD generator does the rest. For example, take a look at the DTD generators at (as of this writing) `http://www.pault.com/pault/dtdgenerator` and `http://www.hitsw.com/xml_utilites`.

Workshop

This workshop tests whether you understand the concepts discussed today. It's a good idea to make sure you can answer these questions before pressing on to tomorrow's work. Answers to the quiz can be found in Appendix A, "Quiz Answers."

5

Quiz

1. What keyword do you use in an `<!ATTLIST>` element to make an attribute optional?
2. What keyword do you use in an `<!ATTLIST>` element to make sure an attribute always has the same value?
3. How can you declare a required `name` attribute, an optional `address` attribute, and an optional `phone` attribute for an element named `<friend>`? Each of these attributes should hold simple character data.
4. How can you restrict an attribute named `married` in an element named `<relative>` to values of `"yes"` or `"no"`, making the default `"no"`?
5. How can you declare an external unparsed entity named `mountains` that corresponds to the image file `mountains.jpg`?

Exercises

1. Create a new XML document that uses a DTD to declare an optional `CDATA` attribute named `date` that holds dates in the form 4/1/05, an attribute called `sex` that can take the values `"male"` and `"female"` only, and a required `CDATA name` attribute. Test your work by using an online XML validator.
2. Parameterize the DTD you created in Exercise 1 so that you can include all the attributes created in that exercise by setting a parameter named `includer` to `INCLUDE` or exclude them by setting that parameter to `IGNORE`.

PART I

DAY 6

Creating Valid XML Documents: XML Schemas

Yesterday and on Day 4, "Creating Valid XML Documents: DTDs," you took a look at working with DTDs to validate XML documents. Today and tomorrow you'll get a look at the other way of validating XML documents: using XML schemas. XML schemas allow you considerably more precision than DTDs do, as you're about to see. Here's an overview of today's topics:

- Validating XML documents by using XML schemas
- Creating XML schemas
- Using XML schema-generating tools
- Declaring elements
- Declaring simple and complex types
- Creating sequences of elements
- Setting the number of times elements may occur
- Giving elements default values
- Specifying attributes
- Specifying default values for attributes

As of this writing, this quote is available on the W3C XML Activity Page (`http://www.w3.org/XML/Activity.html`):

> While XML 1.0 supplies a mechanism, the document type definition (DTD) for declaring constraints on the use of markup, automated processing of XML documents, requires more rigorous and comprehensive facilities in this area.

For the past two days, you've been working with DTDs, but DTDs are actually pretty basic. As XML developed, XML authors asked the W3C for a more comprehensive and detailed way of specifying the syntax of XML documents, and the W3C responded with XML schemas. The W3C XML schema working group was originally created to tackle a number of issues that DTDs didn't handle well—handling namespaces when validating documents, allowing data typing, allowing and restricting inheritance for validation methods, creating our own data types, and other issues. As you're going to see, XML schemas let you spell out the syntax of XML documents far more precisely than DTDs ever could. Originally, there was very little software that could handle XML schemas, but today you'll find more and more XML schema-aware software available.

XML schemas are a W3C recommendation, and that recommendation is available in these three documents:

- **`http://www.w3.org/TR/xmlschema-0`**—This XML schema primer is a tutorial introduction to schemas.
- **`http://www.w3.org/TR/xmlschema-1`**—This document covers XML schema structures, including the formal details on creating schemas.
- **`http://www.w3.org/TR/xmlschema-2`**—This document discusses the data types you can use in schemas.

TIP

> Another good resource on XML schemas is the W3C XML Schema Activity Page, `http://www.w3.org/XML/Schema`, which lists everything that's going on with schemas these days.

Right now, the XML schema recommendation is in version 1.0, but the W3C is starting to think about version 1.1. Nothing's been firmed up at this point, however. Here's what W3C says about version 1.1:

> The XML Schema WG is currently working to develop a set of requirements for XML Schema 1.1, which is intended to be mostly compatible with XML Schema 1.0 and to have approximately the same scope, but also to fix bugs and make whatever improvements you can, consistent with the constraints on scope and compatibility.

Using XML Schema Tools

Today and tomorrow you're going to see how to write XML schemas, but before you dig into the details (and there are plenty of them), it's worth noting that more and more software tools are appearing that can generate XML schemas for you. Although XML authors should know how to write XML schemas, tools that do the work for you can be very handy, so you'll start by introducing them.

Creating Schemas by Using XML Schema-Creation Tools

A growing number of XML schema-creation tools are becoming available; here's a sampling of the ones that are out there as of this writing:

- **HiT Software**(`http://www.hitsw.com/xml_utilites/`)—This is an online automatic XML schema generator and DTD to XML schema converter. You just let it upload a document, and it creates an XML schema for free.
- **xmlArchitect** (`http://www.sysonyx.com/products/xmlArchitect`)—This is an XML editor for creating schemas.
- **XMLspy** (`http://www.xmlspy.com`)—XMLspy is a product family of tools that aid in the creation of XML schemas.
- `XRay (http://architag.com/xray)`—This tool provides support for XML schemas and has an integrated online XML tutorial system.
- **Microsoft Visual Studio .NET** (`http://www.microsoft.com`)—Visual Studio .NET can also generate XML schemas for you automatically.

As an example of the schema-creation process, let's take a look at the XML schema generator in the Microsoft Visual Studio .NET development tool. Take a look at this XML document:

```
<?xml version="1.0"?>
<document xmlns="http://xmlpowercorp">
    <text>
        Welcome to XML Schemas!
    </text>
</document>
```

6

What if you want to automatically generate an XML schema for this document? You start by opening the XML document in Visual Studio .NET (that is, in Visual Studio .NET, you create a new project and then select Project, Add Existing Item to open the Add Existing Item dialog box, where you can browse to the XML document for which you want to create a schema). Figure 6.1 shows the short sample XML document opened in Visual Studio .NET.

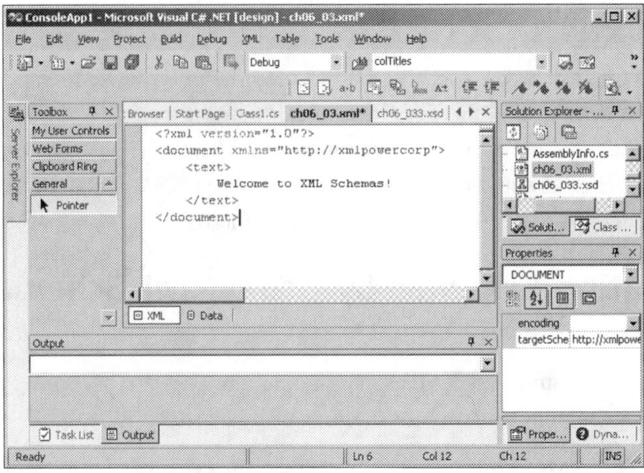

FIGURE 6.1

An XML document in Visual Studio .NET.

Next, you select XML, Create Schema to create an XML schema for the document. The XML that is generated is shown in Figure 6.2.

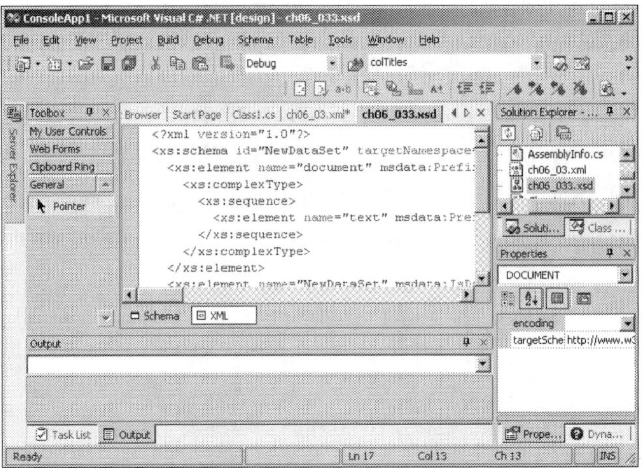

FIGURE 6.2

Creating an XML schema in Visual Studio .NET.

Here's what the generated XML schema looks like (note that it's about four times as long as the original XML document) :

```
<?xml version="1.0"?>
<xs:schema id="NewDataSet"
targetNamespace="http://xmlpowercorp"
xmlns:mstns="http://xmlpowercorp" xmlns="http://xmlpowercorp"
xmlns:xs="http://www.w3.org/2001/XMLSchema"
xmlns:msdata="urn:schemas-microsoft-com:xml-msdata"
```

```
attributeFormDefault="qualified" elementFormDefault="qualified">
  <xs:element name="document" msdata:Prefix="ch06">
    <xs:complexType>
      <xs:sequence>
        <xs:element name="text" msdata:Prefix="ch06"
            type="xs:string" minOccurs="1" />
      </xs:sequence>
    </xs:complexType>
  </xs:element>
  <xs:element name="NewDataSet" msdata:IsDataSet="true"
    msdata:Prefix="ch06" msdata:EnforceConstraints="False">
    <xs:complexType>
      <xs:choice maxOccurs="unbounded">
        <xs:element ref="document" />
      </xs:choice>
    </xs:complexType>
  </xs:element>
</xs:schema>
```

This is a valid XML schema, although it uses a namespace for Microsoft-specific data types that you're not going to use, and it adds more elements than you'll need.

As mentioned earlier today, you can also use free online XML schema generators such as the one at `http://www.hitsw.com/xml_utilities/` to upload XML documents and create XML schemas. Figure 6.3 shows the XML schema that this generator creates for the sample XML document.

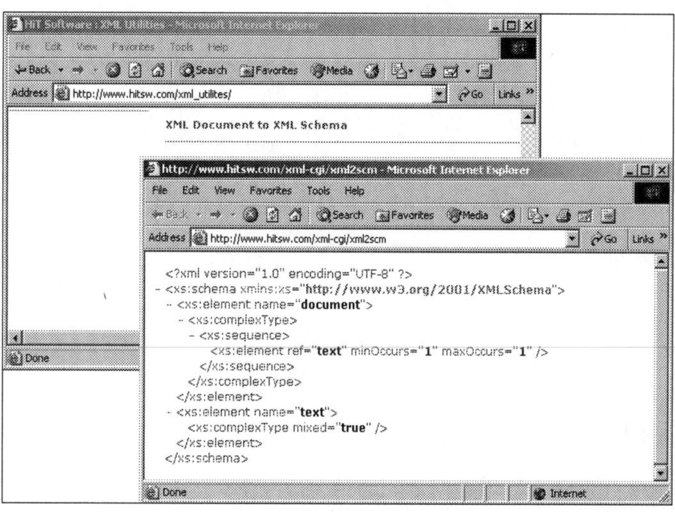

FIGURE 6.3

Using an online XML schema generator.

Validating XML Documents by Using XML Schemas

When you want to validate an XML document by using an XML schema, you can choose from the many XML validators that are available. Here's a starter list:

- **Visual Studio .NET** (`http://www.microsoft.com`)—You just select XML, Validate XML Data to begin validating an XML document.
- **Topologi Schematron Validator** (`http://www.topologi.com`)—This is a free Windows-based tool that validates XML schemas.
- **XML Schema Quality Checker** (`http://www.alphaworks.ibm.com/tech/xmlsqc`)—This is the IBM AlphaWorks XML schema validator.
- **Xerces** (`http://xml.apache.org/xerces2-j/index.html`)—The Apache Project's Xerces 2 XML processor includes XML schema validation.
- **XSD Schema Validator** (`http://apps.gotdotnet.com/xmltools/xsdvalidator`)—This tool is a .NET-based XML schema validator.
- **XSV** (`http://www.w3.org/2001/03/webdata/xsv`)—This is the online W3C XML schema validator.
- **Xerces J** (`http://tools.decisionsoft.com/schemaValidate.html`)—This is a DecisionSoft XML validator.
- **Internet Explorer** (`http://www.microsoft.com/windows/ie/default.asp`)—You can use Microsoft Internet Explorer to validate schemas.

The most widely used of these XML schema validation tools is Internet Explorer. The XML support in Internet Explorer is built into the MSXML package (which was called the Microsoft XML Parser until MSXML version 4.0, when it was named the Microsoft XML Core Services). MSXML version 4.0 is the version that supports XML Schema Definition Language (XSD) schemas. (Note that before version 4.0, MSXML only supported a smaller and different version of XML schemas, which Microsoft called XML-Data Reduced [XDR] schemas.) Table 6.1 lists support for XML schemas, by MSXML version.

TABLE 6.1 XML Schema Support by MSXML Version

Version	*Support*
MSXML	No support.
MSXML 2.0	Support only for XDR schemas.
MSXML 2.6	Support only for XDR schemas.
MSXML 3.0	Support only for XDR schemas.
MSXML 4.0	Support for XSD and XDR schemas. Note that XSD support is not yet complete.

TIP

> If you have Internet Explorer and you're running Windows, you can determine what version of MSXML you have by looking in the directory where Windows stores dynamic link library (DLL) files, which is either `system` or `system32` under the main Windows directory, depending on your version of Windows. For example, if you see `msxml3.dll` and you don't see any later version, you have MSXML 3.0. If you see `msxml4.dll` and no later version, you have version 4.0. To work with full XML schemas, you need MSXML version 4.0 or later. (Microsoft's XDR version of schemas is very different from the W3C XSD type of schemas.) If you don't already have it installed, you can download MSXML 4.0 from Microsoft for free from the Microsoft XML site, currently at `http://msdn.microsoft.com/library/default.asp?url=/nhp/Default.asp?contentid=28000438`.
>
> The direct download site for MSXML 4.0 is `http://msdn.microsoft.com/library/default.asp?url=/downloads/list/xmlgeneral.asp` as of this writing (note that it can change at any time, however) .

Let's put MSXML 4.0 and Internet Explorer 6 to work now. If you want Internet Explorer to validate an XML document by using an XML schema, you have to do a little extra work by using JScript, Internet Explorer's version of JavaScript. You'll take a more detailed look at JavaScript on Day 15, "Using JavaScript and XML," and you don't have to write any JavaScript until then—all the work is already done for you in the HTML document `ch06_01.html`, which is shown in Listing 6.1. You can load this HTML document in an XML document, as stored in a file named `ch06_02.xml`, and validate it.

LISTING 6.1 An HTML Document That Can Validate an XML Document (`ch06_01.xml`)

```
<HTML>
    <HEAD>
        <TITLE>
            Validating With XML Schemas
        </TITLE>
        <SCRIPT LANGUAGE="JavaScript">
            document.write("<H1>Validating With XML Schemas</H1>");
            var parser = new ActiveXObject("MSXML2.DOMDocument.4.0");
            parser.validateOnParse = true;

            if (parser.load("ch06_02.xml")) {
                document.write("The document is valid!");
            } else {
                if (parser.parseError.errorCode != 0) {
                    document.write(parser.parseError.reason);
                }
            }
```

6

LISTING 6.1 continued

```
        </SCRIPT>
    </HEAD>

    <BODY></BODY>
</HTML>
```

As an example, you can validate the following sample XML document, which you have already seen today:

```
<?xml version="1.0"?>
<document xmlns="http://xmlpowercorp">
    <text>
        Welcome to XML Schemas!
    </text>
</document>
```

How do you connect an XML schema to an XML document? Different XML processors do it in different ways, but, slowly, a standard is emerging. If you define a namespace, usually named `xsi`, for the URI `www.w3.org/2001/XMLSchema-instance`, you can then use an attribute named `xsi:schemaLocation` in the document element to specify the URI of the document's XML schema.

Not many XML processors support this attribute yet, but Internet Explorer does. To use this attribute so that Internet Explorer will understand it, you assign it a text string, giving the namespace you're using in our XML document, which is `http://xmlpowercorp` here, and the URI of the XML schema, which is `ch0603.xsd` in this case (assuming that `ch0603.xsd` is in the same directory as the XML document), like this: `xsi:schemaLocation="http://xmlpowercorp ch06_03.xsd"`. (If you're not using a namespace in our XML document, you can use the `xsi:noNamespaceSchemaLocation` attribute.) Listing 6.2 shows how this works in the XML document `ch06_02.xml`.

LISTING 6.2 A Sample XML Document to Verify (`ch06_02.xml`)

```
<?xml version="1.0"?>
<document xmlns="http://xmlpowercorp"
    xmlns:xsi="http://www.w3.org/2001/XMLSchema-instance"
    xsi:schemaLocation="http://xmlpowercorp ch06_03.xsd">
    <text>
        Welcome to XML Schemas!
    </text>
</document>
```

Listing 6.3 shows an XML schema (`ch06_03.xsd`) you can use for this example.

LISTING 6.3 The XML Schema for the First Example (`ch06_03.xsd`)

```
<?xml version="1.0"?>
<xsd:schema targetNamespace="http://xmlpowercorp"
xmlns="http://xmlpowercorp"
xmlns:xsd="http://www.w3.org/2001/XMLSchema"
attributeFormDefault="qualified" elementFormDefault="qualified">
  <xsd:element name="document">
    <xsd:complexType>
      <xsd:sequence>
        <xsd:element name="text" type="xsd:string" minOccurs="1" />
      </xsd:sequence>
    </xsd:complexType>
  </xsd:element>
</xsd:schema>
```

Just by looking at the XML schema in Listing 6.3, you can get an idea of what's going on: You declare an element named `<document>` and another one named `<text>` to match what's in the XML document. Then when you open `ch06_01.html`, Internet Explorer loads in the XML document, `ch06_02.xml`, and then the XML schema, `ch06_03.xsd`, and it validates the XML document, as shown in Figure 6.4. (Note that to run this example, `ch06_01.html`, `ch06_02.xml`, and `ch06_03.xsd` should all be in the same directory.)

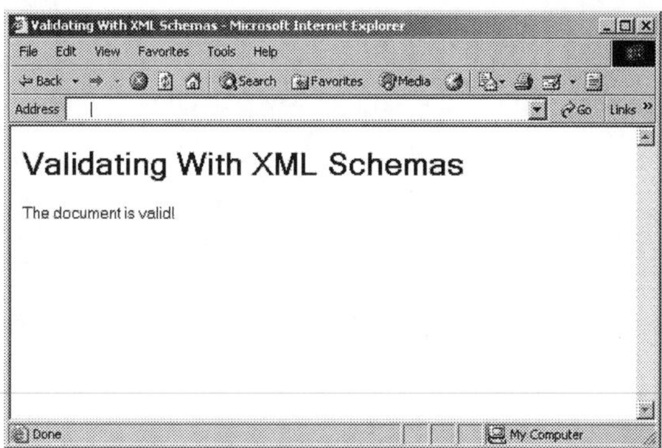

FIGURE 6.4
Validating with an XML schema in Internet Explorer.

On the other hand, what if the XML processor you're using objects to the `xsi:schemaLocation` attribute, which you use to connect the XML schema to an XML document, as nonstandard? It turns out that it's actually not necessary to embed an `xsi:schemaLocation` attribute in an XML document to validate it by using Internet Explorer—you can use JavaScript to tell Internet Explorer where to find the XML schema. Listing 6.4 shows an HTML document (`ch06_04.html`) that does that.

LISTING 6.4 An HTML Document That Verifies an XML Document (`ch06_04.html`)

```
<HTML>
    <HEAD>
        <TITLE>
            Validating With XML Schemas
        </TITLE>
        <SCRIPT LANGUAGE="JScript">
            document.write("<H1>Validating With XML Schemas</H1>");
            var schemaHandler = new ActiveXObject("MSXML2.XMLSchemaCache.4.0");
            schemaHandler.add("http://xmlpowercorp", "ch06_03.xsd");

            var parser = new ActiveXObject("MSXML2.DOMDocument.4.0");
            parser.schemas = schemaHandler;
            parser.validateOnParse = true;

            if (parser.load("ch06_05.xml")) {
                document.write("The document is valid!");
            } else {
                if (parser.parseError.errorCode != 0) {
                    document.write(parser.parseError.reason);
                }
            }
        </SCRIPT>
    </HEAD>

    <BODY></BODY>
</HTML>
```

By using `ch06_04.html`, you don't have to use the `xsi:schemaLocation` attribute, as you can see in the new version of the sample XML document, `ch06_05.xml`, which is shown in Listing 6.5.

LISTING 6.5 The XML Document to Be Verified (`ch06_05.xml`)

```
<?xml version="1.0"?>
<document xmlns="http://xmlpowercorp">
    <text>
        Welcome to XML Schemas!
    </text>
</document>
```

When you open this HTML document, `ch06_04.html`, in Internet Explorer, you get the same results shown in Figure 6.4 as it validates the new version of the XML document. (Note that to run this example, `ch06_04.html`, `ch06_05.xml`, and `ch06_03.xsd` should all be in the same directory.)

Now that you have some experience using software both in generating XML schemas and using them to validate XML, it's time to get into the meat of today's discussion: creating our own XML schemas.

Creating XML Schemas

To create XML schemas ourselves, you're going to need an XML document to practice on—one that will give you some idea of what's possible. For example, say that you're a bank president, and you want to keep track of the mortgage loans you have outstanding. This example involves an XML document that contains the current mortgages held by a real estate investor and records not only data about this investor but also about the bank, and it lists the current mortgages the investor has with our bank, including the mortgage amount, the term of each (in years), and the location of the various properties. This document, `ch06_06.xml`, is shown in Listing 6.6; as shown in the listing, there is a document element named `<document>`, a `<bank>` element that stores data about the bank, a `<mortgagee>` element that stores data about the borrower, and a `<mortgages>` element that lists the mortgages the borrower has with the bank.

LISTING 6.6 An XML Document That Contains Mortgage Information (`ch06_06.xml`)

```
<?xml version="1.0" encoding="UTF-8"?>
<document documentDate="2005-03-02">
    <comment>Good risk</comment>
    <mortgagee phone="888.555.1234">
        <name>James Blandings</name>
        <location>1234 299th St</location>
        <city>New York</city>
        <state>NY</state>
    </mortgagee>
    <mortgages>
        <mortgage loanNumber="66 7777 88">
            <property>The Hackett Place</property>
            <date>2005-03-01</date>
            <loanAmount>80000</loanAmount>
            <term>15</term>
        </mortgage>
        <mortgage loanNumber="11 8888 22">
            <property>123 Acorn Drive</property>
            <date>2005-03-01</date>
            <loanAmount>90000</loanAmount>
            <term>15</term>
        </mortgage>
        <mortgage loanNumber="33 4444 11">
            <property>99 West Pocusset St</property>
            <date>2005-03-02</date>
```

6

LISTING 6.6 continued

```
            <loanAmount>100000</loanAmount>
            <term>30</term>
        </mortgage>
        <mortgage loanNumber="55 3333 88">
            <property>19 Johnson Place</property>
            <date>2005-03-02</date>
            <loanAmount>110000</loanAmount>
            <term>30</term>
        </mortgage>
        <mortgage loanNumber="22 6666 99">
            <property>345 Notingham Court</property>
            <date>2005-03-02</date>
            <loanAmount>120000</loanAmount>
            <term>30</term>
        </mortgage>
    </mortgages>
    <bank phone="888.555.8888">
        <name>XML Bank</name>
        <location>12 Schema Place</location>
        <city>New York</city>
        <state>NY</state>
    </bank>
</document>
```

You're naturally anxious to make sure that the data on our mortgage loans is stored correctly, so you also have a first-class XML schema for this XML document; it is shown in Listing 6.7.

LISTING 6.7 An XML Schema to Validate `ch06_06.xml` (`ch06_07.xsd`)

```
<?xml version="1.0" encoding="UTF-8"?>
<xsd:schema xmlns:xsd="http://www.w3.org/2001/XMLSchema">
    <xsd:annotation>
        <xsd:documentation>
            Mortgage record XML schema.
        </xsd:documentation>
    </xsd:annotation>
    <xsd:element name="document" type="documentType"/>
    <xsd:complexType name="documentType">
        <xsd:sequence>
            <xsd:element ref="comment" minOccurs="1"/>
            <xsd:element name="mortgagee" type="recordType"/>
            <xsd:element name="mortgages" type="mortgagesType"/>
            <xsd:element name="bank" type="recordType"/>
        </xsd:sequence>
        <xsd:attribute name="documentDate" type="xsd:date"/>
```

LISTING 6.7 continued

```
    </xsd:complexType>
    <xsd:complexType name="recordType">
        <xsd:sequence>
            <xsd:element name="name" type="xsd:string"/>
            <xsd:element name="location" type="xsd:string"/>
            <xsd:element name="city" type="xsd:string"/>
            <xsd:element name="state" type="xsd:string"/>
        </xsd:sequence>
        <xsd:attribute name="phone" type="xsd:string"
            use="optional"/>
    </xsd:complexType>
    <xsd:complexType name="mortgagesType">
        <xsd:sequence>
            <xsd:element name="mortgage" minOccurs="1" maxOccurs="8">
                <xsd:complexType>
                    <xsd:sequence>
                        <xsd:element name="property" type="xsd:string"/>
                        <xsd:element name="date" type="xsd:date"
                            minOccurs="0"/>

                        <xsd:element name="loanAmount" type="xsd:decimal"/>
                        <xsd:element name="term">
                        <xsd:simpleType>
                            <xsd:restriction base="xsd:integer">
                                <xsd:maxInclusive value="30"/>
                            </xsd:restriction>
                        </xsd:simpleType>
                        </xsd:element>
                    </xsd:sequence>
                    <xsd:attribute name="loanNumber" type="loanNumberType"/>
                </xsd:complexType>
            </xsd:element>
        </xsd:sequence>
    </xsd:complexType>
    <xsd:simpleType name="loanNumberType">
        <xsd:restriction base="xsd:string">
            <xsd:pattern value="\d{2} \d{4} \d{2}"/>
        </xsd:restriction>
    </xsd:simpleType>
    <xsd:element name="comment" type="xsd:string"/>
</xsd:schema>
```

6

Now that you have a sample XML schema, let's dissect it to see what makes XML schemas tick.

Dissecting an XML Schema

The first thing to note about the XML schema in Listing 6.7 is that it's a well-formed XML document. That is, it uses proper XML elements to declare the syntax of the XML document `ch06_06.xml`. To start, it uses an XML declaration to declare the namespace prefix `xsd` (the usual name for this namespace prefix in XML schemas), and it assigns the URI `www.w3.org/2001/XMLSchema` to that prefix, which is how the W3C says you must do things in XML schemas, in a special element named `<xsd:schema>`:

```
<?xml version="1.0" encoding="UTF-8"?>
<xsd:schema xmlns:xsd="http://www.w3.org/2001/XMLSchema">
        .
        .
        .
</xsd:schema>
```

The items in the schema appear in special elements that are legal to use in XML schemas, like the following, which declares an annotation for the XML schema explaining what it's for:

```
<?xml version="1.0" encoding="UTF-8"?>
<xsd:schema xmlns:xsd="http://www.w3.org/2001/XMLSchema">
    <xsd:annotation>
        <xsd:documentation>
            Mortgage record XML schema.
        </xsd:documentation>
    </xsd:annotation>
        .
        .
        .
</xsd:schema>
```

Here you're putting the `<xsd:documentation>` element with the text "Mortgage record XML schema." inside the `<xsd:annotation>` element, creating a comment in the schema. (You'll hear more about XML schema annotations tomorrow.) Annotations like this one are ignored by XML processors.

Although much of this schema is still unfamiliar to you, you can already see some of what's going on. In particular, note that you use `<xsd:element>` to declare elements and `<xsd:attribute>` to declare attributes:

```
<xsd:schema xmlns:xsd="http://www.w3.org/2001/XMLSchema">
    <xsd:annotation>
        <xsd:documentation>
            Mortgage record XML schema.
        </xsd:documentation>
    </xsd:annotation>
    <xsd:element name="document" type="documentType"/>
```

```
    <xsd:complexType name="documentType">
        <xsd:sequence>
            <xsd:element ref="comment" minOccurs="1"/>
            <xsd:element name="mortgagee" type="recordType"/>
            <xsd:element name="mortgages" type="mortgagesType"/>
            <xsd:element name="bank" type="recordType"/>
        </xsd:sequence>
        <xsd:attribute name="documentDate" type="xsd:date"/>
    </xsd:complexType>
        .
        .
        .
</xsd:schema>
```

As you can see, there are specific elements that are legal in schemas. The following section explains what they are.

The Built-in XML Schema Elements

Table 6.2 lists the elements you can use in XML schemas. These elements are usually used with the namespace `www.w3.org/2001/XMLSchema` and namespace prefix `xsd`, so, for example, the `<all>` element would usually be `<xsd:all>`, and so on.

TABLE 6.2 Legal XML Schema Elements

XML Schema Element	*Description*
`all`	Allows elements in a group to be in any order.
`annotation`	Creates an annotation that lets you add comments to an XML schema.
`any`	Allows any element to appear in a sequence or choice element.
`anyAttribute`	Allows any attribute to appear in the containing complex type or in the containing attribute group.
`appinfo`	Contains information within an annotation element.
`attribute`	Declares an attribute.
`attributeGroup`	Creates an attribute group, which allows attribute declarations to be used as a group for complex type definitions.
`choice`	Allows one, and only one, of the given elements to appear in the containing element.
`complexContent`	Specifies restrictions on a complex type that contains mixed content or elements.
`complexType`	Declares a complex type.
`documentation`	Contains text that can be placed in an annotation element.

6

TABLE 6.2 continued

XML Schema Element	*Description*
`element`	Declares an element.
`extension`	Extends a simple or complex type that has simple content.
`field`	Contains an XML Path Language (XPath) expression that specifies the value for a constraint.
`group`	Groups element declarations together so that they can be used as a group in complex type definitions.
`import`	Imports a namespace whose schema components can be used by a schema.
`include`	Includes the given schema document in the current schema.
`key`	Specifies that an attribute value or element value must be a key.
`keyref`	Specifies that an attribute value or element value must match the value of the given key.
`list`	Declares a simple type element as a list of values of a given data type.
`notation`	Holds a notation to describe the format of non-XML data inside an XML document.
`redefine`	Allows simple and complex types and groups to be redefined in the current schema.
`restriction`	Declares constraints, such as restricting the type of data.
`schema`	Contains a schema definition.
`selector`	Gives an XPath expression that can select elements for an identity constraint.
`sequence`	Constrains the given elements to appear in the given sequence in the XML document.
`simpleContent`	Contains extensions or restrictions on a type.
`simpleType`	Declares a simple type for use with the `type` attribute when you declare elements or attributes.
`union`	Declares a simple type as a collection of values of simple data types.
`unique`	Specifies that an attribute or element value must be unique.

You'll begin putting the elements in Table 6.2 to work next, as you take a look at how to declare elements in XML schemas.

Creating Elements and Types

To declare elements, you use the <xsd:element> element in XML schemas. When you declare an element, you can specify its *type*. For example, the element named <comment> in the sample XML document you've been working with just contains text:

```
<comment>Good risk</comment>
```

You can declare the <comment> element by using <xsd:element> and giving it the name "comment" and the type xsd:string, like this:

```
<xsd:element name="comment" type="xsd:string"/>
```

That was easy enough. In this case, you could use a type that is built into XML schemas, xsd:string. However, you can also define our own types. In fact, there are two types that you can create—simple and complex types.

To create simple types, you use the <xsd:simpleType> element, and to create complex types, you use the <xsd:complexType> element. After you create our own types, you can declare elements by using those types.

Elements that enclose child elements or have attributes are *complex types*. Elements that enclose only simple data, such as numbers, strings, or dates, but do not have any child elements are *simple types*. In other words, complex types can have internal structure, such as child elements and attributes, but simple types cannot. For example, attributes are always simple types because attribute values cannot have any internal structure (such as child elements).

The distinction between simple and complex types is an important one because you declare simple and complex types differently. You declare complex types ourselves, and the XML schema specification comes with many simple types already declared, as you'll see. You can also declare our own simple types, and you'll see how to do that as well.

Using Simple Types

You've already seen that you can use built-in XML schema types when declaring elements, like this:

```
<xsd:element name="comment" type="xsd:string"/>
```

Table 6.3 lists the built-in simple types for XML schemas. Note that if you use the xsd namespace prefix in an XML schema, as is usual, you reference the simple types in the schema as xsd:anyURI, xsd:base64Binary, and so on. Probably the most-used built-in simple type is xsd:string, which is simply a string of text. Other common types are xsd:int for integers, and xsd:date for dates. Note also how detailed these types are compared to DTDs; remember that with DTDs, you can't define data types.

Table 6.3 Simple Types Built into XML Schema

Simple Type	*Examples*
anyURI	http://www.xmlpowercorp.com
base64Binary	GpM6
boolean	true, false, 1, 0
byte	-1, 200
date	2005-03-02
dateTime	2005-03-02T10:14:00.000-05:00
decimal	1.23456, -1.23456, 200000.00
double	12345, 12.345E-6, 3.1415926
duration	P2Y1M3DT10H40M21.7S
ENTITIES	(XML entities)
ENTITY	(An XML entity)
float	12345, 12.345E-6, 3.1415926
gDay	---31
gMonth	--02--
gMonthDay	--04-31
gYear	2005
gYearMonth	2005-07
hexBinary	0EE6
ID	(XML ID)
IDREF	(XML ID REF)
IDREFS	(XML ID REFS)
int	1, 2, -3, 7654321
integer	-12345, -100, 1000
language	en-US, de, fr, jp
long	-1234, 12345678901234
Name	Edward
NCName	Thomas
negativeInteger	-1, -12, -12345
NMTOKEN	CA
NMTOKENS	CA NJ, PA NY MA
nonNegativeInteger	0, 1, 2, 12345
nonPositiveInteger	-12, -33, 0

TABLE 6.3 continued

Simple Type	*Examples*
`normalizedString`	`Welcome to XML Schemas`
`NOTATION`	(XML NOTATION)
`positiveInteger`	`1, 2, 3, 123456`
`QName`	`xml21:Name`
`short`	`-1, 2, 245`
`string`	`Welcome to XML Schemas`
`time`	`10:22:00.000`
`token`	`Hello`
`unsignedByte`	`0, 88, 127`
`unsignedInt`	`0, 1234`
`unsignedLong`	`0, 126789675`
`unsignedShort`	`0, 123`

Usually, when you want to use a simple data type, you use one of the ones listed in Table 6.3. However, you can also use the `<xsd:simpleType>` element to declare our own simple types, as you're going to see tomorrow. If you can't give simple types child elements or attributes and you have a whole selection of predefined simple types to choose from, as shown in Table 6.3, what's the point of declaring our own simple types? Among other things, declaring our own simple types lets you restrict the values those types can take.

For example, take a look at the `<term>` element in the mortgage XML document. This element gives the term (that is, the length) of the mortgage in years, and you want that number to be 30 or less, so you can use a `<xsd:simpleType>` element, enclosing a `<xsd:restriction>` element, to restrict the possible values that can be used in the `<term>` element. Inside the `<xsd:restriction>` element, you can use the `<xsd:maxInclusive>` element to restrict possible values in the `<term>` element to 30 years or less, like this:

```
<xsd:element name="term">
<xsd:simpleType>
    <xsd:restriction base="xsd:integer">
       <xsd:maxInclusive value="30"/>
    </xsd:restriction>
</xsd:simpleType>
```

You'll hear more about this kind of restriction, as well as create our own simple types, tomorrow. at the following section explores how to create our own complex types, which is a far more common thing to do than creating our own simple types.

6

Using Complex Types

You create new complex types by using the <xsd:complexType> element in schemas. A complex type definition can contain element declarations, references to other elements, and attribute declarations. You declare elements by using the <xsd:element> element and attributes by using the <xsd:attribute> element. Like DTDs, element declarations specify the syntax of an element; however, in XML schemas, element and attribute declarations can also specify the element or attribute type.

Here's an example. In the XML document, the document element, which is called <document>, contains <comment>, <mortgagee>, <mortgages>, and <bank> elements, in that order:

```
<document>
    <comment>
        .
        .
        .
    </comment>
    <mortgagee>
        .
        .
        .
    </mortgagee>
    <mortgages>
        .
        .
        .
    </mortgages>
    <bank>
        .
        .
        .
    </bank>
</document>
```

The <document> element can contain other elements, so you need to declare it by using a complex type, which you can call documentType in our XML schema. In the XML schema, you can declare the <document> element to be of the documentType type:

```
<xsd:element name="document" type="documentType"/>
```

You create the documentType type by using an <xsd:complexType> element. In this case, you want to indicate that the subelements in <document> will be <comment>, <mortgagee>, <mortgages>, and <bank> elements, in that order, so you use the <xsd:sequence> element (tomorrow you'll see how you can use <xsd:all>, which enables elements to appear in any order and in any sequence):

```
<xsd:element name="document" type="documentType"/>
<xsd:complexType name="documentType">
    <xsd:sequence>
        <xsd:element ref="comment" minOccurs="1"/>
        <xsd:element name="mortgagee" type="recordType"/>
        <xsd:element name="mortgages" type="mortgagesType"/>
        <xsd:element name="bank" type="recordType"/>
    </xsd:sequence>
</xsd:complexType>
```

The other types you see in this declaration—such as `recordType`, which is the type of the `<mortgagee>` and `<bank>` elements—are also complex types. Here's how `recordType` is declared:

```
<xsd:complexType name="recordType">
    <xsd:sequence>
        <xsd:element name="name" type="xsd:string"/>
        <xsd:element name="location" type="xsd:string"/>
        <xsd:element name="city" type="xsd:string"/>
        <xsd:element name="state" type="xsd:string"/>
    </xsd:sequence>
</xsd:complexType>
```

Note that the elements in this declaration, such as `<name>`, `<location>`, and others, are all of the simple type, `xsd:string`, which is built in to the XML schema specification, so this is all you need to do to declare them.

Using the new type `recordType`, you can create `<bank>` elements, like this:

```
<bank phone="888.555.8888">
    <name>XML Bank</name>
    <location>12 Schema Place</location>
    <city>New York</city>
    <state>NY</state>
</bank>
```

That's how it works: You create a type in an XML schema and then you can declare elements of that type. If you want to use a complex type, you have to create it, and you do that by using the `<xsd:complexType>` element.

One way of declaring elements, as you've seen today, is to specify the element's name and type, as in the following example, which declares the `<comment>` element:

```
<xsd:element name="comment" type="xsd:string"/>
```

Now that you've declared `<comment>`, what if you want to use this element in several places in an XML document? Say, for example, that you want to use `<comment>` elements in various places throughout a document, like this:

```
<customer>
```

```
    <comment>No more credit on this one.</comment>
</customer>
<supplier>
    <comment>Always delivers late.</comment>
</supplier>
```

In this case, you can use the `ref` attribute of the `<xsd:element>` element to indicate that the element you want to use at a particular location has already been declared. You can see an example in the following XML schema for the `<comment>` element:

```
<xsd:complexType name="documentType">
    <xsd:sequence>
        <xsd:element ref="comment" minOccurs="1"/>
        <xsd:element name="mortgagee" type="recordType"/>
        <xsd:element name="mortgages" type="mortgagesType"/>
        <xsd:element name="bank" type="recordType"/>
    </xsd:sequence>
    <xsd:attribute name="documentDate" type="xsd:date"/>
</xsd:complexType>
        .
        .
        .
<xsd:element name="comment" type="xsd:string"/>
```

Using the `ref` attribute lets you make use of an element that has already been declared. Note, however, that you can't just include any element by reference—the element you refer to must have been declared *globally*, which means that it is itself not part of any other complex type. (The other option is to declare elements inside other declarations, which is declaring them *locally*.) A global element or attribute declaration appears as an immediate child element of the `<xsd:schema>` element, and when you declare an element or attribute globally, it can be used in any complex type. Using the `ref` attribute in this way is a powerful technique.

Note also the other attribute here besides `ref`—`minOccurs`. This attribute lets you specify how many of a certain element you'll allow at a specific location. The following section takes a look at that.

Specifying a Number of Elements

The `<document>` element is declared to be of the `documentType` type, and in that type, you use the `minOccurs` attribute to indicate that the `<comment>` element must occur at least once:

```
<xsd:complexType name="documentType">
    <xsd:sequence>
        <xsd:element ref="comment" minOccurs="1"/>
```

```
        <xsd:element name="mortgagee" type="recordType"/>
        <xsd:element name="mortgages" type="mortgagesType"/>
        <xsd:element name="bank" type="recordType"/>
    </xsd:sequence>
    <xsd:attribute name="documentDate" type="xsd:date"/>
</xsd:complexType>
```

To make an element optional, you set `minOccurs` to `0`. You can specify the minimum number of times an element appears by using the `minOccurs` attribute and the maximum number of times it can appear by using the `maxOccurs` attribute. (Keep in mind that you can use `minOccurs` and `maxOccurs` only with local declarations, not global ones.) Here's how you could specify that the `<comment>` element can appear from 0 to 10 times in the `documentType` type:

```
<xsd:complexType name="documentType">
    <xsd:sequence>
        <xsd:element ref="comment" minOccurs="0" maxOccurs="10"/>
        <xsd:element name="mortgagee" type="recordType"/>
        <xsd:element name="mortgages" type="mortgagesType"/>
        <xsd:element name="bank" type="recordType"/>
    </xsd:sequence>
    <xsd:attribute name="documentDate" type="xsd:date"/>
</xsd:complexType>
```

There are built-in default values for `minOccurs` and `maxOccurs` that take effect if you don't specify values. The default value for `minOccurs` is `1`, and the default for `maxOccurs` is the value of `minOccurs`. To specify that there is no upper bound to the `maxOccurs` attribute, you set it to the value `"unbounded"`.

Specifying Element Default Values

The `<xsd:element>` element has two attributes, `fixed` and `default`, that let you specify an element's default values.

The `fixed` attribute sets the value of an element; for example, setting the `<term>` element's `fixed` attribute to an integer value of `800` means that the element will always have that value:

```
<xsd:element name="term" type="xsd:integer" fixed="800"/>
```

The `default` attribute lets you set the default value of an element—that is, the value that the element has if you don't specify any other value. For example, here's how you can specify a value of `800` as a default value instead of fixing this element's value at `800`:

```
<xsd:element name="term" type="xsd:integer" default="800"/>
```

Creating Attributes

As with elements, with XML schemas you can specify the types of attributes. In XML documents, attribute values have to be quoted strings, and if you have, say, a number such as "100", the XML schema is able to indicate that such a number should be interpreted as an integer. To declare an attribute, you use the <xsd:attribute> element as in the following example, which declares an attribute named phone for the recordType type, which means that all elements of this type, such as <bank> in the XML document, will support this attribute:

```
<xsd:complexType name="recordType">
    <xsd:sequence>
        <xsd:element name="name" type="xsd:string"/>
        <xsd:element name="location" type="xsd:string"/>
        <xsd:element name="city" type="xsd:string"/>
        <xsd:element name="state" type="xsd:string"/>
    </xsd:sequence>
    <xsd:attribute name="phone" type="xsd:string"/>
</xsd:complexType>
```

Like <xsd:element>, <xsd:attribute> has a type attribute, and its attributes must always be of a simple type. You can also indicate whether an attribute is required or optional, or whether it has a default value. To do that, you use the <xsd:attribute> element's use and value attributes.

The use attribute specifies whether the attribute is required or optional—and if it is optional, whether the attribute's value is fixed or whether there is a default. For example, you can make the phone attribute optional like this:

```
<xsd:complexType name="recordType">
    <xsd:sequence>
        <xsd:element name="name" type="xsd:string"/>
        <xsd:element name="location" type="xsd:string"/>
        <xsd:element name="city" type="xsd:string"/>
        <xsd:element name="state" type="xsd:string"/>
    </xsd:sequence>
    <xsd:attribute name="phone" type="xsd:string"
        use="optional"/>
</xsd:complexType>
```

Here are the values you can give to the use attribute:

- **default**—If you don't use the use attribute, its value is the default value set with the value attribute. If you do use it, its value is the value you assign it.
- **fixed**—This value makes the attribute fixed. You can set its value by using the value attribute.

- **optional**—This value makes the attribute optional, which means the attribute may have any value.
- **prohibited**—This value means the attribute cannot be used.
- **required**—This value makes the attribute required. The attribute can have any value.

The `value` attribute contains a value if you need to specify one. For example, the following attribute declaration creates an attribute named `year` with the integer fixed value `"2005"`:

```
<xsd:attribute name="year" type="xsd:int" use="fixed" value="2005">
```

Here's another example of an attribute declaration. This example gives the integer attribute `year` the *default* value `"2005"`:

```
<xsd:attribute name="year" type="xsd:int" use="default" value="2005">
```

Summary

Today's discussion provided an introduction to creating XML schemas. You saw that XML schemas are designed to go past DTDs and allow you a great deal more precision—at the cost of some added complexity.

You saw that there are a number of tools available to make working with XML schemas easier. As XML schemas become more complex, XML authors often use XML schema creation tools, and you saw that some of them are available online. You can also check the validity of an XML schema by using a variety of other tools.

You saw that you start an XML schema by using an XML declaration and the `<xsd:schema>` element. In that element, you usually declare a namespace prefix, `xsd`, which is assigned the URI `www.w3.org/2001/XMLSchema`, the official W3C namespace for XML schema. All elements and attributes in the schema then use this prefix.

6

To declare elements and attributes in an XML document by using an XML schema, you can use the XML schema elements `<xsd:element>` and `<xsd:attribute>`. A number of XML schema elements like these two are available, and today you took a brief look at them.

Both `<xsd:element>` and `<xsd:attribute>` support an attribute named `type`, which lets you specify an element's or attribute's type. There are two main types—simple types and complex types. Simple types cannot enclose any child elements or have any attributes, but complex types can. Elements can be declared by using simple or complex types, but attributes can only be declared by using simple types.

A number of simple types are built in to the XML schema specification, and you heard a little about them today. (Microsoft has a set of its own types that extends this built-in set.) Some examples are `xsd:string` for strings of text, `xsd:int` for integers, and `xsd:date` for dates. You can also create your own simple types by using `<xsd:simpleType>`, and you're going to get more experience with `<xsd:simpleType>` tomorrow. You can create complex types by using `<xsd:complexType>`, which may enclose the declarations of child elements. You saw today that enclosing those child elements in an `<xsd:sequence>` element creates an element sequence and that the elements declared in sequence must appear in that sequence in the XML document.

Today you also saw that the `<xsd:element>` element has a `minOccurs` attribute to indicate the minimum number of times an element may appear at the location where it has been declared and a `maxOccurs` attribute to set the maximum number of times it may occur. In addition, you can use the `fixed` and `default` attributes to specify whether an element has a fixed or default value.

Today you've gotten a start with XML schemas today, and you've seen how to declare elements and attributes, as well as how to use the built-in simple types and how to create your own complex types. But there's far more to XML schemas, as you're going to see tomorrow, when you'll take a look at declaring empty elements, mixed content, element groups, and more.

Q&A

Q Does an XML schema really need an XML declaration (such as `<?xml version="1.0" encoding="UTF-8"?>`)? I don't see XML declarations in the examples in the W3C XML schema primer at `http://www.w3.org/TR/xmlschema-0`.

A Oddly, the XML schema examples in the W3C XML schema primer don't have XML declarations. However, it is standard to include an XML declaration at the beginning of each XML schema.

Q I don't want to declare a sequence of XML child elements; I want to declare a list of XML child elements and allow only one to actually be chosen. Can I create choices in XML schema as I can in DTDs?

A Yes. To do this, you use the XML schema `<xsd:choice>` element. You'll hear all the details tomorrow.

Workshop

This workshop tests whether you understand the concepts discussed today. It's a good idea to make sure you can answer these questions before pressing on to tomorrow's work. Answers to the quiz can be found in Appendix A, "Quiz Answers."

Quiz

1. What namespace is used by XML schemas? (Hint: It is the URI that the `xsd` prefix corresponds to.)
2. What XML schema element do you use to declare an XML element in an XML schema? What XML schema element do you use to declare an attribute?
3. How can you use an XML schema to declare an element called `<name>` that holds text content?
4. How can you declare an optional attribute called `language` that holds text?
5. What would the complete declaration of a `<friend>` element that contains `<name>` and `<address>` elements (both of which contain text), in that order, and an attribute named `date` (in the `xsd:date` format) look like?

Exercises

1. Create an XML schema for an XML document that uses the namespace `http://xml21`, with the document element `<document>` and containing both a `<movieTitle>` (content type: `xsd:string`) and `<movieLength>` (content type: `xsd:int`) element. Then, if you have access to Internet Explorer, modify `ch06_04.html` so you can check your work.
2. Modify the XML document you created in Exercise 1 so that the `<movieTitle>` and `<movieLength>` elements can support `date` attributes of the `xsd:date` type. Then, if you have Internet Explorer, validate the new version of the document.

PART I

DAY 7

Creating Types in XML Schemas

Yesterday you got started with XML schemas and heard about some of the basics. Today, you're going to continue with XML schemas, getting a true working knowledge of the subject. Here's an overview of the topics covered today:

- Creating restrictions
- Creating simple types by using facets
- Using anonymous types
- Declaring empty elements
- Declaring mixed-content elements
- Declaring choices
- Grouping elements
- Grouping attributes
- Declaring `all` groups
- Using namespaces in schemas
- Annotating schemas

As you're going to see today, XML schemas give you many options that DTDs don't. Some of what you're going to see was designed for convenience, such as declaring element and attribute groups so you can use such groups throughout a schema; some of the things we'll talk about, such as empty elements and choices, have analogs in DTDs; and things we'll talk about today, such as anonymous types and facets, give you functionality you don't find in DTDs.

Restricting Simple Types by Using XML Schema Facets

One of the most important ways that XML schemas differ from DTDs is that they let you specify data types, such as strings and integers. As you saw yesterday, to do that, XML schemas let you use the data types that are built in to the XML schema specification, such as `xsd:string`, `xsd:integer`, and `xsd:date`. But you can do even more with data types—you can also restrict the values that are acceptable.

For example, take a look at the attribute named `loanNumber`, which is declared to be of type `loanNumberType`:

```
<xsd:complexType name="mortgagesType">
    <xsd:sequence>
        <xsd:element name="mortgage" minOccurs="1" maxOccurs="8">
            <xsd:complexType>
                <xsd:sequence>
                    <xsd:element name="property" type="xsd:string"/>
                    <xsd:element name="date" type="xsd:date" minOccurs="0"/>

                    <xsd:element name="loanAmount" type="xsd:decimal"/>
                    <xsd:element name="term">
                        <xsd:simpleType>
                            <xsd:restriction base="xsd:integer">
                                <xsd:maxInclusive value="30"/>
                            </xsd:restriction>
                        </xsd:simpleType>
                    </xsd:element>
                </xsd:sequence>
                <xsd:attribute name="loanNumber" type="loanNumberType"/>
            </xsd:complexType>
        </xsd:element>
    </xsd:sequence>
</xsd:complexType>
```

The attribute `loanNumber` is not of a predefined type; it's of the `loanNumberType` type, which we've defined ourselves. In particular, we've defined it with the `<simpleType>` element, like this:

```
<xsd:simpleType name="loanNumberType">
    <xsd:restriction base="xsd:string">
        <xsd:pattern value="\d{2} \d{4} \d{2}"/>
    </xsd:restriction>
</xsd:simpleType>
```

As you saw yesterday, you must base your own simple types on the simple types that are built into XML schemas. In this example, you use the `xsd:string` type. What's interesting here is that you can restrict the possible values of a simple type by using the `<xsd:restriction>` element. Here's what's happening: You're using the `<xsd:restriction>` element's `base` attribute to indicate that you are basing this type on the `xsd:string` type. Then you're using an XML schema *facet* to restrict the actual text that can be stored in attributes of the type you're creating.

XML schema facets let you restrict the data that a simple type can hold. In this example, the text in the `loanNumberType` type must match the regular expression pattern `"\d{2} \d{4} \d{2}"`, which matches text strings made up of two digits, a space, four digits, another space, and two more digits (for example, `"22 6666 99"`). You don't have to know how to use regular expressions in this book, but this example shows how powerful facets can be. In this case, you're using the `pattern` facet to specify a regular expression pattern that text used for the `loanNumber` attribute must match: `<xsd:pattern value="\d{2} \d{4} \d{2}"/>`. At this point you've gone far beyond DTDs, which can't even specify data types.

TIP

> Regular expressions used with the XML schema `pattern` facet are the same as those used in the Perl programming language. As of this writing, the complete documentation for Perl regular expressions is at `http://www.perldoc.com/perl5.8.0/pod/perlre.html`.

There are simpler facets than the `pattern` facet. Two popular facets are the `minInclusive` and `maxInclusive` facets, which let you put lower and upper bounds on numeric values. For example, say that you want to create an attribute named `dayNumber` that holds the day of the year and can range from 1 to 366 (to allow for leap years). You might restrict the possible values that `dayNumber` can hold by making it of the type `dayNumberType`, which you can create by using `<xsd:simpleType>` and the `minInclusive` and `maxInclusive` facets, like this:

```
<xsd:simpleType name="dayNumber">
    <xsd:restriction base="xsd:integer">
        <xsd:minInclusive value="1"/>
```

```
        <xsd:maxInclusive value="366"/>
    </xsd:restriction>
</xsd:simpleType>
```

After you declare this new simple type, you can declare elements and attributes of this type.

The following are the available facets and how they constrain data values:

- **totalDigits**—Specifies the maximum number of digits.
- **fractionDigits**—Specifies the maximum number of decimal digits.
- **pattern**—Specifies a regular expression that text must match.
- **whiteSpace**—Can be set to preserve (to preserve white space), replace (to replace all white space with), or collapse (to collapse multiple contiguous whitespace to one).
- **enumeration**—Constrains possible values to a specified set.
- **maxInclusive**—Specifies the maximum possible value, inclusive.
- **maxExclusive**—Specifies the maximum possible value, exclusive.
- **minInclusive**—Specifies the minimum possible value, inclusive.
- **minExclusive**—Specifies the minimum possible value, exclusive.
- **length**—Specifies the data's length, such as number of characters.
- **minLength**—Specifies the minimum possible length.
- **maxLength**—Specifies the maximum possible length.

Which facets apply to which predefined simple types? Can you use a pattern facet with an xsd:int value, for example? Table 7.1 lists what facets you can use with the various simple data types. The numeric simple types and simple types that can be ordered also have some additional facets, as listed in Table 7.2.

TABLE 7.1 The Facets Available for Simple Types

Type	length	minLength	maxLength	pattern	enumeration	whiteSpace
anyURI	×	×	×	×	×	×
base64Binary	×	×	×	×	×	×
boolean				×		×
byte				×	×	×
date				×	×	×
dateTime				×	×	×

TABLE 7.1 continued

Type	`length`	`minLength`	`maxLength`	`pattern`	`enumeration`	`whiteSpace`
`decimal`				×	×	×
`double`				×	×	×
`duration`				×	×	×
`ENTITIES`	×	×	×		×	×
`ENTITX`	×	×	×	×	×	×
`float`				×	×	×
`gDay`				×	×	×
`gMonth`				×	×	×
`gMonthDay`				×	×	×
`gYear`				×	×	×
`gYearMonth`				×	×	×
`hexBinary`	×	×	×	×	×	×
`ID`	×	×	×	×	×	×
`IDREF`	×	×	×	×	×	×
`IDREFS`	×	×	×		×	×
`int`				×	×	×
`integer`				×	×	×
`language`	×	×	×	×	×	×
`long`				×	×	×
`Name`	×	×	×	×	×	×
`NCName`	×	×	×	×	×	×
`negativeInteger`				×	×	×
`NMTOKEN`	×	×	×	×	×	×
`NMTOKENS`	×	×	×		×	×
`nonNegativeInteger`				×	×	×
`nonPositiveInteger`				×	×	×
`normalizedString`	×	×	×	×	×	×
`NOTATION`	×	×	×	×	×	×
`positiveInteger`				×	×	×
`QName`	×	×	×	×	×	×
`short`				×	×	×

TABLE 7.1 continued

Type	length	minLength	maxLength	pattern	enumeration	whiteSpace
string	×	×	×	×	×	×
time				×	×	×
token	×	×	×	×	×	×
unsignedByte				×	×	×
unsignedInt				×	×	×
unsignedLong				×	×	×
unsignedShort				×	×	×

TABLE 7.2 The Facets Available for Simple Ordered Types

Type	max-Inclusive	max-Exclusive	min-Inclusive	min-Exclusive	total-Digits	fraction-Digits
byte	×	×	×	×	×	×
unsignedByte	×	×	×	×	×	×
integer	×	×	×	×	×	×
positiveInteger	×	×	×	×	×	×
negativeInteger	×	×	×	×	×	×
nonNegativeInteger	×	×	×	×	×	×
nonPositiveInteger	×	×	×	×	×	×
int	×	×	×	×	×	×
unsignedInt	×	×	×	×	×	×
long	×	×	×	×	×	×
unsignedLong	×	×	×	×	×	×
short	×	×	×	×	×	×
unsignedShort	×	×	×	×	×	×
decimal	×	×	×	×	×	×
float	×	×	×	×		
double	×	×	×	×		
time	×	×	×	×		
dateTime	×	×	×	×		
duration	×	×	×	×		
date	×	×	×	×		

TABLE 7.2 continued

Type	maxInclusive	maxExclusive	minInclusive	minExclusive	totalDigits	fractionDigits
gMonth	×	×	×	×		
gYear	×	×	×	×		
gYearMonth	×	×	×	×		
gDay	×	×	×	×		
gMonthDay	×	×	×	×		

One of the interesting facets in these tables is `enumeration`, which lets you specify a set of values that a data item can select from. For example, to set up a simple type named `dayOfTheWeek`, whose values can be `"Sunday"`, `"Monday"`, `"Tuesday"`, `"Wednesday"`, `"Thursday"`, `"Friday"`, and `"Saturday"`, you would define the type like this:

```
<xsd:simpleType name="dayOfTheWeek">
    <xsd:restriction base="xsd:string">
        <xsd:enumeration value="Sunday"/>
        <xsd:enumeration value="Monday"/>
        <xsd:enumeration value="Tuesday"/>
        <xsd:enumeration value="Wednesday"/>
        <xsd:enumeration value="Thursday"/>
        <xsd:enumeration value="Friday"/>
        <xsd:enumeration value="Saturday"/>
    </xsd:restriction>
 </xsd:simpleType>
```

NOTE

The extended power of facets, which let you specify and limit the values your data can legally have, is good for the XML author but not so good for programmers who want to support XML schemas. Supporting XML schemas is one thing, but, for example, supporting full regular expressions so you can use facets such as `pattern` is a very difficult thing to do for most programmers. And that's one of the reasons there aren't more validators that use XML schemas and why the implementation of validators that use XML schemas is only partial. Internet Explorer, for example, does not support the `pattern` facet. On the other hand, the Visual Studio .NET programming languages, such as Visual Basic .NET and Visual C# .NET, do support regular expressions, and so they support the `pattern` facet.

Creating XML Schema Choices

Similarly to choices in DTDs, XML schema choices let you specify a number of items, only one of which will be chosen. To create a choice in XML schemas, you use the <xsd:choice> element. Here's an example in which the XML schema currently allows only an element named <property> as the first child element in a <mortgage> element:

```
<xsd:element name="mortgage" minOccurs="1" maxOccurs="8">
    <xsd:complexType>
        <xsd:sequence>
            <xsd:element name="property" type="xsd:string"/>
            <xsd:element name="date" type="xsd:date" minOccurs="0"/>
           <xsd:element name="loanAmount" type="xsd:decimal"/>
            <xsd:element name="term">
                <xsd:simpleType>
                    <xsd:restriction base="xsd:integer">
                        <xsd:maxInclusive value="30"/>
                    </xsd:restriction>
                </xsd:simpleType>
            </xsd:element>
        </xsd:sequence>
        <xsd:attribute name="loanNumber" type="loanNumberType"/>
    </xsd:complexType>
</xsd:element>
```

Let's change this example so that the first child element inside a <mortgage> element can be *either* a <residentialProperty> element or a <commercialProperty> element. Here's how:

```
<xsd:element name="mortgage" minOccurs="1" maxOccurs="8">
    <xsd:complexType>
        <xsd:sequence>
            <xsd:choice>
                <xsd:element name="residentialProperty" type="xsd:string"/>
                <xsd:element name="commercialProperty" type="xsd:string"/>
            </xsd:choice>
            <xsd:element name="date" type="xsd:date" minOccurs="0"/>
            <xsd:element name="loanAmount" type="xsd:decimal"/>
            <xsd:element name="term">
                <xsd:simpleType>
                    <xsd:restriction base="xsd:integer">
                        <xsd:maxInclusive value="30"/>
                    </xsd:restriction>
                </xsd:simpleType>
            </xsd:element>
        </xsd:sequence>
        <xsd:attribute name="loanNumber" type="loanNumberType"/>
    </xsd:complexType>
</xsd:element>
```

Using the <xsd:choice> element this way lets you create choices just as you can in DTDs.

Using Anonymous Type Definitions

Up to this point, when you've created your own types, you've declared elements to be of a certain type and then declared that type. To make use of a type, you give the new type a name and then use that name when declaring an element, as with the documentType type and the <document> element declaration here:

```
<xsd:element name="document" type="documentType"/>
<xsd:complexType name="documentType">
    <xsd:sequence>
        <xsd:element ref="comment" minOccurs="1"/>
        <xsd:element name="mortgagee" type="recordType"/>
        <xsd:element name="mortgages" type="mortgagesType"/>
        <xsd:element name="bank" type="recordType"/>
    </xsd:sequence>
    <xsd:attribute name="documentDate" type="xsd:date"/>
</xsd:complexType>
```

This is fine, and you can go on doing things this way, but there's another way as well: You can use anonymous types. An anonymous type is useful if you want to use a type only once and don't want to create many different elements with the same type. So far, the types you've created ourselves have all had names, but if you want to use a type in only one location, it turns out that you can declare it at that location and you don't need to give it a name. This is called an *anonymous type*.

To create an anonymous type definition, you simply enclose an <xsd:simpleType> or <xsd:complexType> element inside an <xsd:element> element declaration. You don't need to name the type and you don't assign an explicit value to the type attribute in the <xsd:element> element because the anonymous type you're using doesn't have a name.

Here's an example from the XML schema ch06_07.xsd—the <mortgage> element. This element is defined using an anonymous type, which is a child element of the element declaration itself. Here's what it looks like (note that there is no type attribute in the <xsd:element> element because you're using the child <xsd:complexType> element as an anonymous type definition):

```
<xsd:element name="mortgage" minOccurs="1" maxOccurs="8">
    <xsd:complexType>
        .
        .
        .
    </xsd:complexType>
</xsd:element>
```

Now you're free to structure this new anonymous type as you want it, and in doing so, you structure the <mortgage> element declaration, with no named type needed:

```
<xsd:element name="mortgage" minOccurs="1" maxOccurs="8">
    <xsd:complexType>
        <xsd:sequence>
            <xsd:element name="property" type="xsd:string"/>
            <xsd:element name="date" type="xsd:date" minOccurs="0""0"/>
            <xsd:element name="loanAmount" type="xsd:decimal"/>
            <xsd:element name="term">
                <xsd:simpleType>
                    <xsd:restriction base="xsd:integer">
                        <xsd:maxInclusive value="30"/>
                    </xsd:restriction>
                </xsd:simpleType>
            </xsd:element>
        </xsd:sequence>
    </xsd:complexType>
</xsd:element>
```

You can also declare attributes in anonymous types, as is done in the <mortgage> element:

```
<xsd:element name="mortgage" minOccurs="1" maxOccurs="8">
    <xsd:complexType>
        <xsd:sequence>
            <xsd:element name="property" type="xsd:string"/>
            <xsd:element name="date" type="xsd:date" minOccurs="0""0"/>
            <xsd:element name="loanAmount" type="xsd:decimal"/>
            <xsd:element name="term">
                <xsd:simpleType>
                    <xsd:restriction base="xsd:integer">
                        <xsd:maxInclusive value="30"/>
                    </xsd:restriction>
                </xsd:simpleType>
            </xsd:element>
        </xsd:sequence>
        <xsd:attribute name="loanNumber" type="loanNumberType"/>
    </xsd:complexType>
</xsd:element>
```

That's all it takes. This example creates a complex anonymous type, but you can also create simple anonymous types. In fact, you already have. Note the definition of the <term> element in the complex type you just created:

```
<xsd:element name="term">
    <xsd:simpleType>
        <xsd:restriction base="xsd:integer">
            <xsd:maxInclusive value="30"/>
        </xsd:restriction>
    </xsd:simpleType>
</xsd:element>
```

As you can see, this is an anonymous simple type. The idea here is that you want to restrict the possible values that the <term> element can take. In particular, you want to limit those values to 30 years or below for mortgages. To do that, you just use an anonymous simple type, as is done here.

Declaring Empty Elements

Is there a special way to declare empty elements in XML schemas? Not really. You just declare them by using a complex type that has no child elements. In other words, you indicate that these are elements that do not contain any other elements, which means they are empty. Empty elements can have attributes; if you declare them using complex types, you can give them attributes.

For example, say you want to duplicate the HTML empty element <img>, which you use to embed images in Web pages, in XML. You can give this new element some of the same attributes it has in HTML: `src`, `width`, `height`, `name`, `border`, and `alt`. You can start by declaring the <img> element, like this:

```
<xsd:element name="img">
    .
    .
    .
</xsd:element>
```

Now you can use an anonymous complex type to declare the attributes used by this new <img> element:

```
<xsd:element name="img">
    <xsd:complexType>
        .
        .
        .
    </xsd:complexType>
</xsd:element>
```

Then all you need to do is to add the attributes you want:

```
<xsd:element name="img">
    <xsd:complexType>
        <xsd:attribute name="src" type="xsd:string" />
        <xsd:attribute name="width" type="xsd:int" />
        <xsd:attribute name="height" type="xsd:int" />
        <xsd:attribute name="name" type="xsd:string" />
        <xsd:attribute name="alt" type="xsd:string" />
        <xsd:attribute name="border" type="xsd:int" />
    </xsd:complexType>
</xsd:element>
```

That's all you need to do. Now the empty element `<img>`, along with the `src`, `width`, `height`, `name`, `border`, and `alt` attributes, is ready to be used.

Declaring Mixed-Content Elements

XML schemas support true mixed-content elements, in which you can mix text and elements. In other words, character data can appear at the same level as child elements. The following is an example of an XML document with mixed content. It is an invoice from the bank that tells the borrower that the next payment on his or her mortgage is due:

```
<?xml version="1.0" encoding="UTF-8"?>
<invoice>
    To <name>James Blandings</name>:
        Your monthly payment of $2000.00 on
        <property>The Hackett Place</property>
        is due in three weeks. Thanks.
    From your friends at XML Bank.
        <location>12 Schema Place</location>
        <city>New York</city>
        <state>NY</state>
</invoice>
```

As you can see, both text and elements are mixed inside the `<invoice>` element in this example. How can you declare an element like this? You can start by using an anonymous type inside the declaration for the `<invoice>` element. Note that to indicate that this element can handle mixed content, you set the `<complexType>` element's `mixed` attribute to `"true"`:

```
<xsd:element name="invoice">
    <xsd:complexType mixed="true">
        .
        .
        .
    </xsd:complexType>
</xsd:element>
```

All you have to do now is add the declarations for the elements that you can use inside the `<invoice>` element, like this:

```
<xsd:element name="invoice">
    <xsd:complexType mixed="true">
        <xsd:sequence>
            <xsd:element name="name" type="xsd:string"/>
            <xsd:element name="property" type="xsd:string"/>
            <xsd:element name="location" type="xsd:string"/>
            <xsd:element name="city" type="xsd:string"/>
            <xsd:element name="state" type="xsd:string"/>
        </xsd:sequence>
    </xsd:complexType>
</xsd:element>
```

When you were working with DTDs on Day 4, "Creating Valid XML Documents: DTDs," you were able to create mixed-content elements of a sort, but you couldn't specify the order, or the number, of the child elements in an element by using a mixed-content model. With XML schemas, you have more power. You can indeed specify the order and number of child elements in a mixed-content element. That is to say, whereas DTDs provide only partial support for mixed-content models, schemas provide a more complete syntax that allows you to specify the order and number of child elements in mixed-content elements.

However, it is important to note that although you can declare mixed-content elements, you should avoid doing so if possible. In the mixed-content document you just saw, the XML elements such as `<name>` and `<property>` are used almost as you would use HTML elements to format a document for visual display. Ideally in XML documents, all data is enclosed inside elements. Here's how you might restructure the mixed-content document into a standard XML document:

```
<?xml version="1.0" encoding="UTF-8" standalone="yes"?>
<invoice>
    <to>James Blandings</to>
    <for>The Hackett Place</for>
    <amount>$2000.00</amount>
    <text>Your monthly payment is due in three weeks. Thanks.</text>
    <name>XML Bank.</name>
    <location>12 Schema Place</location>
    <city>New York</city>
    <state>NY</state>
</invoice>
```

Grouping Elements Together

Say that as the bank president, you want to extend the credit you offer to borrowers to include not only mortgages but also car loans. To do that, you might create a group named `mortgagesAndCarLoansGroup`. A group like this collects elements together, and you can refer to a group by name. Here's how a group might look in an XML schema example that involves replacing the mortgages element with a group named `mortgagesAndCarLoansGroup`:

```
<xsd:element name="document" type="documentType"/>
<xsd:complexType name="documentType">
    <xsd:sequence>
        <xsd:element ref="comment" minOccurs="1"/>
        <xsd:element name="mortgagee" type="recordType"/>
        <xsd:group ref="mortgagesAndCarLoansGroup"/>
        <xsd:element name="bank" type="recordType"/>
    </xsd:sequence>
    <xsd:attribute name="documentDate" type="xsd:date"/>
</xsd:complexType>
```

7

To create the group named `mortgagesAndCarLoansGroup`, you can use the `<xsd:group>` element. In this example, that group will contain both `<mortgage>` and `<carLoan>` elements, in that sequence. To be flexible, you can set the `minOccurs` attribute of each element to `0` (in case, for example, the borrower has mortgages but no car loan) and the `maxOccurs` attribute to `8`:

```
<xsd:group name="mortgagesAndCarLoansGroup">
    <xsd:sequence>
        <xsd:element name="mortgage" ref="mortgageType"
            minOccurs="0" maxOccurs="8"/>

        <xsd:element name="carLoan" ref="carLoanType"
            minOccurs="0" maxOccurs="8"/>
    </xsd:sequence>
</xsd:group >

<xsd:complexType name="mortgageType">
    <xsd:sequence>
        <xsd:element name="property" type="xsd:string"/>
        <xsd:element name="date" type="xsd:date" minOccurs="0"/>
        <xsd:element name="loanAmount" type="xsd:decimal"/>
        <xsd:element name="term">
            <xsd:simpleType>
                <xsd:restriction base="xsd:integer">
                    <xsd:maxInclusive value="30"/>
                </xsd:restriction>
            </xsd:simpleType>
        </xsd:element>
    </xsd:sequence>
    <xsd:attribute name="loanNumber" type="loanNumberType"/>
</xsd:complexType>

<xsd:complexType name="carLoanType">
    <xsd:sequence>
        <xsd:element name="car" type="xsd:string"/>
        <xsd:element name="date" type="xsd:date" minOccurs="0"/>
        <xsd:element name="loanAmount" type="xsd:decimal"/>
        <xsd:element name="term">
            <xsd:simpleType>
                <xsd:restriction base="xsd:integer">
                    <xsd:maxInclusive value="10"/>
                </xsd:restriction>
            </xsd:simpleType>
        </xsd:element>
    </xsd:sequence>
    <xsd:attribute name="loanNumber" type="loanNumberType"/>
</xsd:complexType>
```

By using groups, you can collect elements together and refer to them by name, which means you can use those groups throughout the XML schema as needed.

Grouping Attributes Together

Besides grouping elements together, you can also group attributes together. You create attribute groups by using the `<xsd:attributeGroup>` element. For example, say that you want to add a set of attributes to the `<mortgage>` element by using a group—specifically, an `xsd:int` attribute named `mortgageID`, an `xsd:date` attribute named `date`, and an enumeration attribute named `secured` that can take the values `"yes"` and `"no"`. To do that, you can use an attribute group named `mortgageAttributeGroup`, and you can refer to that group as follows in the declaration of the `<mortgage>` element:

```
<xsd:complexType name="mortgagesType">
    <xsd:sequence>
        <xsd:element name="mortgage" minOccurs="1" maxOccurs="8">
            <xsd:complexType>
                <xsd:sequence>
                    <xsd:element name="property" type="xsd:string"/>
                    <xsd:element name="date" type="xsd:date" minOccurs="0"/>
                    <xsd:element name="loanAmount" type="xsd:decimal"/>
                    <xsd:element name="term">
                        <xsd:simpleType>
                            <xsd:restriction base="xsd:integer">
                                <xsd:maxInclusive value="30"/>
                            </xsd:restriction>
                        </xsd:simpleType>
                    </xsd:element>
                </xsd:sequence>
                <xsd:attributeGroup ref="mortgageAttributeGroup"/>
            </xsd:complexType>
        </xsd:element>
    </xsd:sequence>
</xsd:complexType>

</xsd:element>
```

To create the attribute group `mortgageAttributeGroup`, you use the `<xsd:attributeGroup>` element, enclosing the `<xsd:attribute>` elements you're going to use to declare the attributes in the group this way:

```
<xsd:attributeGroup name="mortgageAttributeGroup">
    <xsd:attribute name="mortgageID" type="xsd:int"/>
    <xsd:attribute name="date" type="xsd:date"/>
    <xsd:attribute name="secured">
        <xsd:simpleType>
            <xsd:restriction base="xsd:string">
                <xsd:enumeration value="yes"/>
                <xsd:enumeration value="no"/>
            </xsd:restriction>
        </xsd:simpleType>
    </xsd:attribute>
</xsd:attributeGroup>
```

7

By using attribute groups like this, you can collect attributes together and use them in many different elements as needed, simply by referring to the group.

NOTE

The inspiration behind element and attribute groups is parameter entities in DTDs. Parameter entities let you collect declarations together and use them by referring to them simply by using a parameter entity reference.

Declaring `all` Groups

Besides element groups and attribute groups, you can also create `all` groups, by using the `<xsd:all>` element. When you've declared elements so far, you've used the `<xsd:sequence>` element, which creates a set sequence of elements. In an `all` group, elements may appear in any order, but there's a catch: All the elements in this kind of group may appear only once or not at all (which means that the allowed values of `minOccurs` and `maxOccurs` are `0` and `1` only). This kind of group must be used at the top level of the content model, and the group's children must be individual elements—in other words, this group must itself contain no groups.

Let's take a look at an example in which you convert `documentType` (the type for the `<document>` element in this example) from using an internal sequence to using an `all` group instead:

```
<xsd:complexType name="documentType">
    <xsd:all>
        <xsd:element ref="comment" minOccurs="1"/>
        <xsd:element name="mortgagee" type="recordType"/>
        <xsd:element name="mortgages" type="mortgagesType"/>
        <xsd:element name="bank" type="recordType"/>
    </xsd:all>
    <xsd:attribute name="documentDate" type="xsd:date"/>
</xsd:complexType>
```

Now that you're using an `all` group, the elements in the `documentType` type—`<comment>`, `<mortgagee>`, `<mortgages>`, and `<bank>`—may appear in any order, which was not true when you used `<xsd:sequence>`. Although the elements may appear in any order, each element may only appear once at most.

Handling Namespaces in Schemas

DTDs weren't built specially to handle namespaces; as you've seen, they really treat namespace prefixes as part of an element name. XML schemas, on the other hand, were supposed to improve on that situation, and to meet that goal, they support a new attribute: `targetNamespace`.

The `targetNamespace` attribute can hold the namespace the XML schema is targeted toward—that is, the namespace that the elements in the XML document uses. If you use multiple namespaces in the XML document, an XML validator will know what XML schema to use, based on the schema's target namespace. In other words, a target namespace lets an XML validator know what XML schema to use to check XML elements in that namespace.

You saw an example using the `targetNamespace` attribute yesterday in the Internet Explorer examples. In the sample XML document, `ch06_02.xml`, you used the default namespace `"http://xmlpowercorp"` for all elements:

```
<?xml version="1.0"?>
<document xmlns="http://xmlpowercorp"
    xmlns:xsi="http://www.w3.org/2001/XMLSchema-instance"
    xsi:schemaLocation="http://xmlpowercorp ch06_03.xsd">
    <text>
        Welcome to XML Schemas!
    </text>
</document>
```

Then, in the XML schema, `ch06_03.xsd`, you used the `targetNamespace` attribute to indicate that this XML schema is for elements in the `"http://xmlpowercorp"` namespace, which means Internet Explorer will use this schema *only* for elements in that namespace:

```
<?xml version="1.0"?>
<xsd:schema targetNamespace="http://xmlpowercorp"
xmlns="http://xmlpowercorp"
xmlns:xsd="http://www.w3.org/2001/XMLSchema"
attributeFormDefault="qualified" elementFormDefault="qualified">
  <xsd:element name="document">
    <xsd:complexType>
      <xsd:sequence>
        <xsd:element name="text" type="xsd:string" minOccurs="1" />
      </xsd:sequence>
    </xsd:complexType>
  </xsd:element>
</xsd:schema>
```

Working with namespaces in XML schema gets a little complex because you can use namespaces in different ways in both an XML schema and the XML document you're validating. Also, XML schemas support a number of different options that can be combined in various ways. It is important that you know that XML schemas treat global element declarations differently than local element declarations when it comes to working with namespaces; this is because global elements can be used as document elements, whereas local elements can't.

As you've seen, globally declared elements and attributes are declared at the top level in the XML schema, directly under the `<schema>` element. All the other elements and attributes declared in an XML schema are locally declared. When you start working with namespaces, XML schemas allow you to specify whether locals need to be qualified (that is, whether they need a namespace prefix) when used in an XML document.

Declaring Locals Without Qualifying Them

How do you declare locals so that they don't need to be qualified? To specify whether elements need to be qualified, you use the `elementFormDefault` attribute of the `<schema>` element, and to specify whether attributes need to be qualified, you use the `attributeFormDefault` attribute of the same element. You can set the `elementFormDefault` and `attributeFormDefault` attributes to `"qualified"` or `"unqualified"`.

The following example makes both local elements and attributes unqualified:

```
<?xml version="1.0" encoding="UTF-8" ?>
<schema xmlns="http://www.w3.org/2001/XMLSchema"
    targetNamespace="http://xmlpowercorp"
    elementFormDefault="unqualified"
    attributeFormDefault="unqualified">
```

Because you're dealing with namespaces now, let's also take a look at a shortcut way of handling the XML schema URI `"http://www.w3.org/2001/XMLSchema"` in an XML schema. Up to this point, you've been associating the prefix `xsd` with that namespace in the XML schema, as in this example:

```
<xsd:schema xmlns:xsd="http://www.w3.org/2001/XMLSchema">
    <xsd:annotation>
        <xsd:documentation>
            Mortgage record XML schema.
        </xsd:documentation>
    </xsd:annotation>
        .
        .
        .
```

However, if you make `"http://www.w3.org/2001/XMLSchema"` the default namespace in an XML schema (by using an `xmlns` attribute, not an `xmlns:xsd` attribute), you don't need to use a prefix for the XML schema elements:

```
<?xml version="1.0" encoding="UTF-8" ?>
<schema xmlns="http://www.w3.org/2001/XMLSchema"
    targetNamespace="http://xmlpowercorp"
    elementFormDefault="unqualified"
```

```
    attributeFormDefault="unqualified">
    <annotation>
        <documentation>
            Mortgage record XML schema.
        </documentation>
    </annotation>
        .
        .
        .
```

That can save some time, but you have to be a little careful because now the XML validator will assume that everything's in the "http://www.w3.org/2001/XMLSchema" namespace. That's a problem because when you say, for example, that the <document> element is of the documentType type, the XML validator needs to know where to find the documentType type; it won't find that type defined in the default "http://www.w3.org/2001/XMLSchema" namespace. You can indicate that local types are declared locally by using a new namespace prefix, such as xmp (for XML Power Corp.) in this example:

```
<?xml version="1.0" encoding="UTF-8" ?>
<schema xmlns="http://www.w3.org/2001/XMLSchema"
    targetNamespace="http://xmlpowercorp"
    xmlns:xmp="http://xmlpowercorp"
    elementFormDefault="unqualified"
    attributeFormDefault="unqualified">
    <annotation>
        <documentation>
            Mortgage record XML schema.
        </documentation>
    </annotation>
    <element name="document" type="xmp:documentType"/>
    <complexType name="documentType">
        <sequence>
            <element ref="xmp:comment" minOccurs="1"/>
            <element name="mortgagee" type="xmp:recordType"/>
            <element name="mortgages" type="xmp:mortgagesType"/>
            <element name="bank" type="xmp:recordType"/>
        </sequence>
        .
        .
        .
```

Listing 7.1 shows the entire XML schema ch07_01.xsd.

LISTING 7.1 An XML Schema That Has Unqualified Locals (ch07_01.xsd)

```
<?xml version="1.0" encoding="UTF-8" ?>
<schema xmlns="http://www.w3.org/2001/XMLSchema"
    targetNamespace="http://xmlpowercorp"
    xmlns:xmp="http://xmlpowercorp"
    elementFormDefault="unqualified"
    attributeFormDefault="unqualified">
    <annotation>
        <documentation>
            Mortgage record XML schema.
        </documentation>
    </annotation>
    <element name="document" type="xmp:documentType"/>
    <complexType name="documentType">
        <sequence>
            <element ref="xmp:comment" minOccurs="1"/>
            <element name="mortgagee" type="xmp:recordType"/>
            <element name="mortgages" type="xmp:mortgagesType"/>
            <element name="bank" type="xmp:recordType"/>
        </sequence>
        <attribute name="documentDate" type="xmp:date"/>
    </complexType>
    <complexType name="recordType">
        <sequence>
            <element name="name" type="xmp:string"/>
            <element name="location" type="xmp:string"/>
            <element name="city" type="xmp:string"/>
            <element name="state" type="xmp:string"/>
        </sequence>
        <attribute name="phone" type="xmp:string"
            use="optional"/>
    </complexType>
    <complexType name="mortgagesType">
        <sequence>
            <element name="mortgage" minOccurs="0" maxOccurs="8">
                <complexType>
                    <sequence>
                        <element name="property" type="xmp:string"/>
                        <element name="date" type="xmp:date" minOccurs="0"/>
                        <element name="loanAmount" type="xmp:decimal"/>
                        <element name="term">
                        <simpleType>
                            <restriction base="integer">
                                <maxInclusive value="30"/>
                            </restriction>
                        </simpleType>
                        </element>
                    </sequence>
                    <attribute name="loanNumber" type="xmp:loanNumberType"/>
```

LISTING 7.1 continued

```
                </complexType>
            </element>
        </sequence>
    </complexType>
    <simpleType name="loanNumberType">
        <restriction base="string">
            <pattern value="\d{2} \d{4} \d{2}"/>
        </restriction>
    </simpleType>
    <element name="comment" type="xmp:string"/>
</schema>
```

The only two elements that are global in the new XML schema, `ch07_01.xsd`, are `<document>` and `<comment>`, so they're the only ones that need to be qualified with a namespace prefix. Listing 7.2 shows an XML document (`ch07_02.xml`) that `ch07_01.xsd` would validate.

LISTING 7.2 An XML Document That Has Unqualified Locals (`ch07_02.xml`)

```
<?xml version="1.0" encoding="UTF-8"?>
<xmp:document
    xmlns:xmp="http://xmlpowercorp"
    documentDate="2005-03-02">
    <xmp:comment>Good risk</xmp:comment>
    <mortgagee phone="888.555.1234">
        <name>James Blandings</name>
        <location>1234 299th St</location>
        <city>New York</city>
        <state>NY</state>
    </mortgagee>
    <mortgages>
        <mortgage loanNumber="66 7777 88">
            <property>The Hackett Place</property>
            <date>2005-03-01</date>
            <loanAmount>80000</loanAmount>
            <term>15</term>
        </mortgage>
        <mortgage loanNumber="11 8888 22">
            <property>123 Acorn Drive</property>
            <date>2005-03-01</date>
            <loanAmount>90000</loanAmount>
            <term>15</term>
        </mortgage>
        <mortgage loanNumber="33 4444 11">
            <property>99 West Pocusset St</property>
            <date>2005-03-02</date>
```

LISTING 7.2 continued

```
            <loanAmount>100000</loanAmount>
            <term>30</term>
        </mortgage>
        <mortgage loanNumber="55 3333 88">
            <property>19 Johnson Place</property>
            <date>2005-03-02</date>
            <loanAmount>110000</loanAmount>
            <term>30</term>
        </mortgage>
        <mortgage loanNumber="22 6666 99">
            <property>345 Notingham Court</property>
            <date>2005-03-02</date>
            <loanAmount>120000</loanAmount>
            <term>30</term>
        </mortgage>
    </mortgages>
    <bank phone="888.555.8888">
        <name>XML Bank</name>
        <location>12 Schema Place</location>
        <city>New York</city>
        <state>NY</state>
    </bank>
</xmp:document>
```

Declaring and Qualifying Locals

Despite what we discussed in the preceding section, we can require that locals be qualified with a namespace prefix. For example, we can assign the value `"qualified"` to the `elementFormDefault` attribute instead of using `"unqualified"`, as in the XML schema `ch07_01.xsd`. Here's how you do that:

```
<?xml version="1.0" encoding="UTF-8" ?>
<schema xmlns="http://www.w3.org/2001/XMLSchema"
    targetNamespace="http://xmlpowercorp"
    xmlns:xmp="http://xmlpowercorp"
    elementFormDefault="qualified"
    attributeFormDefault="unqualified">
        .
        .
        .
```

Now you have to qualify both locals and globals in the XML document, as shown in `ch07_03.xml` in Listing 7.3.

LISTING 7.3 An XML Document That Has Qualified Locals (`ch07_03.xml`)

```
<?xml version="1.0" encoding="UTF-8"?>
<xmp:document
    xmlns:xmp="http://xmlpowercorp"
    documentDate="2005-03-02">
    <xmp:comment>Good risk</xmp:comment>
    <xmp:mortgagee phone="888.555.1234">
        <xmp:name>James Blandings</xmp:name>

        <xmp:location>1234 299th St</xmp:location>
        <xmp:city>New York</xmp:city>
        <xmp:state>NY</xmp:state>
    </xmp:mortgagee>
    <xmp:mortgages>
        <xmp:mortgage loanNumber="66 7777 88">
            <xmp:property>The Hackett Place</xmp:property>
            <xmp:date>2005-03-01</xmp:date>
            <xmp:loanAmount>80000</xmp:loanAmount>
            <xmp:term>15</xmp:term>
        </xmp:mortgage>
        .
        .
        .
        <xmp:mortgage loanNumber="22 6666 99">
            <xmp:property>345 Notingham Court</xmp:property>
            <xmp:date>2005-03-02</xmp:date>
            <xmp:loanAmount>120000</xmp:loanAmount>
            <xmp:term>30</xmp:term>
        </xmp:mortgage>
    </xmp:mortgages>
    <xmp:bank phone="888.555.8888">
        <xmp:name>XML Bank</name>
        <xmp:location>12 Schema Place</location>
        <xmp:city>New York</xmp:city>
        <xmp:state>NY</xmp:state>
    </xmp:bank>
</xmp:document>
```

You can also require that attributes be qualified by setting `attributeFormDefault` to `"qualified"`:

```
<?xml version="1.0" encoding="UTF-8" ?>
<schema xmlns="http://www.w3.org/2001/XMLSchema"
    targetNamespace="http://xmlpowercorp"
    xmlns:xmp="http://xmlpowercorp"
    elementFormDefault="qualified"
    attributeFormDefault="qualified">
        .
        .
        .
```

7

Now all elements and attributes, both global and local, will have to be qualified. Rather than prefix every element and attribute with `xmp:`, however, you can make things easier by just putting the entire XML document into the `"http://xmlpowercorp"` namespace, as shown in Listing 7.4.

LISTING 7.4 An XML Document That Has Qualified Elements and Attributes (`ch07_04.xml`)

```
<?xml version="1.0" encoding="UTF-8"?>
<document
    xmlns="http://xmlpowercorp"
    documentDate="2005-03-02">
    <comment>Good risk</comment>
    <mortgagee phone="888.555.1234">
        <name>James Blandings</name>
        <location>1234 299th St</location>
        <city>New York</city>
        <state>NY</state>
    </mortgagee>
    <mortgages>
        <mortgage loanNumber="66 7777 88">
            <property>The Hackett Place</property>
            <date>2005-03-01</date>
            <loanAmount>80000</loanAmount>
            <term>15</term>
        </mortgage>
        .
        .
        .
        <mortgage loanNumber="22 6666 99">
            <property>345 Notingham Court</property>
            <date>2005-03-02</date>
            <loanAmount>120000</loanAmount>
            <term>30</term>
        </mortgage>
    </mortgages>
    <bank phone="888.555.8888">
        <name>XML Bank</name>
        <location>12 Schema Place</location>
        <city>New York</city>
        <state>NY</state>
    </bank>
</document>
```

Up to this point, you've specified that all locals must be either qualified or unqualified, but there's also a way of working on locals individually: by using the `form` attribute. For example, in the XML schema `ch07_05.xsd`, you can leave all locals unqualified except for a single attribute, `phone`, which must be qualified (see Listing 7.5).

LISTING 7.5 An XML Schema That Has One Qualified Attribute (`ch07_05.xsd`)

```
<?xml version="1.0" encoding="UTF-8" ?>
<xsd:schema
    xmlns:xsd="http://www.w3.org/2001/XMLSchema"
    elementFormDefault="unqualified"
    attributeFormDefault="unqualified">
    <xsd:annotation>
        <xsd:documentation>
            Mortgage record XML schema.
        </xsd:documentation>
    </xsd:annotation>
    <xsd:element name="document" type="documentType"/>
    <xsd:complexType name="documentType">
        .
        .
        .
    </xsd:complexType>
    <xsd:complexType name="recordType">
        <xsd:sequence>
            <xsd:element name="name" type="xsd:string"/>
            <xsd:element name="location" type="xsd:string"/>
            <xsd:element name="city" type="xsd:string"/>
            <xsd:element name="state" type="xsd:string"/>
        </xsd:sequence>
        <xsd:attribute name="phone" type="xsd:string"
            use="optional" form="qualified"/>
    </xsd:complexType>
    <xsd:complexType name="mortgagesType">
        <xsd:sequence>
            <xsd:element name="mortgage" minOccurs="0" maxOccurs="8">
                <xsd:complexType>
                .
                .
                .
                </xsd:complexType>
            </xsd:element>
        </xsd:sequence>
    </xsd:complexType>
    <xsd:simpleType name="loanNumberType">
        <xsd:restriction base="xsd:string">
            <xsd:pattern value="\d{2} \d{4} \d{2}"/>
        </xsd:restriction>
    </xsd:simpleType>
    <xsd:element name="comment" type="xsd:string"/>
</xsd:schema>
```

Listing 7.6 shows an XML document (`ch07_06.xml`) that this schema would validate. Note that in this example, all locals are unqualified—except the `phone` attribute, which is qualified.

LISTING 7.6 An XML Document That Has One Qualified Attribute (`ch07_06.xml`)

```
<?xml version="1.0" encoding="UTF-8"?>
<xmp:document
    xmlns:xmp="http://xmlpowercorp"
    documentDate="2005-03-02">
    <xmp:comment>Good risk</xmp:comment>
    <mortgagee xmp:phone="888.555.1234">
        <name>James Blandings</name>
        <location>1234 299th St</location>
        <city>New York</city>
        <state>NY</state>
    </mortgagee>
    <mortgages>
        <mortgage loanNumber="66 7777 88">
            <property>The Hackett Place</property>
            <date>2005-03-01</date>
            <loanAmount>80000</loanAmount>
            <term>15</term>
        </mortgage>
        .
        .
        .
        <mortgage loanNumber="22 6666 99">
            <property>345 Notingham Court</property>
            <date>2005-03-02</date>
            <loanAmount>120000</loanAmount>
            <term>30</term>
        </mortgage>
    </mortgages>
    <bank xmp:phone="888.555.8888">
        <name>XML Bank</name>
        <location>12 Schema Place</location>
        <city>New York</city>
        <state>NY</state>
    </bank>
</xmp:document>
```

That finishes our discussion on namespaces and XML schemas. The last topic you'll take a look at today is how to annotate XML schemas.

Annotating an XML Schema

As with DTDs and XML documents, you can add comments to XML schemas. Can you use the XML comments in XML schema? Yes, you can. Here's an example:

```
<?xml version="1.0" encoding="UTF-8" ?>
<xsd:schema xmlns:xsd="http://www.w3.org/2001/XMLSchema">
    <!--Define the document element first -->
    <xsd:element name="document" type="documentType"/>
    <xsd:complexType name="documentType">
        <xsd:sequence>
            <xsd:element ref="comment" minOccurs="1"/>
            <xsd:element name="mortgagee" type="recordType"/>
            <xsd:element name="mortgages" type="mortgagesType"/>
            <xsd:element name="bank" type="recordType"/>
        </xsd:sequence>
        <xsd:attribute name="documentDate" type="xsd:date"/>
    </xsd:complexType>
        .
        .
        .
```

However, as you might expect from the way that you've been extending what you can do in DTDs, there's more to the story. XML schemas also define three new elements that you use to add annotations to schemas: `<xsd:annotation>`, `<xsd:documentation>`, and `<xsd:appInfo>`.

The `<xsd:annotation>` element is a container for the other two, `<xsd:documentation>` and `<xsd:appInfo>`. The `<xsd:documentation>` element holds text intended for human readers, but it's a little more than standard XML comments because the text in `<xsd:documentation>` elements can be stripped out by an XML processor and used to document an XML schema. The `<xsd:appInfo>` element can be used to pass along instructions to the XML processor that is reading the XML schema.

Here's an example from the XML schema you developed yesterday (`ch06_07.xsd`) that uses an `<xsd:documentation>` element, which must be enclosed inside an `<xsd:annotation>` element:

```
<?xml version="1.0" encoding="UTF-8"?>
<xsd:schema xmlns:xsd="http://www.w3.org/2001/XMLSchema">
    <xsd:annotation>
        <xsd:documentation>
            Mortgage record XML schema.
        </xsd:documentation>
    </xsd:annotation>
    .
    .
    .
```

Although you typically add an <xsd:annotation> element at the beginning of an XML schema, you can use these elements anywhere you like in an XML schema, as in this example, where you add an annotation to a complex type declaration:

```
<?xml version="1.0" encoding="UTF-8" ?>
<xsd:schema xmlns:xsd="http://www.w3.org/2001/XMLSchema">
    <xsd:element name="document" type="documentType"/>
    <xsd:complexType name="documentType">
        <xsd:annotation>
            <xsd:documentation>
                This type is used in the document element.
            </xsd:documentation>
        </xsd:annotation>
        <xsd:sequence>
            <xsd:element ref="comment" minOccurs="1"/>
            <xsd:element name="mortgagee" type="recordType"/>
            <xsd:element name="mortgages" type="mortgagesType"/>
            <xsd:element name="bank" type="recordType"/>
        </xsd:sequence>
        <xsd:attribute name="documentDate" type="xsd:date"/>
    </xsd:complexType>
        .
        .
        .
```

The <xsd:appInfo> element, which (like the <xsd:documentation> element) must be enclosed in an <xsd:annotation> element, can pass on information to the XML processor if the XML processor is set up to read that information. For example, if the XML processor expects a set of parameters such as `checkSpelling`, you can enclose those parameters and their settings in an <xsd:appInfo> element:

```
<?xml version="1.0" encoding="UTF-8"?>
<xsd:schema xmlns:xsd="http://www.w3.org/2001/XMLSchema">
    <xsd:annotation>
        <xsd:appInfo>
            checkSpelling="true"
        </xsd:appInfo>
    </xsd:annotation>
    .
    .
    .
```

Summary

There's more about schemas that we haven't covered—for example, one XML schema can *inherit* declarations from another XML schema, and we can specify just how that inheritance process will work. You can also handle keys, IDs, and ID references—and even specify how the validity of the XML schema itself should be checked. (For more details, see `http://www.w3.org/TR/xmlschema-0`, `http://www.w3.org/TR/xmlschema-1`, and `http://www.w3.org/TR/xmlschema-2`.)

The specification for XML schemas is pretty extensive, and it's still under development. From our point of view, this means that XML validators—even the ones from Microsoft—will often only be partial implementations of the full specification. So be warned: If an XML validator doesn't implement the complete XML schema specification, it might simply accept something without comment and without checking its validity—for example, Internet Explorer doesn't implement the `pattern` facet, but if you use it, as you have done in this chapter, it won't complain or generate any errors—it will simply ignore the facet.

Tomorrow, we're going to start handling the visual formatting of the data in XML documents as we use cascading style sheets to work on the presentation of data.

For the second day in a row, today you worked with XML schemas, and you got a good look at what XML schemas can do. You started by taking a look at how to restrict possible data values by using facets.

XML schemas not only let you specify data types for your data, as you saw yesterday, but they also let you impose restrictions on that data. As you saw today, there are 12 facets: `totalDigits`, `fractionDigits`, `pattern`, `whiteSpace`, `enumeration`, `maxInclusive`, `maxExclusive`, `minInclusive`, `minExclusive`, `length`, `minLength`, and `maxLength`. You can use these facets to restrict the possible values you want to allow data to have. The `<xsd:restriction>` element has a base attribute that you can use to set the data type for the data you're restricting.

Today you also saw that you can use the `<xsd:choice>` element to create choices, which work just as choices work in DTDs. Only one item from a choice can be selected and can appear in the XML document you're validating at the location of the `<xsd:choice>` element in the XML schema.

XML schemas support anonymous type definitions, which are simply type definitions that aren't named; as a shortcut, an anonymous type definition appears directly in the element declaration where it will be used. As you saw today, anonymous type definitions are useful if you want to use a type only once and don't need to refer to it in other places in an XML schema.

Today you also saw that empty elements can be declared by using a complex type that simply has no child elements but that may have attributes. You also saw that you can declare mixed-content elements by setting the `mixed` attribute of the `<xsd:complexType>` element to `"true"`.

You can group together elements in the `<xsd:group>` element, and you can group attributes together by using the `<xsd:attributeGroup>` element. These are convenience elements in XML schemas, allowing you to declare groups that you can use throughout an XML schema as you want. You can also create `all` groups instead of just using the sequences you saw yesterday. In an `all` group, elements can appear in any order, but all the elements in this kind of group can appear only once or not at all.

XML schemas also have provisions for handling namespaces—by using the `targetNamespace` attribute, which is an attribute of the `<xsd:schema>` element and can hold the namespace the XML schema is targeted toward. You have seen that you can use the `elementFormDefault` and `attributeFormDefault` attributes to specify whether local elements and attributes need to be qualified with namespace prefixes when used.

As you have seen, XML schemas support three elements that are used to add annotations to schemas: `<xsd:annotation>`, `<xsd:documentation>`, and `<xsd:appInfo>`. The `<xsd:annotation>` element encloses the other two elements; `<xsd:documentation>` holds documentation comments, and the `<xsd:appInfo>` element holds information you want to pass on to the XML processor.

Q&A

Q Is there any way to refer to external XML schemas from the current XML schema, as a DTD can refer to external DTDs?

A Yes. You can use the `<xsd:include>` and `<xsd:import>` elements. The `<xsd:include>` element can include a specified XML schema document in the target namespace of the current schema. The `<xsd:import>` element imports a namespace whose schema components are referenced by the current schema.

Q How can one XML schema inherit declarations from another XML schema?

A Inheritance is a complex topic in XML schema, based on object-oriented programming (OOP) languages such as C++. XML schema inheritance implements many of the features of OOP, all the way up to letting you create abstract types that cannot be instantiated directly but must be implemented locally before they are used. (For the details, you can take a look at `http://www.w3.org/TR/xmlschema-0`.) Not many XML validators or processors support XML schema inheritance yet.

Workshop

This workshop tests whether you understand the concepts discussed today. It's a good idea to make sure you can answer these questions before pressing on to tomorrow's work. Answers to the quiz can be found in Appendix A, "Quiz Answers."

Quiz

1. What element do you use to restrict the possible values data can take? How do you specify the data type you're restricting?
2. What facets do you use to cap allowed vales? What facets do you use to constrain values to be one of a set you specify?
3. How would you declare a simple type named `age` whose integer values are restricted to be between 0 and 125, inclusive?
4. How can you allow either a `<friend>` element or a `<foe>` element to appear at a particular location by using an XML choice element?
5. How can you declare an empty element named `<movie>` with a text attribute named `title` and an integer attribute named `length`?

Exercises

1. Create an XML document that keeps track of the amount of money owed to you by various friends. In the corresponding XML schema, use the appropriate facets to be sure the amount owed is greater than 0 and less than 5,000 (or 500,000—if you really trust your friends).
2. Add another element—the `<repayment>` element—to the XML document you created in Exercise 1. Use the `enumeration` facet to ensure that this element can only take the text values `"Monday"`, `"Tuesday"`, `"Wednesday"`, `"Thursday"`, and `"Friday"`.

PART I

In Review

In Part I, which is all about creating XML documents, you got the basics, including how to write XML documents, how to create well-formed documents, and how to make sure XML documents are valid. You saw that there can be various parts in an XML document, not all of which must appear in all documents:

- XML declarations
- Processing instructions
- Elements and attributes
- Comments
- CDATA sections
- Entities

For example, this XML document, which holds the names of clients for whom you might be doing some programming, begins with an XML declaration, and the document element is <document>:

```
<?xml version = "1.0" standalone="yes"?>
<document>
    <client>
        <name>
            <lastname>Kirk</lastname>
            <firstname>James</firstname>
        </name>
        <contractDate>September 5, 2092</contractDate>
        <contracts>
            <contract>
                <app>Comm</app>
                <id>111</id>
                <fee>$111.00</fee>
            </contract>
            <contract>
                <app>Accounting</app>
```

1

2

3

4

5

6

7

```
                <id>222</id>
                <fee>$989.00</fee>
            </contract>
        </contracts>
    </client>
    <client>
        <name>
            <lastname>McCoy</lastname>
            <firstname>Leonard</firstname>
        </name>
        <contractDate>September 7, 2092</contractDate>
        <contracts>
            <contract>
                <app>Stocker</app>
                <id>333</id>
                <fee>$2995.00</fee>
            </contract>
            <contract>
                <app>Dialer</app>
                <id>444</id>
                <fee>$200.00</fee>
            </contract>
        </contracts>
    </client>
    <client>
        <name>
            <lastname>Spock</lastname>
            <firstname>Mr.</firstname>
        </name>
        <contractDate>September 9, 2092</contractDate>
        <contracts>
            <contract>
                <app>WinHook</app>
                <id>555</id>
                <fee>$129.00</fee>
            </contract>
            <contract>
                <app>MouseApp</app>
                <id>666</id>
                <fee>$25.00</fee>
            </contract>
        </contracts>
    </client>
</document>
```

Each element here has an opening and closing tag, and each element is nested properly.

Well-Formed Documents

Well-formedness is the most basic requirement that a document must fulfill in order to be considered an XML document. You saw on Day 3 that there are a number of requirements for well-formedness: the document must begin with an XML declaration, the document must contain at least one element, one element must contain all the other elements, elements must be nested properly, and so on. For example, this XML document is not well-formed because there's a nesting error with the `<lastName>` and `<firstName>` elements:

```
<?xml version = "1.0" standalone="yes"?>
<document>
    <client>
        <name>
            <lastname>Kirk</firstname>
            <lastname>James</firstname>
        </name>
        <contractDate>September 5, 2092</contractDate>
        .
        .
        .
</document>
```

Valid Documents

Besides being well-formed, XML documents may also be valid. A valid document must conform to a number of syntax rules. There are two ways to specify the syntax of XML documents[md]by using DTDs and XML schemas, each of which has its own syntax.

To declare a DTD, you use the `<!DOCTYPE>` element. That DTD can either be internal to the XML document (in which case you set the XML declaration's `standalone` attribute to `"yes"`), external to the XML document (in which case you give the DTD's URI and set the XML declaration's `standalone` attribute to `"no"`), or a combination of the two.

You can use `<!ELEMENT>` elements to declare XML elements in a DTD. When we use `<!ELEMENT>`, the syntax for elements is `<!ELEMENT` *`name content_model`*`>`. There are also various content models possible when declaring an element. You can use the content model `ANY` to allow any content and to turn off syntax checking, and we can use `EMPTY` to declare an empty element.

You can list possible child elements of an element this way:

```
<!ELEMENT document (client)>
```

This allows a `<document>` element to contain a `<client>` element. In addition, you can list the child elements that an element can contain like this:

```
<!ELEMENT client (name, contractDate, contracts)>
```

And you can specify that an element contains parsed character data by using `#PCDATA`.

In the DTD syntax, you can use the symbols + (one or more), * (zero or more), ? (one or none), and | (choices) to work with multiple child elements. And you can also use these symbols in sequences to specify exactly what child elements, or combinations of child elements, an element can contain.

In Part I you also saw that you declare attributes in a DTD by using an `<!ATTLIST>` element and that you can assign default values to attributes when you declare them. When you declare an attribute, you can assign an explicit default value enclosed in quotation marks, use `#IMPLIED` to make the attribute optional, use `#FIXED` to give it a fixed value, or use `#REQUIRED` to make an attribute required.

And you've also seen in Part I that you can declare the type of an attribute in an `<!ATTLIST>` element. The allowed types are `CDATA`, `ENTITY`, `ENTITIES`, an enumeration, an `ID` value, an `IDREF` value, `IDREFS`, `NMTOKEN`, `NMTOKENS`, and `NOTATION`. Here's what a DTD for your sample document might look like:

```
<?xml version = "1.0" encoding="UTF-8" standalone="yes"?>
<!DOCTYPE document [
<!ELEMENT document (client)*>
<!ELEMENT client (name, contractDate, contracts)>
<!ELEMENT name (lastname, firstname)>
<!ELEMENT lastname (#PCDATA)>
<!ELEMENT firstname (#PCDATA)>
<!ELEMENT contractDate (#PCDATA)>
<!ELEMENT contracts (contract)*>
<!ELEMENT contract (app, id, fee)>
<!ELEMENT app (#PCDATA)>
<!ELEMENT id (#PCDATA)>
<!ELEMENT fee (#PCDATA)>
<!ATTLIST liaison CDATA #IMPLIED>
]>
<document>
    <liaison="no">
        <name>
            <lastname>Kirk</lastname>
            <firstname>James</firstname>
        </name>
        <contractDate>September 5, 2092</contractDate>
        <contracts>
            <contract>
                <app>Comm</app>
```

```
                <id>111</id>
                <fee>$111.00</fee>
            </contract>
            <contract>
                <app>Accounting</app>
                <id>222</id>
                <fee>$989.00</fee>
            </contract>
        </contracts>
    </client>
    <liaison="yes">
        <name>
            <lastname>McCoy</lastname>
            <firstname>Leonard</firstname>
        </name>
        <contractDate>September 7, 2092</contractDate>
        <contracts>
            <contract>
                <app>Stocker</app>
                <id>333</id>
                <fee>$2995.00</fee>
            </contract>
            <contract>
                <app>Dialer</app>
                <id>444</id>
                <fee>$200.00</fee>
            </contract>
        </contracts>
    </client>
</document>
```

In Part I you also got an introduction to creating XML schemas. You saw that you start an XML schema with an XML declaration and an `<xsd:schema>` element, and in this element, you declare a namespace prefix such as `xsd`, which is assigned the URI setting `"http://www.w3.org/2001/XMLSchema"`.

To declare elements and attributes in an XML document using an XML schema, you can use the XML schema elements `<xsd:element>` and `<xsd:attribute>`. Both `<xsd:element>` and `<xsd:attribute>` support an attribute named `type`, which lets you specify an element's or attribute's type.

There are two main types you can use: simple types and complex types. Simple types cannot enclose any child elements or have any attributes, but complex types can. As you've seen, elements can be declared by using simple or complex types, but attributes can only be declared by using simple types.

There are a number of simple types built into the XML schema specification, including `xsd:string` for strings, `xsd:int` for integers, and `xsd:date` for dates. You can also create your own simple types by using `<xsd:simpleType>`.

You can create complex types by using `<xsd:complexType>`, which may enclose the declarations of child elements. You saw on Day 6 that enclosing those child elements in an `<xsd:sequence>` element creates an element sequence and that the elements declared in sequence must appear in that sequence in the XML document.

You also saw that the `<xsd:element>` element has a `minOccurs` attribute to indicate the minimum number of times an element may appear at the location where it has been declared, and a `maxOccurs` attribute to set the maximum number of times it may occur. In addition, you saw that you can use the `fixed` and `default` attributes to specify whether an element has a fixed or default value.

To review how XML schemas work, let's take a look at an XML document that holds data about a property owner who wants to sell his properties:

```
<?xml version="1.0" encoding="UTF-8"?>
<document documentDate="2005-12-02">
    <evaluation>Wants to sell soon.</evaluation>
    <prospect>
        <name>Ralph Kramden</name>
        <location>311 Chauncey Street</location>
        <city>New York</city>
        <state>NY</state>
    </prospect>
    <properties>
        <house listingNumber="111 111 111">
            <address>19 Oak Place</address>
            <sellingPrice>200000</sellingPrice>
            <listingPeriod>3</listingPeriod>
        </house>
        <house listingNumber="222 222 222">
            <address>23 Maple Street</address>
            <sellingPrice>180000</sellingPrice>
            <listingPeriod>3</listingPeriod>
        </house>
        <house listingNumber="333 333 333">
            <address>77 Chestnut Drive</address>
            <sellingPrice>160000</sellingPrice>
            <listingPeriod>6</listingPeriod>
        </house>
        <house listingNumber="444 4444 444">
            <address>677 Pine Place</address>
            <sellingPrice>220000</sellingPrice>
            <listingPeriod>6</listingPeriod>
        </house>
```

```
    </properties>
    <broker>
        <name>XML Broker</name>
        <location>484 Ginko Street</location>
        <city>New York</city>
        <state>NY</state>
    </broker>
</document>
```

The XML schema specifies the syntax of every element in this example in a natural XML way, where elements that enclose various child elements in the XML document also enclose those child elements in the XML schema. Here's what the XML schema that will validate the XML document looks like:

```
<?xml version="1.0" encoding="UTF-8"?>
<xsd:schema xmlns:xsd="http://www.w3.org/2001/XMLSchema">
    <xsd:element name="document" type="documentType"/>
    <xsd:complexType name="documentType">
        <xsd:sequence>
            <xsd:element ref="evaluation" minOccurs="1"/>
            <xsd:element name="prospect" type="recordType"/>
            <xsd:element name="properties" type="propertiesType"/>
            <xsd:element name="broker" type="recordType"/>
        </xsd:sequence>
        <xsd:attribute name="documentDate" type="xsd:date"/>
    </xsd:complexType>
    <xsd:complexType name="recordType">
        <xsd:sequence>
            <xsd:element name="name" type="xsd:string"/>
            <xsd:element name="location" type="xsd:string"/>
            <xsd:element name="city" type="xsd:string"/>
            <xsd:element name="state" type="xsd:string"/>
        </xsd:sequence>
    </xsd:complexType>
    <xsd:complexType name="propertiesType">
        <xsd:sequence>
            <xsd:element name="house" minOccurs="1" maxOccurs="8">
                <xsd:complexType>
                    <xsd:sequence>
                        <xsd:element name="address" type="xsd:string"/>
                        <xsd:element name="sellingPrice" type="xsd:decimal"/>
                        <xsd:element name="listingPeriod">
                        <xsd:simpleType>
                            <xsd:restriction base="xsd:integer">
                                <xsd:maxInclusive value="6"/>
                            </xsd:restriction>
                        </xsd:simpleType>
                        </xsd:element>
                    </xsd:sequence>
                    <xsd:attribute name="listingNumber"
```

```
                        type="listingNumberType"/>
                </xsd:complexType>
            </xsd:element>
        </xsd:sequence>
    </xsd:complexType>
    <xsd:simpleType name="listingNumberType">
        <xsd:restriction base="xsd:string">
            <xsd:pattern value="\d{3} \d{3} \d{3}"/>
        </xsd:restriction>
    </xsd:simpleType>
    <xsd:element name="evaluation" type="xsd:string"/>
</xsd:schema>
```

XML schemas like this aren't necessarily easy to create. However, there are a number of tools out there that can create XML schema for you.

And that's it. Part I helped get you started creating XML documents and making sure they're well-formed and valid. In Part II, you're going to start working on formatting the data in XML documents for presentation.

PART II

At a Glance

Formatting XML Documents

In Part II, you're going to start working with the actual data inside XML documents, but without using programming. You're going to see three ways of formatting XML data in the coming three days.

You'll start by using cascading style sheets (CSS), which are specified by the W3C for formatting both XML and HTML. You can do a lot to format the appearance of XML documents by using CSS. However, CSS aren't native XML.

You'll also take a look at formatting XML by using Extensible Stylesheet Language Transformations (XSLT); XSLT is native XML. By using XSLT you can extract data from XML documents, process it, and create new HTML, RTF, text, and files, as well as files of other formats, including new XML documents—all without programming. However, you can't really format the appearance of XML data directly by using XSLT.

The general version of Extensible Stylesheet Language (XSL) that uses special formatting objects is called XSL-FO, and it can format data down to the smallest spaces and font choices. You'll see XSL-FO in Day 10; although XSL-FO gives you a handle on just about all aspects of displaying XML data, it's pretty complex to work with.

PART II

DAY 8

Formatting XML by Using Cascading Style Sheets

Say that you want to take a look at the data in an XML document by using a browser. You might be out of luck unless you're using a specialized XML browser that can handle the particular XML markup you're using, such as the W3C Amaya browser that handles MathML. However, there are very few specialized XML browsers out there, and there's a great deal of XML. Don't you have any other options? You do. For one, you can use Cascading Style Sheets (CSS). Many browsers, such as Netscape Navigator and Internet Explorer, let you use CSS to format the data in XML documents for display, and today you're going to see how that works. It's getting more and more common to see CSS-formatted XML on the Web, and it often makes sense to display data by using CSS. You might want to create a table, for example, which is a lot easier on the eyes than a 40-page XML document.

Here's an overview of today's topics:

- Creating CSS style sheets and CSS rules
- Using CSS style sheets with XML documents

- Selecting elements in style sheets
- Grouping elements
- Creating CSS classes
- Selecting elements by ID
- Using inline styles
- Using block elements
- Formatting text
- Aligning text
- Creating margins
- Displaying images
- Creating lists
- Creating tables

Our Sample XML Document

You already know that XML provides a good way of storing data; for example, say that you want to store the text of your favorite stoic philosopher in an XML document. Listing 8.1 shows an example of text from the philosopher Epictetus, as `ch08_01.xml`.

LISTING 8.1 An XML Document (`ch08_01.xml`)

```
<?xml version="1.0" standalone="yes"?>
<document>
    <title>The Discourses</title>
    <philosopher>Epictetus</philosopher>
    <book>Book Four</book>
    <paragraph>
        He is free who lives as he wishes to live; who is neither
        subject to compulsion nor to hindrance, nor to force;
        whose movements to action are not impeded, whose desires
        attain their purpose, and who does not fall into that which
        he would avoid.
    </paragraph>
    <paragraph>
        Who, then, chooses to live in error? No man. Who chooses
        to live deceived, liable to mistake, unjust, unrestrained,
        discontented, mean? No man.
    </paragraph>
    <paragraph>
        Not one then of the bad lives as he wishes; nor is he,
        then, free. And who chooses to live in sorrow, fear, envy,
```

LISTING 8.1 continued

```
            pity, desiring and failing in his desires, attempting to
            avoid something and falling into it? Not one.
        </paragraph>
        <paragraph>
            Do we then find any of the bad free from sorrow, free from
            fear, who does not fall into that which he would avoid, and
            does not obtain that which he wishes? Not one; nor then do
            we find any bad man free.
        </paragraph>
</document>
```

The data of Epictetus' text is stored in ch08_01.xml, but it's not exactly presented optimally. Even for a browser that can display XML directly, such as Internet Explorer, this text isn't easy to read because of the embedded markup. Figure 8.1 shows ch08_01.xml in Internet Explorer.

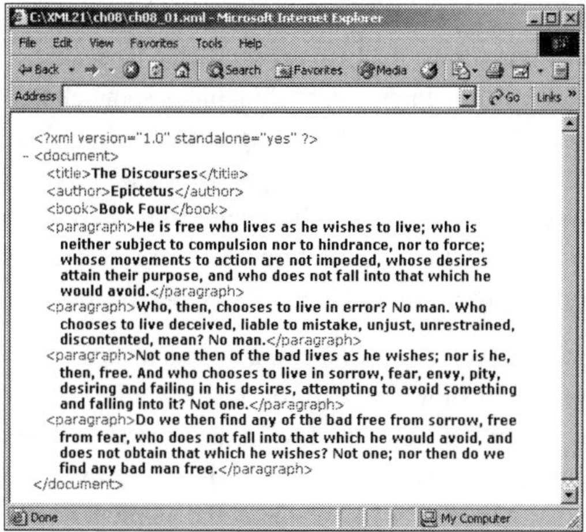

FIGURE 8.1
An XML document displayed in Internet Explorer.

It turns out that you can improve this visual display by telling browsers how to format the XML elements you use for markup—for example, you can say that you want the <title> element to be displayed using a particular font, in a particular size, and even in italics if you want. That's what today's work is all about—convincing standard Web browsers to display XML by telling them how to format the data in various XML elements (and removing all the markup).

To do that, you're going to use CSS today. CSS was first introduced in December 1996. It's now widely in use for HTML browsers, and although it was originally used only to format HTML, thanks to CSS, the major browsers now let you format XML as well. In some ways, CSS works even better with XML than it does with HTML, because in XML you're not limited to the predefined HTML elements and you can style sophisticated nestings of elements and more.

Introducing CSS

CSS has been standardized by the W3C, and as of this writing, there are three levels of CSS available: CSS1, CSS2, and CSS3. You can find the W3C recommendations for CSS1 and CSS2 at `http://www.w3.org/TR/REC-CSS1` and `http://www.w3.org/TR/REC-CSS2`. CSS3 is still under development; it's broken up into many modules, and at this point those modules are at various stages of acceptance, from working drafts to candidate recommendations. You can find more about the many CSS3 modules at `http://www.w3.org/Style/CSS/current-work`. There are also many CSS resources available at the W3C CSS page, `http://www.w3.org/Style/CSS`, including CSS tutorials and links to free tools.

Today you'll be dealing almost exclusively with CSS1 because it gives you all you need in order to present XML documents. CSS2 includes some changes compared to CSS1, but its main thrust is in providing extra features, such as aural stylesheets for sounds and so on; CSS3 is still under development. Support for CSS1 in both Netscape Navigator and Internet Explorer is good—in fact, Internet Explorer supports all of CSS1 (and that was true as of March 27, 2000, when Internet Explorer 5.0 shipped). One notable aspect of CSS2 that you're going to use today is its support for formatting tables.

Formatting using CSS revolves around using style sheets. *Style sheets* are collections of *style rules*, each of which shows how to format an XML element. For example, say that you want to specify how to format the text in the `<title>` element in the `ch08_01.xml` sample XML document shown in Listing 8.1. How could you construct a style rule to do that? A rule is made up of a *selector*, which is the element(s) you want to format, and the *rule specification*, which shows what formatting you want to apply. Here's how a rule might look if you wanted to format the text in the `<title>` element in bold, centered, underlined 36-point font (a point is 1/72 inch):

```
title {display: block; font-size: 36pt; font-weight: bold;
    text-align: center; text-decoration: underline}
```

Note that the rule specification is enclosed in curly braces, `{` and `}`. In this rule, `title` is the selector and `{display: block; font-size: 36pt; font-weight: bold; text-align: center; text-decoration: underline}` is the rule specification.

`display`, `font-size`, `font-weight`, and so on are CSS *properties*, and you're going to see a great many of those properties today. In fact, getting to know CSS largely means getting to know what properties, like these, are available. The second part of today's discussion is devoted to the various CSS properties and what they do for you.

Rule specifications are made up of *property/value* pairs, such as `display: block`, separated with semicolons, as you'll see when you write your own style sheets. The `display: block` property/value pair is a particularly important one because it gives the element you're formatting its own line in the display, creating a *block-level* element, just as the `<H1>` element in HTML is a block-level element. You'll talk more about this in a few pages.

Listing 8.2 shows a CSS style sheet that handles all four of the element types that are in the sample XML document—`<title>`, `<philosopher>`, `<book>`, and `<paragraph>`. Note that CSS style sheet files use the extension `.css`.

LISTING 8.2 A CSS Document (`ch08_02.css`)

```
title {display: block; font-size: 36pt; font-weight: bold;
    text-align: center; text-decoration: underline}
philosopher {display: block; font-size: 16pt;
    text-align: center}
book {display: block; font-size: 28pt; text-align: center;
    font-style: italic}
paragraph {display: block; margin-top: 10}
```

You're going to be writing style sheets of the kind shown in Listing 8.2 throughout today's discussion. Style sheets don't look much like XML documents, but, as with XML, there are a few CSS validators available on the Web to help you check your CSS. Here are two of them:

- The W3C CSS validator, at `http://jigsaw.w3.org/css-validator`, checks the CSS in your pages for you.
- The W3C TIDY program can convert styles in HTML documents to CSS for you. TIDY is available at `http://tidy.sourceforge.net`.

The next step is to connect the CSS style sheet, `ch08_02.css`, to the XML document, `ch08_01.xml`.

Connecting CSS Style Sheets and XML Documents

There are three ways to connect a CSS style sheet with HTML: You can use an internal style sheet, you can use an external style sheet, or you can use the HTML STYLE attribute to associate a CSS style with a particular HTML element. You don't have the luxury of these options in XML, at least not with the current crop of browsers. At this point, there's really only one way of connecting a style sheet to an XML document: by using the `<?xml-stylesheet?>` processing instruction.

Actually, `<?xml-stylesheet?>` isn't built in to the XML specification at all. (As with XML schema, W3C isn't particularly good about indicating how you connect files such as style sheets with XML documents.) It has just become an agreed-upon convention, supported in both Netscape Navigator and Internet Explorer. In HTML browsers, you set the `type` attribute of processing instruction to `"text/css"` and the `href` attribute to the URI of the style sheet. You can see how this works in `ch08_03.xml`, which is the same as `ch08_01.xml` except that it uses a `<?xml-stylesheet?>` processing instruction to connect itself to `ch08_02.css`.

LISTING 8.3 An XML Document That Has an Attached Style Sheet (`ch08_03.xml`)

```
<?xml version="1.0" standalone="yes"?>
<?xml-stylesheet type="text/css" href="ch08_02.css"?>
<document>
    <title>The Discourses</title>
    <philosopher>Epictetus</philosopher>
    <book>Book Four</book>
    <paragraph>
        He is free who lives as he wishes to live; who is neither
        subject to compulsion nor to hindrance, nor to force;
        whose movements to action are not impeded, whose desires
        attain their purpose, and who does not fall into that which
        he would avoid.
    </paragraph>
    <paragraph>
        .
        .
        .
    <paragraph>
        Do we then find any of the bad free from sorrow, free from
        fear, who does not fall into that which he would avoid, and
        does not obtain that which he wishes? Not one; nor then do
        we find any bad man free.
   </paragraph>
</document>
```

When you place ch08_03.xml and ch08_03.css in the same directory and open ch08_03.xml in Internet Explorer, Internet Explorer reads and applies the CSS style rules in ch08_02.css. Figure 8.2 shows the results of doing this.

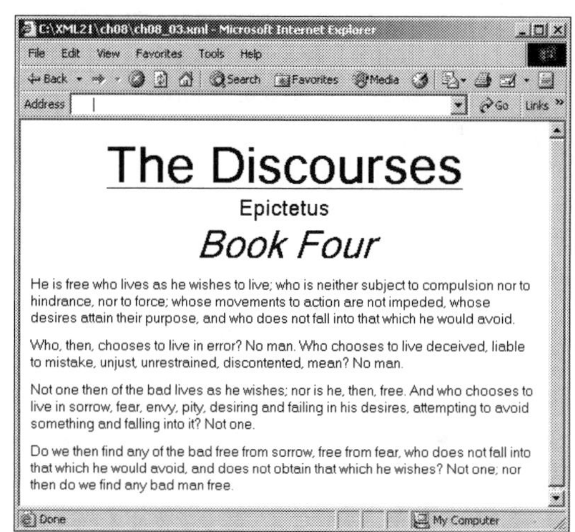

FIGURE 8.2

The sample XML document ch08_03.xml *formatted in Internet Explorer.*

You can see what's happened in Figure 8.2: You told Internet Explorer how to format the <title>, <philosopher>, <book>, and <paragraph> elements, and it did as you wanted, removing all markup from the display. Note that different browsers can give different results for the same CSS formatting. For example, Figure 8.3 shows the same document, ch08_03.xml, in Netscape Navigator. Notice that the text looks different than in Internet Explorer. For one thing, there's no vertical space between paragraphs (because Netscape Navigator doesn't support the margin-top CSS keyword, which specifies how much vertical space to leave between elements) .

TIP

Actually, there is another way to connect styles to XML elements with Internet Explorer. You can create inline styles by using the style attribute, like this:

```
He is free who lives as he <i style="font-style: italic">
wishes to live...</i>
```

This is certainly nonstandard for XML documents in general, but Internet Explorer supports it, as you'll see today.

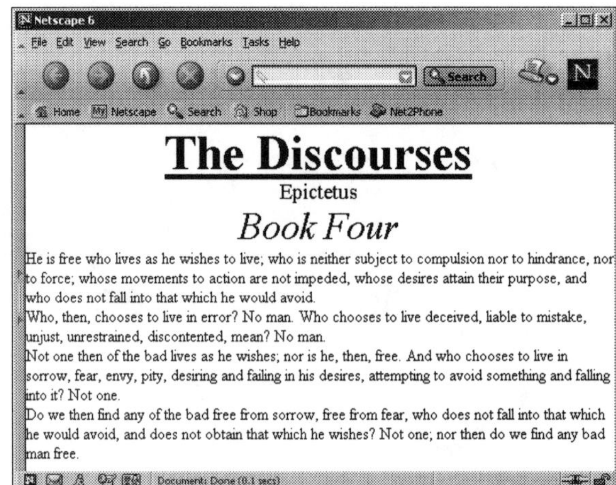

FIGURE 8.3

The sample XML document `ch08_03.xml` *formatted in Netscape Navigator.*

Now that you've gotten some experience with CSS styles sheets and XML, the following section shows how to create style sheets, starting with specifying what elements you want to style.

Creating Style Sheet Selectors

To specify what XML elements you want to format, you use selectors in a XSS style sheet. You've already seen some simple selectors in the style sheet `ch08_02.css`, where each selector is just the name of the element you want to format, such as `title` and `philosopher`:

```
title {display: block; font-size: 36pt; font-weight: bold;
    text-align: center; text-decoration: underline}
philosopher {display: block; font-size: 16pt;
    text-align: center}
book {display: block; font-size: 28pt; text-align: center;
    font-style: italic}
paragraph {display: block; margin-top: 10}
```

In this case, you're applying the style rule specification `{display: block; font-size: 36pt; font-weight: bold; text-align: center; text-decoration: underline}` to the `<title>` element, the style rule specification `{display: block; font-size: 16pt; text-align: center}` to the `<philosopher>` element, and so on. This is the simplest kind of selector, where you just name the element you want to format.

You can also group elements together just by separating them with commas. Listing 8.4 shows an example of this method, in `ch08_04.css`, which formats the `<title>` and `<book>` elements in the same way.

LISTING 8.4 Grouping Selectors (ch08_04.css)

```
title, book {display: block; font-size: 36pt; font-weight: bold;
    text-align: center; text-decoration: underline}
philosopher {display: block; font-size: 16pt;
    text-align: center}
paragraph {display: block; margin-top: 10}
```

Figure 8.4 shows this style sheet applied to the sample XML document. As you can see, the `<title>` and `<book>` elements are formatted the same way.

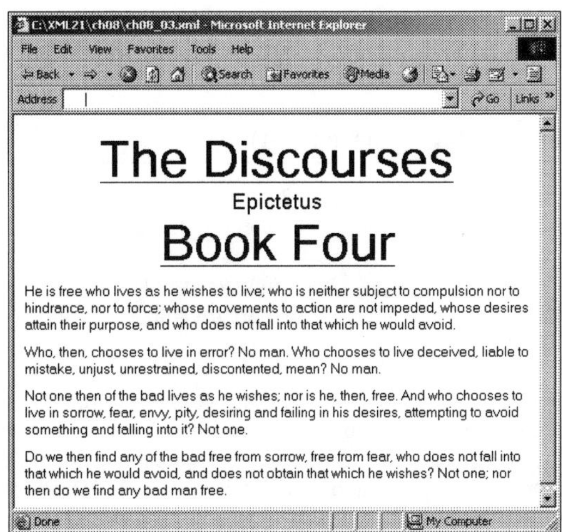

FIGURE 8.4
Formatting by using a group selector.

Creating Style Classes

You don't need to specify an element name or names in order to create a selector; you can instead use a style *class* as a selector. You create a class by preceding its name with a dot (`.`) and using that as a selector. For example, say that you want to create a class named `standout` that formats its text in cyan on a background of coral. You can do that by creating the `standout` class, as shown in Listing 8.5. (This example relies on the fact that the browser you'll use, Internet Explorer, has dozens of colors, including coral and cyan, already built in).

LISTING 8.5 Creating a Style Class (ch08_05.css)

```
title {display: block; font-size: 36pt; font-weight: bold;
    text-align: center; text-decoration: underline}
philosopher {display: block; font-size: 16pt;
```

LISTING 8.5 continued

```
    text-align: center}
book {display: block; font-size: 28pt; text-align: center;
    font-style: italic}
paragraph {display: block; margin-top: 10}
.standout {color:cyan; background-color:coral}
```

You can apply the standout class to elements such as <title> and <philosopher> by using an attribute named class in Internet Explorer (Netscape Navigator doesn't support this attribute). Note that the class attribute isn't built in to XML; it's just used by convention in Internet Explorer for this purpose. Listing 8.6 shows an example of how to style these elements by using the style class ch08_06.css.

LISTING 8.6 Using a Style Class (ch08_06.xml)

```
<?xml version="1.0" standalone="yes"?>
<?xml-stylesheet type="text/css" href="ch08_05.css"?>
<document>
    <title class="standout">The Discourses</title>
    <philosopher class="standout">Epictetus</philosopher>
    <book>Book Four</book>
    <paragraph>
        He is free who lives as he wishes to live; who is neither
        subject to compulsion nor to hindrance, nor to force;
        whose movements to action are not impeded, whose desires
        attain their purpose, and who does not fall into that which
        he would avoid.
    </paragraph>
        .
        .
        .
    <paragraph>
        Do we then find any of the bad free from sorrow, free from
        fear, who does not fall into that which he would avoid, and
        does not obtain that which he wishes? Not one; nor then do
        we find any bad man free.
   </paragraph>
</document>
```

Figure 8.5 shows what this formatted document, ch08_07.xml, looks like in Internet Explorer. Note that the new colors were added to the display; they didn't simply replace the other formatting that was already present.

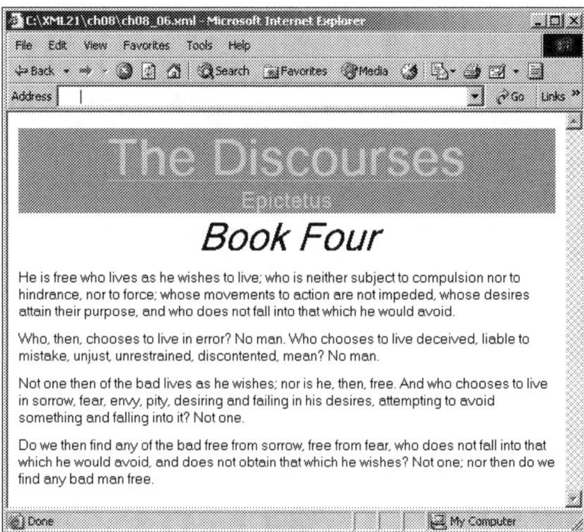

FIGURE 8.5
Using style classes.

TIP

If you want to use the `class` attribute in a valid document, you have to declare it. In a DTD, that might look like this:

```
<!ATTLIST title class CDATA #IMPLIED>
```

In an XML schema, it might look like this:

```
<xsd:attribute name="class" type="xsd:text"/>
```

You can target style classes to specific elements as well. For example, say that you want to format the first paragraph in the text a particular way, indenting it by using the `text-indent` CSS keyword and separating it even more from the previous text by using the `margin-top` keyword. You can do this by creating a new class named, say, `paragraph.first`, which is shown in Listing 8.7. In this case, you're specifying that the new class, `first`, applies only to `<paragraph>` elements.

LISTING 8.7 Creating a Class-Specific Selector (`ch08_07.css`)

```
title {display: block; font-size: 36pt; font-weight: bold;
    text-align: center; text-decoration: underline}
philosopher {display: block; font-size: 16pt;
    text-align: center}
book {display: block; font-size: 28pt; text-align: center;
    font-style: italic}
paragraph {display: block; margin-top: 10}
paragraph.first {text-indent: 40; margin-top: 30}
```

You can put the new style class to work with `<paragraph>` elements as shown in Listing 8.8.

LISTING 8.8 Using a Class-Specific Selector (ch08_08.xml)

```
<?xml version="1.0" standalone="yes"?>
<?xml-stylesheet type="text/css" href="ch08_07.css"?>
<document>
    <title>The Discourses</title>
    <philosopher>Epictetus</philosopher>
    <book>Book Four</book>
    <paragraph class="first">
        He is free who lives as he wishes to live; who is neither
        subject to compulsion nor to hindrance, nor to force;
        whose movements to action are not impeded, whose desires
        attain their purpose, and who does not fall into that which
        he would avoid.
    </paragraph>
        .
        .
        .
    <paragraph>
        Do we then find any of the bad free from sorrow, free from
        fear, who does not fall into that which he would avoid, and
        does not obtain that which he wishes? Not one; nor then do
        we find any bad man free.
   </paragraph>
</document>
```

Figure 8.6 shows how the text looks when you use the class-specific selector. Note in particular that the first paragraph is indeed formatted as you want it—indented and with more vertical space preceding it than the other paragraphs have. You have created a style class that is targeted at one element type alone.

FIGURE 8.6

Using a style targeted to only one element.

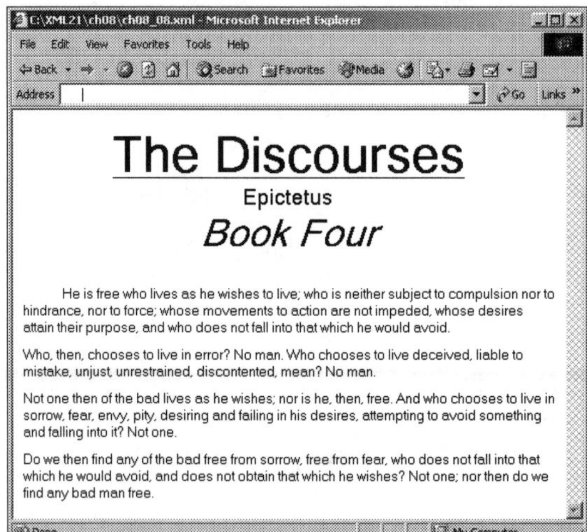

Selecting by ID

Besides creating style classes, there's another way to select XML elements to format: You can use the element's ID value. You can create selectors that target XML elements that have a certain ID by using this syntax:

```
elementName#idValue
```

Listing 8.9 shows an example of this technique. This example, `ch08_09.css`, creates a style rule for `<paragraph>` elements that have the ID `"first"`.

LISTING 8.9 Creating an ID-Based Selector (`ch08_09.css`)

```
title {display: block; font-size: 36pt; font-weight: bold;
    text-align: center; text-decoration: underline}
philosopher {display: block; font-size: 16pt;
    text-align: center}
book {display: block; font-size: 28pt; text-align: center;
    font-style: italic}
paragraph {display: block; margin-top: 10}
paragraph#first {text-indent: 40; margin-top: 30}
```

You can use this new ID-based selector in an XML document as shown in Listing 8.10.

LISTING 8.10 Using an ID-Based Selector (`ch08_10.xml`)

```
<?xml version="1.0" standalone="yes"?>
<?xml-stylesheet type="text/css" href="ch08_09.css"?>
<document>
    <title>The Discourses</title>
    <philosopher>Epictetus</philosopher>
    <book>Book Four</book>
    <paragraph id="first">
        He is free who lives as he wishes to live; who is neither
        subject to compulsion nor to hindrance, nor to force;
        whose movements to action are not impeded, whose desires
        attain their purpose, and who does not fall into that which
        he would avoid.
    </paragraph>
        .
        .
        .
    <paragraph>
        Do we then find any of the bad free from sorrow, free from
        fear, who does not fall into that which he would avoid, and
        does not obtain that which he wishes? Not one; nor then do
        we find any bad man free.
   </paragraph>
</document>
```

When you open `ch08_10.xml` in Internet Explorer (Netscape Navigator does not support the `id` attribute for XML documents), you get the same results shown in Figure 8.6—the first paragraph is indented and given some more vertical space.

Using Inline Styles

In HTML you can create an inline style to format just one particular element. To do this, you simply assign a style rule specification to the `style` attribute of the element. Internet Explorer (but not Netscape Navigator) can do the same thing. For example, to make just the word *wishes* italic in the text "He is free who lives as he wishes to live" in the sample XML document, you can enclose that word in its own element, as shown in Listing 8.11. Figure 8.7 shows the result, with the word *wishes* indeed italicized.

LISTING 8.11 Using Inline Styles (`ch08_11.xml`)

```
<?xml version="1.0" standalone="yes"?>
<?xml-stylesheet type="text/css" href="ch08_02.css"?>
<document>
    <title>The Discourses</title>
    <philosopher>Epictetus</philosopher>
    <book>Book Four</book>
    <paragraph>
        He is free who lives as he
        <i style="font-style: italic">wishes</i>
        to live; who is neither subject to compulsion nor to
        hindrance, nor to force; whose movements to action
        are not impeded, whose desires attain their purpose,
        and who does not fall into that which he would avoid.
    </paragraph>
        .
        .
        .
    <paragraph>
        Do we then find any of the bad free from sorrow, free from
        fear, who does not fall into that which he would avoid, and
        does not obtain that which he wishes? Not one; nor then do
        we find any bad man free.
    </paragraph>
</document>
```

Note that in this case, you're not using `display: block` in the style specification because you want to italicize the word *wishes* in place—not give it its own line. Strictly speaking, this is not valid XML unless you also declare the style attribute in a DTD or an XML schema, of course.

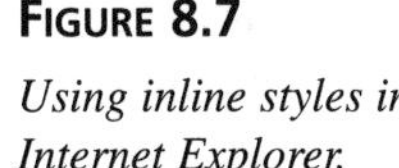

FIGURE 8.7
Using inline styles in Internet Explorer.

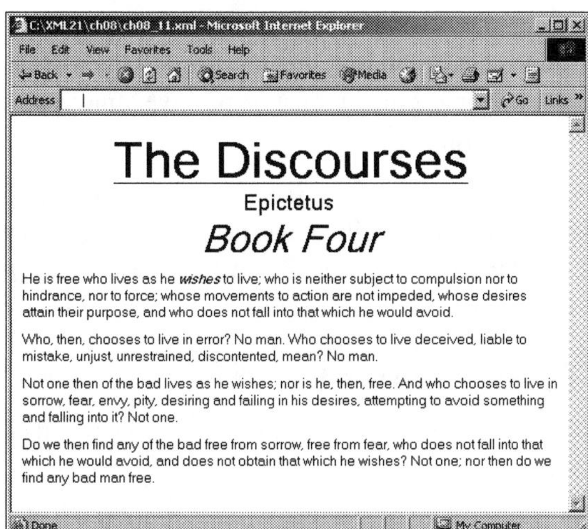

Note that some people recommend not using inline styles in this way because such styles are then spread throughout the document instead of being collected into a single style sheet. On the other hand, Internet Explorer supports inline styles for XML documents, so the choice is up to you.

You now have a good idea of how to create selectors in style sheet rules at this point. Now let's take a look at how to create the other part of style sheet rules: the rule specification itself.

Creating Style Rule Specifications in Style Sheets

As discussed earlier today, a style sheet rule is made up of a selector followed by a style rule specification in curly braces, like this:

```
title {display: block; font-size: 36pt; font-weight: bold;
text-align: center; text-decoration: underline}
```

As mentioned earlier today, the style rule specification is a list of property/value pairs that are separated by semicolons. For example, you can assign the `display` property the value `block`, the `font-size` property the value `36pt` (for 36 points), and so on.

Note that when you assign values to CSS properties, you can specify a size or a length by using points, indicated with the `pt` suffix (for example, `36pt`) or pixels (for example, `20px`). Theoretically, browsers are also supposed to be able to handle measurements in inches (suffix `in`), centimeters (suffix `cm`), millimeters (suffix `mm`), and picas (1/6 inch;

suffix `pc`). If you omit the suffix for a length, pixels are assumed. Also, note that when you specify positions, the origin is at the upper left of the display window (not at the lower right, as many people expect). That is, positive x increases to the right, and positive y increases downward.

To understand how to create style rule specifications, you need to know what CSS properties are available. The CSS specifications list many of them, and only by knowing what properties are available can you know how to create style rule specifications. You'll take a look at some of the possibilities in the rest of today's discussion.

Creating Block Elements

Today you have already used the `display` property, which you can see in action in the following example:

```
title {display: block; font-size: 36pt; font-weight: bold;
    text-align: center; text-decoration: underline}
philosopher {display: block; font-size: 16pt;
    text-align: center}
book {display: block; font-size: 28pt; text-align: center;
    font-style: italic}
paragraph {display: block; margin-top: 10}
```

As mentioned earlier today, when you assign the `display` property the value `block`, the corresponding element will be formatted in a block, which means that the data from the element will start on a new line, and the data from the next element will start on its own line as well. In HTML, this creates what's called a *block-level element.*

Specifying Text Styles

As you might expect, there are plenty of style properties that you can use with text. Here's a sampling:

- **`font-family`**—Specifies the font face. You can list a number of options, separated by commas. The first face supported by the browser will be used.
- **`font-size`**—Specifies the size of the font. You can set this property to a size; for example, `36pt` is 36 points.
- **`font-style`**—Specifies whether to use normal, italic, or oblique face.
- **`font-weight`**—Specifies the boldness of text relative to other fonts in the same font family. You can set it to `bold` for bold text.
- **`line-height`**—Specifies the height of each line of text. You can set it to an absolute size or to a percentage, such as 150% (which creates 1½ spacing).

8

- **`text-align`**—Specifies the alignment of text. You can assign this property values such as `left`, `right`, `center`, and `justify`.
- **`text-decoration`**—Specifies underlining and overlining. You can set it to `underline`, `overline`, `line-through`, or `blink`; to get rid of text inherited decorations, you can set it to `none`.
- **`text-indent`**—Specifies the indentation of the first line of block-level elements. You can set it to a size.
- **`text-transform`**—Specifies whether to display text in all uppercase, in all lowercase, or with initial letters capitalized. The possible values for this property are `capitalize`, `uppercase`, `lowercase`, and `none`.
- **`vertical-align`**—Specifies the vertical alignment of text. You can set this property to `baseline`, `sub`, `super`, `top`, `text-top`, `middle`, `bottom`, or `text-bottom`.

You've already used a number of these properties in style sheets, and now you know what they stand for. You haven't specified the font face yet, however, so take a look at `ch08_12.css` (shown in Listing 8.12), which indicates to use centered 12-point Arial font (or Times New Roman, if the system doesn't have Arial installed).

LISTING 8.12 Using Font Styles (`ch08_12.css`)

```
title {display: block; font-size: 36pt; font-weight: bold;
    text-align: center; text-decoration: underline}
philosopher {display: block; font-size: 16pt;
    text-align: center}
book {display: block; font-size: 28pt; text-align: center;
    font-style: italic}
paragraph {display: block; font-size: 12pt; font-family:
Arial, Times New Roman; text-align: center; margin-top: 10}
```

Figure 8.8 shows what this new style sheet, `ch08_12.css`, looks like applied to an XML document.

Styling Colors and Backgrounds

There are a number of properties that you can use to set color and work with backgrounds; here's a sampling:

- **`background-attachment`**—Specifies whether the background scrolls with the rest of the document.
- **`background-color`**—Specifies the background color. You can set this property to a color.

- **background-image**—Specifies the background image. You can set this property to a URL.
- **background-repeat**—Specifies whether the background image should be tiled. You can set this property to `repeat`, `repeat-x`, `repeat-y`, or `no-repeat`.
- **color**—Specifies the foreground color (that is, the color of text).

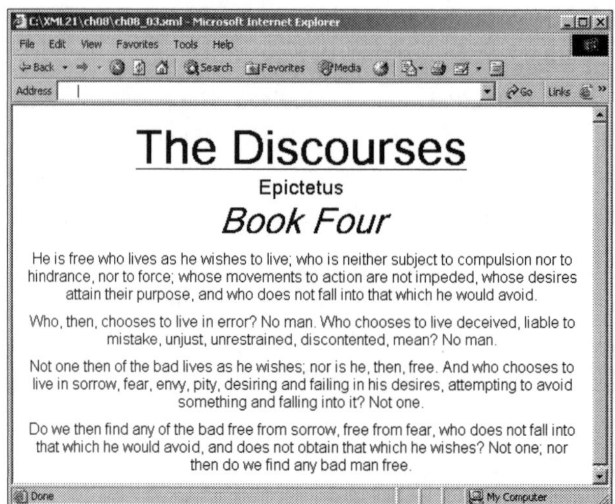

FIGURE 8.8
Using font properties with CSS.

Listing 8.13 shows an example, `ch08_13.css`, in which the style sheet sets the background color of the document to light green. Because all the other elements in the document are child elements of the `<document>` element, they also inherit the same coloring, as shown in Figure 8.9 (in glorious black and white). In fact, that's where the name *cascading* style sheets come from—the *cascading* part means that enclosed elements inherit styles from enclosing elements. This example also sets the color of `<paragraph>` text to red. You can see the style sheet that does all this in Listing 8.13.

LISTING 8.13 Using Color Styles (`ch08_13.css`)

```
document {background-color: lightgreen}
title {display: block; font-size: 36pt; font-weight: bold;
    text-align: center; text-decoration: underline}
philosopher {display: block; font-size: 16pt;
    text-align: center}
book {display: block; font-size: 28pt; text-align: center;
    font-style: italic}
paragraph {display: block; color: red}
```

FIGURE 8.9

Using font properties.

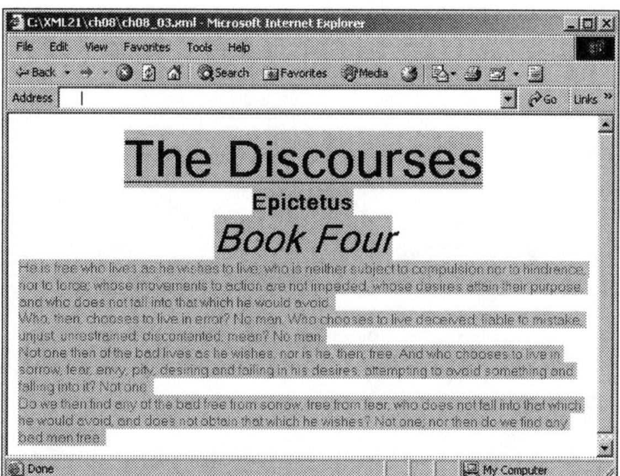

Today you have been using color names such as `cyan`, `coral`, and `lightgreen` because Internet Explorer understands those names. Dozens of these types of color names are built in to browsers such as Internet Explorer and Netscape Navigator, but there are actually only 16 color names built into the CSS standard. Here they are:

- `aqua`
- `black`
- `blue`
- `fuchsia`
- `gray`
- `green`
- `lime`
- `maroon`
- `navy`
- `olive`
- `purple`
- `red`
- `silver`
- `teal`
- `white`
- `yellow`

When you work with HTML browsers, you can define your own colors as standard HTML color triplets, using this syntax:

```
#rrggbb
```

where *rr*, *gg*, and *bb* are two-digit hexadecimal values that you use to specify the red, green, and blue components of a color. For example, black is `#000000`, white is `#ffffff`, pure red is `#ff0000`, and orange is `#ffcc00`. Using colors like these, here's how you might format the background of the `<document>` element and its child elements green:

```
document {background-color: #00ff00}
```

Styling Borders

You can format the borders of block elements by using a number of styles. Here is a sampling of the border properties that are available for block elements:

- **`border-bottom-width`**—Specifies the width of the bottom of the border. You can set this property to a size such as `12px` for 12 pixels, `6pt` for 6 points, or `thin`, `medium`, or `thick`.
- **`border-color`**—Specifies the color to use for the border (using a predefined color or a color triplet). Setting this property sets the color of the whole border.
- **`border-left-width`**—Specifies the width of the left edge of the border. You can set this property to a size such as `12px` for 12 pixels, 6pt for 6 points, or `thin`, `medium`, or `thick`.
- **`border-right-width`**—Specifies the width of the right edge of the border. You can set this property to a size such as `12px` for 12 pixels, `6pt` for 6 points, or `thin`, `medium`, or `thick`.
- **`border-style`**—Specifies the border style. You can set this property to `dotted`, `dashed`, `solid`, `double`, `groove`, `ridge`, `inset`, or `outset`. Most browsers support only `solid`.
- **`border-top-width`**—Specifies the width of the top of the border. You can set this property to a size such as `12px` for 12 pixels, `6pt` for 6 points, or `thin`, `medium`, or `thick`.
- **`border-width`**—Specifies the width of the border. You can set this property to a size such as `12px` for 12 pixels, `6pt` for 6 points, or `thin`, `medium`, or `thick`.

Listing 8.14 shows an example in which you add a solid border to the `<title>` element.

LISTING 8.14 Using Border Styles (ch08_14.css)

```
title {display: block; font-size: 36pt; font-weight: bold;
    text-align: center; text-decoration: underline;
    border-style: solid}
philosopher {display: block; font-size: 16pt;
    text-align: center}
book {display: block; font-size: 28pt; text-align: center;
    font-style: italic}
paragraph {display: block; margin-top: 10}
```

Figure 8.10 shows what Listing 8.14 looks like in Internet Explorer. As the figure shows, the border appears around the title as it should.

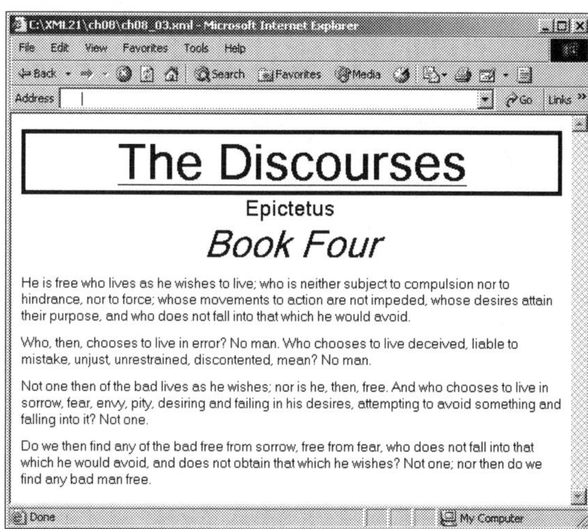

FIGURE 8.10
Giving a block element a border.

It's also worth noting that the `border` style lets you set an element's width, style, and color. For example, here's how you can use it to create a solid 6-point-thick red border:

```
P {border 6pt solid red}
```

Styling Alignments

You can customize alignments and margins. Here's a sampling of applicable properties:

- **`line-height`**—Specifies the height of each line. You can set this property to an absolute size or to a percentage, such as 150% (which creates 1½ spacing).
- **`margin-bottom`**—Specifies the bottom margin of a block element. You can set this property to a size.

- **margin-left**—Specifies the left margin of a block element. You can set this property to a size.
- **margin-right**—Specifies the right margin of a block element. You can set this property to a size.
- **margin-top**—Specifies the top margin of a block element. You can set this property to a size.
- **text-align**—Specifies the alignment of text. You can set this property to `left`, `right`, `center`, or `justify`.
- **text-indent**—Specifies the indentation of the first line of block-level elements. You can set this property to an absolute value such as `12px` (12 pixels) or `6pt` (6 points).
- **vertical-align**—Specifies the vertical alignment of text. You can set this property to `baseline`, `sub`, `super`, `top`, `text-top`, `middle`, `bottom`, or `text-bottom`.

Listing 8.15 shows an example that indents the text in `<paragraph>` elements and moves it all to the right by setting a left margin of 20 pixels.

LISTING 8.15 Using Margin Styles (`ch08_15.css`)

```
title {display: block; font-size: 36pt; font-weight: bold;
    text-align: center; text-decoration: underline}
philosopher {display: block; font-size: 16pt;
    text-align: center}
book {display: block; font-size: 28pt; text-align: center;
    font-style: italic}
paragraph {display: block; text-indent: 30px; margin-left: 20;
    margin-top: 10}
```

Figure 8.11 shows what Listing 8.15 looks like in Internet Explorer. The figure shows that the text is indeed formatted as it should be—each paragraph is indented, and the whole paragraph of text has been moved to the right.

Note that, as with other styles, support for border and margin styles varies by browser. For example, Netscape Navigator doesn't support many margin styles.

Styling Images

You can even display images in some browsers while formatting XML documents. Here's a sampling of the applicable properties:

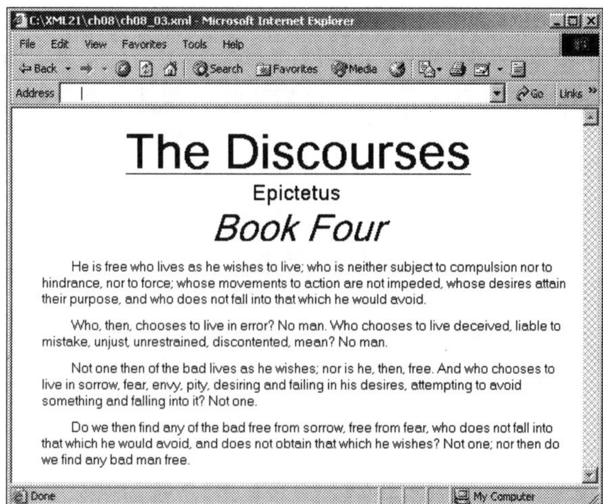

FIGURE 8.11
Indenting text and setting margins.

- **`background-image`**—Specifies a background image for the element. You can set this property to a URL.
- **`background-repeat`**—Specifies whether the background image should be tiled in a repeating fashion. You can set this property to `repeat`, `repeat-x`, `repeat-y`, or `no-repeat`.
- **`background-attachment`**—Specifies whether the background scrolls when the rest of the document is scrolled.
- **`background-position`**—Specifies the initial position of the background image. You can set this property to an x,y coordinate, keeping in mind that the origin is at the upper left (for example, `background-position: 10px 20px`).

For example, you could add a background image when you style the XML document by using the `background-image` property. In this case, you need to supply the URL at which the browser can find the image, and you can do that when you style the `<paragraph>` element, as shown in Listing 8.16.

LISTING 8.16 Using Image Styles (`ch08_16.css`)

```
title {display: block; font-size: 36pt; font-weight: bold;
    text-align: center; text-decoration: underline}
philosopher {display: block; font-size: 16pt;
    text-align: center}
book {display: block; font-size: 28pt; text-align: center;
    font-style: italic}
paragraph {display: block; margin-top: 10px;
    background-image: url(image.jpg);
    background-repeat: repeat}
```

For example, you'll use an image file, `image.jpg`, that displays a star in light gray. (This image file is included in the downloadable code for this book.) Because this image will appear behind paragraph text, you can condense all the `<paragraph>` text into one element for this example (see Listing 8.17) so that you can see the background image clearly.

LISTING 8.17 Using One `<paragraph>` Element (`ch08_17.css`)

```
<?xml version="1.0" standalone="yes"?>
<?xml-stylesheet type="text/css" href="ch08_16.css"?>
<document>
    <title>The Discourses</title>
    <philosopher>Epictetus</philosopher>
    <book>Book Four</book>
    <paragraph>
        He is free who lives as he wishes to live; who is neither
        subject to compulsion nor to hindrance, nor to force;
        whose movements to action are not impeded, whose desires
        attain their purpose, and who does not fall into that which
        he would avoid.
        Who, then, chooses to live in error? No man. Who chooses
        to live deceived, liable to mistake, unjust, unrestrained,
        discontented, mean? No man.
        Not one then of the bad lives as he wishes; nor is he,
        then, free. And who chooses to live in sorrow, fear, envy,
        pity, desiring and failing in his desires, attempting to
        avoid something and falling into it? Not one.
        Do we then find any of the bad free from sorrow, free from
        fear, who does not fall into that which he would avoid, and
        does not obtain that which he wishes? Not one; nor then do
        we find any bad man free.
    </paragraph>
</document>
```

Figure 8.12 shows what Listing 8.17 looks like in Internet Explorer. As the figure shows, the background star appears behind the text.

In addition to using an image as a background image, you can also display an image as a foreground image, as you would in any Web page. To do that, you create a custom element whose express purpose is to display the image.

For example, you'll create an image element named `<image>` and make it display the image by using the CSS property `background-image`. You can also specify the height and width to use when displaying an element by using the CSS properties `height` and `width` (you can use 60×100 pixels, which is the size of `image.jpg`). Finally, you can indicate whether the image will float to the right or left of text by using the `float` property, which is shown to the left in Listing 8.18.

FIGURE 8.12

Displaying a background image.

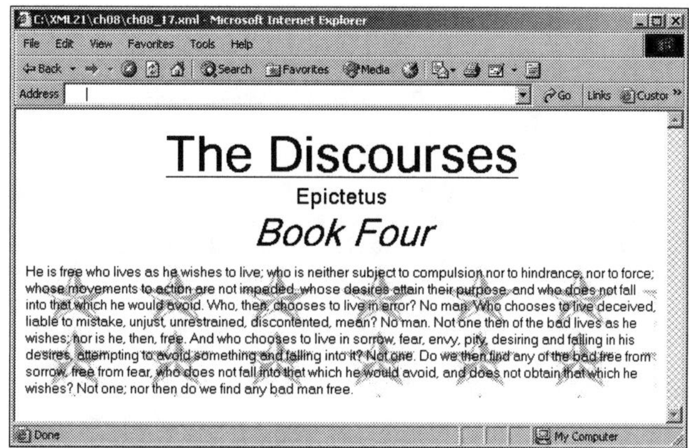

LISTING 8.18 Styling a Foreground Image (ch08_18.css)

```
title {display: block; font-size: 36pt; font-weight: bold;
    text-align: center; text-decoration: underline}
philosopher {display: block; font-size: 16pt;
    text-align: center}
book {display: block; font-size: 28pt; text-align: center;
    font-style: italic}
paragraph {display: block; margin-top: 10}
image {background-image: url(image.jpg);
    height: 60px;
    width: 100px;
    float: left}
```

You can see the new <image> element in the new version of the XML document, ch08_19.xml, in Listing 8.19.

LISTING 8.19 Displaying a Foreground Image (ch08_19.xml)

```
<?xml version="1.0" standalone="yes"?>
<?xml-stylesheet type="text/css" href="ch08_18.css"?>
<document>
    <title>The Discourses</title>
    <philosopher>Epictetus</philosopher>
    <book>Book Four</book>
    <image/>
    <paragraph>
        He is free who lives as he wishes to live; who is neither
        subject to compulsion nor to hindrance, nor to force;
        whose movements to action are not impeded, whose desires
        attain their purpose, and who does not fall into that which
        he would avoid.
```

LISTING 8.19 continued

```
        Who, then, chooses to live in error? No man. Who chooses
        to live deceived, liable to mistake, unjust, unrestrained,
        discontented, mean? No man.
        Not one then of the bad lives as he wishes; nor is he,
        then, free. And who chooses to live in sorrow, fear, envy,
        pity, desiring and failing in his desires, attempting to
        avoid something and falling into it? Not one.
        Do we then find any of the bad free from sorrow, free from
        fear, who does not fall into that which he would avoid, and
        does not obtain that which he wishes? Not one; nor then do
        we find any bad man free.
    </paragraph>
</document>
```

Figure 8.13 shows Listing 8.19 in Internet Explorer. As shown in the figure, the image is now positioned so that it appears in the foreground, and it floats to the left of the text.

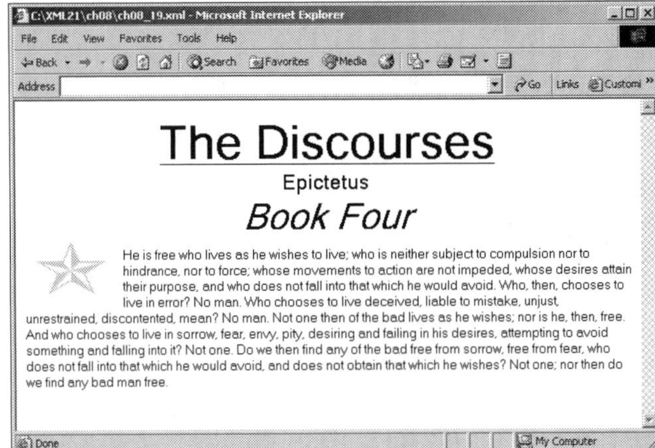

FIGURE 8.13
Styling and showing an image.

All this is fine if you want to let the browser position an image as it likes when it determines the text flow in its display, but you can also specify exactly where you want images and other elements to appear by expressly positioning elements, as discussed in the following section.

Positioning Elements

By using CSS, you can set the positions of elements—and this was a big advance in HTML. Before CSS let you position items in a Web page, HTML authors used HTML tables to make sure that elements were at the correct locations rather than floating as the

Web browser determined. Now, however, you can use CSS to specify positions in HTML and XML.

To specify position, you use the CSS positioning properties. Here's a sampling of the positioning properties that are available:

- **position**—Specifies an element's position. You can set this property to either absolute or relative.
- **top**—Specifies the location of the top of the element.
- **bottom**—Specifies the location the bottom of the element.
- **left**—Specifies the location of the left edge of the element.
- **right**—Specifies the location of the right edge of the element.

For example, say that you want to place the star image right on top of the middle of your text. To do that, you can set the position property of the <image> element to absolute and assign values to the top and left properties, as shown in Listing 8.20.

LISTING 8.20 Positioning a Foreground Image (ch08_20.css)

```
title {display: block; font-size: 36pt; font-weight: bold;
    text-align: center; text-decoration: underline}
philosopher {display: block; font-size: 16pt;
    text-align: center}
book {display: block; font-size: 28pt; text-align: center;
    font-style: italic}
paragraph {display: block; margin-top: 10}
image {background-image: url(image.jpg);
    height: 60px; width: 100px; position:absolute;
    left:250; top:180}
```

Figure 8.14 shows Listing 8.20 in Internet Explorer. In the figure, the image appears right on top of the text. In fact, you can even position text on top of other text. As shown in the figure, absolute positioning lets you specify the exact location of data items from an XML document in the final display.

Besides absolute positioning, there's another option—relative positioning. In relative positioning, you position items relative to the locations they would have in the usual flow of elements as the browser would display them. In this case, you set the position property to relative.

To see how this works, take a look at Listing 8.21, which formats two new elements, <superscript> and <subscript>, to raise and lower text from its normal flow.

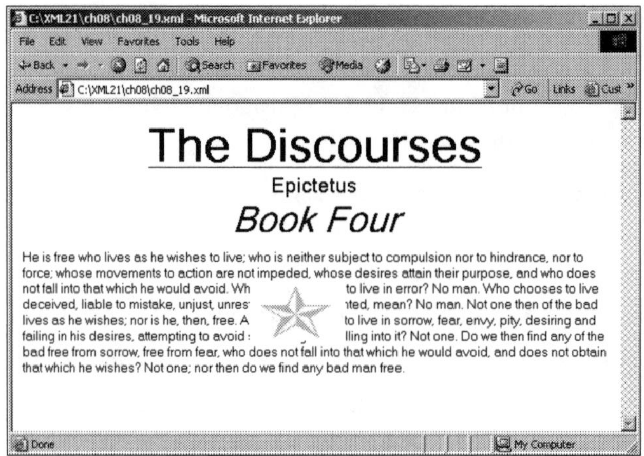

FIGURE 8.14
Positioning an item in absolute terms.

LISTING 8.21 Displaying a Foreground Image (`ch08_21.css`)

```
title {display: block; font-size: 36pt; font-weight: bold;
    text-align: center; text-decoration: underline}
philosopher {display: block; font-size: 16pt;
    text-align: center}
book {display: block; font-size: 28pt; text-align: center;
    font-style: italic}
paragraph {display: block; margin-top: 10}
superscript {position:relative; top:-5}
subscript {position:relative; top:5}
```

Now you can put the `<superscript>` and `<subscript>` elements to work in an XML document, as shown in Listing 8.22, which includes a few changes to Epictetus' original text. Note that because you haven't made `<superscript>` and `<subscript>` block elements, you can use them inline (that is, you don't have to give each of these elements its own line of text, as you do for block elements), as in this example.

LISTING 8.22 Using Relative Positioning (`ch08_22.xml`)

```
<?xml version="1.0" standalone="yes"?>
<?xml-stylesheet type="text/css" href="ch08_21.css"?>
<document>
    <title>The Discourses</title>
    <philosopher>Epictetus</philosopher>
    <book>Book Four</book>
    <paragraph>
        He is free who lives as he wishes to live; who is neither
        subject to compulsion nor to hindrance, nor to force;
```

LISTING 8.22 continued

```
        whose movements to action are not impeded, whose desires
        attain their purpose, and who does not fall into that which
        he would avoid.
    </paragraph>
    <paragraph>
        Who, then, chooses to live on <subscript>roller</subscript>
        <superscript>coasters</superscript>? No man. Who chooses
        to live deceived, liable to mistake, unjust, unrestrained,
        discontented, mean? No man.
    </paragraph>
    <paragraph>
        Not one then of the bad lives as he wishes; nor is he,
        then, free. And who chooses to live in sorrow, fear, envy,
        pity, desiring and failing in his desires, attempting to
        avoid something and falling into it? Not one.
    </paragraph>
    <paragraph>
        Do we then find any of the bad free from sorrow, free from
        fear, who does not fall into that which he would avoid, and
        does not obtain that which he wishes? Not one; nor then do
        we find any bad man free.
    </paragraph>
</document>
```

Figure 8.15 shows Listing 8.22 in Internet Explorer, with the `<superscript>` and `<subscript>` elements used in the first line of the second paragraph.

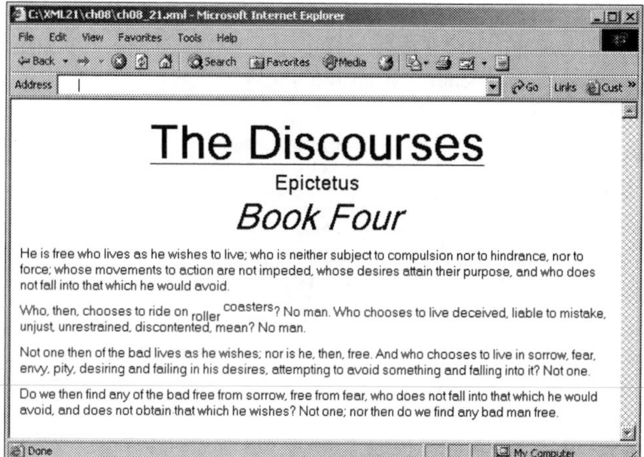

FIGURE 8.15

Positioning elements in relative terms.

Styling Lists

You can show HTML-style lists in some browsers when you format an XML document. Here's a sampling of the applicable properties:

- **`list-item`**—Creates a list when assigned to the `display` property.
- **`list-style-image`**—Specifies the image that should appear in front of each item in the list. This property is not supported by many browsers.
- **`list-style-type`**—Specifies the list item marker, which appears before each list item. You can set this property to various values, such as `disc`, `circle`, `square`, `decimal`, `lowercase Roman`, and `uppercase Roman`. Not all values are supported by all browsers.

For example, you can turn the paragraphs in the earlier example into a list and display a circle before each paragraph. You can see how this works in Listing 8.23.

LISTING 8.23 Using Relative Positioning (`ch08_23.css`)

```
title {display: block; font-size: 36pt; font-weight: bold;
    text-align: center; text-decoration: underline}
philosopher {display: block; font-size: 16pt;
    text-align: center}
book {display: block; font-size: 28pt; text-align: center;
    font-style: italic}
paragraph {display:list-item; margin-left: 10px;
    margin-top:10; list-style-type: circle}
```

Figure 8.16 shows Listing 8.23 in Internet Explorer. As you can see, a small circle does indeed appear before each paragraph's text.

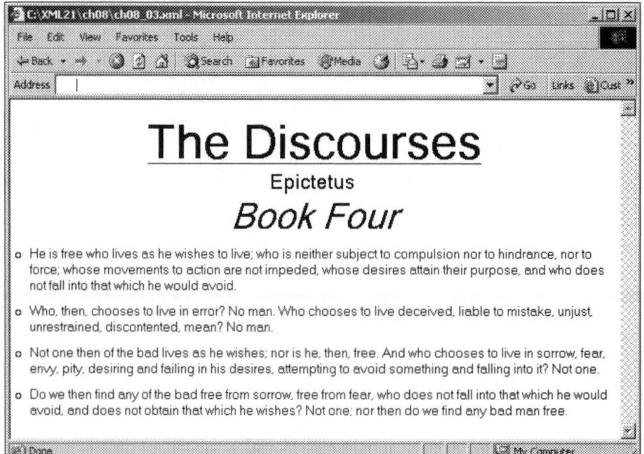

FIGURE 8.16
Displaying a list.

Styling Tables

When it comes to displaying the data in an XML document, using tables is a very popular option. Visually, it's easier to see all your data arrayed horizontally and vertically in tabular format than in an XML document, where you have to look past the markup. Here are the table-styling properties you can assign to the `display` property:

- **`table`**—Indicates that an element encloses a table. Translates to the HTML `<table>` element.
- **`table-caption`**—Gives a caption for the table.
- **`table-cell`**—Creates a table cell. This property translates to the HTML `<td>` element.
- **`table-column`**—Indicates that an element describes a column of cells.
- **`table-column-group`**—Indicates that an element groups one or more columns.
- **`table-footer-group`**—Indicates a table footer group.
- **`table-header-group`**—Indicates a table header group.
- **`table-row`**—Creates an element that contains a row of cells. This property translates to the HTML `<tr>` element.
- **`table-row-group`**—Indicates that an element groups one or more rows.

To see how this works in an example, you need some data that can be displayed as a table. For example, you can use the mortgage data shown in Table 8.1, which lists various borrowers and the amounts they have borrowed. Listing 8.24 shows this data in XML format. As you can see, the XML document doesn't present its data nearly as effectively as the table does. Listing 8.25 converts the XML document into an HTML table.

TABLE 8.1 Mortgage Data

First Name	*Last Name*	*Loan Amount*
Fred	Turner	$100,000
Bill	Saunders	$120,000
Ed	Johnson	$130,000
Sam	Watson	$140,000
James	White	$150,000

LISTING 8.24 An XML Document That Holds Tabular Data (ch08_24.xml)

```
<?xml version="1.0" standalone="yes"?>
<?xml-stylesheet type="text/css" href="ch08_25.css"?>
<document>
  <headers>
    <header>First Name</header>
    <header>Last Name</header>
    <header>Loan Amount</header>
  </headers>
  <mortgages>
    <mortgage>
      <firstName>Fred</firstName>
      <lastName>Turner</lastName>
      <amount>$100,000</amount>
    </mortgage>
    <mortgage>
      <firstName>Bill</firstName>
      <lastName>Saunders</lastName>
      <amount>$120,000</amount>
    </mortgage>
    <mortgage>
      <firstName>Ed</firstName>
      <lastName>Johnson</lastName>
      <amount>$130,000</amount>
    </mortgage>
    <mortgage>
      <firstName>Sam</firstName>
      <lastName>Watson</lastName>
      <amount>$140,000</amount>
    </mortgage>
    <mortgage>
      <firstName>James</firstName>
      <lastName>White</lastName>
      <amount>$150,000</amount>
    </mortgage>
  </mortgages>
</document>
```

LISTING 8.25 Styling XML Data into a Table (ch08_25.css)

```
document {display:table; border-style:solid}
headers {display:table-header-group;}
header {display:table-cell; padding:6px;
    background-color:lightblue; font-weight:bold;
    border-style:solid}
mortgages {display:table-row-group}
mortgage {display:table-row;}
```

LISTING 8.25 continued

```
firstName {display:table-cell; padding:6px;
    border-bottom:solid 1px}
lastName {display:table-cell;
    padding:6px; border-bottom:solid 1px}
amount {display:table-cell;
    border-bottom:solid 1px}
```

As you can see in Listing 8.25, you set the `display` property to `table` for the document element `<document>`, which will be converted to an HTML `<table>` element. Setting the CSS property `display` to `table-row` allows you to convert the `<mortgage>` elements to HTML `<tr>` elements, and so on. Figure 8.17 shows Listing 8.25 in Netscape Navigator. (Note that Internet Explorer doesn't handle this formatting well.) As the figure shows, the data appears in the browser as it should, in tabular form.

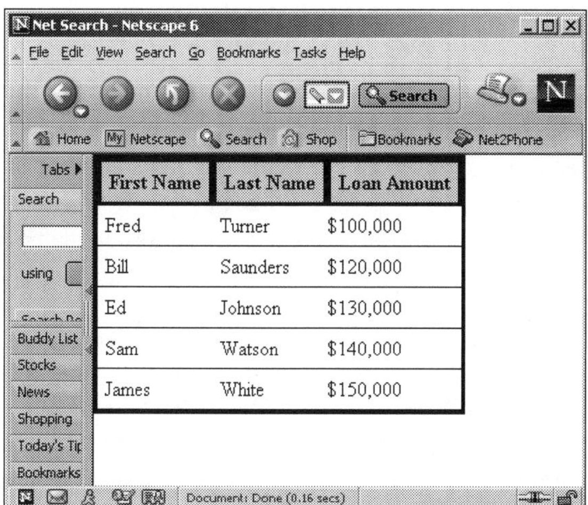

FIGURE 8.17
Displaying a table.

Summary

CSS is a W3C specification, and you can find the W3C recommendations for CSS1 and CSS2 at `http://www.w3.org/TR/REC-CSS1` and `http://www.w3.org/TR/REC-CSS2`; CSS3 is still under development.

Style sheets are collections of style rules, each of which shows how to format an XML element. A rule is made up of a selector, which is the element or elements you want to format, and the rule specification itself, which shows the format.

Today you've seen various ways of creating selectors. You can specify which XML element you want to format directly by name. You can create style classes and use the class attribute in browsers such as Internet Explorer. You can also select elements by ID value.

Rule specifications are made up of CSS property/value pairs in a semicolon-separated list, surrounded by curly braces. There are hundreds of available properties, such as `font-weight`, `text-align`, and `text-decoration`. You can assign values by listing those values after a property name in a rule specification, like this:

```
{font-weight: bold; text-align: center; text-decoration: underline}
```

Knowing which CSS properties are available is essential for effective use of CSS formatting. Today's discussion focuses on the CSS properties you can use and what values you can assign to them.

A style sheet rule includes both a selector and a rule specification, like this:

```
title {display: block; font-size: 36pt; font-weight: bold;
    text-align: center; text-decoration: underline}
```

One important CSS property is `display`, which, among other things, lets you create block elements when you assign the value `block` to it. Block elements are displayed on their own lines. If you don't make an element a block element, it will be an inline element by default; inline elements are arranged by the browser, and they follow the normal flow of items the browser displays. If you want to format elements whose data follows that flow, you should use inline elements. If you want a data item to appear on its own line, you should use a block element.

Today you took a look at text properties, including how to set font face, font size, font weight (such as bold), text alignment, indentation, and decoration (such as underlining and overlining of text). You also saw how to specify colors and backgrounds, as well as how to style borders. And you saw that you can even display images along with your XML data by using CSS properties such `background-image` and `background-repeat`.

You can use CSS to position elements, both in absolute and relative terms. This ability to position what you want where you want in a Web page is responsible for much of CSS's popularity among Web page authors. As you've seen, you can position both text and images as you like by using CSS positioning.

Today you also discussed formatting lists and tables by using CSS. This is particularly useful because it helps you format and display data effectively.

After you've created a CSS style sheet, one way of connecting that style sheet to an XML document is by using the `<?xml-stylesheet?>` processing instruction. Although not an official part of XML, this processing instruction has become an accepted convention. It's important to bear in mind, however, as you use CSS, that different browsers have different levels of support, and the results you get often differ from browser to browser.

As you've seen today, the major HTML browsers are set up to handle and display XML by using CSS, which is a good idea because CSS is in widespread use with HTML. On the other hand, CSS is not an ideal solution for displaying XML data visually because CSS has its own, very non-XML, syntax. There is an XML solution—Extensible Stylesheet Language Transformations (XSLT)—as you'll see tomorrow. XSLT is written in XML, and it lets you target the data in XML documents better than CSS. All the details are coming up tomorrow.

Q&A

Q Is it possible to embed text when using CSS style sheets? For example, what if I want to enclose element names I display in angle brackets, such as `<Jim Thompson>`?

A You can indeed embed text when formatting XML by using CSS. For example, to add < before the data in the `<philosopher>` element, you could use this style rule on its own line in your style sheet:

```
philosopher:before {content:"\003C"}
```

To add > after the data in the `<philosopher>` element, you could use this:

```
philosopher:after {content:"\003E"}
```

Q What are CSS "shortcut" properties?

A Shortcut properties let you specify a number of properties at the same time. For example, by using the `border` shortcut property that you've already seen, you can set `border:inset 1px red;`. You don't need to use a shortcut property for this, of course; the same task can be handled by other properties, such as `border-width` and `border-color`. You have a choice of using the standard properties or using the shortcut properties.

Workshop

This workshop tests whether you understand the concepts discussed today. It's a good idea to make sure you can answer these questions before pressing on to tomorrow's work. Answers to the quiz can be found in Appendix A, “Quiz Answers.”

Quiz

1. How can you set font size to 32 points by using CSS?
2. How can you make an element a block element?
3. How can you center text by using CSS?
4. How can you underline text by using CSS?
5. How can you add 10 pixels of vertical space before an element by using CSS?

Exercises

1. Using `ch08_01.xml` (the original Epictetus example from today’s discussion), create a style sheet that displays all paragraphs as block elements and the text in those paragraphs in 12-point, underlined text.
2. Elaborate the style sheet you created in Exercise 1 so that the paragraph text is colored red and appears in italic, with 15 pixels of vertical space before each paragraph. Also create `<footnote>` and `<footnoteText>` elements that let you add superscript footnote numbering to the text and 10-point explanatory text for each footnote.

PART II

DAY 9

Formatting XML by Using XSLT

Yesterday you saw that you can use CSS to format XML documents in the major browsers (Internet Explorer and Netscape Navigator). However, there's a native XML way to format XML documents for display—using Extensible Stylesheet Language Transformations (XSLT), which is what you'll discuss today. Here's an overview of today's topics:

- Transforming XML in the server, in the client, and with standalone programs
- Creating an XSLT style sheet
- Creating and applying templates
- Getting node values
- Handling multiple selections
- Using the `match` and `select` attributes
- Matching element, processing instructions, and other nodes

- Working with XPath
- Creating XPath node tests
- Copying nodes to the output document
- Making decisions in XSLT based on input data

Introducing XSLT

Today you're going to see how to use XSLT to manipulate, extract, and format data in XML documents without having to resort to programming your own XML processors. XSLT is actually part of the larger specification Extensible Stylesheet Language (XSL). XSLT has become the most popular part of XSL because it's relatively easy to use and it lets you transform XML documents into other formats, such as HTML or plain text. XSL, which you'll see more about tomorrow, is a more general language that lets you format XML in great detail.

XSLT is a specification of the W3C, and in fact it's been a recommendation since November 16, 1999. The W3C recommendation for XSLT 1.0, the current version, is at `http://www.w3.org/TR/xslt`. XSLT 2.0 is in the works, but it's only a working draft at this point. (There actually was an XSLT 1.1, but it was not continued after the working draft stage.) The current version of the XSLT 2.0 Working Draft is at `http://www.w3.org/TR/xslt20`.

TIP

> There is some support for XSLT 2.0 in the Saxon XSLT processor, which you can download for free from `http://saxon.sourceforge.net`. Most XSLT processors only support XSLT 1.0 these days, however.

You use XSLT to transform XML documents, and you can reformat the documents' data as you want. You can use XSLT to transform XML into any text-based format, such as HTML, plain text, rich text format (RTF), and Microsoft Word. The most common transformation is from XML documents to HTML documents, and that's the kind of transformation you'll mainly work with today. XSLT is popular partly because by using it, you can manipulate the data in XML documents without having to write any software.

To transform XML by using XSLT, you need two documents—an XML document you want to transform and an XSLT style sheet. (Note that XSLT style sheets are also XML documents.) Let's start with an example to see how things work. Say that, as a part of a federal watchdog committee, you're in charge of maintaining data about U.S. states, such as what the state's flower is, what their population is, and so on. Listing 9.1 shows an XML document (ch09_01.xml) that does this. ch09_01.xml will be your XML document for today; as you can see, it lists several states, their population, state bird, area, and so on. Today you'll see how to use XSLT to pick data out of this document selectively.

LISTING 9.1 A Sample XML Document (ch09_01.xml)

```
<?xml version="1.0" encoding ="UTF-8"?>
<states>

    <state>
        <name>California</name>
        <population units="people">33871648</population><!--2000 census-->
        <capital>Sacramento</capital>
        <bird>Quail</bird>
        <flower>Golden Poppy</flower>
        <area units="square miles">155959</area>
    </state>

    <state>
        <name>Massachusetts</name>
        <population units="people">6349097</population><!--2000 census-->
        <capital>Boston</capital>
        <bird>Chickadee</bird>
        <flower>Mayflower</flower>
        <area units="square miles">7840</area>
    </state>

    <state>
        <name>New York</name>
        <population units="people">18976457</population><!--2000 census-->
        <capital>Albany</capital>
        <bird>Bluebird</bird>
        <flower>Rose</flower>
        <area units="square miles">47214</area>
    </state>

</states>
```

To extract some data from ch09_01.xml, you need an XSLT style sheet, like the one shown in Listing 9.2, which is called ch09_02.xsl. (XSLT style sheets usually use the extension .xsl.) This example just strips out the names of the states and places them into a basic HTML document.

Listing 9.2 An XSLT Style Sheet (`ch09_02.xsl`)

```
<?xml version="1.0" encoding="UTF-8"?>
<xsl:stylesheet version="1.0" xmlns:xsl="http://www.w3.org/1999/XSL/Transform">

    <xsl:template match="states">
        <HTML>
            <BODY>
                <xsl:apply-templates/>
            </BODY>
        </HTML>
    </xsl:template>

    <xsl:template match="state">
        <P>
            <xsl:value-of select="name"/>
        </P>
    </xsl:template>

</xsl:stylesheet>
```

At this point, then, you have an XML document to work with and a style sheet to transform it. How do you put the two together to actually make the transformation occur?

Transforming XML by Using XSLT

There are three different places where XSLT transformations can happen:

- **In the server**—A server program, such as a .NET or JavaServer Pages (JSP) program, can use XSLT to transform an XML document and send it to the client program (such as a browser).
- **In the client**—A client program, such as an HTML browser, can perform XSLT transformations. For example, Internet Explorer fully supports XSLT 1.0 support.
- **With a separate program**—You can use one of the many standalone programs available to perform XSLT transformations.

The following sections look briefly at these possibilities.

Server-Side XSLT

There are various ways to handle XSLT on Web servers. One of the most popular is to use JSP because Java versions 1.4 and later include complete XSLT 1.0 support. To see how this works, you don't have to write any JSP—it's already been done for you in an example written to work with the Tomcat JSP server in `ch09_03.jsp`, which is shown in Listing 9.3. (Note that you don't have to know any JSP in this book.) Figure 9.1 shows this transformation —which uses the style sheet `ch09_02.xsl` to strip the names of the states out of ch09_01.xml—using ch09_03.jsp and the Tomcat Web server. If you use this method, people who want to look at the results of your XSLT transformations don't have to do anything special—it's all been done for them on the server.

9

LISTING 9.3 A JSP Page (ch09_03.jsp)

```
<%@ page import="javax.xml.transform.*, javax.xml.transform.stream.*,
  java.io.*" %>

<%
    try
    {
        TransformerFactory transformerfactory =
            TransformerFactory.newInstance();
        Transformer transformer = transformerfactory.newTransformer
            (new StreamSource(new File
            (application.getRealPath("/") + "ch09_02.xsl")));

        transformer.transform(new StreamSource(new File(application.getRealPath
            ("/") + "ch09_01.xml")),
        new StreamResult(new File(application.getRealPath("/") +
            "result.html")));

    }
    catch(Exception e) {}

    FileReader filereader = new FileReader(application.getRealPath("/") +
        "result.html");
    BufferedReader bufferedreader = new BufferedReader(filereader);
    String textString;

    while((textString = bufferedreader.readLine()) != null) {
%>
        <%= textString %>
<%
        }
        filereader.close();
%>
```

What's actually happened here is that the names of the states were stripped out and placed into an HTML document, which looks like this (the indentation, which doesn't matter to Web browsers, has been cleaned up here):

```
<HTML>
   <BODY>
        <P>California</P>
        <P>Massachusetts</P>
        <P>New York</P>
    </BODY>
</HTML>
```

FIGURE 9.1
Using XSLT and JSP in the server.

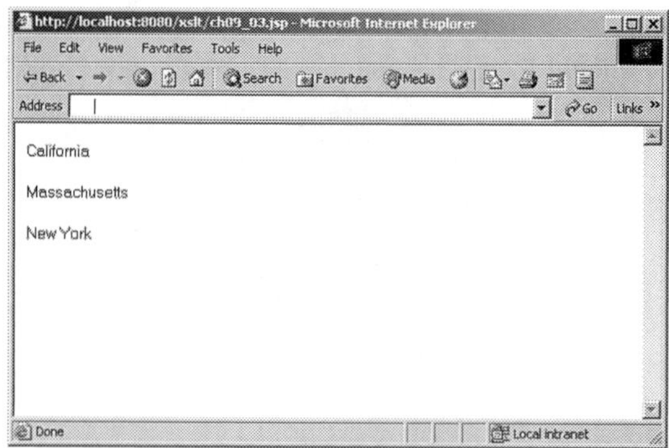

However, server-side programming is not something most XML authors are conversant in. There are other options as well—including using Web browsers such as Internet Explorer, as described in the following section.

Client-Side XSLT

Internet Explorer (but not, unfortunately, Netscape Navigator), lets you perform XSLT 1.0 transformations. All you have to do is connect the XSLT style sheet to the XML document by using an `<?xml-stylesheet?>` processing instruction, like this:

```
<?xml-stylesheet type="text/xsl" href="ch09_02.xsl"?>
```

Note that some other XSLT processors require `type="text/xml"` rather than `type="text/xsl"`. Listing 9.4 shows the Internet Explorer–enabled version of the XML document in `ch09_04.xml`, where you can see the `<?xml-stylesheet?>` processing instruction at work.

LISTING 9.4 An XML Document (`ch09_04.xml`)

```
<?xml version="1.0" encoding ="UTF-8"?>
<?xml-stylesheet type="text/xsl" href="ch09_02.xsl"?>
<states>

    <state>
        <name>California</name>
        <population units="people">33871648</population><!--2000 census-->
        <capital>Sacramento</capital>
        <bird>Quail</bird>
        <flower>Golden Poppy</flower>
        <area units="square miles">155959</area>
    </state>
```

LISTING 9.4 continued

```
        .
        .
        .
    <state>
        <name>New York</name>
        <population units="people">18976457</population><!--2000 census-->
        <capital>Albany</capital>
        <bird>Bluebird</bird>
        <flower>Rose</flower>
        <area units="square miles">47214</area>
    </state>

</states>
```


Figure 9.2 shows Listing 9.4 in Internet Explorer. Note that these results are just like the results shown in Figure 9.1, when using JSP on the server (except for the URL in the title bar, of course). In this case, however, you're using Internet Explorer itself to perform client-side transformations. This is probably the most accessible way to perform XSLT transformations for most people.

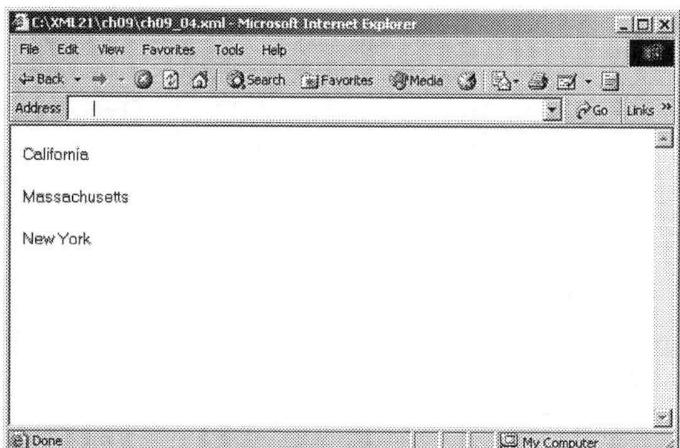

FIGURE 9.2
Using XSLT in the client.

Besides using server-side and client-side XSLT transformations, you can also transform XML by using XSLT with standalone programs.

Standalone Programs and XSLT

Some programs perform XSLT transformations for you. There's a great deal of XSLT support built in to the Java programming language, versions 1.4 and later, so many of the transformation programs use Java. Because I don't expect you to work with Java at this point, I've provided an already written Java example in `ch09_05.java`, which is shown in Listing 9.5, in the downloadable code for this book, along with the compiled Java class file, `ch09_05.class`. If you have Java installed (it's available for free at `http://java.sun.com/j2se/1.4.1/download.html`, as you'll discuss on Day 16, "Using Java and .NET: DOM"), you can transform `ch09_01.xml` by using `ch09_02.xsl` and place the result into a file named `formatted.html`, like this:

```
%java ch09_05 ch09_01.xml ch09_02.xsl formatted.html
```

LISTING 9.5 A Java Program (`ch09_05.java`)

```
import java.io.*;
import javax.xml.transform.*;
import javax.xml.transform.stream.*;

public class ch09_05
{
    public static void main(String args[])
    {

        try
        {
            TransformerFactory tf = TransformerFactory.newInstance();
            Transformer tr = tf.newTransformer(new StreamSource
                (new File(args[1])));

            tr.transform(new StreamSource(new File(args[0])),
            new StreamResult(new File(args[2])));
        }
        catch(Exception ex) {}
    }
}
```

`formatted.html` looks just like the document Internet Explorer created for you in the preceding section:

```
<HTML>
   <BODY>
        <P>California</P>
        <P>Massachusetts</P>
        <P>New York</P>
    </BODY>
</HTML>
```

Writing XSLT Style Sheets

Now that you've seen three different places to create XSLT transformations—on a Web server, in a client browser, and using a standalone program—it's time to see how to create your own XSLT style sheets.

To work with XSLT, you have to know how XSLT views XML documents. In XSLT terms, an XML document is a *tree* of *nodes*. The tree starts with the *root node*, and it branches out from that point. The root node corresponds to the very beginning of the document; it's not the same as the document element. The root node corresponds to the very beginning of the document, so you have access to the document's prolog, which comes before the document element.

Each distinct item in an XML document is considered a node—comments, processing instructions, elements, even the text inside elements. From XSLT's point of view, there are seven types of nodes, and you're going to see how to build style sheets that use all of them:

- **Attribute**—An attribute.
- **Comment**—The text of a comment (excluding the `<!--` and `-->` parts).
- **Element**—An element.
- **Namespace**—The namespace's URI.
- **Processing instruction**—The text of the processing instruction (excluding `<?` and `?>`).
- **Root node**—The very start of the document, before even the document element. XSLT gives you access to the root node, which comes before the document element, in order to give you access to the prolog, such as the XML declaration.
- **Text**—The text of the node.

To handle and search the various nodes in XML documents, the XSLT specification defines a number of elements, just as you saw for XML schemas in Day 6, "Creating Valid XML Documents: XML Schemas." It also uses an XML-specific language, XML Path Language (XPath), to let you specify exactly what nodes you're looking for.

You'll see how this works by dissecting the style sheet `ch09_02.xsl`. You started that document with an XML declaration and by using the `<xsl:stylesheet>` element. (Note that this is *not* the `<?xsl:stylesheet?>` processing instruction you can use in XML documents to connect style sheets to XML documents.) In this element, you associate the `xsl` namespace with the URI `"http://www.w3.org/1999/XSL/Transform"`, which is the official namespace for XSLT:

```
<?xml version="1.0" encoding="UTF-8"?>
<xsl:stylesheet version="1.0" xmlns:xsl="http://www.w3.org/1999/XSL/Transform">
        .
        .
        .
```

To indicate what elements you want to locate and work with, you use the `<xsl:template>` element to create an XSLT template. A *template* lets you match a node or nodes in the XML document and specify what you want to do with the contained data. For example, to match the document element `<states>` in the sample XML document, you can use this `<xsl:template>` element:

```
<?xml version="1.0" encoding="UTF-8"?>
<xsl:stylesheet version="1.0" xmlns:xsl="http://www.w3.org/1999/XSL/Transform">

    <xsl:template match="states">
        .
        .
        .
    </xsl:template>
        .
        .
        .
</xsl:stylesheet>
```

Now the XSLT processor will look through your XML document and match the `<states>` element to the template. Technically speaking, what's happening here is that when the XSLT processor opens the document, it starts at the root node and searches for templates that match the children of the root node, which means that `<xsl:template match="states">` will match because `<states>` is a child of the root node; `<xsl:template match="state">` would not match, however, because `<state>` is a grandchild of the root node.

In the sample template, you specify what you want the matched element to be replaced with in the formatted output document. For example, if you wanted to replace the document element, including all its child nodes, with the HTML `<HTML><BODY><H1>Hello!</H1></BODY></HTML>`, you could use this:

```
<?xml version="1.0" encoding="UTF-8"?>
<xsl:stylesheet version="1.0" xmlns:xsl="http://www.w3.org/1999/XSL/Transform">

    <xsl:template match="states">
        <HTML><BODY><H1>Hello!</H1></BODY></HTML>
    </xsl:template>
        .
        .
        .
</xsl:stylesheet>
```

Now the resulting output document will only hold <HTML><BODY><H1>Hello!</H1></BODY></HTML>. Although this shows how templates work, it's not too useful in itself. In the ch09_02.xsl example, you actually want to produce this kind of output:

```
<HTML>
   <BODY>
        <P>California</P>
        <P>Massachusetts</P>
        <P>New York</P>
    </BODY>
</HTML>
```


To do this, you need to strip data out of the <state> elements in the XML document, and to do that, you can use some additional templates. Now that you've matched the <states> element, you can indicate that you want to match child nodes inside the <states> element by using additional templates. You indicate this by using the <xsl:apply-templates> element:

```
<?xml version="1.0" encoding="UTF-8"?>
<xsl:stylesheet version="1.0" xmlns:xsl="http://www.w3.org/1999/XSL/Transform">

    <xsl:template match="states">
        <HTML>
            <BODY>
                <xsl:apply-templates/>
            </BODY>
        </HTML>
    </xsl:template>
        .
        .
        .
</xsl:stylesheet>
```

This example says is that the XSLT processor should place <HTML><BODY> into the output document, followed by the results of applying any other templates in the style sheet that match the child nodes of the <states> node, followed by </BODY></HTML>.

Using <xsl:apply-templates>

You use the <xsl:apply-templates> element to indicate that you have other templates to use on the child nodes of the current node. For example, say that you just wanted to replace each <state> element with the placeholder text "State data will appear here!" in the output document. How could you do that?

You've already used a template to match the document element <states>. And you've used the <xsl:apply-templates/> element to indicate that you also want the XSLT processor to process the child nodes of the <states> node by searching for additional templates that match those nodes. To match all <state> nodes, you could just use this new template:

```
<?xml version="1.0" encoding="UTF-8"?>
<xsl:stylesheet version="1.0" xmlns:xsl="http://www.w3.org/1999/XSL/Transform">

    <xsl:template match="states">
        <HTML>
            <xsl:apply-templates/>
        </HTML>
  </xsl:template>

    <xsl:template match="state">
        .
        .
        .
    </xsl:template>

</xsl:stylesheet>
```

Note that because <state> nodes are not direct child nodes of the root node, this new template would never match anything unless you specifically used a <xsl:apply-templates/> element in the <states> template to invoke it on the child nodes of the <states> node. (The <states> template, on the other hand, is automatically invoked because it matches a direct child of the root node.) Now you can replace each <state> element with the HTML <P>State data will appear here!</P>, as shown in Listing 9.6.

LISTING 9.6 A Sample XSL Style Sheet (ch09_06.xsl)

```
<?xml version="1.0" encoding="UTF-8"?>
<xsl:stylesheet version="1.0" xmlns:xsl="http://www.w3.org/1999/XSL/Transform">

    <xsl:template match="states">
        <HTML>
            <xsl:apply-templates/>
        </HTML>
  </xsl:template>

    <xsl:template match="state">
        <P>
            State data will appear here!
        </P>
    </xsl:template>

</xsl:stylesheet>
```

When an XSLT processor uses the new XSLT style sheet, this is the result:

```
<HTML>
    <BODY>
        <P>
            State data will appear here!
        </P>

        <P>
            State data will appear here!
        </P>

        <P>
            State data will appear here!
        </P>
    </BODY>
</HTML>
```

Figure 9.3 shows this transformation in Internet Explorer.

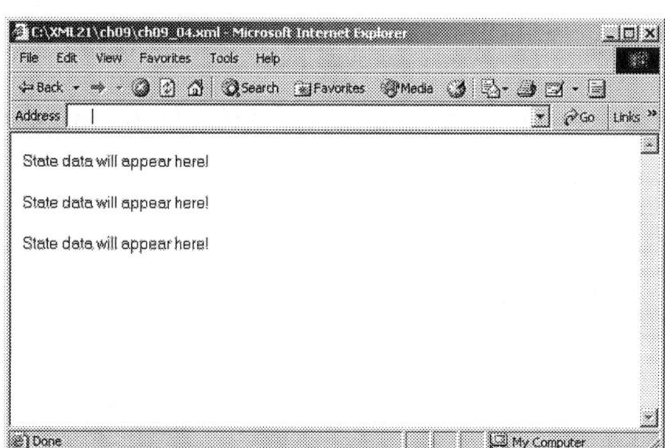

FIGURE 9.3

An elementary XSLT transformation.

This example is fine as far as it goes, but it's not very far. You actually want to pull the name of each state out of the `<state>` element:

```
<?xml version="1.0" encoding ="UTF-8"?>
<?xml-stylesheet type="text/xsl" href="ch09_02.xsl"?>
<states>

    <state>
        <name>California</name>
        <population units="people">33871648</population><!--2000 census-->
        <capital>Sacramento</capital>
        <bird>Quail</bird>
        <flower>Golden Poppy</flower>
```

```
        <area units="square miles">155959</area>
    </state>
        .
        .
        .
```

Using <xsl:value-of> and <xsl:for-each>

To extract the name of each state, you can use the `<xsl:value-of>` element in the template to match every `<state>` element. In particular, you can extract the data in the `<name>` child node inside each `<state>` element by using the `select` attribute, like this:

```
<xsl:value-of select="name"/>
```

Listing 9.7 shows what this looks like, in `ch09_07.xsl`, which encloses each state's name in an HTML `<P>` element.

LISTING 9.7 A Sample XSL Style Sheet That Extracts Data (`ch09_07.xsl`)

```
<?xml version="1.0" encoding="UTF-8"?>
<xsl:stylesheet version="1.0" xmlns:xsl="http://www.w3.org/1999/XSL/Transform">

    <xsl:template match="/">
        <HTML>
            <BODY>
                <xsl:apply-templates/>
            </BODY>
        </HTML>
    </xsl:template>

    <xsl:template match="state">
        <P>
            <xsl:value-of select="name"/>
        </P>
    </xsl:template>

</xsl:stylesheet>
```

Using this new style sheet, `ch09_07.xsl`, gives you the results you want:

```
<HTML>
   <BODY>
        <P>California</P>
        <P>Massachusetts</P>
        <P>New York</P>
    </BODY>
</HTML>
```

Note that the `select` attribute only selects the first node that matches. So what if you have multiple nodes that could match? For example, say you can have multiple <name> elements for each state, as shown in Listing 9.8.

LISTING 9.8 An XML Document That Has Multiple <name> Elements (ch09_08.xml)

```
<?xml version="1.0" encoding ="UTF-8"?>
<states>

    <state>
        <name>California</name>
        <name>Golden State</name>
        <population units="people">33871648</population><!--2000 census-->
        <capital>Sacramento</capital>
        <bird>Quail</bird>
        <flower>Golden Poppy</flower>
        <area units="square miles">155959</area>
    </state>

    <state>
        <name>Massachusetts</name>
        <name>Bay State</name>
        <population units="people">6349097</population><!--2000 census-->
        <capital>Boston</capital>
        <bird>Chickadee</bird>
        <flower>Mayflower</flower>
        <area units="square miles">7840</area>
    </state>

    <state>
        <name>New York</name>
        <name>Empire State</name>
        <population units="people">18976457</population><!--2000 census-->
        <capital>Albany</capital>
        <bird>Bluebird</bird>
        <flower>Rose</flower>
        <area units="square miles">47214</area>
    </state>

</states>
```

To catch all possible matches, you can use the <xsl:for-each> element, as shown in Listing 9.9.

LISTING 9.9 A Sample XSL Style Sheet That Has Multiple Matches (`ch09_09.xsl`)

```
<?xml version="1.0"?>
<xsl:stylesheet version="1.0" xmlns:xsl="http://www.w3.org/1999/XSL/Transform">

    <xsl:template match="states">
        <HTML>
            <xsl:apply-templates/>
        </HTML>
    </xsl:template>

<xsl:template match="state">
    <xsl:for-each select="name">
        <P>
            <xsl:value-of select="."/>
        </P>
    </xsl:for-each>
</xsl:template>

</xsl:stylesheet>
```

This style sheet will catch all `<name>` elements, place their values in a `<P>` element, and add them to the output document, like this:

```
<HTML>
    <BODY>
        <P>California</P>
        <P>Golden State</P>
        <P>Massachusetts</P>
        <P>Bay State</P>
        <P>New York</P>
        <P>Empire State</P>
    </BODY>
</HTML>
```

At this point, you've seen some of the basics of formatting XML by using XSLT. Two of the most important aspects are the `match` attribute in the `<xsl:template>` element and the `select` attribute in the `<xsl:value-of>` element. Working with XSLT involves knowing what values you can assign to these attributes. You can assign XPath expressions to both of these attributes, but there are restrictions on what XPath expressions you can use with the `match` attribute. In the following sections, you'll take a look at the `match` attribute first, followed by the `select` attribute.

Matching Nodes by Using the `match` Attribute

When you create an XSLT template, you need to specify what you want the template to match, and you do that with the `match` attribute. Knowing how to match a node or nodes by using this attribute becomes very important, and there's a whole new syntax here. You'll get the details on what values you can assign to the `match` attribute first because when you know that, you know how to create XSLT templates. Let's start by looking at how to match the root node.

9

Handling the Root Node

As you've seen today, you can match the root node, which corresponds to the very beginning of the document, by assigning a forward slash (`/`) to the `match` attribute in an `<xsl:template>` element:

```
<xsl:template match="/">
    <xsl:apply-templates/>
</xsl:template>
```

Note that XSLT processors start off at the root node level automatically and start searching from that point, so this template is unnecessary. (In fact, you could say that this template is invoked by default in all XSLT processors.)

Handling Elements

As you've seen today, you can match elements simply by using their names:

```
<xsl:template match="states">
  <HTML>
    <xsl:apply-templates/>
  </HTML>
</xsl:template>
```

You can use the `/` operator to separate element names when you want to refer to a child of a particular node. For example, say you want to create a rule that applies only to `<name>` elements that are children of `<state>` elements. In that case, you can match to the expression `"state/name"`. For example, the following rule will surround the text of such elements in a `<P>` element:

```
<xsl:template match="state/name">
    <P><xsl:value-of select="."/></P>
</xsl:template>
```

Note the expression "." here. You use "." with the `select` attribute to specify the current node, as you'll see later today, in the section "Working with the `select` Attribute and XPath."

You can also use `*` character as a wildcard; it can stand for any element (`*` can match only elements). For example, you could use the following to match any child element of the node from which you start searching:

```
<xsl:template match="*">
```

The following rule applies to all <name> elements that are grandchildren of <state> elements:

```
<xsl:template match="state/*/name">
  <P><xsl:value-of select="."/></P>
</xsl:template>
```

Now you've used `"state/name"` to match all <name> elements that are direct children of <state> elements, and you've used `"state/*/name"` to match all <name> elements that are grandchildren of <state> elements. You could also perform both of these matches in an easier way—by simply using the expression `"state//name"`, which matches all <name> elements that are inside <state> elements, no matter how many levels deep (these elements are called *descendants* of the <state> element). Here's how you do it:

```
<xsl:template match="states//name">
  <P><xsl:value-of select="."/></P>
</xsl:template>
```

Handling Attributes

You can handle attributes very much like you handle elements. All that's different is that you have to preface the attribute name with `@`. For example, say that you want to recover the value of the `units` attributes in the <population> and <area> elements of the XML example:

```
<?xml version="1.0" encoding ="UTF-8"?>
<states>

    <state>
        <name>California</name>
        <population units="people">33871648</population><!--2000 census-->
        <capital>Sacramento</capital>
        <bird>Quail</bird>
        <flower>Golden Poppy</flower>
        <area units="square miles">155959</area>
    </state>
        .
        .
        .
```

To get the values of the units attribute, you simply need to refer to it as @units. For example, here's how you might get the population value (using `<xsl:value-of select="."/>`), insert a space (with the `<xsl:text>` element, like this: `<xsl:text> </xsl:text>`), and then add the units for this element (using `<xsl:value-of select="@units"/>`):

```
<xsl:template match="population">
    <xsl:value-of select="."/>
    <xsl:text> </xsl:text>
    <xsl:value-of select="@units"/>
</xsl:template>
```

You can see this at work in Listing 9.10, which reads the data in the XML document and displays it in an HTML table—including the units for various values, as applicable.

9

Listing 9.10 A Sample XSL Style Sheet That Has Multiple Matches (ch09_10.xsl)

```
<?xml version="1.0" encoding="UTF-8"?>
<xsl:stylesheet version="1.0"
xmlns:xsl="http://www.w3.org/1999/XSL/Transform">

    <xsl:template match="/states">
        <HTML>
            <HEAD>
                <TITLE>
                    State Data
                </TITLE>
            </HEAD>
            <BODY>
                <H1>
                    State Data
                </H1>
                <TABLE BORDER="1">
                    <TR>
                        <TD>Name</TD>
                        <TD>Population</TD>
                        <TD>Capital</TD>
                        <TD>Bird</TD>
                        <TD>Flower</TD>
                        <TD>Area</TD>
                    </TR>
                    <xsl:apply-templates/>
                </TABLE>
            </BODY>
        </HTML>
    </xsl:template>

    <xsl:template match="state">
       <TR>
```

LISTING 9.10 continued

```
            <TD><xsl:value-of select="name"/></TD>
            <TD><xsl:apply-templates select="population"/></TD>
            <TD><xsl:apply-templates select="capital"/></TD>
            <TD><xsl:apply-templates select="bird"/></TD>
            <TD><xsl:apply-templates select="flower"/></TD>
            <TD><xsl:apply-templates select="area"/></TD>
        </TR>
    </xsl:template>

    <xsl:template match="population">
        <xsl:value-of select="."/>
        <xsl:text> </xsl:text>
        <xsl:value-of select="@units"/>
    </xsl:template>

    <xsl:template match="capital">
        <xsl:value-of select="."/>
    </xsl:template>

    <xsl:template match="bird">
        <xsl:value-of select="."/>
    </xsl:template>

    <xsl:template match="flower">
        <xsl:value-of select="."/>
    </xsl:template>

    <xsl:template match="area">
        <xsl:value-of select="."/>
        <xsl:text> </xsl:text>
        <xsl:value-of select="@units"/>
    </xsl:template>

</xsl:stylesheet>
```

Here's the HTML you get, including the HTML table:

```
<HTML>
    <HEAD>
        <META http-equiv="Content-Type" content="text/html; charset=UTF-8">
        <TITLE>
            State Data
        </TITLE>
    </HEAD>

    <BODY>
        <H1>
            State Data
```

```
            </H1>
            <TABLE BORDER="1">
                <TR>
                    <TD>Name</TD>
                    <TD>Population</TD>
                    <TD>Capital</TD>
                    <TD>Bird</TD>
                    <TD>Flower</TD>
                    <TD>Area</TD>
                </TR>

                <TR>
                    <TD>California</TD>
                    <TD>33871648 people</TD>
                    <TD>Sacramento</TD>
                    <TD>Quail</TD>
                    <TD>Golden Poppy</TD>
                    <TD>155959 square miles</TD>
                </TR>

                <TR>
                    <TD>Massachusetts</TD>
                    <TD>6349097 people</TD>
                    <TD>Boston</TD>
                    <TD>Chickadee</TD>
                    <TD>Mayflower</TD>
                    <TD>7840 square miles</TD>
                </TR>

                <TR>
                    <TD>New York</TD>
                    <TD>18976457 people</TD>
                    <TD>Albany</TD>
                    <TD>Bluebird</TD>
                    <TD>Rose</TD>
                    <TD>47214 square miles</TD>
                </TR>
            </TABLE>
        </BODY>
    </HTML>
```

Figure 9.4 shows this result in Internet Explorer.

There's another thing you need to know about attributes: You can use the `@*` wildcard to select all attributes of an element. For example, `"state/@*"` would select any attributes of a `<state>` element.

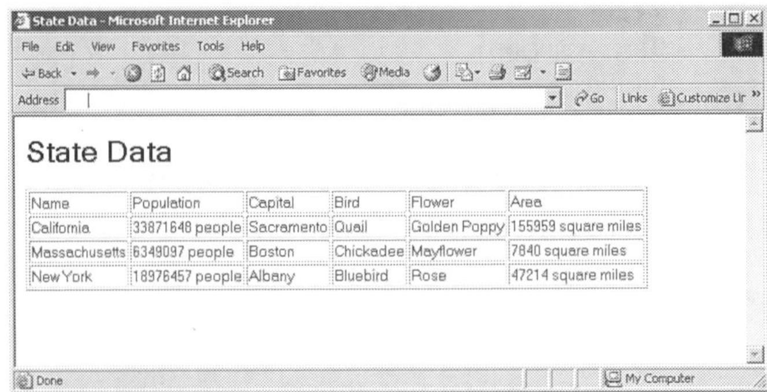

State Data

Name	Population	Capital	Bird	Flower	Area
California	33871648 people	Sacramento	Quail	Golden Poppy	155959 square miles
Massachusetts	6349097 people	Boston	Chickadee	Mayflower	7840 square miles
New York	18976457 people	Albany	Bluebird	Rose	47214 square miles

FIGURE 9.4
Reading attribute values.

Handling ID Attributes

If you have given elements an `ID` attribute and have declared that attribute in a DTD or XML schema, you can match those elements by using the `id()` expression. For example, here's how you might match elements with the `ID` value `Steven`:

```
<xsl:template match="id('Steven')">
    <xsl:value-of select="."/>
</xsl:template>
```

Handling Processing Instructions

You can match processing instructions by using the XPath expression `processing-instruction()`. Here's an example:

```
<xsl:template match="/processing-instruction()">
    <P>
        Matched a processing instruction.
    </P>
</xsl:template>
```

You can specify what processing instruction you want to match if you list its name in the parentheses here. The following example matches the processing instruction `<?xml-stylesheet?>`:

```
<xsl:template match="/processing-instruction(xml-stylesheet)">
    <P>
        Matched an xml-stylesheet processing instruction.
    </P>
</xsl:template>
```

Handling Multiple Matches

You can catch more than one match by using one `match` attribute if you use the Or operator, `|`. For example, say that you want to display the values of the `<bird>` and `<flower>`

elements in bold, using the HTML <B> tag. To do that, you can use a single template to match both elements, as shown in Listing 9.11.

LISTING 9.11 An XSL Style Sheet That Uses Multiple Matches (ch09_11.xsl)

```
<?xml version="1.0"?>
<xsl:stylesheet version="1.0" xmlns:xsl="http://www.w3.org/1999/XSL/Transform">

    <xsl:template match="states">
        <HTML>
            <BODY>
                <xsl:apply-templates/>
            </BODY>
        </HTML>
    </xsl:template>

    <xsl:template match="state">
        <P>
            <xsl:apply-templates/>
        </P>
    </xsl:template>

    <xsl:template match="bird | flower">
        <B>
            <xsl:apply-templates/>
        </B>
    </xsl:template>

</xsl:stylesheet>
```


Here are the results:

```
<HTML>
    <BODY>
        <P>
            California
            33871648
            Sacramento
            <B>Quail</B>
            <B>Golden Poppy</B>
            155959
        </P>

        <P>
            Massachusetts
            6349097
            Boston
            <B>Chickadee</B>
            <B>Mayflower</B>
```

```
            7840
        </P>

        <P>
            New York
            18976457
            Albany
            <B>Bluebird</B>
            <B>Rose</B>
            47214
        </P>
    </BODY>
</HTML>
```

Note that the `<bird>` and `<flower>` values are enclosed in HTML `<B>` elements to make them bold. Also note that the text from elements that didn't even have a template is inserted into the result document as well. The reason for this is that there is a *default template* built in to XSLT for elements, and it just inserts their values into the resulting document. When you used `<xsl:apply-templates>` on the child elements of the `<states>` element, the default template was automatically used for elements, without any explicit template. You'll see the default rules for XSLT later today.

Matching Using XPath Expressions

So far today you've been matching expressions such as `states` and `@units` by assigning those values to `match` attributes. The expressions you've seen have been a subset of the complete XPath syntax (we'll talk more about XPath later today). But oddly enough, you can actually use the full XPath syntax in a value you assign to a `match` attribute if you use it in a *node test*. To create a node test, you use the `[]` operator to test whether a certain condition is true. For example, you can test the value of an element, whether an element has a particular child or attribute, and even the position of a node in the document.

For example, here's how you could match `<state>` elements that have child `<flower>` elements:

```
<xsl:template match = "state[flower]">
```

Here's how you could match any element that has a `<flower>` or `<bird>` child element:

```
<xsl:template match = "*[flower | bird]">
```

Here's how you could match any element that has a `units` attribute:

```
<xsl:template match="*[@units]">
```

These expressions inside the `[` and `]` are full XPath expressions, so it's time to start taking a look at XPath. Up to this point, you've taken a look at the kinds of expressions you can use with the `<xsl:template>` element's `match` attribute. The `select` attribute, which can be used in the `<xsl:apply-templates>`, `<xsl:value-of>`, `<xsl:for-each>`, `<xsl:copy-of>`, and `<xsl:sort>` XSLT elements, however, may be assigned a full XPath expression.

Working with the `select` Attribute and XPath

You can assign the `select` attribute XPath expressions, which are used to indicate exactly what node or nodes you want to use in an XML document. XPath has been a W3C recommendation since November 16, 1999. You can find the XPath recommendation—for the current version, 1.0—at `http://www.w3.org/TR/xpath`. Version 2.0 of XPath is on the way, and it's currently in working draft form at this point; see `http://www.w3.org/TR/xpath20`. (Very little software supports XPath 2.0 yet; the Saxon XSLT processor—at `http://saxon.sourceforge.net`—provides some support for it.)

XPath expressions are more powerful than the `match` expressions you've already seen; for one thing, they're not restricted to working with the current node or direct child nodes; you can use them to work with parent nodes, ancestor nodes, and more.

To specify a node or set of nodes in XPath, you use a location path. A *location path* consists of one or more *location steps*, separated by `/` (to refer to a child node) or `//` (to refer to any descendant node). If you start the location path with `/`, the location path is called an *absolute location path* because you're specifying the path from the root node; otherwise, the location path is *relative*. And the node an XPath expression is working on is called the *context node*.

Location steps are made up of an *axis*, a *node test*, and zero or more *predicates*. For example, in the expression `child::state[position() = 2]` (which picks out the second `<state>` child of the context node), `child` is the name of the axis, `state` is the node test, and `[position() = 2]` is a predicate. You can create location paths with one or more location steps. For example, `/descendant::state/child::name` selects all the `<name>` elements that have a `<state>` parent. You'll get the details about what kind of axes, node tests, and predicates XPath supports in the following sections.

TIP

As you'll soon see, you can often omit the axis name if you use abbreviated XSLT syntax, which is why the earlier examples could use elements like `<xsl:value-of select="name"/>`. Unabbreviated, that would actually be `<xsl:value-of select="child::name"/>`, but the abbreviation rules say that `child::` may be omitted.

Using Axes

In the location step `child::bird`, which refers to a `<bird>` element that is a child of the current node, `child` is called the *axis*. XPath supports many different axes, and it's important to know what they are. Here's the list:

- **`ancestor`**—This axis contains the ancestors of the context node. An ancestor node is the parent of the context node, the parent of the parent, and so forth, back to (and including) the root node.
- **`ancestor-or-self`**—This axis contains the context node and the ancestors of the context node.
- **`attribute`**—This axis contains the attributes of the context node.
- **`child`**—This axis contains the children of the context node.
- **`descendant`**—This axis contains the descendants of the context node. A *descendant* is a child or a child of a child and so on.
- **`descendant-or-self`**—This axis contains the context node and the descendants of the context node.
- **`following`**—This axis contains all nodes that come after the context node.
- **`following-sibling`**—This axis contains all the following siblings of the context node.
- **`namespace`**—This axis contains the namespace nodes of the context node.
- **`parent`**—This axis contains the parent of the context node.
- **`preceding`**—This axis contains all nodes that come before the context node.
- **`preceding-sibling`**—This axis contains all the preceding siblings of the context node.
- **`self`**—This axis contains the context node.

Note that although the `match` attribute can only use the `child` or `attribute` axes in location steps (that's the major restriction on the `match` attribute compared to the `select` attribute), the `select` attribute can use any of the 13 axes. (The term *sibling* in XML refers to an item on the same level as the current item.)

For example, this template extracts the value of the `<name>` element by using the location path `child::name`:

```
<xsl:template match="state">
    <HTML>
        <BODY>
            <xsl:value-of select="child::name"/>
        </BODY>
    </HTML>
</xsl:template>
```

This is really the same as the version you've already been using because, as mentioned, you can abbreviate it by omitting the `child::` part:

```
<xsl:template match="state">
    <HTML>
        <BODY>
            <xsl:value-of select="name"/>
        </BODY>
    </HTML>
</xsl:template>
```


In the location step `child::name`, `child` is the axis and `name` is the node test, which is described in the following section.

Using Node Tests

After you specify the axis you want to use in a location step, you specify the node test. A *node test* indicates what type of node you want to match. You can use names of nodes as node tests, or you can use the wildcard `*` to select element nodes. For example, the expression `child::*/child::flower` selects all `<flower>` elements that are grandchildren of the current node. Besides nodes and the wildcard character, you can also use these node tests:

- **`comment()`**—This node test selects comment nodes.
- **`node()`**—This node test selects any type of node.
- **`processing-instruction()`**—This node test selects a processing instruction node. You can specify, in the parentheses, the name of the processing instruction to select.
- **`text()`**—This node test selects a text node.

Using Predicates

The last part of a location step is the *predicate*. In a location step, the (optional) predicate narrows the search down even more. For example, the location step `child::state[position() = 1]` uses the predicate `[position() = 1]` to select not just a child `<state>` element but the *first* `<state>` child element.

Predicates can get pretty involved because there are all kinds of XPath expressions that you can work with in predicates. And there are various types of legal XPath expressions; here are the possible types:

- Booleans
- Node sets
- Numbers
- Strings

NOTE

There's also another type of XPath expression—result tree fragments—that you can work with in predicates. A *result tree fragment* is a part of an XML document that is not a complete node or complete set of nodes. There are really only two things to do with result tree fragments: You can use the `string()` function or the `boolean()` function to turn them into strings or Booleans (that is, true/false values). Because they don't represent legal XML, they've fallen into disuse.

The following sections look at how expressions help you in XSLT.

Boolean Expressions

XPath Boolean values are true/false values, and you can use the built-in XPath logical operators to produce Boolean results. These are the logical operators:

- `!=`—This stands for "is not equal to."
- `<`—This stands for "is less than." (You use `<` for this in XML documents.)
- `<=`—This stands for "is less than or equal to."
- `=`—This stands for "is equal to."
- `>`—This stands for "is greater than."
- `>=`—This stands for "is greater than or equal to."

For example, here's how to use a logical operator to match all `<state>` elements after the first three, using the `position()` function (which you'll see in the next section):

```
<xsl:template match="state[position() > 3]">
    <xsl:value-of select="."/>
</xsl:template>
```

You can also use the keywords `and` and `or` to connect Boolean expressions. The following example selects all `<state>` elements after the first three and before the tenth one:

```
<xsl:template match="state[position() > 3 and position() < 10]">
    <xsl:value-of select="."/>
</xsl:template>
```

In addition, you can use the `not()` function to reverse the logical sense of an expression. The following example selects all `<state>` elements *except* the last one, using the `last()` function (which you'll see in the next section):

```
<xsl:template match="state[not(position() = last())]">
    <xsl:value-of select="."/>
</xsl:template>
```

Node Sets

Besides Boolean values, XPath can also work with node sets. A node set is just a set of nodes. By collecting nodes into a set, XPath lets you work with multiple nodes at once. For example, the location step `child::state/child::bird` returns a node list of all `<bird>` elements that are children of `<state>` elements.

You can use various XPath functions to work with node sets. For example, the `last()` function picks out the last node in the node set. The following are the node set functions:

- **`last()`**—Returns the number of nodes in the node set.
- **`position()`**—Returns the position of the context node in the node set. (The first node is Node 1.)
- **`count(`*`node-set`*`)`**—Returns the number of nodes in *node-set*.
- **`id(`*`ID`*`)`**—Returns a node set that contains the element whose ID value matches *ID*.
- **`local-name(`*`node-set`*`)`**—Returns the name of the first node in *node-set*.
- **`namespace-uri(`*`node-set`*`)`**—Returns the URI of the namespace of the first node in *node-set*.
- **`name(`*`node-set`*`)`**—Returns the qualified name of the first node in *node-set*.

Some of these functions can be very useful. For example, you can number the states in the XML sample from earlier today by using the `position()` function, as shown in Listing 9.12.

LISTING 9.12 An XSL Style Sheet That Uses `position()` (`ch09_12.xsl`)

```
<?xml version="1.0"?>
<xsl:stylesheet version="1.0" xmlns:xsl="http://www.w3.org/1999/XSL/Transform">

    <xsl:template match="states">
        <HTML>
            <HEAD>
                <TITLE>
                    The States
                </TITLE>
            </HEAD>
            <BODY>
                <H1>
                    The States
                </H1>
                <xsl:apply-templates select="state"/>
            </BODY>
        </HTML>
    </xsl:template>
```

LISTING 9.12 continued

```
    <xsl:template match="state">
        <P>
            <xsl:value-of select="position()"/>.
            <xsl:value-of select="name"/>
        </P>
    </xsl:template>

</xsl:stylesheet>
```

Here's what an XSLT processor produces when you use this style sheet on the sample XML document:

```
<HTML>
    <HEAD>
        <META http-equiv="Content-Type" content="text/html; charset=UTF-8">
        <TITLE>
            The States
        </TITLE>
    </HEAD>

    <BODY>
        <H1>
            The States
        </H1>
        <P>1. California</P>
        <P>2. Massachusetts</P>
        <P>3. New York</P>
    </BODY>
</HTML>
```

Note that the states are indeed numbered. Also, as with today's other examples, the whitespace and indenting here have been cleaned up. Figure 9.5 shows the result of this transformation.

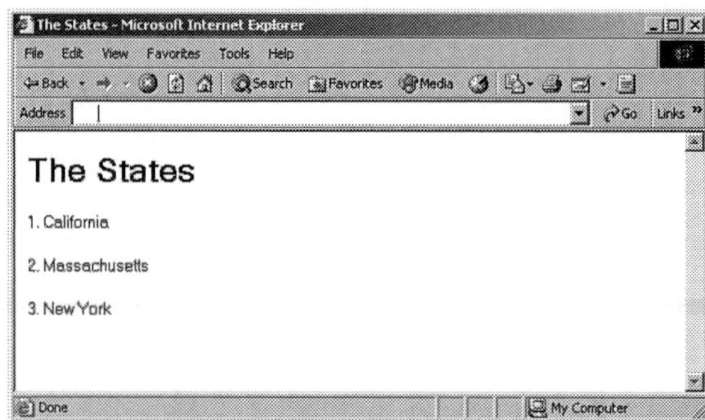

FIGURE 9.5
Numbering items by using XSLT.

When you're working on the nodes in a node set, you can use functions such as `position()` to target specific nodes. For example, `child::state[position() = 1]` selects the first `<state>` child of the node, where you apply this location step, and `child::state[position() = last()]` selects the last.

Numbers

XPath can use numbers in expressions (for example, the `1` in the expression `child::state[position() = 1]`). There are also some operators that you can use to work with numbers:

9

- **+**—Addition.
- **-**—Subtraction.
- *****—Multiplication.
- **div**—Division. Note that the `/` character that stands for division in other languages is used for other purposes in XML and XPath.
- **mod**—Modulus. This operation returns the remainder after one number is divided by another.

For example, if you use `<xsl:value-of select="2 + 2"/>`, you get the string `"4"` in the output document. The following example selects all states that have at least 200 people per square mile:

```
<xsl:template match="states">
    <HTML>
        <BODY>
            <P>
                <xsl:apply-templates select="state[population div area > 200]"/>
            </P>
        </BODY>
    </HTML>
</xsl:template>
```

Besides the numeric operators, XPath also has these functions that work with numbers:

- **ceiling()**—Returns the smallest integer larger than the number you pass in the parentheses. For example, `ceiling(4.6)` returns 5.
- **floor()**—Returns the largest integer smaller than the number you pass it. For example, `floor(4.6)` returns 4.
- **round()**—Rounds the number you pass it to the nearest integer. For example, `round(4.6)` returns 6.
- **sum()**—Returns the sum of the numbers you pass it.

For example, here's how to find the total population of the states in `ch09_01.xml` by using `sum()`:

```
<xsl:template match="states">
    <HTML>
        <BODY>
            <P>
                The total population is:
                <xsl:value-of select="sum(child::population)"/>
            </P>
        </BODY>
    </HTML>
</xsl:template>
```

Strings

Strings in XPath are treated as Unicode characters. A number of XPath functions are specially designed to work on strings. Here they are:

- **`concat(`*`string1`*`, `*`string2`*`, ...)`**—Returns the strings joined together.
- **`contains(`*`string1`*`, `*`string2`*`)`**—Returns `true` if the first string contains the second one.
- **`format-number(`*`number1`*`, `*`string2`*`, `*`string3`*`)`**—Returns a string that holds the formatted string version of *`number1`*, using *`string2`* as a formatting string, and *`string3`* as an optional locale string. (You create formatting strings as you would for Java's `java.text.DecimalFormat` method.)
- **`normalize-space(`*`string1`*`)`**—Returns *`string1`* after stripping leading and trailing whitespace and replacing multiple consecutive empty spaces with a single space.
- **`starts-with(`*`string1`*`, `*`string2`*`)`**—Returns `true` if the first string starts with the second string.
- **`string-length(`*`string1`*`)`**—Returns the number of characters in *`string1`*.
- **`substring(`*`string1`*`, `*`offset`*`, `*`length`*`)`**—Returns *`length`* characters from the string, starting at *`offset`*.
- **`substring-after(`*`string1`*`, `*`string2`*`)`**—Returns the part of *`string1`* after the first occurrence of *`string2`*.
- **`substring-before(`*`string1`*`, `*`string2`*`)`**—Returns the part of *`string1`* up to the first occurrence of *`string2`*.
- **`translate(`*`string1`*`, `*`string2`*`, `*`string3`*`)`**—Returns *`string1`* with all occurrences of the characters in *`string2`* replaced with the matching characters in *`string3`*.

Now you know what items can go into location steps—axes, node tests, and predicates. XPath syntax is far from intuitive, so let's see some more examples as you take a look at XPath abbreviations and default rules.

9

XPath Abbreviations and Default Rules

So far you have specifically indicated what axis you wanted to use when writing location steps, but there are ways to abbreviate location steps to make things easier. For example, as mentioned earlier, the location step `child::state` points to a `<state>` element that is a child element of the context node, but you can abbreviate that location step simply as `state`. These are the legal abbreviations:

Location Step	*Abbreviation*
`self::node()`	`.`
`parent::node()`	`..`
`child::`*`childname`*	*`childname`*
`attribute::`*`childname`*	`@`*`childname`*
`/descendant-or-self::node()/`	`//`

You can also abbreviate predicate expressions. For example, you can abbreviate `[position() = 8]` as `[8]`.

Here are some examples of location paths using abbreviated syntax:

- **`*`**—Matches all element children of the context node.
- **`*/*/state`**—Matches all `<state>` great-grandchildren of the context node.
- **`.`**—Matches the context node.
- **`..`**—Matches the parent of the context node.
- **`../@units`**—Matches the `units` attribute of the parent of the context node.
- **`.//state`**—Matches all `<state>` element descendants of the context node.
- **`//state`**—Matches all `<state>` descendants of the root node.
- **`//state/name`**—Matches all `<name>` elements that have a `<state>` parent.
- **`/states/state[4]/name[3]`**—Matches the third `<name>` element of the fourth `<state>` element of the `<states>` element.
- **`@*`**—Matches all the attributes of the context node.
- **`@units`**—Matches the `units` attribute of the context node.
- **`state`**—Matches the `<state>` element children of the context node.
- **`state[@nickname and @units]`**—Matches all the `<state>` children of the context node that have both a `nickname` attribute and a `units` attribute.
- **`state[@units = "people"]`**—Matches all `<state>` children of the context node that have a `units` attribute that has the value `"people"`.

- **state[7]**—Matches the seventh `<state>` child of the context node.
- **state[7][@units = "people"]**—Matches the seventh `<state>` child of the context node if that child has a `units` attribute with the value `"people"`.
- **state[last()]**—Matches the last `<state>` child of the context node.
- **state[name]**—Matches the `<state>` children of the context node that themselves have `<name>` children.
- **state[name="Massachusetts"]**—Matches the `<state>` child nodes of the context node that have `<name>` children whose text value is `"Massachusetts"`.
- **states//state**—Matches all `<state>` element descendants of the `<states>` element children of the context node.
- **text()**—Matches all child text nodes of the context node.

Listing 9.13 shows an example that uses abbreviated syntax. This example picks out the state bird for each state and lists it by using text such as "The Quail is the California state bird." When you're inside a `<state>` element's `<bird>` template, you can reach the `<name>` element of the state by using `../name`, as shown in this example.

LISTING 9.13 An XSL Style Sheet That Uses Abbreviated Syntax (`ch09_13.xsl`)

```
<?xml version="1.0"?>
<xsl:stylesheet version="1.0"
xmlns:xsl="http://www.w3.org/1999/XSL/Transform">

    <xsl:template match="states">
        <HTML>
            <BODY>
                <xsl:apply-templates select="state"/>
            </BODY>
        </HTML>
    </xsl:template>

    <xsl:template match="state">
        <P>
            <xsl:apply-templates select="bird"/>
        </P>
    </xsl:template>

    <xsl:template match="bird">
        The <xsl:value-of select="."/>
        is the <xsl:value-of select="../name"/>
        state bird.
    </xsl:template>

</xsl:stylesheet>
```

Here are the results of applying this style sheet to the sample XML document:

```
<HTML>
    <BODY>
        <P>
            The Quail
            is the California
            state bird.
        </P>
        <P>
            The Chickadee
            is the Massachusetts
            state bird.
        </P>
        <P>
            The Bluebird
            is the New York
            state bird.
        </P>
    </BODY>
</HTML>
```

Figure 9.6 shows these results in Figure 9.6. This is a good example that shows how to extract and work with data from XML documents by using XSLT.

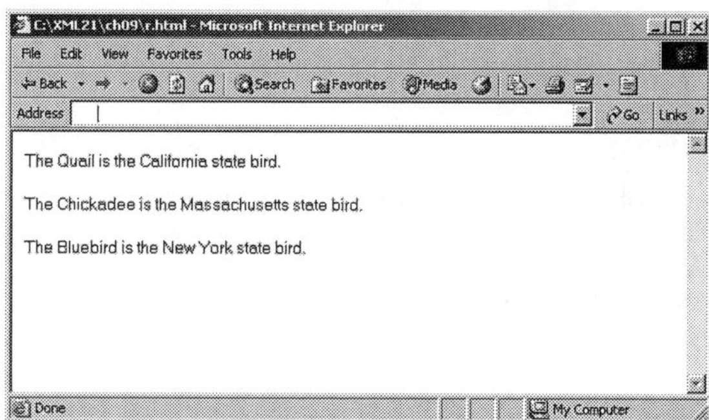

FIGURE 9.6
Using abbreviated syntax.

While you're discussing built-in abbreviated syntax, it's also worth noting that XSLT also has some built-in default rules, some of which you've already seen in action.

The most important default rule applies to elements, and here's how you might put it in XSLT syntax:

```
<xsl:template match="/ | *">
    <xsl:apply-templates/>
</xsl:template>
```

What this means is that if you don't supply a template for an element, that element is still processed with `<xsl:apply-templates/>` to handle the element's child nodes.

Similarly, the default rule for attributes is to place the value of the attribute in the output document, as in this example:

```
<xsl:template match="@*">
    <xsl:value-of select="."/>
</xsl:template>
```

The default rule for text is to just insert the text into the output document. That rule can be expressed like this, where the XPath `text()` function just returns the text in a text node:

```
<xsl:template match="text()">
    <xsl:value-of select="."/>
</xsl:template>
```

However, the content of processing instructions (which may be matched by using the XPath `processing-instruction()` function) and comments (which may be matched by using the XPath `comment()` function) is not inserted into the output document by default. You might express their default rules like this:

```
<xsl:template match="processing-instruction()"/>
<xsl:template match="comment()"/>
```

In fact, you can create whole style sheets that rely entirely on default rules. Here's what that might look like:

```
<?xml version="1.0"?>
<xsl:stylesheet version="1.0" xmlns:xsl="http://www.w3.org/1999/XSL/Transform">
</xsl:stylesheet>
```

Here's what you get when you apply this default-rules-only style sheet to `ch09_01.xml`:

```
<?xml version="1.0" encoding="UTF-8"?>

    California
    33871648
    Sacramento
    Quail
    Golden Poppy
    155959

    Massachusetts
    6349097
    Boston
    Chickadee
    Mayflower
    7840
```

```
New York
18976457
Albany
Bluebird
Rose
47214
```

Note that just the raw data in the document is transferred to the output document, which is the way things work by default in XSLT.

9

XPath Tools

There's no question that it can take some time to get used to XPath syntax. Fortunately, there are some good tools out there to help, such as the XPath Visualiser by Dimitre Novatchev, which you can get for free at `http://www.vbxml.com/downloads/default.asp?id=visualiser`. To use this tool, you just have to browse to the XML document you want to work with and enter the XPath expression you want to check. The XPath Visualiser then highlights in yellow nodes that match your expression. For example, Figure 9.7 shows this tool working on the sample XML document with the XPath expression `//*[@units]`. This is a great way to test your XPath expressions until you get them to do what you want; all you need in order to use this tool is a browser.

FIGURE 9.7

Using the XPath Visualiser.

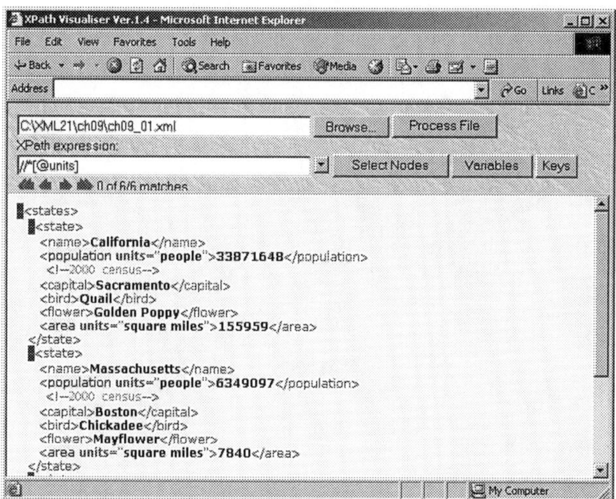

Using <xsl:copy>

The `<xsl:copy>` element lets you copy nodes; it copies only the nodes that match the XPath expression you want. By using `<xsl:copy>`, you can copy whatever child elements, text nodes, or attributes you need.

Listing 9.14 shows an example that copies elements and the text in those elements by using <xsl:copy> just in a template that matches "* | text()" (that is, elements and text).

LISTING 9.14 An XSL Style Sheet That Copies Data (ch09_14.xsl)

```
<?xml version="1.0" encoding="UTF-8"?>
<xsl:stylesheet version="1.0" xmlns:xsl="http://www.w3.org/1999/XSL/Transform">

<xsl:template match="* | text()">
    <xsl:copy>
        <xsl:apply-templates select="* | text()"/>
    </xsl:copy>
</xsl:template>

</xsl:stylesheet>
```

Here are the results of applying this new style sheet to the sample XML document:

```
<?xml version="1.0" encoding="UTF-8"?>
<states>

    <state>
        <name>California</name>
        <population>33871648</population>
        <capital>Sacramento</capital>
        <bird>Quail</bird>
        <flower>Golden Poppy</flower>
        <area>155959</area>
    </state>
        .
        .
        .
    <state>
        <name>New York</name>
        <population>18976457</population>
        <capital>Albany</capital>
        <bird>Bluebird</bird>
        <flower>Rose</flower>
        <area>47214</area>
    </state>

</states>
```

Note that all but the elements and text have been stripped out—no attributes and no comments remain.

Using <xsl:if>

You can use the `<xsl:if>` element to make choices that depend on the data in an XML document. All you have to do to use this element is assign its `test` attribute a value that evaluates to a Boolean value of `true` or `false`.

Listing 9.15 shows an example that lists the states in an XML document, and to set off the list, it adds a horizontal rule element, `<HR>`, before and after the list of states. The example checks whether you're at the beginning or end of the states list by using `<xsl:if test="position() = 1">`, and if you're at the beginning or end, it creates a new `<HR>` element with the `<xsl:element>` element, like this:

```
<xsl:element name="HR"/>
```

9

LISTING 9.15 An XSL Style Sheet That Uses `<xsl:if>` (`ch09_15.xsl`)

```
<?xml version="1.0" encoding="UTF-8"?>
<xsl:stylesheet version="1.0" xmlns:xsl="http://www.w3.org/1999/XSL/Transform">

    <xsl:template match="states">
        <HTML>
            <HEAD>
                <TITLE>
                    The States
                </TITLE>
            </HEAD>
            <BODY>
                <H1>
                    The States
                </H1>
                <xsl:apply-templates select="state"/>
            </BODY>
        </HTML>
    </xsl:template>

    <xsl:template match="state">
        <xsl:if test="position() = 1"><xsl:element name="HR"/></xsl:if>
        <P>
            <xsl:value-of select="position()"/>. <xsl:value-of select="name"/>
        </P>
        <xsl:if test="position() = last()"><xsl:element name="HR"/></xsl:if>
    </xsl:template>

</xsl:stylesheet>
```

Here's what you get when you use this new style sheet:

```
<HTML>
    <HEAD>
        <META http-equiv="Content-Type" content="text/html; charset=UTF-8">
        <TITLE>
            The States
        </TITLE>
    </HEAD>

    <BODY>
        <H1>
            The States
        </H1>
        <HR>
        <P>1. California</P>
        <P>2. Massachusetts</P>
        <P>3. New York</P>
        <HR>
    </BODY>
</HTML>
```

Note the <HR> elements before and after the list of states. Figure 9.8 shows what this looks like.

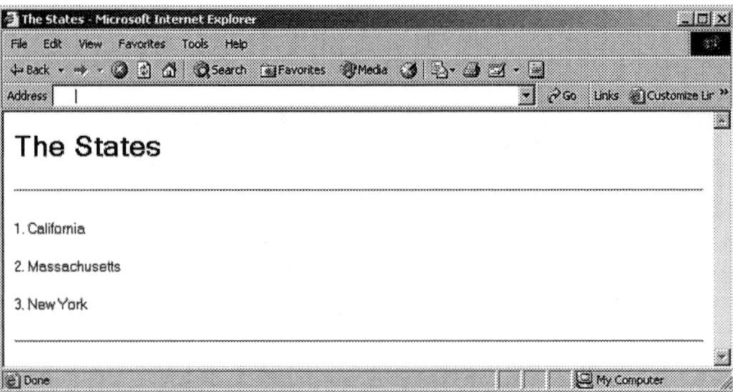

FIGURE 9.8

Making decisions by using <xsl:if>.

Using <xsl:choose>

In addition to using <xsl:if> to make decisions, you can also use <xsl:choose>. This element lets you compare a test value against several possibilities.

Listing 9.16 shows an example that displays the names of the states in the sample XML document in red, white, and blue. This example uses <xsl:when> elements inside an <xsl:choose> element and sets the test attribute in those elements to the Boolean expression you want to test. For example, California is first in the list, so you can display it in red this way:

```
<xsl:template match="state">
    <xsl:choose>
        <xsl:when test="name = 'California'">
            <P>
                <FONT COLOR="RED">
                    <xsl:value-of select="name"/>
                </FONT>
            </P>
        </xsl:when>
    .
    .
    .
```


You can see the whole style sheet in Listing 9.16. Note that at the end of the group of `<xsl:when>` elements, there's an (optional) `<xsl:otherwise>` element; if none of the `<xsl:when>` elements match their test conditions, the `<xsl:otherwise>` element is chosen.

LISTING 9.16 An XSL Style Sheet That Uses `<xsl:choose>` (`ch09_16.xsl`)

```
<?xml version="1.0" encoding="UTF-8"?>
<xsl:stylesheet version="1.0" xmlns:xsl="http://www.w3.org/1999/XSL/Transform">

    <xsl:template match="states">
        <HTML>
            <HEAD>
                <TITLE>
                    The States
                </TITLE>
            </HEAD>
            <BODY BGCOLOR="BLACK">
                <xsl:apply-templates select="state"/>
            </BODY>
        </HTML>
    </xsl:template>

    <xsl:template match="state">
        <xsl:choose>
            <xsl:when test="name = 'California'">
                <P>
                    <FONT COLOR="RED">
                        <xsl:value-of select="name"/>
                    </FONT>
                </P>
            </xsl:when>
            <xsl:when test="name = 'Massachusetts'">
```

LISTING 9.16 continued

```
                <P>
                    <FONT COLOR="WHITE">
                        <xsl:value-of select="name"/>
                    </FONT>
                </P>
            </xsl:when>
            <xsl:when test="name = 'New York'">
                <P>
                    <FONT COLOR="BLUE">
                        <xsl:value-of select="name"/>
                    </FONT>
                </P>
            </xsl:when>
            <xsl:otherwise>
                 <P>
                     <xsl:value-of select="."/>
                 </P>
            </xsl:otherwise>
        </xsl:choose>
    </xsl:template>

</xsl:stylesheet>
```

Here's what you get when you use this style sheet on the sample XML document:

```
<HTML>
    <HEAD>
        <META http-equiv="Content-Type" content="text/html; charset=UTF-8">
        <TITLE>
            The States
        </TITLE>
    </HEAD>

    <BODY BGCOLOR="BLACK">
        <P>
            <FONT COLOR="RED">California</FONT>
        </P>
        <P>
            <FONT COLOR="WHITE">Massachusetts</FONT>
        </P>
        <P>
            <FONT COLOR="BLUE">New York</FONT>
        </P>
    </BODY>
</HTML>
```

Figure 9.9 shows what this looks like (in black and white, of course). Note that this style sheet makes the background color of the whole page black so that the styling (in particular, the white text) will stand out.

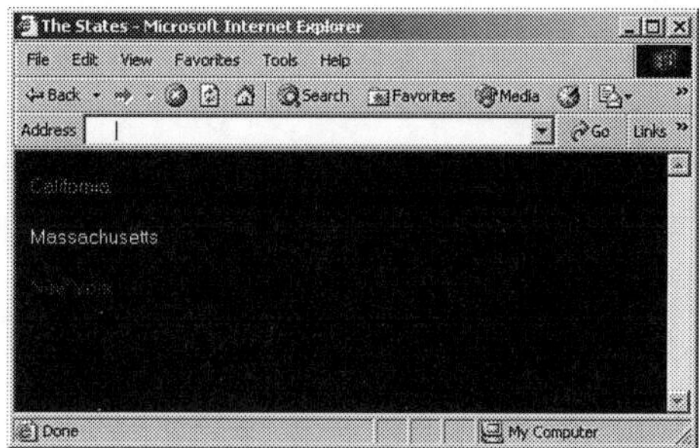

FIGURE 9.9
Making decisions by using `<xsl:choose>`.

Specifying the Output Document Type

Today you've been creating HTML documents from XML documents. You might wonder how the XSLT processor knows not to add an XML declaration at the beginning of the output HTML document. There's actually a special rule about this: If the document node of the output document is `<HTML>`, XSLT processors are supposed to treat the output document as HTML.

In fact, you can specify the type of output document you want by using the XSLT `<xsl:output>` element. Here are the built-in possibilities:

- **`xml`**—This is the default. It makes the output documents start with an `<?xml?>` declaration.
- **`html`**—This makes the output document standard HTML 4.0, without an XML declaration.
- **`text`**—This makes the output document simple text.

To choose from these options, you set the `<xsl:output>` element's `method` attribute to `xml`, `html`, or `text`. For example, if you want to create a plain-text document, you can use this `<xsl:output>` element:

```
<xsl:output method = "text"/>
```

Here are some additional useful `<xsl:output>` attributes:

- **`encoding`**—Indicates the value of the XML declaration's `encoding` attribute.
- **`indent`**—Indicates whether the XSLT processor should indent the output (many don't, even if you ask them to). You can set this attribute to `"yes"` or `"no"`.

- **omit-xml-declaration**—Indicates whether the processor should omit the XML declaration. You can set this attribute to "yes" or "no".
- **standalone**—Indicates the value for the XML declaration's standalone attribute. You can set this attribute to "yes" or "no".
- **version**—Indicates the value for the XML declaration's version attribute.
- **doctype-system and doctype-public**—Let you specify an external DTD for XML documents. For example, <xsl:output doctype-system = "states.dtd"/> produces <!DOCTYPE states SYSTEM "states.dtd">.

You're not restricted to creating XML, HTML, or text output files. You can use the media-type attribute of <xsl:output> to specify the MIME type of the output document. Here's how that might look:

```
<xsl:output media-type="text/rtf"/>
```

Summary

As you have seen today, XSLT gives you a lot of power in terms of handling the data in XML documents. There's a lot more to XSLT than is covered today. Many entire books have been written on the subject. For more details, take a look at both the XSLT specification, at http://www.w3.org/TR/xslt, and the XPath specification, at http://www.w3.org/TR/xpath.

You use XSLT to manipulate, extract, and format data from XML documents. It's an attractive option because it means you don't have to resort to creating your own XML processors. XSLT is a specification of the W3C. The W3C recommendation for XSLT 1.0 is at http://www.w3.org/TR/xslt.

XSLT has its own syntax, and today you've examined it. You now know how to use that syntax in XSLT style sheets, which start with the XML declaration and the element <xsl:stylesheet version="1.0" xmlns:xsl="http://www.w3.org/1999/XSL/Transform">.

XSLT style sheets are made up of templates that match the nodes you want to work with. As you saw today, you use the match attribute in the <xsl:template> element to match nodes. You can also select the values of nodes by using the <xsl:value-of> element and setting the select attribute to the XPath expression you want to use.

XSLT handles XML documents as trees of nodes, and you saw that the XPath language lets you target those nodes with XPath expressions. By using XPath, you can locate exactly the node or nodes in an XML document that you want to work with and specify exactly what you want to do with the node(s).

XPath location paths are made up of location steps, and each location step is made up of an axis, a node test, and an optional predicate. There are 13 axes in XPath 1.0, and you took a look at all of them today. Node tests let you identify specific nodes, and the predicate part of XPath expressions lets you use an extensive range of XPath data values, operators, and functions to pin down the data you're interested in.

XSLT is actually a subpart of XSL. And you're going to take a look at XSL in depth tomorrow.

Q&A

Q Is it possible to sort nodes by using XSLT?

A Yes. You can use the `<xsl:sort>` element, which copies over nodes sorted according to the value that you specify with the `select` attribute. For example, to sort by names as stored in `<name>` elements, you use `<xsl:sort select="name"/>` inside an `<xsl:apply-templates>` element.

Q How can I create whole new elements in the output document by using data from the input document?

A You briefly saw how you can do this today by using the <xsl:element> element. Here's a more in-depth example. If you wanted to create new elements by using the names of the states `<California>`, `<Massachusetts>`, and so on (although note that `<New York>` is not a legal XML element name!), where each element contains a `<population>` element, you could use this XSLT in a template that matches `"state"`:

```
<xsl:element name="{name}">
    <population><xsl:value-of select="population"/></population>
</xsl:element>
```

Note that you surround `name` with curly braces to indicate that it's an XPath expression that you want evaluated—not simply the name you want to use in the new element.

Workshop

This workshop tests whether you understand the concepts discussed today. It's a good idea to make sure you can answer these questions before pressing on to tomorrow's work. Answers to the quiz can be found in Appendix A, "Quiz Answers."

Quiz

1. What element(s) does the XPath expression `*` pick out in the XML document `ch09_01.xml`?
2. What element(s) does the XPath expression `//*` pick out in the XML document `ch09_01.xml`?
3. Using `ch09_01.xml`, what would an XSLT template that inserts the value of `<name>` elements that are children of `<state>` elements into the output document look like?
4. Using `ch09_01.xml`, what would an XSLT template that inserts the value of any element that has a `units` attribute into the output document look like?
5. What would a template that matches both the `<population>` and `<area>` elements look like?

Exercises

1. Using `ch09_01.xml` and XSLT, create an HTML document that displays the names of all the states in an HTML list, using HTML `<UL>` and `<LI>` tags.
2. Using XSLT, convert `ch09_01.xml` into an XML (not HTML) document that does not contain any `<bird>` or `<flower>` elements.

PART II

DAY 10

Working with XSL Formatting Objects

Yesterday you began using XSLT to extract and format the data in XML documents into other forms. Today, you're going to take a look at the rest of the XSL specification: XSL Formatting Objects (XSL-FO). XSL-FO, which is far more involved than XSLT, lets you format data down to the last little detail, such as what font size to use and what margin size.

Today you'll see how to use software to format the data in an XML document into an Adobe Portable Data Format (PDF) file, and you'll be responsible for the complete visual formatting of data. However, note that although XSL deserves a place in Part II, "Formatting XML Documents," of this book, XSL is not in as widespread use as XSLT, so you shouldn't feel that you have to master today's discussion in order to master XML.

Here's an overview of today's topics:

- Using the XSL formatting language
- Formatting objects

- Understanding the `fo` namespace
- Formatting properties
- Using Apache's Formatting Objects Processor (FOP)
- Doing page layout
- Using master pages
- Understanding page sequences
- Using block-level formatting
- Using inline formatting objects
- Using table-formatting objects
- Using rules
- Using graphics
- Using links
- Using lists
- Using tables

Introducing XSL-FO

XSL-FO was created to let you extract the data in an XML document and format it visually as you want it to appear. This is different from yesterday's discussion, where the idea was to use the data in an XML document and simply create a new document.

To let you format individual sections of an output document, the W3C has defined formatting objects such as `root` and `block` that you use as elements (for example, `<root>` and `<block>`) that XSL-FO processors support. By using these elements, you can specify what parts of the output document you want to format. So that you can actually do the formatting, each object has built-in properties (for example, `font-weight`, `line-height`, `border`), which you use as attributes in the corresponding element.

When you use these predefined XSL-FO objects to identify what part of the document you want to format and use their properties to do the actual formatting, you can format your XML data visually. The formatted document can be a Microsoft Word document, a PDF document, or anything that supports the visual formatting you've created. Today you're going to create PDF documents and view them in the Adobe Acrobat PDF viewer.

Like XSLT and the other XML specifications from the W3C, XSL formatting objects have their own namespace, `http://www.w3.org/1999/XSL/Format`. This namespace is usually given the prefix `fo:`, for *formatting objects*, not the `xsl:` prefix you saw yesterday. The current version of XSL-FO is 1.0, and you can find the specification at http://www.w3.org/TR/xsl. The specification for XSL-FO is at http://www.w3.org/TR/xsl/slice6.html, and the specification of the properties you can use with the XSL-FO objects is at http://www.w3.org/TR/xsl/slice7.html. XSL-FO 1.1 is being discussed, as is XSL-FO 2.0, but nothing about them has appeared yet, not even a working draft.

Let's take a look at an example to see what you're working with here. In XSL-FO 1.0, there are 56 formatting objects and 177 properties that apply to those objects. Each of the XSL-FO objects has its own XML tag, and the properties it supports are attributes of that tag; in fact, many of these properties come from CSS2. You can specify how you want the formatting to look by using these objects and properties. For example, here's how you might format the text "XSL-FO Rocks!" in 18-point type in a block (recall that blocks are given their own line in the display):


```
<fo:block font-family="arial" line-height="24pt" font-size="18pt">
    XSL-FO Rocks!
</fo:block>
```

This example uses the <fo:block> element to create a block in the output document, where the font will be Arial, the height of each line will be 24 points, and the font size will be 18 points. When you run this example through an XSL-FO processor, the processor produces a PDF document or another type of document, using the formatting you've specified. Interest in XSL-FO has picked up lately, and a growing number of software packages support it. Here's a sampling:

- Adobe Document Server 5.0 from Adobe Systems (http://www.adobe.com)
- E3 from Arbortext (http://www.arbortext.com)
- FOP from Apache (http://xml.apache.org/fop)
- PassiveTeX from TEI (http://www.tei-c.org.uk/Software/passivetex)
- XEP from RenderX (http://www.renderx.com)
- XSL Formatter from AntennaHouse (http://www.antennahouse.com), which is a commercial product
- XSL-FO Renderer from Advent (http://www.3b2.com)

As with the rest of this book, the best way to see what's going on with XSL-FO objects is by working through an example. The following section takes a look at an in-depth one.

Using XSL-FO

You've already seen a short XSL-FO example, but in fact, XML documents are only rarely formatted by directly using formatting objects as in the example you've seen because the process becomes too complex. What usually happens is that you take an

XML document (with the extension `.xml`), run it through an XSLT processor to create a new XML document that uses XSL-FO (with the extension `.fo`), and then use an XSL-FO processor to create the formatted display document (with the extension `.pdf` in today's discussion). You do things this way because any document except a nontrivial one has many paragraphs of text or data, and to format each one by hand would be a time-consuming process.

In fact, XSLT was originally developed for formatting XML documents by using XSL-FO objects. Since then, being able to access XML data without writing software using XSLT in itself has become so powerful that XSLT has outstripped XSL-FO in popularity.

For example, say that you want to use XSL-FO to format the XML document with state data that you worked with yesterday. Let's use that document today, renaming it `ch10_01.xml`, as shown in Listing 10.1.

LISTING 10.1 An Example of an XML Document (`ch10_01.xml`)

```
<?xml version="1.0" encoding ="UTF-8"?>
<states>

    <state>
        <name>California</name>
        <population units="people">33871648</population><!--2000 census-->
        <capital>Sacramento</capital>
        <bird>Quail</bird>
        <flower>Golden Poppy</flower>
        <area units="square miles">155959</area>
    </state>

    <state>
        <name>Massachusetts</name>
        <population units="people">6349097</population><!--2000 census-->
        <capital>Boston</capital>
        <bird>Chickadee</bird>
        <flower>Mayflower</flower>
        <area units="square miles">7840</area>
    </state>

    <state>
        <name>New York</name>
        <population units="people">18976457</population><!--2000 census-->
        <capital>Albany</capital>
        <bird>Bluebird</bird>
        <flower>Rose</flower>
        <area units="square miles">47214</area>
    </state>

</states>
```

As you'll see later today, the XSL-FO document holding this data that you're going to feed into an XSL-FO processor is about three times the length of ch10_01.xml, which is why it makes sense to use XSLT to convert ch10_01.xml into a document that uses XSL-FO. Let's take a look at the XSLT style sheet that will do that.

Using XSLT to Create an XSL-FO Document

Although you could format ch10_01.xml by hand, it's easier to use an XSLT style sheet to do so. Listing 10.2 contains the style sheet (ch10_02.xml) that you're going to use in this example. In this case, you're just going to extract the state data from ch10_01.xml and present that data in a list form, using 18-point font.

LISTING 10.2 An XSL Document That Adds XSL-FO Formatting (ch10_02.xsl)

```
<?xml version='1.0'?>
<xsl:stylesheet xmlns:xsl="http://www.w3.org/1999/XSL/Transform"
    xmlns:fo="http://www.w3.org/1999/XSL/Format"
    version='1.0'>

    <xsl:template match="states">
        <fo:root>

            <fo:layout-master-set>
                 <fo:simple-page-master master-name="mainPage"
                     page-height="300mm" page-width="200mm"
                     margin-top="20mm" margin-bottom="20mm"
                     margin-left="20mm" margin-right="20mm">

                     <fo:region-body
                       margin-top="0mm" margin-bottom="10mm"
                       margin-left="0mm" margin-right="0mm"/>

                     <fo:region-after extent="20mm"/>
                 </fo:simple-page-master>
             </fo:layout-master-set>

             <fo:page-sequence master-reference="mainPage">
                 <fo:flow  flow-name="xsl-region-body">
                     <xsl:apply-templates/>
                 </fo:flow>
             </fo:page-sequence>

        </fo:root>
    </xsl:template>

    <xsl:template match="state/name">
        <fo:block font-weight="bold" font-size="18pt"
            line-height="24pt" font-family="sans-serif"
```

LISTING 10.2 continued

```
            text-decoration="underline">
            Name:
            <xsl:value-of select="."/>
        </fo:block>
    </xsl:template>

    <xsl:template match="state/population">
        <fo:block font-size="18pt" line-height="24pt"
            font-family="sans-serif">
            Population (people):
            <xsl:value-of select="."/>
        </fo:block>
    </xsl:template>

    <xsl:template match="state/capital">
        <fo:block font-size="18pt" line-height="24pt" font-family="sans-serif">
            Capital:
            <xsl:value-of select="."/>
        </fo:block>
    </xsl:template>

    <xsl:template match="state/bird">
        <fo:block font-size="18pt" line-height="24pt" font-family="sans-serif">
            Bird:
            <xsl:value-of select="."/>
        </fo:block>
    </xsl:template>

    <xsl:template match="state/flower">
        <fo:block font-size="18pt" line-height="24pt" font-family="sans-serif">
            Flower:
            <xsl:value-of select="."/>
        </fo:block>
    </xsl:template>

    <xsl:template match="state/area">
        <fo:block font-size="18pt" line-height="24pt" font-family="sans-serif">
            Area (square miles):
            <xsl:value-of select="."/>
        </fo:block>
    </xsl:template>

</xsl:stylesheet>
```

Today you'll see how `ch10_02.xsl` works and what it does. The first step, as described in the following section, is to put this style sheet to work and create the XSL-FO document.

Creating an XSL-FO Document by Using an XSLT Style Sheet

You're ready to create an XSL-FO document, which you can call ch10_03.fo. This document is the one you'll feed into an XSL-FO processor to create a formatted PDF document that will display the data from the XML document ch10_01.xml. To create ch10_03.fo, you only need to apply the XSLT style sheet ch10_02.xsl to the XML document ch10_01.xml. For example, if you have Java 1.4 or later installed, you can use the Java file ch09_05.class that is in the code download area for this book that you used yesterday, like this:

```
%java ch09_05 ch10_01.xml ch10_02.xsl ch10_03.fo
```

This creates ch10_03.fo, which is ch10_01.xml formatted with XSL-FO. Listing 10.3 presents ch10_03.fo; note the length of it compared to the original XML document, ch10_01.xml, and you can see why it's a good idea to use XSLT to create XSL-FO documents if you're working with data of any significant length.

LISTING 10.3 An XSL-FO Document (ch10_03.fo)

```
<?xml version="1.0" encoding="UTF-8"?>
<fo:root xmlns:fo="http://www.w3.org/1999/XSL/Format">
    <fo:layout-master-set>
        <fo:simple-page-master margin-right="20mm"
            margin-left="20mm" margin-bottom="20mm" margin-top="20mm"
            page-width="200mm" page-height="300mm" master-name="mainPage">
            <fo:region-body margin-right="0mm" margin-left="0mm"
                margin-bottom="10mm" margin-top="0mm"/>
            <fo:region-after extent="20mm"/>
        </fo:simple-page-master>
    </fo:layout-master-set>

    <fo:page-sequence master-reference="mainPage">
        <fo:flow flow-name="xsl-region-body">

            <fo:block text-decoration="underline" font-family="sans-serif"
                line-height="24pt" font-size="18pt" font-weight="bold">
                Name:
                California
            </fo:block>
            <fo:block font-family="sans-serif" line-height="24pt"
                font-size="18pt">
                Population (people):
                33871648
            </fo:block>
            <fo:block font-family="sans-serif" line-height="24pt"
                font-size="18pt">
```

LISTING 10.3 continued

```
        Capital:
        Sacramento
    </fo:block>
    <fo:block font-family="sans-serif" line-height="24pt"
        font-size="18pt">
        Bird:
        Quail
    </fo:block>
    <fo:block font-family="sans-serif" line-height="24pt"
        font-size="18pt">
        Flower:
        Golden Poppy
    </fo:block>
    <fo:block font-family="sans-serif" line-height="24pt"
        font-size="18pt">
        Area (square miles) :
        155959
    </fo:block>

    <fo:block text-decoration="underline" font-family="sans-serif"
        line-height="24pt" font-size="18pt" font-weight="bold">
        Name:
        Massachusetts
    </fo:block>
    <fo:block font-family="sans-serif" line-height="24pt"
        font-size="18pt">
        Population (people):
        6349097
    </fo:block>
    <fo:block font-family="sans-serif" line-height="24pt"
        font-size="18pt">
        Capital:
        Boston
    </fo:block>
    <fo:block font-family="sans-serif" line-height="24pt"
        font-size="18pt">
        Bird:
        Chickadee
    </fo:block>
    <fo:block font-family="sans-serif" line-height="24pt"
        font-size="18pt">
        Flower:
        Mayflower
    </fo:block>
    <fo:block font-family="sans-serif" line-height="24pt"
        font-size="18pt">
        Area (square miles):
        7840
    </fo:block>
```

LISTING 10.3 continued

```
            <fo:block text-decoration="underline" font-family="sans-serif"
                line-height="24pt" font-size="18pt" font-weight="bold">
                Name:
                New York
            </fo:block>
            <fo:block font-family="sans-serif" line-height="24pt"
                font-size="18pt">
                Population (people):
                18976457
            </fo:block>
            <fo:block font-family="sans-serif" line-height="24pt"
                font-size="18pt">
                Capital:
                Albany
            </fo:block>
            <fo:block font-family="sans-serif" line-height="24pt"
                font-size="18pt">
                Bird:
                Bluebird
            </fo:block>
            <fo:block font-family="sans-serif" line-height="24pt"
                font-size="18pt">
                Flower:
                Rose
            </fo:block>
            <fo:block font-family="sans-serif" line-height="24pt"
                font-size="18pt">
                Area (square miles):
                47214
            </fo:block>

        </fo:flow>
    </fo:page-sequence>
</fo:root>
```

You now have `ch10_03.fo`, which is ready to feed into an XSL-FO processor.

Creating a PDF Document

To use `ch10_03.fo` and convert it into a PDF file, `ch10_04.pdf`, you can use what is probably the most popular XSL-FO processor, the Apache XML Project's FOP. You can get FOP for free at `http://xml.apache.org/fop`; just click the Download button. The current version as of this writing is 0.20.4 (0.20.5 is available in a release candidate version, but it's not yet official), and it's written in Java, which means you have to have Java installed in order to use it. The compressed file you download is `fop-0.20.4-bin.tar.gz`.

(`.tar.gz` files are targeted to Unix, but Windows unzip utilities, such as WinZip, from `http://www.winzip.com`, can unzip them as well.)

Here's how to use FOP to convert `ch10_03.fo` into `ch10_04.pdf`, assuming that `ch10_03.fo` is in the same directory where you unzipped FOP (the `-cp` switch here sets the Java `classpath` variable, which you'll discuss further on Day 16, "Using Java and .NET: DOM"):

```
%java -cp build\fop.jar;lib\batik.jar;lib\xalan-2.3.1.jar;
lib\xercesImpl-2.0.1.jar;lib\xml-apis.jar;
lib\avalon-framework-cvs-20020315.jar;lib\logkit-1.0.jar;
lib\jimi-1.0.jar org.apache.fop.apps.Fop ch10_03.fo ch10_04.pdf
```

This is not very easy to type, so FOP also supplies shell scripts for most shells, including a `.bat` file for Windows, which means that the following is usually all you have to type:

```
%fop ch10_03.fo ch10_04.pdf
```

This creates `ch10_04.pdf`, which is the goal you've been working toward. To view this PDF document, you can use the Adobe Acrobat PDF viewer, which you can download for free from Adobe at `http://www.adobe.com` (currently, Adobe Acrobat reader is available at `http://www.adobe.com/products/acrobat/readermain.html`). Figure 10.1 shows `ch10_04.pdf` in Adobe Acrobat. As you can see in the figure, the data from the XML document has indeed been formatted into a PDF document.

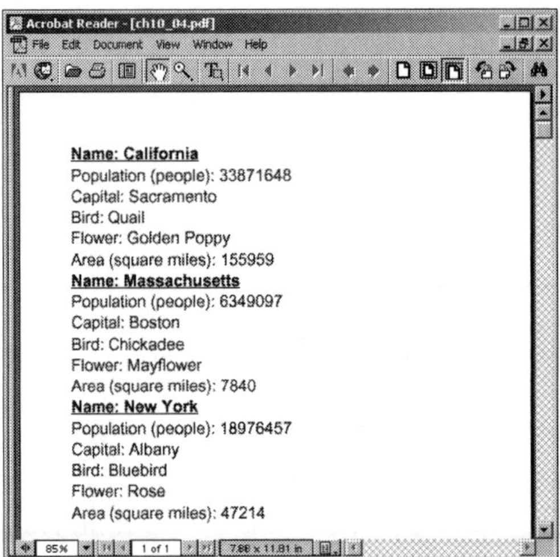

FIGURE 10.1
Formatting XML data in PDF format.

Now take a look at how to create your own XSL-FO formatting.

Using XSL Formatting Objects and Properties

Each of the 56 XSL-FO formatting objects has a corresponding element that you use in XSL-FO documents. Here they are:

- **<fo:bidi-override>**—Lets you overrides the default Unicode bidirectionality algorithm.
- **<fo:block>**—Creates a display block on its own line.
- **<fo:block-container>**—Creates a block-level container.
- **<fo:character>**—Accesses characters.
- **<fo:color-profile>**—Creates a color profile.
- **<fo:conditional-page-master-reference>**—Creates a page master that is used when the specified conditions are met.
- **<fo:declarations>**—Lets you group global declarations together.
- **<fo:external-graphic>**—Embeds an inline image in a document.
- **<fo:float>**—Lets content position float.
- **<fo:flow>**—Creates content flow.
- **<fo:footnote>**—Creates a footnote citation as well as the associated footnote.
- **<fo:footnote-body>**—Holds the content of a footnote.
- **<fo:initial-property-set>**—Formats the first line of a block.
- **<fo:inline>**—Creates an inline formatting area.
- **<fo:inline-container>**—Creates an inline container.
- **<fo:instream-foreign-object>**—Inserts an image or another binary object into an output document.
- **<fo:layout-master-set>**—Creates a set of masters.
- **<fo:leader>**—Creates a rule, a row of repeating characters, or a repeating pattern of characters.
- **<fo:list-block>**—Formats a list.
- **<fo:list-item>**—Contains the label and the body of a list item.
- **<fo:list-item-body>**—Contains the content of the body of a list item.
- **<fo:list-item-label>**—Contains the content of the label of a list item.
- **<fo:marker>**—Together with `<fo:retrieve-marker>`, creates headers and/or footers.

- **<fo:multi-case>**—Is used in a <fo:multi-switch> element for objects that may be displayed or hidden.
- **<fo:multi-properties>**—Lets you switch between property sets.
- **<fo:multi-property-set>**—Creates a set of formatting properties.
- **<fo:multi-switch>**—Lets you switch between formatting objects.
- **<fo:multi-toggle>**—Is used in an <fo:multi-case> element to switch to another <fo:multi-case> element.
- **<fo:page-number>**—Inserts the current page number.
- **<fo:page-number-citation>**—References the page number for a page that contains a citation.
- **<fo:page-sequence>**—Creates a sequence of pages within a document.
- **<fo:page-sequence-master>**—Contains sequences of page masters and is used to create sequences of pages.
- **<fo:region-after>**—Creates a footer.
- **<fo:region-before>**—Creates a header.
- **<fo:region-body>**—Creates the body of a <fo:simple-page-master>.
- **<fo:region-end>**—Creates a sidebar to the right of the page body.
- **<fo:region-start>**—Creates a sidebar to the left of the page body.
- **<fo:repeatable-page-master-alternatives>**—Creates a subsequence made up of repeated alternative page masters.
- **<fo:repeatable-page-master-reference>**—Creates a subsequence of single page masters.
- **<fo:retrieve-marker>**—Is used with <fo:marker> to create headers or footers.
- **<fo:root>**—Contains all the other XSL-FO document elements.
- **<fo:simple-link>**—Contains the start position in a simple link.
- **<fo:simple-page-master>**—Creates a page, which may be divided into up to five regions.
- **<fo:single-page-master-reference>**—Creates a subsequence made up of one single-page master.
- **<fo:static-content>**—Holds elements that must be presented as formatted, not in a flow.
- **<fo:table>**—Creates a table.
- **<fo:table-and-caption>**—Formats both the data and caption of a table.

- **<fo:table-body>**—Contains the table body.
- **<fo:table-caption>**—Contains a block-level caption for a table.
- **<fo:table-cell>**—Creates a table cell.
- **<fo:table-column>**—Formats a table column.
- **<fo:table-footer>**—Creates a table footer.
- **<fo:table-header>**—Creates a table header.
- **<fo:table-row>**—Creates a table row.
- **<fo:title>**—Creates a title for a document.
- **<fo:wrapper>**—Contains inherited properties for a group of objects.

You use these formatting objects with the 177 formatting properties. Many of the formatting properties are the same one you saw on Day 8, "Formatting XML by Using Cascading Style Sheets," such as `background-color` and `background-repeat`. And as in CSS, you can use measurements such as `px` for pixels, `pt` for points, and `mm` for millimeters when you need to specify a size. The following are a sampling of the XSL-FO formatting properties (for all the properties, see `http://www.w3.org/TR/xsl/slice7.html`):

The XSL Formatting Properties

absolute-position	background	background-color
background-image	background-position	background-repeat
border	border-bottom	border-collapse
border-color	border-left	border-right
border-separation	border-spacing	border-style
border-top	border-width	bottom
color	display-align	font
font-family	font-size	font-size-adjust
font-stretch	font-style	font-variant
font-weight	force-page-count	height
last-line-end-indent	left	letter-spacing
linefeed-treatment	line-height	margin
margin-bottom	margin-left	margin-right
margin-top	master-name	max-height
maximum-repeats	max-width	min-height
min-width	padding	padding-after

padding-before	padding-bottom	padding-end
padding-left	padding-right	padding-start
padding-top	page-break-after	page-break-before
page-break-inside	page-height	page-position
page-width	region-name	right
rule-style	rule-thickness	size
source-document	space-after	space-before
space-end	space-start	space-treatment
span	text-align	text-align-last
text-decoration	text-indent	text-shadow
text-transform	top	vertical-align
visibility	white-space	white-space-collapse
width	word-spacing	wrap-option

To see how to use these objects and properties, the following sections dissect the example you've already worked with today.

Building an XSL-FO Document

Now you've seen XSL-FO and gotten an overview of what objects and properties are available; the next step is to see how XSL-FO works by understanding the XSL-FO example. The following sections describe the elements that are involved in the example.

Using `<fo:root>`

The document element of XSL-FO documents has to be `<fo:root>` (although, of course, you can give the namespace any name, not just `fo:`). In the sample XSLT style sheet, you converted the sample XML document's document element, `<states>`, into `<fo:root>` this way:

```
<?xml version='1.0'?>
<xsl:stylesheet xmlns:xsl="http://www.w3.org/1999/XSL/Transform"
    xmlns:fo="http://www.w3.org/1999/XSL/Format"
    version='1.0'>

    <xsl:template match="states">
        <fo:root>
            .
            .
            .
```

The <fo:root> element can contain both a master set layout and page sequences.

The *master set layout*, which uses the <fo:layout-master-set> element, describes the *masters*, or templates, that you want to use in the document. You can specify the default page layout, such as margin sizes, here.

The *page sequences*, which use the <fo:page-sequence> element, specify the format for a sequence of pages. For example, you might give a series of pages the same headers and footers.

The example uses both a master set layout and page sequences, so you can see what they both do.

Using <fo:layout-master-set>

In XSL-FO you can use a *master* as a template for a page, a sequence of pages, or a region on a page. After you create a master, including specifying fonts and margin sizes, you can use it in a page sequence. For example, to create master templates, you can use the <fo:layout-master-set> element:

```
<?xml version='1.0'?>
<xsl:stylesheet xmlns:xsl="http://www.w3.org/1999/XSL/Transform"
    xmlns:fo="http://www.w3.org/1999/XSL/Format"
    version='1.0'>

    <xsl:template match="states">
        <fo:root>

            <fo:layout-master-set>
    .
    .
    .
```

Now you list the masters you want to use in the document in the <fo:layout-master-set> element. For example, you can create a master for each page by using the <fo:simple-page-master> element. You can also create page sequence masters to format pages in a sequence (as when you alternate odd/even page formatting for the left and right sides of a book). In this case, you can format the main page by using an <fo:simple-page-master> element, as described in the next section.

Using <fo:simple-page-master>

You use the page master <fo:simple-page-master> to create a template for a page and outline what goes where. After you create a page master, you can use it where you want in a document. Currently, the XSL specification supports only the <fo:simple-page-master> page master. These are the properties you can use in this element to define the page master:

- Block margin properties: margin-top, margin-bottom, margin-left, margin-right, space-before, space-after, start-indent, and end-indent
- master-name
- page-height
- page-width
- reference-orientation
- writing-mode

In today's example, the page master is named mainPage. You can set the page height, width, and margins like this:

```
<?xml version='1.0'?>
<xsl:stylesheet xmlns:xsl="http://www.w3.org/1999/XSL/Transform"
    xmlns:fo="http://www.w3.org/1999/XSL/Format"
    version='1.0'>

    <xsl:template match="states">
        <fo:root>

            <fo:layout-master-set>
                <fo:simple-page-master master-name="mainPage"
                    page-height="300mm" page-width="200mm"
                    margin-top="20mm" margin-bottom="20mm"
                    margin-left="20mm" margin-right="20mm">
    .
    .
    .
```

That lays out the overall geometry of the page, but there's more to the story: You can also lay out regions in a page, such as the header, footer, and body. You can have up to five regions in a page master in the XSL-FO 1.0 specification:

- **Body**—The body region is the body of the page. To create this region, you use <fo:region-body>.
- **Before**—The before region is the header. To create this region, you use <fo:region-before>.
- **After**—The after region is the footer. To create this region, you use <fo:region-after>.
- **Start**—The start region appears to the left of the body. To create this region, you use <fo:region-start>.
- **End**—The end region appears to the right of the body. To create this region, you use <fo:region-end>.

NOTE

> Note that in languages that read right to left, the start and end regions are reversed.

Each of the region elements also has a number of properties that you can use, as listed here:

- Border, padding, and background properties: `background-attachment`, `background-color`, `background-image`, `background-repeat`, `background-position-horizontal`, `background-position-vertical`, `border-before-color`, `border-before-style`, `border-before-width`, `border-after-color`, `border-after-style`, `border-after-width`, `border-start-color`, `border-start-style`, `border-start-width`, `border-end-color`, `border-end-style`, `border-end-width`, `border-top-color`, `border-top-style`, `border-top-width`, `border-bottom-color`, `border-bottom-style`, `border-bottom-width`, `border-left-color`, `border-left-style`, `border-left-width`, `border-right-color`, `border-right-style`, `border-right-width`, `padding-before`, `padding-after`, `padding-start`, `padding-end`, `padding-top`, `padding-bottom`, `padding-left`, and `padding-right`
- Block margin properties: `margin-top`, `margin-bottom`, `margin-left`, `margin-right`, `space-before`, `space-after`, `start-indent`, and `end-indent`
- `clip`
- `column-count`
- `column-gap`
- `display-align`
- `extent`
- `overflow`
- `region-name`
- `reference-orientation`
- `writing-mode`

10

Using <fo:region-body> and <fo:region-after>

In today's example, you set the margins of the body region by using the available margin properties. In addition, you can set the width or height of the other four regions by using the `extent` property, as in the following markup, which sets the footer region to 20mm height:

```
<xsl:template match="states">
    <fo:root>
```

```
<fo:layout-master-set>
     <fo:simple-page-master master-name="mainPage"
         page-height="300mm" page-width="200mm"
         margin-top="20mm" margin-bottom="20mm"
         margin-left="20mm" margin-right="20mm">

         <fo:region-body
           margin-top="0mm" margin-bottom="10mm"
           margin-left="0mm" margin-right="0mm"/>

         <fo:region-after extent="20mm"/>
     </fo:simple-page-master>
 </fo:layout-master-set>
  .
  .
  .
```

You have now completed the page master you'll use in this document. Besides a page master, you also need to define a page sequence when you format documents in XSL-FO, and that's coming up next.

Using `<fo:page-sequence>`

A *page sequence* is a run of pages that are part of a group, such as a chapter in a book or a section in a report. You create page sequences by using the `<fo:page-sequence>` element. You can use page sequences to alternate page number for even/odd pages in a book, for example. Each such element refers to a page master such as the one you've already created and uses that page master to format its pages.

These are the properties you can use with the `<fo:page-sequence>` element:

- `country`
- `format`
- `language`
- `letter-value`
- `grouping-separator`
- `grouping-size`
- `id`
- `initial-page-number`
- `force-page-count`
- `master-name`
- `master-reference`

You specify the name of the page master you want to use in a page sequence by using the `master-reference` attribute. In today's example, the page master is named `mainPage`, so here's how the page sequence starts out:

```
<?xml version='1.0'? >
<xsl:stylesheet xmlns:xsl="http://www.w3.org/1999/XSL/Transform"
    xmlns:fo="http://www.w3.org/1999/XSL/Format"
    version='1.0'>

    <xsl:template match="states">
        <fo:root>

            <fo:layout-master-set>
                <fo:simple-page-master master-name="mainPage"
                    page-height="300mm" page-width="200mm"
                    margin-top="20mm" margin-bottom="20mm"
                    margin-left="20mm" margin-right="20mm">

                    <fo:region-body
                      margin-top="0mm" margin-bottom="10mm"
                      margin-left="0mm" margin-right="0mm"/>

                    <fo:region-after extent="20mm"/>
                </fo:simple-page-master>
             </fo:layout-master-set>

             <fo:page-sequence master-reference="mainPage">
                .
                .
                .
```

10

The next step is to specify the content of the page sequence, and you do that with the `<fo:flow>` element, as described in the next section.

Using `<fo:flow>`

You use `<fo:flow>` to create a text flow, much like the flow in browsers, where the browser decides how to arrange elements. To create a flow, you specify a region, and the document content flows into that region.

You don't need to let text flow as the XSL-FO processor chooses. Besides `<fo:flow>`, you can also use `<fo:static-content>` in page sequences. The content in `<fo:static-content>` is static, which means it stays as you've arranged it. Static content is often used for headers and footers, where you want to dictate the text content and position, such as page numbers that you might always want centered or on the right.

The <fo:flow> element supports a property named flow-name, and you can use that property to indicate that you want text content to flow into the body region of pages like this, finishing off the <fo:root> element:

```
<?xml version='1.0'?>
<xsl:stylesheet xmlns:xsl="http://www.w3.org/1999/XSL/Transform"
    xmlns:fo="http://www.w3.org/1999/XSL/Format"
    version='1.0'>

    <xsl:template match="states">
        <fo:root>
             .
             .
             .
             <fo:page-sequence master-reference="mainPage">
                 <fo:flow  flow-name="xsl-region-body">
                     <xsl:apply-templates/>
                 </fo:flow>
             </fo:page-sequence>

        </fo:root>
    </xsl:template>
    .
    .
    .
```

Note that the <fo:flow> element, which handles the XML document's content, has an <xsl:apply-templates/> element in it. This means that the XML elements in the XML document will be matched with templates in the XSLT style sheet. For example, to match the <name> elements, you use this template:

```
<xsl:template match="state/name">
        .
        .
        .
```

Now you've matched a <name> element. You want to display its text in bold, underlined text, as shown in Figure 10.1. How do you do that? You start by using <fo:block> to create a block element.

Using <fo:block>

In XSL-FO you can use the <fo:block> element to create block-level elements, much like the ones you created on Day 6, when working with CSS. You use this element to create your own rectangular region that appears on its own line. You can use it to give each data item from ch10_01.xml its own line in the output document.

You can use these properties with `<fo:block>` elements:

- Accessibility properties: source-document and role
- Aural properties: azimuth, cue-after, cue-before, elevation, pause-after, pause-before, pitch, pitch-range, play-during, richness, speak, speak-header, speak-numeral, speak-punctuation, speech-rate, stress, voice-family, and volume
- Border, padding, and background properties: background-attachment, background-color, background-image, background-repeat, background-position-horizontal, background-position-vertical, border-before-color, border-before-style, border-before-width, border-after-color, border-after-style, border-after-width, border-start-color, border-start-style, border-start-width, border-end-color, border-end-style, border-end-width, border-top-color, border-top-style, border-top-width, border-bottom-color, border-bottom-style, border-bottom-width, border-left-color, border-left-style, border-left-width, border-right-color, border-right-style, border-right-width, padding-before, padding-after, padding-start, padding-end, padding-top, padding-bottom, padding-left, and padding-right
- Font properties: font-family, font-size, font-stretch, font-size-adjust, font-style, font-variant, and font-weight
- Hyphenation properties: country, language, script, hyphenate, hyphenation-character, hyphenation-push-character-count, and hyphenation-remain-character-count
- Block margin properties: margin-top, margin-bottom, margin-left, margin-right, space-before, space-after, start-indent, and end-indent
- break-after
- break-before
- color
- font-height-override-after
- font-height-override-before
- hyphenation-keep
- hyphenation-ladder-count
- id
- keep-together
- keep-with-next
- keep-with-previous

- last-line-end-indent
- linefeed-treatment
- line-height
- line-height-shift-adjustment
- line-stacking-strategy
- orphans
- relative-position
- space-treatment
- span
- text-align
- text-align-last
- text-indent
- visibility
- white-space-collapse
- widows
- wrap-option
- z-index

To handle the data in the `<name>`, `<population>`, `<capital>`, and other elements in the XML document, you can use the following templates in `ch10_02.xsl`, which uses `<fo:block>` to create blocks displaying that data:

```
<xsl:template match="state/name">
    <fo:block font-weight="bold" font-size="18pt"
        line-height="24pt" font-family="sans-serif"
        text-decoration="underline">
        Name:
        <xsl:value-of select="."/>
    </fo:block>
</xsl:template>

<xsl:template match="state/population">
    <fo:block font-size="18pt" line-height="24pt"
        font-family="sans-serif">
        Population (people):
        <xsl:value-of select="."/>
    </fo:block>
</xsl:template>

<xsl:template match="state/capital">
    <fo:block font-size="18pt" line-height="24pt"
```

```
            font-family="sans-serif">
            Capital:
            <xsl:value-of select="."/>
        </fo:block>
    </xsl:template>

    <xsl:template match="state/bird">
        <fo:block font-size="18pt" line-height="24pt"
            font-family="sans-serif">
            Bird:
            <xsl:value-of select="."/>
        </fo:block>
    </xsl:template>

    <xsl:template match="state/flower">
        <fo:block font-size="18pt" line-height="24pt" font-family="sans-serif">
            Flower:
            <xsl:value-of select="."/>
        </fo:block>
    </xsl:template>

    <xsl:template match="state/area">
        <fo:block font-size="18pt" line-height="24pt" font-family="sans-serif">
            Area (square miles):
            <xsl:value-of select="."/>
        </fo:block>
    </xsl:template>
```

Now you have created the XSLT style sheet, `ch10_02.xsl`, which converts `ch10_01.xml` into the XSL-FO document `ch10_03.fo`. Congratulations! You've created an XSLT style sheet that transforms an XML document into XSL-FO form, which the FOP XSL-FO processor can now translate into a PDF file.

Handling Inline Formatting

So far today you have created only block elements, but you can also create *inline* formatting. With inline formatting, you format items inline, without giving them their own display block.

A number of XSL-FO elements are designed to handle inline formatting:

- `<fo:bidi-override>`
- `<fo:character>`
- `<fo:initial-property-set>`
- `<fo:external-graphic>`
- `<fo:instream-foreign-object>`

- `<fo:inline>`
- `<fo:inline-container>`
- `<fo:leader>`
- `<fo:page-number>`
- `<fo:page-number-citation>`

The following sections cover some of the most useful of these elements.

Using <fo:inline>

The <fo:inline> element lets you perform inline formatting with text, as when you might want to underline a specific word or even give a word a border. These are the properties you can use with <fo:inline>:

- Accessibility properties: source-document and role
- Aural properties: azimuth, cue-after, cue-before, elevation, pause-after, pause-before, pitch, pitch-range, play-during, richness, speak, speak-header, speak-numeral, speak-punctuation, speech-rate, stress, voice-family, and volume
- Border, padding, and background properties: background-attachment, background-color, background-image, background-repeat, background-position-horizontal, background-position-vertical, border-before-color, border-before-style, border-before-width, border-after-color, border-after-style, border-after-width, border-start-color, border-start-style, border-start-width, border-end-color, border-end-style, border-end-width, border-top-color, border-top-style, border-top-width, border-bottom-color, border-bottom-style, border-bottom-width, border-left-color, border-left-style, border-left-width, border-right-color, border-right-style, border-right-width, padding-before, padding-after, padding-start, padding-end, padding-top, padding-bottom, padding-left, and padding-right
- Font properties: font-family, font-size, font-stretch, font-size-adjust, font-style, font-variant, and font-weight
- Inline margin properties: space-end and space-start
- alignment-adjust
- baseline-identifier
- baseline-shift
- color
- dominant-baseline

- `id`
- `keep-together`
- `keep-with-next`
- `keep-with-previous`
- `line-height`
- `line-height-shift-adjustment`
- `relative-position`
- `text-decoration`
- `visibility`
- `z-index`

For example, Listing 10.4 shows how you can underline the title text Population (people), Capital, and so on by using `<fo:inline>`.

LISTING 10.4 An XSLT Document That Uses `<fo:inline>` (`ch10_05.xsl`)

```
<?xml version='1.0'?>
<xsl:stylesheet xmlns:xsl="http://www.w3.org/1999/XSL/Transform"
    xmlns:fo="http://www.w3.org/1999/XSL/Format"
    version='1.0'>

    <xsl:template match="states">
        <fo:root>

            <fo:layout-master-set>
                 <fo:simple-page-master master-name="mainPage"
                     page-height="300mm" page-width="200mm"
                     margin-top="20mm" margin-bottom="20mm"
                     margin-left="20mm" margin-right="20mm">

                     <fo:region-body
                       margin-top="0mm" margin-bottom="10mm"
                       margin-left="0mm" margin-right="0mm"/>

                     <fo:region-after extent="20mm"/>
                 </fo:simple-page-master>
             </fo:layout-master-set>

             <fo:page-sequence master-reference="mainPage">
                 <fo:flow  flow-name="xsl-region-body">
                     <xsl:apply-templates/>
                 </fo:flow>
             </fo:page-sequence>
```

LISTING 10.4 continued

```
        </fo:root>
    </xsl:template>

    <xsl:template match="state/name">
        <fo:block font-weight="bold" font-size="18pt"
            line-height="24pt" font-family="sans-serif">
            <fo:inline text-decoration="underline">
            Name:
            </fo:inline>
            <xsl:value-of select="."/>
        </fo:block>
    </xsl:template>

    <xsl:template match="state/population">
        <fo:block font-size="18pt" line-height="24pt"
            font-family="sans-serif">
            <fo:inline text-decoration="underline">
            Population (people):
            </fo:inline>
            <xsl:value-of select="."/>
        </fo:block>
    </xsl:template>

    <xsl:template match="state/capital">
        <fo:block font-size="18pt" line-height="24pt" font-family="sans-serif">
            <fo:inline text-decoration="underline">
            Capital:
            </fo:inline>
            <xsl:value-of select="."/>
        </fo:block>
    </xsl:template>

    <xsl:template match="state/bird">
        <fo:block font-size="18pt" line-height="24pt" font-family="sans-serif">
            <fo:inline text-decoration="underline">
            Bird:
            </fo:inline>
            <xsl:value-of select="."/>
        </fo:block>
    </xsl:template>

    <xsl:template match="state/flower">
        <fo:block font-size="18pt" line-height="24pt" font-family="sans-serif">
            <fo:inline text-decoration="underline">
            Flower:
            </fo:inline>
            <xsl:value-of select="."/>
        </fo:block>
```

LISTING 10.4 continued

```
    </xsl:template>

    <xsl:template match="state/area">
        <fo:block font-size="18pt" line-height="24pt" font-family="sans-serif">
            <fo:inline text-decoration="underline">
            Area (square miles):
            </fo:inline>
            <xsl:value-of select="."/>
        </fo:block>
    </xsl:template>

</xsl:stylesheet>
```


Figure 10.2 shows the result. In this figure, the title text is indeed underlined using inline formatting.

FIGURE 10.2
Using inline formatting.

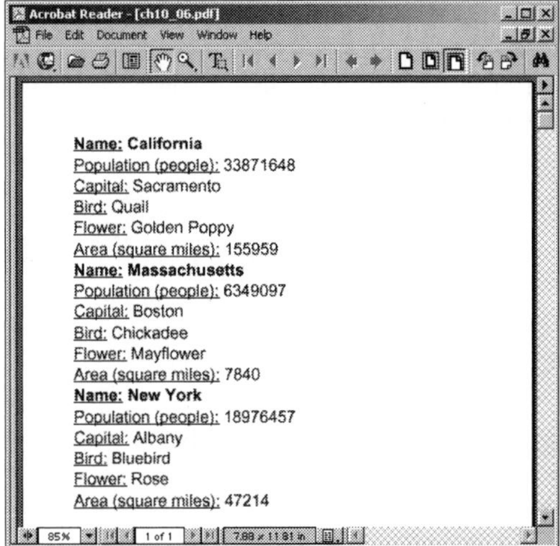

Using `<fo:external-graphic>`

You can use the `<fo:external-graphic>` element to embed image files in output documents. You use the `src` property to specify the URI of the image file, and you can set the size of the image in the document by using the `content-height`, `content-width`, and `scaling` properties (note that if you don't set these properties, the image will be displayed in its original size). Listing 10.5 shows an example, `ch10_07.fo`, that displays the image `image.jpg`, which is included in the download for this book.

LISTING 10.5 An XSLT Document That Uses an Image (ch10_07.fo)

```
<?xml version="1.0" encoding="UTF-8"?>
<fo:root xmlns:fo="http://www.w3.org/1999/XSL/Format">

    <fo:layout-master-set>
        <fo:simple-page-master margin-right="20mm" margin-left="20mm"
            margin-bottom="10mm" margin-top="10mm" page-width="300mm"
            page-height="400mm" master-name="mainPage">
            <fo:region-body margin-right="0mm" margin-left="0mm"
                margin-bottom="10mm" margin-top="0mm"/>
            <fo:region-after extent="10mm"/>
        </fo:simple-page-master>
    </fo:layout-master-set>

    <fo:page-sequence master-reference="mainPage">
        <fo:flow flow-name="xsl-region-body">
            <fo:block>
                <fo:external-graphic src="file:image.jpg"/>
            </fo:block>

            <fo:block space-before="10pt" start-indent="10mm"
                end-indent="0mm" font-size="24pt">
                Images and XSL-FO
            </fo:block>
        </fo:flow>
    </fo:page-sequence>
</fo:root>
```

Figure 10.3 shows the results. In the figure the image `image.jpg` appears in the output PDF file. And that's all it takes.

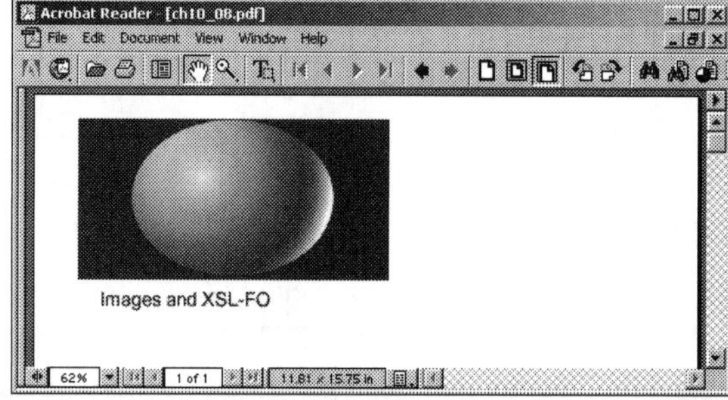

FIGURE 10.3 *Displaying images by using XSL-FO.*

These are the properties you can use with `<fo:external-graphic>`:

- Accessibility properties: `source-document` and `role`
- Aural properties: `azimuth`, `cue-after`, `cue-before`, `elevation`, `pause-after`, `pause-before`, `pitch`, `pitch-range`, `play-during`, `richness`, `speak`,

speak-header, speak-numeral, speak-punctuation, speech-rate, stress, voice-family, and volume

- Border, padding, and background properties: background-attachment, background-color, background-image, background-repeat, background-position-horizontal, background-position-vertical, border-before-color, border-before-style, border-before-width, border-after-color, border-after-style, border-after-width, border-start-color, border-start-style, border-start-width, border-end-color, border-end-style, border-end-width, border-top-color, border-top-style, border-top-width, border-bottom-color, border-bottom-style, border-bottom-width, border-left-color, border-left-style, border-left-width, border-right-color, border-right-style, border-right-width, padding-before, padding-after, padding-start, padding-end, padding-top, padding-bottom, padding-left, and padding-right
- Inline margin properties: space-end and space-start
- alignment-adjust
- baseline-identifier
- baseline-shift
- block-progression-dimension
- content-height
- content-type
- content-width
- dominant-baseline
- height
- id
- inline-progression-dimension
- keep-with-next
- keep-with-previous
- line-height
- line-height-shift-adjustment
- relative-position
- overflow
- scaling
- scaling-method
- src
- width

Using <fo:page-number>

You can use the `<fo:page-number>` element to add page numbers to a document. For example, you might add page numbers to the previous example, which displays an image. Listing 10.6 shows an example of this that aligns the page number at the upper right in the page.

LISTING 10.6 An FO Document That Uses Page Numbers (ch10_09.fo)

```
<?xml version="1.0" encoding="UTF-8"?>
<fo:root xmlns:fo="http://www.w3.org/1999/XSL/Format">

    <fo:layout-master-set>
        <fo:simple-page-master margin-right="20mm" margin-left="20mm"
            margin-bottom="10mm" margin-top="10mm" page-width="300mm"
            page-height="400mm" master-name="mainPage">
            <fo:region-body margin-right="0mm" margin-left="0mm"
                margin-bottom="10mm" margin-top="0mm"/>

            <fo:region-after extent="10mm"/>
        </fo:simple-page-master>
    </fo:layout-master-set>

    <fo:page-sequence master-reference="mainPage">
        <fo:flow flow-name="xsl-region-body">
            <fo:block text-align="right" line-height="24pt" font-size="18pt">
                <fo:page-number/>
            </fo:block>
            <fo:block>
                <fo:external-graphic src="file:image.jpg"/>
            </fo:block>

            <fo:block space-before="10pt" start-indent="10mm"
                end-indent="0mm" font-size="24pt">
                Images and Page Numbers and XSL-FO
            </fo:block>
        </fo:flow>
    </fo:page-sequence>
</fo:root>
```

Figure 10.4 shows the results. As you can see, the page number appears at the upper right.

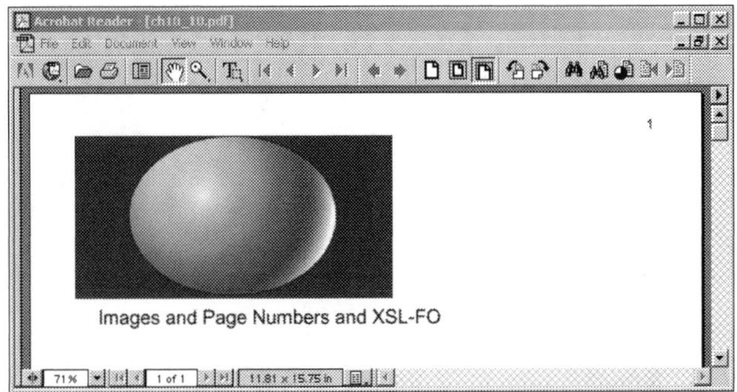

FIGURE 10.4
Displaying page numbers by using XSL-FO.

You can use these properties with the `<fo:page-number>` element:

- Accessibility properties: `source-document` and `role`
- Aural properties: `azimuth`, `cue-after`, `cue-before`, `elevation`, `pause-after`, `pause-before`, `pitch`, `pitch-range`, `play-during`, `richness`, `speak`, `speak-header`, `speak-numeral`, `speak-punctuation`, `speech-rate`, `stress`, `voice-family`, and `volume`
- Border, padding, and background properties: `background-attachment`, `background-color`, `background-image`, `background-repeat`, `background-position-horizontal`, `background-position-vertical`, `border-before-color`, `border-before-style`, `border-before-width`, `border-after-color`, `border-after-style`, `border-after-width`, `border-start-color`, `border-start-style`, `border-start-width`, `border-end-color`, `border-end-style`, `border-end-width`, `border-top-color`, `border-top-style`, `border-top-width`, `border-bottom-color`, `border-bottom-style`, `border-bottom-width`, `border-left-color`, `border-left-style`, `border-left-width`, `border-right-color`, `border-right-style`, `border-right-width`, `padding-before`, `padding-after`, `padding-start`, `padding-end`, `padding-top`, `padding-bottom`, `padding-left`, and `padding-right`
- Font properties: `font-family`, `font-size`, `font-stretch`, `font-size-adjust`, `font-style`, `font-variant`, and `font-weight`
- Inline margin properties: `space-end` and `space-start`
- `alignment-adjust`
- `baseline-identifier`
- `baseline-shift`
- `dominant-baseline`
- `id`

- `keep-with-next`
- `keep-with-previous`
- `letter-spacing`
- `line-height`
- `line-height-shift-adjustment`
- `relative-position`
- `score-spaces`
- `text-decoration`
- `text-shadow`
- `text-transform`
- `word-spacing`

Formatting Lists

XSL-FO lets you format data in lists, by using these four list elements:

- `<fo:list-block>`
- `<fo:list-item>`
- `<fo:list-item-label>`
- `<fo:list-item-body>`

To create a list, you use the `<fo:list-block>` element. You use an `<fo:list-item>` element to create an item in the list. To create a label for each item, you can use the `<fo:list-item-label>` element, and to create the body of the list item, you can use the `<fo:list-item-body>` element. It all sounds simple enough, but as with most things in XSL-FO, even simple things can end up being pretty lengthy. For example, say you want to format and display this short list:

```
1. No
2. worries
3. at
4. all
```

Listing 10.7 shows the XSL-FO to do this. As you can see, you need a lot of XSL-FO to format this list.

LISTING 10.7 Creating a List by Using XSL-FO (ch10_11.fo)

```
<?xml version="1.0" encoding="UTF-8"?>
<fo:root xmlns:fo="http://www.w3.org/1999/XSL/Format">
    <fo:layout-master-set>
        <fo:simple-page-master master-name="mainPage"
            page-height="300mm" page-width="200mm"
            margin-top="20mm" margin-bottom="20mm"
            margin-left="20mm" margin-right="20mm">

            <fo:region-body
                margin-top="0mm" margin-bottom="10mm"
                margin-left="0mm" margin-right="0mm"/>

            <fo:region-after extent="20mm"/>
        </fo:simple-page-master>
    </fo:layout-master-set>

    <fo:page-sequence master-reference="mainPage">
        <fo:flow flow-name="xsl-region-body">
            <fo:block font-size="28pt" line-height="36pt">
                Creating XSL-FO Lists
            </fo:block>
            <fo:list-block
                provisional-distance-between-starts="10mm"
                provisional-label-separation="5mm" font-size="36pt">
                <fo:list-item line-height="24pt">
                    <fo:list-item-label>
                        <fo:block font-family="sans-serif"
                            font-size="18pt">
                            1.
                        </fo:block>
                    </fo:list-item-label>
                    <fo:list-item-body start-indent="body-start()">
                        <fo:block font-family="sans-serif"
                            font-size="18pt">
                            No
                        </fo:block>
                    </fo:list-item-body>
                </fo:list-item>
                <fo:list-item line-height="24pt">
                    <fo:list-item-label>
                        <fo:block font-family="sans-serif"
                            font-size="18pt">
                            2.
                        </fo:block>
                    </fo:list-item-label>
```

10

LISTING 10.7 continued

```
                    <fo:list-item-body start-indent="body-start()">
                        <fo:block font-family="sans-serif"
                            font-size="18pt">
                            worries
                        </fo:block>
                    </fo:list-item-body>
                </fo:list-item>
                 <fo:list-item line-height="24pt">
                    <fo:list-item-label>
                        <fo:block font-family="sans-serif"
                            font-size="18pt">
                            3.
                        </fo:block>
                    </fo:list-item-label>
                    <fo:list-item-body start-indent="body-start()">
                        <fo:block font-family="sans-serif"
                            font-size="18pt">
                            at
                        </fo:block>
                    </fo:list-item-body>
                </fo:list-item>
                 <fo:list-item line-height="24pt">
                    <fo:list-item-label>
                        <fo:block font-family="sans-serif"
                            font-size="18pt">
                            4.
                        </fo:block>
                    </fo:list-item-label>
                    <fo:list-item-body start-indent="body-start()">
                        <fo:block font-family="sans-serif"
                            font-size="18pt">
                            all
                        </fo:block>
                    </fo:list-item-body>
                </fo:list-item>
            </fo:list-block>
        </fo:flow>
    </fo:page-sequence>
</fo:root>
```

Figure 10.5 shows the result of formatting `ch10_11.fo`.

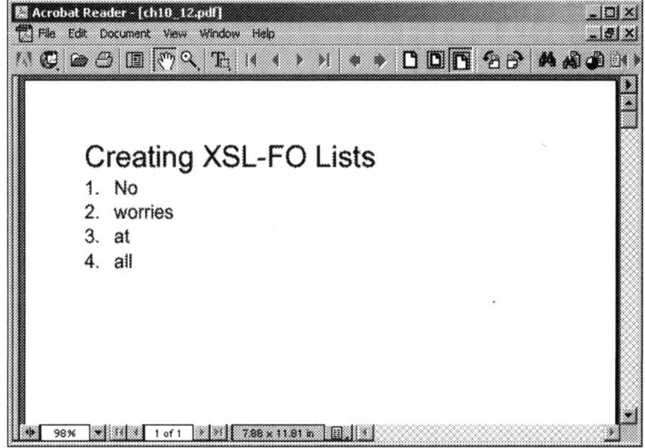

FIGURE 10.5
Creating a list by using XSL-FO.

Formatting Tables

In addition to lists, you can also format tables by using XSL-FO. Tables in XSL-FO work something like tables in HTML. These are the XSL-FO elements that you use to create tables:

- `<fo:table-and-caption>`
- `<fo:table>`
- `<fo:table-column>`
- `<fo:table-caption>`
- `<fo:table-header>`
- `<fo:table-footer>`
- `<fo:table-body>`
- `<fo:table-row>`
- `<fo:table-cell>`

You create a table by using the `<fo:table>` element, and then you format each column by using `<fo:table-column>` elements. Next, you create a table body by using the `<table-body>` element, and you add rows to the table body by using `<table-row>` elements. Finally, you add cells to each row by using the `<table-cell>` element. Listing 10.8 shows an example that displays the flowers and birds for the states example. (Note that you're simply using boldface on text to make a table header in this example because FOP doesn't fully support the `<table-header>` element.)

LISTING 10.8 Creating a Table by Using XSL-FO (ch10_13.fo)

```
<?xml version="1.0" encoding="UTF-8"?>
<fo:root xmlns:fo="http://www.w3.org/1999/XSL/Format">
    <fo:layout-master-set>
        <fo:simple-page-master margin-right="20mm"
            margin-left="20mm" margin-bottom="20mm" margin-top="20mm"
            page-width="200mm" page-height="300mm" master-name="mainPage">
            <fo:region-body margin-right="0mm" margin-left="0mm"
                margin-bottom="10mm" margin-top="0mm"/>
            <fo:region-after extent="20mm"/>
        </fo:simple-page-master>
    </fo:layout-master-set>

    <fo:page-sequence master-reference="mainPage">
        <fo:flow flow-name="xsl-region-body">
            <fo:block font-size="28pt" line-height="36pt" padding-after="12pt">
                Creating XSL-FO Tables
            </fo:block>
            <fo:table width="16cm" table-layout="fixed">
                <fo:table-column column-number="1" column-width="30mm">
                </fo:table-column>
                <fo:table-column column-number="2" column-width="30mm">
                </fo:table-column>
                <fo:table-column column-number="3" column-width="30mm">
                </fo:table-column>
                <fo:table-body>
                     <fo:table-row line-height="26pt">
                         <fo:table-cell column-number="1" border-style="solid">
                             <fo:block font-family="sans-serif"
                                 font-size="20pt" font-weight="bold">
                                 State
                             </fo:block>
                         </fo:table-cell>
                         <fo:table-cell column-number="2" border-style="solid">
                             <fo:block font-family="sans-serif"
                                 font-size="20pt" font-weight="bold">
                                 Flower
                             </fo:block>
                         </fo:table-cell>
                         <fo:table-cell column-number="3" border-style="solid">
                             <fo:block font-family="sans-serif"
                                 font-size="20pt" font-weight="bold">
                                 Bird
                             </fo:block>
                         </fo:table-cell>
                     </fo:table-row>
                     <fo:table-row line-height="26pt">
                         <fo:table-cell column-number="1" border-style="solid">
                             <fo:block font-family="sans-serif"
```

LISTING 10.8 continued

```
                    font-size="20pt">
                    California
                </fo:block>
            </fo:table-cell>
            <fo:table-cell column-number="2" border-style="solid">
                <fo:block font-family="sans-serif"
                    font-size="20pt">
                    Quail
                </fo:block>
            </fo:table-cell>
            <fo:table-cell column-number="3" border-style="solid">
                <fo:block font-family="sans-serif"
                    font-size="20pt">
                    Golden Poppy
                </fo:block>
            </fo:table-cell>
        </fo:table-row>
        <fo:table-row line-height="26pt">
            <fo:table-cell column-number="1" border-style="solid">
                <fo:block font-family="sans-serif"
                    font-size="20pt">
                    Massachusetts
                </fo:block>
            </fo:table-cell>
            <fo:table-cell column-number="2" border-style="solid">
                <fo:block font-family="sans-serif"
                    font-size="20pt">
                    Chickadee
                </fo:block>
            </fo:table-cell>
            <fo:table-cell column-number="3" border-style="solid">
                <fo:block font-family="sans-serif"
                    font-size="20pt">
                    Mayflower
                </fo:block>
            </fo:table-cell>
        </fo:table-row>
        <fo:table-row line-height="26pt">
            <fo:table-cell column-number="1" border-style="solid">
                <fo:block font-family="sans-serif"
                    font-size="20pt">
                    New York
                </fo:block>
            </fo:table-cell>
            <fo:table-cell column-number="2" border-style="solid">
                <fo:block font-family="sans-serif"
                    font-size="20pt">
                    Bluebird
```

LISTING 10.8 continued

```
                            </fo:block>
                        </fo:table-cell>
                        <fo:table-cell column-number="3" border-style="solid">
                            <fo:block font-family="sans-serif"
                                font-size="20pt">
                                Rose
                            </fo:block>
                        </fo:table-cell>
                    </fo:table-row>
                </fo:table-body>
            </fo:table>
        </fo:flow>
    </fo:page-sequence>
</fo:root>
```

Figure 10.6 shows this table after `ch10_13.fo` is processed into `ch10_14.pdf`. As the figure shows, the table appears as you've designed it to appear.

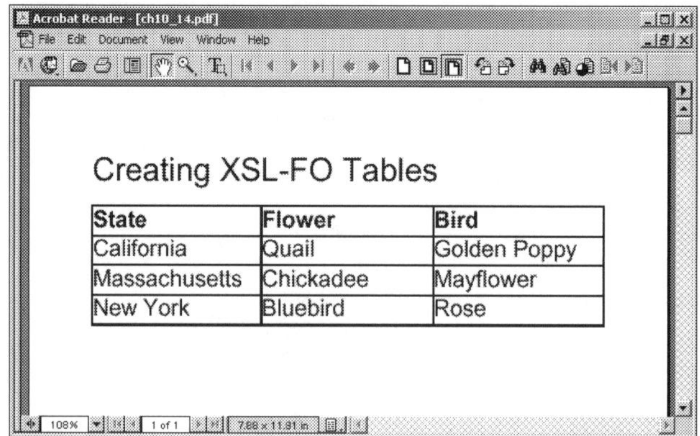

Creating XSL-FO Tables

State	Flower	Bird
California	Quail	Golden Poppy
Massachusetts	Chickadee	Mayflower
New York	Bluebird	Rose

FIGURE 10.6
Creating a table by using XSL-FO.

This completes your look at formatting XML with XSL-FO, and your look at formatting XSL in general. Starting tomorrow you'll see XML in action in the real world, beginning with Extensible Hypertext Markup Language (XHTML) .

Summary

You can use XSL-FO to format every visual detail of the data from an XML document. XSL-FO is more intricate than XSLT because with it you are responsible for the complete visual formatting of your data. Today you saw that there are some XSL-FO formatting processors available, and you put one of them, FOP, to work. Because

XSL-FO–formatted documents are often very long, XSLT style sheets are often used to convert XML documents into XSL-FO documents, which can then be processed by XSL-FO processors into various visual formats, such as .PDF, .RTF, and .DOC.

The XSL-FO 1.0 specification has 56 predefined elements and 177 properties that are attributes of those elements. To master XSL-FO you need to master these elements and attributes, which is no small task.

To start an XSL-FO document, you use an XSML declaration followed by the XSL-FO root element, `<fo:root>`, where the `fo` namespace prefix is `"http://www.w3.org/1999/XSL/Format"`, like this: `<fo:root xmlns:fo="http://www.w3.org/1999/XSL/Format">`.

The `<fo:root>` element can contain both a master set layout and page sequences. The master set layout, which is defined by the `<fo:layout-master-set>` element, describes the masters, or templates, that you want to use in the document. You specify general page layout, such as the margins, in this master. In addition, a master has five regions: the body, before, after, start, and end regions.

Page sequences, which specify the format for a sequence of pages, use the `<fo:page-sequence>` element. You can specify the name of the page master you want to use in a page sequence by using the `master-reference` attribute.

There are two elements you can use to structure the content in a page sequence. The `<fo:flow>` element creates a flow of text and other visual elements that is similar to the content flow in a browser. The `<fo:static-content>` element creates static formatted content, such as headers and footers.

To create a block-level element in a content flow, you can use the `<fo:block>` element. You use attributes such as `line-height`, `font-size`, `font-family`, and `text-decoration` to format the text in a block. You can also perform inline formatting, not just block-level formatting. A number of XSL-FO elements are designed to handle inline formatting, including `<fo:inline>`, which lets you apply formatting to text in place, without having to create a separate block. You can also use the inline element `<fo:external-graphic>` to embed graphics in an XSL-FO document.

You can format data into lists in XSL-FO by using the `<fo:list-block>` element. You can use `<fo:list-item>` elements to create items in the list. You can use the `<fo:list-item-label>` element to create labels for the items in the lists, and you can use the `<fo:list-item-body>` element to specify the body of the list item.

Today you also saw how to format tables by using XSL-FO. You create a table by using the `<fo:table>` element, you format the columns by using the `<fo:table-column>` element, and you create a table body by using the `<table-body>` element. To structure the table body, you can add rows by using `<table-row>` elements, and you can add cells to each row by using the `<table-cell>` element.

Q&A

Q Is there any way of formatting the first line in a block differently than the following lines—for example, to format a paragraph's first line differently?

A Yes. To do this, you can use the `<fo:initial-property-set>`. For example, to use small uppercase letters in the first line, you could use this element inside the `<fo:block>` element:

```
<fo:initial-property-set font-variant="small-caps" />
```

Q Is there any way to work character-by-character in XSL-FO?

A Yes. To do this, you can use the `<fo:character>` element. For example, if you want to replace all the matched text data in an XSLT template with asterisks, `*` (as for passwords), you could use this:

```
<fo:character character="*"><xsl:value-of select="."/></fo:character>
```

Workshop

This workshop tests whether you understand the concepts discussed today. It's a good idea to make sure you can answer these questions before pressing on to tomorrow's work. Answers to the quiz can be found in Appendix A, "Quiz Answers."

Quiz

1. What is the first XSL-FO element you must use in an XSL-FO document?
2. What two items can the `<fo:root>` element contain?
3. What element refers to the header in a page master?
4. What attribute do you use in the `<fo:block>` element to specify the vertical distance each line should get?
5. What attribute do you use in an `<fo:page-sequence>` element to indicate what master you want to use in the sequence?

Exercises

1. Write an XSL-FO document that displays the text of `ch08_01.xml` from Day 8, which is from the stoic philosopher Epictetus. Format this text in 18-point font, and underline the text in the `<title>`, `<philosopher>`, and `<book>` elements. If you have installed FOP, use it to create a PDF file that displays the data in that document.
2. Create an XSLT style sheet that converts the sample XML document `ch10_01.xml` to an XSL-FO table. If you have installed FOP, use it to create a PDF file that displays the data in that document.

PART II

In Review

In Part II we took a look at three ways of formatting and working with XML data without having to do any programming: CSS, XSLT, and XSL-FO. All these techniques have their uses with XML.

Using CSS

CSS lets you format the visual appearance of HTML and CSS by using style sheets. Style sheets are collections of style rules, and each rule shows how to format an XML element. A rule is made up of a selector, which is the element or elements you want to format, and the rule specification, which shows the format you want.

There are a number of ways of creating selectors. For example, you can list an XML element by name, you can create style classes, you can select elements by ID value, and so on.

The second part of a rule, the rule specification, is made up of CSS property/value pairs in a semicolon-separated list, surrounded by curly braces. Many CSS properties are available, such as `text-align`, `text-decoration`, and so forth. You can assign values to those properties by listing those values after a property name, like this, in a rule specification:

```
{text-align: center; text-decoration: underline}
```

You saw in Part II that you can create block-level elements by using the CSS `display` property when you assign the value `block` to it. Block elements are displayed on their own lines. If you don't make an element a block element, it will be an inline element by default; inline elements are arranged by the browser following the normal flow of items that the browser displays.

In Part II you took a look at various text properties, such as those for selecting fonts, font size, font weight, text alignment, indentation, and decoration. And you also saw how to specify colors, backgrounds, and borders and even how to display images. CSS is also good at positioning elements, in both absolute and relative terms.

There are various ways to connect a CSS to an XML document. The most usual in XML documents is by using the `<?xml-stylesheet?>` processing instruction. This example ties an XML document to a CSS by using that processing instruction:

```
<?xml version="1.0" standalone="yes"?>
<?xml-stylesheet type="text/css" href="dickens.css"?>
<document>
    <title>Bleak House</title>
    <author>Charles Dickens</author>
    <chapter>1</chapter>
    <paragraph>
London. Michaelmas term lately over, and the Lord Chancellor sitting in
Lincoln's Inn Hall. Implacable November weather. As much mud in the streets
as if the waters had but newly retired from the face of the earth, and it
would not be wonderful to meet a Megalosaurus, forty feet long or so,
waddling like an elephantine lizard up Holborn Hill. Smoke lowering down
from chimney-pots, making a soft black drizzle, with flakes of soot in it
as big as full-grown snowflakes—gone into mourning, one might imagine, for
the death of the sun. Dogs, undistinguishable in mire. Horses, scarcely better;
splashed to their very blinkers. Foot passengers, jostling one another's
umbrellas in a general infection of ill temper, and losing their foot-hold
at street-corners, where tens of thousands of other foot passengers have been
slipping and sliding since the day broke (if this day ever broke), adding new
deposits to the crust upon crust of mud, sticking at those points tenaciously
to the pavement, and accumulating at compound interest.
    </paragraph>
    <paragraph>
Fog everywhere. Fog up the river, where it flows among green aits and meadows;
fog down the river, where it rolls deified among the tiers of shipping and the
waterside pollutions of a great (and dirty) city. Fog on the Essex marshes,
fog on the Kentish heights. Fog creeping into the cabooses of collier-brigs;
fog lying out on the yards and hovering in the rigging of great ships; fog
drooping on the gunwales of barges and small boats. Fog in the eyes and throats
of ancient Greenwich pensioners, wheezing by the firesides of their wards; fog
in the stem and bowl of the afternoon pipe of the wrathful skipper, down in his
close cabin; fog cruelly pinching the toes and fingers of his shivering little
'prentice boy on deck. Chance people on the bridges peeping over the parapets
into a nether sky of fog, with fog all round them, as if they were up in a
balloon and hanging in the misty clouds.
    </paragraph>
    <paragraph>
Gas looming through the fog in divers places in the streets, much as the sun
may, from the spongey fields, be seen to loom by husbandman and ploughboy.
```

```
Most of the shops lighted two hours before their time—as the gas seems to
know, for it has a haggard and unwilling look.
    </paragraph>
</document>
```

Here's an example of a style sheet, `dickens.css`, that specifies exactly how to format each of the various elements in the XML document by using one style rule for each element type:

```
title {display: block; font-size: 36pt; font-weight: bold;
    text-align: center; text-decoration: underline}
author {display: block; font-size: 16pt;
    text-align: center}
chapter {display: block; font-size: 28pt; text-align: center;
    font-style: italic}
paragraph {display: block; margin-top: 10}
```

Using XSLT

Using XSLT is a powerful way of working with the data in an XML document without having to use any programming code. By using XSLT, you can extract data from an XML document and manipulate it to create a new document in an entirely different format if you choose.

Like CSS, XSLT style sheets are made up of templates. In XSLT, however, you work with nodes in an XML document, not the elements you work with in CSS. XSLT handles XML documents as trees of nodes. In particular, you can use the `match` attribute in the `<xsl:template>` element to match nodes.

By using XPath expressions, you can target nodes you want to work with when using XSLT. XPath location paths are made up of location steps, and each location step is made up of an axis, a node test, and an optional predicate. There are 13 axes in XPath 1.0. Node tests let you identify specific nodes, and the predicate part of an XPath expression lets you use XPath data values, operators, and functions to pin down the data you're interested in.

For example, you can extract the data from this XML document by using XSLT:

```
<?xml version="1.0" encoding ="UTF-8"?>
<inventory>

    <item>
        <name>Widget 1</name>
        <number>10</number>
        <color>blue</color>
    </item>
```

```
    <item>
        <name>Widget 2</name>
        <number>15</number>
        <color>red</color>
    </item>

    <item>
        <name>Widget 3</name>
        <number>5</number>
        <color>green</color>
    </item>

</inventory>
```

Here's an XSLT style sheet that extracts just the names of the items in our inventory and formats them into an HTML document:

```
<?xml version="1.0" encoding="UTF-8"?>
<xsl:stylesheet version="1.0" xmlns:xsl="http://www.w3.org/1999/XSL/Transform">

    <xsl:template match="inventory">
        <HTML>
            <BODY>
                <xsl:apply-templates/>
            </BODY>
        </HTML>
    </xsl:template>

    <xsl:template match="item">
        <P>
            <xsl:value-of select="name"/>
        </P>
    </xsl:template>

</xsl:stylesheet>
```

A more advanced XSLT style sheet might extract all the data from the XML document and format it by using HTML tables, like this:

```
<?xml version="1.0" encoding="UTF-8"?>
<xsl:stylesheet version="1.0"
xmlns:xsl="http://www.w3.org/1999/XSL/Transform">

    <xsl:template match="/inventory">
        <HTML>
            <HEAD>
                <TITLE>
                    Item Data
                </TITLE>
            </HEAD>
            <BODY>
```

```
                <H1>
                    Item Data
                </H1>
                <TABLE BORDER="1">
                    <TR>
                        <TD>Name</TD>
                        <TD>Number</TD>
                        <TD>Color</TD>
                    </TR>
                    <xsl:apply-templates/>
                </TABLE>
            </BODY>
        </HTML>
    </xsl:template>

    <xsl:template match="item">
       <TR>
          <TD><xsl:value-of select="name"/></TD>
          <TD><xsl:apply-templates select="number"/></TD>
          <TD><xsl:apply-templates select="color"/></TD>
       </TR>
   </xsl:template>

    <xsl:template match="number">
        <xsl:value-of select="."/>
    </xsl:template>

    <xsl:template match="color">
        <xsl:value-of select="."/>
    </xsl:template>

</xsl:stylesheet>
```

Using XSL-FO

CSS lets you format XML data visually, and XSLT lets you transform the data in an XML document into other formats. But the only native XML specification that lets you format every visual detail of your XML data is XSL-FO. XSL-FO can be very complex, however; the XSL-FO 1.0 specification has 56 pre-defined elements and 177 properties that are attributes of these elements. Mastering XSL-FO means mastering these elements and attributes.

The `<fo:root>` element can contain both a master set layout and page sequences. The master set layout is defined by the `<fo:layout-master-set>` element and describes the "masters," or templates, that you want to use in the document. Page sequences, on the other hand, use the `<fo:page-sequence>` element and specify the format for a sequence of pages. You can create a flow of text in a page sequence by using the <fo:flow> element. Or you can use the <fo:static-content> element, which creates static content, including headers and footers.

It's difficult to write XSL-FO documents from scratch. Instead, you typically use an XSLT style sheet to format XML into an XSL-FO document, which is what XSLT was originally designed to do. Here's an example of an XSLT style sheet that transforms the XML document containing item data into an XSL-FO document that is suitable for use with XSL-FO processors:

```
<?xml version='1.0'?>
<xsl:stylesheet xmlns:xsl="http://www.w3.org/1999/XSL/Transform"
    xmlns:fo="http://www.w3.org/1999/XSL/Format"
    version='1.0'>

    <xsl:template match="inventory">
        <fo:root>

            <fo:layout-master-set>
                 <fo:simple-page-master master-name="mainPage"
                     page-height="300mm" page-width="200mm"
                     margin-top="20mm" margin-bottom="20mm"
                     margin-left="20mm" margin-right="20mm">

                     <fo:region-body
                       margin-top="0mm" margin-bottom="10mm"
                       margin-left="0mm" margin-right="0mm"/>

                     <fo:region-after extent="20mm"/>
                 </fo:simple-page-master>
             </fo:layout-master-set>

             <fo:page-sequence master-reference="mainPage">
                 <fo:flow  flow-name="xsl-region-body">
                     <xsl:apply-templates/>
                 </fo:flow>
             </fo:page-sequence>

        </fo:root>
    </xsl:template>

    <xsl:template match="item/name">
        <fo:block font-weight="bold" font-size="18pt"
            line-height="24pt" font-family="sans-serif"
            text-decoration="underline">
            Name:
            <xsl:value-of select="."/>
        </fo:block>
    </xsl:template>
```

```
    <xsl:template match="item/number">
        <fo:block font-size="18pt" line-height="24pt"
            font-family="sans-serif">
            Number (people):
            <xsl:value-of select="."/>
        </fo:block>
    </xsl:template>

    <xsl:template match="item/color">
        <fo:block font-size="18pt" line-height="24pt" font-family="sans-serif">
            Color:
            <xsl:value-of select="."/>
        </fo:block>
    </xsl:template>

</xsl:stylesheet>
```

An XSL-FO processor can convert the generated XSL-FO document and into various formats, the most common of which these days is PDF.

In Part III you're going to see how XML is put to work.

Part III

At a Glance

XML at Work

In Part III, you'll see XML at work, as it's used every day around the world. You're going to start by taking an in-depth look at one of the most popular uses of XML around—Extensible Hypertext Markup Language (XHTML).

XHTML is W3C's XML-based version of HTML. As you're going to see, the idea behind making XHTML XML-based is so that you can validate XHTML documents as you would HTML ones; this means you can remove a lot of the sloppiness that's crept into HTML authorship. And you'll see how to extend XHTML with your own elements (something you can't do with HTML).

You're going to take a look at Synchronized Multimedia Integration Language (SMIL), which lets you create XML-based multimedia shows, and Scalable Vector Graphics (SVG), which lets you create graphics images in browsers.

In this part you'll also take a look at XLinks and XPointers, which you use in XML to handle hyperlinks and URIs. XLinks and XPointers can get quite involved; they let you pick out specific parts of documents at will.

Finally, in this part you'll see how to work with the relatively new XForms specification, which lets you display controls such as buttons, list boxes, and check boxes by using XML documents.

PART III

DAY 11

Extending HTML with XHTML

Over the next few days, you'll begin to see XML at work. You'll start with the XML application that has probably the most authors today—Extensible Hypertext Markup Language (XHTML). XHTML is the W3C's version of HTML 4.0, written entirely in XML (and the W3C is responsible for HTML in the first place, so it knows something about the subject). By using XHTML, you can create Web pages that not only work in today's browsers but can also be checked to make sure they're well-formed and valid. You'll put XHTML to work today and tomorrow.

Here's an overview of today's topics:

- XHTML basics
- How XHTML differs from HTML
- The XHTML versions
- XHTML validation
- The `<html>` element
- The `<head>` element

- The <body> element
- The <title> element
- Headings
- How to organize text
- How to display text

Why XHTML?

The main reason the W3C introduced XHTML was that HTML has gotten pretty sloppy. In an effort to serve everybody, HTML browsers tolerate more and more mistakes in HTML; some people say that more than 50% of the code in modern browsers is there to deal with buggy HTML. To fix that, the W3C created XHTML, which uses stricter rules. XHTML is XML, after all, so XHTML documents must be at least well-formed to be considered XHTML (in fact, the W3C also says they should be valid).

Another reason that XHTML was introduced was that, as its name indicates, it can be extended. HTML is limited by the HTML specification (see `http://www.w3.org/TR/html4`) to a fixed set of tags. In XHTML, the idea is that you can define and add your own tags, such as <author>, <data>, <phoneNumber>, and so on. (Note, however, that HTML browsers won't know how to deal with those new XHTML tags yet.)

Let's take a look at an example to see what XHTML looks like. Let's start with the standard HTML document in Listing 11.1.

LISTING 11.1 An Example of an HTML Document (`ch11_01.html`)

```
<HTML>
    <HEAD>
        <TITLE>
            An HTML Document
        </TITLE>
    </HEAD>

    <BODY>
        <H1>
            Long Live HTML!
        </H1>
        This is an HTML document.
        <BR>
        Pretty good, eh?
    </BODY>
</HTML>
```

Figure 11.1 shows this HTML document in an HTML browser.

FIGURE 11.1

An HTML document in a Web browser.

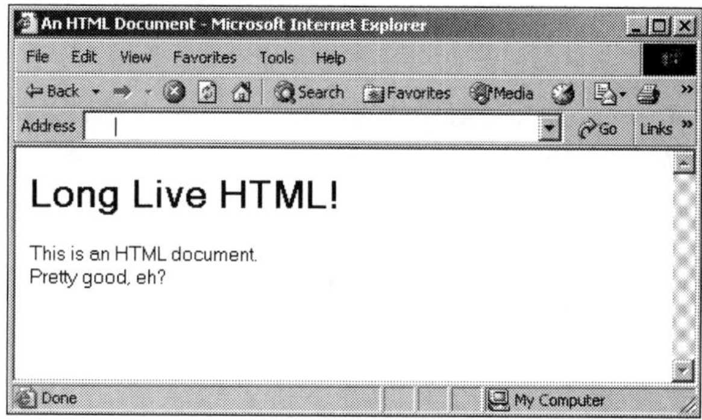

Now take a look at `ch11_02.html` in Listing 11.2, which is the same HTML document as in Listing 11.1, rewritten in XHTML. (You can give an XHTML document the extension `.html` when you want to view it in a browser, or you can give it the extension `.xml` when you want to use it with an XML processor.) There are some differences here from Listing 11.1.

11

LISTING 11.2 An Example of an XHTML Document (`ch11_02.html`)

```
<?xml version="1.0" encoding="UTF-8"?>
<!DOCTYPE html PUBLIC "-//W3C//DTD XHTML 1.0 Transitional//EN"
"http://www.w3.org/TR/xhtml1/DTD/xhtml1-transitional.dtd">
<html xmlns="http://www.w3.org/1999/xhtml">
    <head>
        <title>
            An XHTML Document
        </title>
    </head>

    <body>
        <h1>
            Long Live XHTML!
        </h1>
        This is an XHTML document.
        <br/>
        Pretty good, eh?
    </body>
</html>
```

Figure 11.2 shows this new XHTML document in a browser. As the figure shows, despite the differences between the two documents, the XHTML document works just as the HTML one does, and it looks very much like the HTML document.

FIGURE 11.2

An XHTML document in a Web browser.

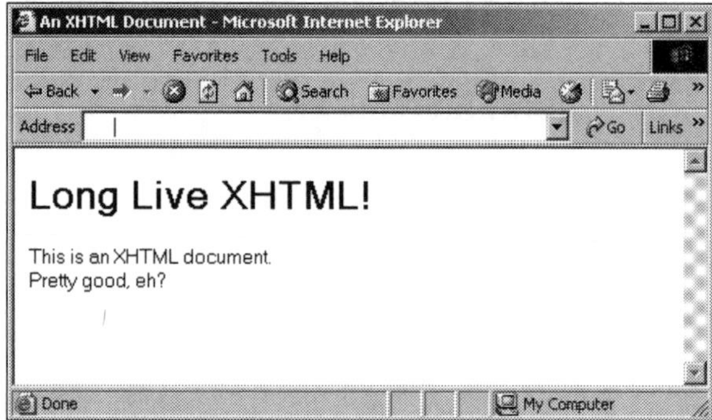

Let's take apart this XHTML example in the following sections to see what's going on here. The first step is to take a look at XHTML itself.

Introducing XHTML 1.0

XHTML 1.0 is the current version of XHTML. XHTML is a rewritten version of HTML 4.0. (HTML is locked now; no future versions will be created; the final recommendation is at `http://www.w3.org/TR/html4`.) The official recommendation for XHTML 1.0 is at `http://www.w3.org/TR/xhtml1`.

The W3C anticipated that it would take some time for XHTML to be accepted, so there are really three versions of XHTML 1.0: Strict (omits all elements and attributes deprecated [that is, made obsolete]in HTML 4.0), Transitional (a looser version, more like HTML as it's used today), and Frameset (the same as transitional, but for use with frames instead of the `<body>` element). Each of these versions has its own DTD, and that DTD can be used by XML processors to validate XHTML document. Here's an overview of these DTDs:

- **The Strict XHTML 1.0 DTD**—This DTD is based on HTML 4.0, and it omits support for elements and attributes that the W3C deprecated in HTML 4.0. This DTD is at `http://www.w3.org/TR/2000/REC-xhtml1-20000126/DTD/xhtml1-strict.dtd`.
- **The Transitional XHTML 1.0 DTD**—This DTD, which is based on the Transitional HTML 4.0 DTD, supports many elements and attributes that were deprecated in HTML 4.0, but are still popular, such as the `<CENTER>` element. Also called the "loose" DTD, this is the most popular version of XHTML. This DTD is

at `http://www.w3.org/TR/2000/REC-xhtml1-20000126/DTD/xhtml1-transitional.dtd`.

- **The Frameset XHTML 1.0 DTD**—This DTD is the same as the Transitional DTD, but it uses the `<frameset>` element for frames rather than the `<body>` element. This DTD is at `http://www.w3.org/TR/2000/REC-xhtml1-20000126/DTD/xhtml1-frameset.dtd`.

Because the most popular version of XHTML today is the Transitional version, you'll use that version today.

Introducing XHTML 1.1

XHTML version 1.1 exists as a W3C recommendation, which is at `http://www.w3.org/TR/xhtml11`. XHTML 1.1 is a strict version of XHTML, and has yet to be really accepted among Web page authors. XHTML 1.1 eliminates all the elements and attributes that were deprecated in HTML 4.0—and a few more as well. The differences between XHTML 1.0 and XHTML 1.1 are listed at `http://www.w3.org/TR/xhtml11/changes.html#a_changes`.

XHTML 1.1's major difference from XHTML 1.0 is that its DTD is designed to be modular. (The W3C refers to XHTML 1.1 as "modular XHTML.") This means that the XHTML 1.1 DTD is really very short; it's simply a DTD driver (refer to Day 5, "Handling Attributes and Entities in DTDs") and just includes other DTDs as needed. It is available at `http://www.w3.org/TR/xhtml11/xhtml11_dtd.html#a_xhtml11_driver`. The idea here is that you can tailor XHTML 1.1 as you like for specific devices, which might not support all XHTML. For example, a PDA or cell phone might not support hyperlinks, and so you can omit those in a DTD driver, as discussed on Day 5. (However, several modules are marked "required" in the XHTML 1.1 DTD, and they cannot be omitted.)

11

Introducing XHTML 2.0

The newest version of XHTML is XHTML 2.0, currently in working draft form. The XHTML 2.0 Working Draft is at `http://www.w3.org/TR/xhtml2`.

Like XHTML 1.1, XHTML 2.0 is modular. However, it appears to be a radical rethinking of the HTML world; XHTML 2.0 strips out all display elements, for example. Here's what the current working draft says:

> The original version of HTML was designed to represent the structure of a document, not its presentation. Even though presentation-oriented elements were later added to the language by browser manufacturers, HTML is at heart a document structuring

language. XHTML2 takes HTML back to these roots, by removing all presentation elements, and subordinating all presentation to stylesheets. This gives greater flexibility, and more powerful presentation possibilities, since CSS can do more than the presentational elements of HTML ever did.

The XHTML 2.0 DTD is not yet published fully; the closest you can come right now is a selection of modules, which are available at `http://www.w3.org/TR/xhtml2/xhtml2-doctype.html#s_doctype`.

XHTML 2.0 is not designed to be backward compatible with HTML or earlier versions of XHTML. In addition, there are new parts to XHTML 2.0 that don't appear in earlier versions, such as support for XForms and XML Events. However, there's little support for these items as yet.

Introducing XHTML Basic

There's one more version XHTML, now a W3C recommendation—XHTML Basic. XHTML Basic is a very small subset of XHTML, reduced to a very minimum so that it can be supported by devices considerably simpler than standard PCs, such as PDAs and cell phones. The recommendation for XHTML Basic is at `http://www.w3.org/TR/xhtml-basic`. Its DTD appears at `http://www.w3.org/TR/xhtml-basic/#a_driver`.

Now that you've been introduced to XHTML, let's start using it.

Writing XHTML Documents

As an XML author, there are a few rules you need to know when it comes to writing XHTML documents. The following are the requirements a document must meet to be an XHTML document, according to the W3C:

- The document element must be `<html>`.
- The XHTML document must validate against one of the W3C XHTML DTDs.
- The document element, `<html>`, must use the `http://www.w3.org/1999/xhtml` namespace, using the `xmlns` attribute.
- The document must have a `<!DOCTYPE>` element, and it must appear before the document element.

Here's a list of some of the main things you, as HTML authors, need to watch out for when creating XHTML documents:

- Element and attribute names have to be in lowercase.
- Attribute values must be in quotes.

- Non-empty elements need end tags. While you can sometimes omit end tags for non-empty elements in HTML, you can't in XHTML.
- You cannot use *standalone attributes* (that is, attributes that are not assigned values) in XHTML. If you have to, you can assign a dummy value to an attribute (for example, noborder = "noborder").
- An empty element needs to be ended with />. The HTML browsers don't have a problem with this ending (as opposed to just >).
- The <a> element may not contain other <a> elements.
- The <button> element may not contain the <input>, <select>, <textarea>, <label>, <button>, <form>, <fieldset>, <iframe>, or <isindex> elements.
- The <form> element may not contain other <form> elements.
- The <label> element may not contain other <label> elements.
- The <pre> element may not contain <img>, <object>, <big>, <small>, <sub>, or <sup> elements.
- You can use the id attribute, but you cannot use the name attribute. In XHTML 1.0, the name attribute of the <a>, <applet>, <form>, <frame>, <iframe>, <img>, and <map> elements has been deprecated. This can be a problem because browsers such as Netscape Navigator support name but not id (in which case the best solution is to use both attributes in the same element, even though it's not legal XHTML) .
- You must escape sensitive characters. For example, when an attribute value contains an ampersand (&), the ampersand should be given as the entity reference &.

Tomorrow you'll talk about a few more requirements (for example, if you use < characters in <SCRIPT> elements, you should either escape such characters as < or, if the browser can't handle that, place the script in an external file) .

Dissecting the Example

Now let's start taking apart the XHTML document ch11_02.html to see what makes XHTML tick.

You start as you would in any XML document, with an XML declaration:

```
<?xml version="1.0" encoding="UTF-8"?>
    .
    .
    .
```

The next element is the <!DOCTYPE> element, to indicate which XHTML DTD you're using—in this case, XHTML 1.0 Transitional (which is the closest to the version of HTML in general use):

```
<?xml version="1.0" encoding="UTF-8"?>
<!DOCTYPE html PUBLIC "-//W3C//DTD XHTML 1.0 Transitional//EN"
"http://www.w3.org/TR/xhtml1/DTD/xhtml1-transitional.dtd">
    .
    .
    .
```

This is just a standard `<!DOCTYPE>` element, and it indicates that the document element in the XHTML document is `<html>`. Remember that there is a different DTD for each version of XHTML, and they're all public DTDs, created by the W3C. The formal public identifier (FPI) for this DTD is `"-//W3C//DTD XHTML 1.0 Transitional//EN"`, which is the DTD for XHTML 1.0 Transitional. You also list the URI for this DTD, for the benefit of XML processors:

```
"http://www.w3.org/TR/xhtml1/DTD/xhtml1-transitional.dtd"
```

These are the `<!DOCTYPE>` elements you should use in XHTML 1.0 for the Strict, Transitional, and Frameset DTDs, respectively:

```
<!DOCTYPE html
     PUBLIC "-//W3C//DTD XHTML 1.0 Strict//EN"
     "http://www.w3.org/TR/xhtml1/DTD/xhtml1-strict.dtd">

<!DOCTYPE html
     PUBLIC "-//W3C//DTD XHTML 1.0 Transitional//EN"
     "http://www.w3.org/TR/xhtml1/DTD/xhtml1-transitional.dtd">

<!DOCTYPE html
     PUBLIC "-//W3C//DTD XHTML 1.0 Frameset//EN"
     "http://www.w3.org/TR/xhtml1/DTD/xhtml1-frameset.dtd">
```

Note that if you're validating XHTML documents against these DTDs, you can download them and store them locally for faster access. For example, if you store these DTDs in a directory named `storage`, it might look like this:

```
<!DOCTYPE html
     PUBLIC "-//W3C//DTD XHTML 1.0 Strict//EN"
     "storage/xhtml1-strict.dtd">

<!DOCTYPE html
     PUBLIC "-//W3C//DTD XHTML 1.0 Transitional//EN"
     "storage/xhtml1-transitional.dtd">

<!DOCTYPE html
     PUBLIC "-//W3C//DTD XHTML 1.0 Frameset//EN"
     "storage/xhtml1-frameset.dtd">
```

Here's the `<!DOCTYPE>` element for XHTML 1.1 (there's only one XHTML 1.1 DTD, not three, as in XHTML 1.0, because XHTML uses Strict XHTML and doesn't have any Transitional forms):

```
<!DOCTYPE html PUBLIC "-//W3C//DTD XHTML 1.1//EN"
     "http://www.w3.org/TR/xhtml11/DTD/xhtml11.dtd">
```

Here's the `<!DOCTYPE>` element for XML Basic:

```
<!DOCTYPE html PUBLIC "-//W3C//DTD XHTML Basic 1.0//EN"
     "http://www.w3.org/TR/xhtml-basic/xhtml-basic10.dtd">
```

And here's the `<!DOCTYPE>` element for XHTML 2.0 (note that the XHTML 2.0 DTD hasn't been posted yet, so the W3C lists the URI as to-be-determined, `"TBD"`):

```
<?xml version="1.0" encoding="UTF-8"?>
<!DOCTYPE html PUBLIC "-//W3C//DTD XHTML 2.0//EN" "TBD">
```

The DTDs at the URIs given by these `<!DOCTYPE>` elements are real DTDs and will work in XML processors. If possible, you should download them and use them locally, however. Imagine the bottleneck that would result from a million browsers all trying to download these DTDs at once.

Following the `<!DOCTYPE>` element is the `<html>` element, which is the document element for all XHTML documents. Note the lowercase here—`<html>`, not `<HTML>`. All elements in XHTML (except the `<!DOCTYPE>` element) are lowercase. That's the way XHTML works, and if you're used to using uppercase HTML tag names, XHTML tags will take a little adjustment. Here's what the `<html>` element looks like:

```
<?xml version="1.0" encoding="UTF-8"?>
<!DOCTYPE html PUBLIC "-//W3C//DTD XHTML 1.0 Transitional//EN"
"http://www.w3.org/TR/xhtml1/DTD/xhtml1-transitional.dtd">
<html xmlns="http://www.w3.org/1999/xhtml">
        .
        .
        .
```

In this case, you're putting the entire document into the `http://www.w3.org/1999/xhtml` namespace, which is the official W3C namespace for XHTML documents. This element also has an `xml:lang` attribute, to set the language for the document when it's interpreted as XML, and the standard HTML attribute `lang`, to set the language when the document is treated as HTML.

The rest of this XHTML example is very much like its HTML counterpart, with the exceptions that all element names are in lowercase and the `<BR>` element has become the more proper `<br/>` XHTML element:

```
<?xml version="1.0" encoding="UTF-8"?>
<!DOCTYPE html PUBLIC "-//W3C//DTD XHTML 1.0 Transitional//EN"
"http://www.w3.org/TR/xhtml1/DTD/xhtml1-transitional.dtd">
<html xmlns="http://www.w3.org/1999/xhtml">
    <head>
```

11

```
        <title>
            An XHTML Document
        </title>
    </head>

    <body>
        <h1>
            Long Live XHTML!
        </h1>
        This is an XHTML document.
        <br/>
        Pretty good, eh?
    </body>
</html>
```

That's your first XHTML document. So how about validating it?

Validating XHTML Documents

To validate XHTML documents, you can use the W3C's own XHTML validator, which is at `http://validator.w3.org`. You just enter the URI of the document or browse to it locally and click the Validate button. The W3C validator checks the document and lets you know how it validates. Figure 11.3 shows how the sample XHTML document does.

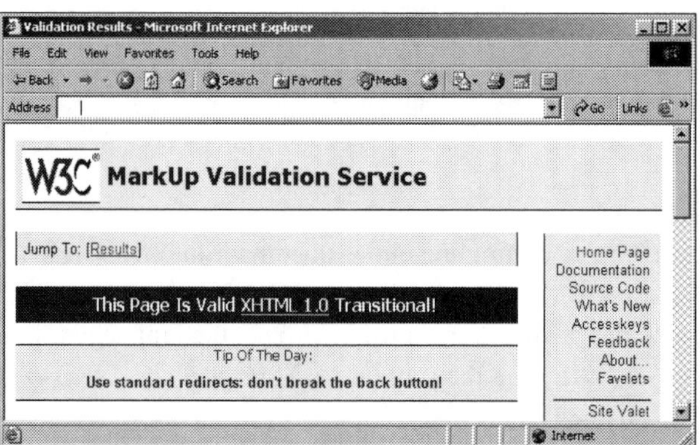

FIGURE 11.3
Validating an XHTML document.

In this case, as shown in Figure 11.4, the document validated properly, and the W3C validator says you can add the official W3C XHTML 1.0 Transitional logo to the document.

FIGURE 11.4
The W3C Transitional XHTML logo.

NOTE

> The W3C XHTML validator doesn't cover all the bases. It doesn't check to make sure that required attributes are present or assigned values, for example. But it's a good place to start.

The Basic XHTML Elements

To be able to use XHTML, you need to know what's available, so the following sections describe the basic XHTML elements and their attributes, with examples. These elements might look like HTML, but they're XHTML, which means they're really XML—and that means that there are rigid rules about which element can or must contain what other elements, which attributes are required, and so on. An HTML author should know these rules when making the transition to XHTML. The following sections list what versions of XHTML support each element and attribute (with the exception of XHTML 2.0, whose list of supported elements isn't even available yet). Let's start with the XHTML document element, `<html>`.

Using the Document Element: `<html>`

As you saw earlier today, the document element for all XHTML elements is `<html>`. This element must contain all other elements in an XHTML document. The `<html>` element is supported in XHTML 1.0 Strict, XHTML 1.0 Transitional, XHTML 1.0 Frameset, and XHTML 1.1. Here are the attributes of the `<html>` element:

- **`dir`**—Sets the direction of text that doesn't have an inherent direction, called *directionally neutral* text. This attribute can be set to `ltr`, for left-to-right text, or `rtl`, for right-to-left text. (Supported in XHTML 1.0 Strict, XHTML 1.0 Transitional, XHTML 1.0 Frameset, and XHTML 1.1.)
- **`lang`**—Specifies the base language of the element. (Supported in XHTML 1.0 Strict, XHTML 1.0 Transitional, XHTML 1.0 Frameset, and XHTML 1.1.)
- **`xml:lang`**—Specifies the base language for the element when the document is treated as XML. (Supported in XHTML 1.0 Strict, XHTML 1.0 Transitional, XHTML 1.0 Frameset, and XHTML 1.1.)
- **`xmlns`**—Is a required attribute that should be set to `"http://www.w3.org/1999/xhtml"`. (Supported in XHTML 1.0 Strict, XHTML 1.0 Transitional, XHTML 1.0 Frameset, and XHTML 1.1.)

As you've already seen today, <html> is the document element for an XHTML document, and it looks like this:

```
<?xml version="1.0" encoding="UTF-8"?>
<!DOCTYPE html PUBLIC "-//W3C//DTD XHTML 1.0 Transitional//EN"
"http://www.w3.org/TR/xhtml1/DTD/xhtml1-transitional.dtd">
<html xmlns="http://www.w3.org/1999/xhtml">
    <head>
        .
        .
        .
    </body>
</html>
```

In HTML, the <HTML> tag is optional because it's the default, and browsers have long come to accept nearly any form of HTML markup. In XHTML, however, the <html> element is required as the document element.

The xmlns attribute is also required, and you use it to set the namespace for the document to "http://www.w3.org/1999/xhtml", as in today's example. The other attributes are optional.

In the XHTML DTDs, the <html> element is declared in such a way that it can contain a <head> element and a <body> element (or a <head> element and a <frameset> element in the XHTML 1.0 Frameset documents). The following section describes the <head> element.

Creating a Document Head: <head>

In an XHTML document, the <head> element contains the document's head, which holds data about the document, scripting elements, and other data not intended for direct display. In XHTML, every XHTML document should have a <head> element, and every <head> element must contain at least a <title> element. The <head> element is supported in XHTML 1.0 Strict, XHTML 1.0 Transitional, XHTML 1.0 Frameset, and XHTML 1.1. Here are the attributes of this element:

- **dir**—Sets the direction of directionally neutral text. This attribute can be set to ltr, for left-to-right text, or rtl, for right-to-left text. (Supported in XHTML 1.0 Strict, XHTML 1.0 Transitional, XHTML 1.0 Frameset, and XHTML 1.1.)
- **lang**—Specifies the base language of the element. (Supported in XHTML 1.0 Strict, XHTML 1.0 Transitional, XHTML 1.0 Frameset, and XHTML 1.1.)
- **profile**—Specifies the location of one or more profile URIs. (Supported in XHTML 1.0 Strict, XHTML 1.0 Transitional, XHTML 1.0 Frameset, and XHTML 1.1.)

- **xml:lang**—Specifies the base language for the element when the document is treated as XML. (Supported in XHTML 1.0 Strict, XHTML 1.0 Transitional, XHTML 1.0 Frameset, and XHTML 1.1.)

You've already seen a <head> element in the sample XHTML document:

```
<?xml version="1.0" encoding="UTF-8"?>
<!DOCTYPE html PUBLIC "-//W3C//DTD XHTML 1.0 Transitional//EN"
"http://www.w3.org/TR/xhtml1/DTD/xhtml1-transitional.dtd">
<html xmlns="http://www.w3.org/1999/xhtml">
    <head>
        <title>
            An XHTML Document
        </title>
    </head>
        .
        .
        .
</html>
```

XHTML specifies that the following elements may appear in the <head> element:

- <base>
- <isindex>
- <link>
- <meta>
- <noscript>
- <object>
- <script>
- <style>
- <title>

11

The only one of these elements that's required in the <head> element is the <title> element, which is described in the following section.

Giving a Document a Title: <title>

The <title> element holds the title of the document. A browser displays the document's title in its title bar. The <title> element is supported in XHTML 1.0 Strict, XHTML 1.0 Transitional, XHTML 1.0 Frameset, and XHTML 1.1. Here are its attributes:

- **dir**—Sets the direction of directionally neutral text. This attribute can be set to ltr, for left-to-right text, or rtl, for right-to-left text. (Supported in XHTML 1.0 Strict, XHTML 1.0 Transitional, XHTML 1.0 Frameset, and XHTML 1.1.)

- **lang**—Specifies the base language of the element. (Supported in XHTML 1.0 Strict, XHTML 1.0 Transitional, XHTML 1.0 Frameset, and XHTML 1.1.)
- **xml:lang**—Specifies the base language for the element when the document is treated as XML. (Supported in XHTML 1.0 Strict, XHTML 1.0 Transitional, XHTML 1.0 Frameset, and XHTML 1.1.)

The W3C XHTML DTDs say that "exactly one title is required per document." You've already seen how to use this element in the XHTML document `ch11_02.html`.

Giving a Document a Body: <body>

The document's body holds the document's content—all the data that the document is meant to display. The `<body>` element is supported in XHTML 1.0 Strict, XHTML 1.0 Transitional, and XHTML 1.1. Here are this element's attributes:

- **alink**—Sets the color of hyperlinks when they're being activated. This attribute was deprecated in HTML 4.0. (Supported in XHTML 1.0 Transitional and XHTML 1.0 Frameset.)
- **background**—Specifies the URI of an image to be used for the browser's background. This attribute was deprecated in HTML 4.0. (Supported in XHTML 1.0 Transitional and XHTML 1.0 Frameset.)
- **bgcolor**—Specifies the color of the browser's background. This attribute was deprecated in HTML 4.0. (Supported in XHTML 1.0 Transitional and XHTML 1.0 Frameset.)
- **class**—Sets the style class of the element. (Supported in XHTML 1.0 Strict, XHTML 1.0 Transitional, XHTML 1.0 Frameset, and XHTML 1.1.)
- **dir**—Sets the direction of directionally neutral text. This attribute can be set to `ltr`, for left-to-right text, or `rtl`, for right-to-left text. (Supported in XHTML 1.0 Strict, XHTML 1.0 Transitional, XHTML 1.0 Frameset, and XHTML 1.1.)
- **id**—Specifies the ID with which to refer to the element. You should set this attribute to a unique identifier. (Supported in XHTML 1.0 Strict, XHTML 1.0 Transitional, XHTML 1.0 Frameset, and XHTML 1.1.)
- **lang**—Sets the base language of the element. (Supported in XHTML 1.0 Strict, XHTML 1.0 Transitional, XHTML 1.0 Frameset, and XHTML 1.1.)
- **link**—Sets the color of hyperlinks that have not yet been visited. This attribute was deprecated in HTML 4.0. (Supported in XHTML 1.0 Transitional and XHTML 1.0 Frameset.)

- **style**—Indicates how a browser should display the element. You should set this to an inline style. (Supported in XHTML 1.0 Strict, XHTML 1.0 Transitional, XHTML 1.0 Frameset, and XHTML 1.1.)
- **text**—Specifies the color of text in the document. This attribute was deprecated in HTML 4.0. (Supported in XHTML 1.0 Transitional and XHTML 1.0 Frameset.)
- **title**—Specifies the title of the body. (Supported in XHTML 1.0 Strict, XHTML 1.0 Transitional, XHTML 1.0 Frameset, and XHTML 1.1.)
- **vlink**—Specifies the color of hyperlinks that have been visited. This attribute was deprecated in HTML 4.0. (Supported in XHTML 1.0 Transitional and XHTML 1.0 Frameset.)
- **xml:lang**—Specifies the base language for the element when the document is treated as XML. (Supported in XHTML 1.0 Strict, XHTML 1.0 Transitional, XHTML 1.0 Frameset, and XHTML 1.1.)

You've seen the `<body>` element in the sample XHTML document already:

```
<?xml version="1.0" encoding="UTF-8"?>
<!DOCTYPE html PUBLIC "-//W3C//DTD XHTML 1.0 Transitional//EN"
"http://www.w3.org/TR/xhtml1/DTD/xhtml1-transitional.dtd">
<html xmlns="http://www.w3.org/1999/xhtml">
    <head>
        .
        .
        .
    </head>

    <body>
        <h1>
            Long Live XHTML!
        </h1>
        This is an XHTML document.
        <br/>
        Pretty good, eh?
    </body>
</html>
```

A number of common attributes of the HTML `<BODY>` element were deprecated in HTML 4.0, so they are not part of either XHTML 1.0 Strict or XHTML 1.1. These attributes include such favorites as `alink`, `background`, `bgcolor`, `link`, `text`, and `vlink`. You're now supposed to use style sheets properties instead of these attributes. Listing 11.3 shows an example that assigns values to some of these properties.

11

LISTING 11.3 An XHTML Document That Uses Styles (`ch11_03.html`)

```
<?xml version="1.0" encoding="UTF-8"?>
<!DOCTYPE html PUBLIC "-//W3C//DTD XHTML 1.0 Transitional//EN"
"http://www.w3.org/TR/xhtml1/DTD/xhtml1-transitional.dtd">
<html xmlns="http://www.w3.org/1999/xhtml">
    <head>
        <title>
            An XHTML Document
        </title>
        <style type="text/css">
            body {background: coral}
            a:link {color: black}
            a:active {color: green}
            a:visited {color: blue}
        </style>
    </head>

    <body>
        <h1>
            Long Live XHTML!
        </h1>
        This is an
        <a href="http://www.w3.org/MarkUp/">XHTML</a>.
        document.
        <br/>
        Pretty good, eh?
    </body>
</html>
```

Figure 11.5 shows the results of Listing 11.3. The W3C's idea in turning toward style sheets to handle the display is that it wants to separate the display details from the data details. That idea is reaching its zenith in XHTML 2.0, which doesn't support even the usual HTML display elements. Theoretically, this transition makes sense, but it has also delayed the acceptance of XHTML by HTML authors.

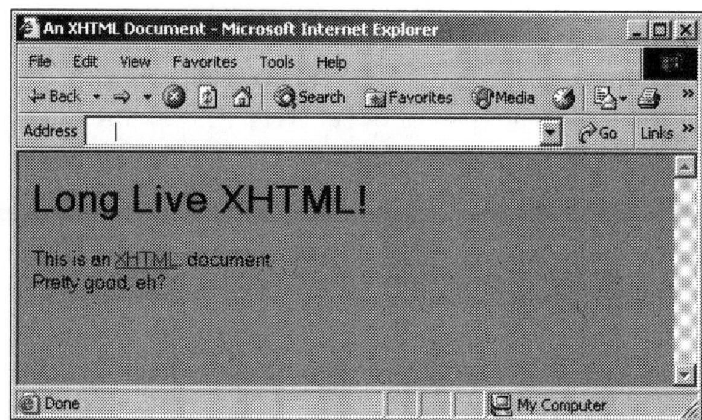

FIGURE 11.5
Using an embedded style sheet.

Note also that if a style sheet contains sensitive characters, such as < or &, you should use external style sheets, as you did on Day 8, "Formatting XML by Using Cascading Style Sheets," because the entire contents of an XHTML document is intended to be valid XML.

Organizing Text

When you want to organize text in an XHTML document, things work very much as they do in HTML. As you've seen, you can place simple text with other elements—in other words, you can use mixed-content models in XHTML:

```
<?xml version="1.0" encoding="UTF-8"?>
<!DOCTYPE html PUBLIC "-//W3C//DTD XHTML 1.0 Transitional//EN"
"http://www.w3.org/TR/xhtml1/DTD/xhtml1-transitional.dtd">
<html xmlns="http://www.w3.org/1999/xhtml">
    <head>
        <title>
            An XHTML Document
        </title>
    </head>

    <body>
        <h1>
            Long Live XHTML!
        </h1>
        This is an XHTML document.
        <br/>
        Pretty good, eh?
    </body>
</html>
```


The five XML predefined entities also work in XHTML:

- `&` is the & character.
- `'` is the ' character.
- `>` is the > character.
- `<` is the < character.
- `"` is the " character.

In fact, there are a great many more character entities in HTML 4.0; they are available at http://www.w3.org/TR/html4/sgml/entities.html, and they're supported in XHTML as well. Here's a sampling:

- `Á` is a Latin capital letter A with an acute accent.
- `α` is a Greek lowercase letter alpha.

- `¢` is a cents sign.
- `€` is a euro symbol.
- `∞` is an infinity symbol.
- `—` is an em dash.
- `Π` is a Greek uppercase letter pi.
- `π` is a Greek lowercase letter pi.
- `®` is a registered trademark sign.

Creating Paragraphs: <p>

The <p> element lets you create block-level paragraphs in XHTML. Note that because <p> is a block-level element, you cannot display other block-level elements inside it. The main difference between <p> in HTML and <p> in XHTML is that in XHTML, every <p> tag needs a closing </p> tag, whereas closing </p> tags are not usually used in HTML. After you've created a paragraph using <p>, you can format it as you like by using style sheets.

The <p> element is supported in XHTML 1.0 Strict, XHTML 1.0 Transitional, XHTML 1.0 Frameset, and XHTML 1.1. Here are this element's attributes:

- **`align`**—Sets the alignment of the text. Possible values include `left` (the default), `right`, `center`, and `justify`. This attribute was deprecated in HTML 4.0. (Supported in XHTML 1.0 Transitional and XHTML 1.0 Frameset.)
- **`class`**—Sets the style class of the element. (Supported in XHTML 1.0 Strict, XHTML 1.0 Transitional, XHTML 1.0 Frameset, and XHTML 1.1.)
- **`dir`**—Sets the direction of directionally neutral text. This attribute can be set to `ltr`, for left-to-right text, or `rtl`, for right-to-left text. (Supported in XHTML 1.0 Strict, XHTML 1.0 Transitional, XHTML 1.0 Frameset, and XHTML 1.1.)
- **`id`**—Specifies the ID with which to refer to the element. You should set this attribute to a unique identifier. (Supported in XHTML 1.0 Strict, XHTML 1.0 Transitional, XHTML 1.0 Frameset, and XHTML 1.1.)
- **`lang`**—Sets the base language of the element. (Supported in XHTML 1.0 Strict, XHTML 1.0 Transitional, XHTML 1.0 Frameset, and XHTML 1.1.)
- **`style`**—Indicates how a browser should display the element. You should set this to an inline style. (Supported in XHTML 1.0 Strict, XHTML 1.0 Transitional, XHTML 1.0 Frameset, and XHTML 1.1.)
- **`title`**—Specifies the title of the element. (Supported in XHTML 1.0 Strict, XHTML 1.0 Transitional, XHTML 1.0 Frameset, and XHTML 1.1.)

- **xml:lang**—Specifies the base language for the element when the document is treated as XML. (Supported in XHTML 1.0 Strict, XHTML 1.0 Transitional, XHTML 1.0 Frameset, and XHTML 1.1.)

Paragraphs are the most basic block elements for text. A browser usually adds some space before and after paragraphs to separate them from other elements, but note that the actual handling varies by browser. Listing 11.4 shows an example that uses both line breaks and paragraphs.

LISTING 11.4 An XHTML Document That Uses Paragraphs and Line Breaks (ch11_04.html)

```
<?xml version="1.0" encoding="UTF-8"?>
<!DOCTYPE html PUBLIC "-//W3C//DTD XHTML 1.0 Transitional//EN"
"http://www.w3.org/TR/xhtml1/DTD/xhtml1-transitional.dtd">
<html xmlns="http://www.w3.org/1999/xhtml">
    <head>
        <title>
            An XHTML Document
        </title>
    </head>

    <body>
        <h1>
            Long Live XHTML!
        </h1>
        <p>
            This is an XHTML document.
        </p>
        Pretty good, eh?
        <br/>
        For more information, see
        <a href="http://www.w3.org/MarkUp/">XHTML</a>.
    </body>
</html>
```

Figure 11.6 shows the XHTML document from Listing 11.4. This example points out the difference between <p> and <br>. The <p> element contains text and makes it into a block-level element; the browser normally uses vertical space to offset it from other elements. The <br> element is an empty element that just makes the browser skip to the next line. You can style the text in a <p> element by styling that element, but you can't style text by using the <br> element.

FIGURE 11.6

Using paragraphs and line breaks.

Skipping a Line: `<br>`

In XHTML, the `<br>` element is an empty element that inserts a line break in text, and you use it like this in XHTML:

```
<br />
```

This element is supported in XHTML 1.0 Strict, XHTML 1.0 Transitional, XHTML 1.0 Frameset, and XHTML 1.1. Here are the attributes of this element:

- **`class`**—Sets the style class of the element. (Supported in XHTML 1.0 Strict, XHTML 1.0 Transitional, XHTML 1.0 Frameset, and XHTML 1.1.)
- **`clear`**—Is used to move past other content. You can set this attribute to `none`, `left`, `right`, or `all`. (Supported in XHTML 1.0 Transitional and XHTML 1.0 Frameset.)
- **`id`**—Specifies the ID with which to refer to the element. You should set this attribute to a unique identifier. (Supported in XHTML 1.0 Strict, XHTML 1.0 Transitional, XHTML 1.0 Frameset, and XHTML 1.1.)
- **`style`**—Indicates how a browser should display the element. You should set this to an inline style. (Supported in XHTML 1.0 Strict, XHTML 1.0 Transitional, XHTML 1.0 Frameset, and XHTML 1.1.)
- **`title`**—Specifies the title of the element. (Supported in XHTML 1.0 Strict, XHTML 1.0 Transitional, XHTML 1.0 Frameset, and XHTML 1.1.)

Using this element as `<br/>` in XHTML doesn't cause any problems in the major browsers.

Centering Text: `<center>`

While HTML was growing up, the `<center>` element was a very popular one. You could use this element to center text and other content in Web pages. Like many other elements and attributes, <center> was deprecated in HTML 4.0 in favor of style sheets, which means that it's only supported in XHTML 1.0 Transitional and XHTML 1.0 Frameset; you won't find it in the XHTML 1.0 Strict, XHTML 1.1, or XHTML 2.0 DTDs. Here are the attributes of this element:

- **class**—Sets the style class of the element. (Supported in XHTML 1.0 Strict, XHTML 1.0 Transitional, XHTML 1.0 Frameset, and XHTML 1.1.)
- **dir**—Sets the direction of directionally neutral text. This attribute can be set to `ltr`, for left-to-right text, or `rtl`, for right-to-left text. (Supported in XHTML 1.0 Strict, XHTML 1.0 Transitional, XHTML 1.0 Frameset, and XHTML 1.1.)
- **id**—Specifies the ID with which to refer to the element. You should set this attribute to a unique identifier. (Supported in XHTML 1.0 Strict, XHTML 1.0 Transitional, XHTML 1.0 Frameset, and XHTML 1.1.)
- **lang**—Sets the base language of the element. (Supported in XHTML 1.0 Strict, XHTML 1.0 Transitional, XHTML 1.0 Frameset, and XHTML 1.1.)
- **style**—Indicates how a browser should display the element. You should set this to an inline style. (Supported in XHTML 1.0 Strict, XHTML 1.0 Transitional, XHTML 1.0 Frameset, and XHTML 1.1.)
- **title**—Specifies the title of the element. (Supported in XHTML 1.0 Strict, XHTML 1.0 Transitional, XHTML 1.0 Frameset, and XHTML 1.1.)
- **xml:lang**—Specifies the base language for the element when the document is treated as XML. (Supported in XHTML 1.0 Strict, XHTML 1.0 Transitional, XHTML 1.0 Frameset, and XHTML 1.1.)

11

Although it has been deprecated, the <center> element is still a very popular one, and it's built into XHTML 1.0 Transitional and XHTML 1.0 Frameset. Listing 11.5 shows an example of using this element in the document `ch11_05.html`.

LISTING 11.5 An XHTML Document That Uses the <center> Element (ch11_05.html)

```
<?xml version="1.0" encoding="UTF-8"?>
<!DOCTYPE html PUBLIC "-//W3C//DTD XHTML 1.0 Transitional//EN"
"http://www.w3.org/TR/xhtml1/DTD/xhtml1-transitional.dtd">
<html xmlns="http://www.w3.org/1999/xhtml">
    <head>
        <title>
            An XHTML Document
        </title>
    </head>

    <body>
```

LISTING 11.5 continued

```
        <center>
            <h1>
                Long Live XHTML!
            </h1>
            This is an XHTML document.
            <br/>
            Pretty good, eh?
            <br/>
            For more information, see
            <a href="http://www.w3.org/MarkUp/">XHTML</a>.
        </center>
    </body>
</html>
```

Figure 11.7 shows what this XHTML document looks like in a browser.

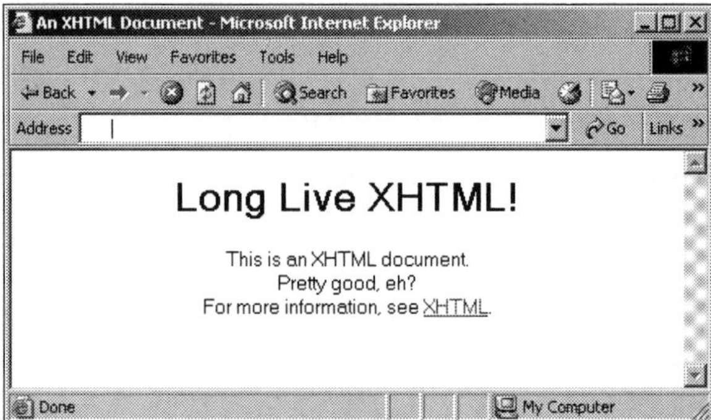

FIGURE 11.7
Centering text by using the `<center>` *element.*

Even though the `<center>` element is still popular, it has been deprecated. So how are you supposed to center text now? You can use the `<div>` element with style sheets, as described in the next section.

Styling Block Content: `<div>`

In XHTML you use the `<div>` element to enclose sections of text or other elements. This lets you style that content as you like. This element is supported in XHTML 1.0 Strict, XHTML 1.0 Transitional, XHTML 1.0 Frameset, and XHTML 1.1. Here are its attributes:

- **`align`**—Specifies the horizontal alignment of the element. This attribute can be set to `left` (the default), `right`, `center`, or `justify`. This attribute was deprecated in HTML 4.0. (Supported in XHTML 1.0 Transitional and XHTML 1.0 Frameset.)

- **class**—Sets the style class of the element. (Supported in XHTML 1.0 Strict, XHTML 1.0 Transitional, XHTML 1.0 Frameset, and XHTML 1.1.)
- **dir**—Sets the direction of directionally neutral text. This attribute can be set to `ltr`, for left-to-right text, or `rtl`, for right-to-left text. (Supported in XHTML 1.0 Strict, XHTML 1.0 Transitional, XHTML 1.0 Frameset, and XHTML 1.1.)
- **id**—Specifies the ID with which to refer to the element. You should set this attribute to a unique identifier. (Supported in XHTML 1.0 Strict, XHTML 1.0 Transitional, XHTML 1.0 Frameset, and XHTML 1.1.)
- **lang**—Sets the base language of the element. (Supported in XHTML 1.0 Strict, XHTML 1.0 Transitional, XHTML 1.0 Frameset, and XHTML 1.1.)
- **style**—Indicates how a browser should display the element. You should set this to an inline style. (Supported in XHTML 1.0 Strict, XHTML 1.0 Transitional, XHTML 1.0 Frameset, and XHTML 1.1.)
- **title**—Specifies the title of the element. (Supported in XHTML 1.0 Strict, XHTML 1.0 Transitional, XHTML 1.0 Frameset, and XHTML 1.1.)
- **xml:lang**—Specifies the base language for the element when the document is treated as XML. (Supported in XHTML 1.0 Strict, XHTML 1.0 Transitional, XHTML 1.0 Frameset, and XHTML 1.1.)

11

The W3C says that you should use the `align` attribute of the `<div>` element to align text. Listing 11.6 shows an example of this.

LISTING 11.6 An XHTML Document That Uses the `<div>` Element (`ch11_06.html`)

```
<?xml version="1.0" encoding="UTF-8"?>
<!DOCTYPE html PUBLIC "-//W3C//DTD XHTML 1.0 Transitional//EN"
"http://www.w3.org/TR/xhtml1/DTD/xhtml1-transitional.dtd">
<html xmlns="http://www.w3.org/1999/xhtml">
    <head>
        <title>
            An XHTML Document
        </title>
    </head>

    <body>
        <div align="center">
            <h1>
                Long Live XHTML!
            </h1>
            This is an XHTML document.
            <br/>
            Pretty good, eh?
```

LISTING 11.6 continued

```
            <br/>
            For more information, see
            <a href="http://www.w3.org/MarkUp/">XHTML</a>.
        </div>
    </body>
</html>
```

This XHTML document gives the same results as shown in Figure 11.7. That's fine, but the W3C seems to have forgotten that it deprecated the `align` attribute in HTML 4.0. To be consistent with the way the W3C has been changing things, you should use a style sheet to style the `<div>` element. Listing 11.7 shows an example of this that gives the same results as Listing 11.6.

LISTING 11.7 An XHTML Document That Uses the `<div>` Element and Styles (`ch11_07.html`)

```
<?xml version="1.0" encoding="UTF-8"?>
<!DOCTYPE html PUBLIC "-//W3C//DTD XHTML 1.0 Transitional//EN"
"http://www.w3.org/TR/xhtml1/DTD/xhtml1-transitional.dtd">
<html xmlns="http://www.w3.org/1999/xhtml">
    <head>
        <title>
            An XHTML Document
        </title>
        <style>
            div {text-align: center}
        </style>
    </head>

    <body>
        <div>
            <h1>
                Long Live XHTML!
            </h1>
            This is an XHTML document.
            <br/>
            Pretty good, eh?
            <br/>
            For more information, see
            <a href="http://www.w3.org/MarkUp/">XHTML</a>.
        </div>
    </body>
</html>
```

You can also position text and other content by using the positioning style properties and the `<div>` element that you saw on Day 6, "Creating Valid XML Documents: XML Schemas." Besides `<div>`, there's another element you can use in XHTML for styling—`<span>`, which you can use for inline styling.

Styling Inline Content: <span>

You can use the `<span>` element to apply inline styles in XHTML. This element is supported in XHTML 1.0 Strict, XHTML 1.0 Transitional, XHTML 1.0 Frameset, and XHTML 1.1. Here are the attributes of this element:

- **class**—Sets the style class of the element. (Supported in XHTML 1.0 Strict, XHTML 1.0 Transitional, XHTML 1.0 Frameset, and XHTML 1.1.)
- **dir**—Sets the direction of directionally neutral text. This attribute can be set to `ltr`, for left-to-right text, or `rtl`, for right-to-left text. (Supported in XHTML 1.0 Strict, XHTML 1.0 Transitional, XHTML 1.0 Frameset, and XHTML 1.1.)
- **id**—Specifies the ID with which to refer to the element. You should set this attribute to a unique identifier. (Supported in XHTML 1.0 Strict, XHTML 1.0 Transitional, XHTML 1.0 Frameset, and XHTML 1.1.)
- **lang**—Sets the base language of the element. (Supported in XHTML 1.0 Strict, XHTML 1.0 Transitional, XHTML 1.0 Frameset, and XHTML 1.1.)
- **style**—Indicates how a browser should display the element. You should set this to an inline style. (Supported in XHTML 1.0 Strict, XHTML 1.0 Transitional, XHTML 1.0 Frameset, and XHTML 1.1.)
- **title**—Specifies the title of the element. (Supported in XHTML 1.0 Strict, XHTML 1.0 Transitional, XHTML 1.0 Frameset, and XHTML 1.1.)
- **xml:lang**—Specifies the base language for the element when the document is treated as XML. (Supported in XHTML 1.0 Strict, XHTML 1.0 Transitional, XHTML 1.0 Frameset, and XHTML 1.1.)

Listing 11.8 shows an example of using the `<span>` element. This example formats the word *XHTML* in red italics (see Figure 11.8) .

11

LISTING 11.8 An XHTML Document That Uses the `<span>` Element (`ch11_08.html`)

```
<?xml version="1.0" encoding="UTF-8"?>
<!DOCTYPE html PUBLIC "-//W3C//DTD XHTML 1.0 Transitional//EN"
"http://www.w3.org/TR/xhtml1/DTD/xhtml1-transitional.dtd">
<html xmlns="http://www.w3.org/1999/xhtml">
    <head>
        <title>
```

LISTING 11.8 continued

```
            An XHTML Document
        </title>
        <style>
            span {color: red; font-style: italic}
        </style>
    </head>

    <body>
        <div>
            <h1>
                Long Live XHTML!
            </h1>
            This is an <span>XHTML</span> document.
            <br/>
            Pretty good, eh?
            <br/>
            For more information, see
            <a href="http://www.w3.org/MarkUp/">XHTML</a>.
        </div>
    </body>
</html>
```

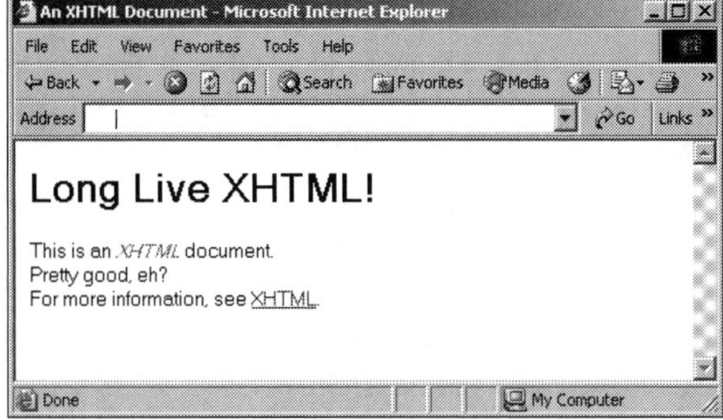

FIGURE 11.8
Using inline formatting.

The <div> and <span> elements are more important in XHTML than they are in HTML because of the reliance on style sheets to handle formatting in XHTML. By handling block styling, the <div> element replaces elements such as <center> in XHTML 1.0 Strict and XHTML 1.1, and by handling inline styling, <span> replaces elements such as <font>.

Creating Headings: <h1> to <h6>

Headings are block elements that present text in bold font of various sizes, allowing you to organize that text into sections. Using headings lets you break up the text flow in

XHTML documents. As in HTML, the <h1> through <h6> elements create headings; <h1> creates the largest text and <h6> the smallest. These elements are supported in XHTML 1.0 Strict, XHTML 1.0 Transitional, XHTML 1.0 Frameset, and XHTML 1.1. Here are the possible attributes of these elements:

- **align**—Specifies the horizontal alignment of the element. This attribute can be set to left (the default), right, center, or justify. It was deprecated in HTML 4.0. (Supported in XHTML 1.0 Transitional and XHTML 1.0 Frameset.)
- **class**—Sets the style class of the element. (Supported in XHTML 1.0 Strict, XHTML 1.0 Transitional, XHTML 1.0 Frameset, and XHTML 1.1.)
- **dir**—Sets the direction of directionally neutral text. This attribute can be set to ltr, for left-to-right text, or rtl, for right-to-left text. (Supported in XHTML 1.0 Strict, XHTML 1.0 Transitional, XHTML 1.0 Frameset, and XHTML 1.1.)
- **id**—Specifies the ID with which to refer to the element. You should set this attribute to a unique identifier. (Supported in XHTML 1.0 Strict, XHTML 1.0 Transitional, XHTML 1.0 Frameset, and XHTML 1.1.)
- **lang**—Sets the base language of the element. (Supported in XHTML 1.0 Strict, XHTML 1.0 Transitional, XHTML 1.0 Frameset, and XHTML 1.1.)
- **style**—Indicates how a browser should display the element. You should set this to an inline style. (Supported in XHTML 1.0 Strict, XHTML 1.0 Transitional, XHTML 1.0 Frameset, and XHTML 1.1.)
- **title**—Specifies the title of the element. (Supported in XHTML 1.0 Strict, XHTML 1.0 Transitional, XHTML 1.0 Frameset, and XHTML 1.1.)
- **xml:lang**—Specifies the base language for the element when the document is treated as XML. (Supported in XHTML 1.0 Strict, XHTML 1.0 Transitional, XHTML 1.0 Frameset, and XHTML 1.1.)

You can see the six heading elements <h1>, <h2>, <h3>, <h4>, <h5>, and <h6> at work in Listing 11.9.

LISTING 11.9 An XHTML Document That Uses Headings (ch11_09.html)

```
<?xml version="1.0" encoding="UTF-8"?>
<!DOCTYPE html PUBLIC "-//W3C//DTD XHTML 1.0 Transitional//EN"
"http://www.w3.org/TR/xhtml1/DTD/xhtml1-transitional.dtd">
<html xmlns="http://www.w3.org/1999/xhtml">
    <head>
        <title>
            Using Headings
        </title>
        <style>
            div {text-align: center}
```

LISTING 11.9 continued

```
        </style>
    </head>

    <body>
        <div>
            <h1>Here is an &lt;h1&gt; heading</h1>
            <h2>Here is an &lt;h2&gt; heading</h2>
            <h3>Here is an &lt;h3&gt; heading</h3>
            <h4>Here is an &lt;h4&gt; heading</h4>
            <h5>Here is an &lt;h5&gt; heading</h5>
            <h6>Here is an &lt;h6&gt; heading</h6>
        </div>
    </body>
</html>
```

Figure 11.9 shows this XHTML document in a browser.

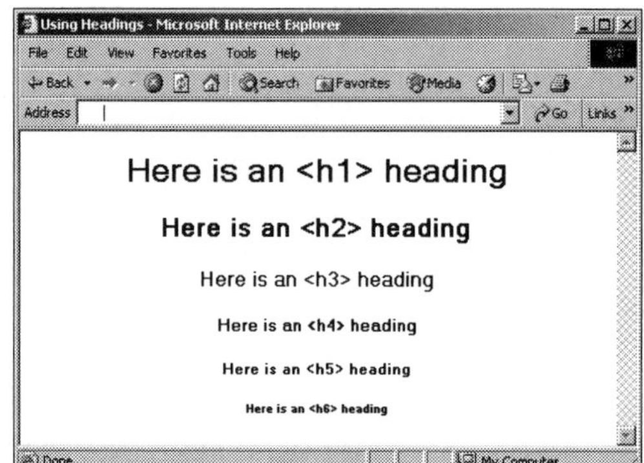

FIGURE 11.9
Using headings in XHTML.

Formatting Text

Although the emphasis in XHTML is turning toward formatting text and other content by using style sheets, XHTML 1.0 and XHTML 1.1 both support the traditional popular HTML formatting elements, such as `<b>` and `<i>`. The following sections take a look at them. Bear in mind that although these elements are still available, they're being phased out of XHTML and won't appear in XHTML 2.0.

Using Bold on Text: <b>

The `<b>` element applies boldface to its enclosed text. This element is supported in XHTML 1.0 Strict, XHTML 1.0 Transitional, XHTML 1.0 Frameset, and XHTML 1.1. Here are its attributes:

- **`class`**—Sets the style class of the element. (Supported in XHTML 1.0 Strict, XHTML 1.0 Transitional, XHTML 1.0 Frameset, and XHTML 1.1.)
- **`dir`**—Sets the direction of directionally neutral text. This attribute can be set to `ltr`, for left-to-right text, or `rtl`, for right-to-left text. (Supported in XHTML 1.0 Strict, XHTML 1.0 Transitional, XHTML 1.0 Frameset, and XHTML 1.1.)
- **`id`**—Specifies the ID with which to refer to the element. You should set this attribute to a unique identifier. (Supported in XHTML 1.0 Strict, XHTML 1.0 Transitional, XHTML 1.0 Frameset, and XHTML 1.1.)
- **`lang`**—Sets the base language of the element. (Supported in XHTML 1.0 Strict, XHTML 1.0 Transitional, XHTML 1.0 Frameset, and XHTML 1.1.)
- **`style`**—Indicates how a browser should display the element. You should set this to an inline style. (Supported in XHTML 1.0 Strict, XHTML 1.0 Transitional, XHTML 1.0 Frameset, and XHTML 1.1.)
- **`title`**—Specifies the title of the element. (Supported in XHTML 1.0 Strict, XHTML 1.0 Transitional, XHTML 1.0 Frameset, and XHTML 1.1.)
- **`xml:lang`**—Specifies the base language for the element when the document is treated as XML. (Supported in XHTML 1.0 Strict, XHTML 1.0 Transitional, XHTML 1.0 Frameset, and XHTML 1.1.)

11

You use a `<b>` element to bold text with inline styling. Listing 11.10 shows a sample XHTML document (`ch11_10.html`) that bolds text by using `<b>`, formats it in italics by using `<i>`, and underlines it by using `<u>`.

LISTING 11.10 An XHTML Document That Displays Bold, Italic, and Underlined Text (`ch11_10.html`)

```
<?xml version="1.0" encoding="UTF-8"?>
<!DOCTYPE html PUBLIC "-//W3C//DTD XHTML 1.0 Transitional//EN"
"http://www.w3.org/TR/xhtml1/DTD/xhtml1-transitional.dtd">
<html xmlns="http://www.w3.org/1999/xhtml">
    <head>
        <title>
            Displaying Bold, Underlined, and Italic Text
        </title>
    </head>

    <body>
        <i>This text is in italics!</i>
        <br />
        <b>This text is bold!</b>
        <br />
        <u>This text is underlined!</u>
    </body>
</html>
```

Figure 11.10 shows this XHTML document in a browser; as you can see, the text the example formats appears in bold, italic, and underlined, as intended.

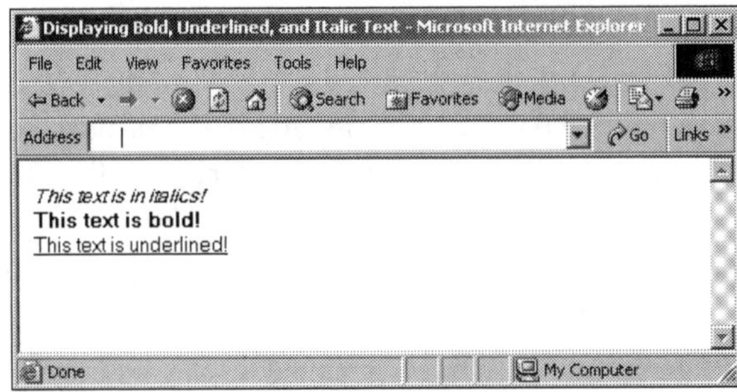

FIGURE 11.10
Displaying italic, bold, and underlined text.

Italicizing Text: `<i>`

The `<i>` element, which supports rudimentary inline text formatting, makes text italic. The `<i>` element is supported in XHTML 1.0 Strict, XHTML 1.0 Transitional, XHTML 1.0 Frameset, and XHTML 1.1. Here are its attributes:

- **`class`**—Sets the style class of the element. (Supported in XHTML 1.0 Strict, XHTML 1.0 Transitional, XHTML 1.0 Frameset, and XHTML 1.1.)
- **`dir`**—Sets the direction of directionally neutral text. This attribute can be set to `ltr`, for left-to-right text, or `rtl`, for right-to-left text. (Supported in XHTML 1.0 Strict, XHTML 1.0 Transitional, XHTML 1.0 Frameset, and XHTML 1.1.)
- **`id`**—Specifies the ID with which to refer to the element. You should set this attribute to a unique identifier. (Supported in XHTML 1.0 Strict, XHTML 1.0 Transitional, XHTML 1.0 Frameset, and XHTML 1.1.)
- **`lang`**—Sets the base language of the element. (Supported in XHTML 1.0 Strict, XHTML 1.0 Transitional, XHTML 1.0 Frameset, and XHTML 1.1.)
- **`style`**—Indicates how a browser should display the element. You should set this to an inline style. (Supported in XHTML 1.0 Strict, XHTML 1.0 Transitional, XHTML 1.0 Frameset, and XHTML 1.1.)
- **`title`**—Specifies the title of the element. (Supported in XHTML 1.0 Strict, XHTML 1.0 Transitional, XHTML 1.0 Frameset, and XHTML 1.1.)
- **`xml:lang`**—Specifies the base language for the element when the document is treated as XML. (Supported in XHTML 1.0 Strict, XHTML 1.0 Transitional, XHTML 1.0 Frameset, and XHTML 1.1.)

In the previous section you saw the <i> element at work, in Listing 11.10 and Figure 11.10.

Underlining Text: <u>

The <u> element performs some rudimentary inline formatting by underlining text. This element was deprecated in HTML 4.0, so it is not supported in XHTML 1.0 Strict or XHTML 1.1. However, it is supported in XHTML 1.0 Transitional and XHTML 1.0 Frameset. Here are the attributes of this element:

- **`class`**—Sets the style class of the element. (Supported in XHTML 1.0 Strict, XHTML 1.0 Transitional, XHTML 1.0 Frameset, and XHTML 1.1.)
- **`dir`**—Sets the direction of directionally neutral text. This attribute can be set to `ltr`, for left-to-right text, or `rtl`, for right-to-left text. (Supported in XHTML 1.0 Strict, XHTML 1.0 Transitional, XHTML 1.0 Frameset, and XHTML 1.1.)
- **`id`**—Specifies the ID with which to refer to the element. You should set this attribute to a unique identifier. (Supported in XHTML 1.0 Strict, XHTML 1.0 Transitional, XHTML 1.0 Frameset, and XHTML 1.1.)
- **`lang`**—Sets the base language of the element. (Supported in XHTML 1.0 Strict, XHTML 1.0 Transitional, XHTML 1.0 Frameset, and XHTML 1.1.)
- **`style`**—Indicates how a browser should display the element. You should set this to an inline style. (Supported in XHTML 1.0 Strict, XHTML 1.0 Transitional, XHTML 1.0 Frameset, and XHTML 1.1.)
- **`title`**—Specifies the title of the element. (Supported in XHTML 1.0 Strict, XHTML 1.0 Transitional, XHTML 1.0 Frameset, and XHTML 1.1.)
- **`xml:lang`**—Specifies the base language for the element when the document is interpreted as an XML document. (Supported in XHTML 1.0 Transitional, and XHTML 1.0 Frameset.)

Like many other formatting elements, the <u> element was deprecated in HTML 4.0 in favor of style sheets (`"text-decoration=underline"`), so it's not available in Strict XHTML 1.0, XHTML 1.1, or XHMTL 2.0. You saw the <u> element at work, in Listing 11.10 and Figure 11.10.

Selecting Fonts: <font>

The <font> element lets you select the font for text, as well as its size and color. This element was deprecated in HTML 4.0 in favor of style sheets, which means it's available in XHTML 1.0 Transitional and XHTML 1.0 Frameset, but not in XHTML 1.1 or XHTML 1.0 Strict. Here are this element's attributes:

- **class**—Sets the style class of the element. (Supported in XHTML 1.0 Strict, XHTML 1.0 Transitional, XHTML 1.0 Frameset, and XHTML 1.1.)
- **color**—Sets the color of the text. This attribute was deprecated in XHTML 4.0. (Supported in XHTML 1.0 Transitional, and XHTML 1.0 Frameset.)
- **dir**—Sets the direction of directionally neutral text. This attribute can be set to `ltr`, for left-to-right text, or `rtl`, for right-to-left text. (Supported in XHTML 1.0 Strict, XHTML 1.0 Transitional, XHTML 1.0 Frameset, and XHTML 1.1.)
- **face**—Specifies a single font name or a list of names, separated by commas. This attribute was deprecated in HTML 4.0. (Supported in XHTML 1.0 Transitional and XHTML 1.0 Frameset.)
- **id**—Specifies the ID with which to refer to the element. You should set this attribute to a unique identifier. (Supported in XHTML 1.0 Strict, XHTML 1.0 Transitional, XHTML 1.0 Frameset, and XHTML 1.1.)
- **lang**—Sets the base language of the element. (Supported in XHTML 1.0 Strict, XHTML 1.0 Transitional, XHTML 1.0 Frameset, and XHTML 1.1.)
- **size**—Specifies the size of the text, from 1 (the smallest) through 7 (the biggest). This attribute was deprecated in HTML 4.0. (Supported in XHTML 1.0 Transitional and XHTML 1.0 Frameset.)
- **style**—Indicates how a browser should display the element. You should set this to an inline style. (Supported in XHTML 1.0 Strict, XHTML 1.0 Transitional, XHTML 1.0 Frameset, and XHTML 1.1.)
- **title**—Specifies the title of the body. (Supported in XHTML 1.0 Strict, XHTML 1.0 Transitional, XHTML 1.0 Frameset, and XHTML 1.1.)
- **xml:lang**—Specifies the base language for the element when the document is treated as XML. (Supported in XHTML 1.0 Strict, XHTML 1.0 Transitional, XHTML 1.0 Frameset, and XHTML 1.1.)

This element was indeed deprecated in HTML 4.0 (you can use `<div>` or `<span>` elements instead, together with the font CSS properties), but it's still in widespread use and available in XHTML 1.0 Transitional and XHTML 1.0 Frameset, so you'll take a quick look at it here. An example is shown in Listing 11.11 and Figure 11.11. This example uses the `<font>` element and its attributes to specify Times New Roman font in blue.

LISTING 11.11 An XHTML Document That Uses the `<font>` Element (`ch11_11.html`)

```
<?xml version="1.0" encoding="UTF-8"?>
<!DOCTYPE html PUBLIC "-//W3C//DTD XHTML 1.0 Transitional//EN"
"http://www.w3.org/TR/xhtml1/DTD/xhtml1-transitional.dtd">
<html xmlns="http://www.w3.org/1999/xhtml">
    <head>
        <title>
            Setting Fonts
        </title>
    </head>

    <body>
        <h1>
            Using the &lt;font&gt; element
        </h1>
        <font size="4" color="blue" face="Times New Roman">
            The &lt;font&gt; element is popular,
            but don't forget that it's deprecated.
        </font>
    </body>
</html>
```

11

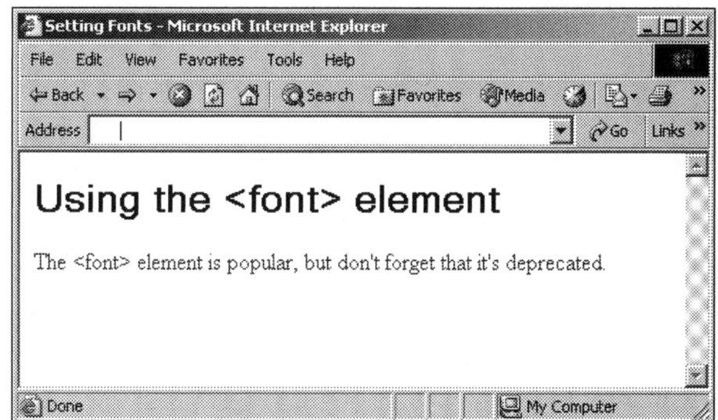

FIGURE 11.11
Using the `<font>` *element in Internet Explorer.*

The font size is set to 4 in `ch11_11.html` (`size="4"`). The `<font>` element lets you set the font sizes from 1 to 7, with 7 being the largest. The example in Listing 11.12 shows all the possible font sizes.

LISTING 11.12 An XHTML Document That Displays Font Sizes (`ch11_12.html`)

```
<?xml version="1.0" encoding="UTF-8"?>
<!DOCTYPE html PUBLIC "-//W3C//DTD XHTML 1.0 Transitional//EN"
"http://www.w3.org/TR/xhtml1/DTD/xhtml1-transitional.dtd">
<html xmlns="http://www.w3.org/1999/xhtml">
```

LISTING 11.12 continued

```
    <head>
        <title>
            Font Sizes
        </title>
        <style>
            div {text-align: center}
        </style>
    </head>

    <body>
        <div>
            <h1>
                Font Sizes
            </h1>
            <font size="7">Here's size 7.</font>
            <br />
            <font size="6">Here's size 6.</font>
            <br />
            <font size="5">Here's size 5.</font>
            <br />
            <font size="4">Here's size 4.</font>
            <br />
            <font size="3">Here's size 3.</font>
            <br />
            <font size="2">Here's size 2.</font>
            <br />
            <font size="1">Here's size 1.</font>
        </div>
    </body>
</html>
```

Figure 11.12 shows this XHTML document, which shows the various font sizes.

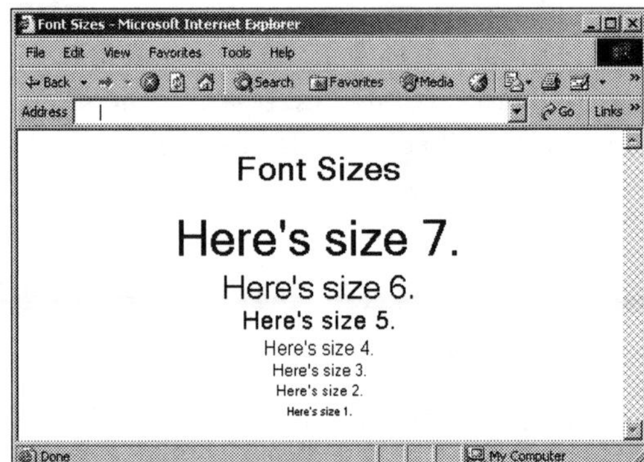

FIGURE 11.12
The available font sizes.

Comments: <!-->

You can use the standard XML- and HTML-style comments in XHTML documents. XHTML comments are supported in XHTML 1.0 Strict, XHTML 1.0 Transitional, XHTML 1.0 Frameset, and XHTML 1.1.

Comments annotate an XHTML document, letting you describe what's happening in the document. A browser strips out comments so that the viewer does not see them. Listing 11.13 shows an XHTML document with embedded comments.

LISTING 11.13 An XHTML Document That Uses Comments (`ch11_13.html`)

```
<?xml version="1.0" encoding="UTF-8"?>
<!--The necessary DOCTYPE element-->
<!DOCTYPE html PUBLIC "-//W3C//DTD XHTML 1.0 Transitional//EN"
"http://www.w3.org/TR/xhtml1/DTD/xhtml1-transitional.dtd">
<html xmlns="http://www.w3.org/1999/xhtml">
<!--XHTML element names are just like HTML element names.-->
<!--But note that XHTML element names are in lower case.-->
    <head>
        <title>
            An XHTML Document
        </title>
    </head>

    <body>
        <h1>
            Long Live XHTML!
        </h1>
        This is an XHTML document.
<!--Here's an empty element.-->
        <br/>
        Pretty good, eh?
    </body>
</html>
```


Summary

XHTML is the reformulation of HTML 4.0 in XML form. XHTML was introduced by the W3C to make HTML documents less sloppy and to enable them to be validated as true XML documents.

There are a number of versions of XHTML: XHTML 1.0 Transitional, the most widespread version, and the closest one to HTML 4.0; XHTML 1.0 Frameset, the same as

XHTML 1.0 Transitional, but targeted to documents that use frames, not a `<body>` element; XHTML 1.1, the module-based version of XHTML; XHTML Basic, targeted to devices that support only smaller implementations of XHTML; and XHTML 2.0, a radical new version that omits all display elements, relying entirely on style sheets instead.

You can find the official recommendation for XHTML 1.0 at `http://www.w3.org/TR/xhtml1`, the recommendation for XHTML 1.1 at `http://www.w3.org/TR/xhtml11`, the XHTML 2.0 Working Draft at `http://www.w3.org/TR/xhtml2`, and the recommendation for XHTML Basic at `http://www.w3.org/TR/xhtml-basic`.

The XHTML document element is `<html>`. The names of XHTML elements and attributes match those in HTML 4.0, but they must be in lowercase. Because an XHTML document is an XML document as well, several rules apply, as you've seen today. For example, non-empty elements need closing tags, you must quote attribute values and not use standalone attributes, and empty elements must end in `/>`.

You also need to use a `<!DOCTYPE>` element, which must appear before the document element. (However, XHTML 2.0 may let you use XML schemas.) In the `<html>` document element, you must declare the XHTML namespace, like this:

```
<html xmlns="http://www.w3.org/1999/xhtml">
```

As you've seen today, the elements you use in XHTML match those in HTML 4.0, with restrictions—for example, the elements and attributes that were deprecated in HTML 4.0 are not part of XHTML 1.0 Strict. You've worked through a number of XHTML elements today and seen how they differ from their HTML counterparts. There's more XHTML coming up tomorrow, when we'll talk about frames, images, hyperlinks, style sheets, tables, forms, and more.

Q&A

Q The `<applet>` element is supported all the way through XHTML 1.1, but I don't see it in the XHTML 2.0 Working Draft. What can I do to replace it?

A You can use the `<object>` element instead. You can find a discussion about how to replace `<applet>` with `<object>` at `http://www.w3.org/TR/xhtml2/mod-object.html#s_objectmodule`.

Q XHTML 1.1 and XHTML 2.0 don't appear to support frames. Why don't they?

A Because frames are formatting elements, they're omitted. However, you can use `<div>` elements to format text into visible areas as you like; you'll hear more about this tomorrow.

Workshop

This workshop tests whether you understand the concepts discussed today. It's a good idea to make sure you can answer these questions before pressing on to tomorrow's work. Answers to the quiz can be found in Appendix A, "Quiz Answers."

Quiz

1. What are the three versions of XHTML 1.0?
2. What is the namespace URI for XHTML 1.0?
3. What standalone XHTML attribute can you use in the `<div>` element to add a border?
4. What element must each `<head>` element contain?
5. What does every `<p>` element in XHTML need that it doesn't need in HTML?

Exercises

1. Write an HTML document that contains a little information about you—your name, educational background, and birth date. Format the text using CSS, as you've done today. Then convert the document into an XHTML 1.0 Transitional document and test it in a browser.
2. Validate the document you created in Exercise 1 by using the W3C XHTML validator. Then convert the document into XHTML 1.0 Strict and check the new results in the validator.

PART III

DAY 12

Putting XHTML to Work

Yesterday, you got a start with XHTML, and you're going to keep going with XHTML today. You're going to really dig into XHTML today.

Here are today's topics:

- Using hyperlinks
- Using images
- Using style sheets
- Using frames
- Using tables
- Extending XHTML by creating custom elements

Let's start today's discussion by working with hyperlinks.

Creating Hyperlinks: <a>

In XHTML, as in HTML, you use the `<a>` element for hyperlinks with the `href` attribute or anchors, using the `id` attribute (and/or the deprecated `name` attribute for browsers like the Netscape Navigator). This element is supported in

XHTML 1.0 Strict, XHTML 1.0 Transitional, XHTML 1.0 Frameset, and XHTML 1.1. Here are this element's attributes:

- **accesskey**—Lets you connect a keyboard access key to a hyperlink. (Supported in XHTML 1.0 Strict and XHTML 1.0 Transitional.)
- **charset**—Specifies the character encoding of the hyperlink's target. The default value is `ISO-8859-1`. (Supported in XHTML 1.0 Strict, XHTML 1.0 Transitional, XHTML 1.0 Frameset, and XHTML 1.1.)
- **class**—Specifies the style class for the element. (Supported in XHTML 1.0 Strict, XHTML 1.0 Transitional, XHTML 1.0 Frameset, and XHTML 1.1.)
- **coords**—Is used with image maps. (Supported in XHTML 1.0 Strict, XHTML 1.0 Transitional, XHTML 1.0 Frameset, and XHTML 1.1.)
- **dir**—Sets the direction of text that doesn't have an inherent direction, called *directionally neutral* text. This attribute can be set to `ltr`, for left-to-right text, or `rtl`, for right-to-left text. (Supported in XHTML 1.0 Strict, XHTML 1.0 Transitional, XHTML 1.0 Frameset, and XHTML 1.1.)
- **href**—Specifies the target URI of the hyperlink. You must assign a value to either this attribute or the `id` attribute. (Supported in XHTML 1.0 Strict, XHTML 1.0 Transitional, XHTML 1.0 Frameset, and XHTML 1.1.)
- **hreflang**—Specifies the base language of the target. You set this attribute to RFC 1766 values. (Supported in XHTML 1.0 Strict, XHTML 1.0 Transitional, XHTML 1.0 Frameset, and XHTML 1.1.)
- **id**—Specifies the ID of the element. (Supported in XHTML 1.0 Strict, XHTML 1.0 Transitional, XHTML 1.0 Frameset, and XHTML 1.1.)
- **lang**—Specifies the base language of the element. (Supported in XHTML 1.0 Strict, XHTML 1.0 Transitional, XHTML 1.0 Frameset, and XHTML 1.1.)
- **name**—Holds the name of the element. This attribute was deprecated in XHTML 1.0, although it is still available. (Supported in XHTML 1.0 Strict, XHTML 1.0 Transitional, and XHTML 1.0 Frameset.)
- **rel**—Specifies the relationship described by the hyperlink. (Supported in XHTML 1.0 Strict, XHTML 1.0 Transitional, XHTML 1.0 Frameset, and XHTML 1.1.)
- **rev**—Acts the same as the `rel` attribute, but the syntax works in the reverse direction. (Supported in XHTML 1.0 Strict, XHTML 1.0 Transitional, XHTML 1.0 Frameset, and XHTML 1.1.)
- **shape**—Specifies the type of region for mapping in an `<area>` element. This attribute is used with the `coords` attribute. Possible values are `rect` (the default), `circ`, `circle`, `POLY`, and `polygon`. (Supported in XHTML 1.0 Strict, XHTML 1.0 Transitional, XHTML 1.0 Frameset, and XHTML 1.1.)

- **`style`**—Indicates how a browser should display the element. You should set this to an inline style. (Supported in XHTML 1.0 Strict, XHTML 1.0 Transitional, XHTML 1.0 Frameset, and XHTML 1.1.)
- **`tabindex`**—Indexes the tab sequence of hyperlinks to facilitate keyboard navigation. (Supported in XHTML 1.0 Strict, XHTML 1.0 Transitional, XHTML 1.0 Frameset.)
- **`target`**—Specifies a named frame that is the target of a hyperlink. (Supported in XHTML 1.0 Transitional and XHTML 1.0 Frameset.)
- **`title`**—Specifies the title of the element. (Supported in XHTML 1.0 Strict, XHTML 1.0 Transitional, XHTML 1.0 Frameset, and XHTML 1.1.)
- **`type`**—Specifies the Multipurpose Internet Mail Extensions (MIME) type of the target given in the `href` attribute. (Supported in XHTML 1.0 Strict, XHTML 1.0 Transitional, XHTML 1.0 Frameset, and XHTML 1.1.)
- **`xml:lang`**—Specifies the base language for the element when the document is treated as XML. (Supported in XHTML 1.0 Strict, XHTML 1.0 Transitional, XHTML 1.0 Frameset, and XHTML 1.1.)

In XHTML, the `<a>` element works much as the `<a>` element does in HTML, except that you need to supply either a value for the `href` attribute or the `id` attribute. Listing 12.1 shows an example that creates a hyperlink to the XHTML Activity page.

LISTING 12.1 An XHTML Document That Uses a Hyperlink (`ch12_01.html`)

```
<?xml version="1.0" encoding="UTF-8"?>
<!DOCTYPE html PUBLIC "-//W3C//DTD XHTML 1.0 Transitional//EN"
"http://www.w3.org/TR/xhtml1/DTD/xhtml1-transitional.dtd">
<html xmlns="http://www.w3.org/1999/xhtml">
    <head>
        <title>
            Hyperlinks in XHTML
        </title>
    </head>

    <body>
       <h1>
            Hyperlinks in XHTML
       </h1>

       This is an
       <a href="http://www.w3.org/MarkUp/Activity.html">XHTML</a>
       document.
    </body>
</html>
```

12

Figure 12.1 shows what this XHTML document looks like in a browser.

FIGURE 12.1

An XHTML hyperlink.

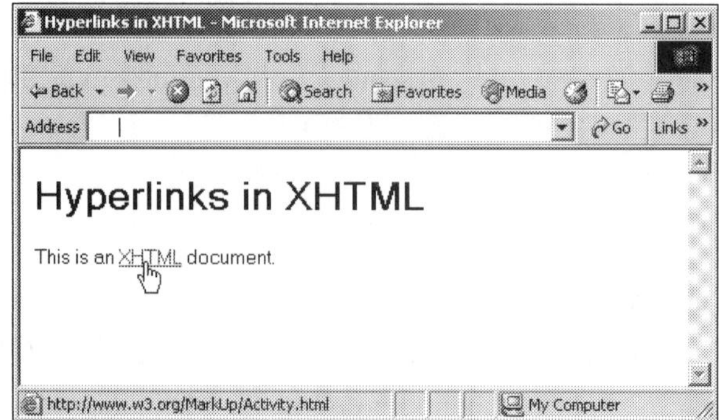

Linking to Other Documents: `<link>`

As you saw when you discussed style sheets and XML schemas, the W3C provides no clear way to connect XML documents to other XML documents yet, so nonstandard elements such as `<?xml-stylesheet?>` are used. However, HTML actually does contain a `<link>` element to link a document to other documents, and there's some hope that it can be used for that purpose in XHTML. This element is empty and appears in the `<head>` section of a document. The `<link>` element is supported in XHTML 1.0 Strict, XHTML 1.0 Transitional, XHTML 1.0 Frameset, and XHTML 1.1. Here are the attributes of `<link>`:

- **`charset`**—Specifies the character encoding of the link's target. The default value is `ISO-8859-1`. (Supported in XHTML 1.0 Strict, XHTML 1.0 Transitional, XHTML 1.0 Frameset, and XHTML 1.1.)
- **`class`**—Specifies the style class for the element. (Supported in XHTML 1.0 Strict, XHTML 1.0 Transitional, XHTML 1.0 Frameset, and XHTML 1.1.)
- **`dir`**—Sets the direction of directionally neutral text. This attribute can be set to `ltr`, for left-to-right text, or `rtl`, for right-to-left text. (Supported in XHTML 1.0 Strict, XHTML 1.0 Transitional, XHTML 1.0 Frameset, and XHTML 1.1.)
- **`href`**—Specifies the target URI of the link. You must assign a value to either this attribute or the `id` attribute. (Supported in XHTML 1.0 Strict, XHTML 1.0 Transitional, XHTML 1.0 Frameset, and XHTML 1.1.)
- **`hreflang`**—Specifies the base language of the target. You set this attribute to RFC 1766 values. (Supported in XHTML 1.0 Strict, XHTML 1.0 Transitional, XHTML 1.0 Frameset, and XHTML 1.1.)

- **`id`**—Specifies the ID of the element. (Supported in XHTML 1.0 Strict, XHTML 1.0 Transitional, XHTML 1.0 Frameset, and XHTML 1.1.)
- **`lang`**—Specifies the base language of the element. (Supported in XHTML 1.0 Strict, XHTML 1.0 Transitional, XHTML 1.0 Frameset, and XHTML 1.1.)
- **`media`**—Specifies the device the document will be displayed on. Possible values are `screen` (the default), `print`, `projection`, `braille`, `speech`, and `all`. Style information should be used for all devices. (Supported in XHTML 1.0 Strict, XHTML 1.0 Transitional, XHTML 1.0 Frameset, and XHTML 1.1.)
- **`rel`**—Specifies the relationship described by the link. (Supported in XHTML 1.0 Strict, XHTML 1.0 Transitional, XHTML 1.0 Frameset, and XHTML 1.1.)
- **`rev`**—Is the same as the `rel` attribute, but the syntax works in the reverse direction. (Supported in XHTML 1.0 Strict, XHTML 1.0 Transitional, XHTML 1.0 Frameset, and XHTML 1.1.)
- **`style`**—Indicates how a browser should display the element. You should set this to an inline style. (Supported in XHTML 1.0 Strict, XHTML 1.0 Transitional, XHTML 1.0 Frameset, and XHTML 1.1.)
- **`target`**—`Specifies` a named frame that is the target of a hyperlink. (Supported in XHTML 1.0 Transitional, XHTML 1.0 Frameset.)
- **`title`**—Specifies the title of the element (which might be displayed in ToolTips). (Supported in XHTML 1.0 Strict, XHTML 1.0 Transitional, XHTML 1.0 Frameset, and XHTML 1.1.)
- **`type`**—Specifies the MIME type of the target given in the `href` attribute. (Supported in XHTML 1.0 Strict, XHTML 1.0 Transitional, XHTML 1.0 Frameset, and XHTML 1.1.)
- **`xml:lang`**—Specifies the base language for the element when the document is treated as XML. (Supported in XHTML 1.0 Strict, XHTML 1.0 Transitional, XHTML 1.0 Frameset, and XHTML 1.1.)

You can specify a relationship between the current document and others by using the `rel` attribute, which can take these values in XHTML:

- **`rel=alternate`**—An alternate resource.
- **`rel=appendix`**—An appendix.
- **`rel=bookmark`**—A bookmark.
- **`rel=chapter`**—A chapter.
- **`rel=contents`**—The contents section.
- **`rel=copyright`**—A copyright document.

- **rel=glossary**—A glossary.
- **rel=help**—A help document.
- **rel=home**—A home page.
- **rel=index**—An index.
- **rel=next**—The next document.
- **rel=previous**—The previous document.
- **rel=section**—A section.
- **rel=start**—The start of a resource.
- **rel=stylesheet**—An external style sheet.
- **rel=subsection**—A subsection.
- **rel=toc**—The table of contents.
- **rel=up**—The parent of the current document.

The `<link>` element deserves a place in our discussion of XHTML because it lets you link documents together, which is very handy in XML, especially because the W3C has so little to say about it. Listing 12.2 shows an example that sets `rel` to `"stylesheet"` to use an external style sheet. The linked-to style sheet appears in `ch12_03.css`, in Listing 12.3.

LISTING 12.2 An XHTML Document That Links to Another Document (`ch12_02.html`)

```
<!DOCTYPE html PUBLIC "-//W3C//DTD XHTML 1.0 Transitional//EN"
"http://www.w3.org/tr/xhtml1/DTD/xhtml1-transitional.dtd">
<html xmlns="http://www.w3.org/1999/xhtml">
    <head>
        <title>
            Linking to External Style Sheets
        </title>
        <link rel="stylesheet" href="ch12_03.css">
    </head>

    <body>
        <h1>
            Linking to External Style Sheets
        </h1>
        <p>
            No problems--now we're linking to external style sheets.
        </p>
    </body>
</html>
```

LISTING 12.3 An External Style Sheet (ch12_03.css)

```
body {background-color: cyan; font-family: Arial}
p {font-size: 18pt; font-style: italic}
```

Figure 12.2 shows the results of Listing 12.3 in a browser.

FIGURE 12.2
Working with external style sheets.

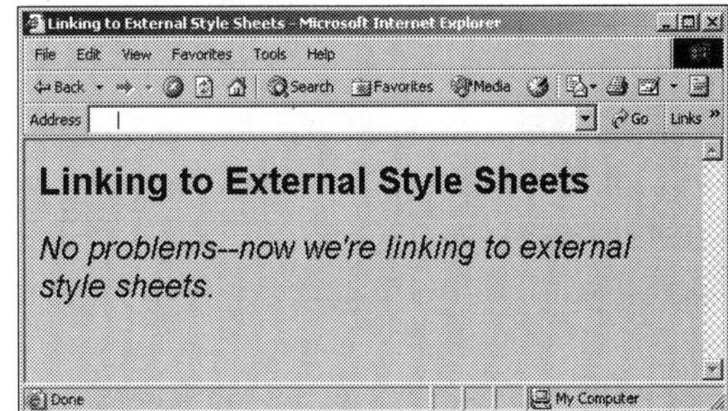

Handling Images: <img>

As you might expect, XHTML supports an `<img>` element, just as XHTML does. The XHTML `<img>` element works much like its counterpart in HTML, except that the `src` and `alt` attributes are required, and you must close this empty element with `/>`, not just `>`. This element is supported in XHTML 1.0 Strict, XHTML 1.0 Transitional, XHTML 1.0 Frameset, and XHTML 1.1. Here are its attributes:

- **`align`**—Specifies the alignment of text relative to the image on the screen. Possible settings are `left`, `right`, `top`, `texttop`, `middle`, `absmiddle`, `baseline`, `bottom`, and `absbottom`. (Supported in XHTML 1.0 Transitional and XHTML 1.0 Frameset.)
- **`alt`**—Specifies the text that should be displayed instead of an image if the image cannot be displayed. This attribute is required. (Supported in XHTML 1.0 Strict, XHTML 1.0 Transitional, XHTML 1.0 Frameset, and XHTML 1.1.)
- **`border`**—Indicates whether the image has a border. You set this attribute to `0` for no border or to a positive integer pixel value. (Supported in XHTML 1.0 Transitional, XHTML 1.0 Frameset.)
- **`class`**—Specifies the style class of the element. (Supported in XHTML 1.0 Strict, XHTML 1.0 Transitional, XHTML 1.0 Frameset, and XHTML 1.1.)
- **`height`**—Specifies the height of the image, in pixels. (Supported in XHTML 1.0 Strict, XHTML 1.0 Transitional, XHTML 1.0 Frameset, and XHTML 1.1.)

- **hspace**—Specifies the horizontal spacing around the image. You set this attribute to pixel measurements. (Supported in XHTML 1.0 Transitional and XHTML 1.0 Frameset.)
- **id**—Specifies the ID of the element. (Supported in XHTML 1.0 Strict, XHTML 1.0 Transitional, XHTML 1.0 Frameset, and XHTML 1.1.)
- **ismap**—Indicates whether this image is to be used as an image map. (Supported in XHTML 1.0 Strict, XHTML 1.0 Transitional, XHTML 1.0 Frameset, and XHTML 1.1.)
- **lang**—Specifies the base language of the element. (Supported in XHTML 1.0 Strict, XHTML 1.0 Transitional, XHTML 1.0 Frameset, and XHTML 1.1.)
- **longdesc**—Holds a longer description of the image. This attribute should be set to a URI. (Supported in XHTML 1.0 Strict, XHTML 1.0 Transitional, XHTML 1.0 Frameset, and XHTML 1.1.)
- **src**—Specifies the URI of the image. This attribute is required. (Supported in XHTML 1.0 Strict, XHTML 1.0 Transitional, XHTML 1.0 Frameset, and XHTML 1.1.)
- **style**—Indicates how a browser should display the element. You should set this to an inline style. (Supported in XHTML 1.0 Strict, XHTML 1.0 Transitional, XHTML 1.0 Frameset, and XHTML 1.1.)
- **title**—Specifies the title of the element. (Supported in XHTML 1.0 Strict, XHTML 1.0 Transitional, XHTML 1.0 Frameset, and XHTML 1.1.)
- **usemap**—Specifies the URI of a client-side image map. (Supported in XHTML 1.0 Strict, XHTML 1.0 Transitional, XHTML 1.0 Frameset, and XHTML 1.1.)
- **vspace**—Sets the vertical spacing around the image. You set this attribute to pixel measurements. (Supported in XHTML 1.0 Transitional, XHTML 1.0 Frameset.)
- **width**—Specifies the width of the image. You set this attribute to pixel measurements. (Supported in XHTML 1.0 Strict, XHTML 1.0 Transitional, XHTML 1.0 Frameset, and XHTML 1.1.)
- **xml:lang**—Specifies the base language for the element when the document is treated as XML. (Supported in XHTML 1.0 Strict, XHTML 1.0 Transitional, XHTML 1.0 Frameset, and XHTML 1.1.)

In XHTML, both the `src` attribute (which contains the image's URI) and the `alt` attribute (which contains alternate text) of the `<img>` element are required. Surprisingly, the `align` attribute was not deprecated in the `<img>` element, as it was for just about every other XHTML element that supported it. Listing 12.4 shows an example that uses the `<img>` element.

LISTING 12.4 Displaying an Image (ch12_04.html)

```
<?xml version="1.0" encoding="UTF-8"?>
<!DOCTYPE html PUBLIC "-//W3C//DTD XHTML 1.0 Transitional//EN"
"http://www.w3.org/TR/xhtml1/DTD/xhtml1-transitional.dtd">
<html xmlns="http://www.w3.org/1999/xhtml">
    <head>
        <title>
            Displaying Images
        </title>
    </head>

    <body>
        <h1>
            Displaying Images
        </h1>
        <img src="image.jpg" width="400" height="200" alt="The Egg!" />
    </body>
</html>
```

Figure 12.3 shows what this document looks like in a browser.

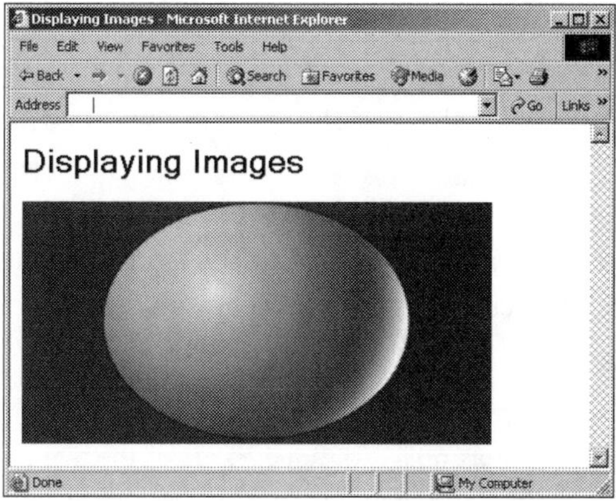

FIGURE 12.3
Displaying an image in XHTML.

12

Creating Frame Documents: <frameset>

In XHTML, like HTML, you use `<frameset>` to display frames. The `<frameset>` element replaces the `<body>` element in XHTML documents with frames, and in XHTML 1.0, that means you use the XHTML 1.0 Frameset DTD because the `<frameset>` element is supported in XHTML 1.0 Frameset only. Note in particular that the `<frame>` and `<frameset>` elements are *not* supported in XHTML 1.1 or XHTML 2.0. Instead, the W3C expects style sheets to handle the presentation techniques you use frames for today (whether or not the Web community will actually do things that way is still an unanswered question). Here are the attributes of the `<frameset>` element:

- **class**—Specifies the style class for the element. (Supported in XHTML 1.0 Frameset.)
- **cols**—Specifies the number of columns in the frameset. (Supported in XHTML 1.0 Frameset.)
- **dir**—Sets the direction of directionally neutral text. This attribute can be set to `ltr`, for left-to-right text, or `rtl`, for right-to-left text. (Supported in XHTML 1.0 Frameset.)
- **id**—Specifies the ID of the element. (Supported in XHTML 1.0 Frameset.)
- **lang**—Specifies the base language of the element. (Supported in XHTML 1.0 Frameset.)
- **rows**—Specifies the number of rows in the frameset. (Supported in XHTML 1.0 Frameset.)
- **style**—Indicates how a browser should display the element. You should set this to an inline style. (Supported in XHTML 1.0 Frameset.)
- **title**—Specifies the title of the element. (Supported in XHTML 1.0 Frameset.)
- **xml:lang**—Specifies the base language for the element when the document is treated as XML. (Supported in XHTML 1.0 Frameset.)

The `<frameset>` element replaces the `<body>` element in an XHTML document that displays frames. To create the frames, you use the `<frame>` element. To format the display into frames, you use the `rows` attribute or the `cols` attribute of the `<frameset>` element. You can specify the number of rows or columns you want to use by listing their heights or widths.

To specify heights or widths, you can specify pixel measurements, or you can use a percentage measurement (such as 60%) to request part of the available display area. If you use an asterisk (`*`), you get the remaining display area; for example, `cols="72, *"` creates one vertical frame of 72 pixels and a second vertical frame that fills the remainder of the display area.

Here's how you might format an XHTML document into two columns using frames by using the XHTML 1.0 Frameset DTD:

```
<?xml version="1.0" encoding="UTF-8"?>
<!DOCTYPE html PUBLIC "-//W3C//DTD XHTML 1.0 Frameset//EN"
"http://www.w3.org/TR/xhtml1/DTD/xhtml1-frameset.dtd">
<html xmlns="http://www.w3.org/1999/xhtml">
    <head>
```

```
        <title>
            Working With Frames
        </title>
    </head>

    <frameset cols = "50%, 50%">
        .
        .
        .
    </frameset>
</html>
```

How to create the frames that you want to have displayed is coming up next.

Creating Frames: <frame>

You use the `<frame>` element to create individual frames. This element is an empty element, and you use it inside the `<frameset>` element. It is supported in XHTML 1.0 Frameset only. Here are its attributes:

- **`class`**—Specifies the style class for the element. (Supported in XHTML 1.0 Frameset.)
- **`dir`**—Sets the direction of directionally neutral text. This attribute can be set to `ltr`, for left-to-right text, or `rtl`, for right-to-left text. (Supported in XHTML 1.0 Frameset.)
- **`frameborder`**—Specifies whether borders should enclose the frame. (Supported in XHTML 1.0 Frameset.)
- **`id`**—Specifies the ID of the element. (Supported in XHTML 1.0 Frameset.)
- **`lang`**—Specifies the base language of the element. (Supported in XHTML 1.0 Frameset.)
- **`longdesc`**—Holds a longer description of the image. This attribute should be set to a URI. (Supported in XHTML 1.0 Frameset.)
- **`marginheight`**—Specifies the height of the top and bottom margins. (Supported in XHTML 1.0 Frameset.)
- **`marginwidth`**—Specifies the width of the right and left margins. (Supported in XHTML 1.0 Frameset.)
- **`name`**—Specifies the name of the frame. This attribute may be used as a target destination for `<a>`, `<area>`, `<base>`, and `<form>` elements. (Supported in XHTML 1.0 Frameset.)

- **noresize**—Specifies that the frame may not be resized. (Supported in XHTML 1.0 Frameset.)
- **scrolling**—Specifies scrollbar action. Possible values are `auto`, `yes`, and `no`. (Supported in XHTML 1.0 Frameset.)
- **src**—Specifies the URI of the frame document. This attribute is required. (Supported in XHTML 1.0 Frameset.)
- **style**—Indicates how a browser should display the element. You should set this to an inline style. (Supported in XHTML 1.0 Strict, XHTML 1.0 Transitional, XHTML 1.0 Frameset, and XHTML 1.1.)
- **title**—Specifies the title of the element. (Supported in XHTML 1.0 Strict, XHTML 1.0 Transitional, XHTML 1.0 Frameset, and XHTML 1.1.)
- **xml:lang**—Specifies the base language for the element when the document is treated as XML. (Supported in XHTML 1.0 Strict, XHTML 1.0 Transitional, XHTML 1.0 Frameset, and XHTML 1.1.)

The one required attribute in the `<frame>` element is the `src` attribute, which specifies the URI of the document you want to display in the frame. Listing 12.5 is an example that uses the `<frameset>` element and two `<frame>` elements to display frames. The documents that will appear in those frames are shown in Listing 12.6 and Listing 12.7.

LISTING 12.5 Using Frames (`ch12_05.html`)

```
<?xml version="1.0" encoding="UTF-8"?>
<!DOCTYPE html PUBLIC "-//W3C//DTD XHTML 1.0 Frameset//EN"
"http://www.w3.org/TR/xhtml1/DTD/xhtml1-frameset.dtd">
<html xmlns="http://www.w3.org/1999/xhtml">
    <head>
        <title>
            Working With Frames
        </title>
    </head>

    <frameset cols = "50%, 50%">
        <frame src="ch12_06.html" />
        <frame src="ch12_07.html" />
    </frameset>
</html>
```

LISTING 12.6 The XHTML for Frame 1 (ch12_06.html)

```
<?xml version="1.0" encoding="UTF-8"?>
<!DOCTYPE html PUBLIC "-//W3C//DTD XHTML 1.0 Frameset//EN"
"http://www.w3.org/TR/xhtml1/DTD/xhtml1-frameset.dtd">
<html xmlns="http://www.w3.org/1999/xhtml">
    <head>
        <title>
            Working With Frames
        </title>
    </head>

    <body>
    <h1>
        <center>
        Frame 1 says, "I've been framed! "
        </center>
    </h1>
    </body>
</html>
```

LISTING 12.7 The XHTML for Frame 2 (ch12_07.html)

```
<?xml version="1.0" encoding="UTF-8"?>
<!DOCTYPE html PUBLIC "-//W3C//DTD XHTML 1.0 Frameset//EN"
"http://www.w3.org/TR/xhtml1/DTD/xhtml1-frameset.dtd">
<html xmlns="http://www.w3.org/1999/xhtml">
    <head>
        <title>
            Working With Frames
        </title>
    </head>

    <body>
    <h1>
        <center>
        Frame 2 says, "Me too!"
        </center>
    </h1>
    </body>
</html>
```

Figure 12.4 shows what this XHTML looks like in a browser. This example uses the XHTML 1.0 Frameset DTD to create a document that displays documents in frames.

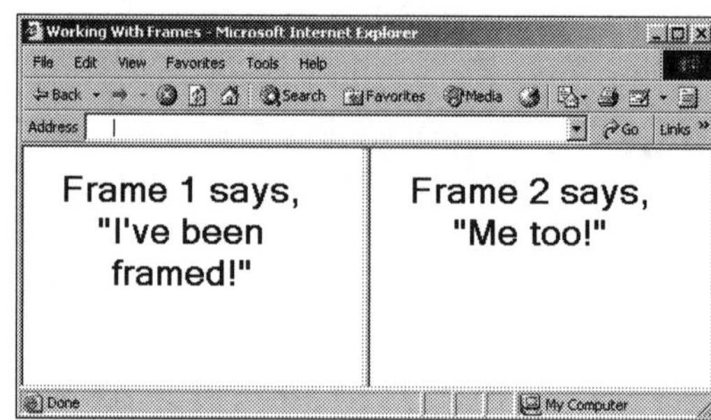

FIGURE 12.4
Handling frames in XHTML.

Before you start relying on frames too much, though, you should keep in mind that the W3C is trying to get rid of them. Whether they'll go quietly, or go at all, is anyone's guess.

Creating Embedded Style Sheets: `<style>`

As you've seen today, you can use the `<link>` element to connect an external style sheet to a document. You can also treat XHTML documents as XML, in which case, you can use the XML processing instruction `<?xml-stylesheet?>` to connect to an external style sheet, as you did in this example on Day 8, "Formatting XML by Using Cascading Style Sheets":

```
<?xml version="1.0" standalone="yes"?>
<?xml-stylesheet type="text/css" href="ch08_05.css"?>
<document>
    <title class="standout">The Discourses</title>
    <philosopher class="standout">Epictetus</philosopher>
    <book>Book Four</book>
    <paragraph>
        He is free who lives as he wishes to live; who is neither
        subject to compulsion nor to hindrance, nor to force;
        whose movements to action are not impeded, whose desires
        attain their purpose, and who does not fall into that which
        he would avoid.
    </paragraph>
        .
        .
        .
    <paragraph>
        Do we then find any of the bad free from sorrow, free from
        fear, who does not fall into that which he would avoid, and
        does not obtain that which he wishes? Not one; nor then do
        we find any bad man free.
   </paragraph>
</html>
```

In addition to using external style sheets in this way, you can also use the `<style>` element to create an internal, or *embedded*, style sheet. The `<style>` element is supported in XHTML 1.0 Strict, XHTML 1.0 Transitional, XHTML 1.0 Frameset, and XHTML 1.1. Here are the attributes of this element:

- **`dir`**—Sets the direction of directionally neutral text. This attribute can be set to `ltr`, for left-to-right text, or `rtl`, for right-to-left text. (Supported in XHTML 1.0 Strict, XHTML 1.0 Transitional, XHTML 1.0 Frameset, and XHTML 1.1.)
- **`lang`**—Specifies the base language of the element. (Supported in XHTML 1.0 Strict, XHTML 1.0 Transitional, XHTML 1.0 Frameset, and XHTML 1.1.)
- **`media`**—Specifies the target media. Possible values are `screen` (the default), `print`, `projection`, `braille`, `speech`, and `all`. (Supported in XHTML 1.0 Strict, XHTML 1.0 Transitional, XHTML 1.0 Frameset, and XHTML 1.1.)
- **`title`**—Specifies the title of the element. (Supported in XHTML 1.0 Strict, XHTML 1.0 Transitional, XHTML 1.0 Frameset, and XHTML 1.1.)
- **`type`**—Specifies the MIME type of the target given in the `href` attribute. This is a required attribute. (Supported in XHTML 1.0 Strict, XHTML 1.0 Transitional, XHTML 1.0 Frameset, and XHTML 1.1.)
- **`xml:lang`**—Specifies the base language for the element when the document is interpreted as an XML document. (Supported in XHTML 1.0 Strict, XHTML 1.0 Transitional, XHTML 1.0 Frameset, and XHTML 1.1.)
- **`xml:space`**—Preserves the current spacing when assigned the value `"preserve"`. (Supported in XHTML 1.0 Strict, XHTML 1.0 Transitional, XHTML 1.0 Frameset, and XHTML 1.1.)

12

You usually put the `<style>` element in an XHTML document's head. Listing 12.8 shows an example that uses the same styles you used when you linked to an external style sheet, but in this case, you're using an internal style sheet. Note that the `type` attribute is required in XHTML, but not in HTML.

LISTING 12.8 Using an Internal Style Sheet (`ch12_08.html`)

```
<!DOCTYPE html PUBLIC "-//W3C//DTD XHTML 1.0 Transitional//EN"
"http://www.w3.org/tr/xhtml1/DTD/xhtml1-transitional.dtd">
<html xmlns="http://www.w3.org/1999/xhtml">
    <head>
        <title>
            Using Internal Style Sheets
        </title>
        <style type="text/css">
            body {background-color: cyan; font-family: Arial}
```

LISTING 12.8 continued

```
            p {font-size: 18pt; font-style: italic}
        </style>
    </head>

    <body>
        <h1>
            Using Internal Style Sheets
        </h1>
        <p>
            No problems--now we're using internal style sheets.
        </p>
    </body>
</html>
```

TIP

> Note that if style sheets include sensitive characters, such as < or &, you should use external style sheets in XHTML, not internal ones.

You can see this XHTML at work in Figure 12.5.

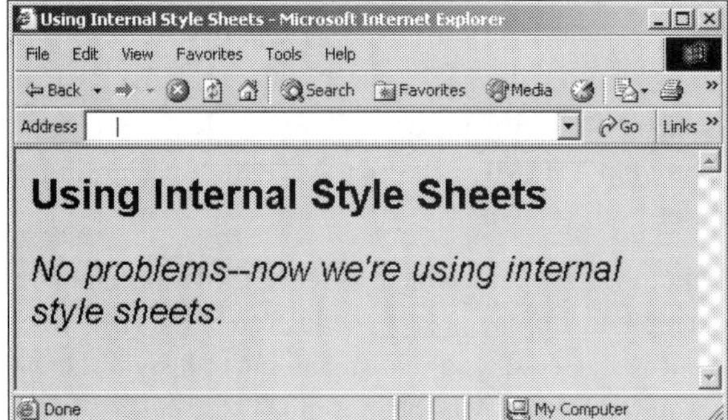

FIGURE 12.5
Using internal style sheets.

In XHTML you can also create *inline styles*, which means you apply styles to one XHTML element only. You create inline styles by using the `style` attribute that most XHTML elements support. Listing 12.9 shows an example that uses the same style formatting as in the previous example, `ch12_08.html`, but this time, you're doing it by using the `style` attribute, not the `<style>` element.

Listing 12.9 Using the <style> Attribute (ch12_09.html)

```
<!DOCTYPE html PUBLIC "-//W3C//DTD XHTML 1.0 Transitional//EN"
"http://www.w3.org/tr/xhtml1/DTD/xhtml1-transitional.dtd">
<html xmlns="http://www.w3.org/1999/xhtml">
    <head>
        <title>
            Using the style Attribute
        </title>
    </head>

    <body style="background-color: cyan; font-family: Arial">
        <h1>
            Using the style Attribute
        </h1>
        <p style="font-size: 18pt; font-style: italic">
            No problems--now we're using the style attribute.
        </p>
    </body>
</html>
```

Style purists frown on the `style` element because, as you can see, using it means you end up mixing presentation details with data. Instead, such purists recommend that you stick with style sheets, which centralize styling information.

Formatting Tables: <table>

12

You use the <table> element to create a table, just as in HTML. To format a table, you use various child elements in <table>, such as <caption>, <tr>, <th>, <td>, <colspan>, <col>, <thead>, <tbody>, and <tfoot>. This element is supported in XHTML 1.0 Strict, XHTML 1.0 Transitional, XHTML 1.0 Frameset, and XHTML 1.1. Here are its attributes:

- **`align`**—Specifies the horizontal alignment of the table in the browser. This attribute can be set to `left`, `center`, or `right`. This attribute was deprecated in HTML 4.0. (Supported in XHTML 1.0 Transitional and XHTML 1.0 Frameset.)
- **`bgcolor`**—Specifies the background color of table cells. This attribute was deprecated in HTML 4.0. (Supported in XHTML 1.0 Transitional and XHTML 1.0 Frameset.)
- **`border`**—Specifies the border width, as measured in pixels. You can set this attribute to 0 for no border or to a positive integer pixel value. (Supported in XHTML 1.0 Transitional and XHTML 1.0 Frameset.)

- `cellpadding`—Specifies the spacing between cell walls and cell contents in pixels. (Supported in XHTML 1.0 Strict, XHTML 1.0 Transitional, XHTML 1.0 Frameset, and XHTML 1.1.)
- `cellspacing`—Specifies the distance between cells. You set this attribute to a value in pixels. (Supported in XHTML 1.0 Strict, XHTML 1.0 Transitional, XHTML 1.0 Frameset, and XHTML 1.1.)
- `class`—Specifies the style class of the element. (Supported in XHTML 1.0 Strict, XHTML 1.0 Transitional, XHTML 1.0 Frameset, and XHTML 1.1.)
- `dir`—Sets the direction of directionally neutral text. This attribute can be set to `ltr`, for left-to-right text, or `rtl`, for right-to-left text. (Supported in XHTML 1.0 Strict, XHTML 1.0 Transitional, XHTML 1.0 Frameset, and XHTML 1.1.)
- `frame`—Creates a frame. Possible values are `void` (no borders), `above` (border on top side only), `below` (border on bottom side only), `hsides` (horizontal borders only), `vsides` (vertical borders only), `lhs` (border on left side only), `rhs` (border on right side only), `box` (border on all four sides), and `border` (the default; the same as `box`). (Supported in XHTML 1.0 Strict, XHTML 1.0 Transitional, XHTML 1.0 Frameset, and XHTML 1.1.)
- `id`—Specifies the ID of the element. (Supported in XHTML 1.0 Strict, XHTML 1.0 Transitional, XHTML 1.0 Frameset, and XHTML 1.1.)
- `lang`—Specifies the base language of the element. (Supported in XHTML 1.0 Strict, XHTML 1.0 Transitional, XHTML 1.0 Frameset, and XHTML 1.1.)
- `rules`—Uses the Complex Table Model to indicate the interior struts in a table. Possible values are `none` (no interior struts), `groups` (horizontal struts), `rows` (horizontal struts displayed between all table rows), `cols` (vertical struts displayed between all table columns), and `all` (struts displayed between all table cells). (Supported in XHTML 1.0 Strict, XHTML 1.0 Transitional, XHTML 1.0 Frameset, and XHTML 1.1.)
- `style`—Indicates how a browser should display the element. You should set this to an inline style. (Supported in XHTML 1.0 Strict, XHTML 1.0 Transitional, XHTML 1.0 Frameset, and XHTML 1.1.)
- `summary`—Holds summary information. (Supported in XHTML 1.0 Strict, XHTML 1.0 Transitional, XHTML 1.0 Frameset, and XHTML 1.1.)
- `title`—Specifies the title of the element. (Supported in XHTML 1.0 Strict, XHTML 1.0 Transitional, XHTML 1.0 Frameset, and XHTML 1.1.)
- `width`—Specifies the width of the table. You can set this to a pixel value or to a percentage of the display area. (Supported in XHTML 1.0 Strict, XHTML 1.0 Transitional, XHTML 1.0 Frameset, and XHTML 1.1.)

- **xml:lang**—Specifies the base language for the element when the document is treated as XML. (Supported in XHTML 1.0 Strict, XHTML 1.0 Transitional, XHTML 1.0 Frameset, and XHTML 1.1.)

To start formatting a table, you need to use the <table> element:

```
<table>
    .
    .
    .
</table>
```

This XHTML alone doesn't display anything visual. To format the data in the table, you use other elements, such as <tr>, which you'll see next.

Creating Table Rows: <tr>

As in HTML, the <tr> element is used in XHTML to create rows in a table. In XHTML this element can contain <th> (table header) and <td> (table data) elements. The <tr> element is supported in XHTML 1.0 Strict, XHTML 1.0 Transitional, XHTML 1.0 Frameset, XHTML 1.1. Here are this element's attributes:

- **align**—Specifies the horizontal alignment of the text in a row. This attribute can be set to `left`, `center`, `right`, `justify`, or `char`. (Supported in XHTML 1.0 Strict, XHTML 1.0 Transitional, XHTML 1.0 Frameset, and XHTML 1.1.)
- **bgcolor**—Specifies the background color of the table cells. This attribute was deprecated in HTML 4.0. (Supported in XHTML 1.0 Transitional and XHTML 1.0 Frameset.)
- **char**—Specifies a character to align text with respect to. (Supported in XHTML 1.0 Strict, XHTML 1.0 Transitional, XHTML 1.0 Frameset, and XHTML 1.1.)
- **charoff**—Sets the alignment offset. (Supported in XHTML 1.0 Strict, XHTML 1.0 Transitional, XHTML 1.0 Frameset, and XHTML 1.1.)
- **class**—Specifies the style class of the element. (Supported in XHTML 1.0 Strict, XHTML 1.0 Transitional, XHTML 1.0 Frameset, and XHTML 1.1.)
- **dir**—Sets the direction of directionally neutral text. This attribute can be set to `ltr`, for left-to-right text, or `rtl`, for right-to-left text. (Supported in XHTML 1.0 Strict, XHTML 1.0 Transitional, XHTML 1.0 Frameset, and XHTML 1.1.)
- **id**—Specifies the ID of the element. (Supported in XHTML 1.0 Strict, XHTML 1.0 Transitional, XHTML 1.0 Frameset, and XHTML 1.1.)
- **lang**—Specifies the base language of the element. (Supported in XHTML 1.0 Strict, XHTML 1.0 Transitional, XHTML 1.0 Frameset, and XHTML 1.1.)

- **style**—Indicates how a browser should display the element. You should set this to an inline style. (Supported in XHTML 1.0 Strict, XHTML 1.0 Transitional, XHTML 1.0 Frameset, and XHTML 1.1.)
- **title**—Specifies the title of the element. (Supported in XHTML 1.0 Strict, XHTML 1.0 Transitional, XHTML 1.0 Frameset, and XHTML 1.1.)
- **valign**—Specifies the vertical alignment of the data in the row. Possible values are `top`, `middle`, `bottom`, and `baseline`. (Supported in XHTML 1.0 Strict, XHTML 1.0 Transitional, XHTML 1.0 Frameset, and XHTML 1.1.)
- **xml:lang**—Specifies the base language for the element when the document is treated as XML. (Supported in XHTML 1.0 Strict, XHTML 1.0 Transitional, XHTML 1.0 Frameset, and XHTML 1.1.)

Here's how you might add a table row to the table you're constructing:

```
<table>
    <tr>
        .
        .
        .
    </tr>
    .
    .
    .
</table>
```

Remember that every row of data in a table needs a `<tr>` element. The `<tr>` element can contain `<th>` elements to create table headers and `<td>` elements to hold the data in the cells in a table.

Formatting Table Headers: <th>

The `<th>` element creates table headers, which are usually displayed centered and in bold text. These headers label the columns in a table. The `<th>` element is supported in XHTML 1.0 Strict, XHTML 1.0 Transitional, XHTML 1.0 Frameset, and XHTML 1.1. Here are its attributes:

- **abbr**—Specifies an abbreviated name for a header. (Supported in XHTML 1.0 Strict, XHTML 1.0 Transitional, XHTML 1.0 Frameset, and XHTML 1.1.)
- **align**—Specifies the horizontal alignment. Possible values are `left`, `center`, `right`, `justify`, and `char`. (Supported in XHTML 1.0 Strict, XHTML 1.0 Transitional, XHTML 1.0 Frameset, and XHTML 1.1.)

- **axis**—Specifies a name for a cell. This attribute is normally used only with table heading cells. (Supported in XHTML 1.0 Strict, XHTML 1.0 Transitional, XHTML 1.0 Frameset, and XHTML 1.1.)
- **bgcolor**—Specifies the background color of table cells. This attribute was deprecated in HTML 4.0. (Supported in XHTML 1.0 Transitional and XHTML 1.0 Frameset.)
- **char**—Specifies a character to align text with respect to. (Supported in XHTML 1.0 Strict, XHTML 1.0 Transitional, XHTML 1.0 Frameset, and XHTML 1.1.)
- **charoff**—Sets the alignment offset. (Supported in XHTML 1.0 Strict, XHTML 1.0 Transitional, XHTML 1.0 Frameset, and XHTML 1.1.)
- **class**—Specifies the style class of the element. (Supported in XHTML 1.0 Strict, XHTML 1.0 Transitional, XHTML 1.0 Frameset, and XHTML 1.1.)
- **colspan**—Specifies the number of columns of the table that the header should span. (the default is 1). (Supported in XHTML 1.0 Strict, XHTML 1.0 Transitional, XHTML 1.0 Frameset, and XHTML 1.1.)
- **dir**—Sets the direction of directionally neutral text. This attribute can be set to `ltr`, for left-to-right text, or `rtl`, for right-to-left text. (Supported in XHTML 1.0 Strict, XHTML 1.0 Transitional, XHTML 1.0 Frameset, and XHTML 1.1.)
- **headers**—Specifies a list of header cells. (Supported in XHTML 1.0 Strict, XHTML 1.0 Transitional, XHTML 1.0 Frameset, and XHTML 1.1.)
- **height**—Specifies the height of the header, in pixels. This attribute was deprecated in HTML 4.0. (Supported in XHTML 1.0 Transitional, XHTML 1.0 Frameset.)
- **id**—Specifies the ID of the element. (Supported in XHTML 1.0 Strict, XHTML 1.0 Transitional, XHTML 1.0 Frameset, and XHTML 1.1.)
- **lang**—Specifies the base language of the element. (Supported in XHTML 1.0 Strict, XHTML 1.0 Transitional, XHTML 1.0 Frameset, and XHTML 1.1.)
- **nowrap**—Specifies that the browser should not wrap text by adding line breaks. This attribute was deprecated in HTML 4.0. (Supported in XHTML 1.0 Transitional and XHTML 1.0 Frameset.)
- **rowspan**—Specifies the number of rows of the table that the header should span. (Supported in XHTML 1.0 Strict, XHTML 1.0 Transitional, XHTML 1.0 Frameset, and XHTML 1.1.)
- **scope**—Specifies a set of data cells for which the header cell gives header information. Possible values are `row`, `col`, `rowgroup`, and `colgroup`. (Supported in XHTML 1.0 Strict, XHTML 1.0 Transitional, XHTML 1.0 Frameset, and XHTML 1.1.)

- **style**—Indicates how a browser should display the element. You should set this to an inline style. (Supported in XHTML 1.0 Strict, XHTML 1.0 Transitional, XHTML 1.0 Frameset, and XHTML 1.1.)
- **title**—Specifies the title of the element. (Supported in XHTML 1.0 Strict, XHTML 1.0 Transitional, XHTML 1.0 Frameset, and XHTML 1.1.)
- **valign**—Specifies the vertical alignment of the data in the cell. Possible values are `top`, `middle`, `bottom`, and `baseline`. (Supported in XHTML 1.0 Strict, XHTML 1.0 Transitional, XHTML 1.0 Frameset, and XHTML 1.1.)
- **width**—Specifies the width of the header. This attribute was deprecated in HTML 4.0. (Supported in XHTML 1.0 Transitional, XHTML 1.0 Frameset.)
- **xml:lang**—Specifies the base language for the element when the document is treated as XML. (Supported in XHTML 1.0 Strict, XHTML 1.0 Transitional, XHTML 1.0 Frameset, and XHTML 1.1.)

Here's how you might create headers if you wanted to display data from the states example from Day 9, "Formatting XML by Using XSLT":

```
<table>
    <tr>
       <th>State</th>
       <th>Bird</th>
       <th>Flower</th>
    </tr>
    .
    .
    .
</table>
```

This example creates three table headers on top of three columns: State, Bird, and Flower.

TIP

XHTML headers can span several columns if you use the `colspan` attribute.

Formatting Table Data: <td>

Data in the cells of a table goes into the `<td>` element, which appears inside the `<tr>` element. The `<td>` element is supported in XHTML 1.0 Strict, XHTML 1.0 Transitional, XHTML 1.0 Frameset, and XHTML 1.1. Here are this element's attributes:

- **abbr**—Specifies an abbreviated name for a cell. (Supported in XHTML 1.0 Strict, XHTML 1.0 Transitional, XHTML 1.0 Frameset, and XHTML 1.1.)

- `align`—Specifies the horizontal alignment of content in the table cell. Possible values are `left`, `center`, `right`, `justify`, and `char`. (Supported in XHTML 1.0 Strict, XHTML 1.0 Transitional, XHTML 1.0 Frameset, and XHTML 1.1.)
- `axis`—Specifies a name for a cell—normally a table heading cell. This attribute allows the table to be mapped to a tree hierarchy. (Supported in XHTML 1.0 Strict, XHTML 1.0 Transitional, XHTML 1.0 Frameset, and XHTML 1.1.)
- `bgcolor`—Specifies the background color of table cells. This attribute was deprecated in HTML 4.0. (Supported in XHTML 1.0 Transitional and XHTML 1.0 Frameset.)
- `char`—Specifies a character to align text with respect to. (Supported in XHTML 1.0 Strict, XHTML 1.0 Transitional, XHTML 1.0 Frameset, and XHTML 1.1.)
- `charoff`—Sets the alignment offset. (Supported in XHTML 1.0 Strict, XHTML 1.0 Transitional, XHTML 1.0 Frameset, and XHTML 1.1.)
- `class`—Specifies the style class of the element. (Supported in XHTML 1.0 Strict, XHTML 1.0 Transitional, XHTML 1.0 Frameset, and XHTML 1.1.)
- `colspan`—Specifies the number of columns this cell should span. (Supported in XHTML 1.0 Strict, XHTML 1.0 Transitional, XHTML 1.0 Frameset, and XHTML 1.1.)
- `dir`—Sets the direction of directionally neutral text. This attribute can be set to `ltr`, for left-to-right text, or `rtl`, for right-to-left text. (Supported in XHTML 1.0 Strict, XHTML 1.0 Transitional, XHTML 1.0 Frameset, and XHTML 1.1.)
- `headers`—Specifies a list of header cells that supply header information. (Supported in XHTML 1.0 Strict, XHTML 1.0 Transitional, XHTML 1.0 Frameset, and XHTML 1.1.)
- `height`—Specifies the height of the cell, in pixels. This attribute was deprecated in HTML 4.0. (Supported in XHTML 1.0 Transitional and XHTML 1.0 Frameset.)
- `id`—Specifies the ID of the element. (Supported in XHTML 1.0 Strict, XHTML 1.0 Transitional, XHTML 1.0 Frameset, and XHTML 1.1.)
- `lang`—Specifies the base language of the element. (Supported in XHTML 1.0 Strict, XHTML 1.0 Transitional, XHTML 1.0 Frameset, and XHTML 1.1.)
- `nowrap`—Specifies that the browser should not wrap text by adding line breaks. This attribute was deprecated in HTML 4.0. (Supported in XHTML 1.0 Transitional and XHTML 1.0 Frameset.)
- `rowspan`—Specifies the number of rows in the table that the header should span. (Supported in XHTML 1.0 Strict, XHTML 1.0 Transitional, XHTML 1.0 Frameset, and XHTML 1.1.)

- **scope**—Specifies a set of data cells for which the header cell gives header information. Possible values are `row`, `col`, `rowgroup`, and `colgroup`. (Supported in XHTML 1.0 Strict, XHTML 1.0 Transitional, XHTML 1.0 Frameset, and XHTML 1.1.)
- **style**—Indicates how a browser should display the element. You should set this to an inline style. (Supported in XHTML 1.0 Strict, XHTML 1.0 Transitional, XHTML 1.0 Frameset, and XHTML 1.1.)
- **title**—Specifies the title of the element. (Supported in XHTML 1.0 Strict, XHTML 1.0 Transitional, XHTML 1.0 Frameset, and XHTML 1.1.)
- **valign**—Specifies the vertical alignment of the data in the cell. Possible values are `top`, `middle`, `bottom`, and `baseline`. (Supported in XHTML 1.0 Strict, XHTML 1.0 Transitional, XHTML 1.0 Frameset, and XHTML 1.1.)
- **width**—Specifies the width of the header. This attribute was deprecated in HTML 4.0. (Supported in XHTML 1.0 Transitional and XHTML 1.0 Frameset.)
- **xml:lang**—Specifies the base language for the element when the document is treated as XML. (Supported in XHTML 1.0 Strict, XHTML 1.0 Transitional, XHTML 1.0 Frameset, and XHTML 1.1.)

Listing 12.10 shows an example that uses `<td>` elements to create cells in XHTML. Note that this example gives the table a border by setting the `border` attribute to `"1"`.

LISTING 12.10 Using Tables in XHTML (`ch12_10.html`)

```
<!DOCTYPE html PUBLIC "-//W3C//DTD XHTML 1.0 Transitional//EN"
"http://www.w3.org/tr/xhtml1/DTD/xhtml1-transitional.dtd">
<html xmlns="http://www.w3.org/1999/xhtml">
    <head>
        <title>
            Formatting Tables in XHTML
        </title>
    </head>

    <body>
        <h1>
            Formatting Tables in XHTML
        </h1>
        <table border="1">
            <tr>
                <th>State</th>
                <th>Bird</th>
                <th>Flower</th>
            </tr>
            <tr>
```

LISTING 12.10 continued

```
                <td>California</td>
                <td>Quail</td>
                <td>Golden Poppy</td>
            </tr>
            <tr>
                <td>Massachusetts</td>
                <td>Chickadee</td>
                <td>Mayflower</td>
            </tr>
            <tr>
                <td>New York</td>
                <td>Bluebird</td>
                <td>Rose</td>
            </tr>
        </table>
    </body>
</html>
```

Figure 12.6 shows what this table looks like; as you can see, the state data is in the table, arranged properly.

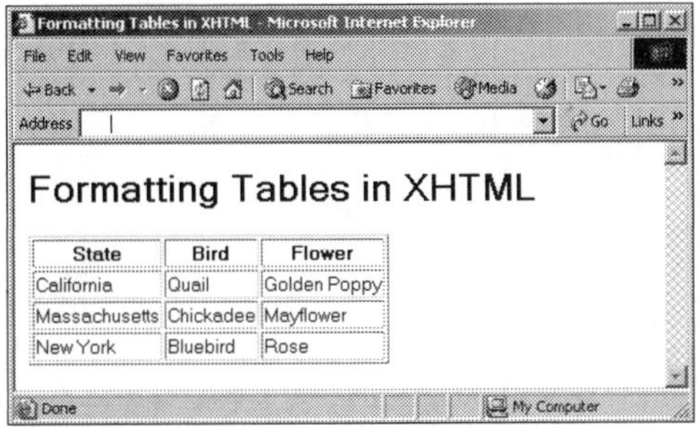

FIGURE 12.6
Creating a table in XHTML.

Extending XHTML

The name *Extensible Hypertext Markup Language* might give you the impression that XHTML is designed to be extended. That's true. However, although you can technically extend XHTML, HTML browsers won't understand what you're doing. Let's take a look at an example.

In this example, you'll extend XHTML by adding to it a new element, `<bold>`, that will display its text in bold. Here's how you might declare this element in a DTD:

```
<!ELEMENT bold (#PCDATA)>
```

You also need the rest of the XHTML 1.0 Transitional DTD, so you start by creating a new parameter entity, which you can call `XHTML1.0DTDEntity`:

```
<!ELEMENT bold (#PCDATA)>
<!ENTITY % XHTML1.0DTDEntity PUBLIC "-//W3C//DTD XHTML 1.0 Transitional//EN"
"http://www.w3.org/TR/xhtml1/DTD/xhtml1-transitional.dtd">
```

Now to include the entire XHTML 1.0 Transitional DTD in the new DTD, you just use a reference to this parameter entity. Listing 12.11 shows how this works.

LISTING 12.11 Extending the XHTML 1.0 Transitional DTD (`ch12_11.dtd`)

```
<!ELEMENT bold (#PCDATA)>
<!ATTLIST bold boldattribute CDATA #IMPLIED >
<!ENTITY % XHTML1.0DTDEntity PUBLIC "-//W3C//DTD XHTML 1.0 Transitional//EN"
"http://www.w3.org/TR/xhtml1/DTD/xhtml1-transitional.dtd">
%XHTML1.0DTDEntity;
```

Now you have a new DTD that supports not only the `<bold>` element, but also the rest of XHTML 1.0 Transitional. So you've extended XHTML. You can see this new DTD at work in Listing 12.12.

LISTING 12.12 Extending XHTML 1.0 Transitional as HTML (`ch12_12.html`)

```
<?xml version="1.0" encoding="UTF-8"?>
<!DOCTYPE html SYSTEM "ch12_11.dtd">
<html xmlns="http://www.w3.org/1999/xhtml">
    <head>
        <title>
            Extending XHTML
        </title>
        <link rel="stylesheet" href="ch12_13.css" />
    </head>

    <body>
        <p>
            This version of XHTML can make text <bold>bold</bold>.
        </p>
    </body>
</html>
```

To style the new `<bold>` element, you can use a CSS, such as the one in Listing 12.13.

LISTING 12.13 A Style Sheet for Extending XHTML 1.0 Transitional (ch12_13.css)

```
bold {font-weight: bold}
```

However, neither Internet Explorer nor Netscape Navigator will understand what to do with your extended XHTML. The reason for this is that you've given the XHTML document, ch12_12.html, the extension .html, which means that browsers will assume the fixed HTML element set and not even try to read in the DTD.

You can do a better job in this case if you treat ch12_12.html as XML instead of HTML. Listing 12.14 shows how that might work. In this version of the document, you're using an internal DTD (so as not to confuse Internet Explorer, which can't handle the DTD here as an external one) and the <?xml-stylesheet?> XML processing instruction to include a new version of the style sheet, ch12_15.css (to make sure the text in the <title> element will also be formatted for display), which is shown in Listing 12.15.

LISTING 12.14 Extending XHTML 1.0 Transitional as XML (ch12_14.xml)

```
<?xml version="1.0" encoding="UTF-8"?>
<?xml-stylesheet type="text/css" href="ch12_15.css"?>
<!DOCTYPE html [
<!ELEMENT bold (#PCDATA)>
<!ENTITY % XHTML1.0DTDEntity PUBLIC "-//W3C//DTD XHTML 1.0 Transitional//EN"
"http://www.w3.org/TR/xhtml1/DTD/xhtml1-transitional.dtd">
%XHTML1.0DTDEntity;
]>
<html xmlns="http://www.w3.org/1999/xhtml">
    <head>
        <title>
            Extending XHTML
        </title>
    </head>

    <body>
        <p>
            This version of XHTML can make text <bold>bold</bold>.
        </p>
    </body>
</html>
```

LISTING 12.15 A Style Sheet Used to Extend XHTML 1.0 Transitional as XML (ch12_15.css)

```
bold {font-weight: bold}
title {display:block; font-size: 24pt}
```

Figure 12.7 shows the results of Listings 12.14 and 12.15. in Internet Explorer. Internet Explorer indeed downloads the XHTML 1.0 Transitional DTD, extends it with the new `<bold>` element, and produces the results shown in Figure 12.7.

FIGURE 12.7 *Extending XHTML.*

By treating the markup as XML, you are able to extend XHTML. That's not too bad because the XHTML DTDs still contain all the XHTML rules, such as which elements can contain which other elements and which attributes are required. The drawback is that you need to define from scratch all the formatting you want to use; you do this by defining your own style sheets or using someone else's.

Summary

In your two-day look at XHTML, you've gotten a good introduction to the subject, and you've seen the major differences between XHTML and HTML. However, there are more than 100 elements in XHTML, and this book doesn't have the space to cover them all. You can get all the details in the W3C XHTML specifications themselves.

Today, you took a look at a number of XHTML elements and their attributes. You've seen that hyperlinks are supported by the `<a>` element. You must supply a value for either the `href` or `id` attribute. Using the `id` attribute can be problematic in browsers that don't support it (such as Netscape Navigator), in which case you use both the `id` and `name` attributes, assigned the same value.

The <link> element lets you link to other documents, which is very useful in XML because the W3C doesn't usually specify how other documents, such as style sheets or XML schemas, may be associated with the current XML document. The <link> element goes in the <head> element of an XHTML document, and you can use the rel and rev attributes to specify relationships with other documents. Some browsers support the <link> element for connecting style sheets to an XHTML (or HMTL) document.

The <img> element displays images in XHTML, just as in HTML. In XHTML, the src and alt attributes are both required. <img> is an empty element, so unlike in HTML, you need to end this element with /> in XHTML.

You can create frames in XHTML by using the <frameset> and <frame> elements, which are supported only in the XHTML 1.0 Frameset DTD. In the <frame> element, the src attribute is required.

Today you saw that there are three ways to associate styles with XHTML. You can use an external style sheet with the <link> element (or the XML processing instruction <?xml-stylesheet?>, if you're treating the XHTML document as XML), you can create an internal style sheet by using the <style> element, or you can style individual elements by using the style attribute.

XHTML also supports the HTML way of formatting tables—using the <table>, <caption>, <tr>, <th>, <td>, <colspan>, <col>, <thead>, <tbody>, and <tfoot> elements.

Today you saw how to extend XHTML. You extended XHTML by creating a DTD that defined a new element and that also included the XHTML 1.0 Transitional DTD. You then used that new DTD in an XHTML document, but HTML browsers couldn't handle the new element when you gave it the extension .html because they treated the document as HTML and didn't understand the new element. You had better luck treating the extended version of XHTML as XML, but doing so meant that you had to style each element individually.

Tomorrow you're going to take a look at two more popular uses for XML as you start to create graphics and handle multimedia: SVG and SMIL.

Q&A

Q I notice that the W3C recommendation for XHTML suggests that I enclose the text content of XHTML `<script>` elements in `CDATA` sections, but my browser freaks out when I do. Any ideas?

A The goal of the `CDATA` suggestion is to let you avoid having the browser interpret sensitive characters such as < that are valid in JavaScript but problematic in XML. This solution is not supported in any HTML browser yet, however; a better solution is to make your scripts external, like this:

```
<script type = "text/javascript" language="javascript" src="script.js">
```

Note that in XHTML, the `type` attribute, which you set to `"text/javascript"` in JavaScript, is required.

Q When you extended XHTML today, you used the `SYSTEM` keyword, which essentially created a private DTD. Can I also extend XHTML in public DTDs?

A Yes, absolutely. But you need to create your own FPI to do that. Review the rules from Day 4, "Creating Valid XML Documents: DTDs," about FPI creation.

Workshop

This workshop tests whether you understand the concepts discussed today. It's a good idea to make sure you can answer these questions before pressing on to tomorrow's work. Answers to the quiz can be found in Appendix A, "Quiz Answers."

Quiz

1. What attributes are required in the XHTML `<a>` element?
2. What attributes are required in the XHTML `<img>` element?
3. What versions of XHTML support the `<frame>` and `<frameset>` elements?
4. How are you supposed to replace the `<frame>` and `<frameset>` elements in versions of XHTML that don't support them?
5. Is the `<table>` element supported in XHTML 1.0 Strict? How about in XHTML 1.1?

Exercises

1. Combine the `<img>` and `<a>` elements we talked about today in an XHTML 1.0 Transitional document that displays an image you can click to be taken to the W3C XHTML 1.0 specification (`http://www.w3.org/TR/xhtml1`).
2. Extend the XHTML 1.0 Transitional DTD to include a new element named `<red>` that styles its text in red. Treating an XHTML document as XML, test your new element.

PART III

DAY 13

Creating Graphics and Multimedia: SVG and SMIL

Today you're going to take a look at two XML applications—Scalable Vector Graphics (SVG) and Synchronized Multimedia Integration Language (SMIL)—both of whose specifications are published by the W3C. SVG lets you create two-dimensional graphics, and SMIL lets you create multimedia presentations, including images, text, and music.

Here's an overview of today's topics:

- Basic shapes in SVG
- SVG hyperlinks
- SVG animation
- SVG text
- SVG gradients
- SVG scripting

- SMIL documents
- SMIL images
- SMIL text

You'll start today's discussion with SVG.

Introducing SVG

There have been a number of XML-based 2D graphics languages over the years. One of them—Vector Markup Language (VML)—is supported only in Internet Explorer. It's more correct to call VML a semi-XML language, actually. Listing 13.1 shows an example of VML that is embedded in HTML. VML has a major drawback: It is supported only in Internet Explorer.

LISTING 13.1 Using VML (ch13_01.html)

```
<HTML xmlns:v="urn:schemas-microsoft-com:vml">

    <HEAD>
        <TITLE>
            Vector Markup Language Example
        </TITLE>

        <STYLE>
        v\:* {behavior: url(#default#VML);}
        </STYLE>
    </HEAD>

    <BODY>
        <CENTER>
            <H1>
                Vector Markup Language Example
            </H1>
        </CENTER>
        <v:rect style='width:80pt; height:60pt' fillcolor="green"
            strokecolor="red" strokeweight="4pt"/>
        <v:oval style='width:80pt; height:60pt' fillcolor="red"/>
    </BODY>
</HTML>
```

Figure 13.1 shows what this example looks like in Internet Explorer.

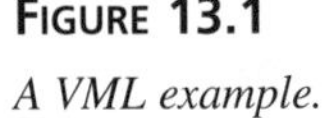

FIGURE 13.1

A VML example.

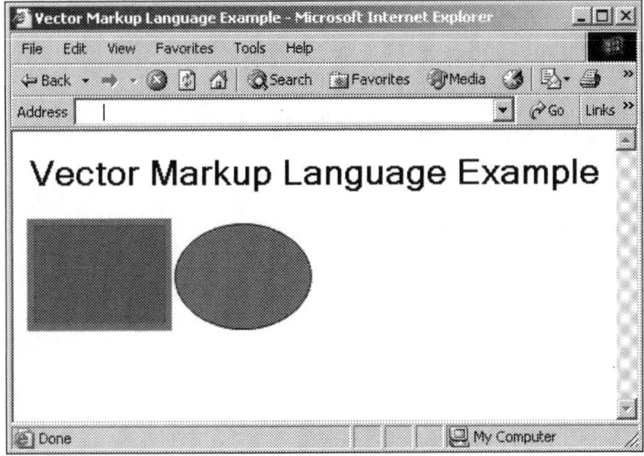

Whereas VML is a proprietary semi-XML application that works only in Internet Explorer, SVG is more broadly based, and by using the SVG Viewer plug-in from Adobe, you can use SVG in browsers such as Netscape Navigator as well as Internet Explorer.

NOTE

> The W3C recommendation for SVG 1.0 is at `http://www.w3.org/TR/SVG` and the W3C recommendation for SVG 1.1 (which is the current version as of January 14, 2003) at `http://www.w3.org/TR/SVG11`. The Adobe plug-in you'll work with today (SVG Viewer) supports only SVG 1.0. In fact, work has started on SVG 1.2, and it includes SVG for mobile devices and printing. An overview of SVG is at `http://www.w3.org/Graphics/SVG/Overview.htm8`.

SVG is a general-purpose 2D graphics language that supports all kinds of powerful tools. It lets you draw basic shapes such as ellipses, rectangles, lines, and polygons, as well as display text, gradients, and so on. You can also create hyperlinks, script SVG by using languages such as JavaScript, and create animation. Here's how W3C describes SVG:

> SVG is a language for describing two-dimensional graphics in XML. SVG allows for three types of graphic objects: vector graphic shapes (e.g., paths consisting of straight lines and curves), images and text. Graphical objects can be grouped, styled, transformed and composited into previously rendered objects. Text can be in any XML namespace suitable to the application, which enhances searchability and accessibility of the SVG graphics. The feature set includes nested transformations, clipping paths, alpha masks, filter effects, template objects and extensibility.
>
> SVG drawings can be dynamic and interactive. The Document Object Model (DOM) for SVG, which includes the full XML DOM, allows for straightforward and efficient

vector graphics animation via scripting. A rich set of event handlers such as `onmouseover` and `onclick` can be assigned to any SVG graphical object. Because of its compatibility and leveraging of other Web standards, features like scripting can be done on SVG elements and other XML elements from different namespaces simultaneously within the same Web page.

SVG includes the following built-in elements:

`a`	`altGlyph`	`altGlyphDef`
`altGlyphItem`	`animate`	`animateColor`
`animateMotion`	`animateTransform`	`circle`
`clipPath`	`color-profile`	`cursor`
`definition-src`	`defs`	`desc`
`ellipse`	`feBlend`	`feColorMatrix`
`feComponentTransfer`	`feComposite`	`feConvolveMatrix`
`feDiffuseLighting`	`feDisplacementMap`	`feDistantLight`
`feFlood`	`feFuncA`	`feFuncB`
`feFuncG`	`feFuncR`	`feGaussianBlur`
`feImage`	`feMerge`	`feMergeNode`
`feMorphology`	`feOffset`	`fePointLight`
`feSpecularLighting`	`feSpotLight`	`feTile`
`feTurbulence`	`filter`	`font`
`font-face`	`font-face-format`	`font-face-name`
`font-face-src`	`font-face-uri`	`foreignObject`
`g`	`glyph`	`glyphRef`
`hkern`	`image`	`line`
`linearGradient`	`marker`	`mask`
`metadata`	`missing-glyph`	`mpath`
`path`	`pattern`	`polygon`
`polyline`	`radialGradient`	`rect`
`script`	`set`	`stop`
`style`	`svg`	`switch`
`symbol`	`text`	`textPath`
`title`	`tref`	`tspan`
`use`	`view`	`vkern`

SVG is actually a language of considerable depth; it includes all kinds of advanced features, such as spotlighting of elements and abstract shape modeling. Although today's discussion doesn't have the space to cover everything about SVG, you'll get a good SVG foundation.

Besides all the built-in elements, SVG also has the following colors predefined and ready for use:

aliceblue	antiquewhite	aqua
aquamarine	azure	beige
bisque	black	blanchedalmond
blue	blueviolet	brown
burlywood	cadetblue	chartreuse
chocolate	coral	cornflowerblue
cornsilk	crimson	cyan
darkblue	darkcyan	darkgoldenrod
darkgray	darkgreen	darkgrey
darkkhaki	darkmagenta	darkolivegreen
darkorange	darkorchid	darkred
darksalmon	darkseagreen	darkslateblue
darkslategray	darkslategrey	darkturquoise
darkviolet	deeppink	deepskyblue
dimgray	dimgrey	dodgerblue
firebrick	floralwhite	forestgreen
fuchsia	gainsboro	ghostwhite
gold	goldenrod	gray
grey	green	greenyellow
honeydew	hotpink	indianred
indigo	ivory	khaki
lavender	lavenderblush	lawngreen
lemonchiffon	lightblue	lightcoral
lightcyan	lightgoldenrodyellow	lightgray
lightgreen	lightgrey	lightpink
lightsalmon	lightseagreen	lightskyblue

`lightslategray`	`lightslategrey`	`lightsteelblue`
`lightyellow`	`lime`	`limegreen`
`linen`	`magenta`	`maroon`
`mediumaquamarine`	`mediumblue`	`mediumorchid`
`mediumpurple`	`mediumseagreen`	`mediumslateblue`
`mediumspringgreen`	`mediumturquoise`	`mediumvioletred`
`midnightblue`	`mintcream`	`mistyrose`
`moccasin`	`navajowhite`	`navy`
`oldlace`	`olive`	`olivedrab`
`orange`	`orangered`	`orchid`
`palegoldenrod`	`palegreen`	`paleturquoise`
`palevioletred`	`papayawhip`	`peachpuff`
`peru`	`pink`	`plum`
`powderblue`	`purple`	`red`
`rosybrown`	`royalblue`	`saddlebrown`
`salmon`	`sandybrown`	`seagreen`
`seashell`	`sienna`	`silver`
`skyblue`	`slateblue`	`slategray`
`slategrey`	`snow`	`springgreen`
`steelblue`	`tan`	`teal`
`thistle`	`tomato`	`turquoise`
`violet`	`wheat`	`white`
`whitesmoke`	`yellow`	`yellowgreen`

In addition, you can specify colors by using hexadecimal numbers as in HTML. For example, `#000000` is black, `#0000FF` is blue, and `#FFFFFF` is white.

Now that you've gotten an overview of SVG, you can start putting it to work by creating and testing your own SVG documents. You can use the free-to-download Adobe SVG Viewer to see what your documents look like in a browser.

Creating an SVG Document

Unlike VML, SVG really is XML. You use an XML declaration at the beginning of an SVG document. Each SVG document should be in the official namespace http://www.w3.org/2000/svg. The public identifier for SVG 1.0 is "PUBLIC "-//W3C//DTD SVG 1.0//EN". The DTD for SVG is at http://www.w3.org/TR/2001/REC-SVG-20010904/DTD/svg10.dtd. The MIME type for SVG (which is important if you want to create SVG documents on a Web server and send them to a browser) is image/svg+xml. And you give SVG documents the extension .svg.

Start by using the <rect> element to create and display a simple rectangle. Begin with an XML declaration:

```
<?xml version="1.0" encoding="UTF-8"?>
        .
        .
        .
```

Next comes the SVG document element, <svg>. Along with this element, you also indicate that the namespace is "http://www.w3.org/2000/svg":

```
<?xml version="1.0" encoding="UTF-8"?>

<svg xmlns="http://www.w3.org/2000/svg">
        .
        .
        .
</svg>
```

TIP

You can use the <svg> element's height and width attributes to limit an SVG display to a specific box.

If you want to check your SVG documents for validity, you can also use a <!DOCTYPE> element, listing the SVG DTD like this:

```
<?xml version="1.0" encoding="UTF-8"?>

<svg xmlns="http://www.w3.org/2000/svg">
    <!DOCTYPE svg "PUBLIC "-//W3C//DTD SVG 1.0//EN"
      "http://www.w3.org/TR/2001/REC-SVG-20010904/DTD/svg10.dtd">
        .
        .
        .
</svg>
```


All the SVG will go inside the <svg> document element, beginning with the <title> element, which gives the document a title that a browser can display, just as in HTML:

```
<?xml version="1.0" encoding="UTF-8"?>

<svg xmlns="http://www.w3.org/2000/svg">
```

```
<title>Creating a rectangle</title>
        .
        .
        .
</svg>
```

Now it's time to create the rectangle itself, by using the `<rect>` element, as described in the following section.

Creating Rectangles

To create rectangles, you can use the `<rect>` element. Here are the required attributes of this element in SVG 1.0:

- **`height`**—Specifies the height of the rectangle.
- **`width`**—Specifies the width of the rectangle.

As in CSS, dimensions in SVG can be specified with `px`, `pt`, `in`, or `cm`; the default measurement is pixels. In addition, you can use abstract units in SVG. To create the rectangle for this example, you can use the `height` and `width` attributes, as well as the `x` and `y` attributes to specify the location of the upper-left corner of the rectangle. (Note that, as in CSS, the coordinate system's origin is at the upper left; positive y goes downward, and positive x goes to the right.) Listing 13.2 shows how to use the `<rect>` element to draw the rectangle.

LISTING 13.2 Using SVG (`ch13_02.svg`)

```
<?xml version="1.0" encoding="UTF-8"?>

<svg xmlns="http://www.w3.org/2000/svg">
   <title>Creating a rectangle</title>
   <rect x="100" y="100" width="300" height="100"/>
</svg>
```

Now that you have your first SVG document, how do you display it? Read on.

Adobe's SVG Viewer

To get a look at your SVG document, you can use Adobe's free SVG viewer, SVG Viewer, which you can download from `www.adobe.com/svg/viewer/install` for many platforms (Macintosh, Windows, Linux, and so on) and operating system versions. The

SVG viewer comes complete with instructions on how to install it, which usually just means running the installer program.

After you install SVG Viewer, you can view SVG documents in a browser; for example, Figure 13.2 shows what `ch13_02.svg` looks like in Internet Explorer. As you can see, the rectangle appears in solid black (and the document's title appears in the browser's title bar).

FIGURE 13.2
Viewing an SVG document.

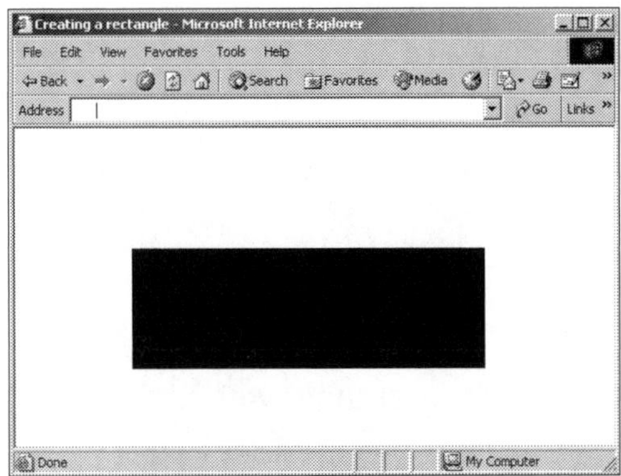

What if you don't want the rectangle to be filled in? What if you would like to specify the colors used instead of using black? As described in the following section, you can use CSS styles with your SVG figures.

Using CSS Styles

It turns out that SVG elements have a style attribute that you can assign CSS styles to. For example, if you want to create a rectangle that is not filled in, you can assign the CSS property `fill` the value `"none"`. To set the color of the rectangle, you can use the `stroke` property, setting it to one of the color names listed earlier today, in the section "Introducing SVG." You could also set the `stroke-width` property to the width of the rectangle's border, like this:

```
<rect x="100" y="100" width="300" height="100"
    style="fill:none; stroke:royalblue; stroke-width:2"/>
```

13

Listing 13.3 shows a new version of the rectangle. This listing also adds some descriptive text by using the `<text>` element, and it styles that text by using CSS styling to set the position and size.

LISTING 13.3 Using SVG with CSS (`ch13_03.svg`)

```
<?xml version="1.0" encoding="UTF-8"?>

<svg xmlns="http://www.w3.org/2000/svg">
    <title>Creating a rectangle with styles</title>
    <text y="40" style="font-size:24pt">
        Creating a rectangle with styles
    </text>
    <rect x="100" y="100" width="300" height="100"
        style="fill:none; stroke:royalblue; stroke-width:2"/>
</svg>
```

Figure 13.3 shows the new version of the rectangle.

FIGURE 13.3

An empty rectangle.

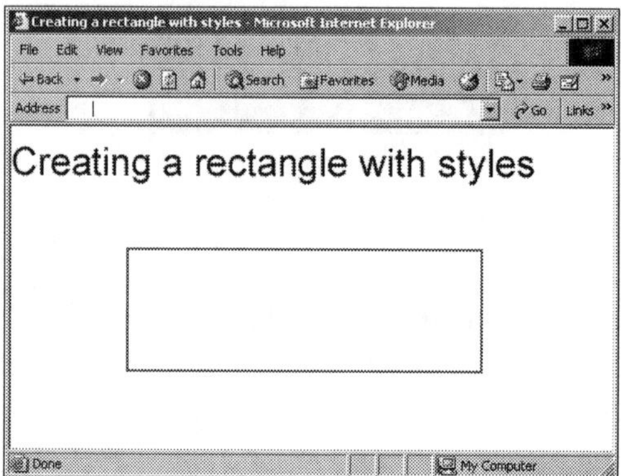

If you want to fill in the rectangle with color, you assign the appropriate color to the `fill` CSS property. Here's how you might fill in the rectangle with `mediumaquamarine`:

```
<?xml version="1.0" encoding="UTF-8"?>

<svg xmlns="http://www.w3.org/2000/svg">
    <title>Creating a rectangle with styles</title>
    <text y="40" style="font-size:24pt">
        Creating a rectangle with styles
    </text>
    <rect x="100" y="100" width="300" height="100"
        style="fill:mediumaquamarine; stroke:royalblue; stroke-width:2"/>
</svg>
```

You can also use many CSS properties directly as attributes of SVG elements, like this:

```
<?xml version="1.0" encoding="UTF-8"?>

<svg xmlns="http://www.w3.org/2000/svg">
    <title>Creating a rectangle with styles</title>
    <text y="40" style="font-size:24pt">
        Creating a rectangle with styles
    </text>
    <rect x="100" y="100" width="300" height="100"
        fill="mediumaquamarine" stroke="royalblue" stroke-width="2"/>
</svg>
```

SVG shares the following CSS properties as attributes:

- clip
- color
- cursor
- direction
- display
- fill
- font
- font-family
- font-size
- font-size-adjust
- font-stretch
- font-style
- font-variant
- font-weight
- letter-spacing
- overflow

SVG also shares the following CSS text properties as attributes:

- text-decoration
- unicode-bidi
- visibility
- word-spacing

13

Creating Circles

You use the <circle> SVG element to create circles. Here are the attributes for this element:

- **r**—Specifies the radius of the circle. This attribute is required.
- **cx**—Sets the horizontal location of the center of the circle.
- **cy**—Sets the vertical location of the center of the circle.

Listing 13.4 shows an example that creates a circle centered at (150,150) with a radius of 100 pixels.

LISTING 13.4 Creating a Circle (ch13_04.svg)

```
<?xml version="1.0" encoding="UTF-8"?>

<svg xmlns="http://www.w3.org/2000/svg">
    <title>Creating a circle</title>
    <text y="40" style="font-size:24pt">
        Creating a circle
    </text>
    <circle r="100" cx="150px" cy="150px"
        style="fill:deepskyblue; stroke:royalblue; stroke-width:2"/>
</svg>
```

Figure 13.4 shows the results of this SVG. As you can see, the circle appears with the fill color, size, and location specified in Listing 13.4.

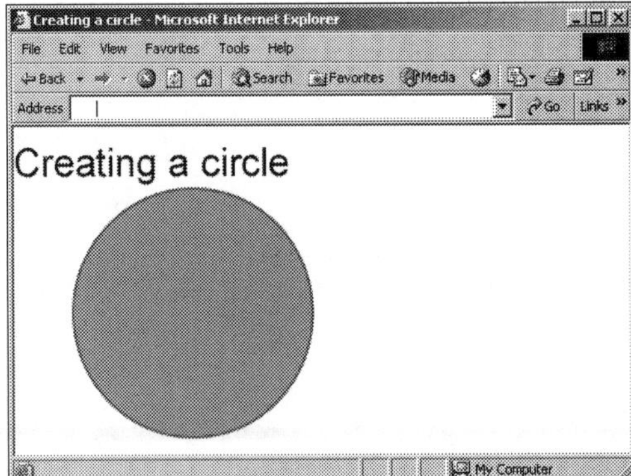

FIGURE 13.4
Creating a circle.

Creating Ellipses

You can create an ellipse by using the SVG `<ellipse>` element. Here are the required attributes for this element:

- **rx**—Specifies one-half the width of the ellipse. This attribute is required.
- **ry**—Specifies one-half the height of the ellipse. This attribute is required.
- **cx**—Sets the horizontal location of the center of the ellipse.
- **cy**—Sets the vertical location of the center of the ellipse.

Listing 13.5 shows an example that takes advantage of the color possibilities in SVG to create an ellipse in blanched almond, with a fill color of dark salmon.

LISTING 13.5 Creating an Ellipse (ch13_05.svg)

```
<?xml version="1.0" encoding="UTF-8"?>

<svg xmlns="http://www.w3.org/2000/svg">
    <title>Creating an ellipse</title>
    <text y="40" style="font-size:24pt">
        Creating an ellipse
    </text>
    <ellipse cx="150" cy="150" rx="150" ry="80"
        style="fill:darksalmon; stroke:blanchedalmond; stroke-width:2"/>
</svg>
```

Figure 13.5 shows this SVG at work.

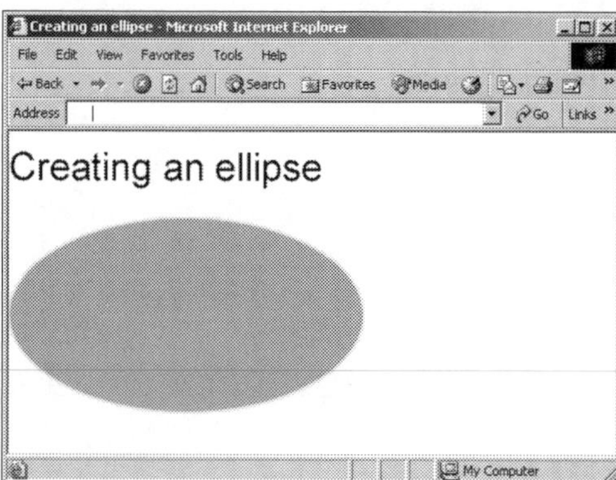

FIGURE 13.5
Creating an ellipse by using SVG.

Creating Lines

The SVG <line> element lets you draw lines. This element doesn't have any required attributes, but you can use the x1, y1, x2, and y2 attributes to draw a line from (x1,y1) to (x2,y2). An example is shown in Listing 13.6, which draws lines in various colors.

LISTING 13.6 Creating Lines (ch13_06.svg)

```
<?xml version="1.0" encoding="UTF-8"?>

<svg xmlns="http://www.w3.org/2000/svg">
  <title>Creating lines</title>
    <text y="40" style="font-size:24pt">
        Creating lines
    </text>
  <line x1="80" y1="80" x2="190" y2="50"
    style="stroke:goldenrod; stroke-width:2"/>
  <line x1="140" y1="60" x2="240" y2="180"
    style="stroke:forestgreen; stroke-width:2"/>
  <line x1="30" y1="50" x2="310" y2="200"
    style="stroke:moccasin; stroke-width:2"/>
  <line x1="30" y1="200" x2="310" y2="30"
    style="stroke:turquoise; stroke-width:2"/>
</svg>
```

You can see the results of this SVG in Figure 13.6.

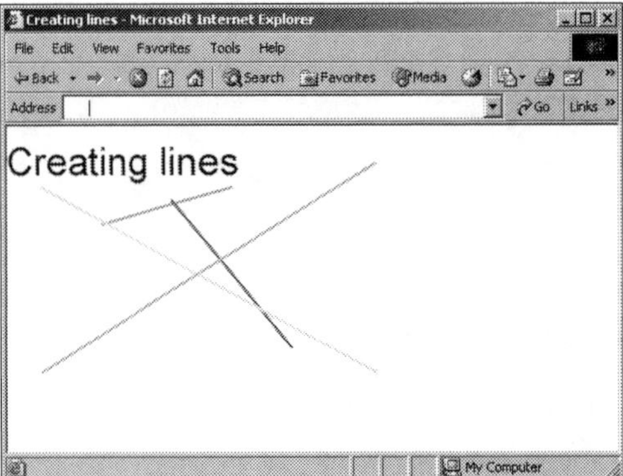

FIGURE 13.6
Creating lines by using SVG.

Creating Polylines

SVG has a <polyline> element that lets you draw multiple lines in connect-the-dots fashion. There's only one required attribute here:

- **points**—Specifies the list of points to be connected.

The `points` attribute is assigned a list of points like this: `"x1,y1 x2,y2, x3,y3 x4,y4..."`. SVG will connect the dots. Listing 13.7 shows an example that connects the dots by using a line in the SVG color fire brick and fills the resulting figure in with the SVG color lemon chiffon.

LISTING 13.7 Creating Polylines by Using SVG (`ch13_07.svg`)

```
<?xml version="1.0" encoding="UTF-8"?>

<svg xmlns="http://www.w3.org/2000/svg">
  <title>Creating polylines</title>
    <text y="40" style="font-size:24pt">
        Creating polylines
    </text>
    <polyline points="80,80 80,100 200,250 250,150 350,200
      360,220 320,300 380,320 420,210 340,250 80,80"
      style="fill:lemonchiffon; stroke:firebrick; stroke-width:2"/>
</svg>
```

You can see the result of Listing 13.7 in Figure 13.7.

FIGURE 13.7

Creating polylines.

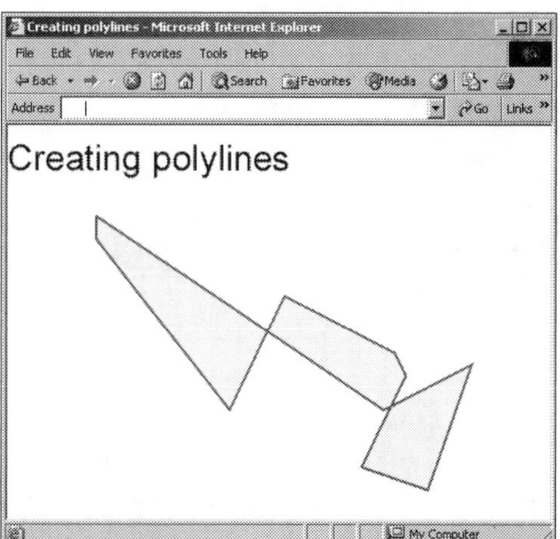

Creating Polygons

The `<polygon>` element is the last of the basic shape elements in SVG. Like the `<polyline>` element, this one requires a `points` attribute that holds a list of points. The `<polygon>` element connects the dots and creates a closed figure; you can see an example in Listing 13.8.

LISTING 13.8 Creating Polygons by Using SVG (ch13_08.svg)

```
<?xml version="1.0" encoding="UTF-8"?>

<svg xmlns="http://www.w3.org/2000/svg">
    <title>Creating polygons</title>
    <text y="40" style="font-size:24pt">
        Creating polygons
    </text>
    <polygon points="30,120 70,80 110,120 90,180 50,180 30,120"
        style="fill:papayawhip; stroke:blue; stroke-width:4"/>
</svg>
```

Figure 13.8 shows this polygon.

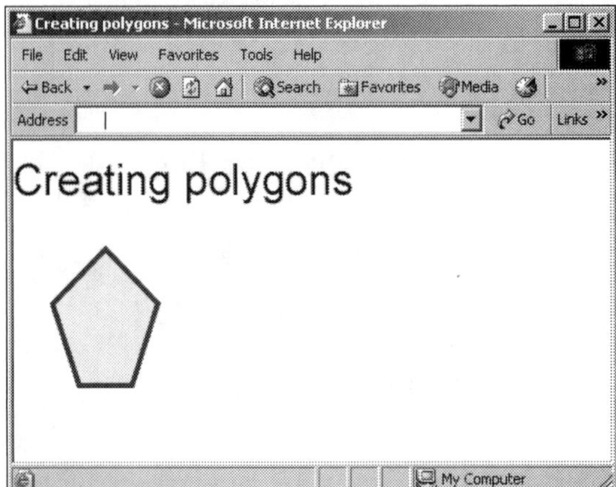

FIGURE 13.8
Creating polygons.

Creating Text

You use the <text> element, as you have already done today, to display text. Unlike the basic shape elements you've seen so far, the <text> element isn't empty; you enclose the text you want to display in it. This element has no required attributes, but to position text, you can use the x and y attributes to specify the location of the upper-left corner of the text.

Listing 13.9 shows an example that shows how to format text in SVG by using CSS styles, covered on Day 8, "Formatting XML by Using Cascading Style Sheets."

LISTING 13.9 Creating Text by Using SVG (`ch13_09.svg`)

```
<?xml version="1.0" encoding="UTF-8"?>

<svg xmlns="http://www.w3.org/2000/svg">
    <title>Creating text</title>
    <text x="40" y="100" style="font-family:sans-serif; font-size:16pt">
        An example of
    </text>
    <text x="180" y="100" style="font-family:courier; font-weight: bold;
        font-size:16pt; font-style:italic; text-decoration:underline">
        formatted text.
    </text>
</svg>
```

You can see what this text looks like in Figure 13.9.

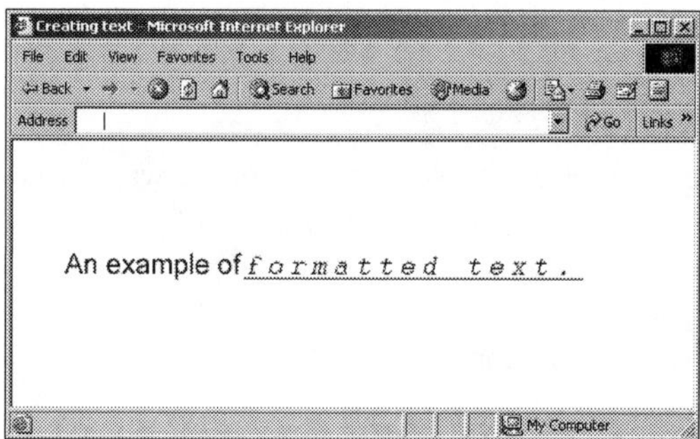

FIGURE 13.9
Handling text.

Note that although you use the `style` attribute in this example to specify CSS styles because you discussed it on Day 8, you can also use CSS properties directly as attributes of SVG elements, like this (note that not all such attributes are supported by Adobe's SVG Viewer):

```
<?xml version="1.0" encoding="UTF-8"?>

<svg xmlns="http://www.w3.org/2000/svg">
    <title>Creating text</title>
    <text x="40" y="100" font-family="sans-serif" font-size="16pt">
        An example of
    </text>
    <text x="180" y="100" font-family="courier" font-weight="bold"
        font-size="16pt" font-style="italic" text-decoration="underline">
        formatted text.
    </text>
</svg>
```

13

Creating Gradients

SVG supports many sophisticated graphics effects, such as color gradients. For example, you can create a linear color gradient that goes from black to blue. You start out by defining a gradient in an element named <defs>, which holds definitions:

```
<defs>
    .
    .
    .
</defs>
```

In this case, you're going to create a linear gradient and name it gradient1, and you can do this by using the <linearGradient> element and its id attribute:

```
<defs>
    <linearGradient id="gradient1">
        .
        .
        .
    </linearGradient>
</defs>
```

This gradient starts with black at a location 5% of the way through the figure, which you can specify with a <stop> element. Here's what that looks like:

```
<defs>
    <linearGradient id="gradient1">
        <stop offset="5%" stop-color="#000000" />
        .
        .
        .
    </linearGradient>
</defs>
```

The gradient becomes pure blue at 95% through the figure:

```
<defs>
    <linearGradient id="gradient1">
        <stop offset="5%" stop-color="#000000" />
        <stop offset="95%" stop-color="#0000FF" />
        .
        .
        .
    </linearGradient>
</defs>
```

Now that you've defined the gradient `gradient1`, all that remains is to put it to work, and you can do that by referencing it in the `fill` attribute as `"url(#gradient1)"`, as shown in Listing 13.10.

LISTING 13.10 Creating Gradients by Using SVG (`ch13_10.svg`)

```
<?xml version="1.0" encoding="UTF-8"?>
<svg xmlns="http://www.w3.org/2000/svg">
    <text y="40" style="font-size:24pt">
        Creating gradients
    </text>
    <defs>
        <linearGradient id="gradient1">
            <stop offset="5%" stop-color="#000000" />
            <stop offset="95%" stop-color="#0000FF" />
        </linearGradient>
    </defs>

    <rect fill="url(#gradient1)" stroke="blue" stroke-width="10"
        x="40" y="100" width="300" height="150"/>
</svg>
```

The result of Listing 13.10 is in Figure 13.10, where, as you can see, the gradient does indeed appear in the figure.

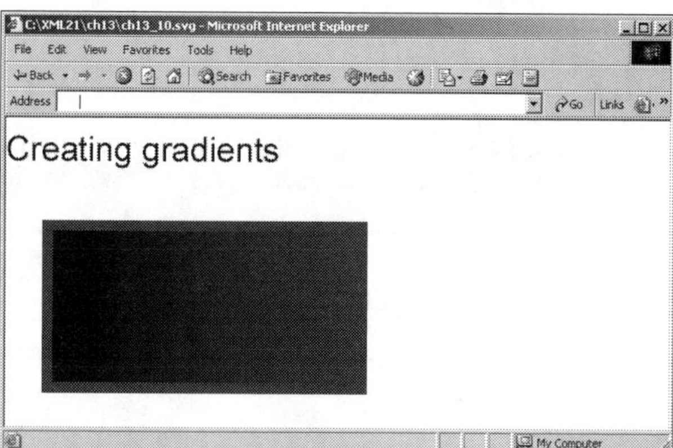

FIGURE 13.10
Creating a gradient.

13

Creating Paths

Another sophisticated aspect of SVG is that it enables you to create visual paths, which you do by using the `<path>` element. This element has one required attribute, `d`, which defines the path. The syntax of this attribute is a little involved; it consists of coordinates and single-letter commands. The list of commands is also a long one. Here are a few favorites:

- **M**—Indicates a "move to" operation.
- **L**—Indicates a "line to" operation.
- **H**—Draws a horizontal line.
- **V**—Draws a vertical line.
- **S**—Draws a cubic Bézier curve from the current point to (x,y). The first control point is assumed to be the reflection of the second control point in the previous command.
- **C**—Draws a cubic Bézier curve from the current point to (x,y), using (x1,y1) as the control point at the beginning of the curve and (x2,y2) as the control point at the end of the curve.

For example, Listing 13.11 draws a curved figure by using the `<path>` element, assigning the path definition "`M100,160 C100,60 250,60 250,140 S400,260 400,160`" to the `d` attribute. To give this path a visual appearance, you set its `stroke-width` and `stroke` CSS properties as shown in Listing 13.11.

LISTING 13.11 Creating a Path by Using SVG (`ch13_11.svg`)

```
<?xml version="1.0" encoding="UTF-8"?>

<svg xmlns="http://www.w3.org/2000/svg">
    <text y="40" style="font-size:24pt">
        Creating paths
    </text>
    <path style="fill:none; stroke-width:4; stroke:#000000"
        d="M100,160 C100,60 250,60 250,140 S400,260 400,160"/>
</svg>
```

You can see what this path looks like in Figure 13.11.

There's more you can do with paths. For example, you can create text paths, as described in the following section.

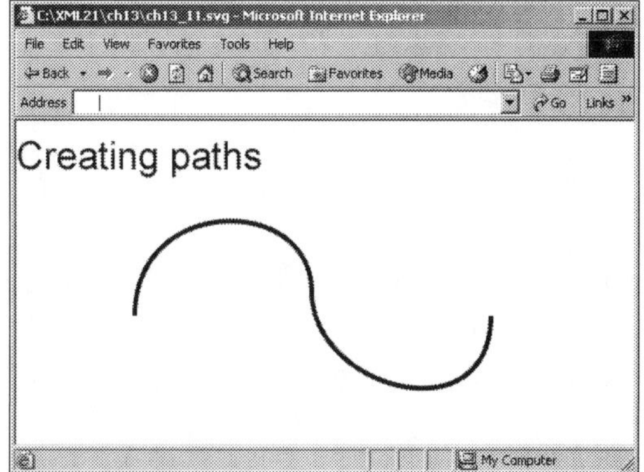

FIGURE 13.11
Drawing a path.

Creating Text Paths

You can create text paths to make text flow as you want it to by using the `<textPath>` and `<path>` elements. To show how this works, you can make some text flow along the path you just created (refer to Figure 13.11).

First, you define the path, giving it the ID `path1`:

```
<path id="path1" style="fill:none"
    d="M100,160 C100,60 250,60 250,140 S400,260 400,160"/>
        .
        .
        .
```

Next, you add a `<text>` element to enclose the text:

```
<path id="path1" style="fill:none"
    d="M100,160 C100,60 250,60 250,140 S400,260 400,160"/>
<text x="40" y="100" font-family="sans-serif" font-size="16pt">
        .
        .
        .
</text>
```

Next, you use an enclosed `<textPath>` element to define the path you want the text to follow. To do that, reference the path, `path1`, by using an XLink (which you'll see more about tomorrow) :

```
<path id="path1" style="fill:none"
    d="M100,160 C100,60 250,60 250,140 S400,260 400,160"/>
<text x="40" y="100" font-family="sans-serif" font-size="16pt">
```

13

```
    <textPath xlink:href="#path1"
        xmlns:xlink="http://www.w3.org/1999/xlink">
        .
        .
        .
    </textPath>
</text>
```

Finally, enclose the text in the <textPath> element. Listing 13.12 shows how this works.

LISTING 13.12 Creating a Text Path in SVG (ch13_12.svg)

```
<?xml version="1.0" encoding="UTF-8"?>

<svg xmlns="http://www.w3.org/2000/svg">
    <text y="40" style="font-size:24pt">
        Creating paths
    </text>
    <path id="path1" style="fill:none"
        d="M100,160 C100,60 250,60 250,140 S400,260 400,160"/>
    <text x="40" y="100" font-family="sans-serif" font-size="16pt">
        <textPath xlink:href="#path1"
        xmlns:xlink="http://www.w3.org/1999/xlink">
            Here's how to create an artful curved text path.
        </textPath>
    </text>
</svg>
```

Figure 13.12 shows what this text path looks like. As you can see, the text does indeed follow the path you defined.

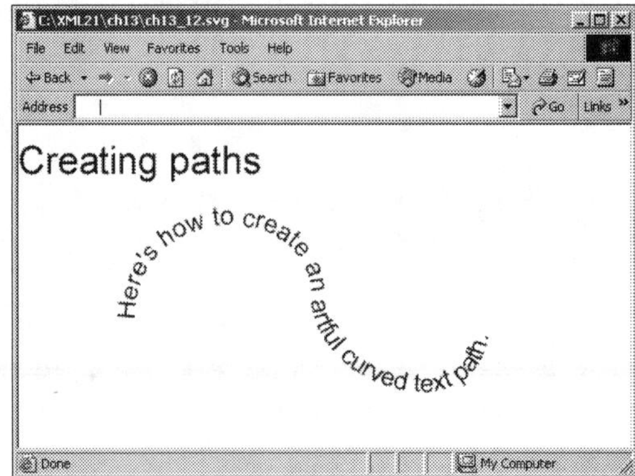

FIGURE 13.12 *Creating a text path.*

Creating Groups and Transformations

SVG allows you to group visual items together by using the <g> element and treat them as one item. To see how this works, you can create a group of visual items and use the <g> element's `transform` attribute to translate (that is, move) and rotate that group.

For this example, you can rotate and translate a group that consists of an ellipse and some text. Rotating and translating are separate operations, and you start by translating the group by +20 pixels in the x direction and +10 pixels in the y direction:

```
<g transform="translate(20, 10)">
    .
    .
    .
</g>
```

Next, you rotate the group by 20 degrees:

```
<g transform="translate(20, 10)">
    <g transform="rotate(20)">
    .
    .
    .
    </g>
</g>
```

Finally, you're ready to put the items you want—an ellipse and some text—into the group, as shown in Listing 13.13.

LISTING 13.13 Creating a Transformation (`ch13_13.svg`)

```
<?xml version="1.0" encoding="UTF-8"?>

<svg xmlns="http://www.w3.org/2000/svg">
    <text y="40" style="font-size:24pt">
        Using groups
    </text>
    <g transform="translate(20, 10)">
        <g transform="rotate(20)">
            <ellipse cx="150" cy="100" rx="100" ry="50"
                fill="none" stroke="darkmagenta" stroke-width="4"/>
            <text x="100" y="100" font-size="20"
                font-family="sans-serif" fill="navy" >
                Rotations!
            </text>
        </g>
    </g>
</svg>
```

This SVG, including the transformation and rotation, appears in Figure 13.13.

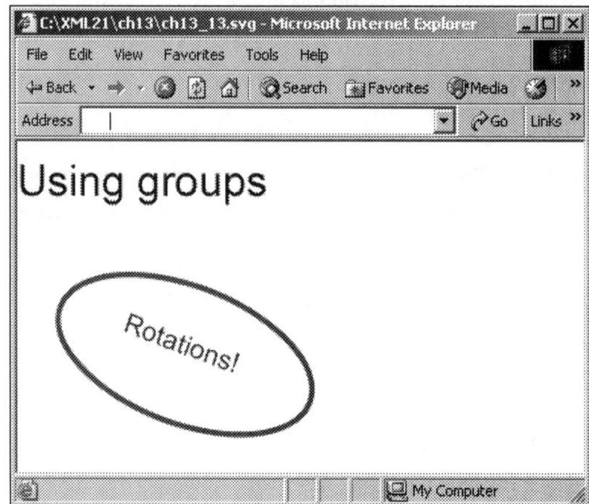

FIGURE 13.13
Creating a transformation by using SVG.

Creating Animation

SVG not only draws static 2D images, but it allows you to animate them as well, and Adobe's SVG Viewer supports animation. To animate graphics, you use the `<animate>` element, along with various attributes (none of which are required). In the following, draw a blue rectangle and then animate it, making it appear to rise and stretch as the user watches. The blue rectangle is originally 100 pixels high and 200 wide:

```
<rect x="200" y="100" width="200" height="100" fill="blue">
        .
        .
        .
</rect>
```

Now you use `<animate>` elements inside the `<rect>` element to animate the rectangle. When you animate an element such as `<rect>`, you really animate its attributes, such as `x`, `y`, `width`, and `height`, over a period of time. In this case, you can use four `<animate>` elements to animate those four attributes. For example, to animate the `x` attribute of the `<rect>` element, making it change from a value of 200 to 100 over a period of 10 seconds, starting when the rectangle first appears, you could use this `<animate>` element:

```
<rect x="200" y="100" width="200" height="100" fill="blue">
    <animate attributeName="x" attributeType="XML"
        begin="0s" dur="10s" fill="freeze" from="200" to="100" />
        .
        .
        .
</rect>
```

Set the `attributeName` attribute to the name of the attribute you want to work with, `x`, and then set the `attributeType` attribute to `"XML"`, meaning that this is an SVG attribute (the other option is `"CSS"`, which means you want to work with a CSS property). The `freeze` attribute lets you specify whether you want the results of the animation to stick around after the animation process is over. Setting `freeze` to `"fill"` means that you don't want the graphics element you're working with to return to its original appearance when the animation is done.

Listing 13.14 shows how to animate all four size attributes of the `<rect>` element—`x`, `y`, `width`, and `height`—by using `<animate>` elements.

LISTING 13.14 Creating Animation by Using SVG (`ch13_14.svg`)

```
<?xml version="1.0" standalone="no"?>
<svg xmlns="http://www.w3.org/2000/svg">
    <text y="40" style="font-size:24pt">
        Using animation
    </text>

    <rect x="200" y="100" width="200" height="100" fill="blue">
        <animate attributeName="x" attributeType="XML"
            begin="0s" dur="10s" fill="freeze" from="200" to="100" />
        <animate attributeName="y" attributeType="XML"
            begin="0s" dur="10s" fill="freeze" from="100" to="50" />
        <animate attributeName="width" attributeType="XML"
            begin="0s" dur="10s" fill="freeze" from="200" to="400" />
        <animate attributeName="height" attributeType="XML"
            begin="0s" dur="10s" fill="freeze" from="100" to="50" />
    </rect>
</svg>
```

You can see this example at work in Figure 13.14. When the animation starts, the rectangle rises and stretches.

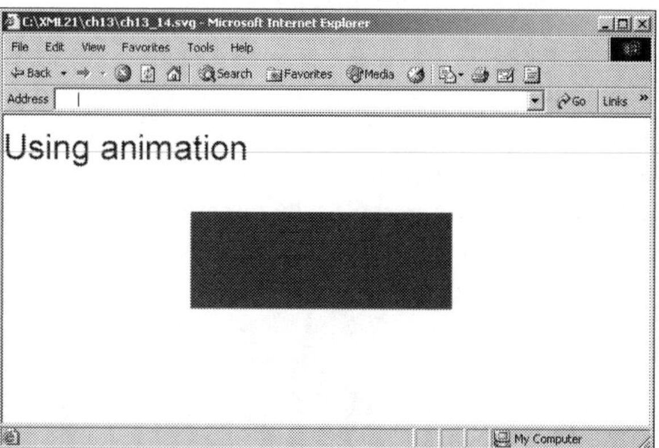

FIGURE 13.14
Animation with SVG.

Besides SVG attributes such as `x`, `y`, `width`, and `height`, you can also work with CSS properties. Here's an example using CSS properties to make the sample rectangle fade away over 10 seconds:

```
<rect x="200" y="100" width="200" height="100" fill="blue">
    <animate attributeType="CSS" attributeName="opacity"
        from="1" to="0" dur="10s"/>
</rect>
```

Creating Links

Just as in HTML, you can create hyperlinks by using the <a> element in SVG. However, SVG uses XLinks, which we'll talk about tomorrow. The XLink namespace is "`http://www.w3.org/1999/xlink`", and you need to define a namespace prefix, `xlink`, to go with that namespace:

```
<?xml version="1.0" standalone="no"?>
<svg xmlns="http://www.w3.org/2000/svg"
    xmlns:xlink="http://www.w3.org/1999/xlink">
    <text y="40" style="font-size:24pt">
        Using links
    </text>
        .
        .
        .
```

Then use the <a> element's required XLink `href` attribute to specify the URI to link to. In this case, you can link to the SVG 1.0 page, `http://www.w3.org/TR/SVG`:

```
<?xml version="1.0" standalone="no"?>
<svg xmlns="http://www.w3.org/2000/svg"
    xmlns:xlink="http://www.w3.org/1999/xlink">
    <text y="40" style="font-size:24pt">
        Using links
    </text>

  <a xlink:href="http://www.w3.org/TR/SVG/">
        .
        .
        .
  </a>
```

The graphical element you're using as a hyperlink doesn't need to be just underlined text; it can be anything. For example, you might use an ellipse as a hyperlink and dis play some underlined text in it to make it clear that the ellipse is, in fact, a hyperlink. Listing 13.15 shows how this might work.

LISTING 13.15 Creating a Hyperlink by Using SVG (ch13_15.svg)

```
<?xml version="1.0" standalone="no"?>
<svg xmlns="http://www.w3.org/2000/svg"
    xmlns:xlink="http://www.w3.org/1999/xlink">
    <text y="40" style="font-size:24pt">
        Using links
    </text>

  <a xlink:href="http://www.w3.org/TR/SVG/">
    <g>
        <ellipse cx="200" cy="100" rx="100" ry="50"
             fill="cyan" />
        <text y="105" x="125" style="font-size:24pt"
            text-decoration="underline">
            Click here!
        </text>
    </g>
  </a>
</svg>
```

You can see the results of Listing 13.15 in Figure 13.15. Note that when the mouse cursor is over the ellipse, it changes to a pointing hand, as is usual for hyperlinks, and as you can see in the figure. All you have to do to jump to the hyperlink target is click the hyperlink. (Unfortunately, right-clicking the hyperlink, as you might do when you want to open the target in a new window, doesn't work.)

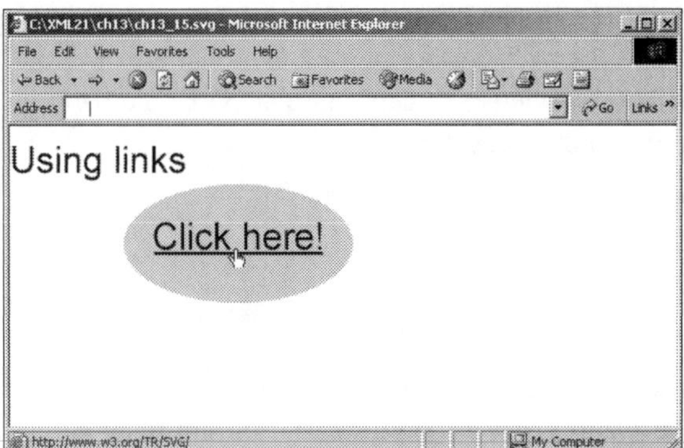

FIGURE 13.15
Creating a hyperlink.

So now not only are you creating animation, but you're also creating hyperlinks by using SVG. There's even more to come—you can also support scripting, as described in the next section.

Creating Scripts

You can use JavaScript to work with SVG. For example, you can add to a rectangle a script that causes the rectangle to grow when it is clicked. You start by creating the rectangle itself:

```
<rect onclick="click_handler(evt)" x="100" y="100"
    width="100" height="50" fill="steelblue"/>
```

Note in particular the `onclick` attribute, which lets the rectangle handle mouse-click events. These are the event attributes that elements such as `<rect>` let you handle:

- `onfocusin`
- `onfocusout`
- `onactivate`
- `onclick`
- `onmousedown`
- `onmouseup`
- `onmouseover`
- `onmousemove`
- `onmouseout`
- `onload`

To handle the mouse-click event in the rectangle, you connect a JavaScript event handler called `click_handler` to the click event, using the `<rect>` element's `onclick` attribute. You're going to work with JavaScript in more detail on Day 15, "Using JavaScript and XML," but here's a preview. You can set up an SVG `<script>` element and enclose the JavaScript code in a `CDATA` section:

```
<script type="text/javascript"> <![CDATA[
    .
    .
    .
]]> </script>
```

To get a JavaScript object that corresponds to the rectangle, you can use the `target` property of the event object passed to the JavaScript function:

```
<script type="text/javascript"> <![CDATA[
    function click_handler(evt)
    {
```

```
        var rect = evt.target;
          .
          .
          .
    }
]]> </script>
```

Now that you have a JavaScript object that corresponds to the rectangle, you can use its `setAttribute` method to set the width of the rectangle to 200 pixels, as shown in Listing 13.16.

LISTING 13.16 Creating a Script in SVG (`ch13_16.svg`)

```
<?xml version="1.0" standalone="no"?>
<svg xmlns="http://www.w3.org/2000/svg">

    <script type="text/javascript"> <![CDATA[
        function click_handler(evt)
        {
            var rect = evt.target;
            rect.setAttribute("width", 200);
        }
    ]]> </script>

    <text y="40" style="font-size:24pt">
        Using JavaScript
    </text>

    <rect onclick="click_handler(evt)" x="100" y="100"
        width="100" height="50" fill="steelblue"/>
</svg>
```

As shown in Figure 13.16, when you click the rectangle, it grows so its new width is 200 pixels.

FIGURE 13.16
Using JavaScript with SVG.

Besides using the `setAttribute` method to set the value of an SVG attribute in a script, you can also use the `getAttribute` method to get the value of an attribute, like this:

```
var w = rect.getAttribute("width");
```

Embedding SVG in HTML

So far today, the SVG documents have been dedicated SVG, but by using the HTML `<EMBED>` element, you can embed SVG documents in HTML pages. Listing 13.17 provides an example that shows how to use this element to embed one of the SVG examples, `ch13_02.svg`, in an HTML page. Note that the `PLUGINSPAGE` attribute lets the browser download the plug-in (after asking the user), if needed.

LISTING 13.17 Embedding SVG in HTML (`ch13_17.html`)

```
<HTML>
    <HEAD>
        <TITLE>
            Embedding SVG in HTML
        </TITLE>
    </HEAD>

    <BODY>
        <H1>Embedding SVG in HTML</H1>
        <EMBED WIDTH="500" HEIGHT="500" SRC="ch13_03.svg"
            PLUGINSPAGE="http://www.adobe.com/svg/viewer/install/">
    </BODY>
</HTML>
```

As shown in Figure 13.17, the SVG document has indeed been embedded in the HTML page.

That's it for your coverage of SVG today. Next, the discussion turns to SMIL.

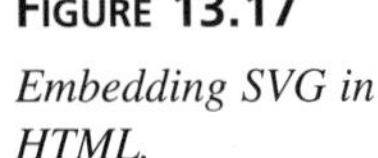

FIGURE 13.17
Embedding SVG in HTML.

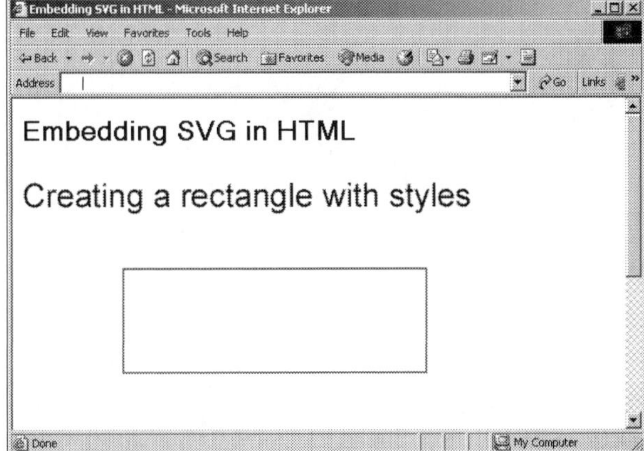

Introducing SMIL

SMIL is all about creating multimedia presentations in XML. Here's what the W3C says about it on its SMIL page, `http://www.w3.org/AudioVideo`:

> The Synchronized Multimedia Integration Language (SMIL, pronounced "smile") enables simple authoring of interactive audiovisual presentations. SMIL is typically used for "rich media"/multimedia presentations which integrate streaming audio and video with images, text or any other media type. SMIL is an easy-to-learn HTML-like language, and many SMIL presentations are written using a simple text-editor.

You can find the W3C recommendation for SMIL 1.0 at `http://www.w3.org/TR/REC-smil` and the W3C recommendation for SMIL 2.0 at `http://www.w3.org/TR/smil20`.

You'll create a SMIL document to see how it works. For this example, you'll create a document, `ch13_18.smil`, that can be opened in RealPlayer (now called RealOne; available from `http://www.real.com` for free). In this example, you will display "SMIL" letter by letter—S, then SM, then SMI, and then SMIL, as the user watches.

SMIL is an HTML-like language, and you start by creating a layout in the `<head>` element of the document. This layout will create two regions, `slide` and `caption`; the `slide` region will display the letters in SMIL, and the `caption` region will display text:

```
<smil>
    <head>
        <layout>
            <root-layout width="400" height="250" background-color="white"/>
            <region id="slide" title="slide" left="0" top="0"
                width="400" height="200"/>
            <region id="caption" title="caption" left="0" top="201"
                width="400" height="50"/>
        </layout>
    </head>
        .
        .
        .
```

You use the <par> element to group presentations together, and use the <seq> element to create a multimedia sequence. In this example, you can start by creating a sequence that shows a preliminary image (`image0.jpg`) that is just a blue background and that you want to display in the `slide` region:

```
<smil>
    <head>
        <layout>
            <root-layout width="400" height="250" background-color="white"/>
            <region id="slide" title="slide" left="0" top="0"
                width="400" height="200"/>
            <region id="caption" title="caption" left="0" top="201"
                width="400" height="50"/>
        </layout>
    </head>

    <body>
        <par>
            <seq>
                <par>
                    <img region="slide" src="image0.jpg"
                        type="image/jpeg" dur="2s"/>
                </par>
                .
                .
                .
            </seq>
        </par>
    </body>
</smil>
```

Now you can continue creating the multimedia sequence, displaying additional images and some text as well. The images appear in the region named `slide`, and the text in region named `caption`, as shown in Listing 13.18.

LISTING 13.18 A SMIL Document (ch13_18.smil)

```
<smil>
    <head>
        <layout>
            <root-layout width="400" height="250" background-color="white"/>
            <region id="slide" title="slide" left="0" top="0"
                width="400" height="200"/>
            <region id="caption" title="caption" left="0" top="201"
                width="400" height="50"/>
        </layout>
    </head>

    <body>
        <par>
            <seq>
                <par>
                    <img region="slide" src="image0.jpg"
                        type="image/jpeg" dur="2s"/>
                </par>
                <par>
                    <img region="slide" src="image1.jpg"
                        type="image/jpeg" dur="2s"/>
                    <text region="caption" src="image1.txt"
                        type="text/plain" dur="2s"/>
                </par>
                <par>
                    <img region="slide" src="image2.jpg"
                        type="image/jpeg" dur="2s"/>
                    <text region="caption" src="image2.txt"
                        type="text/plain" dur="2s"/>
                </par>
                <par>
                    <img region="slide" src="image3.jpg"
                        type="image/jpeg" dur="2s"/>
                    <text region="caption" src="image3.txt"
                        type="text/plain" dur="2s"/>
                </par>
                <par>
                    <img region="slide" src="image4.jpg"
                        type="image/jpeg" dur="2s"/>
                    <text region="caption" src="image4.txt"
                        type="text/plain" dur="2s"/>
                </par>
            </seq>
        </par>
    </body>
</smil>
```

There are a variety of ways to display `ch13_18.smil`. For example, you could use RealPlayer/RealOne or you could use the SOJA Player, which you can get at `http://www.helio.org/products/smil` (SOJA stands for SMIL Output in Java Applets). You can see the SMIL example in RealPlayer/RealOne in Figure 13.18. When you open this document, the letters S, M, I, and L appear one-by-one in the `slide` region, and the text appears in the `caption` region.

FIGURE 13.18
Using SMIL.

Summary

Today, you took a look at SVG and SMIL.

As you've seen, SVG is all about creating 2D graphics. Today you took a look at how to create SVG documents by using the `<svg>` document element. To create basic shapes, you used the `<rect>` element to create rectangles, the `<circle>` element to create circles, the `<ellipse>` element to create ellipses, the `<line>` element to create lines, the `<polyline>` element to create polyline figures, and the `<polygon>` element to create polygons.

Besides these simple shapes, you saw that you can use the `<text>` SVG element to display text, and you can use the `<path>` SVG element to create paths. And, you saw, you can even combine the two to make text follow a path.

The `<group>` SVG element lets you group visual elements together and treat them as a group, including moving and rotating those elements at the same time. The `<animate>` SVG element lets you animate SVG elements by specifying how to change the values of their attributes over time. By using this element, you were able to stretch a rectangle before the user's eyes. The <a> SVG element creates links, and you saw how to use <a> to make the browser navigate to new URIs. Finally, you talked about the <script> element, which lets you use scripting languages such as JavaScript to make your SVG come alive.

As discussed today, SMIL lets you create multimedia presentations by using XML. SMIL is patterned after HTML, and you took a look today at how to create SMIL documents. In particular, you took a look at how to create a SMIL document that displays the letters S, M, I, and L to build up the display "SMIL." To do that, you created display regions and used a SMIL sequence to display successive images in one region and text in another.

Tomorrow, you're going to start talking about two other XML applications: XLinks and XPointers.

Q&A

Q I would like to repeat the same SVG image over and over in a certain area. Any ideas?

A You can use the SVG <pattern> element, which lets you create a pattern by using SVG elements and then use that pattern to paint an area.

Q Can I use audio in SMIL documents?

A Absolutely. Here's an example:

```
<head>
    <layout>
        <region id="audio" title="audio"/>
    </layout>
</head>

<body>
    <par>
        <audio src="mountains.au" region="audio"
            type="audio/x-au" dur="60s"/>
            .
            .
            .
```


Workshop

This workshop tests whether you understand the concepts discussed today. It's a good idea to make sure you can answer these questions before pressing on to tomorrow's work. Answers to the quiz can be found in Appendix A, "Quiz Answers."

Quiz

1. What attributes are required in the SVG `<rect>` element?
2. What attributes are required in the SVG `<circle>` element?
3. What would a `<polyline>` element that drew a line from (0,0) to (100,100) and then to (200,0) look like?
4. How would you move to the location (200,300) in the `d` attribute of a `<path>` element?
5. How can you specify where an image in a SMIL document should appear?

Exercises

1. Create an SVG document that displays eight ellipses in different colors. Next, animate one or all of them to move when the user clicks the display.
2. Create a SMIL document that makes a rectangle flash, alternating between red and blue. (Tip: To create the images, use a paint program if you have one available.) Next, add some text that asks, “Did I get your attention?”

PART III

DAY 14

Handling XLinks, XPointers, and XForms

Today you're going to take a look at three more XML applications: XLinks, XPointers, and XForms. In HTML, you can use hyperlinks to link documents, but in XML, you have more options, which is what the XLink and XPointer specifications are all about. XForms are designed to replace the standard forms you see in Web pages, which display buttons, text fields, and so on; XForms is designed to bring that kind of functionality into the XML world.

Here's an overview of today's topics:

- XLinks
- XBase
- XLink attributes
- Using `xlink:href`
- Extended links and arcs
- XPointers

- XPointer node tests
- XPointer predicates
- XForms
- Separation of data and presentations in XForms
- XForms types
- XForms controls

Today's discussion focuses on concepts taken over from HTML into XML (and often XHTML) by the W3C. You use XLinks to create hyperlinks in XML and XPointers to get even more specific than that: XPointers can build on XPath expressions, allowing you to point at a specific node or node set. XForms brings the idea of Web controls—such as buttons, text fields, and list boxes—to XML. Although XLink, XPointer, and XForms are all accepted W3c specifications, the actual implementation of each is spotty. More software is coming, but it's not here yet. Today, you'll see what you can do with the available software, with some good examples, such as the XSmiles XML browser, which supports XForms.

Introducing XLinks

Where would the Web be without hyperlinks? You find them all over. Here's an example of an HTML hyperlink:

```
<A HREF = "http://www.XMLPowerCorp.com/reviews.html#insurance">
    Health Insurance
<A>
```

This hyperlink appears as the text "Health Insurance" in an HTML document, and when you click it, the browser navigates to (the fictitious) `http://www.XMLPowerCorp.com/reviews.html#insurance`. XLinks work in much the same way as this, except they're the XML version of the familiar HTML construct.

The XLink 1.0 specification is a W3C recommendation that was released June 27, 2001. (The most current version of this recommendation is at `http://www.w3.org/TR/xlink`.) You use XLinks to link one document to another or to link one location inside a document to another.

You saw one of the relatively few software implementations of XLinks in SMIL yesterday, when in the process of creating a text path, you defined a path named `path1` and used an XLink to refer to that path:

```
<path id="path1" style="fill:none"
    d="M100,160 C100,60 250,60 250,140 S400,260 400,160"/>
<text x="40" y="100" font-family="sans-serif" font-size="16pt">
    <textPath xlink:href="#path1"
        xmlns:xlink="http://www.w3.org/1999/xlink">
        .
        .
        .
    </textPath>
</text>
```

This a very simple example of an XLink; it simply defines a namespace called `xlink` with the URI `http://www.w3.org/1999/xlink`. Then it uses an `xlink:href` attribute to connect to the `path1` path. This example works in the Adobe SVG plug-in, as you saw yesterday, but it's a very simple version of an XLink. Here's a more standard example, which converts the HTML `<A>` hyperlink from earlier today into an XLink:

```
<link xmlns:xlink = "http://www.w3.org/1999/xlink"
    xlink:type = "simple"
    xlink:show = "new"
    xlink:href = "http://www.XMLPowerCorp.com/insurance.xml">
    Health Insurance
</link>
```

This is a simple XLink, which is the closest you can get to a standard HTML hyperlink by using XLink. In this example you set the `xlink:type` attribute to `"simple"` and the `xlink:show` attribute to `"new"`; this means the browser should open the linked-to document in a new window and set the `xlink:href` attribute to the URI of the new document. (Bear in mind that the form of XML URIs isn't settled yet either and may grow more complex and comprehensive in time.)

XLinks can go far beyond the simple. In fact, the XLink conception is very ambitious. You might want to link to not one but multiple documents, for example. Or you might want to link to a set of documents and have the link know which document comes next and which document was the previous document in the set. Or you might want a link to be able to search for more recent resources or set up an abstract series of paths that a link could follow, depending on the user's context. XLinks can do all that—theoretically.

Here are a few of the current implementations of XLinks:

- X2X (`http://www.empolis.co.uk/products/prod_X2X.asp`), from empolis GmbH, is an XML XLink engine. It allows linking between documents and information resources.
- Fujitsu XLink Processor (`http://www.labs.fujitsu.com/free/xlip/en/index.html`), developed by Fujitsu Laboratories, Ltd., is an implementation of XLink and XPointer.

- xlinkit.com (`http://www.xlinkit.com`) is a lightweight application service that provides rule-based XLink generation.
- Mozilla (`http://www.mozilla.org`) is a browser that supports simple XLinks.
- Amaya (`http://www.w3c.org/Amaya`), the W3C test browser, supports simple XLinks .

Listing 14.1 puts a health insurance example to work in an XML document. This example is written for XLink-aware browsers such as the W3C's Amaya browser, and it also includes some JavaScript (for example, the `onClick` attribute in this example), which is not XML but is honored by browsers such as Internet Explorer, enabling a simple XLink in that browser.

LISTING 14.1 Emulating XLinks (`ch14_01.xml`)

```
<?xml version="1.0" encoding="UTF-8"?>
<?xml-stylesheet type="text/css" href="ch14_02.css"?>

<insurance>
        <title>
            Supporting XLinks
        </title>
        Looking for
        <link xmlns:xlink = "http://www.w3.org/1999/xlink"
            xlink:type = "simple"
            xlink:show = "new"
            xlink:href = "http://www.w3c.org"
            onClick="location.href='http://www.w3c.org'">
            health insurance
        </link>?
</insurance>
```

You can also use a CSS, `ch14_02.css`, to make the XLink look like a standard HTML hyperlink—blue, underlined, and when the mouse cursor moves across it, it turns to a hand. (However, note that in the Amaya browser, the cursor does not change.)

LISTING 14.2 An XLink Style Sheet (`ch14_02.css`)

```
link {color: #0000FF; text-decoration: underline; cursor: hand}
title {font-size: 24pt}
```

Figure 14.1 shows the results of Listing 14.2 in the Amaya browser. This is a true XLink in a true XLink-enabled browser. When you double-click the XLink, the browser navigates to the target document, `www.w3c.org`.

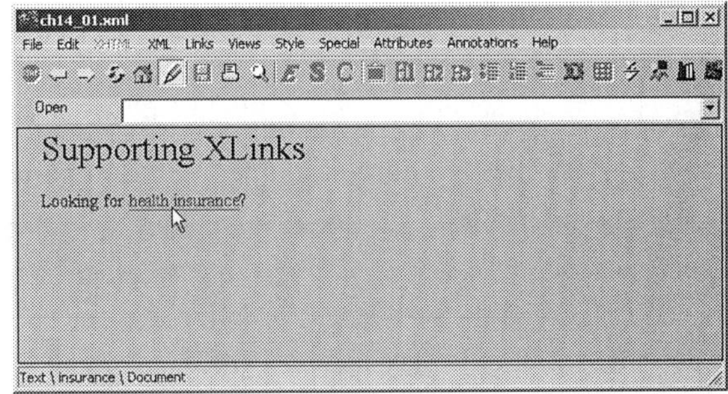

FIGURE 14.1

A simple XLink in the Amaya browser.

This XLink example also works in Internet Explorer, thanks to Internet Explorer's support of the non-XML `onClick` attribute (see Figure 14.2). When you click the XLink, the browser navigates to the target document.

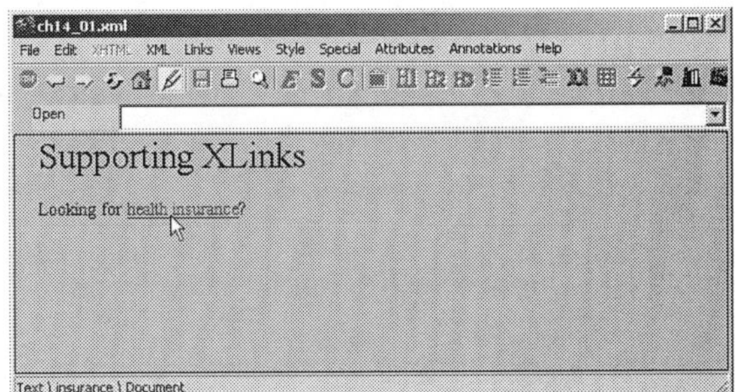

FIGURE 14.2

A simple XLink in Internet Explorer.

As this simple example shows, you don't need an `<A>` element to create an XLink. In fact, any XML element will do. You create an XLink by using attributes, not by using a particular element. You use the `xlink:type` attribute to create an XLink, and you set it to one of the allowable types of XLinks: `"simple"`, `"extended"`, `"locator"`, `"arc"`, `"resource"`, `"title"`, or `"none"`. Here are the available XLink attributes:

- **`xlink:arcrole`**—Contains the link's role in an arc, which can support multiple resources and various traversal paths. (We'll talk more about arcs later today.)
- **`xlink:actuate`**—Specifies when the link should be traversed. You can set this attribute to `"onLoad"`, `"onRequest"`, `"other"`, `"none"`, or other values supported by the software you're using.
- **`xlink:from`**—Defines the starting resources in an arc.

- `xlink:href`—Acts as the locator attribute. This attribute contains the data that allows an XLink to find a remote resource.
- `xlink:label`—Contains a human-readable label for the link.
- `xlink:role`—Describes a remote resource in a machine-readable fashion.
- `xlink:show`—Specifies how to display the linked-to resource. Possible values are `"new"` (open a new display space), `"replace"` (replace the currently displayed data), `"embed"` (embed the new resource in the current one), `"other"` (leave the show function up to the displaying software), and `"none"` (don't show the resource).
- `xlink:title`—Describes a remote resource in a human-readable way.
- `xlink:to`—Defines a target or ending resource in an arc.
- `xlink:type`—Sets the type of the XLink. This is a required attribute, and the possible values are `"simple"`, `"extended"`, `"locator"`, `"arc"`, `"resource"`, `“title"`, and `"none"`.

You don't use all these XLink attributes in the same XLink. Which attributes you use depends on the type of link you're creating, as given by the `xlink:type` attribute. Table 14.1 shows which attributes are required for each type of link.

TABLE 14.1 Required and Optional Attributes by `xlink:type`

	`simple`	`extended`	`locator`	`arc`	`resource`	`title`
`actuate`	Optional	N/A	N/A	Optional	N/A	N/A
`arcrole`	Optional	N/A	N/A	Optional	N/A	N/A
`from`	N/A	N/A	N/A	Optional	N/A	N/A
`href`	Optional	N/A	Required	N/A	N/A	N/A
`label`	N/A	N/A	Optional	N/A	optional	N/A
`role`	Optional	Optional	Optional	Optional	Optional	N/A
`show`	Optional	N/A	N/A	Optional	N/A	N/A
`title`	Optional	Optional	Optional	Optional	Optional	N/A
`to`	N/A	N/A	N/A	Optional	N/A	N/A
`type`	Required	Required	Required	Required	Required	Required

The XLink attributes specify what kind of XLink you're creating. Let's take a closer look at some of them now, starting with `xlink:type`.

Using xlink:type

The `xlink:type` attribute is the most important XLink attribute because it sets the type of XLink you're creating. Here are the possible values:

- **`simple`**—Is used to create a simple link.
- **`extended`**—Is used to create an extended link.
- **`locator`**—Is used to create a locator link that points to a resource.
- **`arc`**—Is used to create an arc with multiple resources and various traversal paths.
- **`resource`**—Is used to create a resource link, which indicates a specific resource.
- **`title`**—Is used to create a title link and can hold the location of element markup for further information on a title (such as with international versions).

You've already seen how to create simple links, which are the most common type of XLinks:

```
<?xml version="1.0" encoding="UTF-8"?>
<?xml-stylesheet type="text/css" href="ch14_02.css"?>

<insurance>
         <title>
             Supporting XLinks
         </title>
         Looking for
         <link xmlns:xlink = "http://www.w3.org/1999/xlink"
             xlink:type = "simple"
             xlink:show = "new"
             xlink:href = "http://www.w3c.org"
             onClick="location.href='http://www.w3c.org'">
             health insurance
         </link>?
</insurance>
```

You'll also see other types of XLinks today.

Using xlink:href

The `xlink:href` attribute is called the *locator* attribute. You use it to give the URI of a remote resource. You've already put this attribute to work today:

```
<?xml version="1.0" encoding="UTF-8"?>
<?xml-stylesheet type="text/css" href="ch14_02.css"?>

<insurance>
         <title>
             Supporting XLinks
         </title>
```

```
        Looking for
        <link xmlns:xlink = "http://www.w3.org/1999/xlink"
            xlink:type = "simple"
            xlink:show = "new"
            xlink:href = "http://www.w3c.org"
            onClick="location.href='http://www.w3c.org'">
            health insurance
        </link>?
</insurance>
```

When you work with simple URLs, the values you can assign to this attribute are fairly simple. But when you work with general URIs, which can include XPointers, things can get pretty complex, as you'll see later today.

Using `xlink:show`

The XLink `xlink:show` attribute specifies how to show the linked resource. The `xlink:show` attribute has five predefined values:

- **`embed`**—Embeds the linked-to resource in the current resource.
- **`new`**—Opens a new display area, such as a new window, to display the new resource.
- **`none`**—Does not show the resource.
- **`other`**—Indicates a setting other than those that are predefined.
- **`replace`**—Replaces the current resource, usually in the same window.

Besides these values, you can also specify your own values as well, as long as the software you're using supports those values. You've put the `xlink:show` attribute to work already today, to indicate that a new window should be opened when the link is activated:

```
<?xml version="1.0" encoding="UTF-8"?>
<?xml-stylesheet type="text/css" href="ch14_02.css"?>

<insurance>
        <title>
            Supporting XLinks
        </title>
        Looking for
        <link xmlns:xlink = "http://www.w3.org/1999/xlink"
            xlink:type = "simple"
            xlink:show = "new"
            xlink:href = "http://www.w3c.org"
            onClick="location.href='http://www.w3c.org'">
            health insurance
        </link>?
</insurance>
```

Using `xlink:actuate`

The `xlink:actuate` attribute specifies when a link should be traversed. The `xlink:actuate` attribute has these predefined values:

- **`onRequest`**—Means that the link should be traversed on the user's request.
- **`onLoad`**—Means that the link should be traversed when the resource is loaded.
- **`other`**—Specifies a custom preference.
- **`none`**—Specifies that there should be no actuation.

You can also set your own values for `xlink:actuate` (as long as your XML application understands them).

Using `xlink:role` and `xlink:title`

You can use the `xlink:role` and `xlink:title` attributes to describe a remote resource. Here's what using these attributes might look like:

```
<?xml version="1.0" encoding="UTF-8"?>
<?xml-stylesheet type="text/css" href="ch14_02.css"?>

<insurance>
        <title>
            Supporting XLinks
        </title>
        Looking for
        <link xmlns:xlink = "http://www.w3.org/1999/xlink"
            xlink:type = "simple"
            xlink:show = "new"
            xlink:role = "insurance "
            xlink:title = "Health Insurance Data"
            xlink:href = "http://www.w3c.org"
            onClick="location.href='http://www.w3c.org'">
            health insurance
        </link>?
</insurance>
```

The `xlink:title` attribute is designed to be read by people, whereas the `xlink:role` attribute is designed to be read by software. A link's role indicates the category of a link; in this example, that's `"insurance "`.

Using `xlink:arcrole` and `xlink:label`

14

The `xlink:label` attribute contains a human-readable label for an XLink. The `xlink:arcrole` attribute works with XLink *arcs*, which are sets of links that can contain multiple resources and various traversal paths. Each XLink can be a member of various arcs and can have different roles in each. For example, a person might be a supervisor in one arc but an employee in another. We'll take a closer look at arcs a little later today.

Beyond Simple XLinks

So far, you've only taken a look at simple XLinks, where the `xlink:type` attribute is set to `"simple"`. In fact, simple links are in practice the only XLinks supported in widely available software. However, more extended links will be supported sooner or later, so it's worth taking a look at them today.

Extended links can involve multiple resources, multiple paths between those resources, and multidirectional paths. Consequently, actual implementations of extended links are a little vague compared to those of simple links because no one has really determined how extended XLinks will really be supported. (In technical terms, an extended link is called a *directed labeled graph*, and they are very general constructs.)

An extended link can really only be characterized as being made up of connections between resources. Those resources may be *local*, which means they're actually part of the extended link element, or *remote*, which means they're not part of the extended link element (but this does not mean they are necessarily in another document). If a link contains resources, it's called an *inline link*; if it does not contain any resources at all, it's called an *out-of-line* link. Inline links havetheir `xlink:type` value set to `"resource"`. Out-of-line links have their `xlink:type` attribute value set to `"locator"`.

Listing 14.3 is an example that shows an extended link. The extended link element, which contains two inline and three out-of-line links, is the `<link>` element (although you could give it any name). This example links to the various `<state>` elements in the `ch10_01.xml` example from Day 1, "Welcome to XML"—California, Massachusetts, and New York. (You might note that to pick out the various states from `ch10_01.xml`, this example uses XPointers, and you'll see how those XPointers work in a few pages.)

LISTING 14.3 Extended XLinks (`ch14_03.xml`)

```
<?xml version="1.0" encoding="UTF-8"?>
<document>
    <link xmlns:xlink="http://www.w3.org/1999/xlink"
             xlink:type="extended" xlink:title="State Data">
        <title xlink:type="resource" xlink:role="Title">
            State Data
        </title>
        <date xlink:type="resource" xlink:role="Date">
            March 1, 2005
        </date>
```

LISTING 14.3 continued

```
        <state xmlns:xlink = "http://www.w3.org/1999/xlink"
            xlink:type = "locator"
            xlink:show = "embed"
            xlink:href = "http://www.XMLPowerCorp.com/ch10_01.xml#xpointer
                (/descendant::state[position() = 1]">
            xlink:title="California"
            xlink:role="State Data"
        </state>
        <state xmlns:xlink = "http://www.w3.org/1999/xlink"
            xlink:type = "locator"
            xlink:show = "embed"
            xlink:href = "http://www.XMLPowerCorp.com/ch10_01.xml#xpointer
                (/descendant::state[position() = 2]">
            xlink:title="Massachusetts"
            xlink:role="State Data"
        </state>
        <state xmlns:xlink = "http://www.w3.org/1999/xlink"
            xlink:type = "locator"
            xlink:show = "embed"
            xlink:href = "http://www.XMLPowerCorp.com/ch10_01.xml#xpointer
                (/descendant::state[position() = 3]">
            xlink:title="New York"
            xlink:role="State Data"
        </state>
    </link>
</document>
```

This example is a start, but it still doesn't do much more than create an extended link with several inline and out-of-line links in it. You can do more if you use the `xlink:from` and `xlink:to` attributes, which allow us to create directed links—that is, *arcs*.

Creating Arcs

When you have a simple XLink, you don't need to worry about how it works; the `xlink:href` attribute tells us all you need to know. On the other hand, what about the extended link you just created? What happens when you activate it? There are many conceivable paths between the resources. To add more direction to what's going on, you can create an arc.

All the possible paths between resources are arcs. You represent those paths in XML elements by setting the `xlink:type` attribute to `"arc"`. Arcs use `xlink:from` and `xlink:to` elements to specify traversal paths. The `xlink:from` attribute indicates what resource an arc comes from, and the `xlink:to` attribute indicates what resource it goes to. You set the values of `xlink:from` and `xlink:to` to match the `xlink:role` attribute of the source and target resources.

Listing 14.4 shows an example that includes three arc elements, <arc1>, <arc2>, and <arc3>. The first arc takes us from California to Massachusetts, the second arc takes us from Massachusetts to New York, and the third arc takes us from New York back to California.

LISTING 14.4 Creating Extended XLinks (ch14_04.xml)

```
<?xml version="1.0" encoding="UTF-8"?>
<document>
    <link xmlns:xlink="http://www.w3.org/1999/xlink"
             xlink:type="extended" xlink:title="State Data">
        <title xlink:type="resource" xlink:role="Title">
            State Data
        </title>
        <date xlink:type="resource" xlink:role="Date">
            March 1, 2005
        </date>
        <state xmlns:xlink = "http://www.w3.org/1999/xlink"
            xlink:type = "locator"
            xlink:show = "embed"
            xlink:href = "http://www.XMLPowerCorp.com/ch10_01.xml#xpointer
                (/descendant::state[position() = 1]">
            xlink:title="California"
            xlink:role="California"
        </state>
        <state xmlns:xlink = "http://www.w3.org/1999/xlink"
            xlink:type = "locator"
            xlink:show = "embed"
            xlink:href = "http://www.XMLPowerCorp.com/ch10_01.xml#xpointer
                (/descendant::state[position() = 2]">
            xlink:title="Massachusetts"
            xlink:role="Massachusetts"
        </state>
        <state xmlns:xlink = "http://www.w3.org/1999/xlink"
            xlink:type = "locator"
            xlink:show = "embed"
            xlink:href = "http://www.XMLPowerCorp.com/ch10_01.xml#xpointer
                (/descendant::state[position() = 3]">
            xlink:title="New York"
            xlink:role="New York"
        </state>

        <arc1 xlink:type = "arc" xlink:from = "California"
            xlink:to = "Massachusetts" xlink:show="new"
            xlink:actuate="onRequest">
        </arc1>

        <arc2 xlink:type = "arc" xlink:from = "Massachusetts"
            xlink:to = "New York" xlink:show="new"
```

LISTING 14.4 continued

```
            xlink:actuate="onRequest">
        </arc2>

        <arc3 xlink:type = "arc" xlink:from = "New York"
            xlink:to = "California" xlink:show="new"
            xlink:actuate="onRequest">
        </arc3>
    </link>
</document>
```

The way these arcs are actually used or activated depends on the software you're working with or that you've created.

Creating Linkbases

When you place out-of-line links in their own documents, those documents are called *linkbases*. The set of out-of-line links in a linkbase is called a *linkset*. You typically have three types of links in a linkbase: extended links, locator links, and arcs. You cannot have any links that are of the resource type.

Here's an example that converts the extended link example into a linkbase:

```
<?xml version="1.0" encoding="UTF-8"?>
<document>
    <link xmlns:xlink="http://www.w3.org/1999/xlink"
            xlink:type="extended" xlink:title="State Data">
        <state xmlns:xlink = "http://www.w3.org/1999/xlink"
            xlink:type = "locator"
            xlink:show = "embed"
            xlink:href = "http://www.XMLPowerCorp.com/ch10_01.xml#xpointer
                (/descendant::state[position() = 1]">
            xlink:title="California"
            xlink:role="California"
        </state>
        <state xmlns:xlink = "http://www.w3.org/1999/xlink"
            xlink:type = "locator"
            xlink:show = "embed"
            xlink:href = "http://www.XMLPowerCorp.com/ch10_01.xml#xpointer
                (/descendant::state[position() = 2]">
            xlink:title="Massachusetts"
            xlink:role="Massachusetts"
        </state>
        <state xmlns:xlink = "http://www.w3.org/1999/xlink"
            xlink:type = "locator"
            xlink:show = "embed"
            xlink:href = "http://www.XMLPowerCorp.com/ch10_01.xml#xpointer
```

```
            (/descendant::state[position() = 3]">
        xlink:title="New York"
        xlink:role="New York"
    </state>

    <arc1 xlink:type = "arc" xlink:from = "California"
        xlink:to = "Massachusetts" xlink:show="new"
        xlink:actuate="onRequest">
    </arc1>

    <arc2 xlink:type = "arc" xlink:from = "Massachusetts"
        xlink:to = "New York" xlink:show="new"
        xlink:actuate="onRequest">
    </arc2>

    <arc3 xlink:type = "arc" xlink:from = "New York"
        xlink:to = "California" xlink:show="new"
        xlink:actuate="onRequest">
    </arc3>
  </link>
</document>
```

Up to this point, you haven't heard very much about the `xlink:href` attribute. You just know that it points at resources. But there's a great deal more to it. You can use this attribute to point to specific locations or sections of a document. And to do that, you use XPointers.

Introducing XPointers

When you use XLinks, you can link to a particular document, but many times, you want to be more precise than that. XPointers let us point to specific locations inside a document, and they are coming into more common use; for example, SMIL 2.0 allows, but does not require, XPointers, and SVG also supports some aspects of XPointers.

There isn't much software that supports XPointers in depth today, although yesterday, when you used XPointers to point to path definitions, you saw that Adobe's SVG Viewer 3 does. Here are two other packages that support XPointers:

- Amaya (`http://www.w3c.org/Amaya`) supports XPointers but does not support the full XPath specification that you can use with general XPointers.
- Fujitsu's XLip (`http://www.labs.fujitsu.com/free/xlip/en/index.html`) has a full implementation.

The XPointer specification has had a contentious past, and it seems to have been one of the W3C specifications that got too complex for itself. It was abandoned at one point and split into parts to make it easier to implement. (You can find the story at `http://www.w3.org/XML/2002/10/LinkingImplementations.html`.) The XPointer specification is now divided into three recommendations and a working draft:

- **`http://www.w3.org/TR/xptr-framework/`**—The XPointer framework, which gives general background and points to the other three schemes.
- **`http://www.w3.org/TR/xptr-element/`**—The element scheme.
- **`http://www.w3.org/TR/xptr-xmlns/`**—The namespace scheme.
- **`http://www.w3.org/TR/xptr-xpointer/`**—The general XPointer scheme.

The XPointer framework specification introduces the idea of XPointers and indicates how to use *barenames* (that is, element names) as XPointers. And it points to the other three parts of the specification that you can use in XPointers: the element scheme, the namespace scheme, and the general XPointer scheme. We'll take a look at these ways of creating XPointers today, starting with barenames.

Using Barenames

The XPointer Framework specification (`http://www.w3.org/TR/xptr-framework`) says that you can use *barenames*—that is, just the names of elements—as XPointers. You can append an XPointer to the end of a URI by preceding it with a `#`, as in the following fictitious example, which points at the `<data>` element in `www.XMLPowerCorp.com/insurance.xml`:

```
<insurance xmlns:xlink = "http://www.w3.org/1999/xlink"
    xlink:type = "simple"
    xlink:show = "new"
    xlink:href = "http://www.XMLPowerCorp.com/insurance.xml#data">
    Health Insurance
</insurance>
```

Besides using barenames like this, you can also use the element, namespace, and general XPointer schemes. They're coming up next.

Using the Element Scheme

The element scheme (`http://www.w3.org/TR/xptr-element`) was broken out of the general XPointer scheme to make XPointer easier to implement. In the element scheme, you use `element()` to identify elements by ID, not by name. For example, to find the element with the ID `"data"`, you could use this expression (technically, you can do this only if the element's ID is declared in an XML schema or a DTD):

14

```
<insurance xmlns:xlink = "http://www.w3.org/1999/xlink"
    xlink:type = "simple"
    xlink:show = "new"
```

```
    xlink:href = "http://www.XMLPowerCorp.com/insurance.xml#element(data)">
    Health Insurance
</insurance>
```

You can also specify child sequences by number; for example, to pick out the `<data>` element's third child element and then identify that element's first child element, you can use this XPath-like expression:

```
<insurance xmlns:xlink = "http://www.w3.org/1999/xlink"
    xlink:type = "simple"
    xlink:show = "new"
    xlink:href = "http://www.XMLPowerCorp.com/insurance.xml#element(data/3/1)">
    Health Insurance
</insurance>
```

As you can see, the element scheme lets you specify an element by ID, and you can also add location steps, by using numbers, to pick out child elements.

Using the Namespace Scheme

The namespace scheme (`http://www.w3.org/TR/xptr-xmlns`) indicates how to use namespaces when pointing to data. For example, if the `<data>` element you want to pick out is part of the `xpc` (for XML Power Corp.) namespace, you could specify that element this way:

```
<insurance xmlns:xlink = "http://www.w3.org/1999/xlink"
    xlink:type = "simple"
    xlink:show = "new"
    xlink:href = "http://www.XMLPowerCorp.com/insurance.xml#xmlns(xpc=
        "http:/XMLPowerCorp)xpc:data">
    Health Insurance
</insurance>
```

This XPointer picks out `<xpc:data>` in the document `www.XMLPowerCorp.com/insurance.xml`.

Using the XPointer Scheme

Because XPointer wasn't gaining much acceptance in its original very general and somewhat complex form, the W3C split the usage for barenames, the element scheme, and the namespace scheme away from the general XPointers to make XPointer easier to implement. However, the original form of XPointers is still part of the XPointer specification, although it's still in working draft form (`http://www.w3.org/TR/xptr-xpointer`). This is where the real meat of XPointer lies because you can use XPath expressions to point to exactly what you want; in fact, the XPointer scheme extends XPath. Here's what a full XPointer might look like—note that you use `xpointer()` here:

```
<insurance xmlns:xlink = "http://www.w3.org/1999/xlink"
    xlink:type = "simple"
    xlink:show = "new"
    xlink:href = "http://www.XMLPowerCorp.com/insurance.xml#xpointer(
        /child::*[position()=119]/child::*[position()=last()])">
    Health Insurance
</insurance>
```

This picks out the last child of the 119th element in `www.XMLPowerCorp.com/insurance.xml`. As you can see, you can use full XPath expressions with general XPointers.

You can also use the `/n/m` type of child identification, as in the element scheme. For example, this long expression:

```
http://www.XMLPowerCorp.com/ch10_01.xml#xpointer(
/child::*[position()=1]/child::*[position()=2]/child::*[position()=3])
```

can be abbreviated as this:

```
http://www.XMLPowerCorp.com/ch10_01.xml#1/2/3
```

In addition, the general XPointer scheme extends XPath by letting us select points and ranges besides normal XPath nodes. A *point* is a specific location in a document, and a *range* is made up of everything between two points. To support points and ranges, the general XPointer scheme extends the concept of nodes to *locations*. A location is an XPath node, a point, or a range. Node sets become *location sets* in the XPointer specification.

Although XPointers use the same axes as XPaths, there are some new node tests. These are the node tests you can use with XPointers:

- **`*`**—Matches any element.
- **`node()`**—Matches any node.
- **`text()`**—Matches a text node.
- **`comment()`**—Matches a comment node.
- **`processing-instruction()`**—Matches a processing instruction node.
- **`point()`**—Matches a point in a resource.
- **`range()`**—Matches a range in a resource.

Note in particular the last two—`point()` and `range()`. These correspond to the two new constructs added in XPointers, points and ranges, and you'll see more on them today.

14

General XPointers also make some additions to the functions that return location sets (that is, node sets in XPath). You can use the `here()` function to refer to the current element. This can be useful when you're working among the nodes of an element and want to refer to the current element or another node in the current element. For example, you might want to refer to the fifth previous `<name>` element of the current element, and you could do that this way:

```
here()/preceding-sibling::name[position() = 5]
```

In addition to `here()`, you can also use the `origin()` function, which is much like the `here()` function but is used with out-of-line links. This function refers to the original element from which the link was activated, even if that element is in another document.

Creating XPointer Points

To define an XPointer point, you use two items—a node and an index that can hold a positive integer or zero. The node specifies an origin for the point, and the index indicates how far the point you want is from that origin.

There are two different ways of measuring the index: in terms of characters in the document and in terms of a number of nodes, and you'll take a look at them here, as well as how to use the functions that work with points.

Measuring in Characters

If the starting node can contain only text, but not any child nodes, then the index is measured in characters. Points like these are called *character-points*. The index of a character-point must be a positive integer or zero and less than or equal to the length of the text string in the node. If the index is zero, the point is immediately before the first character; an index of 5 locates the point immediately after the fifth character. Character-points do not have preceding or following siblings or children.

Here's an example that treats `<DOCUMENT>` as a container node in the document:

```
<data>
Hello!
</data>
```

In this example, there are six character-points, one before each character. The character-point at Index 0 is right before the first character, `H`, the character-point at Index 1 is just before the `e`, and so forth. Note also that the general XPointer specification collapses all consecutive whitespace into a single space for counting purposes.

Measuring in Nodes

When the start node, also called the *container node*, has child nodes (in other words, it's an element node or the root node), the index of a point is measured in child nodes.

For an index of zero, the point is just before any child node. An index of 7 specifies a point immediately after the seventh child node.

Using Point Functions

When it comes to creating points, you can use the `point()` function with a predicate, like this:

```
point()[position()=5]
```

For example, say that you want to locate a point right before the `l` in California in the states example from Day 10, "Working with XSL Formatting Objects," `ch10_01.xml`. You could do that like this:

```
xpointer(/states/state[1]/name/text()/point()[position() = 2])
```

Creating XPointer Ranges

When it comes to creating ranges, all you need are two points: a start point and an end point. This is true as long as they are in the same document and the start point is before or the same as the end point; if the start point and the end point are the same point, the range you create is called a *collapsed range*.

The general XPointer specification adds to the functions in XPath a number of functions to handle ranges:

- **`range(`*`location-set`*`)`**—Takes the locations you passed to it and returns a range that completely covers the locations.
- **`range-inside(`*`location-set`*`)`**—Returns a range or ranges covering each location inside the location set; if you pass an element, the result is a range that encloses all that is inside the element.
- **`range-to(`*`location-set`*`)`**—Returns a range for each location in the location set.

Besides these functions, the XPointer specification includes a function for string matching, `string-range()`. You can use this function to return a range for every match to a search string. Here's how to use `string-range()`:

```
string-range(location-set, string, [index, [length]])
```

For example, the following expression returns a location set of ranges for all matches to the word *Massachusetts*:

```
string-range(/*, "Massachusetts")
```

You can use the `[]` operator to extract a specific match from the location set returned by this function. For example, the following expression returns a range covering the second match to *Massachusetts*:

```
string-range(/*, "Massachusetts")[2]
```

As you've seen so far today, there's a lot more power with XLinks and XPointers than you'll find with simple HTML hyperlinks. The software implementations of XLink and XPointer have been slow in arriving, but more and more are appearing now. XPointer in particular has been slow to be picked up because of the complexity of the general XPointer scheme, which you've just seen, but with the new division into element and namespace schemes, use of XPointer should accelerate.

Introducing XBase

Before you leave our discussion of linking entirely, there's one more W3C specification that you need to know about: XBase. This specification lets us specify a base URI for XML documents, just like the `<BASE>` element in HTML documents. You can use the `xml:base` attribute in an XML document to set the document's base URI. The other URIs in the document are then considered relative URIs, and the URI specified as the base is used to resolve them.

The XBase specification has been W3C recommendation since June 27, 2001, and you can find it at `http://www.w3.org/TR/xmlbase`. The following example uses XBase—note that `xml:base` uses the `xml` namespace, not the `xlink` namespace (the `xml` namespace is predefined in XML as `"http://www.w3.org/XML/1998/namespace"`):

```
<insurance xmlns:xlink = "http://www.w3.org/1999/xlink"
    xlink:type = "simple"
    xlink:show = "new"
    xml:base="http://www.XMLPowerCorp.com"
    xlink:href = "data.xml">
    Health Insurance
</insurance>
```

This example sets the base URI of the document to the fictitious `www.XMLPowerCorp.com`, and the URIs in it, such as the `xlink:href` value of `data.xml`, are resolved with respect to that base.

Introducing XForms

Like the other elements in today's discussion, XForms come from a parallel construct in HTML—Web forms. A Web form lets us display controls such as buttons or list boxes in an HTML page, and XForms are intended to do the same thing in XML. XForms 1.0 is in candidate recommendation form, and you can find the specification at `http://www.w3.org/TR/xforms/`. XForms were originally designed to work with XHTML, but they've been extended to any XML document.

XForms not only bring forms to XML, but they're also designed to improve them. As with style sheets, the emphasis is on separating presentation from data. Here's what W3C says about XForms:

> The current design of Web forms doesn't separate the purpose from the presentation of a form. XForms, in contrast, are comprised of separate sections that describe what the form does, and how the form looks. This allows for flexible presentation options, including classic XHTML forms, to be attached to an XML form definition.

Listing 14.5 shows an example to help you see how XForms work.

LISTING 14.5 Using XForms (`ch14_05.xml`)

```
<?xml version="1.0" encoding="UTF-8"?>
<html xmlns="http://www.w3.org/1999/xhtml"
    xmlns:ev="http://www.w3.org/2001/xml-events"
    xmlns:xforms="http://www.w3.org/2002/xforms/cr">

    <head>
        <xforms:model>
            <xforms:submission localfile="data.xml"/>
            <xforms:instance>
                <data xmlns="">
                    <input>Hello!</input>
                    <select>1</select>
                    <selectboolean>true</selectboolean>
                    <message>Hello!</message>
                </data>
            </xforms:instance>
        </xforms:model>
    </head>

    <body>
        <h1>Using XForms</h1>
        <p>Input Control</p>
        <xforms:input ref="/data/input"></xforms:input>

        <p>Select Control</p>
        <xforms:select appearance="full" ref="/data/select">
            <xforms:item>
                <xforms:value>1</xforms:value>
                <xforms:label>Item 1</xforms:label>
            </xforms:item>
            <xforms:item>
                <xforms:value>2</xforms:value>
                <xforms:label>Item 2</xforms:label>
```

LISTING 14.5 continued

```
            </xforms:item>
            <xforms:item>
                <xforms:value>3</xforms:value>
                <xforms:label>Item 3</xforms:label>
            </xforms:item>
        </xforms:select>

        <p>Button</p>
        <xforms:trigger>
            <xforms:label>Click Me</xforms:label>
            <xforms:message ev:event="click" level="ephemeral"
                ref="/data/message"/>
        </xforms:trigger>

        <p>Select Boolean</p>
        <xforms:selectboolean ref="/data/selectboolean">
            <xforms:label>Click Me</xforms:label>
        </xforms:selectboolean>

        <p>Submit and Reset Buttons</p>
        <xforms:submit>
            <xforms:label>Submit</xforms:label>
        </xforms:submit>

        <xforms:trigger>
            <xforms:label>Reset</xforms:label>
            <xforms:reset ev:event="DOMActivate"/>
        </xforms:trigger>
    </body>
</html>
```

A number of software packages support XForms to some extent; here's a sampling:

- **X-Smiles** (`http://www.x-smiles.org`)—X-Smiles is a Java-based XML browser from Helsinki University of Technology. X-Smiles has good support for the XForms Candidate Recommendation version, and it uses XForms together with XHTML, SMIL, SVG, and XSL-FO.
- **Mozquito XForms** (`http://www.mozquito.com`)—Mozquito XForms is an XForms implementation written in ActionScript for Flash 6.
- **FormsPlayer** (`http://www.FormsPlayer.com`)—FormsPlayer is an XForms processor plug-in for Internet Explorer 6, Service Pack 1.

- **Novell XForms** (`http://www.novell.com/xforms`)—Novell XForms is a Java application that is designed to provide developers with a hands-on introduction to XForms.
- **LiquidOffice** (`http://www.cardiff.com/LiquidOffice`)—LiquidOffice provides support for XForms.
- **Chiba project** (`http://sourceforge.net/projects/chiba`)—Chiba is an implementation of the W3C XForms standard that supports generic, XML-based form processing for the Web.
- **NMatrix** (`http://sourceforge.net/projects/dotnetopensrc`)—NMatrix provides some support for XForms.
- **XMLForm** (`http://xml.apache.org/cocoon/userdocs/concepts/xmlform.html`)—XMLForm is an open-source, server-side implementation of a subset of XForms that is integrated into Apache Cocoon.
- **TrustForm System** (`http://trustform.comsquare.co.kr`)—TrustForm System is a client-side implementation that is based on the XForms Working Draft.
- **AchieveForms** (`http://www.achieveforms.com`)—AchieveForms is a server-based XForms designer with a Web browser interface that can output forms as XForms and can process completed forms from an XForms browser to email recipients and databases and can forward XML files of completed form data.
- **jXForms** (`http://jxforms.cybernd.at`)—jXForms supports working with XForms inside Java-based applications.
- **XServerForms** (`http://sourceforge.net/projects/xserverforms`)—XServerForms is an open-source framework for building Web applications that includes support for XForms.
- **Xero** (`http://typeasoft.com/product/xero`)—Xero is a client-side XForms processor that works in Internet Explorer 6.0 and later.
- **XML Forms Package** (`http://www.alphaworks.ibm.com/tech/xmlforms`)—The IBM XML Forms Package consists of two main components: the data model component and the client component. The data model component supports creating, accessing, and modifying XForms data models. The client component supports an XForms processor control and a Java XForms compiler.
- **FormFaces** (`http://www.formfaces.com`)—FormFaces is a server-side translator to HTML and JavaScript.

Today you'll use the XSmiles XML browser, which you can get for free from `http://www.x-smiles.org`. Figure 14.3 shows `ch14_05.xml` in the XSmiles browser.

FIGURE 14.3

An XForms example in the XSmiles browser.

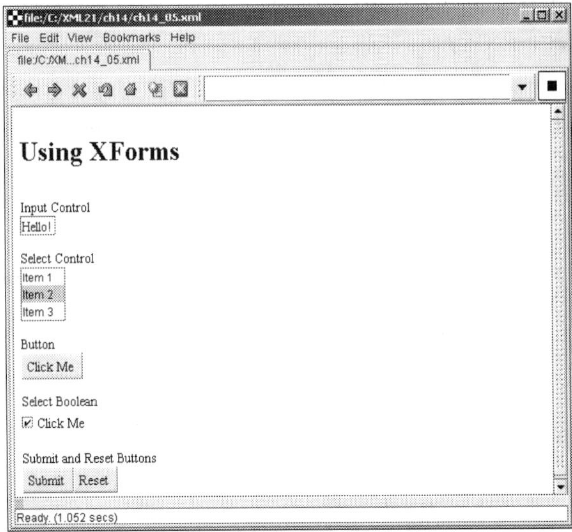

Figure 14.3 shows the various controls you'll work with in this example—an input control (like an HTML text field), a select control (like the HTML select controls), a button, and a select Boolean control (like an HTML check box). When the user makes selections in this XForm and clicks the Submit button at the bottom, a new XML document with the data from those controls is generated, as you can see in Figure 14.4.

Here's what that XML data from the XForm looks like:

```
<?xml version="1.0" encoding="ISO-8859-1"?>
<data xmlns="" xmlns:ev="http://www.w3.org/2001/xml-events"
    xmlns:xforms="http://www.w3.org/2002/xforms/cr">
    <input>Hello!</input>
    <select>2</select>
    <selectboolean>true</selectboolean>
    <message>Hello!</message>
</data>
```

Note that the `<input>` element contains the text data from the input control, the `<select>` element contains the number of the selection the user made in the select control, and the `<selectboolean>` element contains the setting of the select Boolean control, which is `true` because it displays a check mark.

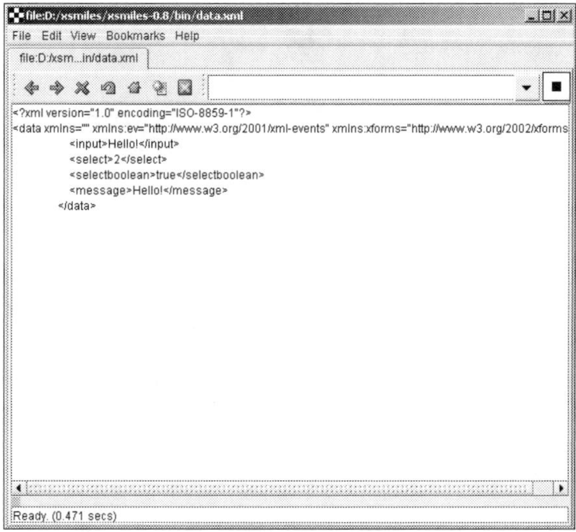

FIGURE 14.4
Data from the XForms example.

An XForm displays controls that you can use, and when you click a Submit button, that data is made accessible to you. Here are the controls you can use in XForms:

- **input control**—Acts like an HTML text field.
- **secret control**—Acts like an HTML hidden field.
- **textarea control**—Acts like an HTML text area control.
- **output control**—Displays output.
- **upload control**—Acts like an HTML upload control.
- **range control**—Allows selection from a sequential range of values.
- **trigger control**—Acts like an HTML `<button>` element.
- **submit control**—Acts like an HTML submit button.
- **select control**—Acts like an HTML select control.
- **select1 control**—Acts like an HTML single-selection HTML control.

To see what's going on here, let's take apart the XForms example `ch14_05.xml` in the following sections.

Writing XForms

XForms are used in XML documents, typically in XHTML, so each one needs to start off with an XML declaration, like this:

```
<?xml version="1.0" encoding="UTF-8"?>
```

If the document is written in XHTML, as this example is, you can include an XHTML <!DOCTYPE> element:

```
<?xml version="1.0" encoding="UTF-8"?>
<!DOCTYPE html PUBLIC "-//W3C//DTD XHTML 1.0 Transitional//EN"
"http://www.w3.org/TR/xhtml1/DTD/xhtml1-transitional.dtd">
        .
        .
        .
```

In this example, however, you're going to omit the XHTML <!DOCTYPE> element for the sake of brevity (so XSmiles won't have to download the entire XHTML 1.0 DTD and check it against the document each time the document is loaded). The next element, the document element, is the <html> element, and you use it to put everything into the XHTML namespace and define two other namespaces—ev for XForms events (such as button clicks) and xforms for XForms elements:

```
<?xml version="1.0" encoding="UTF-8"?>
<html xmlns="http://www.w3.org/1999/xhtml"
    xmlns:ev="http://www.w3.org/2001/xml-events"
    xmlns:xforms="http://www.w3.org/2002/xforms/cr">
        .
        .
        .
</html>
```

Separating Data from a Presentation

A major feature of XForms is the separation of data from presentation; this means that the data for the controls in an XForm is stored separately from the presentation part. You use the <xforms:model> element to specify what data an XForm should hold. For example, you can create an XForms model in the document's <head> element:

```
<?xml version="1.0" encoding="UTF-8"?>
<html xmlns="http://www.w3.org/1999/xhtml"
    xmlns:ev="http://www.w3.org/2001/xml-events"
    xmlns:xforms="http://www.w3.org/2002/xforms/cr">

    <head>
        <xforms:model>
        .
        .
        .
        </xforms:model>
    </head>

</html>
```

Inside the model, you specify the submission mechanism for the data in an `<xforms:submission>` element. Although you could have the data from the XForm sent to a general URI, in this case you should have it stored in a local data file, `data.xml`:

```
<?xml version="1.0" encoding="UTF-8"?>
<html xmlns="http://www.w3.org/1999/xhtml"
    xmlns:ev="http://www.w3.org/2001/xml-events"
    xmlns:xforms="http://www.w3.org/2002/xforms/cr">

    <head>
        <xforms:model>
            <xforms:submission localfile="data.xml"/>
        .
        .
        .
        </xforms:model>
    </head>

</html>
```

You store the actual data in an `<xforms:instance>` element. In this example you'll have an input control whose data will be stored in an `<input>` element, a select control whose data will be stored in a `<select>` element, and so on. Here's what that looks like, with the default data for the controls stored:

```
<?xml version="1.0" encoding="UTF-8"?>
<html xmlns="http://www.w3.org/1999/xhtml"
    xmlns:ev="http://www.w3.org/2001/xml-events"
    xmlns:xforms="http://www.w3.org/2002/xforms/cr">

    <head>
        <xforms:model>
            <xforms:submission localfile="data.xml"/>
            <xforms:instance>
                <data xmlns="">
                    <input>Hello!</input>
                    <select>1</select>
                    <selectboolean>true</selectboolean>
                    <message>Hello!</message>
                </data>
            </xforms:instance>
        </xforms:model>
    </head>
        .
        .
        .
</html>
```

You have now completed the <head> section of the example, where the data is stored. In the <body> section, you'll start creating the controls you'll use, starting with the input control.

Creating Input Controls

You create an input control, much as you do an HTML text field, by using the <input> element. You tie this control to the data you've stored in the <input> element in the <head> element by using the ref attribute, which you'll set to "/data/input" in this example:

```
<?xml version="1.0" encoding="UTF-8"?>
<html xmlns="http://www.w3.org/1999/xhtml"
    xmlns:ev="http://www.w3.org/2001/xml-events"
    xmlns:xforms="http://www.w3.org/2002/xforms/cr">

    <head>
        .
        .
        .
    </head>

    <body>
        <h1>Using XForms</h1>
        <p>Input Control</p>
        <xforms:input ref="/data/input"></xforms:input>
        .
        .
        .
    </body>
</html>
```

Now when the input control first appears, it will display the initial text in the <data> element, "Hello!", as shown in Figure 14.3. If the user changes that text and clicks the Submit button, the new text will be stored in that <data> element in the resulting XML file that the XForm creates, data.xml.

Creating Select Controls

Besides input controls, you can also display select controls, which look much like HTML select controls. A select control can display either a list of items to choose from or a drop-down list, and you create these controls by using the <select> element or the <select1> element (which creates single-selection select controls). In the case of our example, you need to store the current selection number in the select control in the <data> element's <select> element by assigning the select control's ref attribute to "/data/select", and you should display a list of all items in the control by setting the appearance attribute to "full".

To create the items in the select control, you use the <item> element; to label the item, you use the <label> element; and to assign a value to each item, you use the <value> element. When the user selects an item, that item's value is stored in the <select> element in the head's <data> element. Here's what the select control looks like (refer to Figure 14.3):

```
<?xml version="1.0" encoding="UTF-8"?>
<html xmlns="http://www.w3.org/1999/xhtml"
    xmlns:ev="http://www.w3.org/2001/xml-events"
    xmlns:xforms="http://www.w3.org/2002/xforms/cr">

    <head>
        .
        .
        .
    </head>

    <body>
        <h1>Using XForms</h1>
        .
        .
        .
        <p>Select Control</p>
        <xforms:select appearance="full" ref="/data/select">
            <xforms:item>
                <xforms:value>1</xforms:value>
                <xforms:label>Item 1</xforms:label>
            </xforms:item>
            <xforms:item>
                <xforms:value>2</xforms:value>
                <xforms:label>Item 2</xforms:label>
            </xforms:item>
            <xforms:item>
                <xforms:value>3</xforms:value>
                <xforms:label>Item 3</xforms:label>
            </xforms:item>
        </xforms:select>
        .
        .
        .
    </body>
</html>
```

Creating Buttons

XForms also support buttons; in our example, clicking the Click Me button displays a message box that shows the text stored in the <message> element in the document head's <data> element:

```
<xforms:instance>
    <data xmlns="">
        <input>Hello!</input>
        <select>1</select>
        <selectboolean>true</selectboolean>
        <message>Hello!</message>
    </data>
</xforms:instance>
```

To display the text `"Hello!"` in a message box, you can use the XForms `<message>` element. To display the Click Me button, you use a `<trigger>` element and give it a caption by using the `<label>` element. To display a message box when the button is clicked, you set the `<message>` element's event attribute to `"click"`; to display the message, you set the message box's `ref` attribute to `"/data/message"`. To make the message box disappear automatically after a few seconds, you can set its `level` attribute to `"ephemeral"`:

```
<?xml version="1.0" encoding="UTF-8"?>
<html xmlns="http://www.w3.org/1999/xhtml"
    xmlns:ev="http://www.w3.org/2001/xml-events"
    xmlns:xforms="http://www.w3.org/2002/xforms/cr">

    <head>
        .
        .
        .
    </head>

    <body>
        <h1>Using XForms</h1>
        .
        .
        .
        <p>Button</p>
        <xforms:trigger>
            <xforms:label>Click Me</xforms:label>
            <xforms:message ev:event="click" level="ephemeral"
                ref="/data/message"/>
        </xforms:trigger>
        .
        .
        .
    </body>
</html>
```

You can see the results in Figure 14.5. When the user clicks the button, the message box shown in the figure displays the message for a few seconds and then disappears.

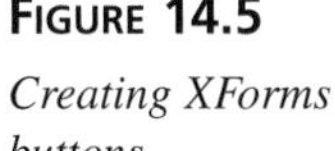

FIGURE 14.5
Creating XForms buttons.

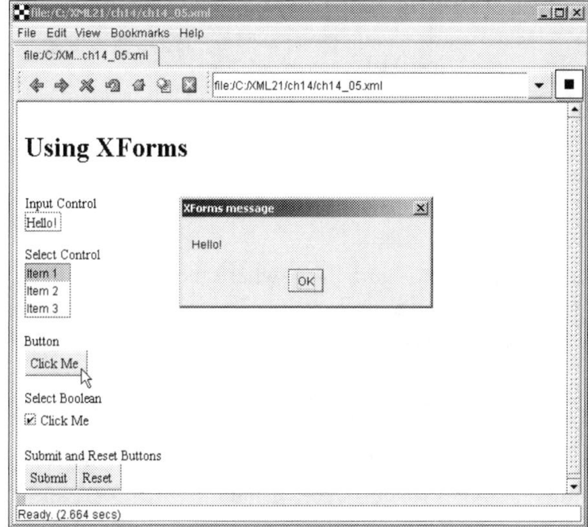

Creating Select Booleans

XForms select Booleans are much like HTML check boxes. They are easy to use: You just use the `<selectboolean>` element to create one and a `<label>` element to give it a label. You can connect the select Boolean to the data in the `<data>` element's `<selectboolean>` element by using the `ref` attribute, like this:

```
<?xml version="1.0" encoding="UTF-8"?>
<html xmlns="http://www.w3.org/1999/xhtml"
    xmlns:ev="http://www.w3.org/2001/xml-events"
    xmlns:xforms="http://www.w3.org/2002/xforms/cr">

    <head>
        .
        .
        .
    </head>

    <body>
        <h1>Using XForms</h1>
        .
        .
        .
```

```
        <p>Select Boolean</p>
        <xforms:selectboolean ref="/data/selectboolean">
            <xforms:label>Click Me</xforms:label>
        </xforms:selectboolean>
        .
        .
        .
    </body>
</html>
```

You can see the results in Figure 14.3, where the select Boolean displays a check box. The setting of this control, `true` or `false`, is stored in the `<selectboolean>` element of the resulting XML document, `data.xml`.

Creating Submit and Reset Buttons

The final controls for the XForms example are Submit and Reset buttons; the Submit button submits the XForm and stores its data in `data.xml`, and the Reset button resets the data in the XForm back to its original value. These controls are supported by their own elements: `<submit>` and `<reset>`. Here's how to use them:

```
<?xml version="1.0" encoding="UTF-8"?>
<html xmlns="http://www.w3.org/1999/xhtml"
    xmlns:ev="http://www.w3.org/2001/xml-events"
    xmlns:xforms="http://www.w3.org/2002/xforms/cr">

    <head>
        .
        .
        .
    </head>

    <body>
        <h1>Using XForms</h1>
        .
        .
        .
        <p>Submit and Reset Buttons</p>
        <xforms:submit>
            <xforms:label>Submit</xforms:label>
        </xforms:submit>

        <xforms:trigger>
            <xforms:label>Reset</xforms:label>
            <xforms:reset ev:event="DOMActivate"/>
        </xforms:trigger>
    </body>
</html>
```

Figure 14.3 shows the Submit and Reset buttons, at the bottom. Clicking the Submit button stores the controls' data in the local file `data.xml`, as you've seen.

That completes your look at XForms and our discussion for today. Tomorrow, you're going to start working with XML and JavaScript.

Summary

Today, you took a look at three XML specifications: XLink, XPointer, and XForms. All three of these XML applications were taken over from HTML into XML by the W3C.

You use XLinks to create hyperlinks in XML. You've seen that any XML element can be an XLink; all you have to do is use the correct attributes. The one required attribute, `xlink:type`, sets the type of XLink; possible values are `"simple"`, `"extended"`, `"locator"`, `"arc"`, `"resource"`, `"title"`, and `"none"`.

Simple XLinks are very much like HTML hyperlinks. To create them, you just set the `xlink:href` and `xlink:type` attributes. Extended XLinks can get quite complex, however, as you've seen today. Today you talked about inline and out-of-line XLinks in extended links, and you created extended links that included arcs, or directional links, by using the `xlink:from` and `xlink:to` attributes.

XPointers let us narrow down searches—down to specific elements or even specific characters in text. The XPointer specification is now divided into three recommendations—the XPointer framework, the element scheme, and the namespace scheme—along with the working draft for the general XPointer scheme. The W3C created this division to make XPointers easier to implement.

Today we talked about how to use the XPointer framework to use element names—barenames—as XPointers; the element scheme to identify elements by ID; and the namespace scheme to use namespaces in XPointers.

The general XPointer scheme is where the full power of XPointers lies, even though there are very few implementations of this scheme yet. General XPointers are powerful because they support full XPath expressions, as well as two more data types—points and ranges.

XForms are the XML analog of HTML Web forms, and you use them to display controls such as buttons and select controls. Today you saw that one of the major ideas behind XForms is to separate data from presentation, and, accordingly, XForms store their data in an XForms model, typically in an XHTML document's `<head>` section. The presentation of the actual controls the XForm displays is done with specialized elements such as `<input>` and `<select>`.

Tomorrow you'll start working with XML and JavaScript.

Q&A

Q How can I declare XLink elements and attributes to make my documents valid?

A Here's an example, which declares a simple XLink element, `<link>`, in a DTD:

```
<!ELEMENT link>
<!ATTLIST link
    xmlns:xlink CDATA #FIXED "http://www.w3.org/1999/xlink"
    xlink:type CDATA #FIXED "simple"
    xlink:href CDATA #REQUIRED
    xlink:show (new | replace | embed | none | other) #IMPLIED "replace">
```

Q An XForm input control handles only a single line of text. What can I use if I want to display multiple lines of text?

A You can use the XForms `<textarea>` element to display multiple lines of text. Here's an example:

```
<xforms:textarea ref="/data/textarea">
    <xforms:label>Textarea</xforms:label>
</xforms:textarea>
```

Workshop

This workshop tests whether you understand the concepts discussed today. It's a good idea to make sure you can answer these questions before pressing on to tomorrow's work. Answers to the quiz can be found in Appendix A, "Quiz Answers."

Quiz

1. What types of XLinks can you create?
2. What attribute is required in every XLink?
3. How would you specify that you want the target document to appear where the current document is now when an XLink is activated?
4. What element do you use in an XHTML document's `<head>` element to specify how an XForm's data should be structured?
5. How can you store data for an input control in an XForm?

Exercises

1. Create an XLink that includes a general XPointer to point to the area of Massachusetts in the `ch10_01.xml` XML document from Day 10.
2. Create an XForms example that uses three input controls to read a user's name, address, and telephone number. Have the XForm store that data in a local file, `userdata.xml`. If you have downloaded the XSmiles XML browser, test your work.

PART III

In Review

In Part III we took a look at some in-depth uses of XML, including XHTML—the reformulation of HTML 4.0 in XML form—SMIL and SVG, XLinks, XPointers, and XForms.

The W3C introduced XHTML with the goal of allowing HTML documents to be validated as true XML documents. There are a number of forms of XHTML:

- XHTML 1.0 Transitional is most like HTML 4.0.
- XHTML 1.0 Frameset is the same as XHTML 1.0 Transitional but is used with documents that use frames.
- XHTML 1.1 is a module-based version of XHTML. XHTML Basic is formulated for devices that will only support smaller implementations of XHTML.
- XHTML 2.0 is a new version that omits all display elements, using style sheets instead.

XHTML 1.0 is built to match HTML closely; for example, the XHTML document element is `<html>`. But because XHTML documents are also XML documents, XML rules apply. For example, elements that are not empty need closing tags, attribute values must be quoted, and empty elements must end in `/>`.

You also need a `<!DOCTYPE>` element in XHTML, and this element must appear before the document element. In the `<html>` document element, you must declare the namespace as `<html xmlns="http://www.w3.org/1999/xhtml">`. Here's an example of an XHTML document:

11

12

13

14

```
<?xml version="1.0" encoding="UTF-8"?>
<!DOCTYPE html PUBLIC "-//W3C//DTD XHTML 1.0 Transitional//EN"
"http://www.w3.org/TR/xhtml1/DTD/xhtml1-transitional.dtd">
<html xmlns="http://www.w3.org/1999/xhtml">
    <head>
        <title>
            Using XHTML
        </title>
    </head>

    <body>
        <h1>
            Welcome to my XHTML-compliant page!
        </h1>
        This is an XHTML document.
        <br/>
        Do you like it?
    </body>
</html>
```

It's apparent how much this document resembles HTML, but it's also apparent that it's XML.

In Part III you saw that XHTML elements mirror HTML elements so well that you can easily convert HTML documents into XHTML if you know the XHTML rules. For example, you can easily convert this HTML document:

```
<HTML>
    <HEAD>
        <TITLE>
            Want to read about HTML?
        </TITLE>
    </HEAD>

    <BODY>
       <H1>
            Want to read about HTML?
       </H1>

       Read all about
       <A HREF="http://www.w3.org/MarkUp/Activity.html">HTML</A>.
    </BODY>
</HTML>
```

into this XHTML document:

```
<?xml version="1.0" encoding="UTF-8"?>
<!DOCTYPE html PUBLIC "-//W3C//DTD XHTML 1.0 Transitional//EN"
"http://www.w3.org/TR/xhtml1/DTD/xhtml1-transitional.dtd">
<html xmlns="http://www.w3.org/1999/xhtml">
```

```
        <title>
            Want to read about XHTML?
        </title>
    </head>

    <body>
       <h1>
            Want to read about XHTML?
       </h1>

       Read all about
       <a href="http://www.w3.org/MarkUp/Activity.html">HTML</a>.
</html>
```

The following is an XHTML example that creates a table by using the HTML analogs `<TABLE>`, `<TR>`, and `<TD>`—that is, `<table>`, `<tr>`, and `<td>`—to hold a tic-tac-toe game:

```
<!DOCTYPE html PUBLIC "-//W3C//DTD XHTML 1.0 Transitional//EN"
"http://www.w3.org/tr/xhtml1/DTD/xhtml1-transitional.dtd">
<html xmlns="http://www.w3.org/1999/xhtml">
    <head>
        <title>
            Formatting Tables in XHTML
        </title>
    </head>

    <body>
        <h1>
            Formatting Tables in XHTML
        </h1>
        <table border="1">
            <tr>
                <th>X</th>
                <th>O</th>
                <th>X</th>
            </tr>
            <tr>
                <td>O</td>
                <td>X</td>
                <td>O</td>
            </tr>
            <tr>
                <td>X</td>
                <td>O</td>
                <td>X</td>
            </tr>
        </table>
    </body>
</html>
```

SVG is all about creating graphics, and you can use a browser plug-in to support SVG, as you did in Part III. SVG documents use the <svg> document element; you were able to create basic shapes by using the <circle> element to create circles, the <line> element to create lines, the <rect> element to create rectangles, the <polyline> element to create polyline figures, the <ellipse> element to create ellipses, and the <polygon> element to create polygons.

Many elements are already built in to SVG. For example, the <group> element lets you group elements together so you can move or rotate them all at once. You can script elements by using the <script> element. The <animate> SVG element lets you animate SVG elements by setting how to change the values of their attributes over time. You can also create all kinds of graphic effects. Here's an SVG example that creates a linear gradient by using the <linearGradient> element:

```
<?xml version="1.0" encoding="UTF-8"?>
<svg xmlns="http://www.w3.org/2000/svg">
    <text y="40" style="font-size:24pt">
        Handling gradients
    </text>
    <defs>
        <linearGradient id="gradient1">
            <stop offset="0%" stop-color="#000000" />
            <stop offset="100%" stop-color="#00FF00" />
        </linearGradient>
    </defs>

    <rect fill="url(#gradient1)" stroke="green" stroke-width="5"
        x="100" y="200" width="200" height="400"/>
</svg>
```

SMIL is designed to create multimedia presentations by using XML. For example, here's how a SMIL presentation might present slides, play music, and display text:

```
<smil>
    <head>
        <layout>
            <root-layout width="400" height="300" background-color="white"/>
            <region id="topRegion" title="topRegion" left="0" top="0"
                width="400" height="200"/>
            <region id="caption" title="caption" left="0" top="201"
                width="400" height="100"/>
        </layout>
    </head>

    <body>
        <par>
            <seq>
                <par>
```

```
                    <img region="topRegion" src="slide1.jpg"
                        type="image/jpeg" dur="20s"/>
                    <text region="caption" src="image1.txt"
                        type="text/plain" dur="20s"/>
                    <audio src="xml1.au" region="audio"
                        type="audio/x-au" dur="20s"/>
                </par>
                <par>
                    <img region="topRegion" src="slide2.jpg"
                        type="image/jpeg" dur="20s"/>
                    <text region="caption" src="image2.txt"
                        type="text/plain" dur="20s"/>
                    <audio src="xml2.au" region="audio"
                        type="audio/x-au" dur="20s"/>
                </par>
                <par>
                    <img region="topRegion" src="slide3.jpg"
                        type="image/jpeg" dur="20s"/>
                    <text region="caption" src="image3.txt"
                        type="text/plain" dur="20s"/>
                    <audio src="xml3.au" region="audio"
                        type="audio/x-au" dur="20s"/>
                </par>
            </seq>
        </par>
    </body>
</smil>
```

XLinks are used to create hyperlinks in XML. Any XML element can be an XLink if you use the correct attributes. In particular, you need to use one attribute, `xlink:type`, to set the type of XLink to one of these values: `"simple"`, `"extended"`, `"locator"`, `"arc"`, `"resource"`, `"title"`, or `"none"`.

Simple XLinks predominate today because they're much like HTML hyperlinks. To create a simple XLink, you set the `xlink:href` and `xlink:type` attributes. The following example, which treats a simple XLink very much like an HTML hyperlink, will work in both XML browsers and HTML browsers that support JavaScript:

```
<?xml version="1.0" encoding="UTF-8"?>
<?xml-stylesheet type="text/css" href="style.css"?>

<insurance>
         <title>
             Markup Information
         </title>
         You can find more about markup languages
         <link xmlns:xlink = "http://www.w3.org/1999/xlink"
             xlink:type = "simple"
             xlink:show = "new"
```

```
            xlink:href = "http://www.w3.org/MarkUp/Activity.html"
            onClick="location.href='http://www.w3.org/MarkUp/Activity.html'">
            here.
        </link>
</insurance>
```

XPointers let you get even more specific than XLinks, but there's currently even less implementation of XPointers than of XLinks. The XPointer specification is now divided into three recommendations—the XPointer framework, the element scheme, and the namespace scheme—along with the working draft for the general XPointer scheme.

XForms show a great deal of promise. XForms are the XML counterpart of HTML Web forms, and you can use them to support controls such as buttons, check boxes, and radio buttons.

A major idea behind XForms is to separate data from presentation, so XForms store their data in an XForms model, typically stored in an XHTML's `<head>` section. The presentation of the actual controls that an XForm displays is done with specialized elements such as `<button>` and `<select>`.

For example, the following example is an XForm that stores its data in the `<head>` section and displays two check boxes as well as Submit and Cancel buttons. Here's what the `<head>` section, which holds the data for the two check boxes, looks like:

```
<?xml version="1.0" encoding="UTF-8"?>
<html xmlns="http://www.w3.org/1999/xhtml"
    xmlns:ev="http://www.w3.org/2001/xml-events"
    xmlns:xforms="http://www.w3.org/2002/xforms/cr">

    <head>
        <xforms:model>
            <xforms:submission localfile="data.xml"/>
            <xforms:instance>
                <data xmlns="">
                    <selectboolean1>true</selectboolean1>
                    <selectboolean2>true</selectboolean2>
                </data>
            </xforms:instance>
        </xforms:model>
    </head>
        .
        .
        .
```

In the presentation of these controls in the `<body>` section, you just refer to the location of their data storage in the `<head>` section:

```
    <body>
        <h1>Using XForms</h1>

        <xforms:selectboolean ref="/data/selectboolean1">
            <xforms:label>Click me</xforms:label>
        </xforms:selectboolean>

        <xforms:selectboolean ref="/data/selectboolean2">
            <xforms:label>Click me too!</xforms:label>
        </xforms:selectboolean>

        <p>Submit and Reset Buttons</p>
        <xforms:submit>
            <xforms:label>Submit</xforms:label>
        </xforms:submit>

        <xforms:trigger>
            <xforms:label>Reset</xforms:label>
            <xforms:reset ev:event="DOMActivate"/>
        </xforms:trigger>
    </body>
</html>
```

And that's it for Part III. In Part IV you're going to start working with programming and XML to take advantage of the full power of XML.

PART IV

At a Glance

Programming and XML

Part IV looks at how to use programming to get the most out of XML. Programming has a great deal to offer the XML author, and you'll start this part by taking a look at working with JavaScript in Web pages.

By using JavaScript, you can load XML documents and parse them, searching through their data for an item. You're going to see how to do that, as well as how to validate XML documents that use either DTDs or XML schemas by using JavaScript.

You'll also take a look at how to use XML with Java in this part. Versions 1.4 and later of Java have a great deal of support for XML built in. You're going to take advantage of that support in both the XML Document Object Model (DOM) and the Simple API for XML (SAX).

In this part you're also going to take a look at how to work with the Simple Object Access Protocol (SOAP). SOAP is an XML-based protocol that lets applications communicate on the Internet, and you'll take a look at working with SOAP both with Java and .NET programming. (If you're a .NET programmer, you should take a look at Day 21, which is dedicated to .NET XML programming.)

PART IV

DAY 15

Using JavaScript and XML

Starting today, we're going to begin working with programming and XML. Today's discussion focuses on JavaScript and XML, and here's a list of today's topics:

- Using the W3C XML DOM
- Using DOM objects
- Using XML data islands
- Accessing data in XML documents
- Parsing XML documents
- Validating XML documents by using a DTD

NOTE

> Today you'll use JavaScript because it's one of the languages commonly used with XML. If you don't know JavaScript but have programmed before, you should be able to easily pick up JavaScript from what you do today. You can also find plenty of JavaScript resources online; a casual search for "JavaScript tutorial" turns up more than 17,000 matches.
>
> The official documentation for JavaScript 1.3 is at `http://developer.netscape.com/docs/manuals/index.html`, and the official documentation for JavaScript 2.0 is at `http://developer.netscape.com/docs/manuals/index.html`. The official documentation for JScript 5.6, the version used in Internet Explorer, is currently at `http://msdn.microsoft.com/library/default.asp?url=/library/en-us/script56/html/js56jsoriJScript.asp` (note, however, that this is a Microsoft URL, and Microsoft reorganizes its sites continuously, which means that by the time you read this book, the URL may be obsolete).

The W3C created the *Document Object Model (DOM)* to let you work with XML documents. Using the DOM is a way of looking at XML documents in programming terms, as you'll see today. Before the DOM standardized things, each XML processor had its own way of handling XML—and all the processors kept changing. Now, things have quieted down and stabilized because of the W3C DOM, and we'll start discussing it today.

Introducing the W3C DOM

When you're dealing with programming, you need some way of working with the data in XML documents, and the W3C DOM gives you that. The DOM lets you consider an XML document as a tree of *nodes*. In the DOM, every data item is a node, and a child element or enclosed text becomes a subnode. When everything in a document—text, attributes, elements, and so on—becomes a node, you can use some well-defined functions to access and work with those nodes in a standard way. These are the node types in the DOM:

- Element
- Attribute
- Text
- `CDATA` section
- Entity reference
- Entity
- Processing instruction

- Comment
- Document
- Document type
- Document fragment
- Notation

Let's take a look at a sample XML document for today's work:

```
<?xml version="1.0" encoding="UTF-8"?>
<document>
    <title>
        The Report
    </title>
    <text>
        All clear on the Western front.
    </text>
</document>
```

This document has an element node, `<document>`, that has two child nodes, `<title>` and `<text>`, and these two nodes are siblings of each other. Each of the `<title>` and `<text>` element nodes contains text, which is treated as a child node. Here's what this document looks like as a tree of nodes:

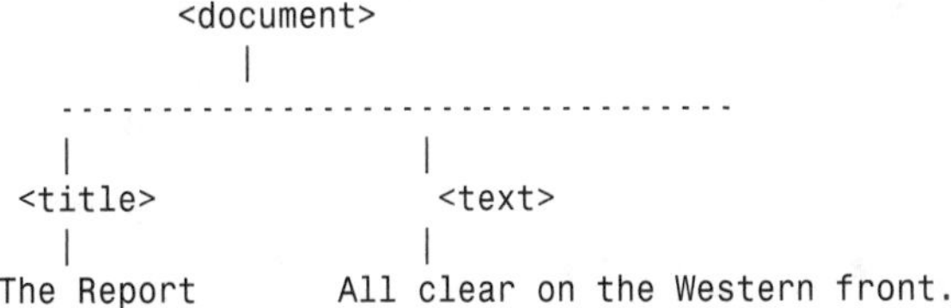

When you use the methods defined in the W3C DOM, you can navigate along the various branches of a document's tree by using methods such as `nextChild` to move to the next child node. Using methods in this way in the W3C DOM and becoming familiar with how they work are a good part of today's work.

The DOM Levels

There are four different levels of the DOM specification:

- **Level 0**—There actually is no DOM Level 0, but that's how W3C refers to the DOM in early versions of the popular browsers—Netscape Navigator 3.0 and Microsoft Internet Explorer 3.0.
- **Level 1**—This level is a W3C recommendation. You can find the documentation for this level at `http://www.w3.org/TR/REC-DOM-Level-1`.

- **Level 2**—Now a recommendation, this level of the DOM is more advanced than Level 1 and includes a style sheet object model. It also lets you traverse a document, has a built-in event model, and supports XML namespaces. You can find the documentation for this level at `http://www.w3.org/TR/DOM-Level-2`.
- **Level 3**—This level is still in the working draft stage and will address document loading and saving. It will also address document views and formatting, event groups, and more. You can find the core working draft at `http://www.w3.org/TR/DOM-Level-3-Core`.

From a JavaScript perspective, the only complete DOM implementation is in Internet Explorer 6 and later, which supports DOM Level 1. You can read all about Internet Explorer's support for the DOM at `http://msdn.microsoft.com/library/default.asp?url=/workshop/author/dom/domoverview.asp`. (Note, however, that Microsoft has the habit of changing its URLs very often, so by the time you read this book, this URL may be out-of-date.)

Today you'll be working with DOM Level 1—the only level of the DOM in widespread use today. You'll also be working with objects in JavaScript today. For example, there's an object that corresponds to the document itself, an object that corresponds to elements, one that corresponds to attributes, and so forth. When you've have an object corresponding to an element, for example, you can use the object's methods and properties to learn all about that element—what its name is, how many children it has, and so on. To dig into the programming, then, you need to understand the objects in the DOM.

Introducing the DOM Objects

Here's an overview of the W3C DOM Level 1 objects:

- **`Document`**—The document object
- **`DocumentFragment`**—A reference to a fragment of a document
- **`DocumentType`**—A reference to the `<!DOCTYPE>` element
- **`EntityReference`**—A reference to an entity
- **`Element`**—An element
- **`Attr`**—An attribute
- **`ProcessingInstruction`**—A processing instruction
- **`Comment`**—The content of an XML comment
- **`Text`**—The text content of an element or attribute
- **`CDATASection`**—A `CDATA` section.

- `Entity`—A parsed or unparsed entity in the XML document
- `Notation`—A notation
- `Node`—A single node in the document tree
- `NodeList`—A list of node objects; allows iteration and indexed access operations
- `NamedNodeMap`—A collection that allows iteration and access by name to the collection of attributes

That's the official list of objects. However, Microsoft, going its own way as usual, supports the W3C DOM but uses its own names for the programming objects:

- `DOMDocument`—The first node of the XML DOM tree
- `XMLDOMNode`—A single node in the document tree
- `XMLDOMNodeList`—A list of node objects
- `XMLDOMNamedNodeMap`—A map of named nodes; supports access by name to a collection of attributes
- `XMLDOMParseError`—Data about an error; includes error number, line number, character position, and a text description
- `XMLHttpRequest`—An object that supports communication with HTTP servers
- `XTLRuntime`—An object that supports methods that you can call from XSL style sheets
- `XMLDOMAttribute`—An attribute object
- `XMLDOMCDATASection`—A CDATA section object
- `XMLDOMCharacterData`—An object that supports methods used for text manipulation
- `XMLDOMComment`—A comment
- `XMLDOMDocumentFragment`—A document fragment object
- `XMLDOMDocumentType`—Data for the document type declaration
- `XMLDOMElement`—An element object
- `XMLDOMEntity`—A parsed or unparsed entity in the XML document
- `XMLDOMEntityReference`—An entity reference node
- `XMLDOMImplementation`—An object that supports general DOM methods
- `XMLDOMNotation`—A notation
- `XMLDOMProcessingInstruction`—A processing instruction
- `XMLDOMText`—The text value of an element or attribute

The list of DOM objects is substantial, so the following sections go through some of the highlights you'll need in code, starting with the main object, the `DOMDocument` object.

Using the `DOMDocument` Object

In the Microsoft version of the DOM, the `DOMDocument` object is the main object, and it represents the top node in every document tree. When we're working with the DOM, this is the only object we create directly. Here's how you might create the `DOMDocument` object in JavaScript:

```
function readXMLData()
{
    var xmlDocumentObject
    xmlDocumentObject = new ActiveXObject("Microsoft.XMLDOM")
    xmlDocumentObject.load("ch15_01.xml")
                    .
                    .
                    .
```

The `Microsoft.XMLDOM` class used here is an early version of Microsoft's XML support, but it's still supported in recent versions of Internet Explorer, which means we can use it as a common denominator in our code. The current version, and the one to use if you can (because it supports the full DOM 1.0 as well as XML schemas), is Microsoft's MSXML version 4.0, which comes with recent versions of Internet Explorer 6. Here's how to use this version:

```
function readXMLData()
{
    var xmlDocumentObject
    xmlDocumentObject = new ActiveXObject("MSXML2.DOMDocument.4.0")
    xmlDocumentObject.load("ch15_01.xml")
                    .
                    .
                    .
```

You can also specify earlier versions of the `Microsoft.XMLDOM` class by using `"MSXML2.DOMDocument.2.0"` or `"MSXML2.DOMDocument.3.0"`.

Here's an overview of the most significant properties of the `DOMDocument` object:

NOTE

> Items that are Microsoft only, not official in the W3C DOM, are marked throughout today's discussion with an asterisk (*).

- **attributes**—Contains the list of attributes for the node. Read-only.
- **childNodes**—Contains a node list of the child nodes of nodes that may have children. Read-only.
- **dataType***—Contains the data type for the node. Read/write.
- **definition***—Contains the definition of the node in the DTD or schema. Read-only.
- **doctype**—Contains the document type node, which is what specifies the DTD for the document. Read-only.
- **documentElement**—Contains the root element of the document. Read/write.
- **firstChild**—Contains the first child of the current node. Read-only.
- **lastChild**—Contains the last child node of the current node. Read-only.
- **namespaceURI***—Contains the URI of a namespace. Read-only.
- **nextSibling**—Contains the next sibling node of the current node. Read-only.
- **nodeName**—Contains the qualified name of the element, attribute, or entity reference. Read-only.
- **nodeType**—Contains the node type. Read-only.
- **nodeTypedValue***—Contains the node's value. Read/write.
- **nodeTypeString***—Contains the node type, expressed as a string. Read-only.
- **nodeValue**—Contains the text of the node. Read/write.
- **ondataavailable***—Sets the event handler for the `ondataavailable` event. Read/write.
- **onreadystatechange***—Sets the event handler that handles `readyState` property changes. Read/write.
- **ontransformnode***—Sets the event handler for the `ontransformnode` event. Read/write.
- **ownerDocument**—Contains the root of the document that contains this node. Read-only.
- **parentNode**—Contains the parent node of the current node. Read-only.
- **parsed***—Is set to true if this node has been parsed; false otherwise. Read-only.
- **parseError***—Contains information about the most recent parsing error. Read-only.
- **prefix***—Contains the namespace prefix. Read-only.

- **preserveWhiteSpace***—Is set to true if processing should preserve whitespace; false otherwise. Read/write.
- **previousSibling**—Contains the previous sibling of this node. Read-only.
- **readyState***—Contains the current browser state of the XML document. Read-only.
- **text***—Contains the text content of the node and its subtrees. Read/write.
- **url***—Contains the URL for the most recently loaded XML document. Read-only.
- **validateOnParse***—Is set to true (the default) if the parser should validate this document on parsing it; false if not. Read/write.
- **xml***—Contains the XML text representation of the node and all of its children. Read-only.

Here is an overview of the significant methods for this object:

- **abort***—Aborts a download.
- **appendChild**—Appends a new child as the last child of the current node.
- **cloneNode**—Returns a node that is a copy of this node.
- **createAttribute**—Returns a new attribute, using the given name.
- **createCDATASection**—Returns a `CDATA` section node that contains the given data.
- **createComment**—Returns a comment node.
- **createDocumentFragment**—Returns an empty `DocumentFragment` object.
- **createElement**—Returns an element node, using the given name.
- **createEntityReference**—Returns a new `EntityReference` object.
- **createNode***—Returns a node, using the given type, name, and namespace.
- **createProcessingInstruction**—Returns a processing instruction node.
- **createTextNode**—Returns a text node that contains the given data.
- **getElementsByTagName**—Yields a collection of elements that have the given name.
- **hasChildNodes**—Returns true if this node has children; false if not.
- **insertBefore**—Inserts a child node before the given node.
- **load***—Loads an XML document from the given location.
- **loadXML***—Loads an XML document, using the given string.
- **nodeFromID***—Yields the node whose `ID` attribute matches the given value.
- **removeChild**—Removes the given child node from the list of children.
- **replaceChild**—Replaces the given child node with the given new child node.

- **save***—Saves an XML document to the given location.
- **transformNode***—Transforms the node and its children by using the given XSL style sheet.

Using the `XMLDOMNode` Object

The Microsoft `XMLDOMNode` object extends the core XML DOM `Node` object by adding support for data types, namespaces, DTDs, and schemas, as implemented in Internet Explorer. It's the generic object used to handle nodes. Here is an overview of the significant properties of this object:

- **attributes**—List of attributes for the node. Read-only.
- **childNodes**—List containing the child nodes of the current node. Read-only.
- **dataType***—Contains the data type for this node. Read/write.
- **firstChild**—Contains the first child of the current node. Read-only.
- **lastChild**—Contains the last child of the current node. Read-only.
- **namespaceURI***—Contains the URI for the namespace. Read-only.
- **nextSibling**—Contains the next sibling of this node. Read-only.
- **nodeName**—Contains the qualified name for an element, attribute, or entity reference, or a string for other node types. Read-only.
- **nodeType**—Contains the node type. Read-only.
- **nodeTypedValue***—Contains the node's value. Read/write.
- **nodeTypeString***—Contains the node type, in string form. Read-only.
- **nodeValue**—Contains the text associated with the node. Read/write.
- **ownerDocument**—Contains the root of the document. Read-only.
- **parentNode**—Contains the parent node. Read-only.
- **parsed***—Returns true if this node has been parsed; false otherwise. Read-only.
- **prefix***—Contains the namespace prefix. Read-only.
- **previousSibling**—Contains the previous sibling of this node. Read-only.
- **text***—Contains the text content of the node and its subtrees. Read/write.
- **xml***—Contains the XML representation of the node and its children. Read-only.

Here is an overview of the significant methods for this object:

- **appendChild**—Appends a new child as the last child of this node.
- **cloneNode**—Creates a new node that is a copy of this node.

- **hasChildNodes**—Returns true if this node has children; false otherwise.
- **insertBefore**—Inserts a child node before the given node.
- **removeChild**—Removes the given child node.
- **replaceChild**—Replaces the given child node with the given new child node.
- **transformNode***—Transforms the node and its children by using the given XSL style sheet.

Using the `XMLDOMElement` Object

The type of node you'll probably work with most often is the element node, which is supported in the Microsoft programming model by the `XMLDOMElement` object. Here are the significant properties of the `XMLDOMElement` object:

- **attributes**—List of attributes for the node. Read-only.
- **childNodes**—Contains a list of the node's children. Read-only.
- **dataType***—Contains the data type for this node. Read/write.
- **firstChild**—Contains the first child node of this node. Read-only.
- **lastChild**—Contains the last child node of this node. Read-only.
- **namespaceURI***—Contains the URI for the namespace. Read-only.
- **nextSibling**—Contains the next sibling of this node. Read-only.
- **nodeName**—Contains the qualified name of an element, attribute, or entity reference, or a string for other node types. Read-only.
- **nodeType**—Contains the node type. Read-only.
- **nodeTypeString***—Contains the node type, in string form. Read-only.
- **nodeValue**—Contains the text associated with the node. Read/write.
- **ownerDocument**—Contains the root of the document. Read-only.
- **parentNode**—Contains the parent node of the current node. Read-only.
- **parsed***—Returns true if this node has been parsed; false otherwise. Read-only.
- **prefix***—Contains the namespace prefix. Read-only.
- **previousSibling**—Contains the previous sibling of this node. Read-only.
- **tagName**—Contains the element name. Read-only.
- **text***—Contains the text content of the node and its subtrees. Read/write.
- **xml***—Contains the XML text representation of the node and all of its children. Read-only.

Here are the significant methods of this object:

- **appendChild**—Appends a new child as the last child of the current node.
- **cloneNode**—Returns a new node that is a copy of this node.
- **getAttribute**—Gets the value of the named attribute.
- **getAttributeNode**—Gets the named attribute node.
- **getElementsByTagName**—Returns a list of all descendant elements that match the given name.
- **hasChildNodes**—Returns true if this node has children; false otherwise.
- **insertBefore**—Inserts a child node before the given node.
- **normalize**—Normalizes all descendent elements by combining two or more text nodes next to each other into one text node.
- **removeAttribute**—Removes or replaces the named attribute.
- **removeAttributeNode**—Removes the given attribute from the element.
- **removeChild**—Removes the given child node.
- **replaceChild**—Replaces the given child node with the given new child node.
- **setAttribute**—Sets the value of a named attribute.
- **setAttributeNode**—Adds or changes the given attribute node on the element.
- **transformNode***—Transforms the node and its children by using the given XSL style sheet.

Using the `XMLDOMAttribute` Object

Attributes are considered nodes in the W3C DOM, but an attribute is not considered a child node of an element. As you'll see today, you use special methods to get the attributes of an element (for example, the `getAttribute` method). Here are the significant properties of the `XMLDOMAttribute` object:

- **attributes**—List of attributes for this node. Read-only.
- **childNodes**—Contains the list of the child nodes. Read-only.
- **dataType***—Contains the data type of this node. Read/write.
- **firstChild**—Contains the first child of the current node. Read-only.
- **lastChild**—Contains the last child of the current node. Read-only.
- **name**—Contains the attribute name. Read-only.
- **namespaceURI***—Contains the URI for the namespace. Read-only.

- **nextSibling**—Contains the next sibling of the node. Read-only.
- **nodeName**—Contains the qualified name for an element, attribute, or entity reference, or a string for other node types. Read-only.
- **nodeType**—Contains the node type. Read-only.
- **nodeTypedValue***—Contains the node's value. Read/write.
- **nodeTypeString***—Contains the node type, in string form. Read-only.
- **nodeValue**—Contains the text associated with the node. Read/write.
- **ownerDocument**—Contains the root of the document. Read-only.
- **parentNode**—Holds the parent node (for nodes that can have parents). Read-only.
- **parsed***—Returns true if this node has been parsed; false otherwise. Read-only.
- **prefix***—Contains the namespace prefix. Read-only.
- **previousSibling**—Contains the previous sibling of this node. Read-only.
- **specified**—Indicates whether the node (usually an attribute) is explicitly specified or derived from a default value. Read-only.
- **text**—Contains the text content of the node and its subtrees. Read/write.
- **value**—Contains the attribute's value. Read/write.
- **xml**—Contains the XML text representation of the node and all its descendants. Read-only.

Here are the significant methods of this object:

- **appendChild**—Appends a new child as the last child of this node.
- **cloneNode**—Returns a new node that is a copy of this node.
- **hasChildNodes**—Is set to true if this node has children.
- **insertBefore**—Inserts a child node before the given node.
- **removeChild**—Removes the given child node from the list.
- **replaceChild**—Replaces the given child node with the new child node.
- **transformNode**—Transforms this node and its children by using the given XSL style sheet.

Using the `XMLDOMText` Object

When it comes time to access the data in an XML document, you'll usually want to work with the text content of an element or an attribute, and you can use the Microsoft `XMLDOMText` object for text nodes. Here are the significant properties of the `XMLDOMText` object:

- **attributes**—Holds the list of attributes for the node. Read-only.
- **childNodes**—Contains the list of the child nodes. Read-only.
- **data**—Contains the node's data. What is actually stored depends on the node type. Read/write.
- **dataType***—Contains the data type for the node. Read/write.
- **firstChild**—Contains the first child of the current node. Read-only.
- **lastChild**—Contains the last child of the current node. Read-only.
- **length**—Contains the length, in characters, of the data. Read-only.
- **namespaceURI***—Contains the URI for the namespace. Read-only.
- **nextSibling**—Contains the next sibling of this node. Read-only.
- **nodeName**—Contains the qualified name of an element, attribute, or entity reference, or a string for other node types. Read-only.
- **nodeType**—Indicates the node type. Read-only.
- **nodeTypedValue***—Contains the node's value. Read/write.
- **nodeTypeString***—Contains the node type, in string form. Read-only.
- **nodeValue**—Contains the text associated with the node. Read/write.
- **ownerDocument**—Contains the root of the document. Read-only.
- **parentNode**—Contains the parent node. Read-only.
- **parsed***—Returns true if this node has been parsed; false otherwise. Read-only.
- **prefix***—Contains the namespace prefix. Read-only.
- **previousSibling**—Contains the previous sibling of this node. Read-only.
- **specified**—Indicates whether the node is explicitly specified or derived from a default value. Read-only.
- **text***—Holds the text content of the node. Read/write.
- **xml***—Holds the XML representation of the node and all of its descendants. Read-only.

Here are the significant methods of this object:

- **appendChild**—Appends a new child as the last child of the node.
- **appendData**—Appends the given string to the existing string data.
- **cloneNode**—Returns a new node that is a copy of this node.
- **deleteData**—Removes the given substring within the string data.
- **hasChildNodes**—Returns true if this node has children; false otherwise.

- **insertBefore**—Inserts a child node before the specified node.
- **insertData**—Inserts the supplied string at the specified offset.
- **removeChild**—Removes the specified child node from the list of children.
- **replaceChild**—Replaces the specified child node with the given new child node.
- **splitText**—Breaks the text node into two text nodes.
- **substringData**—Returns a substring of the full string.
- **transformNode***—Transforms the node and its children by using the given XSL style sheet.

This overview of the JavaScript objects you'll be using today might seem somewhat mysterious, so in the following sections you'll put it to work.

Working with the XML DOM in JavaScript

To put the XML DOM to work with JavaScript, let's start by reading the value of an element in an XML document. Listing 15.1 shows the XML document `ch15_01.xml`, which details the attendance of a senate committee on doughnut consumption. Today you'll extract the name of the third senator, Jay Jones, from it, by using JavaScript.

LISTING 15.1 A Sample XML Document (`ch15_01.xml`)

```
<?xml version="1.0" encoding="UTF-8"?>
<session>
   <committee type="monetary">
       <title>Finance</title>
       <number>17</number>
       <subject>Donut Costs</subject>
       <date>7/15/2005</date>
       <attendees>
           <senator status="present">
               <firstName>Thomas</firstName>
               <lastName>Smith</lastName>
           </senator>
           <senator status="absent">
               <firstName>Frank</firstName>
               <lastName>McCoy</lastName>
           </senator>
           <senator status="present">
               <firstName>Jay</firstName>
               <lastName>Jones</lastName>
           </senator>
       </attendees>
   </committee>
</session>
```

Now you need to build the JavaScript to read the name of the third senator in the example. To start, create a `DOMDocument` object and load in the XML document `ch15_01.xml`, like this:

```
<HTML>
    <HEAD>
        <TITLE>
            Extracting XML Data
        </TITLE>

        <SCRIPT LANGUAGE="JavaScript">
            function readXMLData()
            {
                var xmlDocumentObject
                xmlDocumentObject = new ActiveXObject("Microsoft.XMLDOM")
                xmlDocumentObject.load("ch15_01.xml")
                .
                .
                .
```

Now `ch15_01.xml` is loaded into the `DOMDocument` object. You can use this object's `documentElement` property to get a new node that corresponds to the document element (that is, `<session>`):

```
sessionNode = xmlDocumentObject.documentElement
```

Now you have the `<session>` element's node, and you want to navigate to the third senator's name. Start by getting an `XMLDOMElement` node for the `<committee>` element by using the `<session>` element object's `firstChild` property:

```
committeeNode = sessionNode.firstChild
```

Next, you can get a node object for the `<attendees>` element:

```
attendeesNode = committeeNode.lastChild
```

And then you get a node object for the last `<senator>` element by using the `<attendees>` node's `lastChild` property:

```
senatorNode = attendeesNode.lastChild
```

To get the senator's first name (stored in the `<firstName>` element), you use the `<senator>` element node's `firstChild` property, and to get the senator's last name (stored in the `<lastName>` element), you can get the next sibling element:

```
firstNameNode = senatorNode.firstChild
lastNameNode = firstNameNode.nextSibling
```

Now that you have node objects corresponding to the `<firstName>` and `<lastName>` elements, you can access the text nodes in those elements by using the `firstChild` property, and you can get the actual text by using those nodes' `nodeValue` properties. You can display those values by using Dynamic HTML in an HTML `<DIV>` element, like this:

```
displayText = "Last senator's name: " +
    firstNameNode.firstChild.nodeValue + ' '
    + lastNameNode.firstChild.nodeValue
    displayDIV.innerHTML = displayText
```

Listing 15.2 shows how this all works in `ch15_02.html`, which gives all the HTML and JavaScript you'll need today.

LISTING 15.2 Using JavaScript and XML (`ch15_02.html`)

```
<HTML>
    <HEAD>
        <TITLE>
            Extracting XML Data
        </TITLE>

        <SCRIPT LANGUAGE="JavaScript">
            function readXMLData()
            {
                var xmlDocumentObject, sessionNode, committeeNode,
                    attendeesNode
                var firstNameNode, lastNameNode, displayText
                xmlDocumentObject = new ActiveXObject("Microsoft.XMLDOM")
                xmlDocumentObject.load("ch15_01.xml")

                sessionNode = xmlDocumentObject.documentElement
                committeeNode = sessionNode.firstChild
                attendeesNode = committeeNode.lastChild
                senatorNode = attendeesNode.lastChild
                firstNameNode = senatorNode.firstChild
                lastNameNode = firstNameNode.nextSibling

                displayText = "Last senator's name: " +
                    firstNameNode.firstChild.nodeValue + ' '
                    + lastNameNode.firstChild.nodeValue
                displayDIV.innerHTML = displayText
            }
        </SCRIPT>
    </HEAD>

    <BODY>
        <H1>
            Extracting XML Data
        </H1>

        <INPUT TYPE="BUTTON" VALUE="Get the last senator's name"
            ONCLICK="readXMLData()">
```

LISTING 15.2 continued

```
        <BR>
        <DIV ID="displayDIV"></DIV>
    </BODY>
</HTML>
```

Figure 15.1 shows this page at work in Internet Explorer. When the user clicks the button, the XML document `ch15_01.xml` is read and parsed, and you retrieve and display the third person's name. You've made substantial progress.

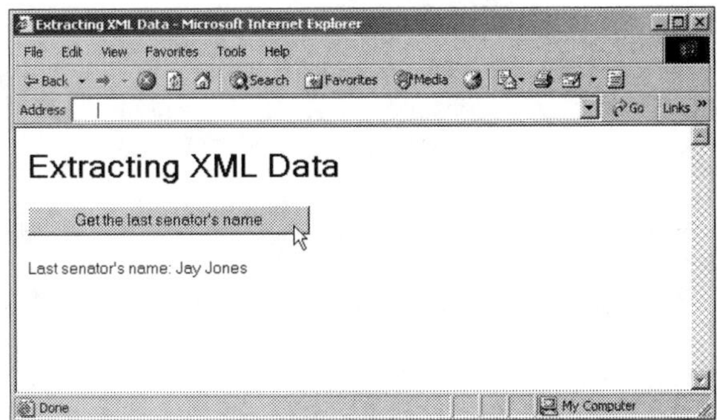

FIGURE 15.1
Reading an XML element in Internet Explorer.

There's another way to do this in Internet Explorer—by using XML data islands. *XML data islands* let us embed XML in an HTML document, and this is how to use them:

```
<HTML>
    <HEAD>
        <TITLE>XML Islands</TITLE>
    </HEAD>

    <BODY>
        <P>This example uses an XML Island.</P>
        <XML>
            <document>
                <title>
                    The Report
                </title>
                <text>
                    All clear on the Western front.
                </text>
            </document>
        </XML>
    </BODY>
</HTML>
```

Here are the attributes you use with the <XML> element:

- **ID**—Contains the ID with which you can refer to the <XML> element in code. This attribute should be set to an alphanumeric string.
- **NS**—Contains the URI of the XML namespace used by the XML content. This attribute should be set to a URI.
- **PREFIX**—Contains the namespace prefix of the XML contents. This attribute should be set to an alphanumeric string.
- **SRC**—Contains the source for the XML document, if the document is external. This attribute should be set to a URI.

You can use the <XML> element, along with the SRC and ID attributes, to read in XML documents and make them accessible. Listing 15.3 shows how this works. This example uses an XML island to get access to the XML document ch15_01.xml.

LISTING 15.3 Using JavaScript and XML Islands (ch15_03.html)

```
<HTML>
    <HEAD>
         <TITLE>
             Extracting XML Data
         </TITLE>

         <XML ID="committeeXML" SRC="ch15_01.xml"></XML>

         <SCRIPT LANGUAGE="JavaScript">
              function readXMLData()
              {
                  var xmlDocumentObject, sessionNode, committeeNode,
                      attendeesNode
                  var firstNameNode, lastNameNode, displayText
                  xmlDocumentObject= document.all("committeeXML").XMLDocument

                  sessionNode = xmlDocumentObject.documentElement
                  committeeNode = sessionNode.firstChild
                  attendeesNode = committeeNode.lastChild
                  senatorNode = attendeesNode.lastChild
                  firstNameNode = senatorNode.firstChild
                  lastNameNode = firstNameNode.nextSibling

                  displayText = "Last senator's name: " +
                        firstNameNode.firstChild.nodeValue + ' '
                      + lastNameNode.firstChild.nodeValue
                  displayDIV.innerHTML = displayText
             }
```

LISTING 15.3 continued

```
        </SCRIPT>
    </HEAD>

    <BODY>
        <H1>
            Extracting XML Data
        </H1>

        <INPUT TYPE="BUTTON" VALUE="Get the last senator's name"
            ONCLICK="readXMLData()">
        <P>
        <DIV ID="displayDIV"></DIV>
    </BODY>
</HTML>
```

This example works just like Listing 15.2. In fact, if you want to, you can enclose the entire text of the XML document, `ch15_01.xml`, in the XML island.

Searching for Elements by Name

Up to this point, you've used JavaScript to navigate through an XML document by brute force, moving from one element to the next by using properties such as `nextSibling` and `nextChild`. However, you can also access individual elements by searching for them by name.

Here's how that works; in this case, you're looking for the third `<firstName>` and `<lastName>` elements in the sample XML document, so you can get a list of them all:

```
<HTML>
    <HEAD>
        <TITLE>
            Searching for Elements
        </TITLE>

        <SCRIPT LANGUAGE="JavaScript">
            function readXMLData()
            {
                var xmlDocumentObject, firstNameNodes, listNodesLastName

                xmlDocumentObject = new ActiveXObject("Microsoft.XMLDOM")
                xmlDocumentObject.load("ch15_01.xml")

                firstNameNodes = xmlDocumentObject.getElementsByTagName(
                    "firstName")
```

```
            lastNameNodes = xmlDocumentObject.getElementsByTagName(
                "lastName")
    .
    .
    .
```

Node lists like the ones here (`firstNameNodes` and `lastNameNodes`) are indexed by number, starting at 0. This means that the third senator's `<firstName>` element can be accessed with `firstNameNodes(2)`. To get the actual name in the element, you access the text node in the element and then get that text node's value, as shown in Listing 15.4.

LISTING 15.4 Searching for Elements (`ch15_04.html`)

```
<HTML>
    <HEAD>
        <TITLE>
             Searching for Elements
        </TITLE>

        <SCRIPT LANGUAGE="JavaScript">
            function readXMLData()
            {
                var xmlDocumentObject, firstNameNodes, listNodesLastName

                xmlDocumentObject = new ActiveXObject("Microsoft.XMLDOM")
                xmlDocumentObject.load("ch15_01.xml")

                firstNameNodes = xmlDocumentObject.getElementsByTagName(
                    "firstName")
                lastNameNodes = xmlDocumentObject.getElementsByTagName(
                    "lastName")

                outputText = "Last senator's name: " +
                    firstNameNodes(2).firstChild.nodeValue + ' '
                    + lastNameNodes(2).firstChild.nodeValue
                displayDIV.innerHTML=outputText
            }
        </SCRIPT>
    </HEAD>

    <BODY>
        <H1>
             Searching for Elements
        </H1>

        <INPUT TYPE="BUTTON" VALUE="Get the last senator's name"
            ONCLICK="readXMLData()">
        <P>
        <DIV ID="displayDIV"></DIV>
    </BODY>
</HTML>
```

You can see the successful results in Figure 15.2.

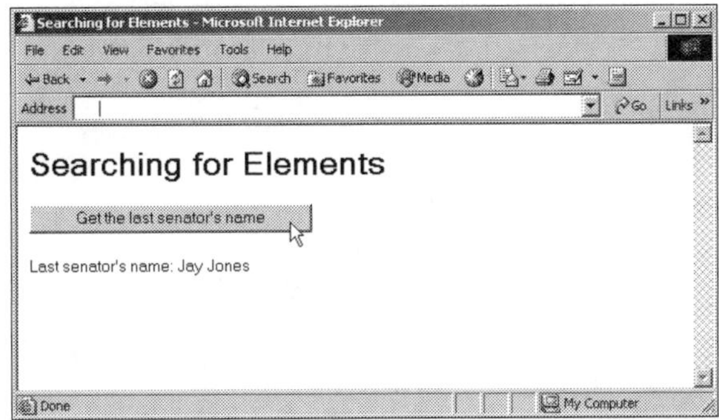

FIGURE 15.2
Accessing data in XML by using Internet Explorer.

Now that you have a handle on elements, let's turn to attributes.

Reading Attribute Values

Next we need to talk about attributes. For example, how can you read the value of the `status` attribute of the third senator in the sample XML document? Here's how:

```
<?xml version="1.0" encoding="UTF-8"?>
<session>
   <committee type="monetary">
       <title>Finance</title>
       <number>17</number>
       <subject>Donut Costs</subject>
       <date>7/15/2005</date>
       <attendees>
           <senator status="present">
               <firstName>Thomas</firstName>
               <lastName>Smith</lastName>
           </senator>
           <senator status="absent">
               <firstName>Frank</firstName>
               <lastName>McCoy</lastName>
           </senator>
           <senator status="present">
               <firstName>Jay</firstName>
               <lastName>Jones</lastName>
           </senator>
       </attendees>
   </committee>
</session>
```

We start by getting a named node map of the attributes of the current element, by using that element's `attributes` property. A map is much like a list, except that you can reference items in a map by name, as you'll soon see. In this case, you want the attributes of the third `<senator>` element, so you get the named node map, which you can call `attributes`, like this:

```
<HTML>
    <HEAD>
        <TITLE>
            Getting attribute values
        </TITLE>

        <SCRIPT LANGUAGE="JavaScript">
            function readXMLData()
            {
                var xmlDocumentObject, sessionNode, committeeNode,
                    attendeesNode
                var firstNameNode, lastNameNode, displayText
                var attributes, statusSenator

                xmlDocumentObject = new ActiveXObject("Microsoft.XMLDOM")
                xmlDocumentObject.load("ch15_01.xml")

                sessionNode = xmlDocumentObject.documentElement
                committeeNode = sessionNode.firstChild
                attendeesNode = committeeNode.lastChild
                senatorNode = attendeesNode.lastChild
                firstNameNode = senatorNode.firstChild
                lastNameNode = firstNameNode.nextSibling

                attributes = senatorNode.attributes
                .
                .
                .
```

Now use the named node map's `getNamedItem` method to search for the value of the `status` attribute (which you can access as `getNamedItem("status")`) and display it, as shown in Listing 15.5.

LISTING 15.5 Reading Attribute Values (`ch15_05.html`)

```
<HTML>
    <HEAD>
        <TITLE>
            Getting attribute values
        </TITLE>
```

LISTING 15.5 continued

```
        <SCRIPT LANGUAGE="JavaScript">
            function readXMLData()
            {
                var xmlDocumentObject, sessionNode, committeeNode,
                    attendeesNode
                var firstNameNode, lastNameNode, displayText
                var attributes, statusSenator

                xmlDocumentObject = new ActiveXObject("Microsoft.XMLDOM")
                xmlDocumentObject.load("ch15_01.xml")

                sessionNode = xmlDocumentObject.documentElement
                committeeNode = sessionNode.firstChild
                attendeesNode = committeeNode.lastChild
                senatorNode = attendeesNode.lastChild
                firstNameNode = senatorNode.firstChild
                lastNameNode = firstNameNode.nextSibling

                attributes = senatorNode. attributes
                statusSenator = attributes.getNamedItem("status")
                outputText = firstNameNode.firstChild.nodeValue
                    + ' ' + lastNameNode.firstChild.nodeValue
                    + "'s status is: " + statusSenator.value
                displayDIV.innerHTML=outputText
            }
        </SCRIPT>
    </HEAD>

    <BODY>
        <H1>
            Getting attribute values
        </H1>

        <INPUT TYPE="BUTTON" VALUE="Get the status of the third senator"
            ONCLICK="readXMLData()">
        <P>
        <DIV ID="displayDIV"></DIV>
    </BODY>
</HTML>
```

Figure 15.3 shows the results, and you can see that the status of the third senator is `present`.

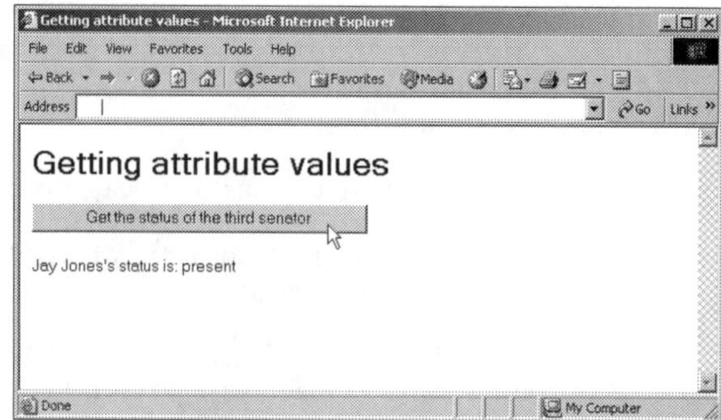

FIGURE 15.3

Reading attribute values.

Getting All XML Data from a Document

So that you can see how to work with all the XML data in an XML document at once, you'll take a look at an example that extracts and displays all the data in the XML sample document by using JavaScript. So far, you've only gone after one element or one attribute, but this example will extract and display all the data in the document. Among other things, this will let you handle general XML documents instead of targeting specific elements. This means you will not have to know the document structure before proceeding, and it will also let you determine node types on-the-fly.

In this example you'll use *recursion*, the technique that allows a method to call itself, to work through an entire document without knowing that document's structure. You'll write a JavaScript method named `childLoop` to do this; when you're at a node, all you will have to do is loop over all of its child nodes by calling `childLoop` on them. All you have to do is pass this method a node and an indentation string, and it will display the current node and all of its children, incrementing the indentation by four spaces for each successive generation to make the display onscreen look good. This means you can start by passing the root node to `childLoop` like this (this method, `readXMLData`, is called when the user clicks a button labeled Get All the Data in this example):

```
<HTML>
    <HEAD>
        <TITLE>
            Getting all XML data
        </TITLE>

        <SCRIPT LANGUAGE="JavaScript">

            function readXMLData()
            {
                xmlDocumentObject = new ActiveXObject("Microsoft.XMLDOM")
                xmlDocumentObject.load("ch15_01.xml")
```

```
                displayDIV.innerHTML = childLoop(xmlDocumentObject, "")
            }
        .
        .
        .
```

Now you need to write the recursive method, `childLoop`. This method has a node and the current indentation (a string of spaces) passed to it, and the first order of business is to discover what kind of node you're dealing with. You can do that by using the node's `nodeType` property, like this:

```
function childLoop(currentNode, indentation)
{
    var typeName

    switch (currentNode.nodeType) {
        case 1:
            typeName = "Element"
            break
        case 2:
            typeName = "Attribute"
            break
        case 3:
            typeName = "Text"
            break
        case 4:
            typeName = "CDATA section"
            break
        case 5:
            typeName = "Entity reference"
            break
        case 6:
            typeName = "Entity"
            break
        case 7:
            typeName = "Processing instruction"
            break
        case 8:
            typeName = "Comment"
            break
        case 9:
            typeName = "Document"
            break
        case 10:
            typeName = "Document type"
            break
        case 11:
            typeName = "Document fragment"
            break
```

```
        case 12:
            typeName = "Notation"
    }
        .
        .
        .
```

Now you know the type of node and have stored the name of the type, such as `"Attribute"` or `"Text"`, in the variable called `typeName`. You can display the type of the current node and its value, if it has a value, like this:

```
var text

if (currentNode.nodeValue != null) {
    text = indentation + "<b>" + typeName +
    "</b>: " + currentNode.nodeValue
} else {
    text = indentation + "<b>" + typeName +
    "</b>: " + currentNode.nodeName
}
```

That takes care of the node and its value, if it has any. If the node is an element, it can also have attributes, so you loop over them like this:

```
if (currentNode.attributes != null) {
    if (currentNode.attributes.length > 0) {
        for (var loopIndex = 0; loopIndex <
            currentNode.attributes.length; loopIndex++) {
            .
            .
            .
        }
    }
}
```

You can display each attribute and its value like this:

```
if (currentNode.attributes != null) {
    if (currentNode.attributes.length > 0) {
        for (var loopIndex = 0; loopIndex <
            currentNode.attributes.length; loopIndex++) {
            text += " <b>Attribute</b>: " +
                currentNode.attributes(loopIndex).nodeName +
                " = \"" +
                currentNode.attributes(loopIndex).nodeValue
                + "\""
        }
    }
}
```

You have completed the display of the current node. Now add a line break and check whether the current node has any children:

```
    text += "<BR>"

    if (currentNode.childNodes.length > 0) {
        .
        .
        .
    }
    return text
}
```

If the current node has any child nodes, you can loop over those child nodes by calling the `childLoop` method recursively, like this:

```
    text += "<BR>"

    if (currentNode.childNodes.length > 0) {
        for (var loopIndex = 0; loopIndex <
            currentNode.childNodes.length; loopIndex++) {
            text += childLoop(currentNode.childNodes(loopIndex),
            indentation + "    ")
        }
    }
    return text
}
```

Note that here you're increasing the indentation by four spaces by using the HTML non-breaking space entity, ` `. Otherwise, the browser would normalize multiple indentation spaces into a single space.

At the end of the `childLoop` method, the code returns the full HTML text to be displayed. The JavaScript in the `readXMLData` method, which is called when the button in this example is clicked, displays that text in the Web page by using a `<DIV>` element:

```
function readXMLData()
{
    xmlDocumentObject = new ActiveXObject("Microsoft.XMLDOM")
    xmlDocumentObject.load("ch15_01.xml")

    displayDIV.innerHTML = childLoop(xmlDocumentObject, "")
}
```

Listing 15.6 shows all the code for this example, as `ch15_06.html`. Note that you've added the code to display the button that the user can click, which calls the `readXMLData` method.

LISTING 15.6 Getting All XML Data from a Document (`ch15_06.html`)

```
<HTML>
    <HEAD>
        <TITLE>
            Getting all XML data
        </TITLE>

        <SCRIPT LANGUAGE="JavaScript">

            function readXMLData()
            {
                xmlDocumentObject = new ActiveXObject("Microsoft.XMLDOM")
                xmlDocumentObject.load("ch15_01.xml")

                displayDIV.innerHTML = childLoop(xmlDocumentObject, "")
            }

            function childLoop(currentNode, indentation)
            {
                var typeName

                switch (currentNode.nodeType)  {
                    case 1:
                        typeName = "Element"
                        break
                    case 2:
                        typeName = "Attribute"
                        break
                    case 3:
                        typeName = "Text"
                        break
                    case 4:
                        typeName = "CDATA section"
                        break
                    case 5:
                        typeName = "Entity reference"
                        break
                    case 6:
                        typeName = "Entity"
                        break
                    case 7:
                        typeName = "Processing instruction"
                        break
                    case 8:
                        typeName = "Comment"
                        break
                    case 9:
                        typeName = "Document"
                        break
```

15

LISTING 15.6 continued

```
                case 10:
                    typeName = "Document type"
                    break
                case 11:
                    typeName = "Document fragment"
                    break
                case 12:
                    typeName = "Notation"
            }
            var text

            if (currentNode.nodeValue != null) {
                text = indentation + "<b>" + typeName +
                "</b>: " + currentNode.nodeValue
            } else {
                text = indentation + "<b>" + typeName +
                "</b>: " + currentNode.nodeName
            }

            if (currentNode.attributes != null) {
                if (currentNode.attributes.length > 0) {
                    for (var loopIndex = 0; loopIndex <
                        currentNode.attributes.length; loopIndex++) {
                        text += " <b>Attribute</b>: " +
                            currentNode.attributes(loopIndex).nodeName +
                            " = \"" +
                            currentNode.attributes(loopIndex).nodeValue
                            + "\""
                    }
                }
            }

            text += "<BR>"

            if (currentNode.childNodes.length > 0)  {
                for (var loopIndex = 0; loopIndex <
                    currentNode.childNodes.length; loopIndex++) {
                    text += childLoop(currentNode.childNodes(loopIndex),
                    indentation + "    ")
                }
            }
            return text
        }

    </SCRIPT>
</HEAD>
```

LISTING 15.6 continued

```
    <BODY>
        <H1>
            Getting all XML data
        </H1>

        <INPUT TYPE="BUTTON" VALUE="Get all the data"
            onClick = "readXMLData()">
        <DIV ID="displayDIV"></DIV>
    </BODY>
</HTML>
```

You can see the results of this JavaScript in Figure 15.4. As you can see, by using JavaScript and the W3C DOM, you've been able to parse an entire XML document and list all of its data independently of the document's structure. Not bad!

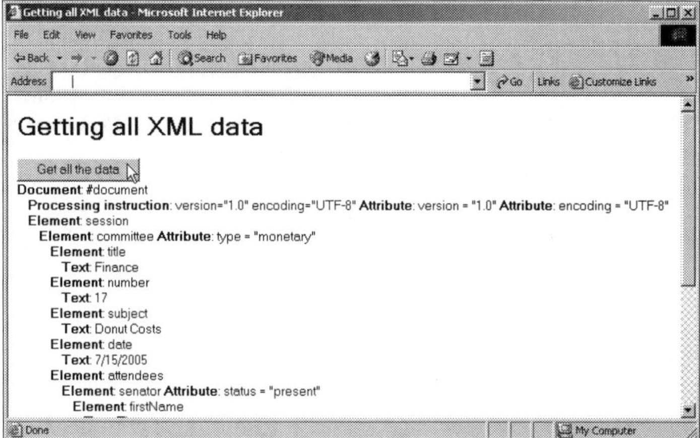

FIGURE 15.4
Parsing an entire XML document.

Validating XML Documents by Using DTDs

On Day 6, "Creating Valid XML Documents: XML Schemas," you saw how to use JavaScript to validate XML documents with XML schemas. Today, you'll see how to validate XML documents with DTDs by using JavaScript. By default, Internet Explorer validates documents by using DTDs. (You can turn validation off if you set the `validateOnParse` property of a document to `false`; it's set to `true` by default). However, you won't know how the validation went unless you check the `parseError` object.

Let's take a look at an example. In this case, you start by giving today's sample XML document, `ch15_01.xml`, a DTD, as shown in Listing 15.7.

LISTING 15.7 Adding a DTD to the XML Sample (`ch15_07.xml`)

```
<?xml version="1.0" encoding="UTF-8"?>
<!DOCTYPE session [
<!ELEMENT session (committee)*>
<!ELEMENT committee (title, number, subject, date, attendees)>
<!ELEMENT title (#PCDATA)>
<!ELEMENT number (#PCDATA)>
<!ELEMENT subject (#PCDATA)>
<!ELEMENT date (#PCDATA)>
<!ELEMENT attendees (senator)*>
<!ELEMENT senator (firstName, lastName)>
<!ELEMENT firstName (#PCDATA)>
<!ELEMENT lastName (#PCDATA)>
<!ATTLIST committee
    type CDATA #REQUIRED>
<!ATTLIST senator
    status CDATA #REQUIRED>
]>
<session>
   <committee type="monetary">
       <title>Finance</title>
       <number>17</number>
       <subject>Donut Costs</subject>
       <date>7/15/2005</date>
       <attendees>
           <senator status="present">
               <firstName>Thomas</firstName>
               <lastName>Smith</lastName>
           </senator>
           <senator status="absent">
               <firstName>Frank</firstName>
               <lastName>McCoy</lastName>
           </senator>
           <senator status="present">
               <firstName>Jay</firstName>
               <lastName>Jones</lastName>
           </senator>
       </attendees>
   </committee>
</session>
```

Now you need to write the code that checks the `parseError` object to see whether there were any validation errors. You can do that by using the `parseError` object's `errorCode`, `url`, `line`, `linepos`, `errorString`, and `reason` properties and displaying the error if there was an error.

First, to be informed of the document's status as validation occurs, you can assign the name of a new method, `changeHandler`, to the document's `onreadystatechange` event:

```
xmlDocumentObject.onreadystatechange = changeHandler
```

Now you need to write the `changeHandler` method. When the document is loaded, you check the `parseError` object's `errorCode` property. If it is nonzero, you know there has been an error, and you can display it this way in the `changeHandler` method:

```
function changeHandler()
{
    if(xmlDocumentObject.readyState == 4){
        var errorText = xmlDocumentObject.parseError.srcText
        errorText = xmlDocumentObject.parseError.srcText.replace(/\</g, "&lt;" )
        errorText = errorText.replace(/\>/g, "&gt;")
        if (xmlDocumentObject.parseError.errorCode != 0) {
            displayDIV.innerHTML = "Error in " +
            xmlDocumentObject.parseError.url +
            " line " + xmlDocumentObject.parseError.line +
            " position " + xmlDocumentObject.parseError.linepos +
            ":<BR>Source: " + errorText +
            "<BR>" + xmlDocumentObject.parseError.reason +
            "<BR>" +  "Error: " +
            xmlDocumentObject.parseError.errorCode
        }
        else {
            displayDIV.innerHTML = "Document validated OK.<BR>"
        }
    }
}
```

Listing 15.8 shows the full code.

LISTING 15.8 Validating an XML Document by Using a DTD (`ch15_08.html`)

```
<HTML>
    <HEAD>
        <TITLE>
            Validation With DTDs
        </TITLE>

        <SCRIPT LANGUAGE="JavaScript">
            var xmlDocumentObject

            function validateDocument()
            {
                xmlDocumentObject = new ActiveXObject("microsoft.XMLDOM")
```

Listing 15.8 continued

```
                xmlDocumentObject.onreadystatechange = changeHandler

                xmlDocumentObject.load('ch15_07.xml')
            }

            function changeHandler()
            {
                if(xmlDocumentObject.readyState == 4){
                    var errorText = xmlDocumentObject.parseError.srcText
                    errorText =
                    xmlDocumentObject.parseError.srcText.replace(/\</g, "&lt;")
                    errorText = errorText.replace(/\>/g, "&gt;")
                    if (xmlDocumentObject.parseError.errorCode != 0) {
                        displayDIV.innerHTML = "Error in " +
                        xmlDocumentObject.parseError.url +
                        " line " + xmlDocumentObject.parseError.line +
                        " position " + xmlDocumentObject.parseError.linepos +
                        ":<BR>Source: " + errorText +
                        "<BR>" + xmlDocumentObject.parseError.reason +
                        "<BR>" +  "Error: " +
                        xmlDocumentObject.parseError.errorCode
                    }
                    else {
                        displayDIV.innerHTML = "Document validated OK.<BR>"
                    }
                }
            }
        </SCRIPT>
    </HEAD>

    <BODY>
        <H1>
            Validation With DTDs
        </H1>

        <INPUT TYPE="BUTTON" VALUE="Validate document"
            ONCLICK="validateDocument()">

        <BR>
        <BR>

        <DIV ID="displayDIV"></DIV>
    </BODY>
</HTML>
```

The document with the DTD, `ch15_07.xml`, validates, as shown in Figure 15.5.

FIGURE 15.5

Validating an XML document by using a DTD.

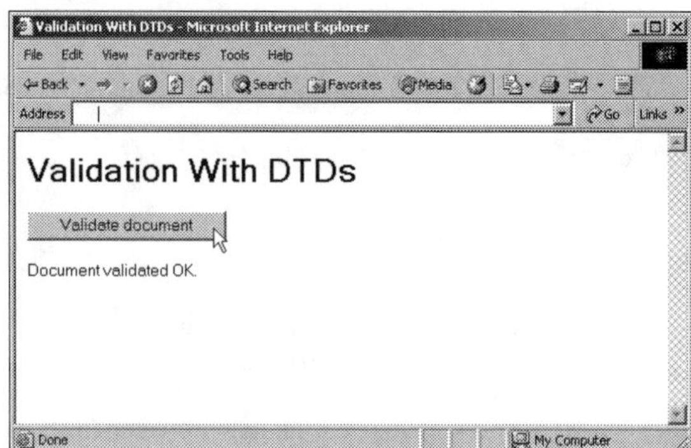

What if there were an error in the DTD? Say that we had omitted the `<attendees>` element from the declaration of the `<committee>` element, like this:

```
<?xml version="1.0" encoding="UTF-8"?>
<!DOCTYPE session [
<!ELEMENT session (committee)*>
<!ELEMENT committee (title, number, subject, date)>
        .
        .
        .
```

Figure 15.6 shows how this error is reported when the document is validated.

FIGURE 15.6

Catching a validation error by using a DTD.

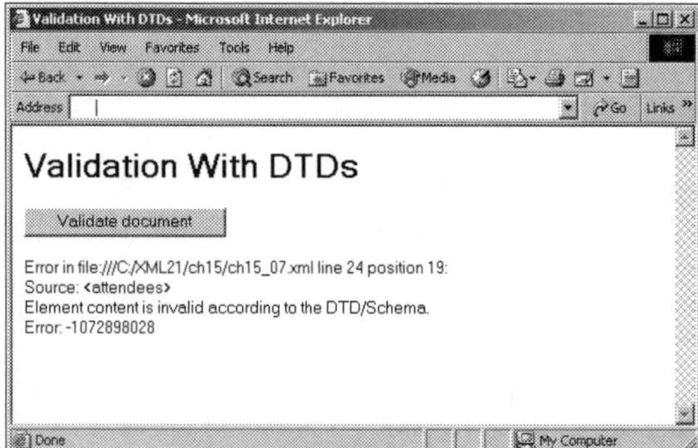

Summary

Today you took at how to use JavaScript with XML. You saw that we can use JavaScript with the W3C DOM, and you saw that various levels of the DOM are available.

The DOM provides a way of treating XML documents as trees of nodes. There are various DOM objects that correspond to the different types of nodes, as well as collections of nodes in lists and named node maps.

After you've loaded an XML document, you can use properties such as `nextChild` and `previousSibling` to navigate through the document's structure. You've seen that you can use these kinds of properties to navigate to a particular node and use the `nodeValue` property to get the value of that node. You can also navigate through a document recursively, as you've done today, which means you don't have to know the document's structure before navigating through it.

Today you also saw how to use JavaScript to find the results of validating an XML document by using a DTD. You saw that you just have to use the various properties of the `parseError` object to learn how a DTD validation went.

Tomorrow we'll talk about how to work with XML and Java.

Q&A

Q Is there a way to monitor the process of loading an XML document in a browser?

A Yes, but only in Internet Explorer. You can use the document object's `ondataavailable` event to watch as data is loaded. In that event's handler, you can use the document object's `readyState` property to check how the loading process is going:

```
xmlDocumentObject = new ActiveXObject("microsoft.XMLDOM")

xmlDocumentObject.ondataavailable = loadingHandler

function loadingHandler()
{
    switch (xmlDocumentObject.readyState)
        case 1:
            displayDIV.innerHTML += "The data is uninitialized.<BR>"
        case 2:
            displayDIV.innerHTML += "The data is loading.<BR>"
        case 3:
            displayDIV.innerHTML += "The data is loaded.<BR>"
        case 4:
            displayDIV.innerHTML += "The data loading process is complete.
            <BR>"
    }
}
```

Q Can I use JavaScript to actually modify the structure of an XML document?

A Yes—in Internet Explorer. The document object supports methods such as `createTextNode` and `createElement` that let you modify an XML document. The new version of the document, however, exists only in the document object. If you want to display the new XML, you can get access to the XML text itself by using a document object's `xml` property, like this:

```
XMLdocumentObject.documentElement.xml
```

What if you want to save the modified XML as a new document? The document object supports a `save` method, but you have to change the security settings of the browser in order to use it. Your best bet is to place the new XML in a hidden HTML field and send it to a server-side script (written in ASP, JSP, Perl, or another language) that reads the text and sends it back as a new XML document.

Workshop

This workshop tests whether you understand the concepts discussed today. It's a good idea to make sure you can answer these questions before pressing on to tomorrow's work. Answers to the quiz can be found in Appendix A, "Quiz Answers."

Quiz

1. What are two ways that you can create a document object from an XML file by using JavaScript in Internet Explorer?
2. What DOM method can you use to move to the next child node?
3. How do you get a node's value by using JavaScript?
4. How can you get a list of all the `<senator>` elements in a document?
5. How can you get a named node map of an element's attributes?

Exercises

1. Create an XML document that lists the names of five of your friends. Use JavaScript to read and display the fourth friend's name.
2. Add a DTD to the XML document you created in Exercise 1 and use Internet Explorer, if you have it, to validate the XML document.

PART IV

DAY 16

Using Java and .NET: DOM

Today, you're going to use Java to work with XML. Yesterday you saw how to work with XML and JavaScript, and today you're going to take the next step and create standalone programs using Java. Today you'll use the built-in Java support for the W3C DOM methods described yesterday. Here's an overview of today's topics:

- Loading XML documents into a Java application
- Parsing XML documents by using Java
- Searching a document for a particular element
- Navigating through an XML document by using Java
- Creating graphical XML browsers by using Java
- Modifying the XML in a document by using Java

Note that we must use Java version 1.4 or later if you want to take advantage of Java's integrated XML support for the W3C DOM, and you'll be using Java 1.4

today. There's all kinds of XML support built into Java 1.4 (with earlier versions, you have to use third-party packages), and you're going to jump right in by seeing how to read in an XML document and extract all the data from it.

TIP

> You'll be using Java 1.4 (or later) today, and I assume that we know how to use Java. To download the latest version of Java, go to `http://java.sun.com/j2se/`. You can find online documentation for Java at `http://developer.java.sun.com/developer/infodocs/`. And you can find more about Java's support for XML at `http://java.sun.com/xml/docs.html`. You can find Java tutorials at `http://developer.java.sun.com/developer/onlineTraining/`.

Using Java to Read XML Data

You're going to create a Java application to read in and extract all the data from the XML document you worked with yesterday, which you can see in Listing 16.1.

LISTING 16.1 A Sample XML Document for Today's Work (`ch16_01.xml`)

```
<?xml version="1.0" encoding="UTF-8"?>
<session>
   <committee type="monetary">
       <title>Finance</title>
       <number>17</number>
       <subject>Donut Costs</subject>
       <date>7/15/2005</date>
       <attendees>
           <senator status="present">
               <firstName>Thomas</firstName>
               <lastName>Smith</lastName>
           </senator>
           <senator status="absent">
               <firstName>Frank</firstName>
               <lastName>McCoy</lastName>
           </senator>
           <senator status="present">
               <firstName>Jay</firstName>
               <lastName>Jones</lastName>
           </senator>
       </attendees>
   </committee>
</session>
```

The Java application you'll create will show how to read in the entire XML document and display it, much as we did in JavaScript yesterday. You start by creating a `DocumentBuilderFactory` object, which you'll use to create a `DocumentBuilder` object, and that object will actually read in the XML document. Here's how to use `DocumentBuilderFactory` in the new application's `main` method, which is called when the application starts:

16

```
import javax.xml.parsers.*;
import org.w3c.dom.*;

public class ch16_02
{
    public static void main(String args[])
    {
        try {
            DocumentBuilderFactory factory =
                DocumentBuilderFactory.newInstance();
            .
            .
            .
    }
```

Table 16.1 lists the methods for the `DocumentBuilderFactory` class.

TABLE 16.1 Methods of the `javax.xml.parsers.DocumentBuilderFactory` Class

Method	*What It Does*
`protected DocumentBuilderFactory()`	Acts as the default `DocumentBuilderFactory` constructor.
`abstract Object getAttribute(String name)`	Returns attribute values.
`boolean isCoalescing()`	Returns `True` if the factory is configured to produce parsers that convert `CDATA` nodes to text nodes.
`boolean isExpandEntityReferences()`	Returns `True` if the factory is configured to produce parsers that expand XML entity reference nodes.
`boolean isIgnoringComments()`	Returns `True` if the factory is configured to produce parsers that ignore comments.
`boolean isIgnoringElementContentWhitespace()`	Returns `True` if the factory is configured to produce parsers that ignore ignorable whitespace (such as that used to indent elements) in element content.

TABLE 16.1 continued

Method	*What It Does*
`boolean isNamespaceAware()`	Returns `True` if the factory is configured to produce parsers that can use XML namespaces.
`boolean isValidating()`	Returns `True` if the factory is configured to produce parsers that validate the XML content during parsing operations.
`abstract DocumentBuilder newDocumentBuilder()`	Returns a new `DocumentBuilder` object.
`static DocumentBuilderFactory newInstance()`	Returns a new `DocumentBuilderFactory` object.
`abstract void setAttribute-(String name, Object value)`	Sets attribute values.
`void setCoalescing(boolean coalescing)`	Specifies that the parser produced will convert `CDATA` nodes to text nodes.
`void setExpandEntityReferences-(boolean expandEntityRef)`	Specifies that the parser produced will expand XML entity reference nodes.
`void setIgnoringComments-(boolean ignoreComments)`	Specifies that the parser produced will ignore comments.
`void setIgnoringElementContentWhitespace-(boolean whitespace)`	Specifies that the parser produced must eliminate ignorable whitespace.
`void setNamespaceAware(boolean awareness)`	Specifies that the parser produced will provide support for XML namespaces.
`void setValidating(boolean validating)`	Specifies that the parser produced will validate documents as they are parsed.

To actually parse the XML document and extract data from it, we need a `DocumentBuilder` object, which is created by the `DocumentBuilderFactory` object. Here's what that looks like in code:

```
public class ch16_02
{
    public static void main(String args[])
    {
        try {
            DocumentBuilderFactory factory =
                DocumentBuilderFactory.newInstance();

            DocumentBuilder builder = null;
```

```
            try {
                builder = factory.newDocumentBuilder();
            }
            catch (ParserConfigurationException e) {}
        .
        .
        .
    }
```

Table 16.2 lists the methods of the `DocumentBuilder` class.

TABLE 16.2 Methods of the `javax.xml.parsers.DocumentBuilder` Class

Method	*What It Does*
`protected DocumentBuilder()`	Acts as the default `DocumentBuilder` constructor.
`abstract boolean isNamespaceAware()`	Returns `True` if this parser is configured to understand namespaces.
`abstract boolean isValidating()`	Returns `True` if this parser is configured to validate XML documents.
`abstract Document newDocument()`	Returns a new instance of a DOM `Document` object to build a DOM tree with.
`Document parse(File f)`	Indicates to parse the content of the file as an XML document and return a new DOM `Document` object.
`Document parse(InputStream is)`	Indicates to parse the content of a given `InputStream` object as an XML document and return a new DOM `Document` object.
`Document parse(InputStream is, String systemId)`	Indicates to parse the content of an `InputStream` object as an XML document and return a new DOM `Document` object.
`Document parse(String uri)`	Indicates to parse the content of a URI as an XML document and return a new DOM `Document` object.
`abstract void setErrorHandler(ErrorHandler eh)`	Sets the `ErrorHandler` object to be used to report errors.

When the user starts the Java application `ch16_02.class`, he or she will type the name of the XML document to read, as we do in the following example, where we want to read and display the data in `ch16_01.xml`:

```
%java ch16_02 ch16_01.xml
```

You can access the name of the XML document the user wants to read as `args[0]`. Here's how to create a Java `Document` object that corresponds to the XML document, using the `DocumentBuilder` object:

```
import javax.xml.parsers.*;
import org.w3c.dom.*;

public class ch16_02
{
    public static void main(String args[])
    {
        try {
            DocumentBuilderFactory factory =
                DocumentBuilderFactory.newInstance();

            DocumentBuilder builder = null;
            try {
                builder = factory.newDocumentBuilder();
            }
            catch (ParserConfigurationException e) {}

            Document document = null;
            document = builder.parse(args[0]);
        .
        .
        .
    }
```

At this point, then, we have a Java `Document` object (actually an `org.w3c.dom.Document` object) that corresponds to the XML document, and we can use the various methods of that object to work with the XML document. Table 16.3 lists the methods of `Document` objects.

TABLE 16.3 Methods of the `org.w3c.dom.Document` Interface

Method	*What It Does*
`Attr createAttribute(String name)`	Returns a new attribute object.
`Attr createAttributeNS-(String namespaceURI, String qualifiedName)`	Returns a new attribute that has the given name and namespace.
`CDATASection createCDATASection(String data)`	Returns a new `CDATASection` node whose value is the given string.

TABLE 16.3 continued

Method	*What It Does*
`Comment createComment(String data)`	Returns a new `Comment` node created using the given string.
`DocumentFragment createDocumentFragment()`	Returns a new empty `DocumentFragment` object.
`Element createElement(String tagName)`	Returns a new element of the type given.
`Element createElementNS-(String namespaceURI, String qualifiedName)`	Returns a new element of the given qualified name and namespace URI.
`ProcessingInstruction createProcessingInstruction-(String target, String data)`	Returns a new `ProcessingInstruction` node.
`Text createTextNode(String data)`	Returns a new text node, given the specified string.
`DocumentType getDoctype()`	Returns the DTD for this document.
`Element getDocumentElement()`	Gives direct access to document element.
`Element getElementById(String elementId)`	Returns an element whose ID is given.
`NodeList getElementsByTagName(String tagname)`	Returns all elements with a given tag name.
`NodeList getElementsByTagNameNS-(String namespaceURI, String localName)`	Returns all elements with a given name and namespace.
`Node importNode(Node importedNode, boolean deep)`	Imports a node from another document.

The next step is to work through the XML document recursively, as you did with JavaScript yesterday. You'll do that in a method named `childLoop` that you can call recursively. Just as you did with JavaScript, you'll also pass an indentation string to this method, which will be increased for each successive generation of a node's children. This method will fill an array of strings, `displayText`, with the XML data from the document and store the total number of strings in the array in a variable named `numberLines`. When `childLoop` is done filling the array of strings, you'll display them, like this:

```
import javax.xml.parsers.*;
import org.w3c.dom.*;

public class ch16_02
{
```

```
    static String displayText[] = new String[1000];
    static int numberLines = 0;

    public static void main(String args[])
    {
        try {
            DocumentBuilderFactory factory =
                DocumentBuilderFactory.newInstance();

            DocumentBuilder builder = null;
            try {
                builder = factory.newDocumentBuilder();
            }
            catch (ParserConfigurationException e) {}

            Document document = null;
            document = builder.parse(args[0]);

            childLoop(document, "");

        } catch (Exception e) {
            e.printStackTrace(System.err);
        }

        for(int loopIndex = 0; loopIndex < numberLines; loopIndex++){
            System.out.println(displayText[loopIndex]);
        }
    }
```

The next order of business is to write `childLoop`, the method that will loop over all nodes in the XML document and store their data in the `displayText` array.

Looping Over Nodes

As in JavaScript, you're using the W3C DOM in Java today, so you're treating our XML document as a tree of nodes. Table 16.4 lists the fields of Java `org.w3c.dom.Node` objects, and Table 16.5 lists the methods of Java `org.w3c.dom.Node` objects.

TABLE 16.4 The Fields of the `org.w3c.dom.Node` Object

Field Summary	*Stands For*
`static short ATTRIBUTE_NODE`	An attribute
`static short CDATA_SECTION_NODE`	A CDATA section
`static short COMMENT_NODE`	A comment
`static short DOCUMENT_FRAGMENT_NODE`	A document fragment
`static short DOCUMENT_NODE`	A document
`static short DOCUMENT_TYPE_NODE`	A DTD

TABLE 16.4 continued

Field Summary	*Stands For*
`static short ELEMENT_NODE`	An element
`static short ENTITY_NODE`	An entity
`static short ENTITY_REFERENCE_NODE`	An entity reference
`static short NOTATION_NODE`	A notation
`static short PROCESSING_INSTRUCTION_NODE`	A processing instruction
`static short TEXT_NODE`	A text node

TABLE 16.5 Methods of the `org.w3c.dom.Node` Interface

Method	*What It Does*
`Node appendChild(Node newChild)`	Appends the given node to the end of the children of the current node.
`NamedNodeMap getAttributes()`	Returns the attributes of an element node.
`NodeList getChildNodes()`	Gets the children of this node.
`Node getFirstChild()`	Gets the first child of this node.
`Node getLastChild()`	Gets the last child of this node.
`String getLocalName()`	Gets the local part of the full name of this node.
`String getNamespaceURI()`	Gets the namespace URI of this node.
`Node getNextSibling()`	Gets the node following this node.
`String getNodeName()`	Gets the name of this node.
`short getNodeType()`	Gets the type of this node .
`String getNodeValue()`	Gets the value of this node.
`Document getOwnerDocument()`	Gets the `Document` object for this node.
`Node getParentNode()`	Gets the parent of this node.
`String getPrefix()`	Gets the namespace prefix of this node.
`Node getPreviousSibling()`	Gets the node preceding the current node.
`boolean hasAttributes()`	Returns `True` if this node has any attributes.
`boolean hasChildNodes()`	Returns `True` if this node has any children.
`Node insertBefore(Node newChild, Node refChild)`	Inserts the new node before a reference child node.

TABLE 16.5 continued

Method	*What It Does*
`void normalize()`	Transforms all text nodes into XML normalized form.
`Node removeChild(Node oldChild)`	Removes a child node and returns it.
`Node replaceChild(Node newChild, Node oldChild)`	Replaces the child node.
`void setNodeValue(String nodeValue)`	Sets the node's value.
`void setPrefix(String prefix)`	Sets the namespace prefix of the node.

The `childLoop` method has a node and an indentation string passed to it. To handle the current node and store its data in the `displayText` array, first check whether the current node is valid, and if it is, get its type by using the `getNodeType` method:

```
public static void childLoop(Node node, String indentation)
{
    if (node == null) {
        return;
    }

    int type = node.getNodeType();
        .
        .
        .
}
```

Now that you know the type of the node you've been passed, how do you handle it and store its data in the array of strings that will be printed out? You have to handle different types of nodes in different ways, and in this case, you'll use a Java `switch` statement to work with different node types, starting with the document node itself.

Handling Document Nodes

You can compare the type of the current node to the fields listed in Table 16.4 to determine what kind of node you're dealing with. For example, if the current node is a document node, you'll just put a generic XML declaration into the display string's array, storing that text in the `displayText` array and incrementing the array's index value, `numberLines`, like this:

```
public static void childLoop(Node node, String indentation)
{
    if (node == null) {
        return;
    }

    int type = node.getNodeType();
```

```
    switch (type) {
        case Node.DOCUMENT_NODE: {
            displayText[numberLines] = indentation;
            displayText[numberLines] += "<?xml version=\"1.0\" encoding=\""+
              "UTF-8" + "\"?>";
            numberLines++;
            childLoop(((Document)node).getDocumentElement(), "");
            break;
        }
        .
        .
        .
```


Now you've displayed a generic XML declaration for the start of the XML document. Next, you'll handle elements.

Handling Elements

Elements have the type `Node.ELEMENT_NODE`, and you can get the name of the element by using the W3C DOM method `getNodeName`. Here's what it looks like in the `childLoop` method's `switch` statement, which lets you handle the various node types:

```
case Node.ELEMENT_NODE: {
    displayText[numberLines] = indentation;
    displayText[numberLines] += "<";
    displayText[numberLines] += node.getNodeName();
        .
        .
        .
```

This gives us the name of the current element, but what if it has attributes? You'll check that next.

Handling Attributes

To see whether the element you're working on has any attributes, you can use the `getAttributes` method, which returns `NamedNodeMap` object, which contains the element's attributes. If there are any attributes, you'll store them in an array and then use the `getNodeName` method to get the attribute's name, and you'll use the `getNodeValue` method to get the attribute's value:

```
int length = (node.getAttributes() != null) ?
    node.getAttributes().getLength() : 0;
Attr attributes[] = new Attr[length];
for (int loopIndex = 0; loopIndex < length; loopIndex++) {
    attributes[loopIndex] = (Attr)node.getAttributes().item(loopIndex);
}
```

```
for (int loopIndex = 0; loopIndex < attributes.length; loopIndex++) {
    Attr attribute = attributes[loopIndex];
    displayText[numberLines] += " ";
    displayText[numberLines] += attribute.getNodeName();
    displayText[numberLines] += "=\"";
    displayText[numberLines] += attribute.getNodeValue();
    displayText[numberLines] += "\"";
}
displayText[numberLines] += ">";

numberLines++;
```

Table 16.6 lists the methods of `NamedNodeMap`.

TABLE 16.6 `NamedNodeMap` Methods

Method	*What It Does*
`int getLength()`	Returns the number of nodes.
`Node getNamedItem(java.lang.String name)`	Gets a node specified by the name.
`Node getNamedItemNS(java.lang.String namespaceURI, java.lang.String localName)`	Gets a node specified by the local name and namespace URI.
`Node item(int index)`	Gets an item in the map by index.
`Node removeNamedItem(java.lang.String name)`	Removes a node.
`Node removeNamedItemNS(java.lang.String namespaceURI, java.lang.String localName)`	Removes the given node with a local name and namespace URI.

Table 16.7 lists the methods of `Attr` objects, which hold attributes.

TABLE 16.7 `Attr` *Interface* Methods

Method	*What It Does*
`java.lang.String getName()`	Gets the name of this attribute.
`Element getOwnerElement()`	Gets this attribute's element node.
`boolean getGiven()`	Returns `True` if this attribute was given a value in the original document.
`java.lang.String getValue()`	Gets the value of the attribute.
`void setValue(String value)`	Sets the value of the attribute.

Now you've handled the current element's name and attributes. But what if the element has child nodes, such as text nodes or child elements? That's coming up next.

Handling Child Nodes

Elements can have child nodes, so before you finish up with elements, you'll also loop over those child nodes by calling the `childLoop` again recursively. You can use the following to get a `NodeList` interface of child nodes by using the `getChildNodes` method, increase the indentation level by four spaces, and call `childLoop` for each child node:

```
    NodeList childNodes = node.getChildNodes();
    if (childNodes != null) {
        length = childNodes.getLength();
        indentation += "    ";
        for (int loopIndex = 0; loopIndex < length; loopIndex++ ) {
           childLoop(childNodes.item(loopIndex), indentation);
        }
    }
    break;
}
```

The `NodeList` interface supports an ordered collection of nodes. Table 26.8 lists the methods of the `NodeList` interface.

TABLE 16.8 `NodeList` Methods

Method	*What It Does*
`int getLength()`	Returns the number of nodes.
`Node item(int index)`	Gets the item at a specified index.

Now that you have handled elements, attributes, and child nodes, you'll take a look at how to work with text nodes.

Handling Text Nodes

Text nodes are of type `Node.TEXT_NODE`, and after you check to make sure a node is a valid text node, you can trim extra spaces (such as indentation text) from the text node's value and add it to the `displayText` array, like this:

```
case Node.TEXT_NODE: {
    displayText[numberLines] = indentation;
    String trimmedText = node.getNodeValue().trim();
    if(trimmedText.indexOf("\n") < 0 && trimmedText.length() > 0) {
        displayText[numberLines] += trimmedText;
        numberLines++;
    }
    break;
}
```

Handling Processing Instructions

Handling processing instructions is not difficult; you just use `getNodeName` to get the processing instruction and the `getNodeValue` method to get the processing instruction's data. Here's how that works in the `childLoop` method's `switch` statement:

```
case Node.PROCESSING_INSTRUCTION_NODE: {
    displayText[numberLines] = indentation;
    displayText[numberLines] += "<?";
    displayText[numberLines] += node.getNodeName();
    String text = node.getNodeValue();
    if (text != null && text.length() > 0) {
        displayText[numberLines] += text;
    }
    displayText[numberLines] += "?>";
    numberLines++;
    break;
}
```

Handling CDATA Sections

Handling CDATA sections is just as easy as handling other nodes: You just use the `getNodeValue` method to get the CDATA section's data. Here's what that looks like in the `childLoop` method's `switch` statement:

```
case Node.CDATA_SECTION_NODE: {
    displayText[numberLines] = indentation;
    displayText[numberLines] += "<![CDATA[";
    displayText[numberLines] += node.getNodeValue();
    displayText[numberLines] += "]]>";
    numberLines++;
    break;
        }
    }
```

Ending Elements

Our last task is to add a closing tag for element nodes. Up to this point, you've only displayed an opening tag for each element and its attributes, but no closing tag. Here's how to add the closing tag with some code at the end of the `childLoop` method:

```
    if (type == Node.ELEMENT_NODE) {
        displayText[numberLines] = indentation.substring(0,
            indentation.length() - 4);
        displayText[numberLines] += "</";
        displayText[numberLines] += node.getNodeName();
        displayText[numberLines] += ">";
        numberLines++;
        indentation += "    ";
    }
}
```

That's it; Listing 16.2 shows all the code in ch16_02.java.

LISTING 16.2 Parsing XML Documents by Using Java (ch16_02.java)

```
import javax.xml.parsers.*;
import org.w3c.dom.*;

public class ch16_02
{
    static String displayText[] = new String[1000];
    static int numberLines = 0;

    public static void main(String args[])
    {
        try {
            DocumentBuilderFactory factory =
                DocumentBuilderFactory.newInstance();

            DocumentBuilder builder = null;
            try {
                builder = factory.newDocumentBuilder();
            }
            catch (ParserConfigurationException e) {}

            Document document = null;
            document = builder.parse(args[0]);

            childLoop(document, "");

        } catch (Exception e) {
            e.printStackTrace(System.err);
        }

        for(int loopIndex = 0; loopIndex < numberLines; loopIndex++){
            System.out.println(displayText[loopIndex]) ;
        }
    }

    public static void childLoop(Node node, String indentation)
    {
        if (node == null) {
            return;
        }

        int type = node.getNodeType();

        switch (type) {
            case Node.DOCUMENT_NODE: {
```

LISTING 16.2 continued

```
        displayText[numberLines] = indentation;
        displayText[numberLines] +=
            "<?xml version=\"1.0\" encoding=\""+
          "UTF-8" + "\"?>";
        numberLines++;
        childLoop(((Document)node).getDocumentElement(), "");
        break;
    }

    case Node.ELEMENT_NODE: {
        displayText[numberLines] = indentation;
        displayText[numberLines] += "<";
        displayText[numberLines] += node.getNodeName();

        int length = (node.getAttributes() != null) ?
            node.getAttributes().getLength() : 0;
        Attr attributes[] = new Attr[length];
        for (int loopIndex = 0; loopIndex < length; loopIndex++) {
            attributes[loopIndex] =
                (Attr)node.getAttributes().item(loopIndex);
        }

        for (int loopIndex = 0; loopIndex < attributes.length;
            loopIndex++) {
            Attr attribute = attributes[loopIndex];
            displayText[numberLines] += " ";
            displayText[numberLines] += attribute.getNodeName();
            displayText[numberLines] += "=\"";
            displayText[numberLines] += attribute.getNodeValue();
            displayText[numberLines] += "\"";
        }
        displayText[numberLines] += ">";

        numberLines++;

        NodeList childNodes = node.getChildNodes();
        if (childNodes != null) {
            length = childNodes.getLength();
            indentation += "    ";
            for (int loopIndex = 0; loopIndex < length; loopIndex++ ) {
               childLoop(childNodes.item(loopIndex), indentation);
            }
        }
        break;
    }

    case Node.TEXT_NODE: {
        displayText[numberLines] = indentation;
```

LISTING 16.2 continued

```
                String trimmedText = node.getNodeValue().trim();
                if(trimmedText.indexOf("\n") < 0 && trimmedText.length() > 0){
                    displayText[numberLines] += trimmedText;
                    numberLines++;
                }
                break;
            }

            case Node.PROCESSING_INSTRUCTION_NODE: {
                displayText[numberLines] = indentation;
                displayText[numberLines] += "<?";
                displayText[numberLines] += node.getNodeName();
                String text = node.getNodeValue();
                if (text != null && text.length() > 0) {
                    displayText[numberLines] += text;
                }
                displayText[numberLines] += "?>";
                numberLines++;
                break;
            }

            case Node.CDATA_SECTION_NODE: {
                displayText[numberLines] = indentation;
                displayText[numberLines] += "<![CDATA[";
                displayText[numberLines] += node.getNodeValue();
                displayText[numberLines] += "]]>";
                numberLines++;
                break;
            }
        }

        if (type == Node.ELEMENT_NODE) {
            displayText[numberLines] = indentation.substring(0,
                indentation.length() - 4);
            displayText[numberLines] += "</";
            displayText[numberLines] += node.getNodeName();
            displayText[numberLines] += ">";
            numberLines++;
            indentation += "    ";
        }
    }
}
```

Now compile `ch16_02.java` by using `javac`, the Java compiler:

```
%javac ch16_02.java
```

This creates `ch16_02.class`, which is ready to be run. Use the following to run this `.class` file to extract all the data from `ch16_01.xml`:

```
%java ch16_02 ch16_01.xml
```

TIP

Depending on how you've set your Java `classpath` environment variable, you might have to include the current directory, which holds `ch16_02.class`, in order to run it. You can do that by using this at the command prompt:

```
set classpath=.
```

Figure 16.1 shows the results of this example in a Windows MS-DOS window. So far today, you've been able to extract all the data in an XML document, format it, and display it.

```
C:\XML21\ch16>java ch16_02 ch16_01.xml
<?xml version="1.0" encoding="UTF-8"?>
<session>
    <committee type="monetary">
        <title>
            Finance
        </title>
        <number>
            17
        </number>
        <subject>
            Donut Costs
        </subject>
        <date>
            7/15/2005
        </date>
        <attendees>
            <senator status="present">
                <firstName>
                    Thomas
                </firstName>
                <lastName>
                    Smith
                </lastName>
            </senator>
            <senator status="absent">
                <firstName>
                    Frank
                </firstName>
                <lastName>
                    McCoy
                </lastName>
            </senator>
            <senator status="present">
                <firstName>
                    Jay
                </firstName>
                <lastName>
                    Jones
                </lastName>
            </senator>
        </attendees>
    </committee>
</session>
```

FIGURE 16.1
Parsing an XML document by using Java.

Finding Elements by Name

As you saw yesterday, we can search for specific elements by using the `getElementsByTagName` method. For example, what if you only want to search for `<senator>` elements in the `ch16_01.xml` document? You can let the user search for `<senator>` elements like this in a new example, `ch16_03.java`:

```
%java ch16_03 ch16_01.xml senator
```

To create this new example, you can build on the one you just created, `ch16_02.java`. All you have to do is get a node list of matches to the element the user is searching for by using `getElementsByTagName`, and you can access that element's name as `args[1]`:

```
public class ch16_03
{
    static String displayText[] = new String[1000];
    static int numberLines = 0;

    public static void main(String args[])
    {
        try {
            DocumentBuilderFactory factory =
            DocumentBuilderFactory.newInstance();

            DocumentBuilder builder = null;
            try {
                builder = factory.newDocumentBuilder();
            }
            catch (ParserConfigurationException e) {}

            Document document = null;
                document = builder.parse(args[0]);

            NodeList nodeList = document.getElementsByTagName(args[1]);
        .
        .
        .
```

Now loop over the matches in the node list. How can you display the elements you've found and all their children and attributes? You can leverage the work you've already done by simply looping over the matches and just calling your `childLoop` method for each one, as shown in Listing 16.3.

LISTING 16.3 Finding Elements in an XML Document (`ch16_03.java`)

```
import javax.xml.parsers.*;
import org.w3c.dom.*;

public class ch16_03
{
    static String displayText[] = new String[1000];
    static int numberLines = 0;

    public static void main(String args[])
    {
        try {
```

LISTING 16.3 continued

```
            DocumentBuilderFactory factory =
            DocumentBuilderFactory.newInstance();

            DocumentBuilder builder = null;
            try {
                builder = factory.newDocumentBuilder();
            }
            catch (ParserConfigurationException e) {}

            Document document = null;
                document = builder.parse(args[0]);

            NodeList nodeList = document.getElementsByTagName(args[1]);

            if (nodeList != null) {
                for (int loopIndex = 0; loopIndex < nodeList.getLength();
                    loopIndex++ ) {
                    childLoop(nodeList.item(loopIndex), "");
                }
            }

        } catch (Exception e) {
            e.printStackTrace(System.err) ;
        }

        for(int loopIndex = 0; loopIndex < numberLines; loopIndex++){
            System.out.println(displayText[loopIndex]);
        }
    }

    public static void childLoop(Node node, String indentation)
    {
        if (node == null) {
            return;
        }

        int type = node.getNodeType();

        switch (type) {
            case Node.DOCUMENT_NODE: {
                displayText[numberLines] = indentation;
                displayText[numberLines] +=
                    "<?xml version=\"1.0\" encoding=\""+
                  "UTF-8" + "\"?>";
                numberLines++;
                childLoop(((Document)node).getDocumentElement(), "");
                break;
             }
```

16

LISTING 16.3 continued

```
case Node.ELEMENT_NODE: {
    displayText[numberLines] = indentation;
    displayText[numberLines] += "<";
    displayText[numberLines] += node.getNodeName();

    int length = (node.getAttributes() != null) ?
        node.getAttributes().getLength() : 0;
    Attr attributes[] = new Attr[length];
    for (int loopIndex = 0; loopIndex < length; loopIndex++) {
        attributes[loopIndex] =
            (Attr)node.getAttributes().item(loopIndex);
    }

    for (int loopIndex = 0; loopIndex < attributes.length;
        loopIndex++) {
        Attr attribute = attributes[loopIndex];
        displayText[numberLines] += " ";
        displayText[numberLines] += attribute.getNodeName();
        displayText[numberLines] += "=\"";
        displayText[numberLines] += attribute.getNodeValue();
        displayText[numberLines] += "\"";
    }
    displayText[numberLines] += ">";

    numberLines++;

    NodeList childNodes = node.getChildNodes();
    if (childNodes != null) {
        length = childNodes.getLength();
        indentation += "    ";
        for (int loopIndex = 0; loopIndex < length; loopIndex++ ){
           childLoop(childNodes.item(loopIndex), indentation);
        }
    }
    break;
}

case Node.TEXT_NODE: {
    displayText[numberLines] = indentation;
    String trimmedText = node.getNodeValue().trim();
    if(trimmedText.indexOf("\n") < 0 && trimmedText.length() > 0){
        displayText[numberLines] += trimmedText;
        numberLines++;
    }
    break;
}
```

LISTING 16.3 continued

```
                case Node.PROCESSING_INSTRUCTION_NODE: {
                    displayText[numberLines] = indentation;
                    displayText[numberLines] += "<?";
                    displayText[numberLines] += node.getNodeName();
                    String text = node.getNodeValue();
                    if (text != null && text.length() > 0) {
                        displayText[numberLines] += text;
                    }
                    displayText[numberLines] += "?>";
                    numberLines++;
                    break;
                }

                case Node.CDATA_SECTION_NODE: {
                    displayText[numberLines] = indentation;
                    displayText[numberLines] += "<![CDATA[";
                    displayText[numberLines] += node.getNodeValue();
                    displayText[numberLines] += "]]>";
                    numberLines++;
                    break;
                }
            }

            if (type == Node.ELEMENT_NODE) {
                displayText[numberLines] = indentation.substring(0,
                    indentation.length() - 4);
                displayText[numberLines] += "</";
                displayText[numberLines] += node.getNodeName();
                displayText[numberLines] += ">";
                numberLines++;
                indentation += "    ";
            }
        }
    }
```

You can see the results—all the senator elements, including their children and attributes—in Figure 16.2.

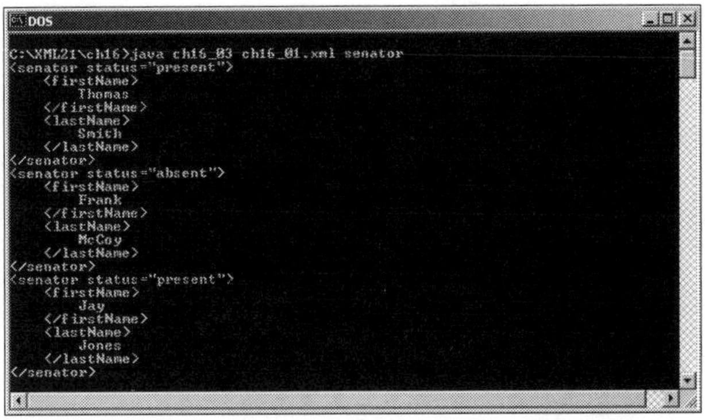

```
C:\XML21\ch16>java ch16_03 ch16_01.xml senator
<senator status="present">
    <firstName>
        Thomas
    </firstName>
    <lastName>
        Smith
    </lastName>
</senator>
<senator status="absent">
    <firstName>
        Frank
    </firstName>
    <lastName>
        McCoy
    </lastName>
</senator>
<senator status="present">
    <firstName>
        Jay
    </firstName>
    <lastName>
        Jones
    </lastName>
</senator>
```

FIGURE 16.2
Searching for elements in an XML document.

Creating an XML Browser by Using Java

Besides letting us work with text, Java also lets us work with graphics. You'll take advantage of that to create a complete XML browser in Java now, using the relatively simple Java Abstract Windowing Toolkit (AWT).

In this example, you're going to read in the XML document shown in Listing 16.4. This document uses a `<square>` element to draw squares in an XML browser. The upper left of each square is set by the `<square>` element's `x` and `y` attributes as the point (x,y), and the width of each square is set by the `width` attribute.

LISTING 16.4 An XML Document for an XML Browser (`ch16_04.xml`)

```
<?xml version = "1.0" encoding="UTF-8"?>
<!DOCTYPE document [
<!ELEMENT document (square)*>
<!ELEMENT square EMPTY>
<!ATTLIST square
    x CDATA #IMPLIED
    y CDATA #IMPLIED
    width CDATA #IMPLIED>
]>
<document>
    <square x='220' y='130' width='50' />
    <square x='140' y='180' width='15' />
    <square x='60' y='100' width='45' />
    <square x='210' y='190' width='35' />
    <square x='20' y='200' width='25' />
    <square x='260' y='280' width='45' />
    <square x='220' y='220' width='25' />
    <square x='90' y='180' width='35' />
    <square x='140' y='290' width='55' />
</document>
```

In your Java code, you need to read in the new XML document, `ch16_04.xml`, and interpret it. You'll store the total number of squares to draw in a variable named `totalFigures`, the x values of the squares in an array named `x`, the y values of the squares in an array named `y`, and the widths of the squares in an array named `width`:

```
import java.awt.*;
import java.awt.event.*;

import javax.xml.parsers.*;
import org.w3c.dom.*;

public class ch16_05
{
    static int totalFigures = 0;
    static  int x[] = new int[100];
    static int y[] = new int[100];
    static int width[] = new int[100];
        .
        .
        .
```

In the `main` method, you'll read in the document and call the `childLoop` method to decode the data in the XML document:

```
import java.awt.*;
import java.awt.event.*;

import javax.xml.parsers.*;
import org.w3c.dom.*;

public class ch16_05
{
    static int totalFigures = 0;
    static  int x[] = new int[100];
    static int y[] = new int[100];
    static int width[] = new int[100];

    public static void main(String args[])
    {
        try {

        DocumentBuilderFactory factory =
            DocumentBuilderFactory.newInstance();

        DocumentBuilder builder = null;
        try {
            builder = factory.newDocumentBuilder();
        }
        catch (ParserConfigurationException e) {}
```

```
        Document document = null;
            document = builder.parse(args[0]);

            childLoop(document);

        } catch (Exception e) {
            e.printStackTrace(System.err);
        }
        .
        .
        .
```

16

After the childLoop method fills the totalFigures variable and the x, y, and width arrays, you can use code in the main method to pass those items to a new Java class, AppFrame, based on the Java Frame class, to create the window and display the data:

```
    AppFrame frame = new AppFrame(totalFigures, x, y, width);

    frame.setSize(400, 400);

    frame.addWindowListener(new WindowAdapter() {public void
        windowClosing(WindowEvent e) {System.exit(0);}});

    frame.show();
}
```

Here's what the AppFrame class, which just uses the Java drawRect method to draw the squares in your new window, looks like:

```
class AppFrame extends Frame
{
    int totalFigures;
    int[] xValues;
    int[] yValues;
    int[] widthValues;

    public AppFrame(int number, int[] x, int[] y, int[] width)
    {
        totalFigures = number;
        xValues = x;
        yValues = y;
        widthValues = width;
    }

    public void paint(Graphics g)
    {
        for(int loopIndex = 0; loopIndex < totalFigures; loopIndex++){
            g.drawRect(xValues[loopIndex], yValues[loopIndex],
                widthValues[loopIndex], widthValues[loopIndex]);
        }
    }
}
```

All that's left is to write the `childLoop` method that does that actual decoding of the data and fills the `totalFigures` variable and the `x`, `y`, and `width` arrays. In this method, you'll look for `<square>` element nodes and decipher their `x`, `y`, and `width` attributes. To do that, you use the `getAttributes` method to get a named node map of each `<square>` element's attributes and then use the `getNamedItem` method to recover the attributes you want. Here's what the `childLoop` method looks like:

```
public static void childLoop(Node node)
{
    if (node == null) {
        return;
    }

    int type = node.getNodeType();

    if (node.getNodeType() == Node.DOCUMENT_NODE) {
        childLoop(((Document)node).getDocumentElement());
    }

    if (node.getNodeType() == Node.ELEMENT_NODE) {

        if (node.getNodeName().equals("square")) {

            NamedNodeMap attrs = node.getAttributes();

            x[totalFigures] =
                Integer.parseInt((String)attrs.getNamedItem("x").
                getNodeValue());

            y[totalFigures] =
                Integer.parseInt((String)attrs.getNamedItem("y").
                getNodeValue());

            width[totalFigures] =
                Integer.parseInt((String)attrs.getNamedItem("width").
                getNodeValue());

            totalFigures++;
        }

        NodeList childNodes = node.getChildNodes();

        if (childNodes != null) {
            int length = childNodes.getLength();
            for (int loopIndex = 0; loopIndex < length; loopIndex++) {
                childLoop(childNodes.item(loopIndex)) ;
            }
        }
    }
}
```

Figure 16.3 shows the results. As the figure shows, the code has indeed read in the XML document `ch16_04.xml`, interpreted it, and displayed the results. Now you've created an XML browser from scratch, using Java. Listing 16.5 shows all the code for it.

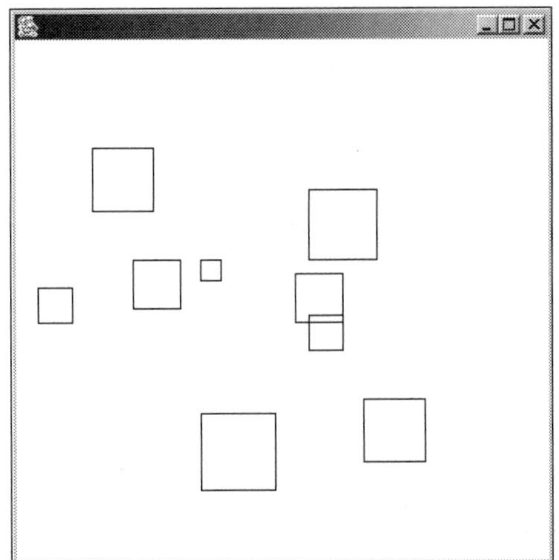

FIGURE 16.3
Creating an XML browser.

LISTING 16.5 An XML Browser (`ch16_05.java`)

```
import java.awt.*;
import java.awt.event.*;

import javax.xml.parsers.*;
import org.w3c.dom.*;

public class ch16_05
{
    static int totalFigures = 0;
    static  int x[] = new int[100];
    static int y[] = new int[100];
    static int width[] = new int[100];

    public static void main(String args[])
    {
        try {

        DocumentBuilderFactory factory =
            DocumentBuilderFactory.newInstance();

        DocumentBuilder builder = null;
        try {
```

LISTING 16.5 continued

```
            builder = factory.newDocumentBuilder();
        }
        catch (ParserConfigurationException e) {}

        Document document = null;
            document = builder.parse(args[0]);

            childLoop(document) ;

        } catch (Exception e) {
            e.printStackTrace(System.err);
        }

        AppFrame frame = new AppFrame(totalFigures, x, y, width);

        frame.setSize(400, 400);

        frame.addWindowListener(new WindowAdapter() {public void
            windowClosing(WindowEvent e) {System.exit(0);}});

        frame.show();
    }

    public static void childLoop(Node node)
    {
        if (node == null) {
            return;
        }

        int type = node.getNodeType();

        if (node.getNodeType() == Node.DOCUMENT_NODE) {
            childLoop(((Document)node).getDocumentElement());
        }

        if (node.getNodeType() == Node.ELEMENT_NODE) {

            if (node.getNodeName().equals("square")) {

                NamedNodeMap attrs = node.getAttributes();

                x[totalFigures] =
                    Integer.parseInt((String)
                    attrs.getNamedItem("x").getNodeValue());
```

Listing 16.5 continued

```
                y[totalFigures] =
                    Integer.parseInt((String)
                    attrs.getNamedItem("y").getNodeValue());

                width[totalFigures] =
                    Integer.parseInt((String)
                    attrs.getNamedItem("width").getNodeValue());

                totalFigures++;
            }

            NodeList childNodes = node.getChildNodes();

            if (childNodes != null) {
                int length = childNodes.getLength();
                for (int loopIndex = 0; loopIndex < length; loopIndex++) {
                    childLoop(childNodes.item(loopIndex));
                }
            }
        }
    }
}

class AppFrame extends Frame
{
    int totalFigures;
    int[] xValues;
    int[] yValues;
    int[] widthValues;

    public AppFrame(int number, int[] x, int[] y, int[] width)
    {
        totalFigures = number;
        xValues = x;
        yValues = y;
        widthValues = width;
    }

    public void paint(Graphics g)
    {
        for(int loopIndex = 0; loopIndex < totalFigures; loopIndex++){
            g.drawRect(xValues[loopIndex], yValues[loopIndex],
                widthValues[loopIndex], widthValues[loopIndex]);
        }
    }
}
```

Navigating Through XML Documents

`Node` objects contain standard W3C DOM methods for navigating in a document, such as `getNextSibling`, `getPreviousSibling`, `getFirstChild`, `getLastChild`, and `getParent`. In this section we'll put these methods to work in the XML document `ch16_01.xml`.

You'll navigate through this document by using navigation methods similar to the ones you used yesterday. You can use the same DOM techniques that you used in JavaScript yesterday, but there is a difference: In Java, even whitespace text is treated as text nodes, and you have to take those nodes into account as you navigate. This means that although you can use almost the same code as in JavaScript, you have to step over the text nodes used for indentation in `ch16_01.xml`. You can see the new navigation code in `ch16_06.java`, shown in Listing 16.6.

LISTING 16.6 Navigating Through an XML Document (`ch16_06.java`)

```
import javax.xml.parsers.*;
import org.w3c.dom.*;

public class ch16_06
{
    public static void main(String args[])
    {
        try {

        DocumentBuilderFactory factory =
            DocumentBuilderFactory.newInstance();

        DocumentBuilder builder = null;
        try {
            builder = factory.newDocumentBuilder();
        }
        catch (ParserConfigurationException e) {}

        Document document = null;
            document = builder.parse("ch16_01.xml");

            childLoop(document);

        } catch (Exception e) {
            e.printStackTrace(System.err);
        }

    }

    public static void childLoop(Node node)
    {
```

LISTING 16.6 continued

```
            Node textNode;
            Node sessionNode = ((Document)node).getDocumentElement();
            textNode = sessionNode.getFirstChild();
            Node committeeNode = textNode.getNextSibling();
            textNode = committeeNode.getLastChild();
            Node attendeesNode = textNode.getPreviousSibling();
            textNode = attendeesNode.getLastChild();
            Node senatorNode = textNode.getPreviousSibling();
            textNode = senatorNode.getFirstChild();
            Node firstNameNode = textNode.getNextSibling();
            textNode = firstNameNode.getNextSibling();
            Node lastNameNode = textNode.getNextSibling();

            System.out.println("Last senator: " +
                firstNameNode.getFirstChild().getNodeValue() + ' '
                + lastNameNode.getFirstChild().getNodeValue());
        }
    }
```

16

Here's what you see when you run this code:

```
%java ch16_06
Last senator: Jay Jones
```

Writing XML by Using Java

The `Node` interface contains a number of methods for editing the XML in XML documents by adding or removing nodes, including methods such as `appendChild`, `insertBefore`, `removeChild`, and `replaceChild`. By using these methods, we can modify our sample XML document, `ch16_01.xml`, on-the-fly. You'll write the new version of our XML document out to a document named `new.xml`.

To make this work, modify your Java XML parsing code to catch the `<senator>` element and add a new child element to it—the `<elected>` element, which indicates when a senator was elected. For example, you're going to change an element like this one:

```
<senator status="present">
    <firstName>
        Jay
    </firstName>
    <lastName>
        Jones
    </lastName>
</senator>
```

to this, where you use 2004 for all senators:

```
<senator status="present">
    <firstName>
        Jay
    </firstName>
    <lastName>
        Jones
    </lastName>
    <elected>
        2004
    </elected>
</senator>
```

Start this example as you have other examples today, by reading in the document to work on in the `main` method and passing it to the `childLoop` method:

```
public static void main(String args[])
{
    try {

        DocumentBuilderFactory factory =
            DocumentBuilderFactory.newInstance();

        DocumentBuilder builder = null;
        try {
            builder = factory.newDocumentBuilder();
        }
        catch (ParserConfigurationException e) {}

        document = builder.parse(args[0]);

        childLoop(document, "");
        .
        .
        .
```

In the `childLoop` method, catch the `<senator>` element and create a new element, `<elected>`:

```
switch (type) {
        .
        .
        .
    case Node.ELEMENT_NODE: {
        if(node.getNodeName().equals("senator")) {
            Element newElement = document.createElement("elected");
        .
        .
        .
    }
```

Then create a new text node that holds the text you want in the <elected> element, "2004":

```
switch (type) {
        .
        .
        .
    case Node.ELEMENT_NODE: {
        if(node.getNodeName().equals("senator")) {
            Element newElement = document.createElement("elected");
            Text textNode = document.createTextNode("2004");
        .
        .
        .
    }
```


Now append the new text node to your new <elected> element by using the appendChild method, and append the new <elected> element to the <senator> element, like this:

```
        .
        .
        .
    case Node.ELEMENT_NODE: {
        if(node.getNodeName().equals("senator")) {
            Element newElement = document.createElement("elected");
            Text textNode = document.createTextNode("2004");
            newElement.appendChild(textNode);
            node.appendChild(newElement) ;
    }
```

You have finished the modifications needed in the childLoop method. Next, back in the main method, write the data we've stored out to a new XML document, which you'll call new.xml here (there is no correspondingly easy way to write out a new XML document in JavaScript, which doesn't allow easy access to the user's disk):

```
        .
        .
        .
        FileWriter filewriter = new FileWriter("new.xml");

        for(int loopIndex = 0; loopIndex < numberLines; loopIndex++){
            filewriter.write(displayText[loopIndex].toCharArray());
            filewriter.write('\n');
        }

        filewriter.close();
    }
    catch (Exception e) {
```

```
        e.printStackTrace(System.err) ;
    }
}
```

That's all there is to it; after you run this code, you get this result, new.xml, complete with the new <elected> elements:

```
<?xml version="1.0" encoding="UTF-8"?>
<session>
    <committee type="monetary">
        <title>
            Finance
        </title>
        <number>
            17
        </number>
        <subject>
            Donut Costs
        </subject>
        <date>
            7/15/2005
        </date>
        <attendees>
            <senator status="present">
                <firstName>
                    Thomas
                </firstName>
                <lastName>
                    Smith
                </lastName>
                <elected>
                    2004
                </elected>
            </senator>
            <senator status="absent">
                <firstName>
                    Frank
                </firstName>
                <lastName>
                    McCoy
                </lastName>
                <elected>
                    2004
                </elected>
            </senator>
            <senator status="present">
                <firstName>
                    Jay
                </firstName>
                <lastName>
                    Jones
```

```
                </lastName>
                <elected>
                    2004
                </elected>
            </senator>
        </attendees>
    </committee>
</session>
```

Listing 16.7 shows the code for this example, `Ch16_07.java`.

LISTING 16.7 Editing an XML Document (`ch16_07.java`)

```
import java.io.*;
import org.w3c.dom.*;
import javax.xml.parsers.*;

public class ch16_07
{
    static String displayText[] = new String[1000];
    static int numberLines = 0;
    static Document document;

    public static void main(String args[])
    {
        try {

            DocumentBuilderFactory factory =
                DocumentBuilderFactory.newInstance();

            DocumentBuilder builder = null;
            try {
                builder = factory.newDocumentBuilder();
            }
            catch (ParserConfigurationException e) {}

            document = builder.parse(args[0]);

            childLoop(document, "");

            FileWriter filewriter = new FileWriter("new.xml");

            for(int loopIndex = 0; loopIndex < numberLines; loopIndex++){
                filewriter.write(displayText[loopIndex].toCharArray());
                filewriter.write('\n');
            }

            filewriter.close();
        }
```

LISTING 16.7 continued

```
        catch (Exception e) {
            e.printStackTrace(System.err);
        }
    }

    public static void childLoop(Node node, String indentation)
    {
        if (node == null) {
            return;
        }

        int type = node.getNodeType();

        switch (type) {
            case Node.DOCUMENT_NODE: {
                displayText[numberLines] = indentation;
                displayText[numberLines] +=
                  "<?xml version=\"1.0\" encoding=\""+
                  "UTF-8" + "\"?>";
                numberLines++;
                childLoop(((Document)node).getDocumentElement(), "");
                break;
             }

             case Node.ELEMENT_NODE: {

                 if(node.getNodeName().equals("senator")) {
                     Element newElement = document.createElement("elected");
                     Text textNode = document.createTextNode("2004");
                     newElement.appendChild(textNode);
                     node.appendChild(newElement);
                 }

                 displayText[numberLines] = indentation;
                 displayText[numberLines] += "<";
                 displayText[numberLines] += node.getNodeName();

                 int length = (node.getAttributes() != null) ?
                     node.getAttributes().getLength() : 0;
                 Attr attributes[] = new Attr[length];
                 for (int loopIndex = 0; loopIndex < length; loopIndex++) {
                     attributes[loopIndex] = (Attr)node.getAttributes().
                     item(loopIndex);
                 }

                 for (int loopIndex = 0; loopIndex < attributes.length;
                     loopIndex++) {
                     Attr attribute = attributes[loopIndex];
```

LISTING 16.7 continued

```
            displayText[numberLines] += " ";
            displayText[numberLines] += attribute.getNodeName();
            displayText[numberLines] += "=\"";
            displayText[numberLines] += attribute.getNodeValue();
            displayText[numberLines] += "\"";
        }
        displayText[numberLines]+=">";

        numberLines++;

        NodeList childNodes = node.getChildNodes();
        if (childNodes != null) {
            length = childNodes.getLength();
            indentation += "    ";
            for (int loopIndex = 0; loopIndex < length;
                loopIndex++ ) {
               childLoop(childNodes.item(loopIndex), indentation);
            }
        }
        break;
    }

    case Node.TEXT_NODE: {
        displayText[numberLines] = indentation;
        String trimmedText = node.getNodeValue().trim();
        if(trimmedText.indexOf("\n") < 0 && trimmedText.length()
            > 0) {
            displayText[numberLines] += trimmedText;
            numberLines++;
        }
        break;
    }

    case Node.PROCESSING_INSTRUCTION_NODE: {
        displayText[numberLines] = indentation;
        displayText[numberLines] += "<?";
        displayText[numberLines] += node.getNodeName();
        String text = node.getNodeValue();
        if (text != null && text.length() > 0) {
            displayText[numberLines] += text;
        }
        displayText[numberLines] += "?>";
        numberLines++;
        break;
    }

    case Node.CDATA_SECTION_NODE: {
```

16

LISTING 16.7 continued

```
                    displayText[numberLines] = indentation;
                    displayText[numberLines] += "<![CDATA[";
                    displayText[numberLines] += node.getNodeValue();
                    displayText[numberLines] += "]]>";
                    numberLines++;
                    break;
                }
            }

            if (type == Node.ELEMENT_NODE) {
                displayText[numberLines] =
                    indentation.substring(0, indentation.length() - 4) ;
                displayText[numberLines] += "</";
                displayText[numberLines] += node.getNodeName();
                displayText[numberLines] += ">";
                numberLines++;
                indentation += "    ";
            }
        }
    }
```

You have completed your Java work with the XML DOM. As you can see, there's plenty of depth here. It turns out that there's another approach to working with XML and Java besides the DOM. The other way is named the Simple API for XML (SAX), and you'll take a look at it tomorrow.

Summary

Today, you looked at how to use Java with the XML DOM. You saw that there's good support for XML DOM handling in Java 1.4 or later. You began today by using a Java `DocumentBuilderFactory` object to create a `DocumentBuilder` object. And you were able to use the `DocumentBuilder` object's `parse` method to parse an XML document and create a Java `Document` object.

The `Document` object corresponds to an entire XML document; it is the top node of the document tree. Today you were able to work with the `Document` node and other nodes in a recursive Java method named `childLoop` that first checked the type of node by using the `getNodeType` method and then handled the different types of nodes by using a Java `switch` statement.

After determining the type of node, you were able to get the node's name by using the `getNodeName` method and get the node's value, if applicable, by using the `getNodeValue` method. And you were able to get an element's attribute nodes by using the `getAttributes` method.

By using the getChildNodes method, you were able to loop over the child nodes of each element node as well, moving through an entire XML document and extracting all the data from it. In this way, you were able to parse whole XML documents by using the DOM and Java.

You were also able to search for specific elements by using the getElementsByTagName method, and navigated through an XML document by using navigation methods such as getNextSibling, getPreviousSibling, getFirstChild, getLastChild, and getParent.

Finally, you saw how to use methods including appendChild, insertBefore, removeChild, and replaceChild, to modify the XML in an XML document, using Java. You were able to modify our sample XML document into a new version by inserting an <elected> element into every <senator> element by using these methods, and were able to write the new version of the document out to disk.

Q&A

Q I don't have version 1.4 (or later) of Java, and I have to stick to my current version for a variety of reasons. Is there no way for me to use the built-in support for XML in Java?

A If you're using a version of Java prior to 1.4, you can download and install the Java XML pack. As of this writing, the download page for that is http://java.sun.com/xml/downloads/javaxmlpack.html. After downloading and unzipping, you have to include the files jaxp-api.jar and xalan.jar in your classpath environment variable. After you do this, you should be able to run today's Java examples.

Q I understand that by default, Java XML parsers treat whitespace nodes, such as the node used for indentation, as text nodes. Isn't there a way to get such parsers to ignore whitespace text nodes so I don't have to worry about them?

A Yes, theoretically, you can use a DocumentBuilderFactory object's setIgnoringElementContentWhitespace method to ignore whitespace nodes:

```
factory.setIgnoringElementContentWhitespace(true)
```

In practice, however, this technique seems to produce inconsistent results.

Workshop

This workshop tests whether you understand the concepts discussed today. It's a good idea to make sure you can answer these questions before pressing on to tomorrow's work. Answers to the quiz can be found in Appendix A, "Quiz Answers."

Quiz

1. How do you read in an XML document and create a Java `Document` object in Java?
2. What DOM method can you use to determine a node's type?
3. How can you determine the name of a node and access its data?
4. How can you get a node list of all the `<senator>` elements in a document?
5. How can you create a new element named `<child>` and make it a child element of an element named `<element>` by using Java?

Exercises

1. Using Java XML DOM navigation methods, determine the last name of the second senator in `ch16_01.xml`.
2. Building on your solution to Exercise 1, use Java to read the value of the second senator's `status` attribute to determine whether he was present or absent for the meeting.

PART IV

DAY 17

Using Java and .NET: SAX

Yesterday, you used Java and the DOM model to work your way through XML documents. Some programmers find the DOM way of doing things pretty complex, however, because it requires us to search out our data in the XML document. Instead of having to go get our data, those programmers say, wouldn't it be easier if that data came to us? That's how the Simple API for XML (SAX) works, as you're going to see today. Today's topics are purposely the same as yesterday's, except today, you're going to do things the SAX way:

- Loading XML documents into a Java application
- Parsing XML documents by using Java
- Searching a document for a particular element
- Navigating through an XML document by using Java
- Creating graphical XML browsers by using Java
- Modifying the XML in a document by using Java

An Overview of SAX

The SAX processor works through a document, and when it finds a node, it calls a method in the code that handles that kind of node. In fact, your DOM code yesterday was set up to do much the same thing. In the `childLoop` method's `switch` statement, set up `case` statements to handle the type of node you were dealing with:

```
public static void childLoop(Node node, String indentation)
{
    if (node == null) {
        return;
    }

    int type = node.getNodeType();

    switch (type) {
        case Node.DOCUMENT_NODE: {
            displayText[numberLines] = indentation;
            displayText[numberLines] += "<?xml version=\"1.0\" encoding=\""+
              "UTF-8" + "\"?>";
            numberLines++;
            childLoop(((Document)node).getDocumentElement(), "");
            break;
         }

         case Node.ELEMENT_NODE: {
             displayText[numberLines] = indentation;
             displayText[numberLines] += "<";
             displayText[numberLines] += node.getNodeName();

             int length = (node.getAttributes() != null) ?
                 node.getAttributes().getLength() : 0;
             Attr attributes[] = new Attr[length];
             for (int loopIndex = 0; loopIndex < length; loopIndex++) {
                 attributes[loopIndex] =
                     (Attr)node.getAttributes().item(loopIndex);
             }

             for (int loopIndex = 0; loopIndex < attributes.length;
                 loopIndex++) {
                 Attr attribute = attributes[loopIndex];
                 displayText[numberLines] += " ";
                 displayText[numberLines] += attribute.getNodeName();
                 displayText[numberLines] += "=\"";
                 displayText[numberLines] += attribute.getNodeValue();
                 displayText[numberLines] += "\"";
             }
             displayText[numberLines] += ">";
```

```
            numberLines++;

            NodeList childNodes = node.getChildNodes();
            if (childNodes != null) {
                length = childNodes.getLength();
                indentation += "    ";
                for (int loopIndex = 0; loopIndex < length; loopIndex++ ) {
                   childLoop(childNodes.item(loopIndex), indentation);
                }
            }
            break;
        }

        case Node.TEXT_NODE: {
            displayText[numberLines] = indentation;
            String trimmedText = node.getNodeValue().trim();
            if(trimmedText.indexOf("\n") < 0 && trimmedText.length() > 0) {
                displayText[numberLines] += trimmedText;
                numberLines++;
            }
            break;
        }

        case Node.PROCESSING_INSTRUCTION_NODE: {
            displayText[numberLines] = indentation;
            displayText[numberLines] += "<?";
            displayText[numberLines] += node.getNodeName();
            String text = node.getNodeValue();
            if (text != null && text.length() > 0) {
                displayText[numberLines] += text;
            }
            displayText[numberLines] += "?>";
            numberLines++;
            break;
        }

        case Node.CDATA_SECTION_NODE: {
            displayText[numberLines] = indentation;
            displayText[numberLines] += "<![CDATA[";
            displayText[numberLines] += node.getNodeValue();
            displayText[numberLines] += "]]>";
            numberLines++;
            break;
        }
    }

    if (type == Node.ELEMENT_NODE) {
        displayText[numberLines] = indentation.substring(0,
            indentation.length() - 4);
        displayText[numberLines] += "</";
```

17

```
            displayText[numberLines] += node.getNodeName();
            displayText[numberLines] += ">";
            numberLines++;
            indentation += "    ";
        }
    }
```

This code handles XML nodes in much the same way that SAX does; the idea is that nodes are fed to the code, and all we have to do is write code for the various different node types that we want to handle. SAX is event based, which means that we write code for the various possible events. For example, we can write our code so that when the SAX parser sees the beginning of an element, it will call the `startElement` method in the code.

Using SAX

Today's first example shows how to work with SAX. You'll start with the same example you used yesterday, except today, you'll use SAX. In particular, you're going to extract all the data from `ch17_01.xml`, which is shown in Listing 17.1.

LISTING 17.1 A Sample XML Document for Use with SAX Methods (`ch17_01.xml`)

```
<?xml version="1.0" encoding="UTF-8"?>
<session>
   <committee type="monetary">
       <title>Finance</title>
       <number>17</number>
       <subject>Donut Costs</subject>
       <date>7/15/2005</date>
       <attendees>
           <senator status="present">
               <firstName>Thomas</firstName>
               <lastName>Smith</lastName>
           </senator>
           <senator status="absent">
               <firstName>Frank</firstName>
               <lastName>McCoy</lastName>
           </senator>
           <senator status="present">
               <firstName>Jay</firstName>
               <lastName>Jones</lastName>
           </senator>
       </attendees>
   </committee>
</session>
```

How do you handle this XML document by using SAX? You start in the `main` method by calling a new version of the `childLoop` method created yesterday. This method will fill the same array of strings, `displayText`, and you'll store the number of strings in a variable named `numberLines`. When the `childLoop` method is done, all you have to do is display all the text in the `displayText` array:

```
import java.io.*;
import org.xml.sax.*;
import javax.xml.parsers.*;
import org.xml.sax.helpers.DefaultHandler;

public class ch17_02 extends DefaultHandler
{
    static int numberLines = 0;
    static String indentation = "";
    static String displayText[] = new String[1000];

    public static void main(String args[])
    {
        ch17_02 parser = new ch17_02();
        parser.childLoop(args[0]);

        for(int loopIndex = 0; loopIndex < numberLines; loopIndex++){
            System.out.println(displayText[loopIndex]);
        }
    }
```

17

In the `childLoop` method, start by creating a `SAXParserFactory` object, using a `DefaultHandler` object. The `DefaultHandler` object tells SAX which object to call when it encounters various nodes, and you'll use the present application object, which you've based on the `DefaultHandler` class:

```
public class ch17_02 extends DefaultHandler
{
        .
        .
        .
```

To refer to the current object, use the Java `this` keyword. Here's how to create the `SAXParserFactory` object:

```
public void childLoop(String uri)
{
    DefaultHandler saxHandler = this;
    SAXParserFactory saxFactory = SAXParserFactory.newInstance();
        .
        .
        .
}
```

Now create a new SAX parser by using this `SAXParserFactory` object, and this SAX parser will parse the XML document `ch17_01.xml`:

```
public void childLoop(String uri)
{
    DefaultHandler saxHandler = this;
    SAXParserFactory saxFactory = SAXParserFactory.newInstance();
    try {
        SAXParser saxParser = saxFactory.newSAXParser();
        saxParser.parse(new File(uri), saxHandler);
    } catch (Throwable t) {}
}
```

Table 17.1 lists the significant methods of the `SAXParserFactory` class, and Table 17.2 lists the significant methods of the `SAXParser` class.

TABLE 17.1 Methods of the `javax.xml.parsers.SAXParserFactory` Interface

Method	*What It Does*
`protected SAXParserFactory()`	Acts as the default constructor for the class.
`boolean isNamespaceAware()`	Returns `True` if the factory is configured to produce parsers that use XML namespaces.
`boolean isValidating()`	Returns `True` if the factory is configured to produce parsers that validate the XML content.
`static SAXParserFactory newInstance()`	Returns a new `SAXParserFactory` object.
`abstract SAXParser newSAXParser()`	Returns a new `SAXParser` object.
`void setNamespaceAware(boolean awareness)`	Requires that the created parser support XML namespaces.
`void setValidating(boolean validating)`	Requires that the parser produced validate XML documents.

TABLE 17.2 Methods of the `SAXParser` Class

Method	*What It Does*
`protected SAXParser()`	Acts as the default class constructor.
`abstract Parser getParser()`	Returns the SAX parser.
`abstract boolean isNamespaceAware()`	Returns `True` if this parser can understand namespaces.
`abstract boolean isValidating()`	Returns `True` if this parser is configured to validate XML documents.

TABLE 17.2 continued

Method	*What It Does*
`void parse(File f, DefaultHandler dh)`	Parses the file specified.
`void parse(InputSource is, DefaultHandler dh)`	Parses the content specified `InputSource` object.
`void parse(InputStream is, DefaultHandler dh)`	Parses the content of the specified `InputStream` object.
`void parse(String uri, DefaultHandler dh)`	Parses the content at the given URI, using the specified `DefaultHandler` object.
`abstract void setProperty(String name, Object value)`	Sets a property in the parser.

17

Now you've connected our SAX parser to our program and launched it, which means it will be calling various methods in your code to handle various types of nodes. It does this because you've based the program's main class on the SAX `DefaultHandler` class:

```
import java.io.*;
import org.xml.sax.*;
import javax.xml.parsers.*;
import org.xml.sax.helpers.DefaultHandler;

public class ch17_02 extends DefaultHandler
        .
        .
        .
```

The `DefaultHandler` class has a number of predefined methods, called *callback methods*, that the SAX parser will call:

- **`characters`**—Called by the SAX parser for text nodes.
- **`endDocument`**—Called by the SAX parser when the end of the document is seen.
- **`endElement`**—Called by the SAX parser when the closing tag of an element is seen.
- **`startDocument`**—Called by the SAX parser when the start of the document is seen.
- **`startElement`**—Called by the SAX parser when the opening tag of an element is seen.

All the required callback methods are already implemented in the `DefaultHandler` class, but they don't do anything. That means we only have to implement the methods we want to use, such as `startDocument` to catch the beginning of the document or `endDocument` to catch the end of the document, as described later today. Table 7.3 lists the significant methods of the `DefaultHandler` class.

TABLE 17.3 Methods of the `DefaultHandler` Class

Method	*What It Does*
`DefaultHandler()`	Acts as the default class constructor.
`void characters(char[] ch, int start, int length)`	Handles text nodes.
`void endDocument()`	Handles the end of the document.
`void endElement(String uri, String localName, String qName)`	Handles the end of an element.
`void error(SAXParseException e)`	Handles a recoverable parser error.
`void fatalError(SAXParseException e)`	Reports a fatal parsing error.
`void ignorableWhitespace(char[] ch, int start, int length)`	Handles ignorable whitespace (such as that used to indent a document) in element content.
`void notationDecl(String name, String publicId, String systemId)`	Handles a notation declaration.
`void processingInstruction(String target, String data)`	Handles an XML processing instruction (such as a JSP directive) .
`InputSource resolveEntity(String publicId, String systemId)`	Resolves an external entity.
`void setDocumentLocator(Locator locator)`	Sets a `Locator` object for document events.
`void skippedEntity(String name)`	Handles a skipped XML entity.
`void startDocument()`	Handles the beginning of the document.
`void startElement(String uri, String localName, String qName, Attributes attributes)`	Handles the start of an element.
`void startPrefixMapping(String prefix, String uri)`	Handles the start of a namespace mapping.
`void unparsedEntityDecl(String name, String publicId, String systemId, String notationName)`	Handles an unparsed entity declaration.
`void warning(SAXParseException e)`	Handles a parser warning.

Let's start by handling the start of the document.

Handling the Start of a Document

To handle the start of a document, you can implement the `DefaultHandler` `startDocument` method:

```
public void startDocument()
{
        .
        .
        .
}
```

When this method is called, the SAX processor has already seen the beginning of the document, so just put a generic XML declaration into the `displayText` array:

```
public void startDocument()
{
    displayText[numberLines] = indentation;
    displayText[numberLines] += "<?xml version=\"1.0\" encoding=\""+
        "UTF-8" + "\"?>";
    numberLines++;
}
```


Handling Processing Instructions

We can handle processing instructions by using the `DefaultHandler` `processingInstruction` method, which is called automatically when the SAX parser finds a processing instruction. The target of the processing instruction is passed to us, as is the data for the processing instruction, which means you can handle processing instructions like this:

```
public void processingInstruction(String target, String data)
{
    displayText[numberLines] = indentation;
    displayText[numberLines] += "<?";
    displayText[numberLines] += target;
    if (data != null && data.length() > 0) {
        displayText[numberLines] += ' ';
        displayText[numberLines] += data;
    }
    displayText[numberLines] += "?>";
    numberLines++;
}
```

Handling the Start of an Element

To handle the start of an element, use the `startElement` SAX method. This method is passed the namespace URI of the element, the local (unqualified) name of the element, the qualified name of the element, and the element's attributes (as an `Attributes` object):

```
public void startElement(String uri, String localName, String qualifiedName,
    Attributes attributes)
{
```

```
        .
        .
        .
}
```

Store the element's name in our `displayText` array, like this:

```
public void startElement(String uri, String localName, String qualifiedName,
    Attributes attributes)
{
    displayText[numberLines] = indentation;

    indentation += "    ";

    displayText[numberLines] += '<';
    displayText[numberLines] += qualifiedName;
        .
        .
        .
    displayText[numberLines] += '>';
    numberLines++;
}
```

So far, so good. But what if the element has attributes?

Handling Attributes

If the element has attributes, loop over them. And the way you determine whether the element has attributes is by checking whether the `Attributes` object passed to you in the `startElement` method is null:

```
public void startElement(String uri, String localName, String qualifiedName,
    Attributes attributes)
{
    displayText[numberLines] = indentation;

    indentation += "    ";

    displayText[numberLines] += '<';
    displayText[numberLines] += qualifiedName;
    if (attributes != null) {
        .
        .
        .
    }
    displayText[numberLines] += '>';
    numberLines++;
}
```

Table 17.4 lists the methods of `Attributes` objects. We can reach the attributes in an object that implements this interface based on index, name, or namespace-qualified name.

TABLE 17.4 `Attributes` Interface Methods

Method	*What It Does*
`int getIndex(java.lang.String uri, java.lang.String localPart)`	Returns the index of an attribute, by namespace and local name.
`int getIndex(java.lang.String qualifiedName)`	Returns the index of an attribute, given its qualified name.
`int getLength()`	Returns the number of attributes in the list.
`java.lang.String getLocalName(int index)`	Returns an attribute's local name, by index.
`java.lang.String getQName(int index)`	Returns an attribute's qualified name, by index.
`java.lang.String getType(int index)`	Returns an attribute's type, by index.
`java.lang.String getType-(java.lang.String qualifiedName)`	Returns an attribute's type, by qualified name.
`java.lang.String getType(java.lang.String uri, java.lang.String localName)`	Returns an attribute's type, by namespace and local name.
`java.lang.String getURI(int index)`	Returns an attribute's namespace URI, by index.
`java.lang.String getValue(int index)`	Returns an attribute's value, by index.
`java.lang.String getValue-(java.lang.String qualifiedName)`	Returns an attribute's value, by qualified name.
`java.lang.String getValue(java.lang.String uri, java.lang.String localName)`	Returns an attribute's value, by namespace name and local name.

Now loop over the attributes and use the `getQName` (get qualified name) and `getValue` methods to store the name and value of each attribute:

```
public void startElement(String uri, String localName, String qualifiedName,
    Attributes attributes)
{
    displayText[numberLines] = indentation;

    indentation += "    ";

    displayText[numberLines] += '<';
    displayText[numberLines] += qualifiedName;
    if (attributes != null) {
```

```
        int numberAttributes = attributes.getLength();
        for (int loopIndex = 0; loopIndex < numberAttributes; loopIndex++) {
            displayText[numberLines] += ' ';
            displayText[numberLines] += attributes.getQName(loopIndex);
            displayText[numberLines] += "=\"";
            displayText[numberLines] += attributes.getValue(loopIndex);
            displayText[numberLines] += '"';
        }
    }
    displayText[numberLines] += '>';
    numberLines++;
}
```

Next, you'll take a look at handling text.

Handling Text

In SAX, you handle text by using the `characters` method. This method is passed an array of characters, the location in that array where the text for the current text node starts, and the length of the text in the text node:

```
public void characters(char characters[], int start, int length)
{
    .
    .
    .
}
```

Here's how to handle the text of a text node, adding it to the `displayText` array:

```
public void characters(char characters[], int start, int length)
{
    String characterData = (new String(characters, start, length)).trim();
    if(characterData.indexOf("\n") < 0 && characterData.length() > 0) {
        displayText[numberLines] = indentation;
        displayText[numberLines] += characterData;
        numberLines++;
    }
}
```

By default, the SAX parser will also call a method named `ignorableWhitespace` when it finds whitespace text nodes, such as whitespace used for indentation. If we want to handle that text like any other text, we can simply pass it on to the `characters` method we just implemented (note that we've commented this line out here because we're supplying our own indentation in this example):

```
public void ignorableWhitespace(char characters[], int start, int length)
{
    //characters(characters, start, length);
}
```

Handling the End of Elements

Besides the `startElement` method, which is called when the SAX parser sees the beginning of an element, we can also implement the `endElement` method to handle an element's closing tag. Here's how that looks in this example:

```
public void endElement(String uri, String localName, String qualifiedName)
{
    indentation = indentation.substring(0, indentation.length() - 4);
    displayText[numberLines] = indentation;
    displayText[numberLines] += "</";
    displayText[numberLines] += qualifiedName;
    displayText[numberLines] += '>';
    numberLines++;
}
```


Handling Errors and Warnings

SAX makes it easy to handle warnings and errors. We can implement the `warning` method to handle warnings, the `error` method to handle errors, and the `fatalError` method to handle errors that the SAX parser considers fatal enough to make it stop processing. Here's what the error handling looks like in this example:

```
public void warning(SAXParseException exception)
{
    System.err.println("Warning: " +
        exception.getMessage());
}

public void error(SAXParseException exception)
{
    System.err.println("Error: " +
        exception.getMessage());
}

public void fatalError(SAXParseException exception)
{
    System.err.println("Fatal error: " +
        exception.getMessage());
}
```

And that's it—now run your new SAX code and parse `ch17_01.xml` like this:

```
%java ch17_02 ch17_01.xml
```

> **TIP**
>
> As in yesterday's discussion, depending on how you've set your Java `classpath` environment variable, you might have to include the current directory, which holds `ch16_02.class`, in order to run it. You can do that by using this at the command prompt:
>
> `set classpath=.`

As shown in Figure 17.1, we've been able to read and extract all the data in the XML document by using SAX methods.

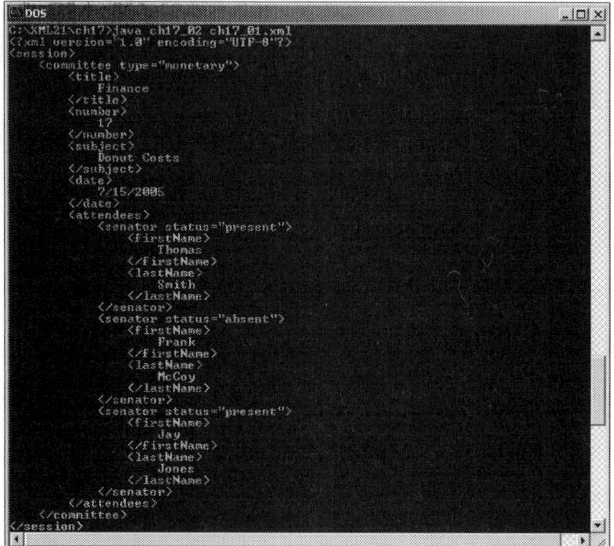

FIGURE 17.1 *Parsing an XML document by using a SAX parser.*

The complete Java code is in Listing 17.2.

LISTING 17.2 Parsing an XML Document by Using Java SAX (`ch17_02.java`)

```
import java.io.*;
import org.xml.sax.*;
import javax.xml.parsers.*;
import org.xml.sax.helpers.DefaultHandler;

public class ch17_02 extends DefaultHandler
{
    static int numberLines = 0;
    static String indentation = "";
    static String displayText[] = new String[1000];
```

LISTING 17.2 continued

```
    public static void main(String args[])
    {
        ch17_02 parser = new ch17_02();
        parser.childLoop(args[0]);

        for(int loopIndex = 0; loopIndex < numberLines; loopIndex++){
            System.out.println(displayText[loopIndex]);
        }
    }

    public void childLoop(String uri)
    {
        DefaultHandler saxHandler = this;
        SAXParserFactory saxFactory = SAXParserFactory.newInstance();
        try {
            SAXParser saxParser = saxFactory.newSAXParser();
            saxParser.parse(new File(uri), saxHandler);
        } catch (Throwable t) {}
    }

    public void startDocument()
    {
        displayText[numberLines] = indentation;
        displayText[numberLines] += "<?xml version=\"1.0\" encoding=\""+
            "UTF-8" + "\"?>";
        numberLines++;
    }

    public void processingInstruction(String target, String data)
    {
        displayText[numberLines] = indentation;
        displayText[numberLines] += "<?";
        displayText[numberLines] += target;
        if (data != null && data.length() > 0) {
            displayText[numberLines] += ' ';
            displayText[numberLines] += data;
        }
        displayText[numberLines] += "?>";
        numberLines++;
    }

    public void startElement(String uri, String localName,
        String qualifiedName, Attributes attributes)
    {
        displayText[numberLines] = indentation;

        indentation += "    ";
```

LISTING 17.2 continued

```
        displayText[numberLines] += '<';
        displayText[numberLines] += qualifiedName;
        if (attributes != null) {
            int numberAttributes = attributes.getLength();
            for (int loopIndex = 0; loopIndex < numberAttributes; loopIndex++){
                displayText[numberLines] += ' ';
                displayText[numberLines] += attributes.getQName(loopIndex);
                displayText[numberLines] += "=\"";
                displayText[numberLines] += attributes.getValue(loopIndex);
                displayText[numberLines] += '"';
            }
        }
        displayText[numberLines] += '>';
        numberLines++;
    }

    public void characters(char characters[], int start, int length)
    {
        String characterData = (new String(characters, start, length)).trim();
        if(characterData.indexOf("\n") < 0 && characterData.length() > 0) {
            displayText[numberLines] = indentation;
            displayText[numberLines] += characterData;
            numberLines++;
        }
    }

    public void ignorableWhitespace(char characters[], int start, int length)
    {
        //characters(characters, start, length);
    }

    public void endElement(String uri, String localName, String qualifiedName)
    {
        indentation = indentation.substring(0, indentation.length() - 4);
        displayText[numberLines] = indentation;
        displayText[numberLines] += "</";
        displayText[numberLines] += qualifiedName;
        displayText[numberLines] += '>';
        numberLines++;
    }

    public void warning(SAXParseException exception)
    {
        System.err.println("Warning: " +
            exception.getMessage());
    }

    public void error(SAXParseException exception)
    {
```

LISTING 17.2 continued

```
            System.err.println("Error: " +
                exception.getMessage());
        }

        public void fatalError(SAXParseException exception)
        {
            System.err.println("Fatal error: " +
                exception.getMessage());
        }
    }
```

Using SAX to Find Elements by Name

Yesterday you were able to use the `getElementsByTagName` method to search an XML document for a particular element, but using that method isn't an option in SAX. Nonetheless, you can search for particular elements when you use SAX—you just have to wait until they come to you when the parser finds them.

You can build on the SAX parsing program you've already written in a new example, `ch17_03.java`. You can let the user enter the name of the XML document to search and the name of the element to search for, like this:

```
%java ch17_03 ch17_01.xml senator
```

In the `main` method, store the name of the element the user wants to search for in a variable called `findNode`:

```
public static void main(String args[])
{
    ch17_03 obj = new ch17_03();
    findNode = args[1];
    obj.childLoop(args[0]);

    for(int index = 0; index < numberLines; index++){
        System.out.println(displayText[index]);
    }
}
```

In the `startElement` method, you'll search for that element, and when you find it, set a Boolean named `displayBoolean` to `true`. When this Boolean is `true`, you know that you're inside the element you're looking for and so should be storing data in the `displayText` array, like this:

```
public void startElement(String uri, String localName,
    String qualifiedName, Attributes attributes)
{
    if(qualifiedName.equals(findNode)){
        displayBoolean=true;
    }
    if (displayBoolean){
        displayText[numberLines] = indentation;

        indentation += "    ";

        displayText[numberLines] += '<';
        displayText[numberLines] += qualifiedName;
        if (attributes != null) {
            int numberAttributes = attributes.getLength();
            for (int loopIndex = 0; loopIndex < numberAttributes; loopIndex++){
                displayText[numberLines] += ' ';
                displayText[numberLines] += attributes.getQName(loopIndex);
                displayText[numberLines] += "=\"";
                displayText[numberLines] += attributes.getValue(loopIndex);
                displayText[numberLines] += '"';
            }
        }
        displayText[numberLines] += '>';
        numberLines++;
    }
}
```

You'll use the `displayBoolean` variable in all the methods that the SAX parser calls in your code to see whether you're in the element the user is searching for and so should be storing text in the `displayText` array. For example, this is how to do that in the `characters` method, which handles text nodes:

```
public void characters(char characters[], int start, int length) {
    if(displayBoolean){
        String characterData = (new String(characters, start, length)).trim();
        if(characterData.indexOf("\n") < 0 && characterData.length() > 0) {
            displayText[numberLines] = indentation;
            displayText[numberLines] += characterData;
            numberLines++;
        }
    }
}
```

When you reach the end of the element you've been searching for, you can set the `displayBoolean` variable to `false`:

```
public void endElement(String uri, String localName, String qualifiedName)
{
    if(displayBoolean){
```

```
            indentation = indentation.substring(0, indentation.length() - 4);
            displayText[numberLines] = indentation;
            displayText[numberLines] += "</";
            displayText[numberLines] += qualifiedName;
            displayText[numberLines] += '>';
            numberLines++;
        }
        if(qualifiedName.equals(findNode)){
            displayBoolean=false;
        }
    }
```

Figure 17.2 shows that we are indeed displaying all the <senator> elements and their contents.

FIGURE 17.2

Searching an XML document for elements by using SAX.

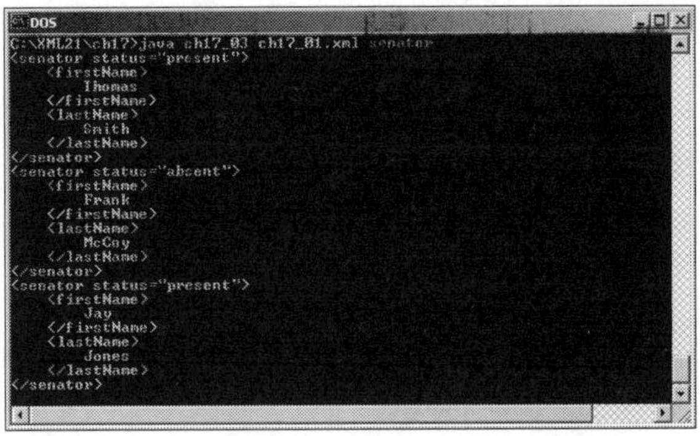

The complete code is shown in Listing 17.3.

LISTING 17.3 Finding XML Elements by Using Java SAX (`ch17_03.java`)

```
import java.io.*;
import org.xml.sax.*;
import javax.xml.parsers.*;
import org.xml.sax.helpers.DefaultHandler;

public class ch17_03 extends DefaultHandler
{
    static int numberLines = 0;
    static String indentation = "";
    static String displayText[] = new String[1000];

    static boolean displayBoolean;
    static String findNode;
```

LISTING 17.3 continued

```
    public static void main(String args[])
    {
        ch17_03 obj = new ch17_03();
        findNode = args[1];
        obj.childLoop(args[0]);

        for(int index = 0; index < numberLines; index++){
            System.out.println(displayText[index]);
        }
    }

    public void childLoop(String uri)
    {
        DefaultHandler saxHandler = this;
        SAXParserFactory saxFactory = SAXParserFactory.newInstance();
        try {
            SAXParser saxParser = saxFactory.newSAXParser();
            saxParser.parse(new File(uri), saxHandler);
        } catch (Throwable t) {}
    }

    public void startDocument()
    {
        if(displayBoolean){
            displayText[numberLines] = indentation;
            displayText[numberLines] += "<?xml version=\"1.0\" encoding=\""+
                "UTF-8" + "\"?>";
            numberLines++;
        }
    }

    public void processingInstruction(String target, String data)
    {
        if(displayBoolean){
            displayText[numberLines] = indentation;
            displayText[numberLines] += "<?";
            displayText[numberLines] += target;
            if (data != null && data.length() > 0) {
                displayText[numberLines] += ' ';
                displayText[numberLines] += data;
            }
            displayText[numberLines] += "?>";
            numberLines++;
        }
    }

    public void startElement(String uri, String localName,
        String qualifiedName, Attributes attributes)
    {
```

LISTING 17.3 continued

```
        if(qualifiedName.equals(findNode)) {
            displayBoolean=true;
        }

        if (displayBoolean){
            displayText[numberLines] = indentation;

            indentation += "    ";

            displayText[numberLines] += '<';
            displayText[numberLines] += qualifiedName;
            if (attributes != null) {
                int numberAttributes = attributes.getLength();
                for (int loopIndex = 0; loopIndex < numberAttributes;
                    loopIndex++) {
                    displayText[numberLines] += ' ';
                    displayText[numberLines] += attributes.getQName(loopIndex);
                    displayText[numberLines] += "=\"";
                    displayText[numberLines] += attributes.getValue(loopIndex);
                    displayText[numberLines] += '"';
                }
            }
            displayText[numberLines] += '>';
            numberLines++;
        }
    }

    public void characters(char characters[], int start, int length) {
        if(displayBoolean){
            String characterData =
                (new String(characters, start, length)).trim();
            if(characterData.indexOf("\n") < 0 && characterData.length() > 0) {
                displayText[numberLines] = indentation;
                displayText[numberLines] += characterData;
                numberLines++;
            }
        }
    }

    public void ignorableWhitespace(char characters[], int start, int length)
    {
        if(displayBoolean){
            //characters(ch, start, length);
        }
    }

    public void endElement(String uri, String localName, String qualifiedName)
    {
        if(displayBoolean){
```

17

LISTING 17.3 continued

```
                indentation = indentation.substring(0, indentation.length() - 4) ;
                displayText[numberLines] = indentation;
                displayText[numberLines] += "</";
                displayText[numberLines] += qualifiedName;
                displayText[numberLines] += '>';
                numberLines++;
            }
            if(qualifiedName.equals(findNode)){
                displayBoolean=false;
            }
        }

        public void warning(SAXParseException exception)
        {
            System.err.println("Warning: " +
                exception.getMessage());
        }

        public void error(SAXParseException exception)
        {
            System.err.println("Error: " +
                exception.getMessage());
        }

        public void fatalError(SAXParseException exception)
        {
            System.err.println("Fatal error: " +
                exception.getMessage());
        }
    }
```

Creating an XML Browser by Using Java and SAX

Yesterday, you were able to create a graphical browser by using DOM methods. You can do the same thing with SAX, but the coding is different. You'll use the same XML document as you did yesterday, `ch17_04.xml` (shown in Listing 17.4), which lets you display a series of squares.

LISTING 17.4 An XML Document with a DTD (`ch17_04.xml`)

```
<?xml version = "1.0" encoding="UTF-8"?>
<!DOCTYPE document [
<!ELEMENT document (square)*>
```

LISTING 17.4 continued

```
<!ELEMENT square EMPTY>
<!ATTLIST square
    x CDATA #IMPLIED
    y CDATA #IMPLIED
    width CDATA #IMPLIED>
]>
<document>
    <square x='220' y='130' width='50' />
    <square x='140' y='180' width='15' />
    <square x='60' y='100' width='45' />
    <square x='210' y='190' width='35' />
    <square x='20' y='200' width='25' />
    <square x='260' y='280' width='45' />
    <square x='220' y='220' width='25' />
    <square x='90' y='180' width='35' />
    <square x='140' y='290' width='55' />
</document>
```


Yesterday you created the visual interface. The trick today will be to extract the x, y, and width data for each square. As you did yesterday, you need to put aside storage space for these items in arrays named `x`, `y`, and `width`:

```
public class ch17_05 extends DefaultHandler
{
    static int totalFigures = 0;
    static int x[] = new int[100];
    static int y[] = new int[100];
    static int width[] = new int[100];
        .
        .
        .
```

Now when you catch a `<square>` element in the `startElement` SAX method, you can get the values we need for each square by using the `Attributes` object's `getValue` method:

```
public void startElement(String uri, String localName,
    String qualifiedName, Attributes attrs)
{
    if (qualifiedName.equals("square")) {
        x[totalFigures] = Integer.parseInt(attrs.getValue("x"));
        y[totalFigures] = Integer.parseInt(attrs.getValue("y"));
        width[totalFigures] = Integer.parseInt(attrs.getValue("width"));
        totalFigures++;
    }
}
```

Then you can draw your squares as you did yesterday, by passing your data to the `AppFrame` object after the `childLoop` method has extracted the needed data:

```
public static void main(String args[])
{
    ch17_05 obj = new ch17_05();
    obj.childLoop(args[0]);

    AppFrame frame = new AppFrame(totalFigures, x, y, width);

    frame.setSize(400, 400);

    frame.addWindowListener(new WindowAdapter() {public void
        windowClosing(WindowEvent e) {System.exit(0);}});

    frame.show();
}
```

Here's how to do the actual drawing in the `AppFrame` object:

```
class AppFrame extends Frame
{
    int totalFigures;
    int[] xValues;
    int[] yValues;
    int[] widthValues;

    public AppFrame(int number, int[] x, int[] y, int[] width)
    {
        totalFigures = number;
        xValues = x;
        yValues = y;
        widthValues = width;
    }

    public void paint(Graphics g)
    {
        for(int loopIndex = 0; loopIndex < totalFigures; loopIndex++){
            g.drawRect(xValues[loopIndex], yValues[loopIndex],
                widthValues[loopIndex], widthValues[loopIndex]);
        }
    }
}
```

Figure 17.3 shows the results. As the figure shows, the SAX graphical browser is indeed displaying the squares as the DOM graphical browser did yesterday.

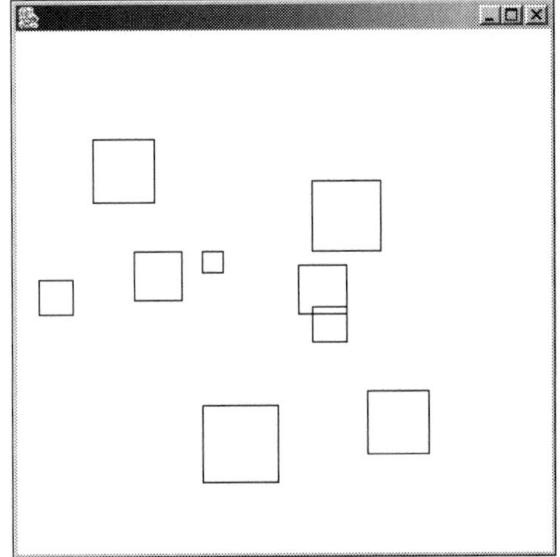

FIGURE 17.3
A graphical XML browser that uses SAX.

Listing 17.5 shows the code for this example.

LISTING 17.5 An XML Browser That Uses SAX (ch17_05.java)

```
import java.io.*;
import java.awt.*;
import org.xml.sax.*;
import java.awt.event.*;
import javax.xml.parsers.*;
import org.xml.sax.helpers.DefaultHandler;

public class ch17_05 extends DefaultHandler
{
    static int totalFigures = 0;
    static int x[] = new int[100];
    static int y[] = new int[100];
    static int width[] = new int[100];

    public static void main(String args[])
    {
        ch17_05 obj = new ch17_05();
        obj.childLoop(args[0]);

        AppFrame frame = new AppFrame(totalFigures, x, y, width);

        frame.setSize(400, 400);
```

LISTING 17.5 continued

```
        frame.addWindowListener(new WindowAdapter() {public void
            windowClosing(WindowEvent e) {System.exit(0);}});

        frame.show();
    }

    public void childLoop(String uri)
    {
        DefaultHandler defaultHandler = this;
        SAXParserFactory factory = SAXParserFactory.newInstance();
        try {
            SAXParser saxParser = factory.newSAXParser();
            saxParser.parse(new File(uri), defaultHandler);
        } catch (Throwable t) {}
    }

    public void startElement(String uri, String localName,
        String qualifiedName, Attributes attrs)
    {
        if (qualifiedName.equals("square")) {
            x[totalFigures] = Integer.parseInt(attrs.getValue("x"));
            y[totalFigures] = Integer.parseInt(attrs.getValue("y"));
            width[totalFigures] = Integer.parseInt(attrs.getValue("width"));
            totalFigures++;
        }
    }

    public void warning(SAXParseException exception)
    {
        System.err.println("Warning: " +
            exception.getMessage());
    }

    public void error(SAXParseException exception)
    {
        System.err.println("Error: " +
            exception.getMessage());
    }

    public void fatalError(SAXParseException exception)
    {
        System.err.println("Fatal error: " +
            exception.getMessage());
    }
}

class AppFrame extends Frame
{
    int totalFigures;
```

LISTING 17.5 continued

```
    int[] xValues;
    int[] yValues;
    int[] widthValues;

    public AppFrame(int number, int[] x, int[] y, int[] width)
    {
        totalFigures = number;
        xValues = x;
        yValues = y;
        widthValues = width;
    }

    public void paint(Graphics g)
    {
        for(int loopIndex = 0; loopIndex < totalFigures; loopIndex++){
            g.drawRect(xValues[loopIndex], yValues[loopIndex],
                widthValues[loopIndex], widthValues[loopIndex]);
        }
    }
}
```


Navigating Through XML Documents by Using SAX

Yesterday you used some W3C DOM methods (for example, `getNextSibling`, `getPreviousSibling`, `getFirstChild`, `getLastChild`, `getParent`) to navigate through an XML document. But you can't do that in SAX because a SAX parser does not create a tree of nodes to support these methods. Instead, you have to wait until what you are searching for comes to you. Yesterday you navigated through an XML document, looking for the last senator in an XML document. You can do the same in SAX; in this case, you just have to wait for the last senator to come to us.

Here's how it looks in code; in the `startElement` method, we count the number of senators we've seen, and if we're on the third and last senator, we set a Boolean variable, `lastSenatorBoolean`, to `true`:

```
public void startElement(String uri, String localName,
    String qualifiedName, Attributes attributes)
{
    if(qualifiedName.equals("senator")) {
        senatorNumber++;
    }
```

```
    if(senatorNumber == 3) {
        lastSenatorBoolean = true;
    }
    .
    .
    .
```

If you're inside the last `<senator>` element, you can catch the `<firstName>` and `<lastName>` elements by setting the Booleans `firstNameBoolean` and `lastNameBoolean` to `true`:

```
public void startElement(String uri, String localName,
    String qualifiedName, Attributes attributes)
{
    if(qualifiedName.equals("senator")) {
        senatorNumber++;
    }

    if(senatorNumber == 3) {
        lastSenatorBoolean = true;
    }

    if(qualifiedName.equals("firstName") && lastSenatorBoolean) {
        firstNameBoolean = true;
    }

    if(qualifiedName.equals("lastName")  && lastSenatorBoolean) {
        firstNameBoolean = false;
        lastNameBoolean = true;
    }
}
```

By using the `firstNameBoolean` and `lastNameBoolean` variables, you can catch the name of the last senator when you handle text nodes:

```
public void characters(char characters[], int start, int length)
{
    String characterData = (new String(characters, start, length)).trim();
    if(characterData.indexOf("\n") < 0 && characterData.length() > 0) {
        if(firstNameBoolean) {
            firstName = characterData;
        }
        if(lastNameBoolean) {
            lastName = characterData;
        }
    }
}
```

Now that you've stored the last senator's first and last names in the variables `firstName` and `lastName`, you can display them when in the `endElement` method:

```
public void endElement(String uri, String localName,
    String qualifiedName)
{
    if(lastSenatorBoolean && lastNameBoolean){
        System.out.println("Last senator: " + firstName +
            " " + lastName);
        lastSenatorBoolean = false;
        firstNameBoolean = false;
        lastNameBoolean = false;
    }
}
```

And that's it—when you run this application, you see this result:

```
%java ch17_06 ch17_01.xml
Last senator: Jay Jones
```


This code gives you the same results as when you used DOM methods yesterday, but instead of going to find the senator as you did yesterday, this time you used SAX methods and let the senator come to you. Listing 17.6 shows the full code for this application, `ch17_06.java`.

LISTING 17.6 Navigating XML by Using SAX (`ch17_06.java`)

```
import java.io.*;
import org.xml.sax.*;
import javax.xml.parsers.*;
import org.xml.sax.helpers.DefaultHandler;

public class ch17_06 extends DefaultHandler
{
    int senatorNumber;
    boolean lastSenatorBoolean = false, firstNameBoolean = false,
        lastNameBoolean = false;
    String firstName, lastName;

    public static void main(String args[])
    {
        ch17_06 obj = new ch17_06();
        obj.childLoop(args[0]);
    }

    public void childLoop(String uri)
    {
        DefaultHandler defaultHandler = this;
        SAXParserFactory factory = SAXParserFactory.newInstance();
        try {
            SAXParser saxParser = factory.newSAXParser();
            saxParser.parse(new File(uri), defaultHandler);
```

LISTING 17.6 continued

```
        } catch (Throwable t) {}
    }

    public void startElement(String uri, String localName,
        String qualifiedName, Attributes attributes)
    {
        if(qualifiedName.equals("senator")) {
            senatorNumber++;
        }

        if(senatorNumber == 3) {
            lastSenatorBoolean = true;
        }

        if(qualifiedName.equals("firstName") && lastSenatorBoolean) {
            firstNameBoolean = true;
        }

        if(qualifiedName.equals("lastName")  && lastSenatorBoolean) {
            firstNameBoolean = false;
            lastNameBoolean = true;
        }

    }

    public void characters(char characters[], int start, int length)
    {
        String characterData = (new String(characters, start, length)).trim();
        if(characterData.indexOf("\n") < 0 && characterData.length() > 0) {
            if(firstNameBoolean) {
                firstName = characterData;
            }
            if(lastNameBoolean) {
                lastName = characterData;
            }
        }
    }

    public void endElement(String uri, String localName,
        String qualifiedName)
    {
        if(lastSenatorBoolean && lastNameBoolean){
            System.out.println("Last senator: " + firstName +
                " " + lastName);
            lastSenatorBoolean = false;
            firstNameBoolean = false;
            lastNameBoolean = false;
        }
    }
```

LISTING 17.6 continued

```
    public void warning(SAXParseException exception)
    {
        System.err.println("Warning: " +
            exception.getMessage());
    }

    public void error(SAXParseException exception)
    {
        System.err.println("Error: " +
            exception.getMessage());
    }

    public void fatalError(SAXParseException exception)
    {
        System.err.println("Fatal error: " +
            exception.getMessage());
    }
}
```


Writing XML by Using Java and SAX

When we're working with DOM, we can use methods such as `createElement`, `insertBefore`, and `addChild` to edit an XML document in memory. On the other hand, in SAX we're not dealing with a tree of nodes, so there are no similar methods.

However, if we want to, we can simulate element creation by calling the `startElement`, `characters`, and `endElement` methods. Listing 17.7 is an example that does the same thing as yesterday's XML-writing example did—inserts an `<elected>2004</elected>` element at the end of each `<senator>` element. The new version of the XML document will be written out as `new.xml`, and Listing 17.7 shows the complete code.

LISTING 17.7 Navigating XML by Using SAX (`ch17_07.java`)

```
import java.io.*;
import org.xml.sax.*;
import javax.xml.parsers.*;
import org.xml.sax.helpers.DefaultHandler;

public class ch17_07 extends DefaultHandler
{
    static String displayText[] = new String[1000];
    static int numberLines = 0;
    static String indentation = "";
```

Listing 17.7 continued

```
    public static void main(String args[])
    {
        ch17_07 obj = new ch17_07();
        obj.childLoop(args[0]);

        try {
            FileWriter filewriter = new FileWriter("new.xml");

            for(int loopIndex = 0; loopIndex < numberLines; loopIndex++){
                filewriter.write(displayText[loopIndex].toCharArray());
                filewriter.write('\n');
            }

            filewriter.close();
        }
        catch (Exception e) {
            e.printStackTrace(System.err);
        }
    }

    public void childLoop(String uri)
    {
        DefaultHandler handler = this;
        SAXParserFactory factory = SAXParserFactory.newInstance();
        try {
            SAXParser saxParser = factory.newSAXParser();
            saxParser.parse(new File(uri), handler);
        } catch (Throwable t) {}
    }

    public void startDocument()
    {
        displayText[numberLines] = indentation;
        displayText[numberLines] += "<?xml version=\"1.0\" encoding=\""+
            "UTF-8" + "\"?>";
        numberLines++;
    }

    public void processingInstruction(String target, String data)
    {
        displayText[numberLines] = indentation;
        displayText[numberLines] += "<?";
        displayText[numberLines] += target;
        if (data != null && data.length() > 0) {
            displayText[numberLines] += ' ';
            displayText[numberLines] += data;
        }
        displayText[numberLines] += "?>";
```

LISTING 17.7 continued

```
            numberLines++;
        }

        public void startElement(String uri, String localName,
            String qualifiedName, Attributes attributes)
        {
            displayText[numberLines] = indentation;

            indentation += "    ";

            displayText[numberLines] += '<';
            displayText[numberLines] += qualifiedName;
            if (attributes != null) {
                int numberAttributes = attributes.getLength();
                for (int loopIndex = 0; loopIndex < numberAttributes; loopIndex++){
                    displayText[numberLines] += ' ';
                    displayText[numberLines] += attributes.getQName(loopIndex);
                    displayText[numberLines] += "=\"";
                    displayText[numberLines] += attributes.getValue(loopIndex);
                    displayText[numberLines] += '"';
                }
            }
            displayText[numberLines] += '>';
            numberLines++;
        }

        public void characters(char characters[], int start, int length)
        {
            String characterData = (new String(characters, start, length)).trim();
            if(characterData.indexOf("\n") < 0 && characterData.length() > 0) {
                displayText[numberLines] = indentation;
                displayText[numberLines] += characterData;
                numberLines++;
            }
        }

        public void ignorableWhitespace(char characters[], int start, int length)
        {
            //characters(characters, start, length);
        }

        public void endElement(String uri, String localName, String qualifiedName)
        {
            indentation = indentation.substring(0, indentation.length() - 4) ;
            displayText[numberLines] = indentation;
            displayText[numberLines] += "</";
            displayText[numberLines] += qualifiedName;
            displayText[numberLines] += '>';
            numberLines++;
```

LISTING 17.7 continued

```
            if (qualifiedName.equals("lastName")) {
                startElement("", "elected", "elected", null);
                characters("2004".toCharArray(), 0, "2004".length());
                endElement("", "elected", "elected");
            }
        }

    public void warning(SAXParseException exception)
    {
        System.err.println("Warning: " +
            exception.getMessage());
    }

    public void error(SAXParseException exception)
    {
        System.err.println("Error: " +
            exception.getMessage());
    }

    public void fatalError(SAXParseException exception)
    {
        System.err.println("Fatal error: " +
            exception.getMessage());
    }
}
```

Here's what the resulting document, `new.xml`, looks like:

```
<?xml version="1.0" encoding="UTF-8"?>
<session>
    <committee type="monetary">
        <title>
            Finance
        </title>
        <number>
            17
        </number>
        <subject>
            Donut Costs
        </subject>
        <date>
            7/15/2005
        </date>
        <attendees>
            <senator status="present">
                <firstName>
                    Thomas
                </firstName>
                <lastName>
```

LISTING 17.7 continued

```
                    Smith
                </lastName>
                <elected>
                    2004
                </elected>
            </senator>
            <senator status="absent">
                <firstName>
                    Frank
                </firstName>
                <lastName>
                    McCoy
                </lastName>
                <elected>
                    2004
                </elected>
            </senator>
            <senator status="present">
                <firstName>
                    Jay
                </firstName>
                <lastName>
                    Jones
                </lastName>
                <elected>
                    2004
                </elected>
            </senator>
        </attendees>
    </committee>
</session>
```


That's it for today's discussion on using XML with Java and SAX. As you can see, SAX provides an alternate way of dealing with XML that is often easier than using the DOM. Tomorrow, you're going to take a look at working with two more popular XML applications: Simple Object Access Protocol (SOAP) and the Resource Description Framework (RDF).

Summary

Today, you took a look at working with SAX and XML in Java. Unlike the DOM techniques discussed yesterday, a SAX parser parses an XML document by itself and calls you when it finds the beginning of a document, the start of an element, and so on. You saw today that you can do all that you did yesterday with DOM techniques by using SAX, although the programming is different.

Today you saw that after you register your code with a SAX handler and parse a document, you get called back as our XML document is parsed. The `startElement` method is called when the beginning of an element is encountered, the `characters` method is called when a text node is encountered, the `processingInstrucion` method is called when a processing method is encountered, the `endElement` method is called when the end of an element is encountered, and so on.

All these SAX methods are called with the data needed from the document you're parsing. For example, the `characters` method is called with the text of a text node, the `endElement` method is called with the local and qualified name of the element, and so on. Note also that attributes are treated as nodes, but SAX doesn't call a separate method for them; instead, use the `Attributes` object passed to the `startElement` method.

Q&A

Q Although the `parse` method returns automatically after parsing a document, isn't there some way to explicitly catch the end of the parsing process, before the `parse` method returns?

A Yes, you can implement the `endDocument` method, called when the end of the document is encountered.

Q Which is better, SAX or DOM?

A As you can guess, that depends. Some people find one easier to use than the other. However, if you want to work directly with document structure, you should consider DOM, which stores the whole document in a reusable tree of nodes. If you just want to pick a few nodes out of an element and don't want to navigate around, you should consider SAX.

Workshop

This workshop tests whether you understand the concepts discussed today. It's a good idea to make sure you can answer these questions before pressing on to tomorrow's work. Answers to the quiz can be found in Appendix A, "Quiz Answers."

Quiz

1. How do you read in an XML document and create a Java `Document` object in Java by using SAX?
2. What SAX method(s) do you implement to handle elements?
3. How can you determine the text in a text node by using SAX?

4. How can you get the attributes of an element by using SAX?
5. What methods can you use with SAX to handle warnings, errors, and fatal errors?

Exercises

1. Using Java XML SAX navigation methods, determine the last name of the second senator in `ch17_01.xml`.
2. Building on your solution to Exercise 1, use Java and SAX to read the value of the second senator's `status` attribute to determine whether he was present or absent for the meeting.

Part IV

Day 18

Working with SOAP and RDF

Today you're going to take a look at two important XML applications—Simple Object Access Protocol (SOAP) and the Resource Description Framework (RDF). SOAP is an XML-based protocol that allows applications to communicate on the Web. RDF lets us describe resources in a standard way that is machine readable, and it's often used to describe Web documents (although we can use it to describe any type of resource). Here's an overview of the topics covered today:

- Using SOAP
- Using SOAP envelopes, headers, and bodies
- Using SOAP to communicate between Web applications
- Using SOAP in .NET
- Using SOAP with Java
- Creating RDF documents
- Using the Dublin Core
- Using abbreviated RDF syntax

Introducing SOAP

SOAP lets Web applications send data back and forth in messages in a platform-independent, language-independent way. SOAP was designed so that distributed applications could communicate through corporate firewalls, allowing applications to work with objects across all kinds of boundaries. In SOAP we send XML-based messages by using HTTP; because it uses widely available HTTP, SOAP has become very popular. SOAP messages can provide a backbone for distributed applications, using existing technologies to connect the parts of those distributed applications. We can also send attachments by using SOAP messages, as you'll see today.

SOAP is a general-purpose XML application that is helping to standardize the way people handle data on the Internet. There are plenty of SOAP resources on the Internet; here's a starter list, including the W3C's documentation on it:

- `http://www.w3.org/TR/SOAP`—The W3C SOAP 1.1 documentation
- `http://www.w3.org/TR/SOAP-attachments`—The W3C "SOAP Messages with Attachments" documentation
- `http://www.javaworld.com/javaworld/jw-03-2001/jw-0330-soap.html`—Part 1 of a SOAP tutorial
- `http://www.javaworld.com/javaworld/jw-04-2001/jw-0427-soap.html`—Part 2 of a SOAP tutorial
- `http://www.javaworld.com/javaworld/jw-06-2001/jw-0601-soap.html`—Part 3 of a SOAP tutorial
- `http://www.javaworld.com/javaworld/jw-07-2001/jw-0706-soap.html`—Part 4 of a SOAP tutorial
- `http://www.w3schools.com/SOAP/default.asp`—A SOAP tutorial
- `http://www.xml.com/pub/a/2000/02/09/feature/index.html`—An article on SOAP from XML.com
- `http://xml.apache.org/soap/faq/index.html`—The Apache project's SOAP FAQ

We'll start digging into SOAP now, beginning with the syntax that makes SOAP work.

Understanding SOAP Syntax

A SOAP message is simply an XML document that uses the SOAP syntax rules. There are three parts of a valid SOAP message:

- **Envelope**—The envelope contains the message itself.
- **Header**—This optional part contains information about and descriptions of the message.
- **Body**—The body contains the actual SOAP message.

As a simple example, here's a SOAP message, complete with an envelope and a body. This message indicates the number of laptops in stock at a warehouse (note that `soap-env` is the usual envelope namespace prefix):

```
<soap-env:Envelope
    xmlns:soap-env="http://www.w3.org/2001/12/soap-envelope"
    soap:soap-enc="http://www.w3.org/2001/12/soap-encoding">
    <soap-env:Header>
        <m:Name xmlns:m="http://www.XMLPowerCorp.com">
            XMLPowerCorp
        </m:Name>
    </soap-env:Header>
    <soap-env:Body>
        <m:numberAvailable xmlns:m="http://www.XMLPowerCorp.com">
            <m:laptops>216</m:laptops>
        </m:numberAvailable>
    </soap-env:Body>
</soap-env:Envelope>
```

18

The default namespace setting for a SOAP envelope is `"http://schemas.xmlsoap.org/soap/envelope/"`. The default namespace setting for the document encoding and data types is `"http://schemas.xmlsoap.org/soap/encoding/"`.

So what elements are already defined in SOAP?

Introducing the SOAP Elements

The root element in a SOAP message is the `<Envelope>` element. There are three possible child elements—`<Header>`, `<Body>`, and `<Fault>`. These elements have to use the names `Header`, `Body`, and `Fault`, respectively, although they can have child elements with any names. For example, here's what a SOAP envelope might look like:

```
<soap-env:Envelope
    xmlns:soap-env="http://schemas.xmlsoap.org/soap/envelope/"
    soap-env:encodingStyle="http://schemas.xmlsoap.org/soap/encoding/">
    .
    .
    .
</soap-env:Envelope>
```

The next element, the `<Header>` element, is optional. It holds information about the SOAP message, as in the following example, where we're setting the language to U.S. English (`<m:locale>` and `<m:language>` are elements we've defined):

```
<soap-env:Envelope
    xmlns:soap-env="http://schemas.xmlsoap.org/soap/envelope/"
    soap-env:encodingStyle="http://schemas.xmlsoap.org/soap/encoding/">
    <soap-env:Header>
        <m:locale xmlns:m="http://www.XMLPowerCorp.com">
            <m:language>en-us</m:language>
        </m:locale>
    </soap-env:Header>
    .
    .
    .
</soap-env:Envelope>
```

Next, the <Body> element holds the actual SOAP message:

```
<soap-env:Envelope
    xmlns:soap-env="http://schemas.xmlsoap.org/soap/envelope/"
    soap-env:encodingStyle="http://schemas.xmlsoap.org/soap/encoding/">
    <soap-env:Header>
        <m:locale xmlns:m="http://www.XMLPowerCorp.com">
            <m:language>en-us</m:language>
        </m:locale>
    </soap-env:Header>

    <soap-env:Body>
        <m:numberAvailable xmlns:m="http://www.XMLPowerCorp.com">
            <m:laptops>216</m:laptops>
        </m:numberAvailable>
    </soap-env:Body>
</soap-env:Envelope>
```

Note that the <Body> element may also contain a <Fault> element, which can hold any errors that occurred:

```
<soap-env:Envelope
    xmlns:soap-env="http://schemas.xmlsoap.org/soap/envelope/"
    soap-env:encodingStyle="http://schemas.xmlsoap.org/soap/encoding/">
    <soap-env:Header>
        <m:locale xmlns:m="http://www.XMLPowerCorp.com">
            <m:language>en-us</m:language>
        </m:locale>
    </soap-env:Header>

    <soap-env:Body>
        <m:numberAvailable xmlns:m="http://www.XMLPowerCorp.com">
            <m:laptops>216</m:laptops>
        </m:numberAvailable>

        <soap-env:Fault>
            <faultcode>1166</faultcode>
```

```
            <faultstring>Batteries are low</faultstring>
        </soap-env:Fault>
    </soap-env:Body>
</soap-env:Envelope>
```

<Fault> elements can have these subelements:

- **<faultcode>**—Contains an error code.
- **<faultstring>**—Contains an error string.
- **<faultactor>**—Specifies the error's source.
- **<detail>**—Contains the details of the error.

A number of fault codes are already defined for use in the <faultcode> element:

- **VersionMismatch**—Means that the namespace for the SOAP <Envelope> element was not correct.
- **MustUnderstand**—Means that an element's content must be understood if this attribute is set to "1".
- **Client**—Means there was a problem with the message as sent from the client.
- **Server**—Means that there was a problem with the server.

In addition, SOAP elements can support various attributes, which we'll look at now.

18

Introducing the SOAP Attributes

The possible attributes we can use in SOAP elements are `actor`, `encodingStyle`, and `mustUnderstand`. For example, the `actor` attribute lists a URI corresponding to the group that is using the SOAP message, like this:

```
<soap-env:Header>
    <m:data xmlns:m="http://www.XMLPowerCorp.com"
        soap-env:actor="http://www.XMLPowerCorp.com/philosophy" />
        <m:language>en-us</m:language>
    </m:data>
</soap-env:Header>
```

The `encodingStyle` attribute indicates the data types used in the message. The W3C provides a default schema for SOAP types, which you can find at `http://schemas.xmlsoap.org/soap/encoding/`:

```
<soap-env:Envelope
    xmlns:soap-env="http://schemas.xmlsoap.org/soap/envelope/"
    soap-env:encodingStyle="http://schemas.xmlsoap.org/soap/encoding/">
    .
    .
    .
</soap-env:Envelope>
```

The `mustUnderstand` attribute is used in the `<Header>` element, and it indicates whether the software interpreting a message must understand a header element or cause a fatal error if it does not. You can set it to a Boolean value, `"1"` for true or `"0"` for false:

```
<soap-env:Header>
    <m:data xmlns:m="http://www.XMLPowerCorp.com"
        soap-env:mustUnderstand="0" />
        <m:language>en-us</m:language>
    </m:data>
</soap-env:Header>
```

Now it's time to see SOAP at work.

A SOAP Example in .NET

You'll start our look at SOAP examples with Microsoft's .NET. In particular, you'll use Microsoft's C# language in Windows. It's a little-known fact that you can get C# for free—to use the C# command-line compiler, `csc`, all you need to do is install the .NET Framework's Software Development Kit (SDK), which you can get for free at `http://msdn.microsoft.com/downloads`.

After you install this download, you can find the `csc` command-line compiler in the system's root directory; for example, in Windows 2000, that is `C:\WINNT\Microsoft.NET\Framework\vxxxxxxxx\csc`, where *xxxxxxxx* is the version of the .NET framework that you downloaded. You can either add `csc` to your computer's path so that you can type it directly at the command line or enter its full path (that is, `C:\WINNT\Microsoft.NET\Framework\vxxxxxxxx\csc`) each time you run it.

You need to know how to use C# for this example. Here, you'll create a SOAP server that will send a message to a client. In this case, you'll use SOAP to send information from the server to the client so that the client will know how to call a method named `upper` in the server, which the client will use to capitalize some text. To describe `upper`, you'll create a C# interface named `IUpper`, which is shown in Listing 18.1.

LISTING 18.1 A SOAP Server (`ch18_01.cs`)

```
public interface IUpper
{
    string upper(string text);
}
```

You can compile `ch18_01.cs` into its own DLL, `ch18_01.dll`, like this:

```
%csc /t:library ch18_01. cs
```

This creates `ch18_01.dll`, which gives you a consistent way of describing the `upper` method to both the client and the server.

Creating a SOAP Server

In the server, you'll implement the `upper` method so it can read the text the client sends you in a class named `Capitalizer`, capitalize that text by using the Java `String` class's `ToUpper` method, and send it back to the client. You do that like this:

```
using System;
using System.IO;
using System.Runtime.Remoting;
using System.Runtime.Remoting.Channels;
using System.Runtime.Remoting.Channels.Http;
using System.Runtime.Serialization.Formatters.Soap;

public class Capitalizer : MarshalByRefObject, IUpper
{
    public string upper(string inText)
    {
        System.Console.WriteLine("Read this: \"{0}\"", inText);
        string outText = inText.ToUpper();
        System.Console.WriteLine("Sending this: \"{0}\"", outText);
        return outText;
    }
}
```

18

To actually send SOAP messages to the client, you'll use an object of the `SoapFormatter` class. In particular, you're going to let the client know how to access an object of your new `Capitalizer` class. Here's what that looks like in the server's main class:

```
public class ch18_02
{
    public static void Main()
    {
        HttpChannel channel = new HttpChannel(65111);
        ChannelServices.RegisterChannel(channel);

        Capitalizer capitalizer = new Capitalizer();

        ObjRef objref = RemotingServices.Marshal(capitalizer);

        FileStream filestream = new FileStream("soap.txt", FileMode.Create);

        SoapFormatter soapformatter = new SoapFormatter();

        soapformatter.Serialize(filestream, objref);
        filestream.Close();
```

```
        System.Console.WriteLine("soap.txt created. Press Enter to quit.");
        System.Console.ReadLine();
    }
}
```

In this case, you're writing a SOAP message that describes the `upper` method in a file, `soap.txt`, which the client will read and use. Listing 18.2 shows the full code for the server.

LISTING 18.2 A SOAP Server (`ch18_02.cs`)

```
using System;
using System.IO;
using System.Runtime.Remoting;
using System.Runtime.Remoting.Channels;
using System.Runtime.Remoting.Channels.Http;
using System.Runtime.Serialization.Formatters.Soap;

public class Capitalizer : MarshalByRefObject, IUpper
{
    public string upper(string inText)
    {
        System.Console.WriteLine("Read this: \"{0}\"", inText);
        string outText = inText.ToUpper();
        System.Console.WriteLine("Sending this: \"{0}\"", outText);
        return outText;
    }
}

public class ch18_02
{
    public static void Main()
    {
        HttpChannel channel = new HttpChannel(65111);
        ChannelServices.RegisterChannel(channel);

        Capitalizer capitalizer = new Capitalizer();

        ObjRef objref = RemotingServices.Marshal(capitalizer);

        FileStream filestream = new FileStream("soap.txt", FileMode.Create);

        SoapFormatter soapformatter = new SoapFormatter();

        soapformatter.Serialize(filestream, objref);
        filestream.Close();

        System.Console.WriteLine("soap.txt created. Press Enter to quit.");
        System.Console.ReadLine();
    }
}
```

You can create the server, `ch18_02.exe`, by linking in the DLL file like this:

```
%csc /t:exe /r:ch18_01.dll ch18_02. cs
```

Creating a SOAP Client

In the client, you can read the SOAP message in `soap.txt` and use it to connect to the server. To do that, we'll need a `SoapFormatter` object, which we create and use to read in `soap.txt` like this:

```
using System;
using System.IO;
using System.Runtime.Remoting;
using System.Runtime.Remoting.Channels;
using System.Runtime.Remoting.Channels.Http;
using System.Runtime.Serialization.Formatters.Soap;

public class ch18_03
{
    public static void Main()
    {
        HttpChannel channel = new HttpChannel();
        ChannelServices.RegisterChannel(channel);

        FileStream filestream = new FileStream ("soap.txt", FileMode.Open);
        SoapFormatter soapformatter = new SoapFormatter();
        .
        .
        .
```

18

Now use the `SoapFormatter` object to create an `IUpper` object named `capper`, and call the `upper` method of this object—which will call the `upper` method in the server remotely—to capitalize the text `"Hello there."`. Here's what it looks like in code:

```
using System;
using System.IO;
using System.Runtime.Remoting;
using System.Runtime.Remoting.Channels;
using System.Runtime.Remoting.Channels.Http;
using System.Runtime.Serialization.Formatters.Soap;

public class ch18_03
{
    public static void Main()
    {
        HttpChannel channel = new HttpChannel();
        ChannelServices.RegisterChannel(channel);

        FileStream filestream = new FileStream ("soap.txt", FileMode.Open) ;
        SoapFormatter soapformatter = new SoapFormatter();
```

```
        try
        {
            IUpper capper = (IUpper)soapformatter.Deserialize(filestream);

            string outText = "Hello there.";
            System.Console.WriteLine("Sending this: \"{0}\"", outText);
            string inText = capper.upper(outText);
        .
        .
        .
    }
}
```

Now all you need to do is display what you got back from the `upper` method, as seen in the client application, `ch18_03.cs`, shown in Listing 18.3.

LISTING 18.3 A SOAP Client (`ch18_03.cs`)

```
using System;
using System.IO;
using System.Runtime.Remoting;
using System.Runtime.Remoting.Channels;
using System.Runtime.Remoting.Channels.Http;
using System.Runtime.Serialization.Formatters.Soap;

public class ch18_03
{
    public static void Main()
    {
        HttpChannel channel = new HttpChannel();
        ChannelServices.RegisterChannel(channel);

        FileStream filestream = new FileStream ("soap.txt", FileMode.Open);
        SoapFormatter soapformatter = new SoapFormatter();

        try
        {
            IUpper capper = (IUpper)soapformatter.Deserialize(filestream);

            string outText = "Hello there.";
            System.Console.WriteLine("Sending this: \"{0}\"", outText) ;
            string inText = capper.upper(outText);
            System.Console.WriteLine("Read this: \"{0}\"", inText);
        }
        catch(System.Exception e)
        {
            System.Console.WriteLine(e.Message);
        }
    }
}
```

You can create the client, `ch18_03.exe`, like this:

```
%csc /t:exe /r:ch18_01.dll ch18_03. cs
```

Using the Server and Client

You're ready to use your two applications and let them communicate with a SOAP message. Start the server, `ch18_02.exe`, in one MS-DOS window, and it displays this text:

```
%ch18_02
soap.txt created. Press Enter to quit.
```

The SOAP message, which tells the client how to connect to the server and use the `upper` method, has now been written to the `soap.txt` file. To read that SOAP message, start the client application in another MS-DOS window. The client then sends the text `"Hello there."` to the server and gets that string back, capitalized:

```
%ch18_03
Sending this text: "Hello there."
Got this text back: "HELLO THERE."
```

The server also indicates what text it got and what text it sent back to the client:

```
%ch18_02
soap.txt created. Press Enter to quit.
Read this: "Hello there."
Sending this: "HELLO THERE."
```


Here's the actual SOAP message that lets the server remotely connect to the `upper` method in the server:

```
<SOAP-ENV:Envelope xmlns:xsi="http://www.w3.org/2001/XMLSchema-instance"
xmlns:xsd="http://www.w3.org/2001/XMLSchema"
xmlns:SOAP-ENC="http://schemas.xmlsoap.org/soap/encoding/"
xmlns:SOAP-ENV="http://schemas.xmlsoap.org/soap/envelope/"
xmlns:clr="http://schemas.microsoft.com/soap/encoding/clr/1.0" SOAP-
ENV:encodingStyle="http://schemas.xmlsoap.org/soap/encoding/">
<SOAP-ENV:Body>
<a1:ObjRef id="ref-1"
xmlns:a1="http://schemas.microsoft.com/clr/ns/System.Runtime.Remoting">
<uri id="ref-2">/23186ad8_d9e2_4018_bcf1_
82cb2b4084c2/UgL21NCXPtdS5ON7digxzBfC_1.rem</uri>
<objrefFlags>0</objrefFlags>
<typeInfo href="#ref-3"/>
<envoyInfo xsi:null="1"/>
<channelInfo href="#ref-4"/>
</a1:ObjRef>
<a1:TypeInfo id="ref-3"
xmlns:a1="http://schemas.microsoft.com/clr/ns/System.Runtime.Remoting">
<serverType id="ref-5">Capitalizer, ch18_02,
Version=0.0.0.0, Culture=neutral, PublicKeyToken=null</serverType>
```

```
<serverHierarchy xsi:null="1"/>
<interfacesImplemented href="#ref-6"/>
</a1:TypeInfo>
<a1:ChannelInfo id="ref-4"
xmlns:a1="http://schemas.microsoft.com/clr/ns/System.Runtime.Remoting">
<channelData href="#ref-7"/>
</a1:ChannelInfo>
<SOAP-ENC:Array id="ref-6" SOAP-ENC:arrayType="xsd:string[1]">
<item id="ref-8">IUpper, ch18_01, Version=0.0.0.0,
Culture=neutral, PublicKeyToken=null</item>
</SOAP-ENC:Array>
<SOAP-ENC:Array id="ref-7" SOAP-ENC:arrayType="xsd:anyType[2]">
<item href="#ref-9"/>
<item href="#ref-10"/>
</SOAP-ENC:Array>
<a3:CrossAppDomainData id="ref-9"
xmlns:a3="http://schemas.microsoft.com/clr/ns/System.Runtime.
Remoting.Channels">
<_ContextID>1345320</_ContextID>
<_DomainID>1</_DomainID>
<_processGuid id="ref-11">f0a6d250_b75d_47be_8df4_5ed8e461af6b</_processGuid>
</a3:CrossAppDomainData>
<a3:ChannelDataStore id="ref-10"
xmlns:a3="http://schemas.microsoft.com/clr/ns/System.Runtime.
Remoting.Channels">
<_channelURIs href="#ref-12"/>
<_extraData xsi:null="1"/>
</a3:ChannelDataStore>
<SOAP-ENC:Array id="ref-12" SOAP-ENC:arrayType="xsd:string[1]">
<item id="ref-13">http://209.177.24.57:65432</item>
</SOAP-ENC:Array>
</SOAP-ENV:Body>
</SOAP-ENV:Envelope>
```

This example shows how C# and .NET use SOAP messages behind-the-scenes. Now let's take a look at a SOAP example in Java.

A SOAP Example in Java

You can use SOAP with Java by using Web services, but doing so is more advanced than the Java work you've already seen in this book. In this example, you're going to use Java servlets on a Web server. For this example you'll use two servlets—one that sends the SOAP message and one that receives that message. The receiving servlet will decode the data in the SOAP message and return a new SOAP message indicating that it has understood.

You need a Web server that can run Java servlets for this example. The Tomcat server is the premier Web server for JavaServer Pages and servlets; you can download it from `http://jakarta.apache.org/tomcat/`. Downloading and installing Tomcat is not difficult; just use the installation directions that come with Tomcat. After you have Tomcat installed and running, navigate to `http://localhost:8080/index.html`, and you should see Tomcat running, as in Figure 18.1.

FIGURE 18.1
Getting the Tomcat server running.

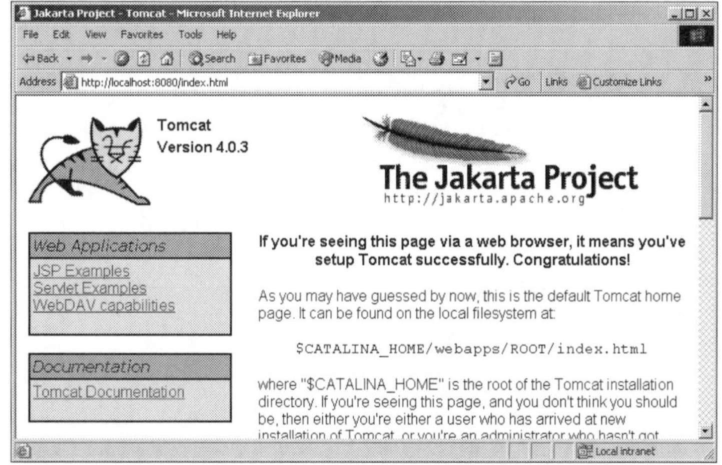

To support Web services, you also need some additional Java packages. There are two options when you're using SOAP with Java—you can download the Java XML pack, which is at (as of this writing) `http://java.sun.com/xml/downloads/javaxmlpack.html`, or you can download the Java Web Services Developer's Pack, which is at (as of this writing) `http://java.sun.com/webservices/webservicespack.html`. It's easiest to download the Java XML pack, which is a simple zipped file that holds the JAR files you'll need: `jaxm-api.jar`, `saaj-api.jar`, and `activation.jar`. You also need `servlet.jar` to create servlets, and this file comes with Tomcat, in the `lib` directory.

There's another step you need to take at this point: You need to set up Tomcat to work with Java XML Messaging (JAXM). You should stop Tomcat if it's running and copy `jaxm-docs.war`, which comes with the Java XML Pack or the Java Web Services Developer's Pack, to the Tomcat `webapps` directory, and then you can restart Tomcat and navigate to `http://localhost:8080/jaxm-docs/tomcat.html` for directions. Setting up Tomcat for JAXM simply involves copying some JAR (Java archive) and WAR (Web archive) files.

With Tomcat set up, you're ready to write the two SOAP servlets you're going to use today: the server, ch18_04, and the client, ch18_05. For this example, you'll start by opening a new Web page, ch18_06.html, that has a link in it to the server servlet, ch18_04. When that link is clicked, the server will send a SOAP message to the client servlet, indicating how many laptops you have in stock, and the client servlet will then send back an acknowledging SOAP message. The actual SOAP messages will also be written to file so you can see what the two servlets sent each other. You'll start by creating the server servlet, ch18_04.

Creating the Server

The first servlet will create and send a SOAP message indicating that you have 216 laptops available. You start by creating a SOAP connection object named connection:

```
package soapExample;

import java.io.*;
import java.net.*;
import javax.servlet.*;
import javax.xml.soap.*;
import javax.activation.*;
import javax.servlet.http.*;

public class ch18_04 extends HttpServlet
{
    private SOAPConnection connection;

    public void init(ServletConfig servletConfig) throws ServletException
    {
        super.init(servletConfig);

        try {
        SOAPConnectionFactory connectionFactory =
                    SOAPConnectionFactory.newInstance();
            connection = connectionFactory.createConnection();
        } catch(Exception e) {}
    }
```

When the servlet is called, its doGet method will be executed, and that's the method where most of your code will go. Here, you create a MessageFactory object and a SOAP message:

```
public void doGet(HttpServletRequest request, HttpServletResponse response)
throws ServletException
{
    String outString ="<HTML><H1>Sending and reading the SOAP Message</H1><P>";
```

```
    try {
        MessageFactory messageFactory = MessageFactory.newInstance();
        SOAPMessage outgoingMessage = messageFactory.createMessage();
        .
        .
        .
```

Create the parts of the message, including the envelope, header, and body, like this:

```
public void doGet(HttpServletRequest request, HttpServletResponse response)
throws ServletException
{
    String outString ="<HTML><H1>Sending and reading the SOAP Message</H1><P>";

    try {
        MessageFactory messageFactory = MessageFactory.newInstance();
        SOAPMessage outgoingMessage = messageFactory.createMessage();

        SOAPPart soappart = outgoingMessage.getSOAPPart();
        SOAPEnvelope envelope = soappart.getEnvelope();
        SOAPHeader header = envelope.getHeader();
        SOAPBody body = envelope.getBody();
    .
    .
    .
```

18

Now you add an element named `<laptops:numberAvailable>` to the SOAP message's body and indicate that there are 216 laptops available, like this:

```
body.addBodyElement(envelope.createName("numberAvailable", "laptops",
"http://www.XMLPowerCorp.com")).addTextNode("216");
```

You can also add attachments to SOAP messages, which you'll do next. In this case, you'll send a text attachment. A handy text file is the `ch18_06.html` document that you browse to in order to run this example, and here's how to attach it to the SOAP message:

```
StringBuffer serverUrl = new StringBuffer();
serverUrl.append(request.getScheme()).append("://")
    .append(request.getServerName());
serverUrl.append(":").append(request.getServerPort())
    .append(request.getContextPath());
String baseUrl = serverUrl.toString();
URL url = new URL(baseUrl + "/ch18_06.html");

AttachmentPart attachmentpart =
    outgoingMessage.createAttachmentPart(new DataHandler(url)) ;
attachmentpart.setContentType("text/html");
outgoingMessage.addAttachmentPart(attachmentpart) ;
```

Now you will write our SOAP message to a file, `out.msg`, so you can look at it later and send that message to the client:

```
URL client = new URL(baseUrl + "/ch18_05");

FileOutputStream outgoingFile = new FileOutputStream("out.msg");
outgoingMessage.writeTo(outgoingFile);
outgoingFile.close();

outString += "SOAP outgoingMessage sent (see out.msg). <BR>";

SOAPMessage incomingMessage = connection.call(outgoingMessage, client);
```

The SOAP message you get back from the client, which should acknowledge that there are 216 laptops available, is in the `incomingMessage` object, which you write to the file `in.msg` so you can take a look at it later:

```
if (incomingMessage != null) {
    FileOutputStream incomingFile = new FileOutputStream("in.msg");
    incomingMessage.writeTo(incomingFile);
    incomingFile.close();
    outString += "SOAP outgoingMessage received (see in.msg).</HTML>";
}
    .
    .
    .
```

That completes the server, which is your `ch18_04` servlet. The server's code, `ch18_04.java`, is shown in Listing 18.4.

LISTING 18.4 SOAP Server (`ch18_04.java`)

```
package soapExample;

import java.io.*;
import java.net.*;
import javax.servlet.*;
import javax.xml.soap.*;
import javax.activation.*;
import javax.servlet.http.*;

public class ch18_04 extends HttpServlet
{
    private SOAPConnection connection;

    public void init(ServletConfig servletConfig) throws ServletException
    {
        super.init(servletConfig);

        try {
        SOAPConnectionFactory connectionFactory =
                    SOAPConnectionFactory.newInstance();
```

LISTING 18.4 continued

```
            connection = connectionFactory.createConnection();
        } catch(Exception e) {}
    }

    public void doGet(HttpServletRequest request, HttpServletResponse response)
    throws ServletException
    {
        String outString =
            "<HTML><H1>Sending and reading the SOAP Message</H1><P>";

        try {
            MessageFactory messageFactory = MessageFactory.newInstance();
            SOAPMessage outgoingMessage = messageFactory.createMessage();

            SOAPPart soappart = outgoingMessage.getSOAPPart();
            SOAPEnvelope envelope = soappart.getEnvelope();
            SOAPHeader header = envelope.getHeader();
            SOAPBody body = envelope.getBody();

            body.addBodyElement(envelope.createName("numberAvailable",
            "laptops",
            "http://www.XMLPowerCorp.com")).addTextNode("216");

            StringBuffer serverUrl = new StringBuffer();
            serverUrl.append(request.getScheme()).append("://").
                append(request.getServerName());
            serverUrl.append(":").append(request.getServerPort()).
                append(request.getContextPath());
            String baseUrl = serverUrl.toString();
            URL url = new URL(baseUrl + "/ch18_06.html");

            AttachmentPart attachmentpart = outgoingMessage.
                createAttachmentPart(new DataHandler(url));
            attachmentpart.setContentType("text/html");
            outgoingMessage.addAttachmentPart(attachmentpart);

            URL client = new URL(baseUrl + "/ch18_05");

            FileOutputStream outgoingFile = new FileOutputStream("out.msg");
            outgoingMessage.writeTo(outgoingFile);
            outgoingFile.close();

            outString += "SOAP outgoingMessage sent (see out.msg). <BR>";

            SOAPMessage incomingMessage = connection.
                call(outgoingMessage, client);

            if (incomingMessage != null) {
```

18

LISTING 18.4 continued

```
                FileOutputStream incomingFile = new FileOutputStream("in.msg");
                incomingMessage.writeTo(incomingFile);
                incomingFile.close();
                outString +=
                    "SOAP outgoingMessage received (see in.msg).</HTML>";
            }

        } catch(Throwable e) {}

        try {
            OutputStream outputStream = response.getOutputStream();
            outputStream.write(outString.getBytes());
            outputStream.flush();
            outputStream.close();
        } catch (IOException e) {}
    }
}
```

Creating the Client

The next step is to create the client, the `ch18_05` servlet, which gets the server's SOAP message, interprets it, and sends a message back, indicating that it has understood the incoming message. Start by basing this servlet on the `JAXMServlet` class so that it can handle SOAP messages and creating a `MessageFactory` object so you can send SOAP messages:

```
package soapExample;

import java.util.*;
import javax.servlet.*;
import javax.xml.soap.*;
import javax.servlet.http.*;
import javax.xml.messaging.*;

public class ch18_05 extends JAXMServlet implements ReqRespListener
{
    static MessageFactory messageFactory = null;

    public void init(ServletConfig servletConfig) throws ServletException
    {
        super.init(servletConfig);
        try {
            messageFactory = MessageFactory.newInstance();
        } catch (Exception ex) {}
    }
        .
        .
        .
```

Now you can decipher the incoming SOAP message by getting the value of the `<laptops:numberAvailable>` element and storing it in a variable named `element`, like this:

```
public SOAPMessage onMessage(SOAPMessage msg)
{
    try {
        SOAPPart soappart = msg.getSOAPPart();
        SOAPEnvelope incomingEnvelope = soappart.getEnvelope();
        SOAPBody body = incomingEnvelope.getBody();

        Iterator iterator = body.getChildElements(
        incomingEnvelope.createName("numberAvailable", "laptops",
            "http://www.XMLPowerCorp.com"));

        SOAPElement element;
        element = (SOAPElement) iterator.next();
        .
        .
        .
```

The number of laptops left in stock can now be accessed with `element.getValue()`, and here's how to create a SOAP message to send back to the server, indicating that you've gotten that data:

```
            SOAPMessage message = messageFactory.createMessage();
            SOAPEnvelope envelope = message.getSOAPPart().getEnvelope();

            envelope.getBody().addChildElement(envelope.
                createName("Response")).addTextNode(
                "Got the SOAP message indicating there are " +
                element.getValue() +
                " laptops available."
            );
        .
        .
        .
}
```

Finally, send the new SOAP message that acknowledges the number of laptops back to the client by returning the new message, which automatically sends it back to the server servlet, `ch18_04`, as you can see in `ch18_05.java`, the SOAP client, in Listing 18.5.

LISTING 18.5 A SOAP Client (`ch18_05.java`)

```
package soapExample;

import java.util.*;
import javax.servlet.*;
import javax.xml.soap.*;
```

LISTING 18.5 continued

```
import javax.servlet.http.*;
import javax.xml.messaging.*;

public class ch18_05 extends JAXMServlet implements ReqRespListener
{
    static MessageFactory messageFactory = null;

    public void init(ServletConfig servletConfig) throws ServletException
    {
        super.init(servletConfig);
        try {
            messageFactory = MessageFactory.newInstance();
        } catch (Exception ex) {}
    }

    public SOAPMessage onMessage(SOAPMessage msg)
    {
        try {
            SOAPPart soappart = msg.getSOAPPart();
            SOAPEnvelope incomingEnvelope = soappart.getEnvelope();
            SOAPBody body = incomingEnvelope.getBody();

            Iterator iterator = body.getChildElements(
            incomingEnvelope.createName("numberAvailable", "laptops",
                "http://www.XMLPowerCorp.com"));

            SOAPElement element;
            element = (SOAPElement) iterator.next();

            SOAPMessage message = messageFactory.createMessage();
            SOAPEnvelope envelope = message.getSOAPPart().getEnvelope();

            envelope.getBody().addChildElement(envelope
                .createName("Response")).addTextNode(
                "Got the SOAP message indicating there are " +
                    element.getValue() +
                " laptops available."
            );

            return message;
        } catch(Exception e) {return null;}
    }
}
```

To compile these new servlets, `ch18_04.java` and `ch18_05.java`, you need to have `servlet.jar`, `jaxm-api.jar`, `saaj-api.jar`, and `activation.jar` in the Java `classpath` environment variable. For example, if those JAR files are in the same directory as `ch18_04.java` and `ch18_05.java`, here's what this looks like:

```
%set classpath=servlet.jar;jaxm-api.jar;saaj-api.jar;activation.jar
%javac ch18_04.java
%javac ch18_05.java
```

If the JAR files are in the same directory as `ch18_04.java` and `ch18_05.java`, you need to make sure to preface every JAR file filename with its correct path.

This gives you the compiled files you need, `ch18_04.class` and `ch18_05.class`. How can you run the server, `ch18_04.class`? Here, you'll use an HTML document, `ch18_06.html`, to call the `ch18_04.class` servlet by using a hyperlink. Listing 18.6 shows how this HTML document works. When the user clicks the hyperlink, the server servlet is called, the server servlet sends a SOAP message to the client servlet, and the client servlet returns a SOAP message to the server.

LISTING 18.6 The SOAP Example Introduction Page (`ch18_06.html`)

```
<HTML>
    <HEAD>
        <TITLE>SOAP and Java</TITLE>
    </HEAD>

    <BODY>
        <H1>SOAP and Java</H1>
        Click <A HREF="ch18_04">here</a> to send the SOAP message.
    </BODY>
</HTML>
```

18

Now you need to install all that you've done in the Tomcat server. To do that, begin by creating a file named `web.xml` that will tell Tomcat about the `ch18_04.class` and `ch18_05.class` files so that you can use those files with Tomcat. Here's what `web.xml` looks like:

```
<?xml version="1.0" encoding="ISO-8859-1"?>

<!DOCTYPE web-app
    PUBLIC "-//Sun Microsystems, Inc.//DTD Web Application 2.2//EN"
    "http://java.sun.com/j2ee/dtds/web-app_2_2.dtd">

<web-app>
    <servlet>
        <servlet-name>
            ch18_04
        </servlet-name>
        <servlet-class>
            soapExample.ch18_04
        </servlet-class>
    </servlet>
```

```
    <servlet>
        <servlet-name>
            ch18_05
        </servlet-name>
        <servlet-class>
            soapExample.ch18_05
        </servlet-class>
    </servlet>

    <servlet-mapping>
        <servlet-name>
            ch18_04
        </servlet-name>
        <url-pattern>
            /ch18_04
        </url-pattern>
    </servlet-mapping>

    <servlet-mapping>
        <servlet-name>
            ch18_05
        </servlet-name>
        <url-pattern>
            /ch18_05
        </url-pattern>
    </servlet-mapping>
</web-app>
```

Now that you have all the files you'll need, you can install them in the Tomcat `webapps` directory in order to make them available through the Tomcat server. You'll install these files in a directory named `JavaSoap` and place your actual servlet code in a directory named `soapExample` (which is the Java package for those servlets). Here's what the completed directory structure looks like:

```
webapps [This is a directory]
|____JavaSoap [This is a directory]
     |____ch18_06.html [Our starting Web page]
     |____WEB-INF [This is a directory]
          |____web.xml [Configures Tomcat]
          |____classes [This is a directory]
               |____soapExample [This is a directory]
                    |____ch18_04.class [The server servlet]
                    |____ch18_05.class [The client servlet]
```

After you copy these files as shown here, start Tomcat (or if it was already started, stop it and start it again). Now all you need to do is navigate a browser to `http://localhost:8080/soap/ch18_06.html`, as shown in Figure 18.2.

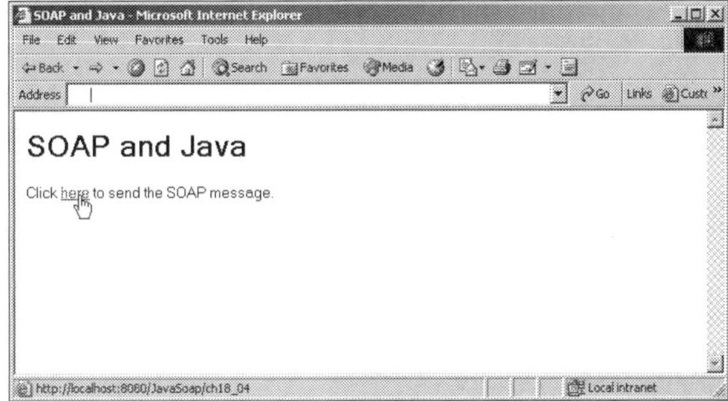

FIGURE 18.2
The Java SOAP example's opening page.

Now click the hyperlink shown in Figure 18.2 in order to call the server servlet, which sends the first SOAP message, stating the number of laptops available in stock, to the client servlet, which sends back an acknowledgement. Figure 18.3 shows the results of calling the server servlet.

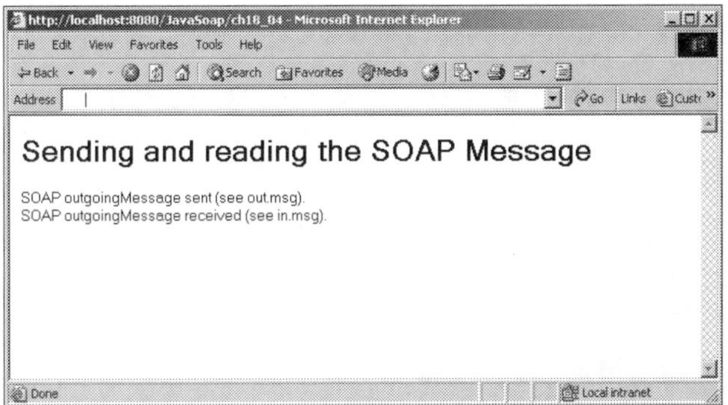

FIGURE 18.3
The results of the Java SOAP example.

18

What does the SOAP message sent from the server to the client look like? You can see it in the file `out.msg`, which is written to the Tomcat `bin` directory. Note that `out.msg` contains not only your SOAP message, but also the attached text, `ch18_06.html`:

```
------=_Part_4_6912871.1056396066449
Content-Type: text/xml

<?xml version="1.0" encoding="UTF-8"?>
<soap-env:Envelope xmlns:soap-env="http://schemas.xmlsoap.org/soap/envelope/">
    <soap-env:Header/>
    <soap-env:Body>
        <laptops:numberAvailable
            xmlns:laptops="http://www.XMLPowerCorp.com">
            216
```

```
        </laptops:numberAvailable>
    </soap-env:Body>
</soap-env:Envelope>
------=_Part_4_6912871.1056396066449
Content-Type: text/html

<HTML>
    <HEAD>
        <TITLE>SOAP and Java</TITLE>
    </HEAD>

    <BODY>
        <H1>SOAP and Java</H1>
        Click <A HREF="ch18_04">here</a> to send the SOAP message.
    </BODY>
</html>

------=_Part_4_6912871.1056396066449--
```

Here's what the SOAP message the client sent back to the server, as the code stored in `in.msg`, looks like (note that the client is acknowledging the data the server sent):

```
<?xml version="1.0" encoding="UTF-8"?>
<soap-env:Envelope
    xmlns:soap-env="http://schemas.xmlsoap.org/soap/envelope/">
    <soap-env:Header/>
    <soap-env:Body>
        <Response>
            Got the SOAP message indicating there are 216 laptops available.
        </Response>
    </soap-env:Body>
</soap-env:Envelope>
```

In this example you've been able to send, interpret, and reply to a SOAP message in Java. You've taken a look at programming examples in both .NET and Java now, and as you can see, both packages give SOAP support. You've just scratched the surface so far—covering the uses of SOAP can take whole books—but you have an idea what SOAP is good for from what you've seen. We'll turn now to RDF.

Introducing RDF

RDF is an XML-based language that we use to describe various resources in a standard way. We can use it to describe any resource, but it's most often used to describe documents on the Web. This is how the W3C describes RDF:

> Resource Description Framework (RDF) is a foundation for processing metadata; it provides interoperability between applications that exchange machine-understandable

information on the Web. RDF emphasizes facilities to enable automated processing of Web resources. RDF can be used in a variety of application areas; for example: in resource discovery to provide better search engine capabilities, in cataloging for describing the content and content relationships available at a particular Web site, page, or digital library, by intelligent software agents to facilitate knowledge sharing and exchange, in content rating, in describing collections of pages that represent a single logical "document", for describing intellectual property rights of Web pages, and for expressing the privacy preferences of a user as well as the privacy policies of a Web site. RDF with digital signatures will be key to building the "Web of Trust" for electronic commerce, collaboration, and other applications.

As expected, RDF is a W3C recommendation. You can find an overview page at `http://www.w3.org/RDF`. The RDF model and syntax specification are at `http://www.w3.org/TR/REC-rdf-syntax` and the RDF schema specification is at `http://www.w3.org/TR/rdf-schema`. And you can find an RDF primer at `http://www.w3.org/TR/rdf-primer`. Here's an overview of some RDF resources that are available:

- **`http://athena.ics.forth.gr:9090/RDF/`**—A validating RDF parser by ICS-FORTH that is based on Java.
- **`http://lists.w3.org/Archives/Public/www-rdf-interest/2000May/0009.html`**—An RDF parser by Dan Connolly that uses XSLT.
- **`http://nestroy.wi-inf.uni-essen.de/xwmf`**—The Extensible Web Modeling Framework (XWMF), which includes an RDF parser.
- **`http://www.w3.org/RDF/Validator`**—A simple RDF validator on the W3C site.
- **`http://www.w3.org/Library/src/HTRDF`**—John Punin's RDF parser, which is written in C.
- **`http://www710.univ-lyon1.fr/~champin/rdf-tutorial`**—An RDF tutorial online. (It's in English, even though the Web page is French.)

18

No major browser has a lot of built-in RDF support right now. Mozilla, Netscape Navigator's open-source test version, has some RDF support built into it. If you want to learn more, take a look at these documents:

- **`http://www.mozilla.org/rdf/50-words.html`**—An overview of RDF and how it fits with Mozilla.
- **`http://www.mozilla.org/rdf/doc/faq.html`**—The RDF Mozilla FAQ, which also includes a little sample code.

- **`http://www.mozilla.org/rdf/doc/datasource-howto.html`**—A cookbook that shows how to create RDF data sources.
- **`http://www.mozilla.org/rdf/rdf-nglayout.html`**—A document that describes how to use RDF in Mozilla.
- **`http://www.mozilla.org/rdf/doc/api.html`**—A technical overview of the Mozilla RDF implementation.
- **`http://www.mozilla.org/rdf/doc/SmartBrowsing.html`**—A page that describes Mozilla's SmartBrowsing system, which allows third-party metadata servers to provide RDF related-link annotations. SmartBrowsing is one of the first true uses of RDF for indexing Web resources on a large scale.

Internet Explorer lags behind Mozilla, although Microsoft does have an RDF viewer available for free. You can find it at (as of this writing) `http://msdn.microsoft.com/downloads/samples/Internet/xml/xml_rdf_viewer/sample.asp`. This viewer can read RDF documents and display the data in them—but note that to run the viewer, you need Internet Explorer 5.0 or later, Visual Basic 6.0, and Windows 98, Windows NT 4.0, or Windows 2000.

What do RDF documents look like? Here's an example of an RDF document that describes the stoic philosopher Epictetus as the creator of a certain resource, which, let's say, is to be found at the (fictitious) URI `http://www.XMLPowerCorp.com/philosophy.html`:

```
<?xml version="1.0" encoding="UTF-8"?>
<rdf:RDF
    xmlns:rdf="http://www.w3.org/1999/02/22-rdf-syntax-ns#">
    <rdf:Description about="http://www.XMLPowerCorp.com/philosophy.html">
        <Creator>Epictetus</Creator>
    </rdf:Description>
</rdf:RDF>
```

RDF is a very general language. In fact, the `<Creator>` element does not exist in standard RDF. However, there are many sublanguages built on RDF, such as one called the Dublin Core. The `<Creator>` element is part of the Dublin Core, which means that Web search engines that support the Dublin Core know enough to search for `<Creator>` elements when they want to find a particular Web resource's author.

We'll start working with RDF by seeing what the rules are.

Understanding How RDF Documents Work

In general, RDF documents are made of RDF statements, each of which has three parts, making each statement a *triple*. Here are the three parts of an RDF statement:

- **A resource**—A resource is typically a Web document that we point to with a URI.
- **A named property**—A named property is a characteristic or an attribute of the resource, such as the resource's creator.
- **A property value**—The property value is the property's content. For example, the value of the `<Creator>` property is often the name of the resource's creator.

In RDF the resource is called the *subject* of the statement, the named property is called the *predicate* of the statement, and the property value is called the *object* of the statement. In the following simple RDF document:

```
<?xml version="1.0" encoding="UTF-8"?>
<rdf:RDF
    xmlns:rdf="http://www.w3.org/1999/02/22-rdf-syntax-ns#">
    <rdf:Description about="http://www.XMLPowerCorp.com/philosophy.html">
        <Creator>Epictetus</Creator>
    </rdf:Description>
</rdf:RDF>
```

the subject is the document `http://www.XMLPowerCorp.com/philosophy.html`, the predicate is the named property `Creator`, and the object is the name of the document's creator, Epictetus. We'll take this document apart in detail now.

18

Creating RDF Root Elements

RDF documents are XML documents, of course, so start each one with an XML declaration. The root element is `<RDF>`:

```
<?xml version="1.0" encoding="UTF-8"?>
<RDF
        .
        .
        .
</RDF>
```

RDF documents must use the RDF namespace setting, which is `"http://www.w3.org/1999/02/22-rdf-syntax-ns#"`. (The `#` on the end, which might look odd, is not an error; the idea is that it can help applications create XPointers.) The usual prefix for this namespace is `rdf`, and you'll use that here:

```
<?xml version="1.0" encoding="UTF-8"?>
<rdf:RDF
    xmlns:rdf="http://www.w3.org/1999/02/22-rdf-syntax-ns#">
        .
        .
        .
</rdf:RDF>
```

Creating Description Elements

When you describe a resource, it gets its own `<rdf:Description>` element. Here are the attributes you can use with this element:

- **about**—Specifies what resource the element describes.
- **aboutEach**—Specifies statements about each of the element's children.
- **aboutEachPrefix**—Specifies RDF container items, by prefix.
- **bagID**—Specifies the ID of an associated bag container.
- **ID**—Gives the element an ID value.
- **type**—Specifies the description's type.

In this example, the resource you are describing is `http://www.XMLPowerCorp.com/philosophy.html`, so assign that URI to the `about` attribute of the `<rdf:Description>` element:

```
<?xml version="1.0" encoding="UTF-8"?>
<rdf:RDF
    xmlns:rdf="http://www.w3.org/1999/02/22-rdf-syntax-ns#">
    <rdf:Description about="http://www.XMLPowerCorp.com/philosophy.html">
    .
    .
    .
    </rdf:Description>
</rdf:RDF>
```

To store the actual description of the resource, we use property elements, which are described next.

Creating Property Elements

The `<rdf:Description>` element contains the elements that contain the actual description. For example, for the document you're describing, you can use a `<Creator>` element:

```
<?xml version="1.0" encoding="UTF-8"?>
<rdf:RDF
    xmlns:rdf="http://www.w3.org/1999/02/22-rdf-syntax-ns#">
    <rdf:Description about="http://www.XMLPowerCorp.com/philosophy.html">
        <Creator>Epictetus</Creator>
    </rdf:Description>
</rdf:RDF>
```

There are no properties, like `Creator`, built into RDF, per se. We can create whatever properties we like. There are a number of RDF applications already available, however, and the most popular and well supported of these is the Dublin Core. You'll take a look at it next—and it does have a `<Creator>` element built into it.

Using the Dublin Core

All the details about the Dublin Core are available at http://dublincore.org/. The Dublin Core provides a set of elements for use in RDF, and it is being used in many places—government agencies, libraries, corporations, on the Web. The Dublin Core calls itself a "metadata initiative," and it's a strongly supported concern; you'll find frequent updates to what's going on at its Web site.

The Dublin Core namespace setting is "http://purl.org/DC/" (note that this namespace is usually associated with the prefix dc). You should use this namespace setting if you're going to use the Dublin Core. Here's how that looks in our RDF example:

```
<?xml version="1.0" encoding="UTF-8"?>
<rdf:RDF
    xmlns:rdf="http://www.w3.org/1999/02/22-rdf-syntax-ns#"
    xmlns:dc="http://purl.org/DC/">
    <rdf:Description about="http://www.XMLPowerCorp.com/philosophy.html">
        <dc:Creator>Epictetus</dc:Creator>
    </rdf:Description>
</rdf:RDF>
```

Besides <Creator>, there are plenty of other elements in the Dublin Core, as listed in Table 18.1.

TABLE 18.1 The Dublin Core Elements

Element	*What It Means*
Contributor	A person or an organization that has contributed to this resource.
Coverage	The extent or scope of the resource.
Creator	Usually refers to the resource's author.
Date	A date connected to the resource, such as its last update or its creation date. It uses the YYYY-MM-DD format.
Description	A description of the resource.
Format	The format used for the resource. It is usually a MIME type.
Identifier	An ID value for the resource in its context.
Language	The language of the resource. It uses values defined by RFC 1766 and includes a two-letter language code with an optional two-letter country code (from the ISO 3166 standard), such as "en-us".
Publisher	The entity responsible for the resource.
Relation	A reference to a related resource or relationship type.
Rights	Rights information for the resource.
Source	The source from which the current resource is derived.

TABLE 18.1 continued

Element	*What It Means*
`Subject`	The topic of the content of the resource.
`Title`	A name given to the resource.
`Type`	The content type of the resource.

Also, each of the Dublin Core elements has 10 attributes:

- **`Comment`**—Provides a comment about the use of the data in the element.
- **`Datatype`**—Specifies the type of data in the element.
- **`Definition`**—Defines the concept behind the data in the element.
- **`Identifier`**—Specifies a unique identifier assigned to the element that identifies it.
- **`Language`**—Specifies the language of the data in the element.
- **`Maximum Occurrence`**—Puts a limit on how many times the element may occur.
- **`Name`**—Specifies the name assigned to the data element.
- **`Obligation`**—Specifies whether the element is required.
- **`Registration Authority`**—Refers to the agency or group authorized to register the element.
- **`Version`**—Specifies the version of the element.

Six of these attributes have fixed values:

- **`Version`**—`1.1`
- **`Registration Authority`**—`Dublin Core Metadata Initiative`
- **`Language`**—`en` (that is, English)
- **`Obligation`**—`Optional`
- **`Datatype`**—`Character String`
- **`Maximum Occurrence`**—`Unlimited`

In addition, the Dublin Core also lists a set of default resource types that we can use with the `<Type>` element:

- `collection`
- `dataset`
- `event`

- `image`
- `interactive resource`
- `model`
- `party`
- `physical object`
- `place`
- `service`
- `software`
- `sound`
- `text`

Up to this point, you've only used one property, `Creator`, to describe the resource, but you can use multiple resources at the same time. For example, Listing 18.7 shows an example of an RDF document that uses multiple properties to describe a single resource.

LISTING 18.7 An RDF Example (`ch18_07.rdf`)

```
<?xml version="1.0" encoding="UTF-8"?>
<rdf:RDF
    xmlns:rdf="http://www.w3.org/1999/02/22-rdf-syntax-ns#"
    xmlns:dc="http://purl.org/DC/">

    <rdf:Description about="http://www.XMLPowerCorp.com/philosophy.html">
        <dc:Creator>Epictetus</dc:Creator>
        <dc:Description>The stoic philosopher's teachings</dc:Description>
        <dc:Title>The Discourses</dc:Title>
        <dc:Type>text</dc:Type>
    </rdf:Description>

</rdf:RDF>
```

18

Working with Multiple Resources

Besides using multiple properties for each description, you can also use one single RDF document to describe multiple resources; in this case, each description has its own `<rdf:Description>` element. Listing 18.8 shows an example that describes various chapters from Book III of Epictetus' Discourses.

Listing 18.8 An RDF Example That Describes Multiple Resources (ch18_08.rdf)

```
<?xml version="1.0" encoding="UTF-8"?>
<rdf:RDF
    xmlns:rdf="http://www.w3.org/1999/02/22-rdf-syntax-ns#"
    xmlns:dc="http://purl.org/DC/">

    <rdf:Description about="http://www.XMLPowerCorp.com/chapter1.html">
        <dc:Creator>Epictetus</dc:Creator>
        <dc:Language>en</dc:Language>
        <dc:Title>Of personal adornment</dc:Title>
        <dc:Type>text</dc:Type>
    </rdf:Description>

    <rdf:Description about="http://www.XMLPowerCorp.com/chapter2.html">
        <dc:Creator>Epictetus</dc:Creator>
        <dc:Language>en</dc:Language>
        <dc:Title>The fields of study</dc:Title>
        <dc:Type>text</dc:Type>
    </rdf:Description>

    <rdf:Description about="http://www.XMLPowerCorp.com/chapter3.html">
        <dc:Creator>Epictetus</dc:Creator>
        <dc:Language>en</dc:Language>
        <dc:Title>What is the subject-matter?</dc:Title>
        <dc:Type>text</dc:Type>
    </rdf:Description>

</rdf:RDF>
```

We can also nest RDF descriptions. For example, if we want to describe three chapters of Epitectus' Book III by using nested RDF, we just have to nest `<rdf:Resource>` elements appropriately. Listing 18.9 shows how this works.

Listing 18.9 A Nested RDF Example (ch18_09.rdf)

```
<?xml version="1.0" encoding="UTF-8"?>
<rdf:RDF xmlns:rdf="http://www.w3.org/1999/02/22-rdf-syntax-ns#"
    xmlns:dc="http://www.purl.org/DC/">

    <rdf:Description about="http://www.XMLPowerCorp.com/bookIII.html">
        <dc:Title>Book III</dc:Title>
        <dc:Creator>Epictetus</dc:Creator>
        <rdf:Description about="http://www.XMLPowerCorp.com/chapter1.html">
            <dc:Creator>Epictetus</dc:Creator>
            <dc:Language>en</dc:Language>
            <dc:Title>Of personal adornment</dc:Title>
            <dc:Type>text</dc:Type>
```

LISTING 18.9 continued

```
        </rdf:Description>

        <rdf:Description about="http://www.XMLPowerCorp.com/chapter2.html">
            <dc:Creator>Epictetus</dc:Creator>
            <dc:Language>en</dc:Language>
            <dc:Title>The fields of study</dc:Title>
            <dc:Type>text</dc:Type>
        </rdf:Description>

        <rdf:Description about="http://www.XMLPowerCorp.com/chapter3.html">
            <dc:Creator>Epictetus</dc:Creator>
            <dc:Language>en</dc:Language>
            <dc:Title>What is the subject-matter?</dc:Title>
            <dc:Type>text</dc:Type>
        </rdf:Description>
    </rdf:Description>
</rdf:RDF>
```


Using Resource Attributes

In RDF, there's another valid way of referring to a resource that a property describes: using the `rdf:resource` attribute. Listing 18.10 shows an example that uses this attribute to tie various RDF elements to the resources they describe.

LISTING 18.10 An RDF Resource Attribute Example (`ch18_10.rdf`)

```
<?xml version="1.0" encoding="UTF-8"?>
<rdf:RDF
    xmlns:rdf="http://www.w3.org/1999/02/22-rdf-syntax-ns#"
    xmlns:dc="http://www.purl.org/DC/">

    <rdf:Description about="http://www.XMLPowerCorp.com/chapter1.html">
        <dc:Title>Chapter 1</dc:Title>
        <dc:Creator rdf:resource="http://www.XMLPowerCorp.com/epictetus.html"/>
    </rdf:Description>

    <rdf:Description about="http://www.XMLPowerCorp.com/chapter2.html">
        <dc:Title>Chapter 2</dc:Title>
        <dc:Creator rdf:resource="http://www.XMLPowerCorp.com/epictetus.html"/>
    </rdf:Description>

    <rdf:Description about="http://www.XMLPowerCorp.com/chapter3.html">
        <dc:Title>Chapter 3</dc:Title>
        <dc:Creator rdf:resource="http://www.XMLPowerCorp.com/epictetus.html"/>
    </rdf:Description>

</rdf:RDF>
```

Using the `rdf:resource` attribute is a shortcut way to connect a resource to an RDF that makes such a connection easy to implement.

Using XML in RDF Elements

It's not uncommon to use XML inside RDF elements to store data. Unfortunately, although we can set the `Type` property `to "text"`, there is no official `"xml"` setting for this property. Instead, we can set up our software to treat the XML data as XML. As far as RDF is concerned, we can set the `parseType` attribute of the property to `"Literal"`, as shown in Listing 18.11.

LISTING 18.11 A Nested RDF Example (`ch18_11.rdf`)

```
<?xml version="1.0" encoding="UTF-8"?>
<rdf:RDF
    xmlns:rdf="http://www.w3.org/1999/02/22-rdf-syntax-ns#"
    xmlns:dc="http://www.purl.org/DC/"
    xmlns:nsp="http://www.XMLPowerCorp.com/namespace/">

    <rdf:Description about="http://www.XMLPowerCorp.com/philosophy.html">
        <dc:Creator parseType="Literal">
            <nsp:name>Epictetus</nsp:name>
            <nsp:occupation>Philosopher</nmp:occupation>
            <nsp:type>Stoic</nsp:type>
            <nsp:locale>Italy</nsp:locale>
        </dc:Creator>
    </rdf:Description>

</rdf:RDF>
```

Another way of doing this is to use the Dublin Core `<Format>` element and use an XML MIME type, like this:

```
<?xml version="1.0" encoding="UTF-8"?>
<rdf:RDF
    xmlns:rdf="http://www.w3.org/1999/02/22-rdf-syntax-ns#"
    xmlns:dc="http://www.purl.org/DC/"
    xmlns:nsp="http://www.XMLPowerCorp.com/namespace/">

    <rdf:Description about="http://www.XMLPowerCorp.com/philosophy.html">
        <dc:Format>application/xml</dc:Format>
        <dc:Creator parseType="Literal">
            <nsp:name>Epictetus</nsp:name>
            <nsp:occupation>Philosopher</nmp:occupation>
            <nsp:type>Stoic</nsp:type>
            <nsp:locale>Italy</nsp:locale>
```

```
        </dc:Creator>
    </rdf:Description>

</rdf:RDF>
```

Using Abbreviated RDF

There's also an abbreviated RDF syntax that can make writing RDF documents easier. When we abbreviate RDF, we just change property elements into attributes of the `<rdf:Description>` element. Say, for example, that you have this RDF document:

```
<?xml version="1.0" encoding="UTF-8"?>
<rdf:RDF
    xmlns:rdf="http://www.w3.org/1999/02/22-rdf-syntax-ns#"
    xmlns:dc="http://purl.org/DC/">

    <rdf:Description about="http://www.XMLPowerCorp.com/chapter1.html">
        <dc:Creator>Epictetus</dc:Creator>
        <dc:Language>en</dc:Language>
        <dc:Title>Chapter 1</dc:Title>
        <dc:Type>text</dc:Type>
    </rdf:Description>

    <rdf:Description about="http://www.XMLPowerCorp.com/chapter2.html">
        <dc:Creator>Epictetus</dc:Creator>
        <dc:Language>en</dc:Language>
        <dc:Title>Chapter 2</dc:Title>
        <dc:Type>text</dc:Type>
    </rdf:Description>
    .
    .
    .
```

You could abbreviate the RDF this way:

```
<?xml version="1.0" encoding="UTF-8"?>
<rdf:RDF
    xmlns:rdf="http://www.w3.org/1999/02/22-rdf-syntax-ns#"
    xmlns:dc="http://purl.org/DC/">

    <rdf:Description about="http://www.XMLPowerCorp.com/chapter1.html">
        dc:Creator = "Epictetus"
        dc:Language = "en"
        dc:Title = "Chapter 1"
        dc:Type = "text">
    </rdf:Description>

    <rdf:Description about="http://www.XMLPowerCorp.com/chapter2.html">
        dc:Creator = "Epictetus">
        dc:Language = "en"
```

```
        dc:Title = "Chapter 2"
        dc:Type = "text">
    </rdf:Description>
    .
    .
    .
```

This type of abbreviating can be especially useful with RDF that is embedded in an HTML document because HTML browsers convert elements they don't understand into simple text. If we want to hide RDF data, we can put that data into attributes, not RDF elements, because the data in the attributes won't be shown.

Summary

Today you took a look at two important XML applications: SOAP and RDF. SOAP lets applications work with objects across programming boundaries, and RDF lets us describe resources in a flexible way, allowing software to read and handle those descriptions.

SOAP messages are made up of three parts: an envelope (with the namespace `http://schemas.xmlsoap.org/soap/envelope/`), which contains the whole message, an optional header, which holds information about the message itself, and a body, which is where the message goes. SOAP messages can also have attachments.

The root element in a SOAP message is the `<Envelope>` element. And there are three possible child elements—`<Header>`, `<Body>`, and `<Fault>`—each of which may have various child elements, as described today.

Today you put SOAP to work in both Java and .NET. The .NET example used C# to give one application access to an object in another application. The Java example let you explicitly construct a SOAP message, including the envelope, header, and body, and send data to and from another servlet by using the Tomcat server.

RDF is all about describing resources, and today you saw that it provides a framework for handling general descriptions. RDF can be used to describe any resource that can be described in words, but it's used most often to describe resources on the Web. By using RDF, search engines can access and store information on Web resources.

RDF statements typically have three parts: the resource itself, located with a URI; a named property that indicates what aspect of the resource we're describing; and a property value, which is the description itself.

Today you saw that the root element is `<RDF>`, and it must be in the RDF namespace, which is `"http://www.w3.org/1999/02/22-rdf-syntax-ns#"`. You usually use the RDF `<Description>` element to create a description of a resource.

The Dublin Core provides a set of elements for use with RDF (for example, `<Creator>`, `<Contributor>`, `<Format>`, `<Subject>`) to help describe a resource.

As you have seen today, SOAP and RDF are two powerful XML applications, and they are also two of the most popular. Tomorrow, you're going to take a look at another powerful XML technique: data binding.

Q&A

Q I know that SOAP messages can have attachments, but how can I check what type an attachment is—text, image, and so on—before I try to read it?

A In Java, you can use the `javax.xml.soap.AttachmentPartgetContentType` method, which returns the MIME type of the SOAP message's attachment.

Q What if a resource I'm trying to describe in RDF can take multiple values?

A RDF allows you to handle that case by defining property containers. There are three containers:

- **`Bag`**—A simple group of properties, in no particular order.
- **`Seq`**—A sequence of properties in a particular order.
- **`Alt`**—A list of properties that specify alternate choices, only one of which may be chosen.

These property containers are supported with the `<rdf:Bag>`, `<rdf:Seq>`, and `<rdf:Alt>` elements.

18

Workshop

This workshop tests whether you understand the concepts discussed today. It's a good idea to make sure you can answer these questions before pressing on to tomorrow's work. Answers to the quiz can be found in Appendix A, "Quiz Answers."

Quiz

1. What are the three parts of a SOAP message?
2. What three child elements can you use in a SOAP envelope?
3. What attribute and attribute value do you use in a SOAP element if you want to insist that the element be interpreted correctly?
4. What element do you use in RDF to hold the description of a resource?
5. If someone is not a main author of a resource but has worked on it, which Dublin Core element would you use to indicate that fact?

Exercises

1. If you have access to C#, modify today's SOAP example to convert it into a calculator. For this calculator, various values should be sent to the remote server to be added, and the server should return the sum.
2. Create an RDF document that describes the SOAP example you created in Exercise 1. Make sure you include a `<Description>` element and use various Dublin Core elements to contain the actual description.

PART IV

In Review

In Part IV we took a look at programming with XML, beginning with JavaScript. We saw that you can use JavaScript with the W3C DOM, and we saw that there are various levels of the DOM available.

When you load an XML document, you can use JavaScript properties such as `nextChild` and `previousSibling` to move through the document. It's also common to loop over nodes and search for the data you want. Let's look at an example that illustrates looping over nodes. Say you have the following XML document, which contains data about some of your clients and the programming applications you're writing for them:

```
<?xml version = "1.0" standalone="yes"?>
<document>
    <client>
        <name>
            <lastname>Kirk</lastname>
            <firstname>James</firstname>
        </name>
        <contractDate>September 5, 2092</contractDate>
        <contracts>
            <contract>
                <app>Comm</app>
                <id>111</id>
                <fee>$111.00</fee>
            </contract>
            <contract>
                <app>Accounting</app>
                <id>222</id>
                <fee>$989.00</fee>
            </contract>
        </contracts>
    </client>
    <client>
        <name>
            <lastname>McCoy</lastname>
```

15

16

17

18

```
                <firstname>Leonard</firstname>
            </name>
            <contractDate>September 7, 2092</contractDate>
            <contracts>
                <contract>
                    <app>Stocker</app>
                    <id>333</id>
                    <fee>$2995.00</fee>
                </contract>
                <contract>
                    <app>Dialer</app>
                    <id>444</id>
                    <fee>$200.00</fee>
                </contract>
            </contracts>
        </client>
        <client>
            <name>
                <lastname>Spock</lastname>
                <firstname>Mr.</firstname>
            </name>
            <contractDate>September 9, 2092</contractDate>
            <contracts>
                <contract>
                    <app>WinHook</app>
                    <id>555</id>
                    <fee>$129.00</fee>
                </contract>
                <contract>
                    <app>MouseApp</app>
                    <id>666</id>
                    <fee>$25.00</fee>
                </contract>
            </contracts>
        </client>
    </document>
```

You can use JavaScript to strip out the data you want from documents like this. For example, if you're interested in the last names of your clients, you might want to catch all `<lastname>` elements. When you catch each element, you could set a Boolean flag to `true` to indicate that you want to catch the following text node, which holds the last name:

```
if(currentNode.nodeName == "lastname") {
    catchNext = true
}
```

Then you would loop over all child nodes of the present node:

```
if (currentNode.childNodes.length > 0) {
    for (var loopIndex = 0; loopIndex <
        currentNode.childNodes.length; loopIndex++) {
        text += childLoop(currentNode.childNodes(loopIndex), catchNext)
    }
}
```

If `catchNext` was `true` when dealing with a child node, you would know that you were dealing with a text node whose text you need, so you could save that text this way:

```
if(catchNext) {
    text = currentNode.nodeValue + "<BR>"
    catchNext = false
}
```

Here's what the whole HTML page, including the needed JavaScript, looks like (in this case, we've named the XML document we're working with `projects.xml`):

```
<HTML>
    <HEAD>
        <TITLE>
            Getting the last names
        </TITLE>

        <SCRIPT LANGUAGE="JavaScript">

            function readXMLData()
            {
                xmlDocumentObject = new ActiveXObject("Microsoft.XMLDOM")
                xmlDocumentObject.load("projects.xml")

                displayDIV.innerHTML = childLoop(xmlDocumentObject, false)
            }

            function childLoop(currentNode, catchNext)
            {
                var text = ""

                    if(catchNext) {
                        text = currentNode.nodeValue + "<BR>"
                        catchNext = false
                    }

                    if(currentNode.nodeName == "lastname") {
                        catchNext = true
                    }
```

```
                if (currentNode.childNodes.length > 0) {
                    for (var loopIndex = 0; loopIndex <
                        currentNode.childNodes.length; loopIndex++) {
                        text += childLoop(currentNode.childNodes(loopIndex),
                            catchNext)
                    }
                }
                return text
            }

        </SCRIPT>
    </HEAD>

    <BODY>
        <H1>
            Getting the last names
        </H1>

        <INPUT TYPE="BUTTON" VALUE="Get last names"
            onClick = "readXMLData()">
        <DIV ID="displayDIV"></DIV>
    </BODY>
</HTML>
```

This example displays the last names of your clients in a Web page, like this:

```
Kirk
McCoy
Spock
```

In Part IV we also looked at how to use Java with the XML DOM. There's an immense amount of support for XML DOM handling in Java 1.4 and later. You can use a Java `DocumentBuilderFactory` object to create a `DocumentBuilder` object, and you can use the `DocumentBuilder` object's `parse` method to parse an XML document and create a Java `Document` object.

The `Document` object corresponds to the top node of the document tree. You can move from node to node by using methods such as `getChildNodes`. You can check the type of a node by using the `getNodeType` method, a node's name by using the `getNodeName` method, and a node's value by using the `getNodeValue` method. And you can get an element's attribute nodes by using the `getAttributes` method.

For instance, here's what the JavaScript example we just saw looks like converted into Java—the logic is the same, but this time, the implementation is in Java:

```
import javax.xml.parsers.*;
import org.w3c.dom.*;
```

```
public class t
{
    static String displayText[] = new String[1000];
    static int numberLines = 0;

    public static void main(String args[])
    {
        try {
            DocumentBuilderFactory factory =
                DocumentBuilderFactory.newInstance();

            DocumentBuilder builder = null;
            try {
                builder = factory.newDocumentBuilder();
            }
            catch (ParserConfigurationException e) {}

            Document document = null;
            document = builder.parse(args[0]);

            childLoop(document, false);

        } catch (Exception e) {
            e.printStackTrace(System.err);
        }

        for(int loopIndex = 0; loopIndex < numberLines; loopIndex++){
            System.out.println(displayText[loopIndex]);
        }
    }

    public static void childLoop(Node node, boolean catchNext)
    {
        if (node == null) {
            return;
        }

        int type = node.getNodeType();

        switch (type) {

            case Node.DOCUMENT_NODE: {
                childLoop(((Document)node).getDocumentElement(), false);
                break;
             }

             case Node.ELEMENT_NODE: {
                 if(node.getNodeName().equals("lastname")) {
                     catchNext = true;
                 }
```

```
                NodeList childNodes = node.getChildNodes();
                if (childNodes != null) {
                    int length = childNodes.getLength();
                    for (int loopIndex = 0; loopIndex < length;
                        loopIndex++ ) {
                       childLoop(childNodes.item(loopIndex), catchNext);
                    }
                }
                break;
            }

            case Node.TEXT_NODE: {
                if(catchNext){
                    String trimmedText = node.getNodeValue().trim();
                    if(trimmedText.indexOf("\n") < 0 && trimmedText.length()
                        > 0) {
                        displayText[numberLines] = trimmedText;
                        numberLines++;
                    }
                    catchNext = false;
                }
                break;
            }
        }
    }
}
```

This application gives you the same result as the previous example:

```
Kirk
McCoy
Spock
```

By using the DOM and Java, you can also search for specific elements by using the `getElementsByTagName` method or move through an XML document by using methods such as `getNextSibling`, `getPreviousSibling`, `getFirstChild`, `getLastChild`, and `getParent`. You can even edit the contents of an XML document by using methods such as `appendChild`, `insertBefore`, `removeChild`, and `replaceChild`.

Besides using the DOM in Java, you can also work with SAX to parse XML documents. A SAX parser is event driven—that is, it parses an XML document and calls code when it find the beginning of a document, the start of an element, a text node, and so on.

When you register your code with a SAX handler and parse a document, the `startElement` method is called when the beginning of an element is encountered, the `characters` method is called when a text node is encountered, the `processingInstruction` method is called when a processing method is encountered, the `endElement` method is called when the end of an element is encountered, and so forth. These SAX methods are called with the data you need from the document you're parsing.

We ended Part IV with a look at two important XML applications: SOAP and RDF. SOAP enables applications to communicate by working with objects across programming boundaries. A SOAP message is made up of three parts: an envelope that contains the message, an optional header that holds data about the message, and a body that holds the actual message. SOAP messages can also have attachments, and we took a look at an example of a SOAP message that did.

RDF lets you describe resources. In theory, RDF can be used to describe any resource that you can describe in words. However, it's used mostly to describe Web resources. RDF gives search engines easy and uniform access to information on Web resources. RDF is not widely implemented today yet, but it's gaining ground.

There are usually three parts to an RDF statement: the resource itself, which you point to with a URI, a name that shows what property of the resource you want to describe, and the description itself.

That's it for Part IV. You have a great deal of power when you write programming code to work with XML. Although working with XSLT and CSS to handle XML is fine up to a point, to really get into your data, extract what you want, and process it, you need to write your own code. And now that you have the fundamentals down and have seen examples, it's not all that difficult. In Part V you're going to work with another popular XML topic—using XML and databases.

PART V

At a Glance

Data Handling and XML

Part V examines how to work with XML and databases. You'll start by taking a look at the extensive data-binding techniques available in Internet Explorer. These techniques let you treat XML documents like databases by treating elements as database records and connecting the data in the child elements of each record in HTML controls.

You're also going to see how various true database systems use XML behind-the-scenes by writing database tables out in XML and reading them back in as well. And you'll see that some database systems let you address the data in XML documents by using XPath expressions.

Treating XML documents like databases with standard database software is okay, but it doesn't go too far. We're going to go farther. In particular, you'll see how a relatively new XML specification, XQuery, provides a native-XML way of working with XML documents as if they were databases.

In addition, you're going to take a look at working with XML in .NET. There's a great deal of built-in support for XML in the .NET programming languages, and you'll see what they have to offer.

PART V

DAY 19

Handling XML Data Binding

Today's and tomorrow's discussions focus on database handling with XML, and, of course, data is what XML is all about. Today, you're going to see the various ways of binding XML data to controls in Internet Explorer, and tomorrow, you'll deal with working with XML and true databases. Today, you're going to use Internet Explorer to bind XML data to HTML text fields, select controls, and more, making that data appear in those controls automatically. Here's an overview of today's topics:

- Binding HTML data to HTML controls
- Binding XML data to HTML controls
- Navigating through XML data
- Displaying XML data in tables
- Using the XML data source object (DSO)
- Searching XML data
- Displaying hierarchical XML data

We'll start with the basis of data binding—DSOs.

Introducing DSOs

We can use Internet Explorer for all kinds of data binding, as you're going to see today, and that's great if data is stored in XML format and we want to display it to the user on the Internet. Internet Explorer connects to XML and HTML documents that store data using the ActiveX Data Objects (ADO) protocol (not the ADO.NET protocol of the .NET Framework).

We'll start by taking a look at general data binding in Internet Explorer, and then we'll examine more specialized data binding in XML. To bind the data in an XML or HTML document to HTML controls in a Web page, we use one of the four DSOs available in Internet Explorer—the Microsoft HTML (MSHTML) control, XML data islands, the tabular data control (TDC), or the XML DSO applet. Two of these DSOs, the XML DSO and XML data islands, support XML documents.

DSOs don't appear visually themselves—they just connect to a document and make the data in that document available to the controls in a Web page. For example, let's take a look at the HTML document in Listing 19.1 (`ch19_01.html`). This HTML document holds the states data you saw on Day 10, "Working with XSL Formatting Objects" (compare `ch19_01.html` to `ch10_01.xml`, for example)—the names of various states, their populations, capitals, state birds, and so on. In HTML we use `<SPAN>` or `<DIV>` elements to mimic XML elements, naming the "element" by assigning a value to the `ID` attribute. For example, the `<name>` element in `ch10_01.xml` becomes the `<SPAN ID="name">` element here.

Listing 19.1 An HTML Document That Holds Data (`ch19_01.html`)

```
<HTML>
    <HEAD>
        <TITLE>
            State Data
        </TITLE>
    </HEAD>

    <BODY>
        Name:
        <SPAN ID="name">
            California
        </SPAN><BR>
        Population:
        <SPAN ID="population">
            33871648
        </SPAN><BR>
        Capital:
```

Listing 19.1 continued

```
            <SPAN ID="Capital">
                Sacramento
            </SPAN><BR>
            Bird:
            <SPAN ID="bird">Quail</SPAN><BR>
            Flower:
            <SPAN ID="flower">
                Golden Poppy
            </SPAN><BR>

            Name:
            <SPAN ID="name">
                Massachusetts
            </SPAN><BR>
            Population:
            <SPAN ID="population">
                6349097
            </SPAN><BR>
            Capital:
            <SPAN ID="Capital">
                Boston
            </SPAN><BR>
            Bird:
            <SPAN ID="bird">Chickadee</SPAN><BR>
            Flower:
            <SPAN ID="flower">
                Mayflower
            </SPAN><BR>

            Name:
            <SPAN ID="name">
                New York
            </SPAN><BR>
            Population:
            <SPAN ID="population">
                18976457
            </SPAN><BR>
            Capital:
            <SPAN ID="Capital">
                Albany
            </SPAN><BR>
            Bird: <SPAN ID="bird">Bluebird</SPAN><BR>
            Flower:
            <SPAN ID="flower">
                Rose
            </SPAN><BR>
        </BODY>
    </HTML>
```

19

We'll use the MSHTML DSO, the simplest of the DSOs, to read in the data from `ch19_01.html` and bind that data to HTML controls so we can display that data in those controls. When we bind the data in a document such as `ch19_01.html` with a DSO, that DSO handles the data in *records* and creates a *record set* that is accessible from the HTML control in the Web page. For example, here's what the record for New York looks like:

```
Name:
<SPAN ID="name">
    New York
</SPAN><BR>
Population:
<SPAN ID="population">
    18976457
</SPAN><BR>
Capital:
<SPAN ID="Capital">
    Albany
</SPAN><BR>
Bird: <SPAN ID="bird">Bluebird</SPAN><BR>
Flower:
<SPAN ID="flower">
    Rose
</SPAN>
```

This record has five *fields*—`name`, `population`, `capital`, `bird`, and `flower`—each of which store data. By using Internet Explorer `<OBJECT>` element, create an MSHTML DSO and bind it to `employee.htm`; here, you'll name this DSO `states`:

```
<OBJECT ID="states" DATA="ch19_01.html" HEIGHT="0" WIDTH="0">
</OBJECT>
```

The DSO will read and interpret `ch19_01.html` and convert that document into an ADO record set, making that record set available to the rest of the HTML page. (The record set that is created is read-only, and it is called an ADOR record set.) The DSO holds data from only one record at a time, and that record is called the *current record*. We can use the built-in methods of a record set to navigate through data by making other records the current record; some common methods are `moveFirst`, `moveLast`, `moveNext`, and `movePrevious`, which let us navigate from record to record, and you're going to see these methods today. To actually display the data from this DSO, we can bind it to HTML elements.

Binding HTML Elements to HTML Data

Many of the HTML elements supported in Internet Explorer can be bound to DSOs. We use the `DATASRC` and `DATAFLD` attributes to bind an element to a DSO; to do so, we assign the DATASRC attribute to the name of a DSO and the DATAFLD attribute to the name of the data field we want to bind the element to. After it's been bound, the element will display the data in the current record in the DSO. In code, we can use the moveFirst, moveLast, moveNext, and movePrevious methods to make other records the current record, and the data in the bound elements is updated automatically.

Say, for instance, that we've bound an HTML text field to the states DSO and to the name field in the DSO's records. When the page first loads, that control will display the name "California". Executing the moveNext method will make the next record in the record set the current record, and the text field will display the name "Massachusetts".

Here's a list of HTML elements in Internet Explorer, indicating what elements may be bound and what property is bound when we use the DATASRC and DATAFLD attributes:

- **A**—Data is bound to the href property; changes are not automatically updated.
- **APPLET**—Data is bound to the param property; changes are automatically updated.
- **BUTTON**—Data is bound to the value property; changes are not automatically updated.
- **DIV**—Data is bound to the innerText and innerHTML properties; changes are not automatically updated.
- **FRAME**—Data is bound to the src property; changes are not automatically updated.
- **IFRAME**—Data is bound to the src property; changes are not automatically updated.
- **IMG**—Data is bound to the src property; changes are not automatically updated.
- **INPUT TYPE=BUTTON**—Data is bound to the value property; changes are not automatically updated.
- **INPUT TYPE=CHECKBOX**—Data is bound to the checked property; changes are automatically updated.
- **INPUT TYPE=HIDDEN**—Data is bound to the value property; changes are automatically updated.
- **INPUT TYPE=PASSWORD**—Data is bound to the value property; changes are automatically updated.
- **INPUT TYPE=RADIO**—Data is bound to the checked property; changes are automatically updated.
- **INPUT TYPE=TEXT**—Data is bound to the value property; changes are automatically updated.
- **LABEL**—Data is bound to the value property; changes are not automatically updated.

- **MARQUEE**—Data is bound to the `innerText` and `innerHTML` properties; changes are not automatically updated.
- **OBJECT**—Data is bound to the `objects` property; changes are automatically updated.
- **PARAM**—Data is bound to the `param` property; changes are automatically updated.
- **SELECT**—Data is bound to the `text` property of an option; changes are automatically updated.
- **SPAN**—Data is bound to the `innerText` and `innerHTML` properties; changes are not automatically updated.
- **TABLE**—This element constructs an entire table; changes are not automatically updated.
- **TEXTAREA**—Data is bound to the `value` property; changes are automatically updated.

Let's put all this to work. You'll start by creating a DSO and using it to read the data from `ch19_01.html`. You'll navigate through that data by using buttons. Begin by creating the DSO by using the `<OBJECT>` element, naming it `states`, and connecting it to your data file, `ch19_01.html`:

```
<HTML>
    <HEAD>
        <TITLE>
            Using the MSHTML Data Source Object
        </TITLE>
    </HEAD>

    <BODY>
        <H1>
            Using the MSHTML Data Source Object
        </H1>

        <OBJECT ID="states" DATA="ch19_01.html"
        HEIGHT="0" WIDTH="0"></OBJECT>
        .
        .
        .
```

Now connect the various data fields in the `states` DSO to HTML text fields by using the `DATASRC` and `DATAFLD` attributes—here's how that works for the `name` and `population` fields:

```
Name: <INPUT TYPE="TEXT" DATASRC="#states"
    DATAFLD="name" SIZE="10">
```

```
<BR><BR>
Population: <INPUT TYPE="TEXT" DATASRC="#states"
    DATAFLD="population" SIZE="10">
```

You can also bind data to other elements. Here's how to bind the data in the `capital` and `flower` fields to the text in `<SPAN>` elements:

```
<BR><BR>
Capital: <SPAN DATASRC="#states"
    DATAFLD="capital"></SPAN>

<BR><BR>
Flower: <SPAN DATASRC="#states" DATAFLD="flower">
</SPAN>
```

In fact, you can even bind the data in the `bird` fields to a `<SELECT>` control, which will display the state's bird by using a drop-down list:

```
<BR><BR>
Bird: <SELECT DATASRC="#states"
    DATAFLD="bird" SIZE="1">
    <OPTION VALUE="Quail">Quail
    <OPTION VALUE="Chickadee">Chickadee
    <OPTION VALUE="Bluebird">Bluebird
</SELECT>
```

When this page first appears, the data from the first record will appear in the bound controls. To let the user navigate to other records, you can use buttons and some JavaScript. These buttons will display a caption of << to move to the first record, > to move to the next record, and so on. For example, to let the user navigate to the first record, you'll use the states DSO's record set's `moveFirst` method, like this:

```
<BR><BR>
<BUTTON ONCLICK=
    "states.recordset.moveFirst()"> &lt;&lt; 
</BUTTON>
```

To navigate to the previous record, first check whether you're at the beginning of the record set by checking whether the `states.recordset.BOF` property is `true`. If it is not, navigate to the previous record like this:

```
<BUTTON ONCLICK="if (!states.recordset.BOF)
    states.recordset.movePrevious()"> &lt; 
</BUTTON>
```

Similarly, you can navigate to the next record if you're not already at the end of the record set, which you check by seeing whether the `states.recordset.EOF` property is `true`. If it is not, move to the next record with the `moveNext` method:

19

```
<BUTTON ONCLICK="if (!states.recordset.EOF)
    states.recordset.moveNext()"> &gt; 
</BUTTON>
```

To move to the last record in the record set, use the `moveLast` method:

```
<BUTTON ONCLICK=
    "states.recordset.moveLast()"> &gt;&gt; 
</BUTTON>
```

Listing 19.2 shows the full code for your HTML DSO document (`ch19_02.html`).

LISTING 19.2 An HTML DSO Document (`ch19_02.html`)

```
<HTML>
    <HEAD>
        <TITLE>
            Using the MSHTML Data Source Object
        </TITLE>
    </HEAD>

    <BODY>
        <H1>
            Using the MSHTML Data Source Object
        </H1>

        <OBJECT ID="states" DATA="ch19_01.html"
        HEIGHT="0" WIDTH="0"></OBJECT>

        Name: <INPUT TYPE="TEXT" DATASRC="#states"
            DATAFLD="name" SIZE="10">

        <BR><BR>
        Population: <INPUT TYPE="TEXT" DATASRC="#states"
            DATAFLD="population" SIZE="10">

        <BR><BR>
        Capital: <SPAN DATASRC="#states"
            DATAFLD="capital"></SPAN>

        <BR><BR>
        Bird: <SELECT DATASRC="#states"
            DATAFLD="bird" SIZE="1">
            <OPTION VALUE="Quail">Quail
            <OPTION VALUE="Chickadee">Chickadee
            <OPTION VALUE="Bluebird">Bluebird
        </SELECT>

        <BR><BR>
        Flower: <SPAN DATASRC="#states" DATAFLD="flower">
```

LISTING 19.2 continued

```
        </SPAN>

        <BR><BR>
        <BUTTON ONCLICK=
            "states.recordset.moveFirst()"> &lt;&lt; 
        </BUTTON>
        <BUTTON ONCLICK="if (!states.recordset.BOF)
            states.recordset.movePrevious()"> &lt; 
        </BUTTON>
        <BUTTON ONCLICK="if (!states.recordset.EOF)
            states.recordset.moveNext()"> &gt; 
        </BUTTON>
        <BUTTON ONCLICK=
            "states.recordset.moveLast()"> &gt;&gt; 
        </BUTTON>
    </BODY>
</HTML>
```

Figure 19.1 shows `ch19_02.html` at work. As shown in the figure, the data from `ch19_01.html` is indeed bound to your controls. The user can move from record to record easily by using the buttons at the bottom of the page.

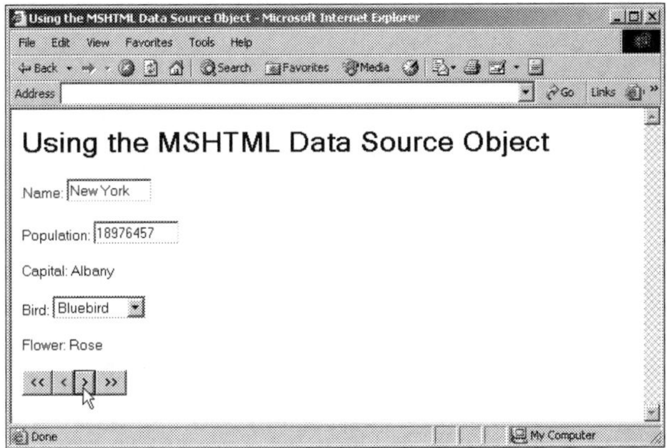

FIGURE 19.1
Data binding with the MSHTML control.

The record set object in a DSO has these properties:

- **`absolutePosition`**—Specifies the position of the current record in a record set.
- **`BOF`**—Is set to `true` if the current record position in a record set is the first record.
- **`cacheSize`**—Specifies the number of records from a record set that are cached locally.

19

- `cursorLocation`—Specifies the location of the record set cursor for the record set.
- `editMode`—Indicates whether editing is in progress.
- `EOF`—Is set to `true` if the current record is the last record in the record set.
- `lockType`—Specifies the type of database locking used.
- `maxRecords`—Specifies the maximum number of records a record set can contain.
- `pageCount`—Specifies the number of pages of data a record set contains.
- `pageSize`—Specifies the number of records that make up one page of data.
- `recordCount`—Specifies the number of records in the current record set.
- `state`—Indicates whether a record set is open or closed.
- `status`—Indicates the status of the current record.
- `stayInSync`—Indicates whether a hierarchical record set should stay in sync with the data source.

Here are the methods of the record set objects inside DSOs:

- `addNew`—You use this method to add a new record to the record set.
- `cancel`—You use this method to cancel execution of a pending `Execute` or `Open` request.
- `cancelUpdate`—You use this method to cancel an update operation.
- `clone`—You use this method to create a copy of the record set.
- `close`—You use this method to close a record set.
- `delete`—You use this method to delete the current record (or group of records).
- `find`—You use this method to search the record set. (Note that you use SQL to perform the search, which is not supported in Internet Explorer.)
- `getRows`—You use this method to read records and store them in an array.
- `getString`—You use this method to get the record set as a string.
- `move`—You use this method to move the position of the current record.
- `moveFirst`, `moveLast`, `moveNext`, **and** `movePrevious`—You use this method to navigate to various positions in the record set.
- `nextRecordSet`—You use this method to clear the current record set object and return the next record set when working with hierarchical record sets.
- `open`—You use this method to open a database.
- `requery`—You use this method to re-execute the command that created a record set.

- **save**—You use this method to save a record set in a file.
- **supports**—You use this method to determine the features the record set supports.

In addition, DSOs support a number of events we can handle in scripting code. Here they are:

- **onDataAvailable**—Occurs when data is downloaded.
- **onDatasetChanged**—Occurs when the record set is changed.
- **onDatasetComplete**—Occurs when the data is downloaded and ready to be used.
- **onReadyStateChange**—Occurs when the `ReadyState` property changes.
- **onRowEnter**—Occurs when a new record becomes the current one.
- **onRowExit**—Occurs just before exiting the current record.
- **onRowsDelete**—Occurs when a row is deleted.
- **onRowsInserted**—Occurs when a row is inserted.
- **onCellChange**—Occurs when the data in a bound control changes and the focus leaves that cell.

Now that we've explored how to do data binding in HTML, let's do this kind of data binding directly with XML.

Binding HTML Elements to XML Data

To bind XML data to controls in Internet Explorer, use your standard XML document that contains the state data, which is shown in Listing 19.3. (Note that we've removed the `units` attribute from the `<population>` element because Internet Explorer can't convert that element's data into readable form when XML elements use attributes.)

19

LISTING 19.3 An XML Data Document (`ch19_03.xml`)

```
<?xml version="1.0" encoding ="UTF-8"?>
<states>

    <state>
        <name>California</name>
        <population>33871648</population>
        <capital>Sacramento</capital>
        <bird>Quail</bird>
        <flower>Golden Poppy</flower>
        <area units="square miles">155959</area>
    </state>

    <state>
        <name>Massachusetts</name>
```

LISTING 19.3 continued

```
        <population>6349097</population>
        <capital>Boston</capital>
        <bird>Chickadee</bird>
        <flower>Mayflower</flower>
        <area units="square miles">7840</area>
    </state>

    <state>
        <name>New York</name>
        <population>18976457</population>
        <capital>Albany</capital>
        <bird>Bluebird</bird>
        <flower>Rose</flower>
        <area units="square miles">47214</area>
    </state>
</states>
```

You'll start by using XML data islands to bind to the data in `ch19_03.xml`. All you need to do is change the DSO you're using to an XML island by using the `<XML>` element, as shown in Listing 19.4.

LISTING 19.4 Reading XML Data with XML Islands (`ch19_04.html`)

```
<HTML>
    <HEAD>
        <TITLE>
            Binding with XML data islands
        </TITLE>
    </HEAD>

    <XML SRC="ch19_03.xml" ID="states"></XML>

    <BODY>
        <H1>
            Binding with XML data islands
        </H1>

        Name: <INPUT TYPE="TEXT" DATASRC="#states"
            DATAFLD="name" SIZE="10">

        <BR><BR>
        Population: <INPUT TYPE="TEXT" DATASRC="#states"
            DATAFLD="population" SIZE="10">

        <BR><BR>
        Capital: <SPAN DATASRC="#states"
            DATAFLD="capital"></SPAN>
```

LISTING 19.4 continued

```
        <BR><BR>
        Bird: <SELECT DATASRC="#states"
            DATAFLD="bird" SIZE="1">
            <OPTION VALUE="Quail">Quail
            <OPTION VALUE="Chickadee">Chickadee
            <OPTION VALUE="Bluebird">Bluebird
        </SELECT>

        <BR><BR>
        Flower: <SPAN DATASRC="#states" DATAFLD="flower">
        </SPAN>

        <BR><BR>
        <BUTTON ONCLICK=
            "states.recordset.moveFirst()"> &lt;&lt; 
        </BUTTON>
        <BUTTON ONCLICK="if (!states.recordset.BOF)
            states.recordset.movePrevious()"> &lt; 
        </BUTTON>
        <BUTTON ONCLICK="if (!states.recordset.EOF)
            states.recordset.moveNext()"> &gt; 
        </BUTTON>
        <BUTTON ONCLICK=
            "states.recordset.moveLast()"> &gt;&gt; 
        </BUTTON>
    </BODY>
</HTML>
```

19

The results are the same as when you used the MSHTML DSO and HTML data, as shown in Figure 19.2.

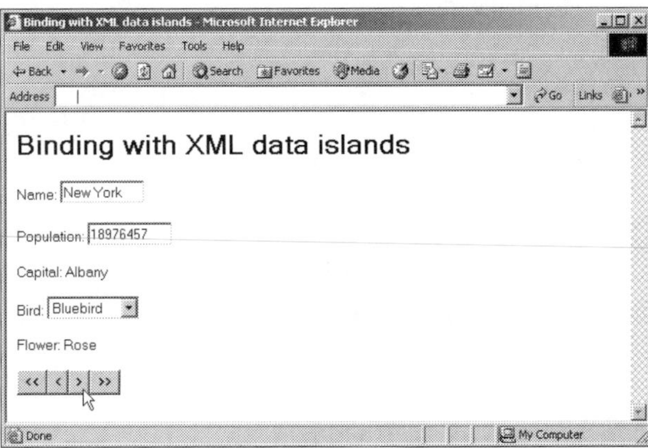

FIGURE 19.2
Data binding with XML data islands.

Now you have a way to display XML data in HTML controls in Internet Explorer.

Binding HTML Tables to XML Data

Besides simple HTML controls, you can also bind data to more advanced HTML controls, such as tables. The following example shows how to bind your state data to an HTML table, using an XML data island:

```
<HTML>
    <HEAD>
        <TITLE>
            Displaying XML data using XML data islands
        </TITLE>
    </HEAD>

    <BODY>
        <H1>
            Displaying XML data using XML data islands
        </H1>

        <XML SRC="ch19_03.xml" ID="states"></XML>
        .
        .
        .
```

To connect the `states` DSO to the table, you'll use the `<TABLE>` element's `DATASRC` attribute, like this:

```
<TABLE DATASRC="#states" BORDER="1">
     <THEAD>
         <TR>
             <TH>Name</TH>
             <TH>Population</TH>
             <TH>Capital</TH>
             <TH>Bird</TH>
             <TH>Flower</TH>
         </TR>
     </THEAD>
         .
         .
         .
```

Now, in the body of the table, tie each table cell to a data field by using the `DATAFLD` attribute of a `<SPAN>` element in each `<TD>` element:

```
<TABLE DATASRC="#states" BORDER="1">
     <THEAD>
         <TR>
             <TH>Name</TH>
```

```
            <TH>Population</TH>
            <TH>Capital</TH>
            <TH>Bird</TH>
            <TH>Flower</TH>
        </TR>
    </THEAD>

    <TBODY>
        <TR>
            <TD>
                <SPAN DATAFLD="name">
                </SPAN>
            </TD>
            <TD>
                <SPAN DATAFLD="population">
                </SPAN>
            </TD>
            <TD>
                <SPAN DATAFLD="capital">
                </SPAN>
            </TD>
            <TD>
                <SPAN DATAFLD="bird">
                </SPAN>
            </TD>
            <TD>
                <SPAN DATAFLD="flower">
                </SPAN>
            </TD>
        </TR>
    </TBODY>
</TABLE>
```


And that's all there is to it. The whole example is shown in Listing 19.5.

LISTING 19.5 Displaying XML Data in a Table (ch19_05.html)

```
<HTML>
    <HEAD>
        <TITLE>
            Displaying XML data using XML data islands
        </TITLE>
    </HEAD>

    <BODY>
        <H1>
            Displaying XML data using XML data islands
        </H1>
```

LISTING 19.5 continued

```
            <XML SRC="ch19_03.xml" ID="states"></XML>

            <TABLE DATASRC="#states" BORDER="1">
                 <THEAD>
                     <TR>
                         <TH>Name</TH>
                         <TH>Population</TH>
                         <TH>Capital</TH>
                         <TH>Bird</TH>
                         <TH>Flower</TH>
                     </TR>
                  </THEAD>

                  <TBODY>
                      <TR>
                          <TD>
                              <SPAN DATAFLD="name">
                              </SPAN>
                          </TD>
                          <TD>
                              <SPAN DATAFLD="population">
                              </SPAN>
                          </TD>
                          <TD>
                              <SPAN DATAFLD="capital">
                              </SPAN>
                          </TD>
                          <TD>
                              <SPAN DATAFLD="bird">
                              </SPAN>
                          </TD>
                          <TD>
                              <SPAN DATAFLD="flower">
                              </SPAN>
                          </TD>
                      </TR>
                  </TBODY>
            </TABLE>
        </BODY>
    </HTML>
```

The results of Listing 19.5 appear in Figure 19.3. As the figure shows, the data from your sample XML document, `ch19_03.xml`, is displayed in an HTML table.

FIGURE 19.3

Binding data to a table.

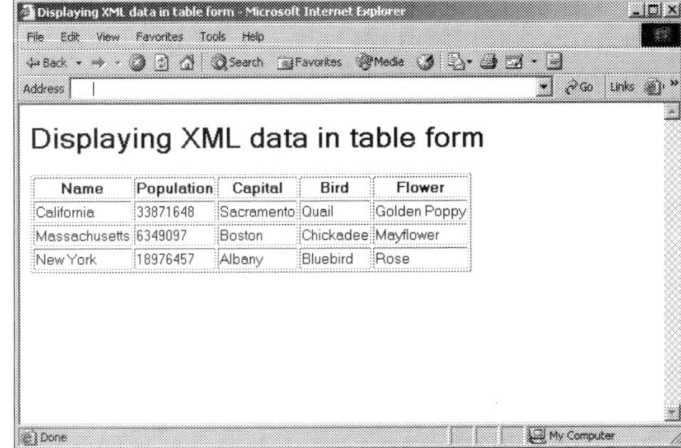

Accessing Individual Data Fields

Besides displaying data by binding it to HTML controls, we can also access the data in the fields of a DSO by using JavaScript. For example, you can access the value of the current record's `name` field in the `states` DSO as `states.recordset("name")` in JavaScript.

In the following example, you'll use JavaScript to display data from the various states in a text sentence, not in HTML controls. Start by looping over the records in the DSO:

```
<SCRIPT LANGUAGE="JavaScript">
    function displayData()
    {
        while (!states.recordset.EOF) {
        .
        .
        .
            states.recordset.moveNext()
        }
    }
</SCRIPT>
```


Now all you have to do is grab your data from the DSO by using JavaScript:

```
<SCRIPT LANGUAGE="JavaScript">
    function displayData()
    {
        while (!states.recordset.EOF) {
            displayDIV.innerHTML +=
            states.recordset("name") +
            "'s population is " +
            states.recordset("population") +
            ", its bird is the " +
```

```
                states.recordset("bird") +
                ", and its flower is the " +
                states.recordset("flower") +
                ".<BR><BR>"
                states.recordset.moveNext()
            }
        }
</SCRIPT>
```

And that's all you need to do to complete this example of accessing XML data from a DSO using JavaScript directly. The results appear in Figure 19.4.

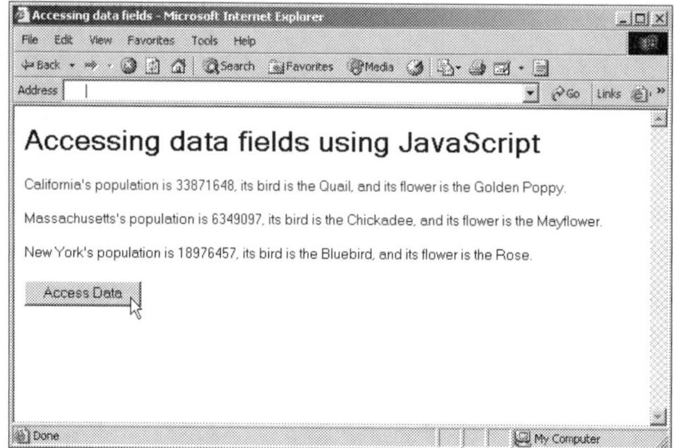

FIGURE 19.4
Accessing data by using JavaScript.

Listing 19.6 shows the complete code for this example.

LISTING 19.6 Accessing Individual XML Data Fields (`ch19_06.html`)

```
<HTML>
    <HEAD>
        <TITLE>
            Accessing data fields
        </TITLE>

        <XML ID="states" SRC="ch19_03.xml"></XML>

        <SCRIPT LANGUAGE="JavaScript">
            function displayData()
            {
                while (!states.recordset.EOF) {
                    displayDIV.innerHTML +=
                    states.recordset("name") +
                    "'s population is " +
```

Listing 19.6 continued

```
                    states.recordset("population") +
                    ", its bird is the " +
                    states.recordset("bird") +
                    ", and its flower is the " +
                    states.recordset("flower") +
                    ".<BR><BR>"
                    states.recordset.moveNext()
                }
            }
        </SCRIPT>
    </HEAD>

    <BODY>
        <H1>
            Accessing data fields
        </H1>

        <DIV ID="displayDIV"></DIV>
        <FORM>
            <INPUT TYPE="BUTTON" VALUE="Access Data"
                ONCLICK="displayData()">
        </FORM>
    </BODY>
</HTML>
```

You've been using XML islands up to this point, but now you'll take a look at another DSO: the XML DSO.

19

Binding HTML Elements to XML Data by Using the XML DSO

Beginning in version 4, Internet Explorer has included an XML DSO designed to be used only with XML. This DSO is unique because it's not internal to Internet Explorer and it's not an ActiveX control—it's a Java applet. Embed this applet in a page and create an XML DSO by using the HTML <APPLET> element, like this:

```
<APPLET
    CODE="com.ms.xml.dso.XMLDSO.class"
    ID="IDNAME"
    WIDTH="0"
    HEIGHT="0"
    MAYSCRIPT="true">
    <PARAM NAME="URL" VALUE="XMLPageURL">
</APPLET>
```

The URI of the XML document is passed as a parameter to the XML DSO applet, using the `<PARAM>` element. Let's take a look at the XML DSO at work in an example. Here's how to connect this DSO to your XML document `ch19_03.xml`:

```
<HTML>
    <HEAD>
        <TITLE>
            Using the XML Data Source Object
        </TITLE>
    </HEAD>

    <BODY>
        <H1>
            Using the XML Data Source Object
        </H1>

        <APPLET CODE="com.ms.xml.dso.XMLDSO.class"
            ID="states"
            WIDTH="0" HEIGHT="0"
            MAYSCRIPT="true">
            <PARAM NAME="URL" VALUE="ch19_03.xml">
        </APPLET>
        .
        .
        .
```

You can now use this DSO to bind to various controls, similarly to how you have before:

```
Name: <INPUT TYPE="TEXT" DATASRC="#states"
    DATAFLD="name" SIZE="10">

<BR><BR>
Population: <INPUT TYPE="TEXT" DATASRC="#states"
    DATAFLD="population" SIZE="10">

<BR><BR>
Capital: <SPAN DATASRC="#states"
    DATAFLD="capital"></SPAN>

<BR><BR>
Bird: <SELECT DATASRC="#states"
    DATAFLD="bird" SIZE="1">
    <OPTION VALUE="Quail">Quail
    <OPTION VALUE="Chickadee">Chickadee
    <OPTION VALUE="Bluebird">Bluebird
</SELECT>

<BR><BR>
Flower: <SPAN DATASRC="#states" DATAFLD="flower">
</SPAN>
```

Finally, use the methods of the record set object contained in the XML DSO (such as `moveNext`, `moveFirst`, and so on) to navigate through the record set with buttons, as shown in Listing 19.7.

LISTING 19.7 Using the XML DSO (`ch19_07.html`)

```
<HTML>
    <HEAD>
        <TITLE>
            Using the XML Data Source Object
        </TITLE>
    </HEAD>

    <BODY>
        <H1>
            Using the XML Data Source Object
        </H1>

        <APPLET CODE="com.ms.xml.dso.XMLDSO.class"
            ID="states"
            WIDTH="0" HEIGHT="0"
            MAYSCRIPT="true">
            <PARAM NAME="URL" VALUE="ch19_03.xml">
        </APPLET>

        Name: <INPUT TYPE="TEXT" DATASRC="#states"
            DATAFLD="name" SIZE="10">

        <BR><BR>
        Population: <INPUT TYPE="TEXT" DATASRC="#states"
            DATAFLD="population" SIZE="10">

        <BR><BR>
        Capital: <SPAN DATASRC="#states"
            DATAFLD="capital"></SPAN>

        <BR><BR>
        Bird: <SELECT DATASRC="#states"
            DATAFLD="bird" SIZE="1">
            <OPTION VALUE="Quail">Quail
            <OPTION VALUE="Chickadee">Chickadee
            <OPTION VALUE="Bluebird">Bluebird
        </SELECT>

        <BR><BR>
        Flower: <SPAN DATASRC="#states" DATAFLD="flower">
        </SPAN>
```

19

LISTING 19.7 continued

```
        <BR><BR>
        <BUTTON ONCLICK=
            "states.recordset.moveFirst()"> &lt;&lt; 
        </BUTTON>
        <BUTTON ONCLICK="if (!states.recordset.BOF)
            states.recordset.movePrevious()"> &lt; 
        </BUTTON>
        <BUTTON ONCLICK="if (!states.recordset.EOF)
            states.recordset.moveNext()"> &gt; 
        </BUTTON>
        <BUTTON ONCLICK=
            "states.recordset.moveLast()"> &gt;&gt; 
        </BUTTON>
    </BODY>
</HTML>
```

Figure 19.5 shows this example at work. This example looks just the same as if you had used XML islands.

FIGURE 19.5

Data binding with the XML DSO.

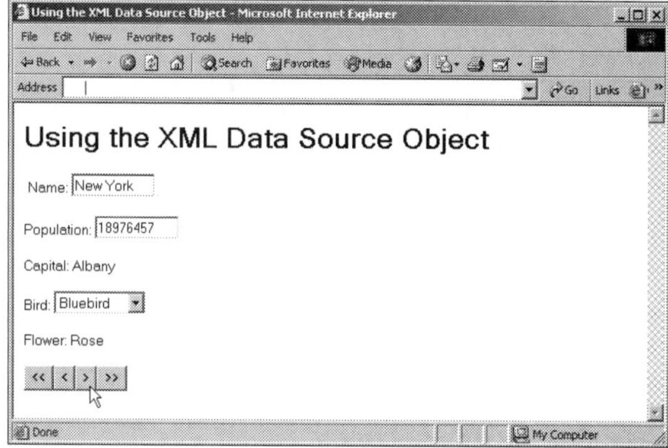

And you can also bind the XML DSO to HTML tables.

Binding HTML Tables to XML Data by Using the XML DSO

It's as easy to bind the XML DSO to tables as it is to bind XML data islands to tables. The following example shows how this works. In Listing 19.8, you're binding ch19_03.xml to a table by using the XML DSO, and you're displaying all the fields in the various records of ch19_03.xml all at once.

LISTING 19.8 Binding Tables by Using the XML DSO (ch19_08.html)

```
<HTML>
    <HEAD>
        <TITLE>
            The XML Data Source Object and Tables
        </TITLE>
    </HEAD>

    <BODY>
        <H1>
            The XML Data Source Object and Tables
        </H1>

        <APPLET CODE="com.ms.xml.dso.XMLDSO.class"
            ID="states"
            WIDTH="0" HEIGHT="0"
            MAYSCRIPT="true">
            <PARAM NAME="URL" VALUE="ch19_03.xml">
        </APPLET>

        <TABLE DATASRC="#states" BORDER="1">
             <THEAD>
                 <TR>
                     <TH>Name</TH>
                     <TH>Population</TH>
                     <TH>Capital</TH>
                     <TH>Bird</TH>
                     <TH>Flower</TH>
                 </TR>
              </THEAD>

              <TBODY>
                  <TR>
                      <TD>
                          <SPAN DATAFLD="name">
                          </SPAN>
                      </TD>
                      <TD>
                          <SPAN DATAFLD="population">
                          </SPAN>
                      </TD>
                      <TD>
                          <SPAN DATAFLD="capital">
                          </SPAN>
                      </TD>
```

LISTING 19.8 continued

```
                    <TD>
                        <SPAN DATAFLD="bird">
                        </SPAN>
                    </TD>
                    <TD>
                        <SPAN DATAFLD="flower">
                        </SPAN>
                    </TD>
                </TR>
            </TBODY>
        </TABLE>
    </BODY>
</HTML>
```

That's all it takes. Figure 19.6 shows this page in action.

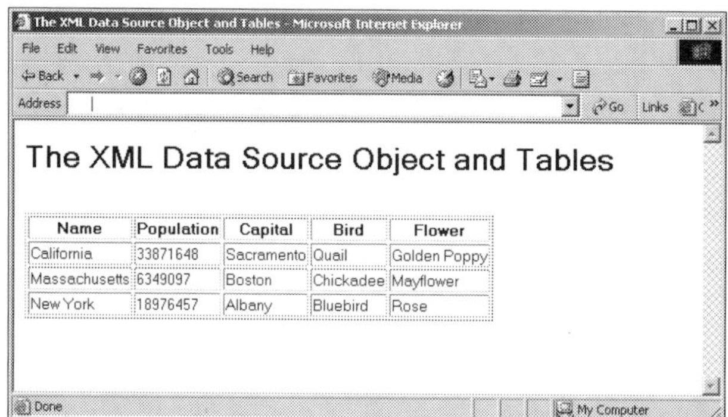

FIGURE 19.6
Tabular data binding with the XML DSO in Internet Explorer.

Searching XML Data by Using a DSO and JavaScript

As you've already seen, you don't have to bind the data from a DSO to HTML controls at all; you can work with that data from a scripting language such as JavaScript. That makes it easy to handle data in various ways, such as searching for a particular data item behind-the-scenes and displaying the results of the search in a Web page.

For example, say that a user wants to search for all the data about a particular state rather than having to navigate through all the states to find the one she wants. We can let her simply enter the name of the state in a text field, search for the matching state, and display the data if a match occurs. In this example, you'll use the XML DSO to point out another feature of that DSO: If you give it a size (not just zero width and height), it will display status and error messages. Here's how that might look:

```
<APPLET CODE="com.ms.xml.dso.XMLDSO.class"
    ID="states"
    WIDTH="400" HEIGHT="20"
    MAYSCRIPT="true">
    <PARAM NAME="URL" VALUE="ch19_03.xml">
</APPLET>
```

To make your search case-insensitive, you'll read the state name the user has entered, convert it to lowercase, and store it in the JavaScript variable `findMe`:

```
function search()
{
    var findMe = form1.text1.value.toLowerCase()
        .
        .
        .
```

Then you can loop over the states in code (converting their names to lowercase for the comparison), and check whether you find the matching state:

```
function search()
{
    var findMe = form1.text1.value.toLowerCase()

    while (!states.recordset.EOF) {
        .
        .
        .
        }
        states.recordset.moveNext()
    }
}
```

If you find a match, display the matching state's data:

```
function search()
{
    var findMe = form1.text1.value.toLowerCase()

    while (!states.recordset.EOF) {
        var stateName = new String(states.recordset("name"))
        stateName = stateName.toLowerCase()
        if (stateName.indexOf(findMe) >= 0) {
            displayDIV.innerHTML +=
            states.recordset("name") +
            "'s population is " +
            states.recordset("population") +
            ", its bird is the " +
```

19

```
                states.recordset("bird") +
                ", and its flower is the " +
                states.recordset("flower") +
                ".<BR><BR>"
        }
        states.recordset.moveNext()
    }
}
```

All that's left to do is display the text field for the user to enter the state's name and a button to click to start the search. That looks like this:

```
<DIV ID="displayDIV"></DIV>
<FORM ID="form1">
    State to find: <INPUT TYPE="TEXT" NAME="text1">
    <BR>
    <BR>
    <INPUT TYPE="BUTTON" VALUE="Find state"
        ONCLICK="search()">
</FORM>
```

Figure 19.7 shows how this works; in this figure, you have gotten the goods on New York State. Also note in this figure that the XML DSO is displaying a status message indicating that it successfully loaded the XML document `ch19_03.xml`. If you give it space in your Web pages, this DSO will let you know what's going on, and if a parsing error occurs, it will give you all the details.

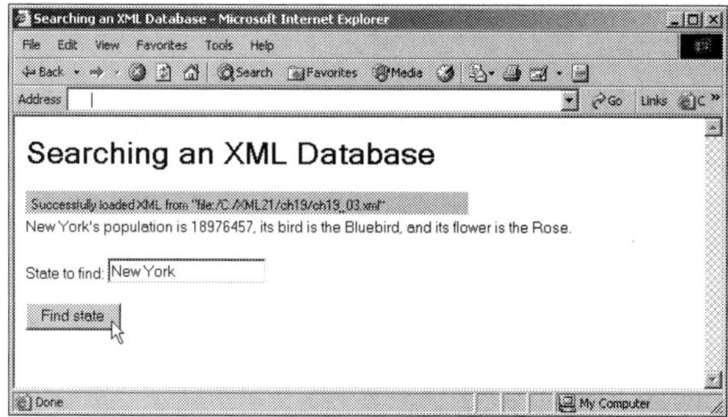

FIGURE 19.7
Searching an XML database.

Listing 19.9 shows the full code for this example.

LISTING 19.9 Searching XML Data (`ch19_09.html`)

```
<HTML>
    <HEAD>
        <TITLE>
            Searching an XML Database
```

LISTING 19.9 continued

```
        </TITLE>

        <SCRIPT LANGUAGE="JavaScript">
            function search()
            {
                var findMe = form1.text1.value.toLowerCase()

                while (!states.recordset.EOF) {
                    var stateName = new String(states.recordset("name"))
                    stateName = stateName.toLowerCase()
                    if (stateName.indexOf(findMe) >= 0) {
                        displayDIV.innerHTML +=
                        states.recordset("name") +
                        "'s population is " +
                        states.recordset("population") +
                        ", its bird is the " +
                        states.recordset("bird") +
                        ", and its flower is the " +
                        states.recordset("flower") +
                        ".<BR><BR>"
                    }
                    states.recordset.moveNext()
                }
            }
        </SCRIPT>
    </HEAD>

    <BODY>
        <H1>
            Searching an XML Database
        </H1>

        <APPLET CODE="com.ms.xml.dso.XMLDSO.class"
            ID="states"
            WIDTH="400" HEIGHT="20"
            MAYSCRIPT="true">
            <PARAM NAME="URL" VALUE="ch19_03.xml">
        </APPLET>

        <BR>
        <DIV ID="displayDIV"></DIV>
        <FORM ID="form1">
            State to find: <INPUT TYPE="TEXT" NAME="text1">
            <BR>
            <BR>
            <INPUT TYPE="BUTTON" VALUE="Find state"
                ONCLICK="search()">
        </FORM>
    </BODY>
</HTML>
```

19

Handling Hierarchical XML Data

The last topic today concerns hierarchical record sets, where one field can contain an entire child record set. As data evolves, it becomes very useful; it means we can organize our data into project records, for example, and each project record can have a field that contains a record set listing personnel, parts needed, or code files.

XML documents let us store hierarchical data, and all we have to do to make it happen is nest elements. For example, say that you want to keep track of your friends in the various states in your states XML document. To do that, add a new element, `<friends>`, which contains various `<friend>` elements, like this:

```
<state>
    <name>California</name>
    <population>33871648</population>
    <capital>Sacramento</capital>
    <bird>Quail</bird>
    <flower>Golden Poppy</flower>
    <area units="square miles">155959</area>
    <friends>
        <friend>
            <firstName>Tom</firstName>
            <lastName>Marshall</lastName>
        </friend>
        <friend>
            <firstName>Ed</firstName>
            <lastName>Norton</lastName>
        </friend>
    </friends>
</state>
```

The `friends` field, which contains multiple `friend` records, now contains a record set and is arranged hierarchically. You can add a `friends` record to every state in your sample XML document, as shown in Listing 19.10.

LISTING 19.10 XML with Hierarchical Data (`ch19_10.xml`)

```
<?xml version="1.0" encoding ="UTF-8"?>
<states>

    <state>
        <name>California</name>
        <population>33871648</population>
        <capital>Sacramento</capital>
        <bird>Quail</bird>
        <flower>Golden Poppy</flower>
        <area units="square miles">155959</area>
        <friends>
```

LISTING 19.10 continued

```
            <friend>
                <firstName>Tom</firstName>
                <lastName>Marshall</lastName>
            </friend>
            <friend>
                <firstName>Ed</firstName>
                <lastName>Norton</lastName>
            </friend>
        </friends>
    </state>

    <state>
        <name>Massachusetts</name>
        <population>6349097</population>
        <capital>Boston</capital>
        <bird>Chickadee</bird>
        <flower>Mayflower</flower>
        <area units="square miles">7840</area>
        <friends>
            <friend>
                <firstName>Frank</firstName>
                <lastName>Stein</lastName>
            </friend>
            <friend>
                <firstName>Britta</firstName>
                <lastName>Regensburg</lastName>
            </friend>
            <friend>
                <firstName>Ralph</firstName>
                <lastName>Kramden</lastName>
            </friend>
        </friends>
    </state>

    <state>
        <name>New York</name>
        <population>18976457</population>
        <capital>Albany</capital>
        <bird>Bluebird</bird>
        <flower>Rose</flower>
        <area units="square miles">47214</area>
        <friends>
            <friend>
                <firstName>Trixie</firstName>
                <lastName>Norton</lastName>
            </friend>
        </friends>
    </state>
</states>
```

Now each `friends` field contains a record set. The best way to see how this works is by using an HTML table that displays your data in a hierarchical fashion. You'll start with an XML island connected to your new XML document, `ch19_10.xml`, and a table connected to that XML island that is set up to display the names of the states:

```
<XML SRC="ch19_10.xml" ID=states></XML>

<TABLE DATASRC="#states" BORDER="1">
    <TR>
        <TH><DIV DATAFLD="name"></DIV></TH>
        .
        .
        .
```

Now you'll display the data in the `friends` field, which you can handle as a record set itself. You can refer to that record set as `friends.friend`, which makes sense in a hierarchy. In this case, you'll display the contents of each `friends.friend` record set in its own nested table:

```
<XML SRC="ch19_10.xml" ID=states></XML>

<TABLE DATASRC="#states" BORDER="1">
    <TR>
        <TH><DIV DATAFLD="name"></DIV></TH>
        <TD>
            <TABLE DATASRC="#states"
            DATAFLD="friends">
                <TR>
                    <TD>
                    <TABLE BORDER="1">
                        <TR ALIGN = "LEFT">
                            <TH WIDTH="128">First Name</TH>
                            <TH WIDTH="128">Last Name</TH>
                        </TR>
                    </TABLE>
                    <TABLE DATASRC="#states"
                        CELLPADDING = "5"
                        DATAFLD="friends.friend"
        .
        .
        .
```

Now that you've tied this new table to the `friends.friend` records set, display the data from the fields in that record set, like this:

```
<XML SRC="ch19_10.xml" ID=states></XML>

<TABLE DATASRC="#states" BORDER="1">
    <TR>
        <TH><DIV DATAFLD="name"></DIV></TH>
        <TD>
```

```
            <TABLE DATASRC="#states"
            DATAFLD="friends">
                <TR>
                    <TD>
                    <TABLE BORDER="1">
                        <TR ALIGN = "LEFT">
                            <TH WIDTH="128">First Name</TH>
                            <TH WIDTH="128">Last Name</TH>
                        </TR>
                    </TABLE>
                    <TABLE DATASRC="#states"
                        CELLPADDING = "5"
                        DATAFLD="friends.friend"
                        BORDER="1">
                        <TR ALIGN = "LEFT">
                            <TD WIDTH="120"><DIV
                            DATAFLD="firstName">
                            </DIV></TD>
                            <TD WIDTH="120"><DIV
                            DATAFLD="lastName">
                            </DIV></TD>
                        </TR>
                    </TABLE>
                    </TD>
                </TR>
            </TABLE>
        </TD>
    </TR>
</TABLE>
```

Figure 19.8 shows the results; as the figure shows, you've been able to display all the child record sets for each state, treating your record sets as hierarchical.

19

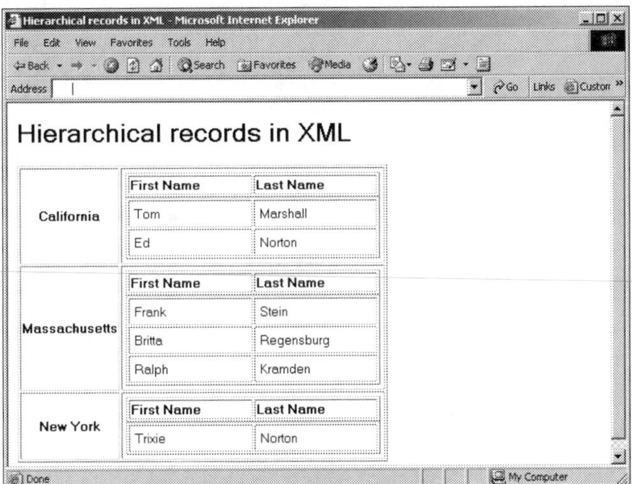

FIGURE 19.8
Handling hierarchical record sets.

Listing 19.11 shows the complete code for this example.

LISTING 19.11 Displaying Hierarchical XML Data (`ch19_11.html`)

```
<HTML>
    <HEAD>
        <TITLE>
            Hierarchical records in XML
        </TITLE>
    </HEAD>

    <BODY>
        <H1>
            Hierarchical records in XML
        </H1>

        <XML SRC="ch19_10.xml" ID=states></XML>

        <TABLE DATASRC="#states" BORDER="1">
            <TR>
                <TH><DIV DATAFLD="name"></DIV></TH>
                <TD>
                    <TABLE DATASRC="#states"
                    DATAFLD="friends">
                        <TR>
                            <TD>
                            <TABLE BORDER="1">
                                <TR ALIGN = "LEFT">
                                    <TH WIDTH="128">First Name</TH>
                                    <TH WIDTH="128">Last Name</TH>
                                </TR>
                            </TABLE>
                            <TABLE DATASRC="#states"
                                CELLPADDING = "5"
                                DATAFLD="friends.friend"
                                BORDER="1">
                                <TR ALIGN = "LEFT">
                                    <TD WIDTH="120"><DIV DATAFLD="firstName">
                                    </DIV></TD>
                                    <TD WIDTH="120"><DIV
                                    DATAFLD="lastName">
                                    </DIV></TD>
                                </TR>
                            </TABLE>
                            </TD>
                        </TR>
                    </TABLE>
                </TD>
```

LISTING 19.11 continued

```
            </TR>
        </TABLE>
    </BODY>
</HTML>
```

That's it for today's discussion on data binding. There's a lot going on here, but for now, we're limited to the support in Internet Explorer. Tomorrow, we'll talk about more ways of handling XML data as we start discussing XML and databases.

Summary

Today you took a look at binding XML data in Internet Explorer. You saw that there are various DSOs that you can use to connect to data sources and make XML data accessible to HTML controls and scripting code.

We started by taking a look at the MSHTML DSO, which lets us handle data formatted in HTML by using `<SPAN>` or `<DIV>` elements. You saw that you can create an MSHTML DSO by using the `<OBJECT>` element and the `DATA` attribute.

Then we discussed two XML DSOs: XML data islands and the XML DSO applet. You can connect an XML data island to an XML document by using the `<XML>` element and the `SRC` attribute. And you can connect an XML DSO to an XML document by using a `<PARAM>` element inside the `<APPLET>` element.

To bind an HTML element such as a text field or table to a DSO, use the element's `DATASRC` and `DATAFLD` attributes; the `DATASRC` attribute contains the name of the DSO, and the `DATAFLD` attribute gives the name of the field in the DSO's current record to connect to. The data in the bound field or fields is automatically displayed in the bound controls. And when you change the current record by using DSO methods such as `moveNext` or `moveLast`, the data in all controls bound to that DSO is also updated.

Today you also saw that you can access the data in a DSO by using JavaScript, without having to bind that data to controls, and that you can also work with hierarchical record sets in Internet Explorer.

Q&A

Q The XML DSO is based on an applet. Can I count on it being released with future versions of Internet Explorer?

A The answer is probably no. Indications are that the XML DSO is still being released with Internet Explorer only for the sake of backward compatibility. But it's not even an ActiveX control, and Microsoft might stop supporting it at any time.

Q How can I be notified of errors when a DSO tries to load an XML document?

A You can use code to handle the DSO's `onerrorupdate` event.

Workshop

This workshop tests whether you understand the concepts discussed today. It's a good idea to make sure you can answer these questions before pressing on to tomorrow's work. Answers to the quiz can be found in Appendix A, "Quiz Answers."

Quiz

1. How would you create an XML island that makes the XML data in a document named `data.xml` available as a DSO named `data`?
2. What two HTML attributes do you normally use to bind an HTML control to a DSO?
3. How can you bind an HTML table to a DSO?
4. How can you determine when you're at the beginning or end of a record set?
5. How would you access the `address` field in the current record in a DSO in JavaScript?

Exercises

1. Use JavaScript and a DSO to extract the data in `ch19_01.xml` and display it in an HTML table—without binding the table directly to the DSO.
2. Create an XML document that holds phone numbers of relatives or acquaintances, using hierarchical data, and bind it to an HTML table, making sure the hierarchical data is displayed correctly.

PART V

DAY 20

Working with XML and Databases

The connection between XML and databases is a natural one, and we're going to take a look at this field today. We'll also take a look at the XQuery language that is now being developed as a W3C recommendation and that is designed to work with XML and databases. In fact, today you'll use one of the few XQuery software implementations available to get all the details. Here's an overview of today's topics:

- Handling XML databases
- Using XML for database storage with Visual Basic .NET 2003
- Using XPath in Visual Basic .NET 2003 databases
- Working with XQuery
- Using XQuery to query an XML document

The way XML is implemented by database providers varies widely, which means the coverage today will be in many different areas. First, we're going to take a look at a brute-force method of working with XML and databases, and then we'll examine some integrated XML support in a database provider, and finally we'll talk about W3C's XQuery, which provides a query language (much like SQL for database applications) to work with databases from XML's point of view.

XML, Databases, and ASP

The brute-force way of extracting data from a database by using XML is to use intermediate code to access the data in the database and return the results in XML format. Let's look at an example that uses Active Server Pages (ASP) and Microsoft Internet Information Server (IIS). In this case, you'll use an ASP page `ch20_01.asp` to read the data in the Microsoft Access database `ch20_02.mdb`. The sample database in this example, `ch20_02.mdb`, which is shown in Access in Figure 20.1, contains the grades of a number of students.

FIGURE 20.1

A sample Access database.

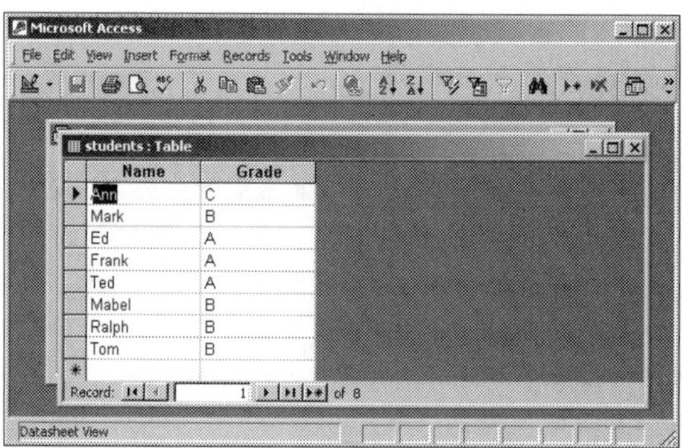

The `ch20_01.asp` page will act as the intermediary between the database provide, Access, and the XML results, which you'll see in a Web page. The internal workings of ASP are beyond the scope of this book, but we'll take a look at this in overview. The plan here will be to extract the names in the database and display them in an XML document you send to a client browser.

You start the ASP page by indicating that you're creating an XML document so the browser will know how to handle it:

```
<% Response.ContentType = "application/xml" %>
        .
        .
        .
```

Now embed the beginning of the XML document you want to send back:

```
<% Response.ContentType = "application/xml" %>

<?xml version="1.0" encoding="UTF-8"?>
<document>
        .
        .
        .
```

Now connect to the database and read it in to an ActiveX Data Objects (ADO) record set, like this:

```
<% Response.ContentType = "application/xml" %>

<?xml version="1.0" encoding="UTF-8"?>
<document>

DIM adoConnect
DIM adoRecordset

Set adoConnect = Server.CreateObject("ADODB.Connection")

adoConnect.open "Provider=Microsoft.Jet.OLEDB.4.0;" _
    & "Data Source=C:\xml21\ch20\ch20_02.mdb"

Set adoRecordset = adoConnect.Execute("SELECT * FROM Students")
        .
        .
        .
```

You can access the name of each student and add those names to your XML document by looping over the record set, as shown in Listing 20.1.

LISTING 20.1 Using ASP to Access Data (ch20_01.asp)

```
<% Response.ContentType = "application/xml" %>

<?xml version="1.0" encoding="UTF-8"?>
<document>

<%

DIM adoConnect
DIM adoRecordset

Set adoConnect = Server.CreateObject("ADODB.Connection")
```

LISTING 20.1 continued

```
adoConnect.open "Provider=Microsoft.Jet.OLEDB.4.0;" _
    & "Data Source=C:\xml21\ch20\ch20_02.mdb"

Set adoRecordset = adoConnect.Execute("SELECT * FROM Students")

Do While Not adoRecordset.EOF
    Response.Write "<student>" + adoRecordset("Name") + "</student>"
    adoRecordset.MoveNext
Loop

adoRecordset.Close

set adoRecordset = Nothing

%>

</document>
```

Use an ASP-aware Web server, such as Microsoft's IIS, to display the resulting XML document. Figure 20.2 shows what this looks like.

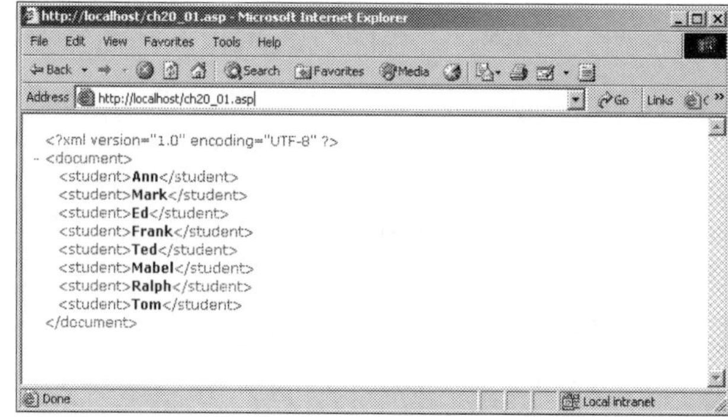

FIGURE 20.2
Brute-force XML database handling with ASP.

Here's the XML document this example generates and sends back to the browser:

```
<?xml version="1.0" encoding="UTF-8" ?>
<document>
    <student>Ann</student>
    <student>Mark</student>
    <student>Ed</student>
    <student>Frank</student>
    <student>Ted</student>
    <student>Mabel</student>
    <student>Ralph</student>
    <student>Tom</student>
</document>
```

You've just used a brute-force way of working with databases and XML. All we did here was to use some intermediary code to gather the data we wanted from the database, package it as XML, and send that XML back to the client. We don't always have to use this brute-force method because some database packages come with a great deal of XML support built in, as we'll discuss next.

Storing Databases as XML

Microsoft has added a great deal of XML support to its database products—far more than any other provider out there, so like it or not, we're in Microsoft territory here. In particular, Microsoft's ADO.NET database protocol uses XML to send data back and forth between databases and applications.

For example, let's examine how to use a Visual Basic .NET application to interact with a database by using SQL Server and see how the data is actually transferred with XML. Figure 20.3 shows a step in the process of creating a new Visual Basic .NET Windows application named `ch20_03`.

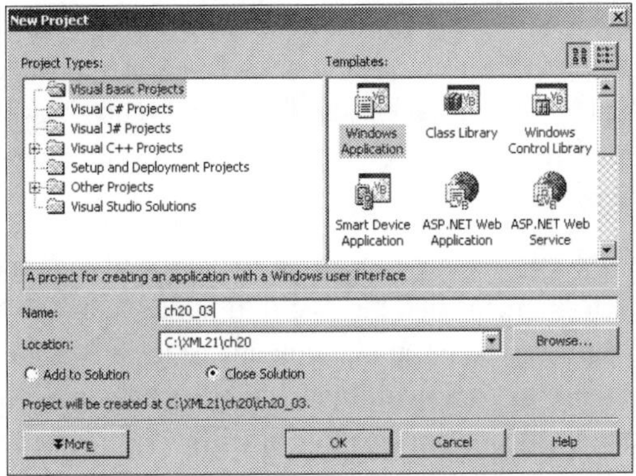

FIGURE 20.3
Creating a Visual Basic .NET Windows application.

Figure 20.4 shows the new Windows application that we create, complete with the two buttons Store XML Data and Read XML Data. Because ADO.NET datasets are sent back and forth by using XML, we can create a dataset when the user clicks the Store XML Data button and store it in XML; then we can create a new dataset by using that XML data when the user clicks the Read XML Data button. After we create the second dataset, we'll bind that data to a data grid control, so let's add a data grid to the Windows form now, as shown in Figure 20.4.

FIGURE 20.4

Creating the `ch20_03` *application.*

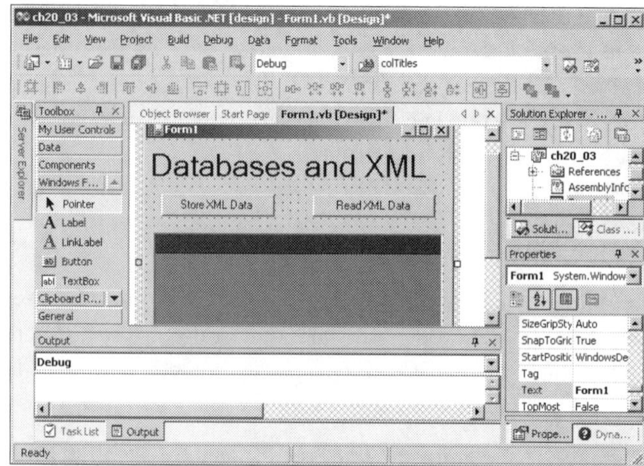

We'll need a connection to a data source, and in this case we can use Microsoft SQL Server, which is often used in .NET data work. In this case, we'll use a data connection to the `pubs` SQL Server sample database and extract the data from the `employee` table in that database. To create that data connection, right-click the Data Connections icon in the Visual Basic .NET Server Explorer (the tab for this tool appears at the left in the Visual Basic .NET development environment, as shown in Figure 20.4), and select the Add Connection item; or select Tools, Connect to Database. In either case, the Data Link Properties dialog box appears.

In the Data Link Properties dialog box, enter the name of the server you want to work with, as well as the login name and password, if applicable—or select the Windows NT integrated security option if your application and SQL Server are on the same machine. Next, choose a database to work with by using either the Select the Database on the Server option or the Attach a Database File as a Database Name option. In this case, we'll use the `pubs` sample database that comes with SQL Server, so let's select the first option and choose the `pubs` database. Then you need to click OK to close this dialog box.

This new data connection appears in the Visual Basic .NET Server Explorer. Now that we've created a data connection to the `pubs` database, we can drag an `OleDbDataAdapter` control from the Visual Basic .NET toolbox to the Visual Basic .NET form we're creating; this opens the Data Adapter Configuration Wizard. You need to click Next to move to the second pane of this wizard, as shown in Figure 20.5. Then select the data connection to the `pubs` database (it is named `STEVE.pubs.dbo` on the machine this example is being developed on, as shown in the figure), and then click Next twice, to open the Data Adapter Configuration Wizard's fourth pane.

FIGURE 20.5

Connecting to the `pubs` *database.*

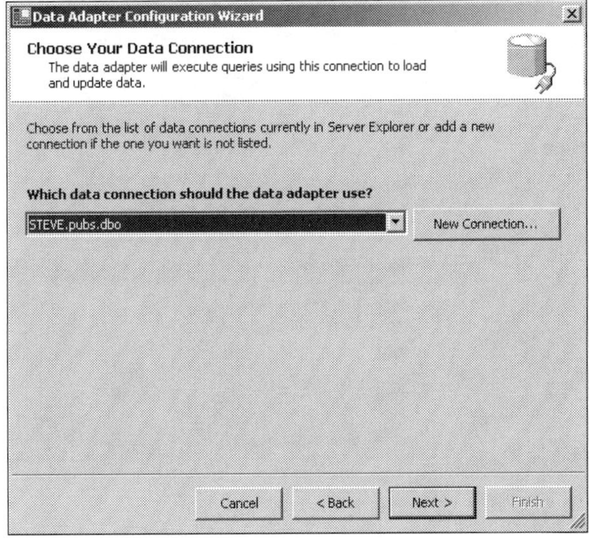

To indicate that you want to connect to the `employee` table, you need to click the Query Builder button in the fourth pane of the wizard, select the employee item in the Add Table dialog box that appears, click the Add button and then the Close button. The Query Builder appears, as shown in Figure 20.6.

FIGURE 20.6

The Query Builder.

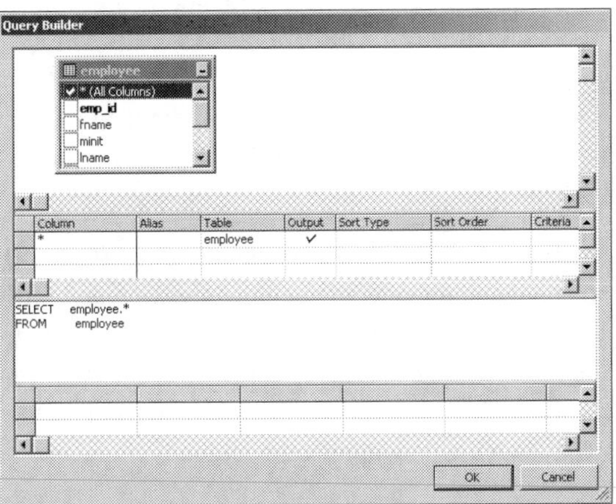

The Query Builder lets us generate the SQL needed to extract the `employee` table from the `pubs` database. To generate that SQL, click the All Columns check box in the employee table's window, as shown in Figure 20.6, and then click OK. As you can see in the Data Adapter Configuration Wizard in Figure 20.7, this generates the following SQL statement:

```
SELECT
    employee.*
FROM
    employee"
```

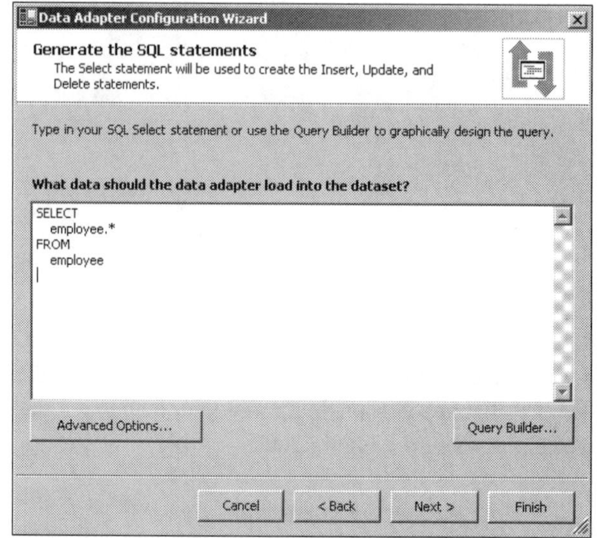

FIGURE 20.7

A new SQL statement in the Query Builder.

Now you need to click Next and then Finish to complete the creation of the data adapter you'll need to connect to the `employee` table. This creates both an `OleDbDataAdapter` object and an `OleDbConnection` object.

The connection object will maintain the connection to SQL Server, and the adapter object will be responsible for activating the connection and retrieving data. Both connection and adapter objects are important in ADO.NET work. Table 20.1 lists the significant properties of the `OleDbDataAdapter` objects, and Table 20.2 lists the significant methods of these objects. Table 20.3 lists the significant properties of the `OleDbConnection` objects, and Table 20.4 lists the significant methods of these objects.

TABLE 20.1 Significant Public Properties of `OleDbDataAdapter` Objects

Property	*Description*
`DeleteCommand`	Returns or sets the SQL for deleting records.
`InsertCommand`	Returns or sets the SQL for inserting new records.
`SelectCommand`	Returns or sets the SQL for selecting records.
`UpdateCommand`	Returns or sets the SQL for updating records.

TABLE 20.2 Significant Public Methods of `OleDbDataAdapter` Objects

Method	*Description*
`Fill`	Adds rows to or refreshes rows in a dataset to make them match the rows in a data store.

TABLE 20.3 Significant Public Properties of `OleDbConnection` Objects

Property	*Description*
`ConnectionString`	Returns or sets the connection string to open a database.
`ConnectionTimeout`	Returns the time to wait while trying to make a connection (in seconds).
`Database`	Returns the name of the database to open.
`DataSource`	Returns the data source (usually the location and filename of the file to open).
`Provider`	Returns the OLE DB provider's name.
`ServerVersion`	Returns the version of the server.
`State`	Returns the connection's current state.

TABLE 20.4 Significant Public Methods of `OleDbConnection` Objects

Method	*Description*
`BeginTransaction`	Starts a database transaction.
`ChangeDatabase`	Changes the current database.
`Close`	Closes the connection to the data provider.
`CreateCommand`	Creates an `OleDbCommand` object for this connection.
`GetOleDbSchemaTable`	Returns the current schema table.
`Open`	Opens a database connection.

We're going to connect the `employee` table to a dataset object so we can access that table's data. To create a dataset based on the data supplied by our `OleDeDataAdapter` object, you need to select Data, Generate Dataset in Visual Basic .NET. This opens the Generate Dataset dialog box, and you need to click OK to create a new dataset object, `DataSet11` (that is, the first object of the automatically generated `DataSet1` class). Datasets act as repositories of data in .NET, and they give us direct local access to the data from a data provider. Table 20.5 lists the significant properties of the `DataSet` class, and Table 20.6 lists the significant methods of the `DataSet` class.

TABLE 20.5 Significant Public Properties of the `DataSet` Class

Property	*Description*
`DataSetName`	Returns or sets the name of the dataset.
`EnforceConstraints`	Returns or sets whether constraint rules are enforced.
`HasErrors`	Indicates whether there are errors in any row in the table.
`Relations`	Gets relation objects that link tables.
`Tables`	Returns tables in the dataset.

TABLE 20.6 Significant Public Methods of the `DataSet` Class

Method	*Description*
`AcceptChanges`	Accepts (commits) the changes made to the dataset.
`Clear`	Clears the dataset by removing all rows in all tables.
`Copy`	Copies the dataset.
`GetChanges`	Returns a dataset that contains all changes made to the current dataset.
`GetXml`	Returns the data in the dataset in XML.
`GetXmlSchema`	Returns the XSD schema for the dataset.
`HasChanges`	Indicates whether the dataset has changes that have not yet been accepted.
`Merge`	Merges this dataset with another dataset.
`ReadXml`	Reads data into a dataset from XML.
`ReadXmlSchema`	Reads an XML schema into a dataset.
`RejectChanges`	Rolls back the changes made to the dataset since it was created or since the `AcceptChanges` method was last called.
`Reset`	Resets the dataset to the original state.
`WriteXml`	Writes the dataset's schema and data to XML.
`WriteXmlSchema`	Writes the dataset schema to XML.

Now double-click the Store XML Data button to open the handler function that holds the code that will be executed when the button is clicked:

```
Private Sub Button1_Click(ByVal sender As System.Object,
        .
        .
        .
End Sub
```

Begin this code by using the data adapter object to fill the dataset object with data from the `employee` table:

```
Private Sub Button1_Click(ByVal sender As System.Object,
    ByVal e As System.EventArgs) Handles Button1.Click
    DataSet11.Clear()
    OleDbDataAdapter1.Fill(DataSet11)
        .
        .
        .
End Sub
```

Next store the `employee` table from the dataset as an XML document, `data.xml`, by using the dataset's `WriteXml` method:

```
Private Sub Button1_Click(ByVal sender As System.Object,
    ByVal e As System.EventArgs) Handles Button1.Click
    DataSet11.Clear()
    OleDbDataAdapter1.Fill(DataSet11)
    DataSet11.WriteXml("data.xml")
        .
        .
        .
End Sub
```

In fact, ADO.NET uses XML and XML schemas to transfer data in .NET, so write the current schema out to a file, `dataSchema.xml`, as well, by using the `WriteXmlSchema` method:

```
Private Sub Button1_Click(ByVal sender As System.Object,
    ByVal e As System.EventArgs) Handles Button1.Click
    DataSet11.Clear()
    OleDbDataAdapter1.Fill(DataSet11)
    DataSet11.WriteXml("data.xml")
    DataSet11.WriteXmlSchema("dataSchema.xml")
End Sub
```


Now you'll read this XML back in and use it to create a new dataset object. First, create that dataset object by adding this code to the handler method that is called when the Read XML Data button is clicked:

```
Private Sub Button2_Click(ByVal sender As System.Object,
    ByVal e As System.EventArgs) Handles Button2. Click
    Dim ds As New DataSet()
        .
        .
        .
End Sub
```

Now use this dataset object's `ReadXML` method to read the XML document that holds the entire `employee` table:

```
Private Sub Button2_Click(ByVal sender As System.Object,
    ByVal e As System.EventArgs) Handles Button2.Click
    Dim ds As New DataSet()
    ds.ReadXml("data.xml")
        .
        .
        .
End Sub
```

Because you've read the XML holding the `employee` table back in, bind it to your `DataGrid` control:

```
Private Sub Button2_Click(ByVal sender As System.Object,
    ByVal e As System.EventArgs) Handles Button2.Click
    Dim ds As New DataSet()
    ds.ReadXml("data.xml")
    DataGrid1.SetDataBinding(ds, "employee")
End Sub
```

The `DataGrid` class lets us display entire database tables in .NET applications, and it's designed to be used in data-aware applications. Table 20.7 lists the significant properties of the `DataGrid` class, and Table 20.8 lists the significant methods of this class.

TABLE 20.7 Significant Public Properties of the `DataGrid` Class

Property	*Description*
`AllowNavigation`	Returns or sets whether navigation is allowed in the data grid.
`AllowSorting`	Returns or sets whether the grid can be sorted when the user clicks a column header.
`AlternatingBackColor`	Returns or sets the background color used in alternating rows.
`BackColor`	Returns or sets the background color of the data grid.
`BackgroundColor`	Returns or sets the color of the nondata sections of the data grid.
`BorderStyle`	Returns or sets the data grid's border style.
`CaptionBackColor`	Returns or sets the caption's background color.
`CaptionFont`	Returns or sets the caption's font.
`CaptionForeColor`	Returns or sets the caption's foreground color.

TABLE 20.7 continued

Property	*Description*
`CaptionText`	Returns or sets the caption's text.
`CaptionVisible`	Returns or sets whether the caption is visible.
`ColumnHeadersVisible`	Returns or sets whether the parent rows of a table are visible.
`CurrentCell`	Returns or sets which cell has the focus.
`CurrentRowIndex`	Returns or sets the index of the selected row.
`DataMember`	Returns or sets the table or list of data the data grid should display.
`DataSource`	Returns or sets the data grid's data source, such as a dataset.
`FirstVisibleColumn`	Returns the index of the first column visible in the grid.
`FlatMode`	Returns or sets whether the data grid should be shown flat.
`ForeColor`	Returns or sets the foreground color used in the data grid.
`GridLineColor`	Returns or sets the color of grid lines.
`GridLineStyle`	Returns or sets the grid line style.
`HeaderBackColor`	Returns or sets the background color of headers.
`HeaderFont`	Returns or sets the font used for headers.
`HeaderForeColor`	Returns or sets the foreground color of headers.
`Item`	Returns or sets the value in a particular cell.
`LinkColor`	Returns or sets the color of links to child tables.
`LinkHoverColor`	Returns or sets the color of links to child tables when the mouse moves over it.
`ParentRowsBackColor`	Returns or sets the background color of parent rows.
`ParentRowsForeColor`	Returns or sets the foreground color of parent rows.
`ParentRowsLabelStyle`	Returns or sets the style for parent row labels.
`ParentRowsVisible`	Returns or sets whether parent rows are visible.
`PreferredColumnWidth`	Returns or sets the width of the grid columns (in pixels).
`PreferredRowHeight`	Returns or sets the preferred row height.
`ReadOnly`	Returns or sets whether the grid is read-only.
`RowHeadersVisible`	Returns or sets whether row headers are visible.
`RowHeaderWidth`	Returns or sets the width of row headers.
`SelectionBackColor`	Returns or sets the selected cell's background color.
`SelectionForeColor`	Returns or sets the selected cell's foreground color.
`TableStyles`	Returns the table styles in the data grid.
`VisibleColumnCount`	Returns the number of visible columns.
`VisibleRowCount`	Returns the number of visible rows.

TABLE 20.8 Significant Public Methods of the `DataGrid` Class

Method	*Description*
`BeginEdit`	Makes the data grid allow editing.
`Collapse`	Collapses child table relations.
`EndEdit`	Ends editing operations.
`Expand`	Displays child relations.
`HitTest`	Coordinates the mouse position with points in the data grid.
`IsExpanded`	Returns whether a row is expanded or collapsed.
`IsSelected`	Returns whether a row is selected.
`NavigateBack`	Navigates to the previous table that was shown in the grid.
`NavigateTo`	Navigates to a specific table.
`Select`	Makes a selection.
`SetDataBinding`	Sets both the `DataSource` and `DataMember` properties. This method is used at runtime.
`UnSelect`	Deselects a row.

Now run this application by selecting Debug, Start. Then, when you click the Store XML Data button, the `employee` table is stored in an XML document on disk; when you click the Read XML Data button, that XML document is read back into a new dataset object, which is bound to the `DataGrid` control in this application. Figure 20.8 shows the results, with the `employees` table, fresh from your XML document, appearing in the data grid.

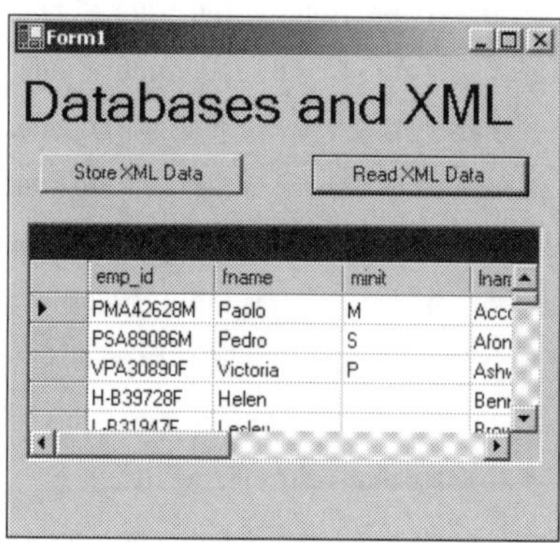

FIGURE 20.8
Writing a database table to XML and reading it back in.

Here's what the `employee` table looks like as stored in XML in your XML document (note that each employee's data is stored in an element named `<employee>`):

```
<?xml version="1.0" standalone="yes"?>
<DataSet1 xmlns="http://www.tempuri.org/DataSet1.xsd">
  <employee>
    <emp_id>PMA42628M</emp_id>
    <fname>Paolo</fname>
    <minit>M</minit>
    <lname>Accorti</lname>
    <job_id>13</job_id>
    <job_lvl>35</job_lvl>
    <pub_id>0877</pub_id>
    <hire_date>1992-08-27T00:00:00.0000000-04:00</hire_date>
  </employee>
  <employee>
    <emp_id>PSA89086M</emp_id>
    <fname>Pedro</fname>
    <minit>S</minit>
    <lname>Afonso</lname>
    <job_id>14</job_id>
    <job_lvl>89</job_lvl>
    <pub_id>1389</pub_id>
    <hire_date>1990-12-24T00:00:00.0000000-05:00</hire_date>
  </employee>
  <employee>
    <emp_id>VPA30890F</emp_id>
    <fname>Victoria</fname>
    <minit>P</minit>
    <lname>Ashworth</lname>
    <job_id>6</job_id>
    <job_lvl>140</job_lvl>
    <pub_id>0877</pub_id>
    <hire_date>1990-09-13T00:00:00.0000000-04:00</hire_date>
  </employee>
  <employee>
    <emp_id>H-B39728F</emp_id>
    <fname>Helen</fname>
    <minit> </minit>
    <lname>Bennett</lname>
    <job_id>12</job_id>
    <job_lvl>35</job_lvl>
    <pub_id>0877</pub_id>
    <hire_date>1989-09-21T00:00:00.0000000-04:00</hire_date>
  </employee>
          .
          .
          .
```

20

Here's what the XML schema for this table looks like:

```
<?xml version="1.0" standalone="yes"?>
<xs:schema id="DataSet1" targetNamespace="http://www.tempuri.org/DataSet1.xsd"
xmlns="http://www.tempuri.org/DataSet1.xsd"
```

```
xmlns:xs="http://www.w3.org/2001/XMLSchema"
xmlns:msdata="urn:schemas-microsoft-com:xml-msdata"
attributeFormDefault="qualified" elementFormDefault="qualified">
  <xs:element name="DataSet1" msdata:IsDataSet="true">
    <xs:complexType>
      <xs:choice maxOccurs="unbounded">
        <xs:element name="authors">
          <xs:complexType>
            <xs:sequence>
              <xs:element name="au_id" type="xs:string" />
              <xs:element name="au_lname" type="xs:string" />
              <xs:element name="au_fname" type="xs:string" />
              <xs:element name="phone" type="xs:string" />
              <xs:element name="address" type="xs:string" minOccurs="0" />
              <xs:element name="city" type="xs:string" minOccurs="0" />
              <xs:element name="state" type="xs:string" minOccurs="0" />
              <xs:element name="zip" type="xs:string" minOccurs="0" />
              <xs:element name="contract" type="xs:boolean" />
            </xs:sequence>
          </xs:complexType>
        </xs:element>
        <xs:element name="employee">
          <xs:complexType>
            <xs:sequence>
              <xs:element name="emp_id" type="xs:string" minOccurs="0" />
              <xs:element name="fname" type="xs:string" minOccurs="0" />
              <xs:element name="minit" type="xs:string" minOccurs="0" />
              <xs:element name="lname" type="xs:string" minOccurs="0" />
              <xs:element name="job_id" type="xs:short" minOccurs="0" />
              <xs:element name="job_lvl" type="xs:unsignedByte"
                  minOccurs="0" />
              <xs:element name="pub_id" type="xs:string" minOccurs="0" />
              <xs:element name="hire_date" type="xs:dateTime" minOccurs="0" />
            </xs:sequence>
          </xs:complexType>
        </xs:element>
      </xs:choice>
    </xs:complexType>
    <xs:unique name="Constraint1" msdata:PrimaryKey="true">
      <xs:selector xpath=".//mstns:authors" />
      <xs:field xpath="mstns:au_id" />
    </xs:unique>
  </xs:element>
</xs:schema>
```

This XML document and XML schema show the actual way that data is transmitted from database to .NET application and back again by using ADO.NET. Listing 20.2 shows the code we've written for this example.

LISTING 20.2 Button-Handling Code in the `ch20_03` Project (from `Form1.vb` in the `ch20_03` Project)

```
Public Class Form1
    Inherits System.Windows.Forms.Form
        .
        .
        .
    Private Sub Button1_Click(ByVal sender As System.Object, _
        ByVal e As System.EventArgs) Handles Button1.Click
        DataSet11.Clear()
        OleDbDataAdapter1.Fill(DataSet11)
        DataSet11.WriteXml("data.xml")
        DataSet11.WriteXmlSchema("dataSchema.xml")
    End Sub

    Private Sub Button2_Click(ByVal sender As System.Object, _
        ByVal e As System.EventArgs) Handles Button2.Click
        Dim ds As New DataSet
        ds.ReadXml("data.xml")
        DataGrid1.SetDataBinding(ds, "employee")
    End Sub
End Class
```

Using XPath with a Database

In addition to storing data by using XML, we can also treat databases as XML in .NET in other ways. For example, we can address the data in a dataset by using XPath expressions, and we'll take a look at how this works here in a new Visual Basic .NET project, `ch20_04`.

Start by creating a new Windows project named `ch20_04`. In this example, you'll use the XPath expression `*` to get a node list of all the child elements of the `<employee>` element. This expression will return all the fields of the various employees in the `employee` table you worked with in the previous example. To create this example, start by adding to the main form in your project a button with the caption Get Names and two text boxes to display the names, as shown in Figure 20.9. You need to make the text boxes multiline text boxes by setting their `Multiline` property to `true` in the properties window at the lower right in the Visual Basic .NET development environment; you need to stretch these boxes as shown in Figure 20.9.

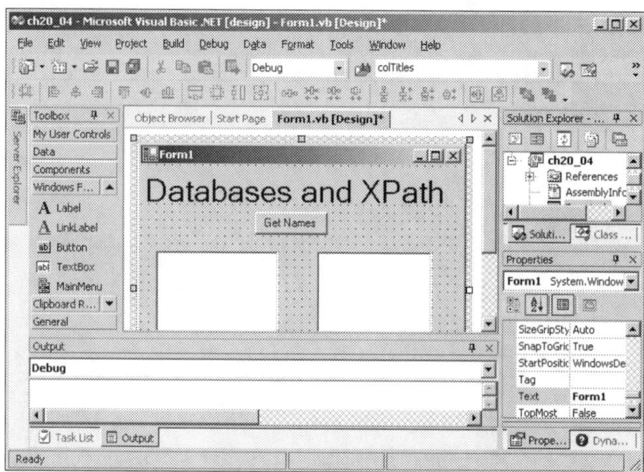

FIGURE 20.9

Creating the `ch20_04` *project.*

In addition, create a dataset object, `DataSet11`, that is connected to the `employee` table in the `pubs` database, as you did in the previous example. That is, drag an `OleDbDataAdapter` object to the main form in the project, use the Data Adapter Configuration Wizard to connect this data adapter to the `employee` table, select Data, Generate Dataset to open the Generate Dataset dialog box, and click OK to create `DataSet11`.

Now double-click the Get Names button to open the handler method in code that will be called when the button is clicked:

```
Private Sub Button1_Click(ByVal sender As System.Object,
    ByVal e As System.EventArgs) Handles Button1.Click
        .
        .
        .
End Sub
```

When the Get Names button is clicked, you'll read the data in the dataset—the `employee` table—into an `XmlDataDocument` object, which will allow you to address that data by using XPath:

```
Private Sub Button1_Click(ByVal sender As System.Object,
    ByVal e As System.EventArgs) Handles Button1.Click
    DataSet11.Clear()
    OleDbDataAdapter1.Fill(DataSet11)

    Dim xmlDoc As New System.Xml.XmlDataDocument(DataSet11)
        .
        .
        .
End Sub
```

Now you have a new `XmlDataDocument` object, `xmlDoc`, that holds the `employee` table, set up explicitly as XML. Table 20.9 lists the significant properties of `XmlDataDocument` objects, and Table 20.10 lists the significant methods of `XmlDataDocument` objects.

TABLE 20.9 Significant Public Properties of `XmlDataDocument` Objects

Property	*Description*
`Attributes`	Returns the attributes of this node.
`BaseURI`	Returns the base URI of the current node.
`ChildNodes`	Returns all the child nodes of the node.
`DataSet`	Returns a dataset that contains the data in the `XmlDataDocument` object.
`DocumentElement`	Returns the root `XmlElement` object for the document.
`DocumentType`	Returns the node that contains the `DOCTYPE` declaration.
`FirstChild`	Returns the first child of the node.
`HasChildNodes`	Returns `true` if this node has any child nodes.
`InnerText`	Returns or sets the concatenated values of the node and all its child nodes.
`InnerXml`	Returns or sets the markup representing the children of the current node.
`IsReadOnly`	Returns `true` if the current node is read-only.
`Item`	Returns the given child element.
`LastChild`	Returns the last child of the node.
`LocalName`	Returns the local name of the node.
`Name`	Returns the qualified name of the node.
`NamespaceURI`	Returns the namespace URI of this node.
`NextSibling`	Returns the node immediately following this node.
`NodeType`	Returns the type of the current node.
`OuterXml`	Returns the markup representing this node and all its child nodes.
`OwnerDocument`	Returns the `XmlDocument` object to which the current node belongs.
`ParentNode`	Returns the parent of this node (for nodes that can have parents) .
`Prefix`	Returns or sets the namespace prefix of this node.
`PreserveWhitespace`	Returns or sets a value indicating whether to preserve whitespace.
`PreviousSibling`	Returns the node immediately preceding this node.
`Value`	Returns or sets the value of the node.

TABLE 20.10 Significant Public Methods of `XmlDataDocument` Objects

Method	*Description*
`AppendChild`	Adds the given node to the end of the list of child nodes of the current node.
`CreateAttribute`	Creates an `XmlAttribute` object with the given name.
`CreateCDataSection`	Creates an `XmlCDataSection` object that contains the given data.
`CreateComment`	Creates an `XmlComment` object that contains the given data.
`CreateDocumentFragment`	Creates an `XmlDocumentFragment` object.
`CreateDocumentType`	Returns a new `XmlDocumentType` object.
`CreateElement`	Creates an `XmlElement` object.
`CreateNode`	Creates an `XmlNode` object.
`CreateProcessingInstruction`	Creates an `XmlProcessingInstruction` object with the given name and data.
`CreateSignificantWhitespace`	Creates an `XmlSignificantWhitespace` node.
`CreateTextNode`	Creates an `XmlText` object with the given text.
`CreateWhitespace`	Creates an `XmlWhitespace` node.
`CreateXmlDeclaration`	Creates an `XmlDeclaration` node with the given values.
`Equals`	Determines whether two object instances are equal.
`GetElementById`	Returns the `XmlElement` object that has the given ID.
`GetElementFromRow`	Retrieves the `XmlElement` object associated with the given `DataRow` object.
`GetElementsByTagName`	Returns an `XmlNodeList` object that contains a list of all descendant elements that match the given name.
`GetRowFromElement`	Retrieves the `DataRow` object associated with the given `XmlElement` object.
`GetType`	Returns the type of the current instance.
`ImportNode`	Imports a node from another document to the current document.
`InsertAfter`	Inserts the given node immediately after the given reference node.
`InsertBefore`	Inserts the given node immediately before the given reference node.
`Load`	Loads the `XmlDataDocument` object by using the given data source.
`LoadXml`	Loads the XML document from the given string.
`PrependChild`	Adds the given node to the beginning of the list of child nodes for this node.

TABLE 20.10 Significant Public Methods of `XmlDataDocument` Objects

Method	*Description*
`RemoveAll`	Removes all the child nodes and/or attributes of the current node.
`RemoveChild`	Removes the given child node.
`ReplaceChild`	Replaces the child node `oldChild` with the `newChild` node.
`Save`	Saves the XML document to the given location.
`SelectNodes`	Selects a list of nodes that match the XPath expression.
`SelectSingleNode`	Selects the first `XmlNode` object that matches the XPath expression.
`WriteTo`	Saves the `XmlDocument` object.

A `XmlDataDocument` object has a `DocumentElement` property that returns the document object of its XML documents as an `XmlElement` object. This `XmlElement` object supports a method called `SelectNodes` that lets us select XML nodes by using XPath expressions. To select all the employee elements in the `employee` table, all you have to do is pass the `SelectNodes` method the XPath expression `*`, and you get back a `NodeList` object back that holds the matching nodes:

```
Private Sub Button1_Click(ByVal sender As System.Object,
    ByVal e As System.EventArgs) Handles Button1.Click
    DataSet11.Clear()
    OleDbDataAdapter1.Fill(DataSet11)

    Dim xmlDoc As New System.Xml.XmlDataDocument(DataSet11)

    Dim nodeList As System.Xml.XmlNodeList =
        xmlDoc.DocumentElement.SelectNodes("*")
        .
        .
        .
End Sub
```

20

Now you have a node list of the `<employee>` elements, extracted from your `XmlDataDocument` using `XPath`. How can you access the data in the corresponding `employee` records in the dataset? You can do that with the `XmlDataDocument` object's `GetRowFromElement` method—all you have to do is to pass an XML element to this method, and it'll return the dataset row containing the employee's record. When you have the employee's data record, you can extract the employee's first and last names (Fields 1 and 3 in each record) this way:

```
Private Sub Button1_Click(ByVal sender As System.Object,
    ByVal e As System.EventArgs) Handles Button1.Click
    DataSet11.Clear()
```

```
    OleDbDataAdapter1.Fill(DataSet11)

    Dim xmlDoc As New System.Xml.XmlDataDocument(DataSet11)

    Dim nodeList As System.Xml.XmlNodeList =
        xmlDoc.DocumentElement.SelectNodes("*")
    Dim tempRow As DataRow
    Dim tempNode As System.Xml.XmlNode

    For Each tempNode In nodeList
        tempRow = xmlDoc.GetRowFromElement(CType(tempNode,
            System.Xml.XmlElement) )

        If Not tempRow Is Nothing Then TextBox1.Text +=
            tempRow(1).ToString() + ControlChars.CrLf
        If Not tempRow Is Nothing Then TextBox2.Text +=
            tempRow(3).ToString() + ControlChars.CrLf
    Next

End Sub
```

When you run this example and click the Get Names button, you get all the employees records by using XPath, and then look up all the employees' first and last names and display them as shown in Figure 20.10.

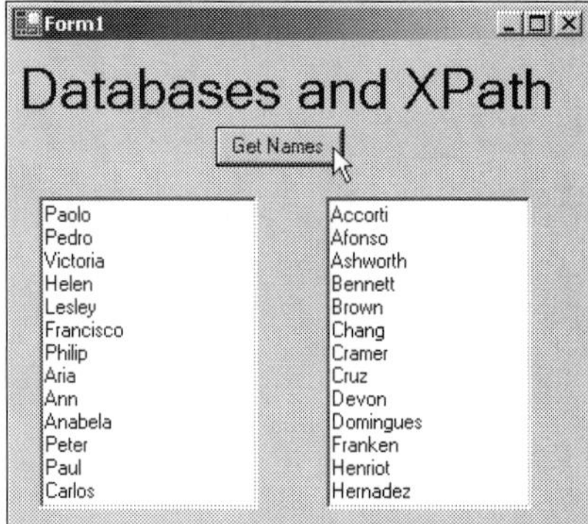

FIGURE 20.10

Running the `ch20_04` *project.*

Today you've used XPath to access records in a dataset, thanks to the `XmlDataDocument` object. Listing 20.3 shows the code that we've written for this example. Although in this example we used only the simple XPath expression `*` to access all the employees in the `employee` table, we can use full XPath expressions as well.

LISTING 20.3 Button-Handling Code in the `ch20_04` Project (from `Form1.vb` in the `ch20_04` Project)

```
Public Class Form1
    Inherits System.Windows.Forms.Form
        .
        .
        .
    Private Sub Button1_Click(ByVal sender As System.Object, _
        ByVal e As System.EventArgs) Handles Button1.Click
        DataSet11.Clear()
        OleDbDataAdapter1.Fill(DataSet11)

        Dim xmlDoc As New System.Xml.XmlDataDocument(DataSet11)

        Dim nodeList As System.Xml.XmlNodeList = _
            xmlDoc.DocumentElement.SelectNodes("*")
        Dim tempRow As DataRow
        Dim tempNode As System.Xml.XmlNode

        For Each tempNode In nodeList
            tempRow = xmlDoc.GetRowFromElement(CType(tempNode, _
            System.Xml.XmlElement))

            If Not tempRow Is Nothing Then TextBox1.Text += _
                tempRow(1).ToString() + ControlChars.CrLf
            If Not tempRow Is Nothing Then TextBox2.Text += _
                tempRow(3).ToString() + ControlChars.CrLf
        Next
    End Sub
End Class
```

Using XPath is one way to address data in databases. However, XPath isn't powerful enough to handle databases, which is why the W3C is introducing XQuery—which is described in the next section.

20

Introducing XQuery

Because XPath isn't really strong enough to let us handle databases, the W3C is creating XQuery. (In fact, the data model at the core of XQuery is going to be the basis of the next version of XPath, version 2.0.) Here's what the W3C says about XQuery:

> XML is a versatile markup language, capable of labeling the information content of diverse data sources including structured and semi-structured documents, relational databases, and object repositories. A query language that uses the structure of XML intelligently can express queries across all these kinds of data, whether physically

> stored in XML or viewed as XML via middleware. This specification describes a query language called XQuery, which is designed to be broadly applicable across many types of XML data sources.

The idea is for XQuery to be a query language something like SQL (which is used in database applications) that we can use with XML documents. XQuery is designed to let us access data much as if we were working with a database, even though we're working with XML. The creation of such a query language was inevitable—after all, XML's whole reason for existence is to provide a way to work with data. XQuery gives us not only a data model to let us interpret XML documents, but also a set of operators and functions to let us extract data from those documents.

Unfortunately, the W3C XQuery specification is very much up in the air at this time. It's been around a long time, but progress has been slow. This specification is divided into several working drafts; the main XQuery 1.0 working draft is at `http://www.w3.org/TR/xquery`, but there are also working drafts for XQuery semantics, the data model, and serialization. Here's a short list of what's available online as of this writing:

- The XQuery Activity Page (`http://www.w3.org/XML/Query`), which provides an overview of XQuery
- The XQuery version 1.0 Working Draft (`http://www.w3.org/TR/xquery`)
- The XQuery 1.0 and XPath 2.0 Data Model (`http://www.w3.org/TR/xpath-datamodel`)
- The XQuery 1.0 and XPath 2.0 Formal Semantics (`http://www.w3.org/TR/xquery-semantics`)
- The XML Syntax for XQuery 1.0 (XQueryX; `http://www.w3.org/TR/xquery/xqueryx`)
- The XQuery 1.0 and XPath 2.0 Functions and Operators (`http://www.w3.org/TR/xquery/xpath-functions`)
- The XML Query Requirements (`http://www.w3.org/TR/xquery-requirements`), which provides an overview of what's going to go into XQuery, in working draft form

Despite its slow progress, XQuery is very popular, and there are a number of implementations of XQuery 1.0 out there. Here's a starter list:

- The XQuery 1.0 Grammar Test Page (`http://www.w3.org/2003/05/applets/xqueryApplet.html`)

- The XPath 2.0 Grammar Test Page (`http://www.w3.org/2003/05/applets/xpathApplet.html`)
- BEA's Liquid Data (`http://edocs.bea.com/liquiddata/docs10/prodover/concepts.html`)
- Bluestream Database Software Corp.'s XStreamDB (`http://www.bluestream.com/dr/?page=Home/Products/XStreamDB`)
- Cerisent's XQE (`http://cerisent.com/cerisent-xqe.html`)
- Cognetic Systems's XQuantum (`http://www.cogneticsystems.com/xquery/xquery.html`)
- Enosys Software's XQuery Demo (`http://xquerydemo.enosyssoftware.com`)
- eXcelon's eXtensible Information Server (XIS 3.1 SP2) (`http://www.exln.com/products/xis`)
- Stylus Studio 4.5, with XQuery and XML Schema support (`http://www.exln.com/products/stylusstudio`)
- E-XMLMedia's XMLizer (`http://www.e-xmlmedia.com/prod/xmlizer.htm`)
- Fatdog's XQEngine (`http://www.fatdog.com`)
- GAEL's Derby (`http://www.gael.fr/derby`)
- GNU's Qexo (Kawa-Query; `http://www.qexo.org`), which compiles XQuery on-the-fly to Java bytecodes
- Ipedo's XML Database v3.0 (`http://www.ipedo.com`)
- IPSI's IPSI-XQ (`http://ipsi.fhg.de/oasys/projects/ipsi-xq/index_e.html`)
- Lucent's Galax (`http://db.bell-labs.com/galax/`), which is open source
- Microsoft's XML Query Language Demo (`http://xqueryservices.com`)
- Neocore's XML management system (XMS; `http://www.neocore.com/products/products.htm`)
- Nimble Technology's Nimble Integration Suite (`http://www.nimble.com`)
- OpenLink Software's Virtuoso Universal Server (`http://demo.openlinksw.com:8890/xqdemo`)
- Oracle's XML DB (`http://otn.oracle.com/tech/xml/xmldb/htdocs/querying_xml.html`)
- Politecnico di Milano's XQBE (`http://dbgroup.elet.polimi.it/xquery/xqbedownload.html`)
- QuiLogic's SQL/XML-IMDB (`http://www.quilogic.cc/xml.htm`)

- Software AG's Tamino XML Server (http://www.softwareag.com/tamino/News/tamino_41.htm)
- Tamino XML Query Demo (http://tamino.demozone.softwareag.com/demoXQuery/index.html)
- Sourceforge's Saxon (http://saxon.sourceforge.net/)
- SourceForge's XQuench (http://xquench.sourceforge.net/), which is open source
- SourceForge's XQuery Lite (http://sourceforge.net/projects/phpxmlclasses/)
- X-Hive's XQuery demo (http://www.x-hive.com/xquery)
- XML Global's GoXML DB (http://www.xmlglobal.com/prod/xmlworkbench)

Today, you're going to take a look at using XQuery with Lucent's Galax XQuery processor, one of the foremost XQuery implementations. You can download Galax for free at http://db.bell-labs.com/galax/, and you can see an online demo at http://db.bell-labs.com/galax/demo/galax_demo.html.

To use XQuery, we'll need an XML document, and we'll use the one shown in Listing 20.4, ch20_05.xml. This document contains data about some friends and a number of meetings arranged for their reunion, stored in <meeting> elements. We're going to use XQuery to extract information about the meetings and meeting locations.

LISTING 20.4 A Sample XML Document (ch20_05.xml)

```
<?xml version="1.0" encoding="UTF-8"?>
<friends>
    <title>List of Friends</title>
    <friend>Ed Banachek</friend>
    <friend>Mark Up</friend>
    <friend>Wendy Thurston</friend>
    <friend>Becki Franks</friend>
    <meeting ID="introduction" time="evening" >
        <title>Introduction</title>
        <p>Getting to know everyone</p>
        <meeting>
            <title>Men</title>
            <p>Men's gathering</p>
        </meeting>
        <meeting>
            <title>Women</title>
            <p>Women's gathering</p>
            <location address="campus">
                <title>Student Center</title>
```

LISTING 20.4 continued

```
                <phone number="555-1111"/>
            </location>
            <p>Just for fun</p>
        </meeting>
    </meeting>
    <meeting ID="breakfast" time="morning" >
        <title>Breakfast</title>
        <p>Breakfast meeting</p>
        <location address="cafeteria">
            <title>Student Cafeteria</title>
                <phone number="555-1112"/>
        </location>
        <p>Just for fun</p>
        <meeting>
            <title>Men</title>
            <p>Men's gathering</p>
        </meeting>
        <meeting>
            <title>Women</title>
            <p>Women's gathering</p>
            <location address="campus">
                <title>Student Dorm</title>
                <phone number="555-1113"/>
            </location>
        </meeting>
        <meeting>
            <title>Good Bye</title>
            <p>So long!</p>
        </meeting>
    </meeting>
</friends>
```

To use Galax, you'll create two XQuery files. The first file will hold XQuery context code, where you'll declare the XML elements in `ch20_05.xml` and the XQuery functions you'll use. The other XQuery file will hold the template you'll use to query your XML document.

Start the XQuery context file, `ch20_06.xq`, by defining all the XML elements in your sample XML document so Galax can check the validity of that document. You can define the elements and attributes in your sample XML document easily, using this DTD-like syntax:

```
define element friends
{
    element title,
    element friend+,
```

```
    element meeting+
}

define element title {xsd:string}
define element friend {xsd:string}

define element meeting
{
    attribute ID {xsd:string}?,
    attribute time {xsd:string}?,
    element title,
      (element p | element location | element meeting) *
}

define element p {xsd:string}

define element location
{
    attribute address { xsd:string },
    element title,
    element phone
}

define element phone
{
    attribute number {xsd:string}
}

define element meetingSummary
{
    attribute ID {xsd:string}?,
    attribute time {xsd:string}?,
    element title,
    element locationCount {xsd:int},
    element meetingSummary*
}
```

This file sets the context for your XQuery work, so you'll connect your XML document `ch20_05.xml` to an XQuery *variable*, `$friendlist`, making the data in that document available to your XQuery code. XQuery variables are used to store data, and the name of an XQuery variable begins with a $ sign. In this case, you'll define a global variable (accessible in your XQuery template file) named `$friendsList` to hold the data from your XML document:

```
define global $friendsList {treat as document friends
(glx:document-validate("ch20_05.xml", "friends"))}
```

We can also define *functions* in XQuery. We pass data to a function, and the code in the function can work on that data with XQuery statements and operators, and it returns the processed results. In this case you'll define a function named summary, which will return a summary of an element and display selected data from that element. You'll pass an element to this function, and start by getting the name of the element by using the built-in local-name function:

```
define function summary($elem as element) as element*
{
    let $name := local-name($elem)
        .
        .
        .
}
```

If you're dealing with a <meeting> element, you'll report this element in the results returned from this function, including its attributes, which you can refer to as $elem/@*. In the XML example, meetings themselves can have submeetings, so you'll loop over all the child elements of the current element and call summary recursively for them (items in curly braces, { and }, are evaluated by the XQuery engine and embedded in the output):

```
define function summary($elem as element) as element*
{
    let $name := local-name($elem)
    return
        if ($name = "meeting")
        then
            <meeting>
                {$elem/@*}
                {for $item in $elem/* return summary($item)}
             </meeting>
        .
        .
        .
}
```

This displays all the <meeting> elements and their <meeting> children. You'll also handle <title> elements in this function by returning the <title> element itself so that the title of any <meeting> elements will appear in the output:

20

```
define function summary($elem as element) as element*
{
    let $name := local-name($elem)
    return
        if ($name = "meeting")
        then
            <meeting>
                {$elem/@*}
                {for $item in $elem/* return summary($item)}
             </meeting>
```

```
            else if ($name = "title")
            then $elem
            else ()
}
```

That's it for your XQuery context file, `ch20_06.xq`, which defines the syntax for your XML document, stores the data in that XML document as a global variable named `$friendsList`, and defines the `summary` function. Listing 20.5 shows the file `ch20_06.xq`.

LISTING 20.5 The XQuery Context Document (`ch20_06.xq`)

```
define element friends
{
    element title,
    element friend+,
    element meeting+
}

define element title {xsd:string}
define element friend {xsd:string}

define element meeting
{
    attribute ID {xsd:string}?,
    attribute time {xsd:string}?,
    element title,
      (element p | element location | element meeting)*
}

define element p {xsd:string}

define element location
{
    attribute address { xsd:string },
    element title,
    element phone
}

define element phone
{
    attribute number {xsd:string}
}

define element meetingSummary
{
    attribute ID {xsd:string}?,
    attribute time {xsd:string}?,
    element title,
```

LISTING 20.5 continued

```
        element locationCount {xsd:int},
        element meetingSummary*
}

define global $friendsList {treat as document friends
(glx:document-validate("ch20_05.xml", "friends"))}

define function summary($elem as element) as element*
{
    let $name := local-name($elem)
    return
        if ($name = "meeting")
        then
            <meeting>
                {$elem/@*}
                {for $item in $elem/* return summary($item)}
             </meeting>
         else if ($name = "title")
         then $elem
         else ()
}
```

Now you'll create an XQuery template file, `ch20_07.xq`, which will extract data from your XML document (stored in the `$friendsList` variable) and present those results as XML. For example, to get a summary of the `<meeting>` elements in your XML document, you'll create an element named `<meetings>` and display a summary of the `<meeting>` child elements of the `<friends>` document element in it. Note in particular the XPath-like syntax to specify the `<meeting>` child elements of the `<friends>` document element—`$friendsList/friends/meeting`:

```
<meetings>
    {
        for $meeting in $friendsList/friends/meeting return summary($meeting)
    }
</meetings>
;
```

This code will strip out and display a summary of each `<meeting>` element—including all child `<meeting>` elements—while also preserving the `<title>` elements. Here's what the results look like:

```
<meetings>
  <meeting time="evening"
    ID="introduction">
    <title>Introduction</title>
    <meeting><title>Men</title></meeting>
```

20

```
    <meeting><title>Women</title></meeting>
  </meeting>
  <meeting time="morning"
    ID="breakfast">
    <title>Breakfast</title>
    <meeting><title>Men</title></meeting>
    <meeting><title>Women</title></meeting>
    <meeting><title>Good Bye</title></meeting>
  </meeting>
</meetings>
```

You'll also display the locations of the various meetings by picking out the `<location>` elements in the XML document, preserving their attributes and titles, and displaying the results in a `<locations>` element, like this:

```
<locations>
    {
        for $location in $friendsList//location
        return
            <location>
                {$location/@*}
                {$location/title}
            </location>
    }
</locations>
;
```

This code gives you the following results in the output, where you're displaying the `<location>` elements and their attributes, as well as any contained `<title>` elements:

```
<locations>
  <location address="campus"><title>Student Center</title></location>
  <location address="cafeteria"><title>Student Cafeteria</title></location>
  <location address="campus"><title>Student Dorm</title></location>
</locations>
```

Use the XQuery `count` function to count the number of `<meeting>` elements. To count all `<meeting>` elements, no matter where they are in the input XML document, use the expression `$friendsList//meeting` (using the XPath-like `//` syntax to indicate any descendent), like this:

```
<meetingCount>{count($friendsList//meeting)}</meetingCount>
;
```

This gives you these results:

```
<meetingCount>7</meetingCount>
```

You can count the total number of <location> elements this way:

```
<locationCount>{count($friendsList//location)}</locationCount>
;
```

Here are the results:

```
<locationCount>3</locationCount>
```

You can also count the number of top-level meetings (remember that the <meeting> elements that themselves contain submeetings), like this:

```
<mainMeetingCount>
    {
        count($friendsList/friends/meeting)
    }
</mainMeetingCount>
;
```

And this is what you'll see in the output:

```
<mainMeetingCount>2</mainMeetingCount>
```

Listing 20.6 shows the complete XQuery template file, ch20_07.xq.

LISTING 20.6 An XQuery Document (ch20_07.xq)

```
<meetings>
    {
        for $meeting in $friendsList/friends/meeting return summary($meeting)
    }
</meetings>
;

<locations>
    {
        for $location in $friendsList//location
        return
            <location>
                {$location/@*}
                {$location/title}
            </location>
    }
</locations>
;

<meetingCount>{count($friendsList//meeting)}</meetingCount>
;

<locationCount>{count($friendsList//location)}</locationCount>
;
```

LISTING 20.6 continued

```
<mainMeetingCount>
    {
        count($friendsList/friends/meeting)
    }
</mainMeetingCount>
;
```

Now you'll pull it all together by using Galax on your context and template XQuery files. Here's how you do this:

```
%galax -context ch20_06.xq ch20_07.xq
```

And here are the results you get, showing how you've been able to extract and handle the data in `ch20_05.xml` and then format the results as XML:

```
%galax -context ch20_06.xq ch20_07.xq
<meetings>
  <meeting time="evening"
    ID="introduction">
    <title>Introduction</title>
    <meeting><title>Men</title></meeting>
    <meeting><title>Women</title></meeting>
  </meeting>
  <meeting time="morning"
    ID="breakfast">
    <title>Breakfast</title>
    <meeting><title>Men</title></meeting>
    <meeting><title>Women</title></meeting>
    <meeting><title>Good Bye</title></meeting>
  </meeting>
</meetings>
<locations>
  <location address="campus"><title>Student Center</title></location>
  <location address="cafeteria"><title>Student Cafeteria</title></location>
  <location address="campus"><title>Student Dorm</title></location>
</locations>
<meetingList>
  <meeting title="Introduction" outsideLocations="0"/>
  <meeting title="Men" outsideLocations="0"/>
  <meeting title="Women" outsideLocations="1"/>
  <meeting title="Breakfast" outsideLocations="1"/>
  <meeting title="Men" outsideLocations="0"/>
  <meeting title="Women" outsideLocations="1"/>
  <meeting title="Good Bye" outsideLocations="0"/>
</meetingList>
<meetingCount>7</meetingCount>
<locationCount>3</locationCount>
<mainMeetingCount>2</mainMeetingCount>
```

You can also write these results to an XML document like this, which creates the document `results.xml`:

```
%galax -context ch20_06.xq ch20_07.xq -output-xml results. xml
```

NOTE

> Unfortunately, it's impossible to get Galax to put an XML declaration at the beginning of its output documents, so although we can create XML element output, as described in this section, the results can't be considered a completely well-formed XML document.

In this section you've used Galax and XQuery to execute queries and extract data from your XML document. Not bad! Bear in mind, however, that XQuery is only at the working draft stage, and the kind of support you see here, and XQuery itself, will probably be changing rapidly.

Summary

Today you took a look at working with XML and databases. This is a widespread field, so you were only able to look at a few examples today. You started with the brute-force method, using software as an intermediary between the user and the data provider. In this case, you used ASP to work with an Access database, extract data from that database, and send it as XML to the user.

Microsoft has integrated a large amount of support for XML in its .NET programming platform, and you took a look at some of that support today. Because the ADO.NET protocol uses XML to transfer data between applications and data sources, you used the `WriteXml` method to write out the XML version of the `employee` table in the SQL Server sample `pubs` database. You also used the `WriteXmlSchema` method to write out the XML schema used for this table. And you used the `ReadXml` method to read the XML for the table back in, creating a dataset from that XML.

Today you also took a look at working with .NET `XmlDataDocument` objects. These objects let you address the data in a database by using XPath expressions. Although the process worked, it was a little awkward because you had to refer to the original database table to extract the data you were looking for. You were able to use XPath expressions to track down your data, but the XPath support felt more like an afterthought, not an integrated technique.

The third technique you looked at today—using XQuery—is really native XML. Although it's still just in the W3C Working Draft stage, there's a lot of excitement about

XQuery, and you got a good introduction to it today. By using the Galax XQuery processor, you were able to create XQuery variables, functions, and templates, and used them to successfully query the data in an XML document and extract what you wanted.

XQuery is designed to be to XML much like SQL is to databases—a query language that you can use to extract the data you want and work with it.

Q&A

Q Can I sort items in XQuery?

A Yes. Currently, you use the `order by` statement to do this. For example, to order items in the `$name` variable by `<lastName>` elements, you could use this code:

```
order by $name/lastName
```

To order by first and last name, you could use

```
order by $name/lastName, $name/firstName
```

Q Can I use XPath-like predicates in XQuery?

A Yes. Here's an example that also uses the `exists` function to test whether you actually matched any elements:

```
let $result := $friends//friend[state = $state and city = $city]
if (exists($result)) then...
```

Workshop

This workshop tests whether you understand the concepts discussed today. It's a good idea to make sure you can answer these questions before pressing on to tomorrow's work. Answers to the quiz can be found in Appendix A, "Quiz Answers."

Quiz

1. What method do you use with an `OleDbDataAdapter` method to retrieve data from the data store and place it into a dataset object?
2. What methods do you use to write and read XML data from a .NET dataset object?
3. How would you create an XQuery variable named `$name` that holds the name of an element stored in `$elem`?
4. How can you include an element's attributes in XQuery output for an element stored in a variable named `$elem`?
5. How would you load an XML document named `data.xml` with a document element named `<document>` into an XQuery variable named `$data` by using the Galax XQuery engine?

Exercises

1. Use the Galax XQuery engine to alter the XQuery example to display the number of <p> elements in `ch20_05.xml`.
2. Give each child <meeting> element in the XQuery example a <refreshment> element that indicates what refreshment was served at the meeting, and add that data to the meeting's data in the `summary` function. Check your work by using Galax.

PART V

DAY 21

Handling XML in .NET

Today we're going to take a look at working with XML in Microsoft's .NET programming. Some people aren't fond of Microsoft applications, but Microsoft provides so much XML support that this book would be seriously remiss if it didn't discuss that support. If you have Visual Studio .NET, you can follow along with today's discussion by creating and implementing the examples we'll develop.

Here's an overview of today's topics:

- Editing XML documents and XML schemas in .NET
- Writing and reading XML documents from code
- Using the XML ASP.NET control to display formatted XML
- Creating XML Web services

Today we're going to look at various ways of working with XML with Visual Studio .NET programming. Some use XML explicitly, as when we create a new XML document with code. Others use XML implicitly, such as XML Web services, which send and receive data from code on the Internet by using XML behind-the-scenes. You're going to get a good introduction to using XML and .NET today, starting by creating and editing an XML document.

Creating and Editing an XML Document in .NET

The .NET Framework has a great deal of XML support built in, including support for creating XML documents, and that's where you're going to start today. You'll use the tools in Microsoft Visual Studio .NET to create an XML document by using an XML schema.

To create a new project, select Visual Basic Projects in the Project Types box and Windows Application in the Templates box and then give the new project the name `ch21_01`, as shown in Figure 21.1.

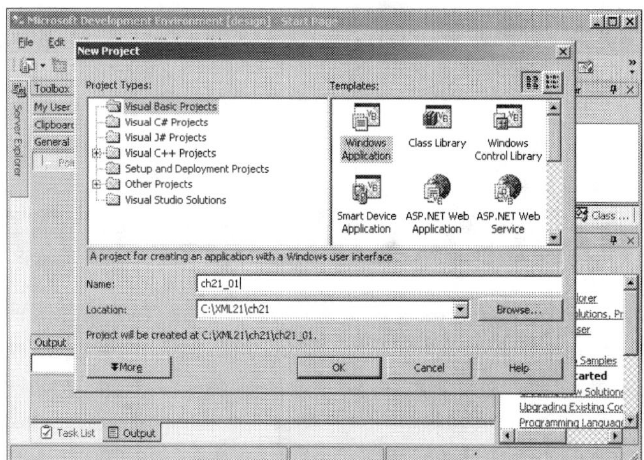

FIGURE 21.1
Creating a .NET project.

Creating a New XML Document in .NET

You can create a new XML document by selecting Project, Add Item to open the Add New Item dialog box, shown in Figure 21.2. Then select the XML File template in the Templates box and name this new file `ch21_01.xml`, as shown in Figure 21.2.

When you click Open, the new XML file is created and opened for editing in a Visual Studio designer (that is, an editor window), as shown in Figure 21.3.

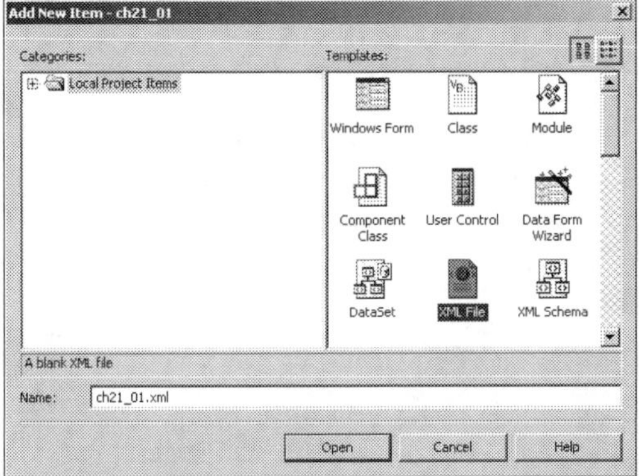

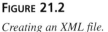

FIGURE 21.2

Creating an XML file.

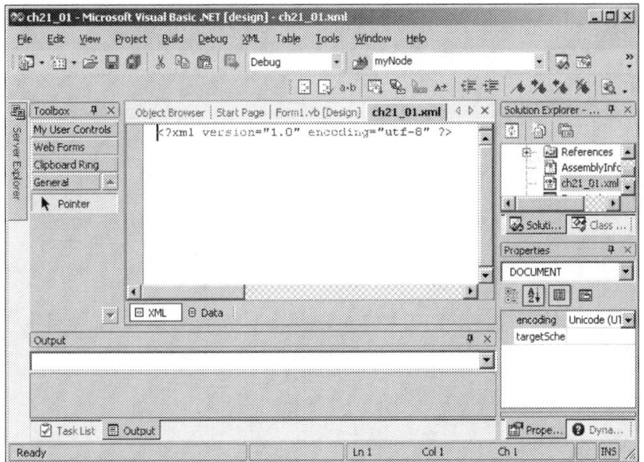

FIGURE 21.3

Editing an XML file.

You'll also create an XML schema for your XML document, and to do so, again select Project, Add Item, but this time select the XML Schema item in the Templates box and name the new XML schema `ch21_01Schema.xsd`, as shown in Figure 21.4.

When you click Open, the new XML schema is created and opened for editing, as shown in Figure 21.5.

FIGURE 21.4

Creating an XML schema.

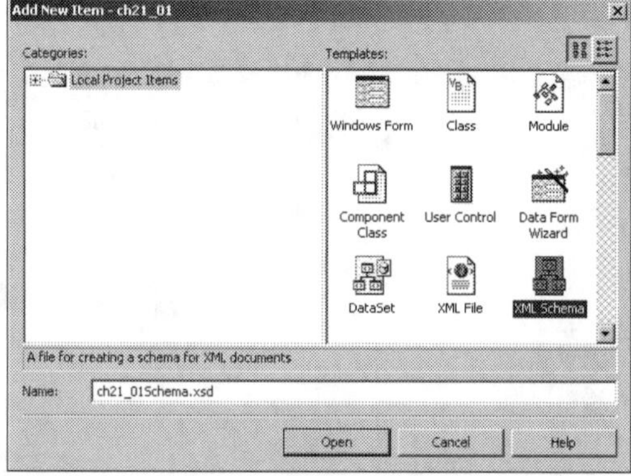

FIGURE 21.5

Editing an XML schema.

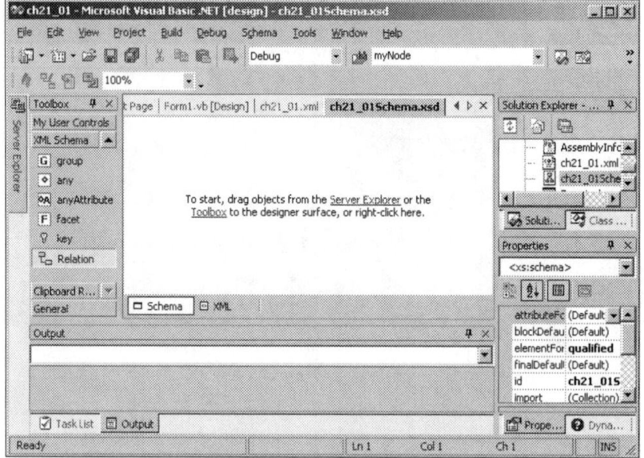

Creating a Simple Type in an XML Schema in .NET

How do you add types to an XML schema in Visual Studio .NET? You can simply drag types from the toolbox to the left of the XML schema onto that XML schema. For example, to create a type that will hold five-digit zip codes, you can drag `simpleType` from the toolbox to the XML schema. This creates a new simple type entry in the XML schema with the default name `simpleType1` highlighted. You can change that name to `zipcode` now and press Tab to move to the next field in the entry.

In the next field, select `positiveInteger` as the new type from the drop-down list box. To make sure your `zipcode` type can take only five-digit values, press Tab to move to the next row in this new entry and select `pattern` from the drop-down list box. This lets you enter a regular expression of the kind you saw on Day 7, "Creating Your Own Types in XML Schemas," that you can use with XML schemas to enforce data typing. In this case, your pattern will be `\d{5}`, ensuring that zip code values have five digits. Press Tab one more time and enter this pattern to complete the entry, as shown in Figure 21.6.

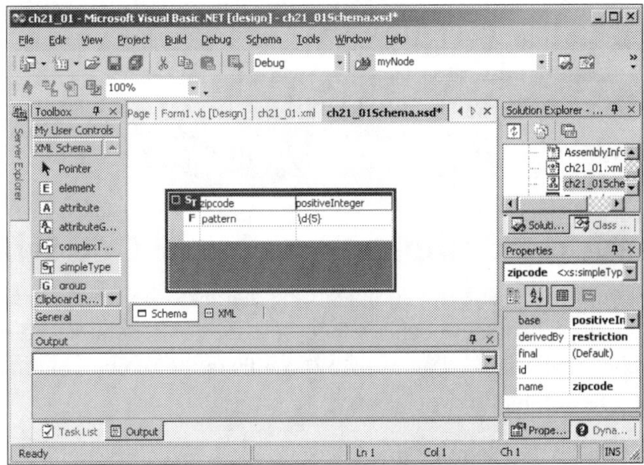

FIGURE 21.6

Creating a simple type.

To see what this new simple type looks like in XML, click the XML button at the bottom of the XML schema designer, and you see the results shown in Figure 21.7.

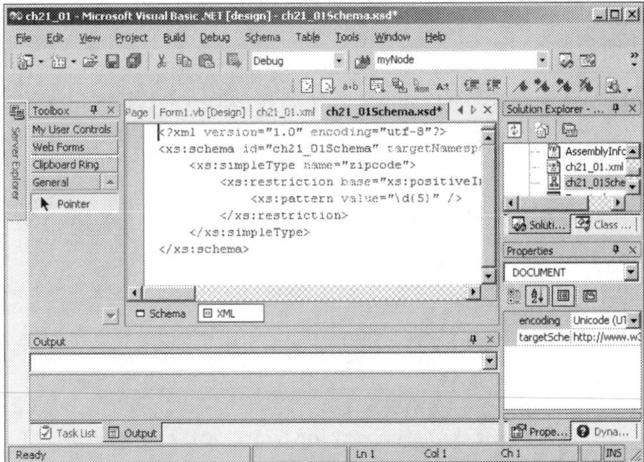

FIGURE 21.7

The XML view of a simple type.

Here's what your XML schema looks like so far:

```
<?xml version="1.0" encoding="utf-8"?>
<xs:schema id="ch21_01Schema"
    targetNamespace="http://tempuri.org/ch21_01Schema.xsd"
    elementFormDefault="qualified" xmlns="http://tempuri.org/ch21_01Schema.xsd"
    xmlns:mstns="http://tempuri.org/ch21_01Schema.xsd"
    xmlns:xs="http://www.w3.org/2001/XMLSchema">
    <xs:simpleType name="zipcode">
        <xs:restriction base="xs:positiveInteger">
            <xs:pattern value="\d{5}" />
        </xs:restriction>
    </xs:simpleType>
</xs:schema>
```

Creating a Complex Type in an XML Schema

Now you'll put together a complex type that uses the simple `zipcode` type you just created. To do so, click the Schema button in the XML schema's designer to switch back to the Schema view, and drag `complexType` from the toolbox onto the XML schema, which opens a new complex type's entry.

Next, replace the default name `complexType1`, which is highlighted, with a new name, `person`; you'll use this to hold data about various people. Instead of selecting a data type for this new type, press Tab twice to move to the next row. Then type `name` to create a name field and press Tab to select the data type for this new field. Next, select the `string` type from the drop-down list box; as you can see in the drop-down list box, there are many different data types available here. Then create a new field named `address` and give it the type `string`.

Press Tab once more to create a new field, `zip`—but this time, select your new simple type, `zipcode`, in the drop-down list box, which produces the results shown in Figure 21.8.

Now when you switch to the XML view, you'll see that your XML schema includes the complex type `person`:

```
<?xml version="1.0" encoding="utf-8"?>
<xs:schema id="ch21_01Schema"
    targetNamespace="http://tempuri.org/ch21_01Schema.xsd"
    elementFormDefault="qualified"
    xmlns="http://tempuri.org/ch21_01Schema.xsd"
    xmlns:mstns="http://tempuri.org/ch21_01Schema.xsd"
    xmlns:xs="http://www.w3.org/2001/XMLSchema">
    <xs:simpleType name="zipcode">
        <xs:restriction base="xs:positiveInteger">
            <xs:pattern value="\d{5}" />
        </xs:restriction>
```

```
    </xs:simpleType>
    <xs:complexType name="person">
        <xs:sequence>
            <xs:element name="name" type="xs:string" />
            <xs:element name="address" type="xs:string" />
            <xs:element name="zip" type="zipcode" />
        </xs:sequence>
    </xs:complexType>
</xs:schema>
```

To save your work so far, select File, Save All.

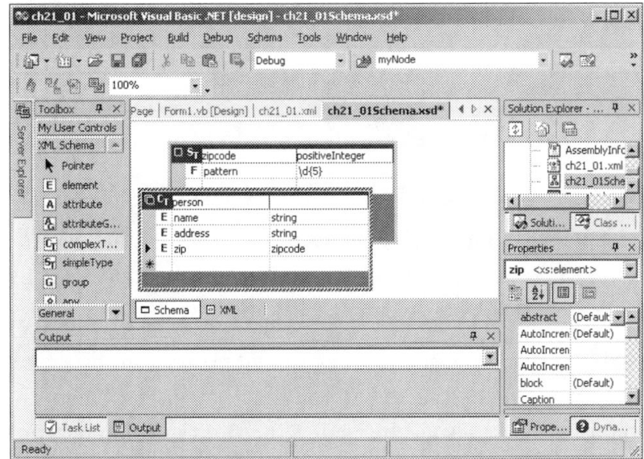

FIGURE 21.8

Creating a complex type.

Creating an Element

At this point, we've created two types—a simple type named `zipcode` and a complex type named `person`. Next we'll create an XML element, named `<project>`, which will hold data about a project we're interested in, including a contact person and the title of the project. To create this element, drag `element` from the toolbox onto the XML schema and open the new element for editing.

Next, give this new element the name `project` and click the middle box in the second row of this element's entry. Type `title` in that box and press Tab to move to the third box, and then select the type `string`. Next, tab to the next line and type `contact` in that line's middle box and select the type `person`, as shown in Figure 21.9.

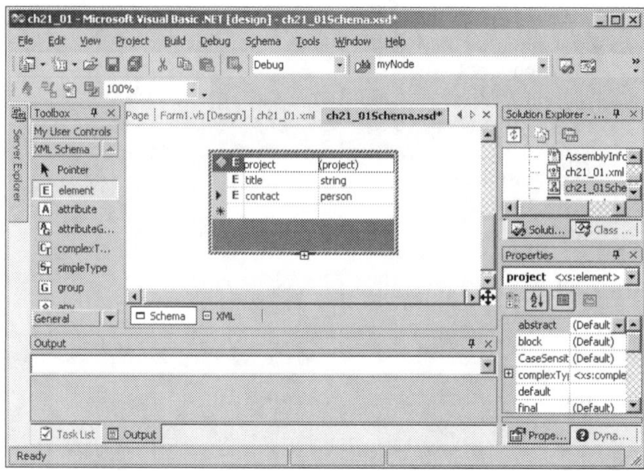

FIGURE 21.9
Creating an element.

Creating a Document Element

Next, we'll create a document element, `<projects>`, that can contain multiple `<project>` elements. To create the `<projects>` element, drag `element` from the toolbox to the XML schema and give this new element the name "projects".

To install the `<project>` element as a child element of the `<projects>` element, just drag the small + sign at the bottom of the `<project>` element (if it's a – sign, click it first to turn it into a + sign) inside the `<projects>` element. The results are shown in Figure 21.10. That's the way you create a document element—by dragging other elements into it. You can create the entire XML element hierarchy this way, simply by dragging elements.

Here's what the new, and final, version of your XML schema looks like:

```
<?xml version="1.0" encoding="utf-8"?>
<xs:schema id="ch21_01Schema"
    targetNamespace="http://tempuri.org/ch21_01Schema.xsd"
    elementFormDefault="qualified"
    xmlns="http://tempuri.org/ch21_01Schema.xsd"
    xmlns:mstns="http://tempuri.org/ch21_01Schema.xsd"
    xmlns:xs="http://www.w3.org/2001/XMLSchema">
    <xs:simpleType name="zipcode">
        <xs:restriction base="xs:positiveInteger">
            <xs:pattern value="\d{5}" />
        </xs:restriction>
    </xs:simpleType>
```

```
    <xs:complexType name="person">
        <xs:sequence>
            <xs:element name="name" type="xs:string" />
            <xs:element name="address" type="xs:string" />
            <xs:element name="zip" type="zipcode" />
        </xs:sequence>
    </xs:complexType>
    <xs:element name="projects">
        <xs:complexType>
            <xs:sequence>
                <xs:element name="project">
                    <xs:complexType>
                        <xs:sequence>
                            <xs:element name="title" type="xs:string" />
                            <xs:element name="contact" type="person" />
                        </xs:sequence>
                    </xs:complexType>
                </xs:element>
            </xs:sequence>
        </xs:complexType>
    </xs:element>
</xs:schema>
```

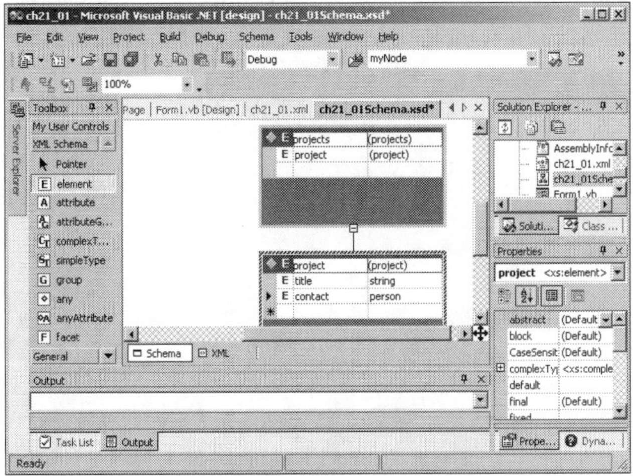

FIGURE 21.10

Creating a document element.

You need to save the XML schema in order to make it accessible to the XML document, so select File, Save All.

Connecting an XML Schema to an XML Document

To connect your new XML schema with your XML document, `ch21_01.xml`, click the `ch21_01.xml` tab to open this XML document. In the properties page at the lower right in

Visual Studio, click the `targetSchema` property and select the `http://tempuri.org/ch21_01Schema.xsd` item in the drop-down list box to associate your new XML schema with this XML document. When you do, Visual Studio adds this XML, getting you started by creating a `<projects>` document element:

```
<?xml version="1.0" encoding="utf-8" ?>
<projects xmlns="http://tempuri.org/ch21_01Schema.xsd">
        .
        .
        .
</projects>
```

Now we're ready to add some data to our XML document.

Working With XML Data

To add some data to your XML document now that you've associated your XML schema with that document, click between the `<projects>` and `</projects>` tags and type <, indicating that you want to start a new element. Doing so displays the possible options, and in this case, the only option is the `<project>` element, as shown in Figure 21.11.

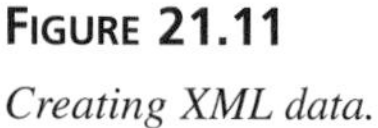

FIGURE 21.11
Creating XML data.

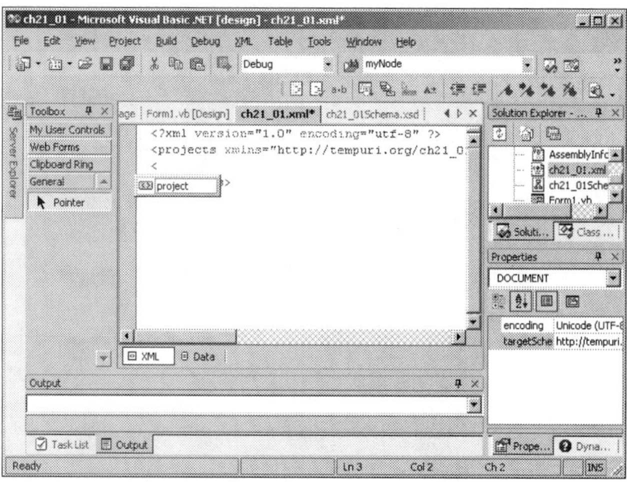

Select the `<project>` element now and type > to close the element. Visual Studio adds the closing tag, so your XML now looks like this:

```
<?xml version="1.0" encoding="utf-8" ?>
<projects xmlns="http://tempuri.org/ch21_01Schema.xsd">
<project></project>
</projects>
```

That's how the editing process works—you type < when you want to be prompted with the acceptable elements, you select an element from the prompt that appears, and you type > to close the element. Using the XML editor and the prompts based on your XML schema, you now enter this XML in your document:

```
<?xml version="1.0" encoding="utf-8" ?>
<projects xmlns="http://tempuri.org/ch21_01Schema.xsd">
    <project>
        <title>The XML Project</title>
        <contact>
            <name>Edward Zip</name>
            <address>0 Disk Drive</address>
            <zip>10001</zip>
        </contact>
    </project>
</projects>
```

To validate this XML document against your XML schema, select XML, Validate XML Data. This evaluates the data you've entered, and if everything checks out against the XML schema, you'll get the message `No validation errors were found.` at lower left in Visual Studio .NET, as shown in Figure 21.12. If you've made a mistake—such as not entering five digits (and only five digits) for the zip code—Visual Studio .NET lets you know with error messages in the Task window.

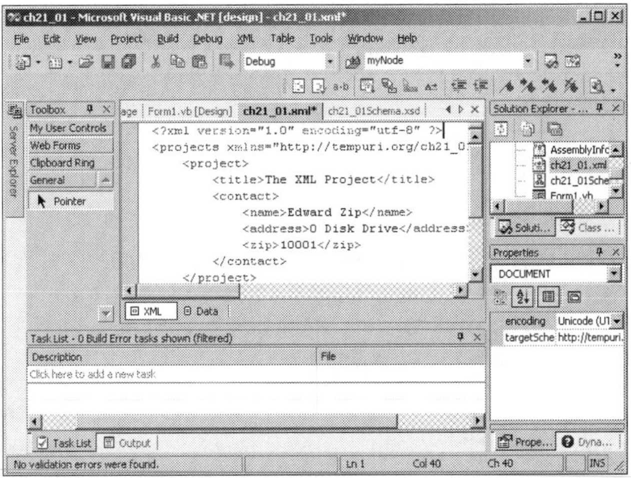

FIGURE 21.12
Validating an XML document.

You have just created and validated a new XML document with an XML schema by using Visual Studio .NET.

From XML to Databases and Back

Data from XML documents and data from databases are often treated in similar ways in .NET. For example, you can handle the data in your new XML document as you might handle data in an application such as Microsoft Access. To see how that works, click the Data button at the bottom of the XML document's designer to switch to Data view, which is shown in Figure 21.13. This view presents XML data in very much the way that Microsoft Access might, and you can edit it as you would in Access.

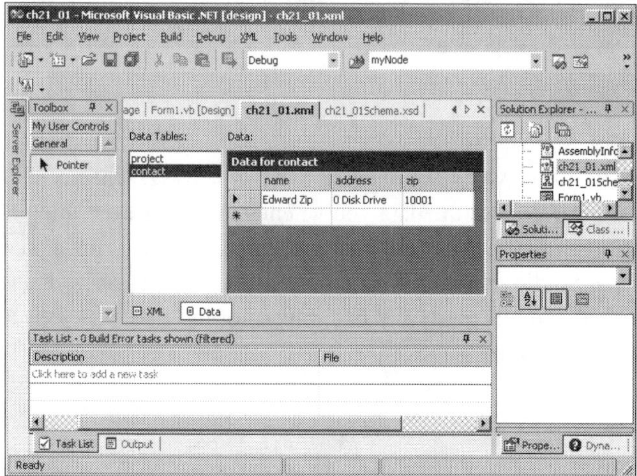

FIGURE 21.13
Examining an XML document's data.

There's another connection you can make between XML data and standard data handling in Visual Studio .NET: You can create .NET dataset objects of the type you saw yesterday when using an XML schema.

For example, open the XML schema in this project again and select the Preview Dataset menu item, which opens the Dataset Properties dialog box shown in Figure 21.14. This shows what fields would appear in the new dataset object and what properties those fields would have.

If you want to create this dataset object for use in code, select Schema, Generate Dataset. After you've created this object, you can use its `ReadXml` method, which you saw yesterday, to fill it with data by reading the XML document you've created using the XML schema.

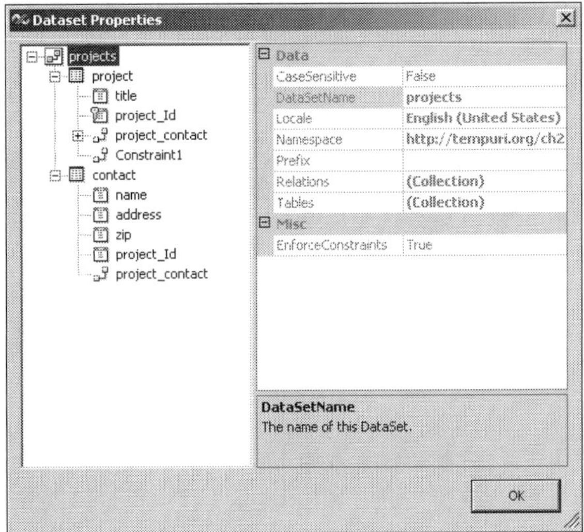

FIGURE 21.14
Creating a dataset from an XML schema.

Reading and Writing XML in .NET Code

Let's look at another example that shows how to work with XML in .NET programming. This time we'll use the `XmlTextWriter` and `XmlTextReader` classes. In this example, we'll use Visual Basic .NET code to write an XML document. We'll write out our sample document from Day 9, "Formatting XML by Using XSLT," which contains data on several states, and read it back in.

Begin by creating a new Windows project named `ch21_02` and adding two buttons to it—Write XML Document and Read XML Document, as shown in Figure 21.15. Also add a multiline text box where we'll display the data we've read in, as shown in the figure.

Next you need to use `XmlTextWriter` to write the XML.

Writing XML in .NET

To write your XML document with `XmlTextWriter`, you need to import `System.Xml` with an `Imports` statement to use this class. You will create a new object of the `XmlTextWriter` class, `xwriter`, and connect it to the XML document you'll create, `data.xml`:

```
Imports System.Xml
        .
        .
        .
Private Sub Button1_Click(ByVal sender As System.Object, _
    ByVal e As System.EventArgs) Handles Button1.Click
```

```
Dim xwriter As New XmlTextWriter("data.xml", System.Text.Encoding.UTF8)
        .
        .
        .
```

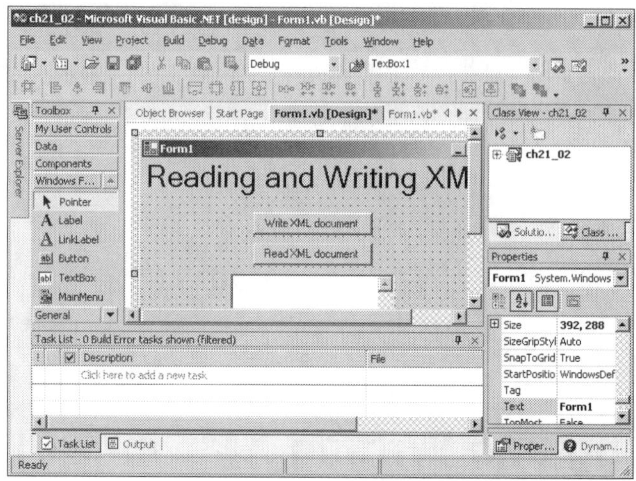

FIGURE 21.15

Creating the `ch21_02` *project.*

Now use the various methods of the `xwriter` object to write your new XML document from code. You'll start with the `WriteStartDocument` method to start the new XML document. Then you'll use the `WriteStartElement` method to create the `<states>` document element, which you'll put in the `"www.XMLPowerCorp.com"` namespace. You'll also create the first `<state>` element by using `WriteStartElement`, like this:

```
Imports System.Xml
        .
        .
        .
Private Sub Button1_Click(ByVal sender As System.Object, _
    ByVal e As System.EventArgs) Handles Button1.Click
    Dim xwriter As New XmlTextWriter("data.xml", System.Text.Encoding.UTF8)

    xwriter.WriteStartDocument(True)

    xwriter.WriteStartElement("states", "www.XMLPowerCorp.com")

    xwriter.WriteStartElement("state", "www.XMLPowerCorp.com")
        .
        .
        .
```

Now write the child elements that contain the document's data, such as `<name>`, `<population>`, and so on. All these elements just contain text, so you can use the `WriteElementString` method to write them. Here's how to write the data for California:

```
xwriter.WriteElementString("name", "www.XMLPowerCorp.com", "California")
xwriter.WriteElementString("population", "www.XMLPowerCorp.com", "33871648")
xwriter.WriteElementString("capital", "www.XMLPowerCorp.com", "Sacramento")
xwriter.WriteElementString("bird", "www.XMLPowerCorp.com", "Quail")
xwriter.WriteElementString("flower", "www.XMLPowerCorp.com", "Golden Poppy")
xwriter.WriteElementString("area", "www.XMLPowerCorp.com", "155959")
```

Now end this first `<state>` element with the `WriteEndElement` method:

```
xwriter.WriteEndElement()
```

Here's how to write the data for the Massachusetts and New York `<state>` elements, and then close those elements, close the `<states>` element, and end the document:

```
    xwriter.WriteStartElement("state", "www.XMLPowerCorp.com")

    xwriter.WriteElementString("name", "www.XMLPowerCorp.com", "Massachusetts")
    xwriter.WriteElementString("population", "www.XMLPowerCorp.com", "6349097")
    xwriter.WriteElementString("capital", "www.XMLPowerCorp.com", "Boston")
    xwriter.WriteElementString("bird", "www.XMLPowerCorp.com", "Chickadee")
    xwriter.WriteElementString("flower", "www.XMLPowerCorp.com", "Mayflower")
    xwriter.WriteElementString("area", "www.XMLPowerCorp.com", "7840")

    xwriter.WriteEndElement()

    xwriter.WriteStartElement("state", "www.XMLPowerCorp.com")

    xwriter.WriteElementString("name", "www.XMLPowerCorp.com", "New York")
    xwriter.WriteElementString("population", "www.XMLPowerCorp.com",
        "18976457")
    xwriter.WriteElementString("capital", "www.XMLPowerCorp.com", "Albany")
    xwriter.WriteElementString("bird", "www.XMLPowerCorp.com", "Bluebird")
    xwriter.WriteElementString("flower", "www.XMLPowerCorp.com", "Rose")
    xwriter.WriteElementString("area", "www.XMLPowerCorp.com", "47214")

    xwriter.WriteEndElement()

    xwriter.WriteEndElement()
    xwriter.WriteEndDocument()

    xwriter.Close()
End Sub
```


That's all you need. When you run this example, you see our states data XML document stored in the project's `bin` directory as `data.xml`—this time created by Visual Basic .NET. Listing 21.1 shows this document.

LISTING 21.1 An XML Document (`data.xml`)

```
<?xml version="1.0" encoding="utf-8" standalone="yes"?>
<states xmlns="www.XMLPowerCorp.com">
    <state>
        <name>California</name>
        <population>33871648</population>
        <capital>Sacramento</capital>
        <bird>Quail</bird>
        <flower>Golden Poppy</flower>
        <area>155959</area>
    </state>

    <state>
        <name>Massachusetts</name>
        <population>6349097</population>
        <capital>Boston</capital>
        <bird>Chickadee</bird>
        <flower>Mayflower</flower>
        <area>7840</area>
    </state>

    <state>
        <name>New York</name>
        <population>18976457</population>
        <capital>Albany</capital>
        <bird>Bluebird</bird>
        <flower>Rose</flower>
        <area>47214</area>
    </state>
</states>
```

Now it's time to read this document back in.

Reading XML

You can read XML documents in with `XmlTextReader` objects, which work something like a SAX parser. You can create a new `XmlTextReader` object, `xreader`, that is tied to the Read XML Document button in the XML document, `data.xml`, like this:

```
Private Sub Button2_Click(ByVal sender As System.Object, _
    ByVal e As System.EventArgs) Handles Button2.Click
    Dim xreader As XmlTextReader = Nothing

    xreader = New XmlTextReader("data.xml")
        .
        .
        .
```

Now loop over all nodes in your document by using a `While` loop and the `XmlTextReader` class's `Read` method. Each time through the loop, check the current node's type by using the `XmlTextReader` object's `NodeType` property; if that property equals `XmlNodeType.XmlDeclaration`, the current node is an XML declaration, if it equals `XmlNodeType.ProcessingInstruction`, it's a processing instruction, and so on. You can format the actual data in the node for display by using a procedure named `Format`, which you'll call for every node type, like this:

```
Private Sub Button2_Click(ByVal sender As System.Object, _
    ByVal e As System.EventArgs) Handles Button2.Click
    Dim xreader As XmlTextReader = Nothing

    xreader = New XmlTextReader("data.xml")

    While xreader.Read()

        Select Case (xreader.NodeType)

            Case XmlNodeType.XmlDeclaration
                Format(xreader, "XmlDeclaration")

            Case XmlNodeType.ProcessingInstruction
                Format(xreader, "ProcessingInstruction")

            Case XmlNodeType.DocumentType
                Format(xreader, "DocumentType")

            Case XmlNodeType.Comment
                Format(xreader, "Comment")

            Case XmlNodeType.Element
                Format(xreader, "Element")

            Case XmlNodeType.Text
                Format(xreader, "Text")

            Case XmlNodeType.Whitespace
        End Select
    End While

End Sub
```

In this example, the `Format` procedure will format and display data from element and text nodes in your application's text box. To get the name of an element, use the `XmlTextReader` object's `Name` property, and to get the value of an element or text node, use the `XmlTextReader` object's `Value` property. Here's what this looks like in code:

```
Sub Format(ByRef reader As XmlTextReader, ByVal nodeType As String)
    If (nodeType = "Element") Then
        TextBox1.Text &= "<" & reader.Name & ">" & reader.Value & _
            ControlChars.CrLf
    End If

    If (nodeType = "Text") Then
        TextBox1.Text &= "    " & reader.Value & ControlChars.CrLf
    End If
End Sub
```

Now when the user clicks the Write XML Document button, your application will write the states data to `data.xml`. When the user clicks the Read XML Document button, the application will read that data back and display it, as shown in Figure 21.16.

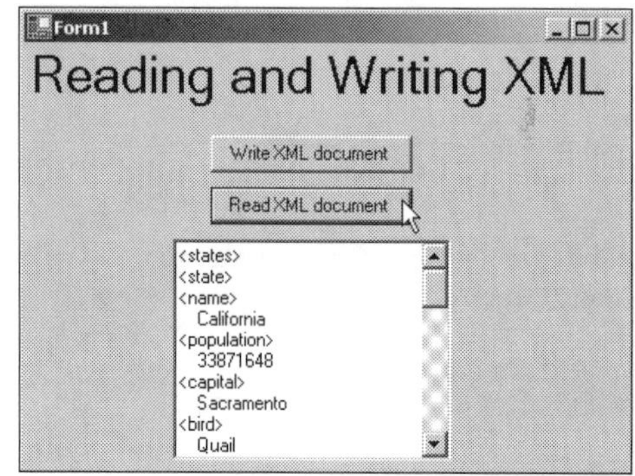

FIGURE 21.16 *Reading XML in Visual Basic .NET code.*

Listing 21.2 shows the code we've written for this example.

LISTING 21.2 Writing and Reading XML in .NET (`Form1.vb` from the `ch21_02` Project)

```
Imports System.Xml
        .
        .
        .
Private Sub Button1_Click(ByVal sender As System.Object, _
    ByVal e As System.EventArgs) Handles Button1.Click
    Dim xwriter As New XmlTextWriter("data.xml", System.Text.Encoding.UTF8)

    xwriter.WriteStartDocument(True)

    xwriter.WriteStartElement("states", "www.XMLPowerCorp.com")

    xwriter.WriteStartElement("state", "www.XMLPowerCorp.com")
```

Listing 21.2 continued

```
        xwriter.WriteElementString("name", "www.XMLPowerCorp.com", "California")
        xwriter.WriteElementString("population", "www.XMLPowerCorp.com",
            "33871648")
        xwriter.WriteElementString("capital", "www.XMLPowerCorp.com", "Sacramento")
        xwriter.WriteElementString("bird", "www.XMLPowerCorp.com", "Quail")
        xwriter.WriteElementString("flower", "www.XMLPowerCorp.com",
            "Golden Poppy")
        xwriter.WriteElementString("area", "www.XMLPowerCorp.com", "155959")

        xwriter.WriteEndElement()

        xwriter.WriteStartElement("state", "www.XMLPowerCorp.com")

        xwriter.WriteElementString("name", "www.XMLPowerCorp.com", "Massachusetts")
        xwriter.WriteElementString("population", "www.XMLPowerCorp.com", "6349097")
        xwriter.WriteElementString("capital", "www.XMLPowerCorp.com", "Boston")
        xwriter.WriteElementString("bird", "www.XMLPowerCorp.com", "Chickadee")
        xwriter.WriteElementString("flower", "www.XMLPowerCorp.com", "Mayflower")
        xwriter.WriteElementString("area", "www.XMLPowerCorp.com", "7840")

        xwriter.WriteEndElement()

        xwriter.WriteStartElement("state", "www.XMLPowerCorp.com")

        xwriter.WriteElementString("name", "www.XMLPowerCorp.com", "New York")
        xwriter.WriteElementString("population", "www.XMLPowerCorp.com",
            "18976457")
        xwriter.WriteElementString("capital", "www.XMLPowerCorp.com", "Albany")
        xwriter.WriteElementString("bird", "www.XMLPowerCorp.com", "Bluebird")
        xwriter.WriteElementString("flower", "www.XMLPowerCorp.com", "Rose")
        xwriter.WriteElementString("area", "www.XMLPowerCorp.com", "47214")

        xwriter.WriteEndElement()

        xwriter.WriteEndElement()
        xwriter.WriteEndDocument()

        xwriter.Close()
    End Sub

    Private Sub Button2_Click(ByVal sender As System.Object, _
        ByVal e As System.EventArgs) Handles Button2.Click

        Dim xreader As XmlTextReader = Nothing

        xreader = New XmlTextReader("data.xml")

        While xreader.Read()
```

Listing 21.2 continued

```
            Select Case (xreader.NodeType)

                Case XmlNodeType.XmlDeclaration
                    Format(xreader, "XmlDeclaration")

                Case XmlNodeType.ProcessingInstruction
                    Format(xreader, "ProcessingInstruction")

                Case XmlNodeType.DocumentType
                    Format(xreader, "DocumentType")

                Case XmlNodeType.Comment
                    Format(xreader, "Comment")

                Case XmlNodeType.Element
                    Format(xreader, "Element")

                Case XmlNodeType.Text
                    Format(xreader, "Text")

                Case XmlNodeType.Whitespace
            End Select
        End While

    End Sub

    Sub Format(ByRef reader As XmlTextReader, ByVal nodeType As String)
        If (nodeType = "Element") Then
            TextBox1.Text &= "<" & reader.Name & ">" & reader.Value &
            ControlChars.CrLf
        End If

        If (nodeType = "Text") Then
            TextBox1.Text &= "    " & reader.Value & ControlChars.CrLf
        End If
    End Sub
```

Using XML Controls to Display Formatted XML

The .NET platform supports an XML control that you can use to format and display XML. In this section you'll take a look at how to use your full states data XML example, which appears in Listing 21.3, in this control.

LISTING 21.3 A Sample XML Document (ch21_03.xml)

```
<?xml version="1.0" encoding ="UTF-8"?>
<states>

    <state>
        <name>California</name>
        <population units="people">33871648</population><!--2000 census-->
        <capital>Sacramento</capital>
        <bird>Quail</bird>
        <flower>Golden Poppy</flower>
        <area units="square miles">155959</area>
    </state>

    <state>
        <name>Massachusetts</name>
        <population units="people">6349097</population><!--2000 census-->
        <capital>Boston</capital>
        <bird>Chickadee</bird>
        <flower>Mayflower</flower>
        <area units="square miles">7840</area>
    </state>

    <state>
        <name>New York</name>
        <population units="people">18976457</population><!--2000 census-->
        <capital>Albany</capital>
        <bird>Bluebird</bird>
        <flower>Rose</flower>
        <area units="square miles">47214</area>
    </state>

</states>
```

You use the XML control in Web applications, not Windows applications; it lets you display XML documents such as ch21_03.xml directly in a Web page. The XML control also lets you use XSLT to format the XML as you want it. Rather than display XML directly, you usually use the XML control with an XSLT style sheet to transform an XML document into HTML to be displayed in a Web page. Listing 21.4 shows the XSLT style sheet, ch21_04.xsl, that you'll use in this case. This XSLT style sheet will extract the data in ch21_03.xml and format it into an HTML table that the XML control can display.

LISTING 21.4 A Sample XSLT Style Sheet (`ch21_04.xsl`)

```
<?xml version="1.0" encoding="UTF-8"?>
<xsl:stylesheet version="1.0"
xmlns:xsl="http://www.w3.org/1999/XSL/Transform">

    <xsl:template match="/states">
        <HTML>
            <HEAD>
                <TITLE>
                    State Data
                </TITLE>
            </HEAD>
            <BODY>
                <BR/>
                <BR/>
                <BR/>
                <TABLE BORDER="1">
                    <TR>
                        <TD>Name</TD>
                        <TD>Population</TD>
                        <TD>Capital</TD>
                        <TD>Bird</TD>
                        <TD>Flower</TD>
                        <TD>Area</TD>
                    </TR>
                    <xsl:apply-templates/>
                </TABLE>
            </BODY>
        </HTML>
    </xsl:template>

    <xsl:template match="state">
       <TR>
          <TD><xsl:value-of select="name"/></TD>
          <TD><xsl:apply-templates select="population"/></TD>
          <TD><xsl:apply-templates select="capital"/></TD>
          <TD><xsl:apply-templates select="bird"/></TD>
          <TD><xsl:apply-templates select="flower"/></TD>
          <TD><xsl:apply-templates select="area"/></TD>
       </TR>
   </xsl:template>

    <xsl:template match="population">
        <xsl:value-of select="."/>
        <xsl:text> </xsl:text>
        <xsl:value-of select="@units"/>
    </xsl:template>
```

LISTING 21.4 continued

```
    <xsl:template match="capital">
        <xsl:value-of select="."/>
    </xsl:template>

    <xsl:template match="bird">
        <xsl:value-of select="."/>
    </xsl:template>

    <xsl:template match="flower">
        <xsl:value-of select="."/>
    </xsl:template>

    <xsl:template match="area">
        <xsl:value-of select="."/>
        <xsl:text> </xsl:text>
        <xsl:value-of select="@units"/>
    </xsl:template>

</xsl:stylesheet>
```

Table 21.1 lists the significant properties of XML controls.

TABLE 21.1 Significant Public Properties of XML Controls

Property	*Description*
`Document`	Returns or sets the `System.Xml.XmlDocument` object to display in the XML control.
`DocumentContent`	Sets a string that contains the XML document to display in the XML control.
`DocumentSource`	Returns or sets the path to an XML document to display in the XML control.
`Transform`	Returns or sets the `System.Xml.Xsl.XslTransform` object that formats the XML document.
`TransformSource`	Returns or sets the path to an XSLT style sheet that formats the XML document.

In our example, all we have to do is assign the name of our XML document to a new XML control's `DocumentSource` property and assign to the `TransformSource` property the name of our XSLT style sheet.

To host the XML control, we'll need a .NET Web application. To create Web applications, you need to use Internet Information Server (IIS) and configure it for use with .NET. The Visual Studio .NET installation documentation describes how to do this.

You can create a new Web application by selecting File, New, Project to open the New Project dialog box. Then you select Visual Basic Projects in the Project Types box and ASP.NET Web Application in the Templates box. Finally, give this new project the name `ch21_05`. Figure 21.17 shows what this looks like.

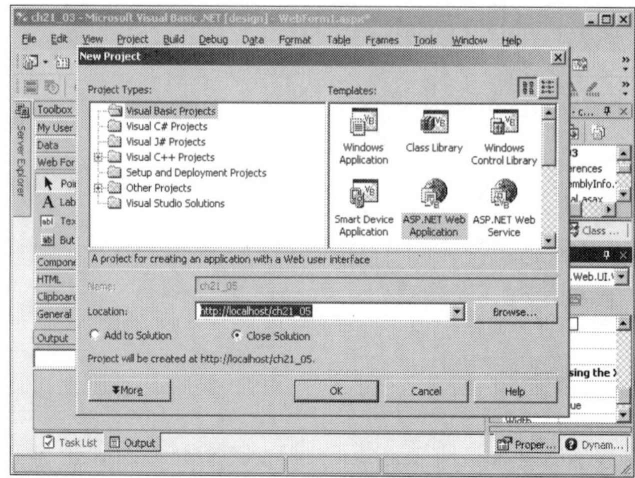

FIGURE 21.17
Creating the `ch21_05` *example.*

When you click the OK button in the New Project dialog box, the new Web application is created on the server you selected, and you can work with this application locally, as shown in Figure 21.18. In this case, you've added a label with the text "Using the XML Control" to your main Web form.

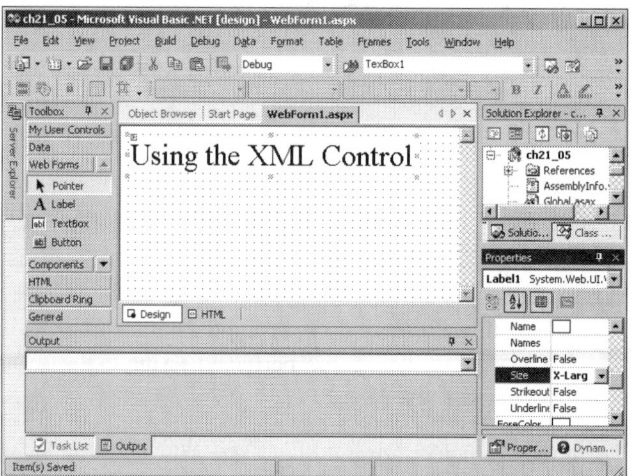

FIGURE 21.18
Editing the `ch21_05` *example.*

Next, drag an XML control from the Web Forms tab in the toolbox to the main Web form. Then select that control and click the `DocumentSource` property in the properties window at the lower right in Visual Studio. Click the ellipsis (...) button that appears in the properties window and browse to your XML document, `ch21_03.xml`. Next, click the `TransformSource` property in the properties window, click the ellipsis button that appears, and browse to your XSLT style sheet, `ch21_04.xsl`.

You're ready to run this example, so select Debug, Start. When you run this application, you'll see the data in `ch21_03.xml` formatted using the XSLT style sheet in `ch21_04.xsl` into an HTML table, as shown in Figure 21.19.

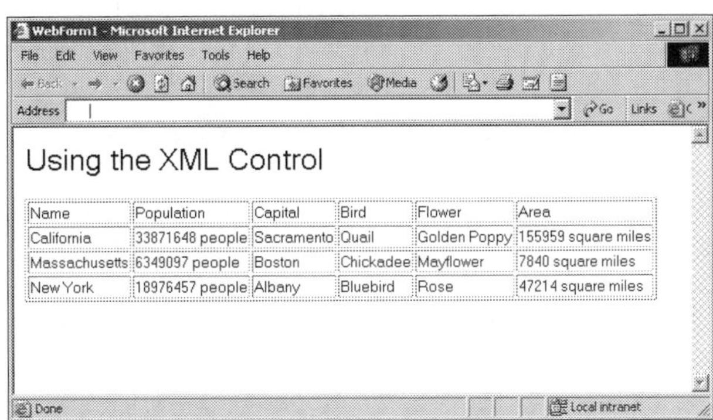

FIGURE 21.19
Using XML controls.

Now you're transforming XML into HTML by using XSLT and an XML control.

Creating XML Web Services

The last .NET XML topic we'll take a look at today are XML Web services. These services let you provide accessible services on the Web, and they can be used by other applications.

For example, say you were in the field and wanted to retrieve data from a database back at the central office. A Web service can help you do that, as long as the Web server the service is on has access to that database. All you have to do is connect to the Web service from a laptop, and you can get all the data you want. Even a Windows application can call the methods you put into a Web service, allowing you to integrate Web access into Windows applications easily. Web services are often used to implement multitiered, distributed data applications, and in the following sections we'll create a Web service much like that. All the data in this example will be passed back and forth by using XML.

Creating a Web Service

Our sample XML Web service is called `ch21_06`, and we'll use it to gain access to the `authors` table in the SQL `pubs` sample database. In particular, we'll implement two methods in this Web service—`GetAuthors`, to return a dataset that holds the `authors` table, and `UpdateAuthors`, to update that table in the `pubs` database when needed. Our XML Web service will be on the Web, so if a Windows application needs that data, it can just use our Windows service.

You can create a new Web service project by selecting File, New, Project, selecting the ASP.NET Web Service icon, making the project a Visual Basic .NET project, and giving this project the name `ch21_06`. When you click the OK button in the New Project dialog box, the new Web service project shown in Figure 21.20 is created.

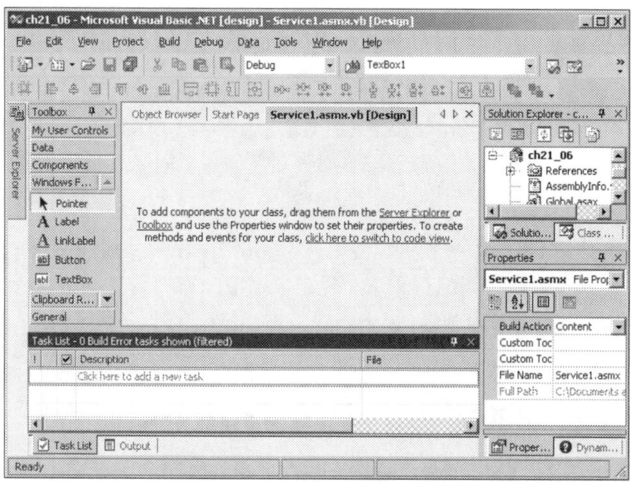

FIGURE 21.20
Creating a new Web service project.

The Visual Basic .NET code file for your new Web service is `Service1.asmx.vb`, and the name of your new Web service is `Service1`. When you open `Service1.asmx.vb` in Visual Studio .NET, you see that this new service is derived from the `WebService` class:

```
Imports System.Web.Services

<System.Web.Services.WebService(Namespace :=
    "http://tempuri.org/ch21_06/Service1")> _
Public Class Service1
    Inherits System.Web.Services.WebService
        .
        .
        .
```

In this Web service, we'll set up our connection to the `authors` table in the `pubs` sample SQL Server database. To do that, drag an `OleDbDataAdapter` data adapter to the Web service designer and use the Data Adapter Configuration Wizard to connect the data adapter to the `authors` table, as you did earlier today for the `employee` table. Then select Data, Generate Dataset to create a new dataset class, `DataSet1`. This is the dataset class you'll use to access the `authors` table in the Web service.

To make the methods in a Web service accessible outside the service, you use the `<WebMethod()>` attribute when declaring those methods. For example, here is how you do this for the `GetAuthors` method:

```
<WebMethod(Description:="Sends the authors table to the client")> _
Public Function GetAuthors() As DataSet1
        .
        .
        .
End Function
```

In the `GetAuthors` method, you want to return a dataset filled with the `authors` table, so add this code in `Service1.asmx.vb`:

```
<WebMethod(Description:="Sends the authors table to the client")> _
Public Function GetAuthors() As DataSet1
    Dim AuthorsDataTable As New DataSet1
    OleDbDataAdapter1.Fill(AuthorsDataTable)
    Return AuthorsDataTable
End Function
```

As you're going to see, the `GetAuthors` method will be available to code in other applications after you've added a Web reference to the Web service in those applications.

You can also implement the `UpdateAuthors` method, which will update the `authors` table with changes the user has made. We can pass this method to a dataset that holds changes to the `authors` table and update the `authors` table by using the data adapter's `Update` method, like this:

```
<WebMethod(Description:="Updates the authors table from the client")> _
Public Function UpdateAuthors(ByVal _
    ChangedAuthorsRecords As DataSet1) As DataSet1
    If (ChangedAuthorsRecords Is Nothing) Then
        Return Nothing
    Else
        OleDbDataAdapter1.Update(ChangedAuthorsRecords)
        Return ChangedAuthorsRecords
    End If
End Function
```

We have now implemented the `GetAuthors` and `UpdateAuthors` methods. To make this Web service available to applications, you should build the service now by selecting Build, Build `ch21_06`. Listing 21.5 shows the code we've developed so far for this example.

LISTING 21.5 An XML Web Service (from `Service1.asmx.vb`, `ch21_06` Project)

```
Imports System.Web.Services
        .
        .
        .
    <WebMethod(Description:="Sends the authors table to the client")> _
    Public Function GetAuthors() As DataSet1
        Dim AuthorsDataTable As New DataSet1
        OleDbDataAdapter1.Fill(AuthorsDataTable)
        Return AuthorsDataTable
    End Function

    <WebMethod(Description:="Updates the authors table from the client")> _
Public Function UpdateAuthors(ByVal _
    ChangedAuthorsRecords As DataSet1) As DataSet1
        If (ChangedAuthorsRecords Is Nothing) Then
            Return Nothing
        Else
            OleDbDataAdapter1.Update(ChangedAuthorsRecords)
            Return ChangedAuthorsRecords
        End If
    End Function

End Class
```

Using a Web Service

Now we'll put our new Web service to work and call it from a Windows application. To make that work, add a new Windows project that will connect to the Web service by selecting File, Add Project, New Project.

In the Add New Project dialog box, select the Windows Application icon, name this new Windows application `ch21_07`, and click OK. The Windows application opens, as shown in Figure 21.21. Because the Web service has no visual interface, you need to make this Windows application the startup project by selecting Project, Set as StartUp Project. Now when you select Debug, Start, the Windows application will appear.

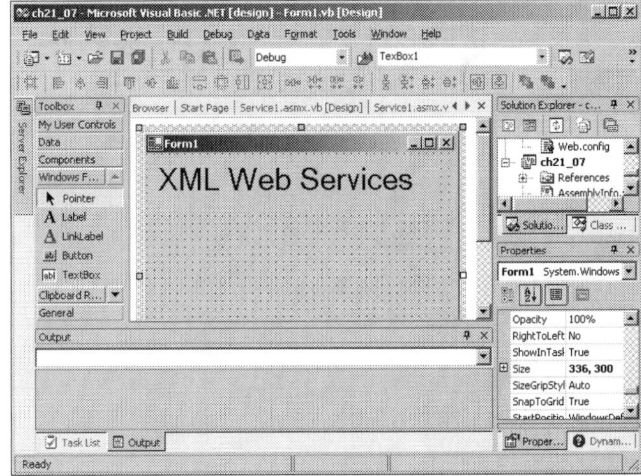

FIGURE 21.21

The `ch21_07` *Windows application.*

We want to call the `GetAuthors` and `UpdateAuthors` methods in our Windows application. To do that, we need to add a Web reference to our Web service. To do this, right-click the `ch21_07` entry in the Solution Explorer at the right in Visual Studio, and then select the Add Web Reference menu item. This opens the Add Web Reference dialog box, which lists the available Web service locations.

To add a reference to a Web service, you can enter the URL for the service's `.vsdisco` (Visual Studio discovery) file in the Address box in the Add Web Reference dialog box. Or you can browse to the service you want to use by clicking the link in the Add Web Reference dialog box for a server and then click the name of the service you want to use (in this case, `Service1`).

Either technique opens your Web service's entry in the Add Web Reference dialog box, as shown in Figure 21.22. To add a reference to this Web service to your Windows application, click the Add Reference button.

The Web reference is added to our Windows application, and this reference will give us access to the `GetAuthors` and `UpdateAuthors` methods. To hold the data returned from the Web service, add a data grid to the Windows application and place above the data grid two buttons with the captions Get the Data and Set the Data.

Next, drag a dataset object—not a data adapter this time—from the Data tab of the toolbox to the main form in the Windows application. When you do, the Add Dataset dialog box opens, as shown in Figure 21.23. In that dialog box, select the dataset object in your Web service, `DataSet1`, from the drop-down list (the fully qualified name of `DataSet1` is `ch21_07.localhost.DataSet1`, as shown in Figure 21.23).

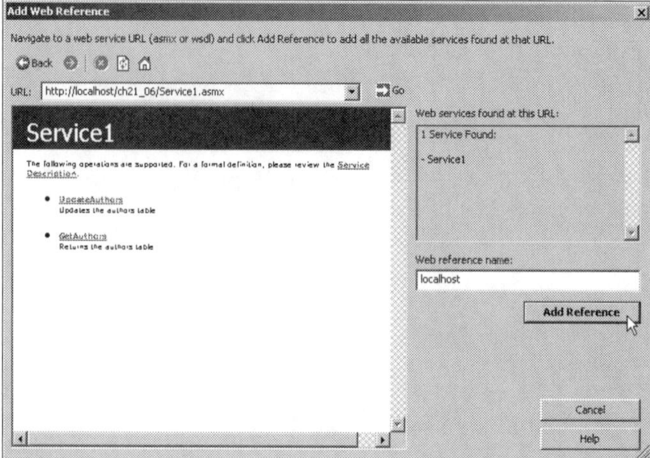

FIGURE 21.22

The Add Web Reference dialog box.

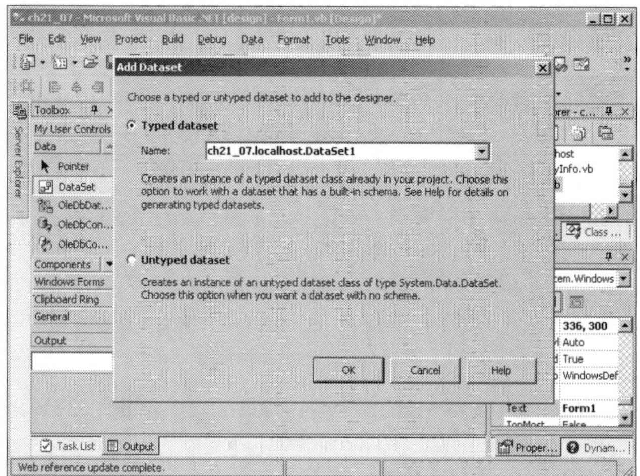

FIGURE 21.23

Using the Add Dataset dialog box.

To create the new dataset we'll use in our Windows application, `DataSet11`, click the OK button in the Add Dataset dialog box. We'll bind `DataSet11` to the data grid in the Windows application, so set the data grid's `DataSource` property to `DataSet11` and its `DataMember` property to `authors` in the properties window.

You're almost done. When you click the Get the Data button, the dataset, `DataSet11`, should fill with data sent to us from the Web service. To do that, you create an object, `service`, of your Web service class:

```
Private Sub Button1_Click(ByVal sender As System.Object, _
    ByVal e As System.EventArgs) Handles Button1.Click
```

```
    Dim service As New ch21_07.localhost.Service1
        .
        .
        .
End Sub
```

The `service` object will let us use the methods we've built into our Web service. We can fill the Windows application's `DataSet11` object with the dataset returned from the Web service's `GetAuthors` method by using the `Merge` method, like this:

```
Private Sub Button1_Click(ByVal sender As System.Object, _
    ByVal e As System.EventArgs) Handles Button1.Click
    Dim service As New ch21_07.localhost.Service1
    DataSet11.Merge(service.GetAuthors())
End Sub
```

That's all it takes—you create an object corresponding to the Web service, and then you can use that object's methods and access the Web service in your code.

We can update the `authors` table as needed. When the user edits the data in the data grid, those changes are also made to the `DataSet11` object. To extract the changed records from that dataset, we can use the dataset's `GetChanges` method, like this:

```
Private Sub Button2_Click(ByVal sender As System.Object, _
    ByVal e As System.EventArgs) Handles Button2.Click
    If DataSet11.HasChanges() Then
        Dim dsUpdates As New _
            Ch21_07.localhost.DataSet1
        dsUpdates.Merge(DataSet11.GetChanges())
        .
        .
        .
    End If
End Sub
```

Now we can use the Web service's `UpdateAuthors` method to update the `authors` table in the `pubs` database. That method returns the changed records, and we can merge them into the Windows application's dataset so those records will no longer be marked as changed:

```
Private Sub Button2_Click(ByVal sender As System.Object, _
    ByVal e As System.EventArgs) Handles Button2.Click
    If DataSet11.HasChanges() Then
        Dim service As New Ch21_07.localhost.Service1
        Dim dsUpdates As New _
            Ch21_07.localhost.DataSet1
        dsUpdates.Merge(DataSet11.GetChanges())
        DataSet11.Merge(service.UpdateAuthors(dsUpdates) )
    End If
End Sub
```

The complete code for this example is shown in Listing 21.6.

LISTING 21.6 Using an XML Web Service (from `Form1.vb`, `ch21_07` Project)

```
Public Class Form1
    Inherits System.Windows.Forms.Form
        .
        .
        .
    Private Sub Button1_Click(ByVal sender As System.Object, _
        ByVal e As System.EventArgs) Handles Button1.Click
        Dim service As New ch21_07.localhost.Service1
        DataSet11.Merge(service.GetAuthors())
    End Sub

    Private Sub Button2_Click(ByVal sender As System.Object, _
        ByVal e As System.EventArgs) Handles Button2.Click
        Dim service As New ch21_07.localhost.Service1
        Dim dsUpdates As New _
            ch21_07.localhost.DataSet1
        dsUpdates.Merge(DataSet11.GetChanges())
        DataSet11.Merge(service.UpdateAuthors(dsUpdates))
    End Sub
End Class
```

When you run this example and click the Get the Data button, the data from the `authors` table should appear in the data grid, as shown in Figure 21.24. If you edit the data in the data grid and click the Set the Data button, your edits will be sent back to the `authors` table in the `pubs` database.

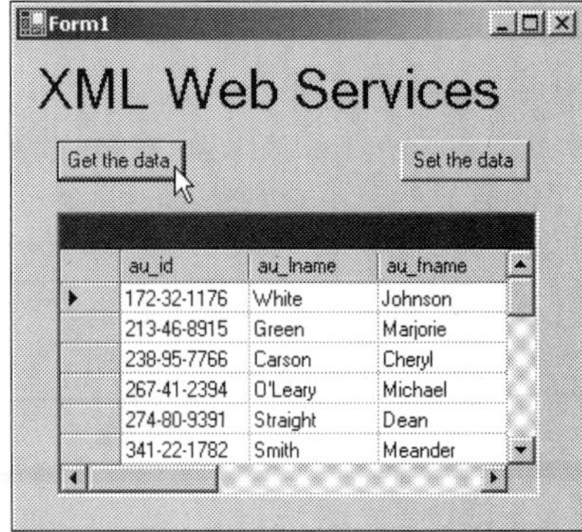

FIGURE 21.24 *Connecting to and using a Web service.*

As far as the users are concerned, the connection to the Web is maintained entirely behind-the-scenes; all the users have to do is click buttons. That's how XML Web services work. Behind-the-scenes in this example, all the data was sent back and forth by using XML. All in all, this is a very impressive showing for .NET programming.

Summary

Today you took a look at working with XML in .NET programming. There's a great deal of support for XML in .NET, and you got a good introduction to the topic today.

You began by seeing how to create and edit a simple XML document by using Visual Studio .NET. To create a new XML document, you just select Project, Add Item in Visual Studio .NET to open the Add new Item dialog box, and you select the XML File template in the Templates box. And you can also create a new XML schema by using the same technique, except that you select the XML Schema item in the Templates box. You saw that you can create an XML schema simply by dragging simple and complex types onto the schema designer and that you can connect a completed XML schema to a new XML document.

Next, you took a look at the `XmlTextWriter` and `XmlTextReader` classes. You used these classes to write an XML document to a file and read that file back in, displaying the data in that document. You saw that the `XmlTextReader` class works much like a SAX parser, letting you loop over nodes, determine their types, and examine their data.

You also took a look at XML Web controls in .NET programming. By using these controls, you can format XML data by using an XSLT style sheet. You do this by assigning an XML control's `DocumentSource` property the name of an XML document and assigning the `TransformSource` property the name of the XSLT style sheet.

You also took a look at working with XML Web services in Visual Basic .NET today. Web services expose methods that may be called by other applications. The example you saw today let you call two methods, `GetAuthors` and `UpdateAuthors`, to get and set the data in the `authors` table of the `pubs` SQL Server sample database.

To expose methods from a Web service and make them accessible outside the service, you use the `<WebMethod()>` attribute. To access a Web method in a Web service from an application, you first have to add a Web reference to that service. You can do that by right-clicking a project in the Visual Studio .NET Solution Explorer, selecting the Add Web Reference menu item, and browsing to the Web service you want in the Add Web Reference dialog box. After you've added the Web reference, you're free to create a new object of that service's class, as you've done today, and call the Web methods of that object. In your code today, you saw how to call the GetAuthors and UpdateAuthors methods this way.

You have now completed our survey of XML. You've come far in this book, from the very basic all the way up to the advanced. All that remains now is for you to put all this XML power to work for yourself—happy programming!

Q&A

Q Do I have to create an XML schema before I can create and enter data into an XML document in Visual Studio .NET?

A Not at all. Even if you want to use an XML schema, you can enter your XML document first and then select XML, Create Schema to create an XML schema from it. (On the other hand, this technique is problematic because Visual Studio .NET can only guess at the data types and data ranges you're using.)

Q I want to use the XMLTextWriter class's WriteElementString method, but my data is not in string format. Is there any way to convert it properly?

A One handy way is to use the XmlConvert.ToString method, like this:

```
xwriter.WriteElementString("data", XmlConvert.ToString(data))
```

Workshop

This workshop tests whether you understand the concepts discussed today. It's a good idea to make sure you can answer these questions before pressing on to tomorrow's work. Answers to the quiz can be found in Appendix A, "Quiz Answers."

Quiz

1. How can you create a new XML document in Visual Studio .NET?
2. What XmlTextWriter method can you use to create the opening tag of an XML element?
3. How do you determine the type of the current node being read by an XmlTextReader object?
4. What attribute do you use when you declare a Web method in a Web service to make that method accessible outside the service?
5. What do you need to do in a Windows application before you work with the methods of a Web service?

Exercises

1. Following the steps outlined today, create a new XML document and XML schema in Visual Studio .NET and store in it the names of five favorite books, their authors, and their publishers.
2. Here's an advanced one: Create a new Web service, and have the Web service implement a Web method named `GetTime` that will return the current time on the Web server as a string. (In Visual Basic .NET, you can use the `TimeString` property to return the current time in a string like this: `"The time is " & TimeString`.)

PART V

In Review

In Part V we took a look at working with databases and XML. This is a natural connection because XML is all about data. We took two main approaches here: treating XML documents as standard databases and using XQuery for the native XML way of handling XML documents as databases.

We started by examining the way you can bind data to Web pages in Internet Explorer. We talked about the various DSOs that you can use to connect to data sources and make XML data accessible to HTML controls and scripting code.

There are two XML DSOs in Internet Explorer: XML data islands and the XML DSO applet. You create an XML data island by using the <XML> element and the SRC attribute to connect it to an XML document. And you can connect a XML DSO to an XML document by using a <PARAM> element in the <APPLET> element.

When you want to bind data from a DSO to HTML controls, you use element attributes such as DATASRC and DATAFLD. You assign the DATASRC attribute the name of the DSO, and you assign the DATAFLD attribute the name of the field in the current record you want to work with. You can also use methods such as moveNext and moveLast to change the current record, and any such change is reflected in all the controls that are bound to that DSO.

Let's look at an example that shows some of the work we did in Day 19. In this case, we're going to search a bound XML document for some data, and we'll bind the results to HTML controls, combining our searching and navigating examples. Here's the XML document we'll use, projects.xml, which holds data about various programming projects you are doing for a set of clients:

```
<?xml version = "1.0" standalone="yes"?>
<document>
    <client>
            <lastname>Kirk</lastname>
            <firstname>James</firstname>
        <contractDate>September 5, 2092</contractDate>
        <contracts>
            <contract>
                <app>Comm</app>
                <id>111</id>
                <fee>$111.00</fee>
            </contract>
            <contract>
                <app>Accounting</app>
                <id>222</id>
                <fee>$989.00</fee>
            </contract>
        </contracts>
    </client>
    <client>
            <lastname>McCoy</lastname>
            <firstname>Leonard</firstname>
        <contractDate>September 7, 2092</contractDate>
        <contracts>
            <contract>
                <app>Stocker</app>
                <id>333</id>
                <fee>$2995.00</fee>
            </contract>
            <contract>
                <app>Dialer</app>
                <id>444</id>
                <fee>$200.00</fee>
            </contract>
        </contracts>
    </client>
    <client>
            <lastname>Spock</lastname>
            <firstname>Mr.</firstname>
        <contractDate>September 9, 2092</contractDate>
        <contracts>
            <contract>
                <app>WinHook</app>
                <id>555</id>
                <fee>$129.00</fee>
            </contract>
            <contract>
                <app>MouseApp</app>
                <id>666</id>
                <fee>$25.00</fee>
```

```
            </contract>
        </contracts>
    </client>
</document>
```

This example lets the user enter the last name of the client he or she wants to search for and click a button; the code will then jump to that record, which means the fields of that client's record will appear in the Web page.

To find the record the user is searching for, we begin by creating a new function, `search`. This function will read the last name the user has entered and find the matching record (in production code, you would add code here to handle problems if there was no match to the last name the user entered):

```
function search()
{
    var findMe = form1.text1.value.toLowerCase()

    while (!clients.recordset.EOF) {
        var clientLastName = new String(clients.recordset("lastname"))
        clientLastName = clientLastName.toLowerCase()
        if (clientLastName.indexOf(findMe) >= 0) {
            return
        }
        else {
            clients.recordset.moveNext()
        }
    }
}
```

After the match is made, the current record will be the record the user was searching for. To display that record's data, all we have to do is bind our DSO to various HTML controls. In this example, we'll just use two `<SPAN>` elements to display the client's first and last names, like this:

```
<APPLET CODE="com.ms.xml.dso.XMLDSO.class"
    ID="clients"
    WIDTH="0" HEIGHT="0"
    MAYSCRIPT="true">
    <PARAM NAME="URL" VALUE="projects.xml">
</APPLET>
        .
        .
        .
<FORM ID="form1">
    Last name to find: <INPUT TYPE="TEXT" NAME="text1">
    <BR>
    <BR>
    <INPUT TYPE="BUTTON" VALUE="Find client"
```

```
        ONCLICK="search()">
    <BR>
    <BR>
    First Name: <INPUT TYPE="TEXT" DATASRC="#clients"
        DATAFLD="firstname" SIZE="10">

    <BR><BR>
    Last Name: <SPAN DATASRC="#clients"
        DATAFLD="lastname"></SPAN>

</FORM>
```

Now when the user enters the last name of a client and clicks the Find Client button, the code moves to the client's record and display the client's first and last names automatically. Here's what the whole Web page looks like:

```
<HTML>
    <HEAD>
        <TITLE>
            Finding a client
        </TITLE>

        <SCRIPT LANGUAGE="JavaScript">
            function search()
            {
                var findMe = form1.text1.value.toLowerCase()

                while (!clients.recordset.EOF) {
                    var clientLastName = new
                        String(clients.recordset("lastname"))
                    clientLastName = clientLastName.toLowerCase()
                    if (clientLastName.indexOf(findMe) >= 0) {
                        return
                    }
                    else {
                        clients.recordset.moveNext()
                    }
                }
            }
        </SCRIPT>
    </HEAD>

    <BODY>
        <H1>
            Finding a client
        </H1>

        <APPLET CODE="com.ms.xml.dso.XMLDSO.class"
            ID="clients"
            WIDTH="0" HEIGHT="0"
```

```
            MAYSCRIPT="true">
            <PARAM NAME="URL" VALUE="projects.xml">
        </APPLET>

        <BR>
        <FORM ID="form1">
            Last name to find: <INPUT TYPE="TEXT" NAME="text1">
            <BR>
            <BR>
            <INPUT TYPE="BUTTON" VALUE="Find client"
                ONCLICK="search()">
            <BR>
            <BR>
            First Name: <INPUT TYPE="TEXT" DATASRC="#clients"
                DATAFLD="firstname" SIZE="10">

            <BR><BR>
            Last Name: <SPAN DATASRC="#clients"
                DATAFLD="lastname"></SPAN>

        </FORM>
    </BODY>
</HTML>
```

The results are shown in the following figure:

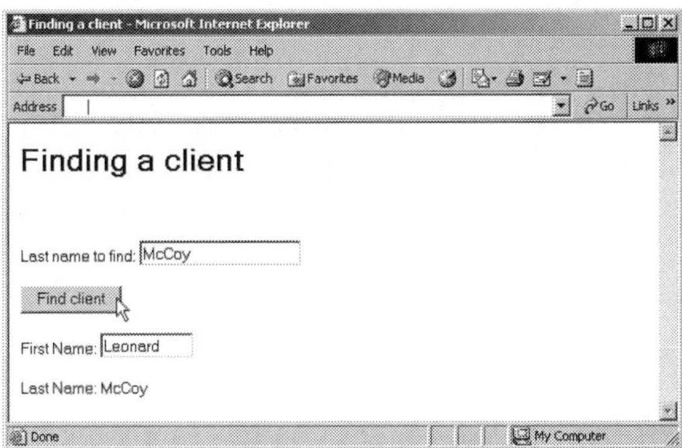

In Part V we also took a look at handling XML documents as true databases. To start, we were able to use an ASP page as an intermediary, letting us connect to a table in a database and getting back an XML document in a Web browser.

There's also a large amount of XML-enabled database support in .NET programming, and we took a look at it in overview in Day 20. For example, you were able to use the `WriteXml` method to write out a database table, the `WriteXmlSchema` method to write out an XML schema for the table, and the `ReadXml` method to read the table back in.

You were also able to use the .NET `XmlDataDocument` class to target the data in a database by using XPath. That can be useful, although XPath as currently supported often can't get the job done when you need database access. That's why XQuery was introduced—to provide a native XML way of working with XML documents and handling them as if they were databases. XQuery is still in the working draft stage, but we were able to use it along with the Galax XQuery engine in Part V.

You can use XQuery to create variables, functions, and templates, and you can then use XQuery to query XML documents to extract or manipulate the data you want. The idea is that XQuery will ultimately provide a true XML way of querying XML documents, much like SQL does for databases.

In addition, there's a great deal of XML support in .NET programming languages, and we got a look at it in overview in Part V. For example, you can create XML documents by using XML designers that are built into Visual Studio .NET, and you can create XML schemas either automatically or by dragging items into other items in an XML schema designer. You did both in Part V.

The .NET `XmlTextWriter` and `XmlTextReader` classes let you write XML documents and read them in. And XML Web controls let you display formatted XML in Web applications. To use an XML control, you use an XSLT style sheet, assigning its location to the control's `TransformSource` property, and you assign the XML document's location to the XML control's `DocumentSource` property.

The final .NET programming topic in Part V involved how to create and work with XML Web services. XML Web services let applications access code on the Web, and they use XML to communicate behind the scenes. Web services are designed to expose methods that you can call from other applications, and they typically involve database access on a Web server. You saw how that works in Part V, where you created an XML Web service that returned an entire database table by using XML on the Web.

APPENDIX A

Quiz Answers

Quiz Answers for Day 1

1. XML gives you a way of packaging your data, and it's taken off largely because XML documents are text, which has meant that you can send them using the existing Internet framework, as built for HTML.
2. Notes, working drafts, candidate recommendations, and recommendations.
3. An XML element is the basic data-holding construct in an XML document. It starts with an opening tag, can contain text or other elements, and ends with a closing tag, like this: `<greeting>hello</greeting>`. An attribute gives you more information, and is always assigned a quoted value in XML. Here's how you might add an attribute named language to this element: `<greeting language = "en">hello</greeting>`.
4. The ones we discussed today are that an XML document must contain one or more elements. One element, the root element, must contain all the other elements. Finally, each element must nest inside any enclosing elements correctly.

5. Document Type Definitions (DTDs—see Days 4 and 5) and XML schemas (see Days 6 and 7).

Quiz Answers for Day 2

1. All XML processors are supposed to implement at least the UTF-8 (compressed Unicode) and UTF-16 (compressed UCS) character encodings. In practice, you can only count on UTF-8, however.
2. You can escape < and > like this: <message>This is a <message> element.</message>.
3. A prolog can contain XML declarations, XML comments (which describe the XML document), processing instructions, whitespace, and doctype declaration(s).
4. The attributes you can use in an XML document are: version (required; the XML version), encoding (optional; the character encoding), and standalone (optional; "yes" if the document does not refer to any external documents or entities, "no" otherwise).
5. There are no processing instructions built into XML already, although some, like <?xml-stylesheet?>, have been generally agreed upon by browser manufacturers.

Quiz Answers for Day 3

1. One. You need at least a root element for an XML document to be well-formed.
2. In a well-formed XML document, there must be one root element that contains all the others.
3. The attribute values are not enclosed in quotation marks.
4. You could use this attribute xmlns:service="http://www.superduperbigco.com/customer_service" in an element. After using this attribute, you can use the service prefix in the current element and any child elements.
5. Use this attribute in the enclosing element: xmlns="http://www.superduperbigco.com/customer_returns".

Quiz Answers for Day 4

1. The <hiredate> and <name> elements are not declared in the DTD.
2. The <hiredate> and <name> elements appear in the wrong order.
3. This DTD uses a choice for the <employee> element, and the choice says that the document can contain either <hiredate> elements or <name> elements—but not both.

A

4. The DTD says there can be at most one `<employee>` element, but there are two.
5. This XML document references an external DTD, so the XML declaration's `standalone` attribute should be set to `"no"`. There may also be errors in the external DTD, of course.

Quiz Answers for Day 5

1. You can use the `#IMPLIED` keyword.
2. You can use the `#FIXED` keyword.
3. Here's one solution:

```
<!ATTLIST friend
    name CDATA #REQUIRED
    address CDATA #IMPLIED
    phone CDATA #IMPLIED
>
```

4. Here's one way of doing it:

```
<!ATTLIST
relative married (yes | no) "no"
>
```

5. This will work:

```
<!NOTATION jpg SYSTEM "image/jpeg">
<!ENTITY mountains SYSTEM "mountains.jpg" NDATA jpg>
```

Quiz Answers for Day 6

1. The namespace that is used by XML schemas is `www.w3.org/2001/XMLSchema`.
2. You can declare elements by using `<xsd:element>` and attributes by using `<xsd:attribute>`.
3. You can declare the element like this:

```
<xsd:element name="name" type="xsd:string"/>
```

4. You can do this in an XML schema:

```
<xsd:attribute name="language" type="xsd:string" use="optional"/>.
```

5. Here's one solution:

```
<xsd:element name="friend" type="friendType"/>

<xsd:complexType name="friendType">
    <xsd:sequence>
        <xsd:element name="name" type="xsd:string"/>
        <xsd:element name="address" type="xsd:string"/>
    </xsd:sequence>
    <xsd:attribute name="date" type="xsd:date"/>
</xsd:complexType>
```

Quiz Answers for Day 7

1. You use the `<xsd:restriction>` element and the `base` attribute.
2. To cap values, you can use the `maxIncusive` and `maxExclusive` facets. To constrain values to be one of a set, you can use the `enumeration` facet.
3. Here's one solution:

```
<xsd:simpleType name="age">
    <xsd:restriction base="xsd:integer">
        <xsd:minInclusive value="0"/>
        <xsd:maxInclusive value="125"/>
    </xsd:restriction>
</xsd:simpleType>
```

4. Here's one solution:

```
<xsd:choice>
    <xsd:element name="friend" type="xsd:string"/>
    <xsd:element name="foe" type="xsd:string"/>
</xsd:choice>
```

5. Here's one solution:

```
<xsd:element name="movie">
    <xsd:complexType>
        <xsd:attribute name="title" type="xsd:string" />
        <xsd:attribute name="length" type="xsd:int" />
    </xsd:complexType>
</xsd:element>
```

Quiz Answers for Day 8

1. You can use this CSS property/value pair: `font-size: 36pt`.
2. You can use this CSS property/value pair: `display: block`.
3. You can use this CSS property/value pair: `text-align: center`.
4. You can use this CSS property/value pair: `text-decoration: underline`.
5. You can use this CSS property/value pair: `margin-top: 10`.

Quiz Answers for Day 9

1. `*` by itself applied to `ch09_01.xml` just picks out the `<states>` element. `*` selects all element children (not grandchildren or any descendents) of the context node, and when you open `ch09_01.xml`, the root node is the context node.
2. The XPath expression `//*` selects all elements in `ch09_01.xml`.

A

3. Here's one solution:

```
<xsl:template match="state">
        <xsl:value-of select="name"/>
</xsl:template>
```

4. Here's one solution:

```
<xsl:template match="*[@units = "people"]">
        <xsl:value-of select="."/>
</xsl:template>
```

5. Here's one solution:

```
<xsl:template match="population | area">
        .
        .
        .
</xsl:template>
```

Quiz Answers for Day 10

1. The first XSL-FO element you must use in an XSL-FO document is the `<fo:root>` element.
2. The `<fo:root>` element can contain both a master set layout and page sequences.
3. The `<fo:region-before>` element.
4. The `line-height` attribute.
5. The `master-reference` attribute.

Quiz Answers for Day 11

1. The three versions of XHTML 1.0 are XHTML 1.0 Transitional, XHTML 1.0 Frameset, and XHTML 1.0 Strict.
2. The namespace is `"http://www.w3.org/1999/xhtml"`.
3. This is a trick question. You can't use standalone attributes in XHTML. Every attribute must be assigned a quoted value.
4. In XHTML, every XHTML document must have a `<head>` element, and every `<head>` element must contain at least a `<title>` element.
5. Every `<p>` element needs a closing tag, `</p>`.

Quiz Answers for Day 12

1. You need to use either the `href` or `id` attribute in the `<a>` element.
2. The `src` and `alt` attributes are required.

3. The <frameset> and <frame> elements are supported in XHTML 1.0 Frameset only.
4. The W3C suggests that you use style sheets instead of the <frame> and <frameset> elements. To replace frames, you can often use a <div> element and position it where you want it.
5. The <table> element is supported in both XHTML 1.0 Strict and XHTML 1.1.

Quiz Answers for Day 13

1. The `height` and `width` attributes are required.
2. The `r` attribute is required.
3. Here's one example: `<polyline points="0,0 100,100 200,0/>`
4. You can use this command: `"M200,300"`.
5. You can use the <img> element's `region` attribute to specify a region that is defined in the <layout> element.

Quiz Answers for Day 14

1. The possible values you can assign to the `xlink:type` attribute, which sets the type of the XLink, are `"simple"`, `"extended"`, `"locator"`, `"arc"`, `"resource"`, `"title"`, and `"none"`.
2. The `xlink:type` attribute is required in every XLink.
3. You can set the `xlink:show` attribute to `"replace"`.
4. You use the <xforms:model> element to specify how an XForm's data should be structured.
5. You can use XML like this:

```
<xforms:instance>
    <data xmlns="">
        <input>Hello!</input>
    </data>
</xforms:instance>
```

   You also need to set the `ref` attribute of the input control to `"/data/input"`.

Quiz Answers for Day 15

1. There are two ways that you can create a document object from an XML file by using JavaScript in Internet Explorer. You can do this:

```
var xmlDocumentObject
xmlDocumentObject = new ActiveXObject("Microsoft.XMLDOM")
xmlDocumentObject.load("ch15_01.xml")
```

or you can use an XML island, like this:

```
<XML ID="committeeXML" SRC="ch15_01.xml"></XML>
        .
        .
        .
var xmlDocumentObject
xmlDocumentObject= document.all("committeeXML").XMLDocument
```

2. You can use the `nextChild` method to move to the next child node.
3. You can use the `nodeValue` property to get a node's value.
4. You can call `xmlDocumentObject.getElementsByTagName("senator")` to get a list of all the `<senator>` elements in a document.
5. To get a named node map of an element's attributes, you simply use the element's `attributes` property.

Quiz Answers for Day 16

1. In Java 1.4 or later, you can use a Java `DocumentBuilderFactory` object to create a `DocumentBuilder` object. Then you can use the `DocumentBuilder` object's `parse` method to parse an XML document and create a Java `Document` object.
2. You can use the node's `getNodeType` method and check the results it returns against fields such as `Node.ELEMENT_NODE`, `Node.TEXT_NODE`, and so on.
3. You can use the `getNodeName` method to get a node's name and its `getNodeValue` method to get its value.
4. You can call a `Document` object's `getElementsByTagName` method like this:

   ```
   document.getElementsByTagName("senator")
   ```

5. You can create the `<child>` element by using a `Document` object's `createElement` method, create the text in it by using the `createTextNode` method, append the text node to the `<child>` element by using the element's `appendChild` method, and append the `<child>` element to the `<element>` element by using the `<child>` element's `appendChild` method.

Quiz Answers for Day 17

1. In Java 1.4 or later, you can derive a class from a SAX handler class, such as `DefaultHandler`, and then use a `SAXParserFactory` object to create a new SAX factory. You create a SAX parser by using the `SAXParserFactory` object, call its `parse` method, and implement the SAX methods you want (for example, the `startElement` method).

2. You can implement the `startElement` and `endElement` methods to catch the starting and closing tags of elements.
3. You can implement the `characters` method and extract the text node's text from the character array passed to you, using the starting position in the array. The length of the text is also passed to you.
4. You can use the `Attributes` object passed to the `startElement` method to handle an element's attributes.
5. You use methods such as the `warning` method to handle warnings, the `error` method to handle errors, and the `fatalError` method to handle fatal errors.

Quiz Answers for Day 18

1. The three parts of a SOAP message are the envelope, header, and body.
2. The `<Header>`, `<Body>`, and `<Fault>` elements are the three child elements you can use in a SOAP envelope.
3. You set the element's `mustUnderstand` attribute to `"1"`.
4. You use the `<Description>` element.
5. A good choice would be the `<Contributor>` element.

Quiz Answers for Day 19

1. You can create an XML island that makes the XML data in a document named `data.xml` available as a DSO named `data` by using this HTML element:

   ```
   <XML SRC="data.xml" ID="data"></XML>
   ```
2. `DATASRC` and `DATAFLD` are the two HTML attributes you normally use to bind an HTML control to a DSO.
3. One way is to use the `DATASRC` attribute of the `<TABLE>` element to connect to a DSO and the `DATAFLD` attribute of a `<SPAN>` element in each `<TD>` element.
4. You can use the *`dso`*`.recordset.BOF` and *`dso`*`.recordset.EOF` properties, where *`dso`* is the name of the DSO.
5. You can access it as *`dso`*`.recordset("address")`, where *`dso`* is the name of the DSO.

Quiz Answers for Day 20

1. You use the `Fill` method.
2. You can use the `WriteXml` and `ReadXml` methods.

3. Here's one solution:

```
let $name := local-name($elem)
```

4. You can use the expression $elem/@*.
5. Here's one way to do it:

```
define global $data {treat as document data
(glx:document-validate("data.xml", "document"))}
```

Quiz Answers for Day 21

1. You can select Project, Add Item in Visual Studio .NET to open the Add new Item dialog box. Then you select the XML File template in the Templates box, give the new document a name, and click the Open button.
2. You use the WriteStartElement method.
3. You can check the XMLTextReader object's NodeType property, which you can compare to fields such as XmlNodeType.XmlDeclaration and XmlNodeType.ProcessingInstruction.
4. To expose methods from a Web service and make them accessible outside the service, you use the <WebMethod()> attribute.
5. You need to add to the Windows application a Web reference to the Web service, and you need to create an object corresponding to that service. Then you can call the Web service's members by using that object.

INDEX

Symbols

A

B

C

D

E

F

G

K-L

M

N

O

P

Q-R

S

T

U

V

W

X-Z

What if Que

joined forces to deliver the
best technology books in a
common digital reference platform?

We have. Introducing
InformIT Online Books
powered by Safari.

- **Specific answers to specific questions.**
InformIT Online Books' powerful search engine gives you relevance-ranked results in a matter of seconds.

- **Immediate results.**
With InformIt Online Books, you can select the book you want and view the chapter or section you need immediately.

- **Cut, paste, and annotate.**
Paste code to save time and eliminate typographical errors. Make notes on the material you find useful and choose whether or not to share them with your workgroup.

- **Customized for your enterprise.**
Customize a library for you, your department, or your entire organization. You pay only for what you need.

informIT Online Books

POWERED BY Safari

As an InformIT partner, Que has shared the knowledge and hands-on advice of our authors with you online. Visit InformIT.com to see what you are missing.

Get your first 14 days FREE!

InformIT Online Books is offering its members a 10-book subscription risk free for 14 days. Visit **http://www.informit.com/onlinebooks** for details.

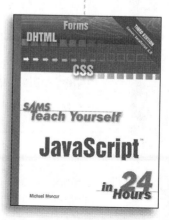